GLOBAL STRATEGIC ASSESSMENT 2009

AMERICA'S SECURITY ROLE
IN A CHANGING WORLD

Edited by Patrick M. Cronin

NDU Press

Published for the Institute for National Strategic Studies
By National Defense University Press
Washington, D.C.
2009

Library of Congress Cataloging-in-Publication Data

Global strategic assessment 2009 : America's security role in a changing world / edited by Patrick M. Cronin.
    p. cm.
 Includes bibliographical references and index.
 1. United States—Foreign relations—2009- 2. United States—Foreign relations—2001-2009. 3. United States—Military policy. 4. National security—United States. I. Cronin, Patrick M., 1958-
 JZ1480.G595 2009
 355'.033073--dc22

                        2009027484

First Printing, September 2009

For sale by the Superintendent of Documents, U.S. Government Printing Office
Internet: bookstore.gpo.gov Phone: toll free (866) 512-1800; DC area (202) 512-1800
Fax: (202) 512-2104 Mail: Stop IDCC, Washington, DC 20402-0001
ISBN 978-0-16-083212-3

Global Strategic Assessment 2009: America's Security Role in a Changing World

Introduction

By Patrick M. Cronin

Although the United States cannot afford to be the world's exclusive security guarantor, the world is ill prepared for U.S. retrenchment. This Global Strategic Assessment offers a conceptual pathway for U.S. policymakers to begin recalibrating America's security role to reverse what has appeared to be a widening gap between U.S. ends and means, now and in the future. International security requires U.S. active engagement, but the character of that engagement is changing along with the global environment. Worldwide trends suggest that the United States will increasingly have to approach complex challenges and surprises through wider and more effective partnerships and more integrated strategies. This volume explains the complex security environment and how in particular the United States can begin the process of strategic adaptation.

Complexity is the watchword of our century. This assessment should be a healthy reminder of just how complex—and dangerous—a world we live in. That complexity was encapsulated by the Greek poet Archilochus, who said that the fox knows many things but the hedgehog had only one big idea. During the previous administration, the United States conflated security under the umbrella of a "global war on terror" and focused on a single big idea. Thus, in this volume a central idea, if not an organizing principle, is that the United States will have to be as clever as the fox, keeping its eye on multiple challenges and taking care not to exert its finite resources on any single problem. Preparing for and dealing with such profound complexity requires particular capabilities, approaches, and proclivities: cultural, developmental, experiential, technical, organizational, political, and operational.

These attributes can be selected, cultivated, and enhanced, and it seems that they will have to be if we are to survive, let alone succeed.

This book attempts to bridge the gap between theory and praxis, but it is not a policy blueprint. As suggested above, its overriding message is to emphasize global complexity and America's vital yet limited role in coping with that complexity. Some critics of this volume will hew to a traditional view of security and the world, claiming that the threats are far more straightforward and the world quite predictable. Indeed, the world of tomorrow will carry on with a great deal of continuity. It is also fair to say that this volume tries harder to identify change than highlight that continuity. Even so, the gist of this research, undertaken by 125 scholars, suggests that policymakers and analysts are only beginning to come to terms with the uncertain, complex world in which we operate. For instance, too little systematic thought has been given to the interactions between state and nonstate actors, between economics and security, and in the "global commons." Moreover, to the extent that officials and analysts are able to stay on top of global trends, they also realize that our prescriptions, policies, and strategies tend to lag woefully behind them.

Today's world is marked by the uneasy coexistence between traditional geopolitics and ever-widening globalization. A fundamental question undergirding this volume is how the United States can best use its essential and yet insufficient influence in a world marked by both rising state power centers and the devolution of power into the hands of more nonstate actors. Clearly, there is no simple prescription for the problem of how the United States can best exert its influence in this dynamic security landscape. Even so, the breadth of threats, challenges, and opportunities that may surface in the coming years will require a comprehensive approach that utilizes the full continuum of power—be it hard, soft, smart, dumb, or fuzzy. Complexity should not be an excuse for ignoring clear, urgent, and obvious dangers, but responses to those threats must better assess the side effects and opportunity costs of neglecting the full array of challenges confronting the United States and the world. In short, there is no substitute for making conscious choices within a grand strategic perspective: the world cannot afford for us to be narrow, near-sighted, or parochial.

Safeguarding U.S. national interests and global security is complex and uncertain today and is only likely to become more so tomorrow. This volume provides departure points for reflecting on challenges, considering remedies, and managing complexity. It is designed to serve the broadest possible community, from officials in the Obama administration and across the U.S. national security community, to elite and public audiences around the world.

There are three sections: first, an overview of eight broad trends shaping the international security environment; second, a global analysis of the world's seven regions, to consider important developments in their distinctive neighborhoods; and, third, an examination of prospective U.S. contributions, military capabilities and force structure, national security organization, alliances and partnerships, and strategies. Every chapter contains at least five succinct essays designed to assess a particular issue and its implications. Thus, while the 20 chapters reflect more than 125 separate issues, they all contribute to a general framework from which policymakers may initiate discussions.

Section I considers eight strategic trends shaping both near- and long-term challenges and opportunities. Economic and political power is shifting; technology is altering political and social patterns of behavior; energy and the environment are looming as larger long-term drivers of security than in the past; permanent fragile states and nonstate actors are creating new dimensions to what had once been seen by many as a big-power chessboard; and the proliferation of weapons and hybrid warfare are likely to change the character of conflict in the future. The world seems stuck in a constant tussle between geopolitics and globalization, between classic state-power contests for competition and cooperation, and emerging dynamics in which

the good and ill effects of globalization take on heightened importance. Policymakers will have to seek the best balance between these traditional and emerging forces.

Section II provides seven regional surveys that highlight the rich and distinctive issues, uncertainties, competitions, and partnerships that characterize each region of the world. Trends may be global, but they affect and shape each region in different ways. Moreover, each region appears to have largely local domestic and regional concerns, even while increasingly intersecting with other regions and global security issues. As for which countries will contribute to regional and international security, there is an obvious gap between the array of challenges transcending narrow national interests and the level of contributions most countries are making. Again, policymakers will have to find a balance between local and regional priorities on the one hand and more global and transnational issues on the other.

Finally, Section III focuses more directly on the implications of global and regional trends for U.S. policy. The complex environment poses a potent set of challenges for how the administration of President Barack Obama seeks to exert America's significant yet finite power to safeguard against a diverse set of traditional and modern threats and challenges, while also seizing as many opportunities as possible to build more durable, peaceful, and collaborative solutions for the 21st century. In his first months in office, President Obama demonstrated a keen ability to change the basic narrative of the United States, placing it in a far less confrontational stance with most of the world, and showing a willingness to give greater weight to local and multilateral solutions.

Although this project was largely accomplished before the beginning of the Obama administration, we know from the first months of its tenure that in many ways the United States has turned the page on its style and narrative in many parts of the world. At the same time, it should be obvious that while diplomacy and rhetoric can provide an important new beginning, the hard work of seeking security, building support, and implementing whole-of-government solutions across a vast number of complex challenges is a never-ending business. The administration has not only embraced the "3 Ds" of diplomacy, development, and defense, but has also recognized that many broad security issues are interwoven with the "3 Es" of economics, energy, and the environment. Other issues, such as democracy and human rights, cannot be divorced from security, whether concerning the future course of Iran or the difficulties democracies have in waging protracted counterinsurgencies without losing popular support or straying from democratic values.

Albert Einstein once said that given an hour to save the world, he would devote 59 minutes to thinking about the problem and 1 minute to resolving it. This volume hews to that advice by allowing some 125 expert authors to contribute to a portrait of the world that pays homage to the breadth and diversity of issues driving tomorrow's security environment in an accessible and constructive way. It presents a coherent whole, but it does not attempt to speak with one voice. The breadth of this approach is meant to provide decisionmakers with a full palette of the circumstances that they face and the options to consider.

This Global Strategic Assessment provides a purposefully broad point of departure for many national security functions: subsequent analysis, interagency coordination, policy derivation, coalition-building, reorganization, long-range planning, and operations. The need for broader U.S. strategic thinking is obvious to me and to my colleagues at the Institute for National Strategic Studies (INSS) at the National Defense University. But equally important is the need to mobilize partners, conduct serious planning, integrate a rich variety of disciplines and actors, follow through on implementation, and then assess actions with an appreciation of history. And all of these steps must then, in turn, inform our education and training. No single essay in the full collection ever provides the depth that some experts require. Instead, the attempt is to cover enough issues and areas of the world to review the intricacies of global security. In so doing, it makes an obvious case for all-of-government and coalition-based solutions. Again, this assessment is not a policy treatise, but it does set out the terms of the debate as a first step to confronting challenges, exploiting opportunities, and keeping the United States secure.

This should be a familiar process: on the modern battlefields of Iraq and Afghanistan, a deep and sober understanding of what U.S. and coalition forces faced had to emerge before any hope of a comprehensive and successful strategy was possible. The Global Strategic Assessment aspires to get this strategic learning process off the battlefield to the maximum extent possible and appropriate.

The challenges are great, but so are the opportunities. The world is changing, but the United States still has the greatest capacity to cope with these vicissitudes, to lead global responses, and to make the world a safer place. Many of the trends are positive, and the contributions of issues as diverse as the information revolution and advances in the life sciences are bringing greater overall good than ill to humankind. Even so, in a volume focused on security risks, it would be a dereliction of duty to avoid difficult questions about better ways to manage the challenges emerging even from positive trends.

In addition to the elaborate interrelatedness of international security, this Global Strategic Assessment should remind the reader of the enduring realities of American power. There is nothing permanent about the U.S. global security role, and there are no guarantees in international security, but no other nation has America's unique attributes: a global zeal to make the world a better place; potent expeditionary forces to project power on all continents and oceans; a large and open economy; and a diverse and ever-changing society built on freedom and the rule of law. As the Nation is refocusing its foreign policy on diplomatic rather than military capabilities, the fact remains that formidable military power has supercharged our diplomacy and remains key to providing the Obama administration with far more purchase than other countries. Whether through settled or ad hoc collective security arrangements, no other country appears ready to mobilize its instruments of power to address threats posed by state and nonstate actors. Even as American power measured as a percentage of the global economy has declined, its comparative advantage in terms of hard military power has expanded.

Although the weight of these diverse essays may leave some wondering about America's future, there is inherent in this document a good deal of optimism: that problems can be resolved or at least better managed; that a more humble America that is more sensitive to diverse views from around the world is ready to work together with others; and that for America's relative decline in perceived and actual influence, perhaps, there is every reason to believe that the United States will remain a powerful and unique contributor—only one, to be sure—to global security.

The effort embodied in this Global Strategic Assessment harkens back to the origins of INSS, which was established 25 years ago by then–Chairman of the Joint Chiefs of Staff General Jack Vessey, who understood long before whole-of-government approaches became fashionable that planning and assessment needed to take full advantage of diverse expertise, cutting-edge research, and a blend of civil-military teamwork. As General Vessey mentioned in early 2009: "the [geographic and functional commanders in chief] were constructing our war plans in basement rooms around the world with, except for Stratcom [U.S. Strategic Command], staffs equipped with #2 pencils and yellow foolscap." Responding to the inherent challenge presented by General Vessey, INSS published a series of annual assessments over the last decade. In 2008, the Office of the Secretary of Defense asked the Institute to prepare another assessment that would provide a broad and diverse understanding of the international security environment in the decade ahead, specifically designed for use early in the term of the new President. It is a great privilege to be able to share this volume with the widest possible audience. **gsa**

Contents

II. Assessing Complex Regional Trends

Introduction

III. Recalibrating American Power

Introduction

Acknowledgements

INSERT

Strategic Atlas: *Executive Branch Geographic Areas of Responsibility*

Section I
Adapting to Eight Global Challenges

Secretary of Defense Robert M. Gates (right) and British Defence Secretary John Hutton talk during the non-NATO International Security Assistance Force meeting in Krakow, Poland, February 2009.

Over the coming decade and beyond, world leaders will face enormously complex global security challenges. A mixture of enduring and emerging threats and challenges will mean that policymakers are increasingly operating in terra incognito. The United States and other states will have to adapt to eight broad trends driving the future security environment:

■ a global redistribution of economic power from the West to the "Rest"

■ the partial emergence of a multipolar world

■ an information revolution that leaves modern societies vulnerable

■ the acceleration of an energy and environmental security tipping point

■ the mounting challenges emanating from many fragile states and ungoverned spaces

■ the increasingly transnational dimensions of terrorism

■ the changing character of conflict from conventional to irregular and hybrid warfare

■ the potential further spread of nuclear and biological weapons.

First, a global redistribution of economic power is under way. The subprime mortgage crisis, the Wall Street meltdown, the temporary freezing of credit markets, and the reverberations around global markets are all reminders that economic power is the bedrock of sustainable military and political power. Much of the past 500 years of history has been dominated by the rise of the West, including the Industrial Revolution. More recently, however, economic power has shifted increasingly to "the Rest," especially Asia. Nations that had spent decades on the periphery of the global economic and trading system, including China, are now critical production centers. Capital is flowing out of emerging nations and into the developed world and is being used to recapitalize the rich nations' foundering banking systems. Even while the Group of 7 or 8 is being enlarged if not overtaken by an emerging Group of 20, there are also roughly a billion people in some 60 countries, mainly but not exclusively in sub-Saharan Africa, who are being left behind.

Second, it is fashionable to point to the declining influence of the United States over the past decade and in the decades ahead. The world is no longer bipolar, as it was during the Cold War's East-West divide, although concerns about the durability of major power peace are far from dormant. It is not unipolar, with the United States a sole superpower convincing other powers to coalesce around Washington's agenda. But it is also not truly multipolar,

Traders deal in crude oil futures pit at New York Mercantile Exchange

Head of Zimbabwe's Movement for Democratic Change announces launch of fund to help displaced victims of political violence

with political power residing in the hands of several world capitals attempting to preserve global order. Many of the emerging or resurgent powers—including China, Russia, India, and Brazil—either lack the desire to assume the mantle of global management or do not enjoy a seat at the international high table. Meanwhile, there are increasingly global and transnational challenges—from nuclear proliferation and climate change to terrorism and global poverty—that make national security interdependent with global security. In short, the post–World War II international security system is in transition, with the key question being, "Toward what?"

Members of Internet Corporation for Assigned Names and Numbers, the key Internet oversight agency, relaxed rules to permit new domain names

A third global trend centers on the information revolution and technology. Modern network technologies are shifting power to the edge, allowing decentralized networked groups to compete with hierarchical structures. The globalization of communications and computing infrastructure is allowing nonstate groups—including terrorists, criminal organizations, antiglobalization movements, pernicious hackers, and others—to directly threaten national security and international stability. Three trends in this information revolution are particularly relevant to strategic concerns: ubiquitous connectivity, transparency, and cyber warfare. In 2008, the number of people owning a cell phone exceeded the number of people who did not. It was only a few years ago when half of the world had never heard a dial tone. Ubiquitous and instantaneous communications are also increasing global transparency; it is not clear how anything on the future urban battlefield can be kept secret for longer than it takes to establish a cell phone connection. But modern information technology and Internet systems are increasingly vulnerable to cyber attack, and new complexities make cyber attack both increasingly possible and hard to trace.

Fourth, the emerging energy system is far more complex and global than the industrial-era system that it is slowly replacing. Today, when security planners talk about energy security, they are as likely to be referring to carbon emissions and diminishing water supplies as energy self-reliance and affordable oil. Moreover, the energy and environmental security problems that are emerging are increasingly beyond the ability of any single country to control. Significant increases in the price of oil have weakened the global economy, contributed to a sharp rise in global food prices, and transferred trillions of dollars to autocratic oil-exporting regimes. Energy diplomacy has become increasingly confrontational as states jockey for control of gas and oil markets and pipelines. Meanwhile, concerns about pollution and greenhouse gases have strained diplomatic relations with other nations and are forcing fundamental changes in energy policy. Water is another critical resource. China has more than 22 percent of the world's population and only 8 percent of the world's fresh water; water shortages are causing rising food prices and migration. In India, urban water demand is expected to double and industrial demand to triple by 2025. And in the Middle East, between 1985 and 2005, the overall per capita fresh water availability was cut in half and was expected to be cut in half again well before 2025.

Brazilian police guard raft loaded with logs illegally cut during government's fight against deforestation in the Amazon

Fifth, since 9/11, fragile states and ungoverned spaces have risen in stature as a serious challenge to security. Everywhere, it seems, the nation-state is under siege: from below by aggrieved national groups pressing upward; from above by international bodies and global advocacy groups; and from the side by global society's empowered private actors, both licit

United Nations personnel help displaced persons return to homes in Pristina, Kosovo

and illicit. There is no easy answer to state weakness and no surefire way to build effective states. Oversimplification of cause-and-effect relationships between weak states as a group and the universe of "spillover" threats often attributed to them forms a poor basis for public policy decisionmaking. Even so, fragile states may aid and abet a host of other problems, from piracy in the Gulf of Aden and Strait of Malacca, to trafficking in illegal commodities, to incubating terrorism and pandemics. Indeed, a nation-state's capacity to govern effectively faces no stiffer test than its ability to manage infectious diseases crises. Pandemics require unprecedented multiagency communication, expertise, and collaboration at the state, regional, and international levels, all of which are crucial for containment of the disease and mitigation of its consequences. A growing need to address state weakness seems a likely bet for the next half-century.

A sixth trend relates to transnational movements and terrorism. National and international security now involves nonstate actors to an extent unprecedented in modern history. Transnational movements and substate actors have tremendous power both to contribute to the greater good and to bring about violence. The most prominent such

threat arises from transnational Salafi jihadism, of which al Qaeda is the standard bearer. Al Qaeda and likeminded groups boast as members only a fraction of 1 percent of the 91 million Muslims who could have potentially celebrated the events of September 11, 2001. While familiarity with al Qaeda tends to breed contempt, there remains a great concern about terrorists acquiring and using weapons of mass destruction (WMD). Successful responses to and prevention of this emerging threat will probably have to be designed as an all-of-society or whole-of-government approach. Ironically, our greatest strength—military power—has become our greatest liability because extensive use of military power can help to mobilize Muslims to become Salafi jihadists. Our most important partners are Muslims, and we will have to continue to find ways to support ongoing Muslim efforts to marginalize the Salafi jihadist ideology across the Islamic world while taking prudent actions to inhibit catastrophic terrorism.

Pigeons scatter as Taj Hotel burns during terror attacks in Mumbai, India, November 2008

Seventh, the character of war is changing. The most complex challenges of the future could involve synergies from the simultaneous application of multiple modes of war. The most capable opponents may seek to pursue what has been called hybrid warfare—the combination of conventional, irregular, and catastrophic forms of warfare. We have certainly seen a recent revival of irregular warfare, and not only in Iraq and Afghanistan. For instance, during the 34-day-long war in southern Lebanon in 2006, Hizballah demonstrated the ability of a nonstate actor to discern the vulnerabilities of Western-style militaries by mixing an organized political

U.S. Navy SEAL trainee in close quarters combat exercise at Naval Special Warfare Center, Campo, California

first state ever to withdraw from the Nuclear Non-proliferation Treaty regime, and the path ahead for denuclearizing the Korean Peninsula remains long and treacherous. Iran's continued highly enriched uranium program has made it a virtual threshold nuclear power, and it is believed to be capable of building a nuclear weapon within the next several years should it so choose. We can prevent a second nuclear age, and perhaps an expansion of a costly proliferation of military platforms in space, but it will take considerable effort. In the meantime, and more ominously, we still do not fully understand how the rapid advances in biological and chemical science and technology will change the landscape for biological and chemical weapons. The nature of life sciences is such that even a few individuals could inflict untold damage if armed with the right unconventional weapon. **gsa**

movement with decentralized cells employing adaptive tactics in zones outside the local government's control. Hizballah, like the jihadist defenders in the battles of Fallujah, Iraq, during April and November of 2004, skillfully exploited the urban terrain to create ambushes, evade detection, and hold strong defensive fortifications in close proximity to non-combatants. But this does not mean that traditional forces are irrelevant—far from it. Beyond the resurgence of ground forces with respect to wars such as those in Iraq and Afghanistan, trends suggest that the importance of seapower in relation to the global economy is growing. Similarly, it can be argued that airpower's ability to contribute to the course and outcome of combat operations at the higher end of the conflict spectrum is also expanding. Meanwhile, at the lower end of the conflict spectrum, complex operations and humanitarian problems have been constant companions of military operations in the past two decades, and this trend is likely to continue in the coming decades, requiring new blends of military and civilian forces acting together.

An eighth trend shaping tomorrow's security environment is WMD proliferation. Our worst fears regarding the proliferation and use of nuclear weapons have not been realized to date, but important developments have made it increasingly possible that nuclear or biological weapons may be used in the next half-century. The absence of catastrophic WMD use is the most positive trend of recent years, and everything should be done to preserve it. As disruptive and costly as the 2001 anthrax letters incident proved, only 5 people are known to have died and 22 to have sustained injury. North Korea became the

North Korean soldier monitors South Korean side of border at Panmunjom

Chapter 1

The Global Redistribution of Economic Power

Economic power is the bedrock of sustainable military and political power. The severity and expected duration of the financial crisis that gripped the world in 2008 make it all the more imperative to understand the national security implications of U.S. and global economic trends. This chapter focuses on selected economic issues from a broad strategic perspective. The topics are diverse, ranging from extreme poverty to high finance, but together they illustrate a key theme of this study: the global redistribution of power.

The chapter begins with a definition of economic power and an exploration of its use and limits. It continues with a historical overview of the rise of the West, beginning with the Industrial Revolution, and the subsequent shift of economic power from the West to "the Rest," mainly Asia. Along the way, living standards on average have vastly improved, and new sources of wealth have arisen. Globalization has greatly accelerated these positive trends, but it has also created new sources of instability.

The third and fourth segments and a sidebar analyze one of these sources of instability: the rapidly changing world of finance. A sound and prospering financial system is an indispensable foundation of economic (and therefore military) power, but the size and speed of borderless financial markets far outstrip the resources available to slow-moving national governments and international institutions. As the current financial crisis has shown so vividly, the speed of global financial flows exposes participating economies to sudden job losses and extreme volatility in equity markets.

Nowhere is the global redistribution of economic power more evident than in the world of finance. Although the role of governments remains crucial, the size and speed of private transactions mean that financial power has largely shifted from public entities to the private sector. In addition, a role reversal has occurred: financial institutions in the developing world have helped rescue Western banks and financial institutions. As of late 2008, China had accumu-

Trader reacts to activities on floor of Indonesia Stock Exchange

AP Images (Achmad Ibrahim)

lated almost $2 trillion of foreign exchange reserves, out of a world total of about $7.3 trillion. Taken together, Taiwan, India, South Korea, Singapore, and Hong Kong accounted for another trillion.

Although the fundamental strengths of the U.S. economy are still in place, American-style capitalism has suffered a loss of prestige. The subprime mortgage crisis of 2007–2008, the Wall Street meltdown that began in September 2008, the collapse or near-bankruptcy of hallowed firms, the freezing of credit markets, the massive size of proposed bailouts, and the gyrations of stock markets around the world—all complicated by a U.S. Presidential transition—damaged U.S. economic power and thus undermined Washington's global influence.

The fifth section of the chapter, on economic security, documents another source of instability: poverty. Within the developing world, economic success is accruing to some countries but not to others. Roughly 1 billion people in some 60 countries, mainly but not exclusively in sub-Saharan Africa, are being left behind. Some of these countries are subject to repeated civil wars; some provide havens for non-traditional threats to U.S. national security, such as terrorism, illegal trafficking, and pandemic disease; and some generate calls for humanitarian intervention. The analysis concludes with several policy recommendations and a plea for the more coordinated use of military and civilian instruments.

The chapter ends with a look at one U.S. reaction to the redistribution of economic power away from the West: protectionism. With the U.S. economy slowing to a crawl, trade is virtually the only source of growth. Measures to restrict trade and investment inflict damage on not only the American economy, but also U.S. power and influence. Vigorous and farsighted leadership will be required to reverse this trend and strengthen America's ability to lead.

What Is Economic Power?

There is general agreement that in the 21st century, economic power is an important strategic asset. But what is economic power? How is it changing? And how can it be measured?

Economic power can be broadly defined as the ability to control or influence the behavior of others through the deliberate and politically motivated use of economic assets. *National economic power* implies that a government is in a position to use, offer, or withhold such assets even when they are in private hands (for example, by mandating trade embargoes or imposing controls on exports to targeted

countries). In fact, the exercise of economic power may well have economic costs because almost by definition it entails interfering with decisions made for economic reasons.

Economic power can also be thought of as the ability to *resist* external control or influence because dependence on external suppliers is sufficiently diverse to preclude vulnerability to outside pressure. The United States, for instance, imports about two-thirds of its oil from foreign sources and is thus vulnerable to oil exporters as a group (although not to any one country). But what is sometimes forgotten is that sellers need markets. If the United States were to significantly reduce its appetite for foreign oil, it would gain relative economic power over these suppliers. Persuading others to establish a "consumer cartel," as some have suggested, would have an even greater effect on the balance of economic power.

An extreme example of the ability to resist external control is economic self-sufficiency. Certain great empires of history, such as imperial China, were almost entirely self-sufficient. But in today's world, the pursuit of economic self-sufficiency results in lower levels of technology and productivity and a greater degree of poverty than would otherwise be the case (North Korea is a perfect example). If market forces are allowed to operate, some countries will be more self-sufficient than others, but none will be completely self-sufficient in all sectors.

National economic power has often been used to punish other governments. Whenever another government behaves in a way that violates international norms, a common U.S. response is a call for economic sanctions. Certain "smart sanctions"—such as denying U.S. visas to family members of dictators and freezing their bank accounts—may have some effect. But efforts to apply trade embargoes and other forms of economic coercion to influence another country's political or military behavior fail more often than not, especially when the targeted regime perceives that the reforms sought by the outside world threaten its survival. Worse still, economic sanctions often end up enriching elites, who have ready access to the black market, and impoverishing everybody else.

Globalization and Economic Power

Throughout much of recorded history, the assets associated with economic power consisted primarily of land, natural resources, and the ability to spend more than one's adversaries spend on weapons and wars. In a global economy, these elements, while still

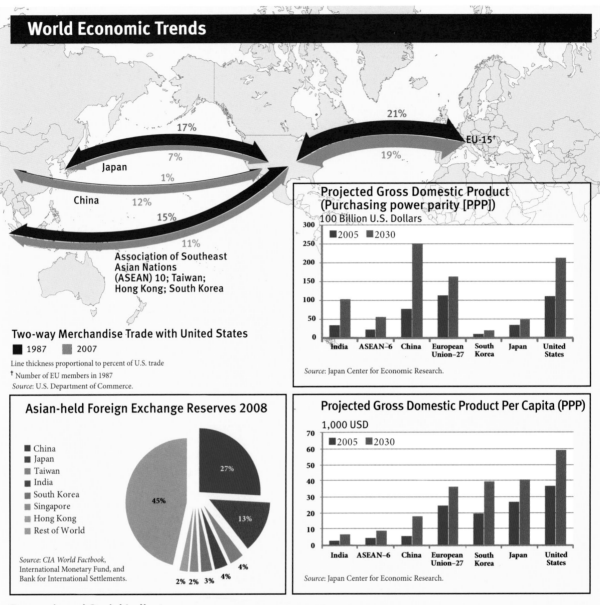

World Economic Trends

17%

21%

Japan

7%

EU-15†

1%

19%

China   12%

15%

11%

Association of Southeast
Asian Nations
(ASEAN) 10; Taiwan;
Hong Kong; South Korea

Two-way Merchandise Trade with United States

■ 1987   ■ 2007

Line thickness proportional to percent of U.S. trade
† Number of EU members in 1987
Source: U.S. Department of Commerce.

Projected Gross Domestic Product (Purchasing power parity [PPP])

100 Billion U.S. Dollars

■ 2005   ■ 2030

India | ASEAN-6 | China | European Union-27 | South Korea | Japan | United States

Source: Japan Center for Economic Research.

Asian-held Foreign Exchange Reserves 2008

■ China
■ Japan
■ Taiwan
■ India
■ South Korea
■ Singapore
■ Hong Kong
■ Rest of World

27%

45%

13%

4%

2% 2% 3% 4%

Source: CIA World Factbook,
International Monetary Fund, and
Bank for International Settlements.

Projected Gross Domestic Product Per Capita (PPP)

1,000 USD

■ 2005   ■ 2030

India | ASEAN-6 | China | European Union-27 | South Korea | Japan | United States

Source: Japan Center for Economic Research.

Economic and Social Indicators

Country	GDP per Capita (PPP)	Broadband (per 100 people)	Cellphones (per 100 people)	Median Age	Population (millions)	Life Expectancy
United States	$45,800	23.9	83.5	36.6	305.7	78.06
Hong Kong	$42,000	26.4	149.2	41.2	7.0	81.77
Canada	$38,600	27.6	61.7	39.1	33.4	80.34
Japan	$33,500	22.1	83.9	43.5	127.7	82.07
Europe / EU	$32,700	14.2	109.6	37.7	494.8	78.70
Taiwan	$30,100	20.9	106.1	35.5	23.0	77.56
South Korea	$25,000	30.5	90.2	35.8	48.2	79.10
Russia	$14,800	2.8	114.6	38.2	141.9	65.87
Mexico	$12,400	4.3	62.5	25.6	106.7	75.84
Brazil	$9,500	0.4	63.1	28.6	188.1	72.70
China	$5,400	5.0	41.2	33.2	1,327.5	72.88
India	$2,600	0.3	20.0	24.8	1,141.1	68.59

Source: Broadband and cellphone data from International Telecommunication Union. All others: *CIA World Factbook*, most recent data as of October 2008.

important, contribute less to overall economic power than what societies and governments can create for themselves: sound financial and macroeconomic policies, an educated and adaptable work force, market-based competition, a supportive infrastructure (including transportation, communications, and energy distribution), and a stable and welcoming investment climate, backed by good governance and predictable rules.

These self-created assets virtually guarantee a competitive niche in the global economy. They fueled the remarkable performance of Japan and the "four tigers" (South Korea, Taiwan, Hong Kong, and Singapore) during the 1970s and 1980s. Similarly, the reforms launched by Deng Xiaoping in the late 1970s transformed China from an autarkic economic backwater to the economic powerhouse that it has become today. Thanks in part to China-centered production networks and widespread pro-market reforms, Asia has experienced robust growth. Its success should not be exaggerated, however; the region suffers from a variety of economic, political, and demographic weaknesses. It is highly dependent on the global economy and remains vulnerable to internal and external shocks.

Just as globalization has altered the content of economic power, so it has limited the sovereignty associated with it. A single nation has only a partial ability to claim autonomous economic power and to use it unilaterally. China, for instance, still depends heavily on markets in North America, Europe, and Japan. This means that China's national economic power cannot be wielded autonomously and at will because doing so would undermine the confidence of foreign investors and thus retard the economic growth that the Chinese leadership needs to maintain its legitimacy. China's alleged "dollar weapon" is not a weapon at all.

Until fairly recently, products were made in one country and sold to customers in another. But thanks to the revolutions in transportation and information technology, most of the world's biggest companies now operate in numerous countries. Although the components of a product may come from multiple sources, that product's label usually records only the point of final assembly and shipment. Interdependence also characterizes the operation of international financial markets. The first decade of the 21st century has witnessed a major shift in financial power from the West to other parts of the world, particularly Asia. Countries in the region hold roughly two-thirds of the world's foreign exchange reserves.

▼ *Continued on p. 13*

Peering into the Abyss: Implications of the Global Financial Crisis

The 2008–2009 global financial crisis may one day be remembered as the greatest setback to the world economy since 1945—and perhaps even the Great Depression. It has already inflicted considerable pain on many countries, thereby jeopardizing their social and political stability as well as their commercial prospects and eroding what was a remarkably widespread consensus in favor of market capitalism. The sudden slump in global growth has also undermined U.S. prestige and influence and will complicate Washington's diplomacy and security relationships for years to come.

Overview
Typical recessions are officially induced. Monetary authorities see that the economy they oversee is overheating and starting to generate inflationary momentum. They react by tightening the flow of credit, which causes corporations and households to curtail their expenditures and hence retards the pace of gross domestic product (GDP) growth. When inflationary pressures abate, the central bank loosens policy and allows private-sector demand to resume its upward trajectory. The present disaster, by contrast, stems from the simultaneous and cataclysmic resolution of two distortions in the global economy. The unique elements of this crisis ensure that its impact will be much deeper and more enduring than that of ordinary recessions.

Of Leverage and Deleverage
The first structural flaw was a gradual rise in leverage—borrowing money to finance extra consumption and investment—that occurred over decades as households, corporations, and governments assumed ever more debt. This phenomenon accelerated in the 1990s and early 2000s, when deregulation and the development of new financial products emboldened financiers to take on more risk and allowed households in the most liberal economies to borrow against the equity in their homes in order to enhance their purchasing power and raise their standards of living. The ratio of debt to global GDP accordingly rose to unprecedented heights. This increase in leverage occurred, furthermore, beyond the ken of regulators who chose to close their eyes to new developments and consequently failed to appreciate the dendritic connections that were forming between the various new markets. So while many observers accurately perceived parts of the problem, few if any understood the combined magnitude of the stresses that were building in the international financial system.

The reversal of that trend through almost universal deleveraging—that is, the attempt by borrowers to reduce their debts to more comfortable levels—is what differentiates the current crisis from normal recessions, and puts it in the same category as the Great Depression and Japan's "lost decade." In this latest instance, the crisis started when the bubble in the American subprime residential market began to deflate in 2006. This damaged the balance sheets of the many American and European banks and non-banks that owned subprime mortgages, and compelled them to seek to strengthen their balance sheets by selling off other assets and calling in loans. In the autumn of 2007, some parts of the credit market therefore froze, causing costs for other corporations and financial institutions to surge even as the stocks, bonds, derivative securities, and real estate in their various portfolios depreciated. Soon, even richly capitalized enterprises with no exposure to dubious American properties were seeing the value of their assets erode, and they felt compelled to join the wave of deleveraging.

As was the case in 1990s Japan, the usual governmental remedies lost their efficacy in the face of such inexorable debt repayment. Lowering short-term interest rates toward zero cannot stimulate credit creation in such an environment because lenders do not want to incur new financial obligations at any price. Nor is bank recapitalization an adequate countermeasure, since banks comprise such a small part of the spectrum of indebted financial and nonfinancial entities—investment banks, credit card companies, consumer financing outfits, automobile manufacturers, and many others—that are withdrawing credit and divesting assets. So conventional efforts must be supplemented with "quantitative easing," the practice whereby monetary authorities stop focusing on short-term interest rates and start trying to reduce long-term rates by purchasing stocks, bonds, currencies, or even real estate and other tangible things. The objective of this "unconventional" policy is to push down credit costs for mortgage holders, corporations that raise their money directly from capital markets, and government. But while this bold approach, in conjunction with aggressive fiscal policy, may cushion the macroeconomic impact of deleveraging and prevent the onset of a depression, it probably cannot precipitate a sustained recovery until firms and households have approached their target debt ratios and are no longer determined to sell off their investments. This adjustment, sadly, probably will not reach completion until at least 2011.

A Precarious Imbalance
The deleveraging process would have been traumatic enough had it not interacted destructively with the extremely rapid resolution of a second structural problem: namely, the global financial imbalances. The consensus view as recently as a year ago was that those imbalances resulted from excessive consumption in the United States and a few other countries. American households, in particular, borrowed and spent so copiously that the country ran an enormous current account deficit—peaking at 6 percent of GDP in 2006—which sucked up the liquidity that the high-saving economies were so much more responsibly and magnanimously providing. An equally valid explanation for the problematic pattern of capital flows, however, works in precisely the opposite direction. In that view, the world suffered from a glut of capital in the 1990s and 2000s, as aging people in China, Japan, and elsewhere saved a disproportionate fraction of their income in anticipation of retirement; and developing economies, frightened by the exchange rate crises of the last decade, insisted on generating current account surpluses and amassing ever larger foreign reserves for use in the event of an emergency. Then came the commodity boom of recent years, in which oil producers and some other exporters of raw materials reaped windfall profits so large that they could not exhaust them domestically and were forced to ship much of their surplus income abroad. But since savings represent foregone consumption and investment, the resulting glut of capital in the international market could easily have caused world demand to fall structurally below supply, and hence caused a protracted recession—and perhaps even deflation. The only way to avoid this outcome would be for someone, somewhere, to absorb the surfeit of capital and expend it on goods and services.

This is where the leverage and current-account stories converge. Over the last two decades, central banks pumped vast amounts of liquidity into the world economy, where financial institutions used new products and ever-increasing leverage to expand the supply of new credit still further. That money poured into the most liberalized national markets, meaning primarily the United States, United Kingdom, Australia, and Spain, where it produced conspicuous bubbles in local real estate markets. The citizens of those countries availed themselves of this appreciation and the availability of home equity loans to finance additional consumption, which pushed their national current accounts into deficit and soaked up the rest of the world's exports of goods and services.

Everyone accepted this situation because it raised standards of living in the deficit countries while permitting the parsimonious countries to achieve rapid GDP growth even as they built up their foreign reserves. The United States and the other spendthrift economies thus served as the engine of global commerce in the 2000s.

A Dismal Outlook

That engine has now stalled. By destroying something approaching $15 trillion in American wealth (a figure that could rise higher), the crisis has impoverished American households and caused them to curtail consumption and to begin ratcheting up their savings rates. This year's current account deficit will accordingly decline by more than two-thirds from the 2006 peak of 6 percent of American GDP. The sharp contraction in demand for foreign exports already has eviscerated international trade, which was increasing at an average annual pace of over 8 percent in 2006 and 2007, but will actually decrease this year and perhaps next year as well. At this point, the data suggest that 2009 will be a dismal year, with GDP contracting by at least 2 percent in the United States, European Union, and United Kingdom—and Japan's economy shrinking by two or three times that figure. Even the speed of China's economic expansion will fall by well over half from its peak early last year of 13 percent. As a result, the global rate of GDP growth this year, measured at prevailing exchange rates, will fall below zero for the first time since World War II.

The immediate recession may end in late 2009 or 2010, but an early return to trend growth will not then ensue. A sustained weakness in international demand is portended by not only the steadily rising savings rate in the United States, but also the much larger loss of one-third of worldwide wealth that has simultaneously occurred. While corporate profitability and savings rates around the globe may fall, newly impoverished households in Japan, China, and the other aging countries will hardly increase their consumption and residential investment. Meanwhile, the 8 to 10 percent shrinkage in Ireland's GDP that seems likely to happen this year cannot help but underscore developing countries' fear of liberalization and their consequent desire to amass more foreign reserves. The global imbalances will doubtless decrease in size, since by definition the sum of all surpluses must fall to the level of the overall deficit registered by the more profligate countries. But this change will occur through an economic slowdown that presumably will last well into the next decade.

Broader Implications

Today's crisis should not prove as disruptive as the Great Depression, but its global scope assuredly entails more international problems than did Japan's 1990s stagnation. Among the most salient of the impending events are changes in the structure of financial markets; more activist and intrusive government; more protectionist sentiment around the world; movement away from American dominance in multilateral forums; and a marginal diminution in global political stability and international cooperation.

Financial Markets. The crisis has virtually wiped out investment banks, whose dependence on short-term funding proved fatal when credit markets seized up in late 2007 and 2008. Even such flagship enterprises as Goldman Sachs have transformed themselves into more conservative institutions with more traditional fundraising and operational schemes. At the same time, the implosion of the worldwide bubble has devastated the private equity and hedge funds, whose portfolios depreciated precipitously and whose sources of capital must inevitably dwindle. All of these industries will revive eventually, albeit in diminished form and with much less leverage, and hence lower profitability. Even the fledgling sovereign wealth funds will lose prominence, both because the trade surpluses

Circuit City store in Richmond, Virginia, advertises going out of business prior to filing bankruptcy

that produced their capital are shrinking, and because they, too, relied on aggressive leverage to improve their returns—leverage that is no longer readily available. The world therefore will emerge from the present crisis with a less dynamic and volatile financial system that also contributes somewhat less to GDP growth.

Governmental Intrusion. To maintain economic stability amid plummeting consumption and investment, the world's governments will expand their spending considerably over the next few years: in the United States and United Kingdom, for instance, official budget deficits could reach 10 percent of GDP in 2009, and will remain voluminous for some time thereafter. Bank recapitalization, meanwhile, will give the authorities big equity stakes in many countries' financial enterprises. Regulators also will become more intrusive in their relations with private enterprise. The virtually universal failure of oversight agencies to monitor and discourage the increase in leverage within and between economies is already perceived as having contributed to the genesis of the crisis. It follows that political pressures will mount for governments to impose new laws and regulations in order to forestall a recurrence of the current disaster. Many of these changes will of course be salubrious, but the adoption of some ill-advised rules seems inevitable. There will, in short, be some degree of retreat from the norms of liberal capitalism.

Protectionism. Before the crisis unfolded, most analysts believed that the global imbalances would eventually resolve in a manner that promoted American exports. As their holdings of U.S. bonds grew ever larger, foreign investors would ultimately lose faith in the United States, sell the dollar, and move their money elsewhere. This sudden loss of confidence would depress the value of that currency, causing imports to decrease and exports to surge. The result would be a contraction in the current account deficit that benefited the American manufacturing sector.

What has now happened, though, is that the adjustment has occurred almost entirely on the import side of the ledger and with no significant benefit to American exporters. By destroying vast sums of American wealth, the crisis has crippled consumption of both domestic and imported goods even as it induced dollar appreciation and thereby disadvantaged manufacturers. The loss of the U.S. increment of international demand, in turn, has harmed the entire world. The volume of global trade was rising at an average of over 8 percent in 2006 and 2007, but decelerated somewhat in 2008 and will actually contract this year

and perhaps next. The upshot is a crushing blow to exporters everywhere, whose employees are understandably prodding their governments to protect what is left of their domestic market. Illustrative of this new mood was the attempt by many Members of Congress, backed by the steel industry, to add "Buy American" language to the infrastructure section of the Obama administration's draft stimulus bill in early February 2009. This protectionist trend will soon become more widespread because of the effect that the rapidly diminishing current account imbalances are having in all but the most isolated of countries.

American Dominance. In the short term, the crisis has reinforced the U.S. position at the heart of the global financial system, for the main beneficiaries of recent events are first the yen and then the dollar. Both currencies are viewed as safe investments that may appreciate as deflationary forces intensify; appreciation in the euro, by contrast, is constrained by rigid labor markets and the relative inflation that they entail. The yen additionally benefits from the reversal of the carry trade, in which foreigners borrowed at cheap rates in Japan and then invested the proceeds at higher rates abroad, while the dollar gains from the general expectation that the United States will be the first big economy to recover. For the time being, therefore, the dollar should retain its place as the preeminent reserve currency.

Yet Washington has certainly lost some of its prestige in the international community. That the crisis originated in U.S. real estate markets and amplified through the most liberal Western markets has, to some extent, discredited the Anglo-American regulatory system. *Dirigisme* of the French variety consequently has reared its head, and Russian and Chinese leaders have used their public pronouncements at the World Economic Forum in Davos and elsewhere to criticize U.S. capitalism. Likewise, calls are multiplying for a stronger developing-country voice in such multilateral organizations as the International Monetary Fund—whose policies in the 1997–1998 Asian financial crisis were widely seen as too austere and which appear largely irrelevant in today's debacle. In this atmosphere of skepticism regarding U.S. values and Western-sponsored organizations, the eminently reasonable and long-overdue process of giving the newly emerging economies more institutional prominence could take on a certain anti-American flavor and thus further vitiate Washington's influence.

Political Stability. While the unfolding crisis will doubtless harm the whole world, its effects on some states will be particularly pronounced. The present trauma may, for instance, be the straw that breaks the back of the Japanese party system, inaugurating a period of even weaker governance in that critically important country. Meanwhile, such commodity producers as Iran, Russia, and Venezuela are already watching their oil revenues collapse and their government budgets deteriorate markedly—with untold implications for their social and political stability as well as their foreign policies. It is true that the erosion of these states' power may advance American interests in the immediate term, but the present regimes could conceivably be replaced by even more minatory leaders. Meanwhile, the governments of such nations as China, where economic development is the main pillar of legitimacy and political stability, may also encounter more difficulty managing their domestic affairs over the next few years. Even Europe will suffer greater political strain as the economic downturn imposes disproportionate pain on the eurozone's poorer members, underscores the divergence of their interests from those of Germany, and raises questions about the utility of the currency union itself.

The 2008–2009 financial crisis will inevitably complicate many forms of international cooperation, and may well threaten stability in some key regions. A number of countries will suffer wrenching economic pain and a degree of social and political unrest, while many more will become more politically self-centered and perhaps even nationalistic. This trend toward introspection will also have economic ramifications as governments, in an understandable attempt to help their peoples in this inclement global environment, become more protectionist and paternalistic. Market-oriented economic reforms will also decelerate in some parts of the world, further stunting opportunities for trade, investment, and improvements in GDP growth. In fact, it would not be surprising to see a range of states react to their straitened conditions by reducing their military budgets, withdrawing from some of their overseas commitments, and scaling back their investments of time and energy in multilateral diplomacy. Overcoming this new reticence and the resentment against the United States engendered by the crisis will be critical to the success of the Obama administration's foreign policy.

▲ *Continued from p. 9*

Well over half of those reserves are denominated in dollars, and much of that is recycled back into the U.S. economy. Foreign governments therefore have a large financial as well as a commercial stake in the health of the American economy.

Security ties help to explain the continuing predominance of the U.S. dollar as a major reserve currency. Other governments' decisions to accumulate dollar reserves and to link the management of their currencies to the movement of the dollar rest in part on the belief that the United States remains the predominant, if not the sole, provider of security. They watched in dismay as the fall in the value of the dollar caused the value of their dollar-denominated assets to tumble. In the future, their mix of reserve currencies may well continue to shift toward the euro and the yen. Nevertheless, security ties with Washington will likely prevent them from tilting too far in this direction.

What governments can do to exercise financial power is extremely limited compared to the burgeoning size, speed, and pace of innovation in private capital markets. In the past, finance more or less followed trade flows, but financial flows now occupy a separate and ever-expanding universe. Private capital resources dwarf anything that governments and international institutions such as the World Bank and the International Monetary Fund (IMF) can provide. Governments with sufficiently good credit ratings prefer to borrow from private sources, thus avoiding the politically onerous conditions often placed on support packages negotiated with the IMF or the World Bank.

Financial flows provide needed liquidity (ready cash) to international markets, but they can be extremely destabilizing. As Asians learned in the financial crisis of 1997–1998, the sudden withdrawal of private capital can topple governments and send economies reeling. The proportion of Indonesians living in absolute poverty, for example, doubled almost overnight, from 13 to 26 percent. The credit crisis of 2008 stemmed from risky behavior on Wall Street, but stock markets around the world plunged.

Measuring Economic Power

The national security implications of economic power transcend the ability to finance a higher defense budget and field expensive weaponry. Signs that a country is on the road to economic power include a strong and stable currency, adequate foreign exchange reserves, inflows of foreign investment, rising productivity, manageable inflation, and a declining level of poverty. Other indicators reflect the degree of urbanization, levels of education, social indicators such as life expectancy, and others. All of these can be measured.

The most common indicator of economic power is the size of a country's *gross domestic product* (GDP), defined as the sum of consumption, gross investment, government spending, and net exports, or alternatively, as the sum of all goods and services produced in a given year. GDP is calculated in two ways: by measuring output in terms of prevailing exchange rates, or by calculating the purchasing power parity of each currency relative to some standard (usually the U.S. dollar). To simplify, one measures how much a nation's output is worth abroad (usually in dollars), and the other measures how much people in one country have to pay for a given basket of goods compared to what people in other countries have to pay.

The rate of GDP growth is also a key measurement. As a general rule, developing countries grow faster than highly industrialized ones, provided that they have reasonably good economic policies and a functioning government in place. Such countries start from a low base; double-digit growth, while impressive, is not uncommon.

GDP per capita is also widely used. Economists have predicted that several decades from now, China's GDP will surpass that of the United States. This achievement certainly signifies China's growing economic power. But because of China's huge population, when this threshold is crossed China's GDP per capita will likely be only about one-quarter to one-third of the U.S. level. Which figure matters more to perceptions of economic power? The answer will vary according to the values and goals of the observer.

Several yardsticks have been developed to measure various other contributors to economic power, such as market-oriented policies and low levels of corruption. The World Economic Forum's *Global Competitiveness Report* measures "the productive potential of nations." Top marks in 2008 went to the United States, Switzerland, Denmark, Sweden, and Singapore, while China came in 30th and India 50th out of 131 countries polled. The International Finance Corporation's 2007–2008 report on the ease or difficulty of doing business abroad names Singapore, New Zealand, and the United States as the top 3 among the 181 economies that were ranked, with Guinea-Bissau, the Central African Republic, and the Democratic Republic of Congo bringing up the rear; China and India are ranked 83d and 120th, respectively. Another index, produced by

the Heritage Foundation and the *Wall Street Journal*, measures "economic freedom": top winners in 2008 are Hong Kong and Singapore, with the United States ranked fifth.

Good governance is a key pillar of durable economic power. Politicians who demand huge bribes and send millions of dollars to foreign bank accounts stunt their countries' development in multiple ways. An index developed by Transparency International measures perceptions of corruption. Based on a scale of 1 to 10 (10 means least corrupt), top prizes in 2008 went to the Nordic countries, New Zealand, and Singapore. The United States trails at 7.3 points, and China and India earned scores of 3.6 and 3.4, respectively.

Concern for the environment has given rise to several indices of "sustainability." The idea here is not only that the environment should be protected, but also that GDP growth will falter if a government depletes its natural resources and sickens its people.

Small countries may get high marks in these various contests, but size matters. It used to be said, for example, that a large population of poor people was a liability. But as markets grow, large numbers of people who are eager for jobs, education, and training are now seen as an asset. From this perspective, China, India, the United States, Russia, and Indonesia all carry economic weight no matter what they do.

Finally, two related elements of economic power are popularity and prestige. If a given country is highly anti-American, resistance to U.S. economic power will be stronger. A trade minister from a country whose press spews forth daily attacks on the United States will have less freedom to make trade "concessions" than a trade minister from a country where the United States is admired and liked.

Prestige has been a longstanding American asset. Thanks to its huge market, skilled manpower, and ever-growing stock of leading-edge technology, the United States is still an economic powerhouse. But huge trade and budget deficits, heavy dependence on imported oil, record-high consumer debt, and rising levels of protectionism have tarnished America's economic reputation and undermined U.S. influence abroad.

American prestige suffered a further blow in 2007, when the U.S. subprime mortgage crisis sent many major U.S. financial institutions to Asian banks for relief. In September 2008, the crisis ballooned. The dramatic financial crash and associated bailouts shook Wall Street to its foundations and seriously undermined America's economic image. Although the shakedown can be seen as a healthy corrective, it has diminished America's near-term economic power.

The Global Redistribution of Economic Power

Economic Power and National Security Strategy

In today's world, economic power has become largely synonymous with successful engagement with the global economy. Paradoxically, the greater such engagement becomes, the more limits governments face when they contemplate using their country's economic resources as a coercive tool to influence the behavior of other governments.

Used constructively, however, U.S. economic power bolsters Washington's influence abroad. But sustaining such influence depends critically on sound policies at home. The risky behavior and lack of oversight that ultimately ignited the financial crash of 2008 damaged America's relative power and influence. Restoring them requires paying heed to the old adage, "Physician, heal thyself."

Sustained economic power is at the root of sustainable military power. Strategic planners need to overcome stovepipe thinking that consigns economic and security issues to different mental boxes. They must understand global economic trends and incorporate them—not as an add-on, but as a core element of their analysis. Drawing on this broader concept of national security, America's elected lead-

ers will be better equipped to make decisions about using economic power. They will also understand that America's economic vitality, flexibility, and spirit of innovation are the true foundation of U.S. economic power, and that adopting the right mix of policies to sustain them is a national security imperative.

The Rise of the Rest

The 1990s were marked in the West by triumphalism. The "end of history" thesis, articulated by Francis Fukuyama, argued that a combination of liberal democracy and market capitalism had become so dominant that, with communism and fascism vanquished, the Western way of governance would no longer face significant challenges. This thesis held that the West, and specifically the United States, had no effective rivals and for the indefinite future could rule at will.

Most noteworthy in the first decade of the new century, however, has been the appearance of nascent power centers outside the traditional Western sphere, especially in Asia. On balance, this is a positive trend, but it poses a long-term challenge to the U.S. global standing.

International Monetary Fund financial committee meets in Washington, 2008

Image Images (Stephen Jaffe)

GLOBAL STRATEGIC ASSESSMENT 2009   **15**

Background

The current dominance of the West has its roots in the Industrial Revolution of the 19th century, and specifically in Britain's newly acquired ability to grow its economy by around 2 percent per year. That capacity spread to much of Europe and the United States on the heels of industry and capital. Britain's capacity for regular growth provided the economic foundation of the British Empire. Broader Western growth at 2 to 4 percent, in contrast with the economic stagnation of most of the Middle Eastern, Asian, African, and Latin American regions, underlay global dominance by the West in the 19th and 20th centuries. The Industrial Revolution was, of course, fueled in large part by the

Executives from Big Three manufacturers and United Auto Workers union testify before Senate Banking Committee on auto industry bailout, December 2008

wealth and raw materials that the colonial powers stripped from those regions. Still, this concatenation of Western dynamism with Confucian and Islamic stagnation was historically unusual. In the pre-Renaissance Middle Ages, the reverse had occurred.

Japan's successful industrialization in the Meiji era created an alternative power center in the first half of the 20th century. Alone among South and East Asian countries (except for Thailand), Japan maintained its independence from Western domination. While Thailand remained poor and underdeveloped, Japan borrowed Western techniques and became a modern power. After its defeat in World War II, the Western consensus was that Japan would remain a backward agricultural economy and a minor power indefinitely. Japan began to grow 10 percent per annum, however,

and quickly became treated as a major power—for instance, as one critical leg in institutions such as the Trilateral Commission and as leader of the Asian Development Bank. Japan's emergence initiated a new era of postwar history.

Gradually, South Korea and Southeast Asia adopted policies that resulted in 7 to 10 percent annual growth, or about three times the rate that underlay Western dominance. In the 1980s, China's new generation of leaders learned to emulate the dynamic growth techniques, and in the 1990s India, responding to the sudden loss of patronage from the Soviet Union, began to emulate China by dismantling the complex and bureaucratic business licensing system called the "license raj," welcoming foreign investment, and abandoning socialist planning. Even Pakistan managed to raise its growth rate. Now nations encompassing about 3 billion people, roughly half the human race, were growing at several times the rate that underlay Western dominance.

Implications

What are the implications of this new era of rapid growth in "the Rest," especially Asia?

First, *the consequences of the "Asian Miracle" have so far been extremely stabilizing.* Rapid growth has stabilized the internal politics of countries from Japan to Indonesia. As late as the mid 1960s, Japan's internal stability seemed to be in doubt. Moreover, Indonesia contained both the world's third largest communist party and more Islamic militants than the rest of the world combined. Following a severe crackdown on the communist party in 1965, the Suharto government launched an era of rapid growth that significantly diminished political unrest in most of the country. Economic growth has also stabilized regional geopolitics. Ideological demagoguery and proselytizing have declined throughout the Asian Miracle region. The ability to achieve national prestige and influence rapidly by focusing on economic growth, together with the costs that modern military technology imposes on any attempt to achieve those goals by military means, has led to a vast shift of strategy from geopolitical aggressiveness and territorial disputes to economic priorities.

This shift has occurred throughout the entire Asian region. South Korea moved from a failed strategy of military priorities under Syngman Rhee to a brilliantly successful economics-focused strategy under Park Chung Hee and his successors, leaving the economy of the once hapless South Korea over 22 times larger than that of its formerly superior northern rival. Other regional successes have included Indonesia, which abandoned territorial claims covering most of Southeast Asia, and China, which has settled 12 of its 14 land border disputes to the satisfaction of the other parties and which has embarked on a remarkably successful campaign of "friendship diplomacy" in order to focus on economic development. India, which has also adopted "friendship diplomacy," shows early signs of making a similar shift, despite greater difficulty. None of the rapidly rising Asian powers has yet shown any inclination to revert to obsolete territorially focused strategies. This shift toward stability appears to belie the argument among prominent realists that rising powers are invariably disruptive. Asia's shift to stability shows that similar economic progress could stabilize other regions.

Second, most of these great economic successes have been based on movement toward integration into the Western-style market economy and acceptance of the basic institutional arrangements that the West created after World War II: relatively open trade and foreign investment, a competitive internal market, market-driven domestic pricing for most things, Western-type law, a substantial degree of freedom of inquiry, considerable freedom to travel and exchange ideas, Western-style capital markets and banking systems, and engagement with the most important Western economic institutions (notably the IMF, the World Bank, and the World Trade Organization [WTO]). None of these movements is irreversible, but the dominant trends in these success stories have included rejection of autarky (Burma vs. Thailand), xenophobia (Sukarno vs. Suharto), the command economy (North Korea vs. South Korea), arbitrary personal rule (Mao Zedong vs. Hu Jintao), and other forms of behavior that are antithetical to the modern market economy.

Third, convergence in economic policy has been accompanied by some elements of convergence in systems of governance. So far, all of the fully successful industrialized Asian economies, from Japan to Indonesia, have adopted variants of democracy from fully competitive democracy (Taiwan, South Korea, Indonesia) to dominant-party democracy or quasi-democracy (Japan, Malaysia, Singapore). Those in earlier stages of development have all had to accept key elements of the Western system of governance, such as some degree of freedom of inquiry, increasing transparency, Western-style legal norms, reduction of arbitrary rule, and the like. But the degree to which China and Vietnam will be compelled to follow the paths of South Korea and Taiwan remains open to question.

Although the eventual degree of convergence remains quite controversial (can China and Russia sustain capitalist autocracies?), the degree that has already been reached constitutes a substantial triumph of Western norms. The argument can be made that, on the one hand, continued success on the part of the rising powers will require a good deal more convergence with Western political norms. On the other hand, the successful emerging economies may also develop competitive advantages that force traditional Western systems to bend some old norms. European-style pension systems and adversarial unionism are potential candidates for Darwinian decline, along with American-style lack of national infrastructure planning and low educational standards.

Finally, the balance of influence in all the major institutions of the post–World War II world—the IMF, World Bank, WTO, United Nations, and others—will have to shift; those institutions must either bend or break.

Crucial Uncertainties

Projecting economic growth is rife with uncertainties. A generation ago, many people believed that Japan's continued success would make it the world's leading economy. There are even greater uncertainties about how economic prowess will translate into geopolitical influence. A few of these uncertainties will be highlighted here.

Most obviously, both the success of the West and the rise of "the Rest" have depended on the steady progress of globalization. So long as globalization advances, the most open economies win, but by the same token, they will be the ones most damaged by a crisis of globalization. Singapore, Hong Kong, South Korea, and Taiwan would be devastated. The trend toward competing geopolitically on the basis of economic priorities rather than military ones would surely be reversed in many places. Raw materials producers would suffer severely from declining demand and radical price collapses. Financial markets would suffer catastrophic reversals, with the United States, Germany, and the United Kingdom probably hurt the most. The reverse sequence is also possible: the financial crisis that exploded in the late summer and early fall of 2008 could deal a serious blow to globalization, depending how quickly recovery proceeds and confidence in the financial system is restored.

A second great source of uncertainty is the impact of demographic differences. Many countries, including most of the rich ones, are graying, meaning that the number of productive workers is declining relative to the number of elderly retirees. In countries such as Japan, where there is resistance to immigration and radical domestic productivity reforms, graying implies relative economic, and probably geopolitical, decline. In the United States, tendencies toward graying have so far been more than offset by immigration and rising productivity.

The greatest contrast in approaches to demographic challenges is between India and China. India is betting on continued population growth to avert graying, but it has so far failed to provide the education and infrastructure to ensure that its large and youthful workforce will have the requisite ability to work competitively and productively. India's risk is that whole population segments and geographic regions will be left out of or prove unable to cope with global competition, and that severe social unrest will ensue. An indigenous Maoist insurgency is already taking advantage of popular disaffection in some of India's poorest states. China, on the other hand, has recently recommitted itself to a "one-child" policy (a partial misnomer) that ensures a rapid decline in the ratio of the working population to the nonworking. China is betting that rapid progress in education, infrastructure, urbanization, and globalization, combined with a relative reduction in environmental stress, will raise productivity and offset the effects of graying. These contrasting strategies comprise one of the most consequential bets in human history and may largely determine Asia's and the world's future economic and geopolitical balance.

A third source of uncertainty centers on energy and food prices. The 2008 upsurge proved a temporary phenomenon, but future spikes are possible once global growth resumes. The effects will vary enormously from country to country. Moreover, the long-term consequences of sustained high prices depend heavily on whether today's primary consumers compete destructively or, for instance, collaborate on clean coal technologies that could shift the economic and geopolitical balance away from the Middle East and toward the United States, China, and India. The world's future economic and political balance hangs on these multiple layers of uncertainty.

Finally, climate change is another great unknown. Desertification, declining fish populations, the melting of the polar ice cap, and other aspects of climate change are to the advantage of some groups economically, while giving the disadvantage to others, and will potentially cause political strife both within and between countries. Governments are already jockeying over competing claims to possible energy resources under the ocean floor, while access to water is an increasingly potential source of conflict across many parts of the world.

Despite these uncertainties, Asia's political evolution and economic success seem almost certain to bring new stability to key areas of the world by persuading its governments to selectively adopt market-oriented economic policies and substantial elements of Western-style political management. Such a transformation will gradually diversify the economic basis of geopolitical influence to an extent that permanently reduces Western dominance of global prestige and power. Paradoxically, the relative decline of the West represents the victory of what Singapore's Kishore Mahbubani calls key Western contributions to the "march to modernity": free markets, science and technology, meritocracy, pragmatism, a culture of peace, the rule of law, and education.

Issues for the New Administration

The rise of new powers and the failure of others to adapt create profound challenges for the new administration. First, continuation of the virtuous circle, whereby globalization creates economic takeoffs, and economic takeoffs in turn stabilize world politics, can only occur if the United States leads. But instead of celebrating their successes, Americans have fallen into a mood that assumes, falsely, that the United States cannot compete successfully against rising economic powers and that the emergence of new powers inevitably brings increased risks of violence and instability. If the current defeatism is not overcome, the United States will suffer disproportionately in any crisis of globalization. Reversing this defeatist mood will require strong, positive political leadership.

More specifically, the executive branch and Congress will have to work together to find new ways to distribute the fruits of globalization. Doing so will require major changes in tax, welfare, and education policies. There will also be a need for a Presidential campaign to educate the public about the changing global economy. The President will have to explain why Americans should welcome, rather than fear, rapid economic growth in China and India. He will need to point out, for example, that surging Asian demand for African energy and raw materials is boosting growth rates in Africa and reducing the risk that jihadism will spread throughout the continent.

Second, economic and geopolitical changes will challenge many assumptions and force many institutional changes. The governance of all major global institutions will have to be revised to accommodate the new powers. Otherwise, these institutions will become ineffective and discredited.

Third, the President will need to find ways to draw more of the Islamic world into the global economy. It was economic globalization that substantially ameliorated radical Islamism in Indonesia, Malaysia, and India.

Finally, there is no possibility that the United States will be able to extend its military dominance to every country in the world. It needs allies more than ever. But the U.S. alliance system will have to adjust to the relative decline of Japan, an important partner that in some ways is failing the test of globalization, and to the emergence of China, which is embracing globalization relatively well and which, despite its serious domestic challenges, will necessarily be a principal U.S. partner on a range of global issues.

Finance and Power

A critical challenge for the new administration will be to reassert American leadership in the international economy and rebuild America's financial health. Economic strength has underpinned the national power and influence of every state in history. Economic strength, in turn, is driven by a strong financial system, capable of raising large amounts of capital and efficiently deploying it. No nation has long maintained its strategic or military dominance after it has ceased to be the world's foremost financial center. If a nation allows its financial system to weaken, it undermines its economic strength, and by extension its ability to project its power and influence into the larger world.[1]

Wars put heavy stress on financial markets and fiscal resources and also put national prestige at risk. Great Britain learned this lesson going into World War II: when combined with economic depression, systemic fiscal and financial frailty, and a decline in the global power of one's currency, war can become a mile marker for hegemonic decline, even in victory.

To some extent, the costs of the conflicts in Iraq and Afghanistan also weigh down U.S. prospects for a quick economic recovery. Although the upfront costs of those wars and related military responses following 9/11 are far less than those of World War I, World War II, or the Vietnam War, they still are considerable, amounting to $859 billion thus far (or roughly 6 percent of GDP).[2] The price tag for rebuilding America's military forces in the wake of this conflict will add greatly to this figure.

In 1992, Clinton administration advisor James Carville said that in his next life, he wanted to come back as the bond market so that he could scare everyone. His comment, although framed as a joke, was a stark admission that finance was already driving U.S. policy and that no major decision could be made without taking the reaction of the bond market into account. When Carville made his comment, global financial assets, including the market for U.S. Government debt, totaled about $42 trillion, and the combined GDP of the world was $21 trillion. If these huge numbers worried Carville in 1992, he would likely be panic-stricken to face a world where financial assets are now over $167 trillion with a global GDP of $48 trillion. These numbers represent not only huge growth in a short time, but also a divergence of the financial market from the underlying real economy.

When Ronald Reagan assumed the Presidency, global GDP and financial assets were relatively equal. By the time Bill Clinton became President, the ratio of financial assets to GDP was 2:1, and by 2008 it was closing in on 4:1. How the United States adjusts to this rapidly changing and little understood world of global finance will determine its strategic influence in the 21st century.

Unfortunately, for at least the past decade, the United States has set itself squarely on the path of wrecking the financial system that has maintained its global prominence for the past seven decades or more. Drastic action is now required in order to change course in time, for once economic rot sets in, it is historically very difficult to reverse. If the United States is to have any chance of doing so, policymakers must first understand how the global financial system works and how much it has changed since Carville first voiced his trepidation about the bond market.

A number of measures reveal that America's leadership position in the international economy has gone through a remarkable period of decline over the last decade. This is best reflected by the value of the dollar, which from 2001 to 2008 depreciated by 56 percent against the euro, 30 percent against the Canadian dollar, 24 percent against the British pound, and 4 percent against the Japanese yen. Remarkably, although the trade-weighted value of the dollar against all currencies declined by over 23 percent in that period—which should have given U.S. exporters a large competitive boost—the U.S. trade deficit nearly doubled before exports began to rise in 2008.

Likewise, the cheapening dollar is becoming progressively less attractive as a store of value for

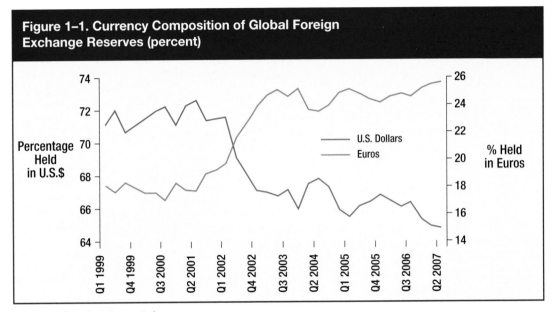

Figure 1–1. Currency Composition of Global Foreign Exchange Reserves (percent)

Source: Independent Strategy Ltd.

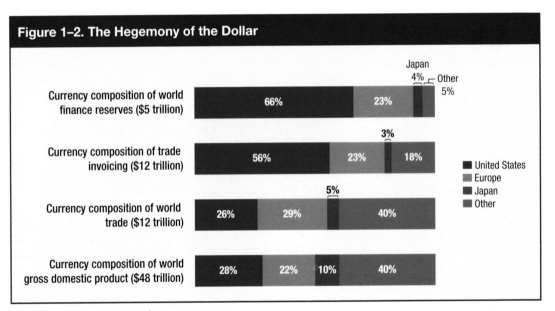

Figure 1–2. The Hegemony of the Dollar

Source: Independent Strategy Ltd.

other central banks. Markets are already adjusting to the fact that a weakening dollar is being increasingly replaced as a reserve currency by a strengthening euro (see figure 1–1). Since the turn of the decade, reserve holdings of the dollar have fallen approximately 8 percent, while euro holdings have risen in rough proportion. Although the dollar remains the chief currency for global trade finance, this leading status has come under stress (see figure 1–2). Presently, the United States accounts for only about a quarter of world trade, while over

half of global commerce is dollar-based. This strategic advantage could dissipate if confidence in its reliability as a storehouse of value slips further. As economist Barry Eichengreen notes, "Never before have we seen the extraordinary situation where the country issuing the international currency is running a current account deficit of 6 percent of GDP. Never before have we seen the reserve currency country so deeply in debt to the rest of the world."[3] By 2008, that ratio had fallen to 5 percent, but unless these trends are more substantially reversed,

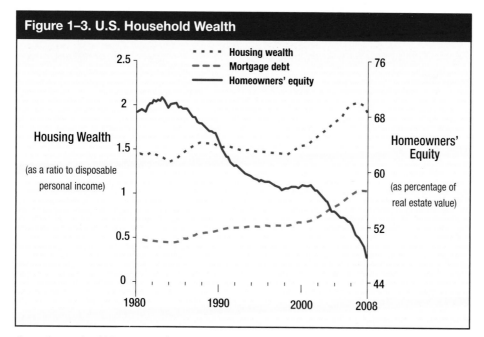

Figure 1–3. U.S. Household Wealth

- - - - Housing wealth
- - - Mortgage debt
—— Homeowners' equity

Source: International Monetary Fund/Haver Analytics.

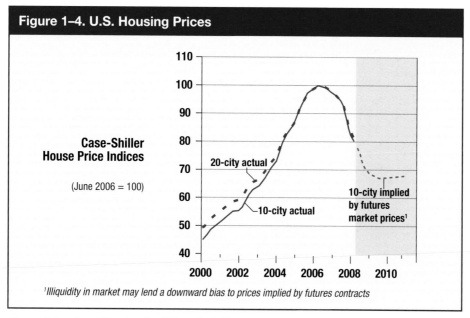

Figure 1–4. U.S. Housing Prices

Case-Shiller
House Price Indices

(June 2006 = 100)

20-city actual

10-city actual

10-city implied
by futures
market prices[1]

[1]*Illiquidity in market may lend a downward bias to prices implied by futures contracts*

Source: International Monetary Fund/Haver Analytics.

the dollar's dominant position in global trade will rapidly erode.

Making matters considerably more challenging, America's financial system and private finances have entered their darkest period in decades. In the last decade, Americans became more financially leveraged than at any time since World War II. Before the housing bubble burst in 2007, consumer and business debt had jumped by nearly 50 percent—twice

the run-up experienced in the 1980s (see figure 1–3). Household mortgage debt accounted for the largest percentage of total private debt by far (see figure 1–4). In turn, the ready availability of subprime and adjustable rate mortgage financing drove a major increase in home ownership and sent property values skyrocketing. Consumers substituted these rising home values for savings, which at both the national and household levels are at 75-year lows. The abil-

Figure 1–5. The U.S. Consumption Binge

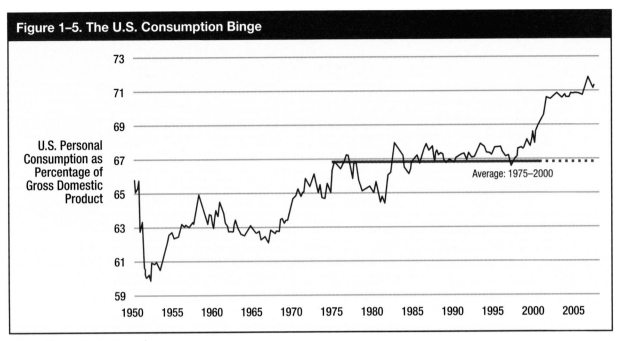

U.S. Personal Consumption as Percentage of Gross Domestic Product

Average: 1975–2000

Source: Morgan Stanley Research.

ity to cash out home equity also drove a personal consumption binge of historical proportions (see figure 1–5). Even as the national savings rate turned negative, consumption accounted for ever greater amounts of GDP (over 71 percent in 2008). Consumption as a percentage of GDP reached 4 percent over its 25-year average, far higher than at any other point in American history.

In June 2007, the housing bubble burst. In the next 15 months, home prices fell by 7 percent nationally—the first sustained decline since the Great Depression. The housing crisis, in turn, triggered a string of bank failures. The first casualties were the large regional bank Indy Mac and the famed investment bank Bear Stearns. Unfortunately, in succeeding months, the Treasury and Federal Reserve still failed to get ahead of a crisis they hardly understood. Two U.S. Government–sanctioned institutions, Freddie Mac and Fannie Mae, saw their capital wiped out and had to be nationalized at a cost to the taxpayer initially estimated at over $200 billion.

Even those steps did not stem the tide. In September 2008, two more large investment banks vanished, and the world's largest insurance company was taken over by the Government. The details of the largest government-led market intervention in history were recently hammered out with Congress. As a result of these negotiations, the U.S. Government initially announced that it would

begin recapitalizing the banking system through a combination of direct capital injections ($250 billion) and purchase of certain financial instruments ($450 billion) currently sitting on banks' books in order to set a price floor under the debt market.

In April 2008, the IMF estimated that the total cost of the U.S. subprime crisis could amount to over $1 trillion, but it is now clear that this was a lowball estimate. Worse still, the subprime blowout is buffeting other financial markets: the Standard & Poor 500 index fell to levels last seen in January 2001.

The U.S. Government can continue to backstop the market without imperiling its fiscal position, as a debt-to-GDP ratio of under 70 percent still gives financial officials some room to maneuver. It will become increasingly difficult, however, for the Government to absorb the costs of the largest financial bailout in history while dealing with slipping tax revenues, slower economic growth, and increasing public sector imbalances. It should be remembered that Japan went from having the best fiscal position in the Group of Seven (G–7) in 1990 to the worst in 2000, because, in response to its own financial and banking crisis, it mismanaged and delayed writeoffs and selloffs. Combined with the long-term funding challenges of entitlement programs such as Social Security and Medicare, the United States may be laying the groundwork for the emergence of an even worse financial crisis.

The implications of America's financial distress for the world economy are considerable, not simply because of the role that U.S. consumers play in driving global growth, but also because the entire global financial system has become leveraged to the U.S. household sector. This situation arose largely as a result of the explosive growth in financial instruments linked or leveraged to U.S. property markets, which were marketed heavily to foreign investors by U.S. investment banks. There were myriad strategies that offered apparently low risks and high returns (but, in hindsight, had high risk and potentially no positive return). These included "structured investment vehicles" that many banks used as a way to earn money off their balance sheet, arbitraging their ability to plow low-cost, short-term capital into longer dated and high-yielding asset-backed securities. These worked until the market for asset-backed securities imploded.

Another supposedly low-risk investment class was in collateralized debt obligations (CDOs), instruments issued by investment banks and backed by U.S. subprime loans, mortgage-backed securities, commercial mortgages, debt financing, and leveraged buyouts. Pools of CDOs were packaged into super-leveraged instruments called "CDO squared" or even "CDO cubed." Incredibly, these CDOs were given AAA ratings by the rating agencies, which implied almost no probability of default, because investors in CDOs had taken out insurance with bond insurers. Ironically, investors would learn, when it was too late to change anything, that these insurers had inadequate capital to cover a default, and that they would head toward bankruptcy themselves. Chasing these Ponzi-like schemes were pension funds, banks, insurance companies, and other supposedly smart institutional investors that bought into the assumption that financial risk could be largely engineered away. Many of these investors came to realize gigantic losses. Investment banks such as Citigroup, Bear Stearns, and Merrill Lynch that were involved in selling CDOs also got clobbered. With the market for selling CDOs gone, Merrill Lynch decided in July 2008 to liquidate its mammoth unsold inventory of CDOs at 20 cents on the dollar.

The financial crisis of 2008 revealed that perhaps the fastest growing segment in the rapidly expanding derivatives universe was also its most dangerous: credit default swaps. In simple terms, they are a type of insurance policy contracted between two parties, whereby one guarantees a payment to the other in the event of a default, in exchange for an insurance

premium paid along the way. The Bank for International Settlements estimated that, as of the end of 2007, there was over $57.8 trillion in credit default swaps outstanding—a fourfold increase over the level at the end of December 2005.[4] Large financial firms such as the now-defunct Lehman Brothers and Bear Stearns issued massive amounts of these swaps to cover their myriad risks. Among the biggest buyers of these default swaps were the banks and insurance companies, which also had snapped up the aforementioned CDOs. The net result was that when Lehman and Bear collapsed, already beleaguered banks and insurers were left holding the bag, with an expected payout on the failure of Lehman's credit default swaps alone of over $365 billion.[5]

Today, the notional value of the derivatives market adds up to 976 percent of world GDP—a nearly tenfold increase since 1990.[6] In Berkshire Hathaway's annual report to shareholders in 2002, Warren Buffett pointedly described derivatives as "financial weapons of mass destruction." Buffett further commented:

Unless derivatives contracts are collateralized or guaranteed, their ultimate value also depends on the creditworthiness of the counterparties to them. In the meantime, though, before a contract is settled, the counterparties record profits and losses—often huge in amount—in their current earnings statements without so much as a penny changing hands. The range of derivatives contracts is limited only by the imagination of man (or sometimes, so it seems, madmen).[7]

As a result of the derivatives boom, financial distress in the U.S. household and banking sectors has been magnified globally, adding to the stresses facing European and Asian economies. The potential unwinding of the globalization of financial leverage threatens the success of economic globalization itself.

At risk is the almost-century-long U.S. primacy as the world's foremost financial power. If that primacy declines, economic growth will slow as capital becomes more costly and harder to obtain. Furthermore, as Cicero pointed out 2,000 years ago, the key to success in war is "endless streams of money." That remains as true today as it was then. If raising capital in vast amounts becomes harder, America's ability to finance the military forces it requires in the future will be more difficult.

The United States has always snapped back following times of economic doubt and apparent decline. The stagflation and stagnation of the 1970s produced in the wake of the Vietnam War, the 1973 oil shock, and the decisive break with the fixed exchange rate system were followed by the economic boom of the 1980s and victory in the Cold War. There is no reason to believe that recovery should be any different in the coming decade. But understanding the scope of the problems—and devising and implementing a strategy to solve them—will be imperative.

Noted economic historian Charles Kindleberger observed that nations that have turned back negative economic tides and emerged stronger from moments of seeming decline are those that possess flexibility and adaptability, rather than passivity and rigidity.[8] Americans are known for being flexible and adaptive. Unfortunately, however, the scale and scope of America's global economic and financial challenges are considerable and they will defy any easy or rapid solution.

Brave New World

What has happened to the American economy?

As of late 2008, four of America's great money center banks had ceased to exist, the entire banking system was going hat in hand to emerging economies to beg for multibillion-dollar bailouts, inflation was rising, housing prices had collapsed, thousands of people were losing their homes, and the U.S. Government had launched the largest market intervention in history. Meanwhile, the price of gasoline soared to over $4 a gallon before falling back to more normal levels.

Eventually, U.S. policymakers will hit upon on the right measures to stabilize the system, and markets will once again demonstrate their remarkable resilience. But a major lesson of the credit crisis is that the monetary and financial levers that policymakers have used for the past generation were rather ineffectual and in some case downright harmful. More importantly, these levers will become ever more obsolete with time, leaving the United States (along with the rest of the global economy) at risk of further financial shocks that will undermine our economic strength. And as goes the U.S. economy, so goes U.S. military strength and strategic influence.

To maintain the United States as the preeminent economic and financial power in the world (and by extension, a global military power), policymakers must come to grips with a financial system unlike anything in their prior experience. If they fail to grasp how financial markets have changed, it will be impossible for them to emplace the regulatory and oversight structure that will allow the financial

system and the economy to adapt to future crises, which are sure to arise as the pace of innovation and change accelerates.

For the past two decades, the world of finance has mutated to the point that an investment banker from 1980 would not recognize it. Innovation has taken place at such a dizzying pace that very few outside of the world's money center institutions understand it at all. This is a remarkably dangerous situation. Policymakers, reeling from the public reaction to the 2007–2008 credit crisis, are promising increased regulation of an industry they do not even comprehend. Too many of them are apparently formulating policy based on the global financial system enshrined in the 1944 Bretton Woods agreements, which fixed exchange rates, established a new gold standard, and created the IMF and World Bank. Globalized markets killed off that orderly world some time ago.

Unfortunately, however, the relics of that era, in the form of the IMF and World Bank, still exist, and their global employees are constantly casting widely for a new mission. Detailing what is wrong with these two entities would fill many books. Suffice it to say that organizations designed to manage global finance and postwar reconstruction while the guns of World War II still pounded are finding it impossible to find relevance today. When they were created, the dollar was king, and a billion dollars was serious money even for Congress. Today, the dollar is in competition with the yuan, the yen, and the euro, in markets that move literally at the speed of light.

When the Bretton Woods agreements were signed, the widespread assumption was that international financial flows would roughly track trade and investment flows, as they had for centuries. International trade on the eve of the financial crisis was about $3.5 trillion a year, but currency flows are $2 trillion a *day*.

Just as financial markets have been diverging from the underlying economy over recent years, international currency movements have decoupled from trade and investment for the first time in history. This development has implications that rival the challenges faced by the Bretton Woods representatives in 1944. Yet hardly any strategists are studying the implications of these changes, an oversight that leaves a giant blind spot in U.S. strategic planning.

There are sure to be new regulations on the U.S. financial system in the wake of the 2007–2008 credit crisis. Before new rules are enacted, someone must step back and ask what effects they will have on a 24-hour trading book, which moves around the world as various markets open and close. Many problems currently plaguing the U.S. financial system, such as capital-draining "structured investment vehicles," are a result of earlier ill-considered regulations. In effect, any new U.S. regulatory regime that tries to constrain traders or place barriers in front of market liquidity can and will be circumvented by traders, who will just move their operations (or simply their domicile) into countries whose regulatory systems are more accommodating. Such "regulatory arbitrage" will further weaken U.S. dominance of the global financial system.

Structural Changes

The last two decades have witnessed a major structural shift in the global economy and a realignment of the relative influence of various countries. Nations that had spent decades on the periphery of the global economic and trading system, China in particular but also several others, are now critical production centers. Although several serious scandals have revealed that its product safety regulations are poorly enforced, China remains highly competitive.

In the years and months leading to the financial meltdown of 2008, a number of new players began to adopt asset allocation programs that shifted capital flows away from traditional avenues. (That is, there was less reliance on safe U.S. Government debt and a greater willingness to seek higher returns through investing in riskier assets.) Some of these new players, such as pension funds and hedge funds, have been part of the financial landscape for a while, but they now make up a much larger and more aggressive share of the market than in the past. Joining this trend toward accepting greater risk were the major banks, which were trading on their own account and employing significant leverage to do it, thus making themselves the functional equivalents of hedge funds.

Moreover, dozens of countries that are typically thought of as perennial debtor nations have now accumulated significant reserves of wealth. Through "sovereign wealth funds," the governments of these countries began to deploy their cash reserves over a range of asset classes and away from U.S. Government debt. In addition, the new players made greater use of highly leveraged and increasingly exotic financial instruments (derivatives), which have deeply altered the character and risk profile of the market in ways not sufficiently understood by policymakers or, in many cases, by the market participants themselves.

Implications

What has gone practically unnoticed in the ongoing credit crisis is the international role reversal that is occurring. As the developed world searches for solutions to the crisis, it is the emerging world that is riding to the economic rescue. In an unprecedented development, capital is flowing out of emerging nations and into the developed world, where it is being used to recapitalize the rich nations' foundering banking systems. In recent months, estimates place emerging nations' sovereign wealth fund investments in rich world banks at over $70 billion. It is worth remembering that it was only just over a decade ago that the financial collapse in Mexico, East Asia, and Russia prompted a call for the rich countries of the world to deploy tens of billions of dollars to contain those multiple crises.

Today, many of these same nations have used a decade of unprecedented growth, thanks in part to soaring oil prices, to build up substantial financial reserves that will have several major effects. They have partly immunized themselves against current

Emma Maersk, owned by A.P. Moller-Maersk Group, is among world's largest container ships

and future financial crises because these reserves give them the means to defend their currency and cushion against any future period of adaptation. An almost unnoticed effect of this development is that the IMF, as it is currently structured, has lost its original raison d'être.[9] Emerging nations will no longer need IMF-coordinated bailouts that come with politically and often socially ruinous conditions attached.

Newly accumulated reserves, coupled with the increasing wealth of many persons in emerging nations (the middle classes of both China and India now exceed the entire U.S. population), will increase the amount of domestic consumption in these countries. This means that many of these nations will start shifting production away from exports and toward domestic consumers. This, in turn, will relieve pressure on politicians to implement new protectionist policies and will help reduce the U.S. current account deficit without having to further erode the dollar's value. Moreover, these nations will begin to break free of their reliance on the United States as their ultimate market as their future growth becomes increasingly driven by internal rather than external demand.

As these accumulated reserves exceed what emerging nations consider prudent cushions against exogenous shocks, they will be deployed through sovereign wealth funds into a variety of asset classes in pursuit of higher returns. This activity presents a new challenge to national security planners. Although such funds in and of themselves are not a *threat* in the classic definition of the term, they do introduce some major concerns if they are used for strategic advantage.

One concern is that sovereign wealth funds will not only seek superior returns, but also will be used to purchase strategic assets that will give the nations controlling these funds access to classified information and critical military technology, diplomatic power over weaker nations, and enhanced access to scarce resources. Moreover, there is a risk that some nations will use their intelligence services to help bolster the returns of the sovereign wealth funds. For instance, if Russia were again to use its control of gas pipelines to limit supplies to Ukraine or threaten cutoffs to Europe, an official might first tip off Russian fund mangers so that they can position themselves for the impact that such a move would have on the energy market. The potential interaction among intelligence services, sovereign wealth funds, and national banks strongly suggests that the United States should redouble its efforts to surveil global financial movements.[10]

What Must Be Done

The United States needs to reorder its policies and diplomatic initiatives to adapt to a world where economic power is shifting from the West to "the Rest," particularly Asia. This new and rapidly changing world will eventually require significant adjustments to the system that emerged as a result of the 1944 Bretton Woods Agreements:

■ The United States must recognize that the economic power of many G–7 members has been eclipsed by several emerging nations who will have considerable impact on the future global economy. Either the G–7 has to be reorganized, or the United States must develop new structures that involve these new financial and economic powers as full members.

■ The Federal Reserve has to complete a full analysis of the global financial system and get legislative approval for the use of new policy levers that are more finely tuned than current instruments and that will be more effective in the new environment. Moreover, the Federal Reserve and U.S. Treasury need to increase levels of international cooperation to ensure a more coordinated approach to future financial imbalances.

■ The IMF and World Bank find themselves in an environment in which emerging nations do not need their services. The IMF is being made obsolete by emerging nations whose reserves are such that they can forego IMF funding and its stringent conditionality clauses. As for the World Bank, the amount of investment funds available to emerging nations through the capital markets dwarfs anything it can bring to the table. The best future for these institutions would likely be to have them reestablish themselves as facilitators of multilateral restructuring endeavors. In effect, they would use their technical expertise and international reputation to provide support and political cover for policymakers to undertake required structural adjustments that might otherwise be politically difficult to enact without the backing of a multilateral institution.

■ The financial plumbing (back room operations) and risk management processes of all major players in the global financial system need to be upgraded and made more transparent through appropriate regulation.

■ Concerns over the use of sovereign wealth funds must be addressed before they kick off a destructive round of financial protectionism and/or increased regulation aimed at limiting global capital flows. Either one of these outcomes would unleash a dangerous reversal of the globalization process, which has raised the living standards of several billion people. As a starting point, managers of these funds need to sign off on an internationally negotiated code of conduct and become more transparent in their activities.

Prospects

Such radical changes in the U.S. and global financial systems will be hard, but they will inevitably be made. The question is whether they will be accomplished in an orderly manner or forced on policymakers in the face of another crisis. As matters stand now, policymakers are trying to deal with the "brave new world" of finance without any real understanding of how the old world is evolving. Even as the 2008 financial crisis is forcing adjustments on its participants, policymakers must undertake a thorough analysis of what the crisis signified, how the financial system is changing, and where it is likely to go.

Once that analysis is complete, strategists can begin to analyze and understand how the developing financial environment affects national security now and in the future. Only then will policymakers be able to get ahead of these changes and avoid reacting to them in ways that further damage America's financial health.

Economic Security

Challenges

Many states are not capable of providing conditions in which the bulk of their citizens can achieve an adequate degree of economic security. Economic insecurity implies poverty so pervasive and persistent that it breeds a wide array of social and personal ills: child malnutrition, low life expectancy, limited education, and little potential for a better future. Societies burdened by economic insecurity are more likely than others to experience civil war and cross-border conflict.

Although there are pockets of such insecurity in most societies, in approximately 60 countries a large majority of people are stuck in these conditions. Their societies are too poor for the redistribution of assets to solve the problem. And they remain stuck because, for the past 40 years, per capita incomes have been practically stagnant. The combined population of these 60 countries is around 1 billion people, sometimes referred to as "the bottom billion." Seventy percent of them live in sub-Saharan Africa. The extent of global poverty is, of course, much wider than just the bottom billion; for example, there are still many poor people living in China and India. There is a strong case, however, for focusing the efforts of the developed world on the bottom billion.

First, a key difference between being poor in China and being poor in Chad is whether a credible basis for hope exists. A poor family in China has reason to hope that its children will grow up in a society that is economically transformed. In contrast, based on the past 40 years' experience, a poor family in Chad does not have good reason for such hope. The critical task is to provide credible hope to such people.

Second, many countries inevitably experience adverse shocks that inflict harm on economically insecure people, who then require assistance from the state. In the societies of the bottom billion, however, the state itself is impoverished and usu-

ally ineffective. Hence, these countries are prone to humanitarian crises that can only be addressed by rapid international intervention. Increasingly, thanks to global media coverage, the citizens of developed countries expect their governments to act, but budgetary and logistical restraints sometimes stymie rapid action. The military is the main governmental organization capable of rapid, large-scale delivery of relief supplies, but recipient governments sometimes resist the entry of foreign military forces, even for humanitarian purposes. In 2008, for example, the Burmese government refused to permit Western military ships and aircraft to deliver relief supplies to victims of a devastating cyclone.

Third, because most citizens of the poorest nations are economically insecure, the state becomes politically insecure. For example, we now know that in years of poor rainfall, the risk of a civil war increases. This may be because rebel organizations find it easier to recruit when conditions get desperate. Once civil wars start, they tend to continue for about a decade, further damaging the economy and thus compounding the problem of insecurity. Where rebellion is easy to ignite, hostile neighboring states tend to use it as a form of clandestine international warfare. For example, for many years Uganda and Sudan engaged in low-level international warfare by supporting each other's rebel groups.

In some cases, the weak state becomes a tempting target for neighbors, as was the case with the Democratic Republic of Congo (formerly Zaire). Taking advantage of Zaire's vicious civil war between the postcolonial dictatorship and a popular insurgency, neighbors Rwanda and Uganda contributed forces that first helped topple the regime and then went after its successor. Several other countries threw their weight in as well, and the fighting spread across the region, devastating already weak societies.

Until the end of the Cold War, the international community was not in a position to intervene to end such wars, and as a result the rate at which they started exceeded the rate at which they stopped. By the end of the 1990s, the international community had succeeded in bringing some pressure to bear to resolve these conflicts, and by the turn of the millennium many were settled.

Unfortunately, postconflict situations are typically even more fragile than the preconflict societies of the bottom billion. In the past, 40 percent of all postconflict situations have reverted to conflict within a decade. The typical postconflict society is critically impoverished, and its state institutions are ineffective.

Afghanistan is one example. There are currently over 100,000 United Nations (UN) peacekeeping troops serving in postconflict situations around the world. Hence, the insecurity of the 60 or so countries housing the bottom billion poses an important security challenge for developed countries.

The fourth, and most basic, reason for focusing on the countries of the bottom billion is that by better understanding them, the developed world will be better able to do something about them. In the past, because these countries have been individually marginal, they have been neglected as a group.

Reasons for Failure to Develop

Most developing countries have done just that: develop. There is no one overarching explanation of why some 60 nations of the world have stagnated.

One problem is the lack of accountability in government. Even where elections are held, the elites who run in them have learned how to game them with a mixture of bribery, ballot fraud, and intimidation, as happened in Kenya and Zimbabwe in 2008. Because governments have avoided being accountable, they are not forced to provide effective economic policies.

The problem of unaccountable government is particularly severe in countries with large revenues from exports of valuable natural resources. Potentially, this is an opportunity for transformation, but because the revenues accrue to the government, harnessing the opportunity for development depends on good governance. To date, the possession of valuable resources has usually proved to be a curse. Nigeria, a major oil exporter, is probably the most obvious example: by any reasonable counterfactual, its citizens are now poorer than they would have been if oil had not been discovered there 40 years ago. The key problem is that valuable resources controlled by the government become a honeypot contested by different groups, usually organized along ethnic lines. Not needing broad-based taxation, the state never provokes citizen scrutiny; in many cases, mechanisms for such scrutiny do not exist. Rival elites jockey for power, divorced from the interests and concerns of ordinary citizens.

At a deeper level, the problem is that these countries are structurally insecure. On the one hand, many African countries are too large to be unified by a sense of nationhood, in that their citizens identify more strongly with subnational ethnic and religious groupings than with the nation. This situation is a result of the artificial borders imposed by the European colonial powers, without regard to historical tribal and ethnic boundaries, during the land grabs of the

18th and 19th centuries; Kenya is an example. On the other hand, the countries of the bottom billion are too small to be effective states. They have tiny, typically agrarian and extractive economies—often smaller than a medium-sized American city—and so cannot reap economies of scale in the provision of key public goods such as military security.

A further problem is geography. Many of the poorest countries are landlocked, which makes it difficult for them to integrate into the global economy. Their access to major roads and ports may depend on hostile neighbors; for example, Ethiopia cannot use the closest port because it lies in Eritrea, which is a bitter enemy. Many of them suffer from widespread disease (notably malaria and AIDS), which drains manpower and resources and thus inflicts high economic costs.

Issues Deserving Early Attention

The international community has four policy instruments for dealing with these problems: foreign aid (publicly funded development assistance); trade policy; military security; and rules and codes of governance. To date it has relied excessively upon foreign aid relative to the other three. Multilateral leadership in the provision of foreign aid has shifted from the United States to Europe and Japan: for example, Britain now provides the most money for the World Bank's International Development Association, which is the main multilateral source of grants and soft loans for the world's poorest countries.

Trade policy has never been effectively focused on the poorest countries; the WTO is basically a bargaining forum in which the countries of the bottom billion have little influence and the developed countries have other priorities than assisting them. The international provision of military security has lurched between excessive caution, as in Rwanda, and military intervention, as in Somalia and Haiti. The international provision of rules and norms of governance has largely bypassed the countries of the bottom billion: the ruling elites have preferred to protect their power by hiding behind national sovereignty, and the international community has not assigned a high priority to overcoming economic security.

Although there is plenty of scope for using all four policy instruments more effectively, four issues seem ripe for action.

Improving the Conduct of Elections. Three recent African elections (Nigeria in 2007 and Kenya and Zimbabwe in 2008) have all been fiascos. Kenya and Zimbabwe were such high-profile disasters that they provoked international outrage and eventual intervention by members of the African Union. The African Union alone is unlikely to resolve the problems entirely, however, because it harbors too many vested interests in preserving business as usual. While international action in support of democratic institutions is necessary, the United Nations is unlikely to be a viable route because China routinely opposes any action that it believes infringes on national sovereignty; in the case of Zimbabwe, for example, Beijing blocked proposed UN Security Council decisions aimed at putting pressure on the Robert Mugabe government to honor the country's election laws.

The international community has probably oversold elections relative to other important attributes of good governance, such as the rule of law and financial transparency. Because elections are such high-profile events, they have come to be seen as the defining feature of good governance. It would be helpful to shift the prestige away from elections per se, to elections that are reliably judged to meet international standards.

On this issue, it should be feasible to get Europe, Japan, and the large emerging market democracies such as India and Brazil to be supportive. A possible way forward is to encourage a "democracy club," not in the form of a military alliance such as the North

Atlantic Treaty Organization, but rather as a group committed to enforcing democratic standards and norms among its own members. Countries that claimed to be democracies could join, thus committing themselves to certain minimum standards. Their electoral performance would then be monitored by election supervisors.

The principle of supervised elections is already well established, but at present there is no coordinated assessment. (The European Union conducts an official assessment, but no larger group does so.) Nor is an adverse assessment linked to any consequences, such as expulsion from a group; the worst that an offending government can expect is international condemnation. Whether such an approach can work would depend in part on whether governments other than established democracies chose to sign up to the commitments. It can be assumed that some would. For example, President Mwai Kibaki of Kenya would probably have committed himself to signing when he was running for office in 2002 in order to reassure voters of his willingness to abide by democratic norms.

However, elections, even if well conducted, are not enough to guarantee real democracy; it is important to supplement them with checks and balances on government power. In some societies, elections can

Workers process piles of carrots in China as wholesale market price hit lowest point in 15 years

be polarizing because leaders have yet to build a sense of common nationhood. Nevertheless, improving the conduct of elections is both highly topical and supportive of many other reforms, and so it is a good place to start the long process of making democracy work.

Securing Postconflict Societies. Postconflict societies are fragile. Currently, there are a lot of them, so developed countries should do what they can to avoid a repeat of past disasters. For example, southern Sudan may well head back into war.

Three types of actor determine whether postconflict situations result in a durable peace: providers of peacekeeping troops, providers of postconflict aid, and postconflict governments. The actions of these three are mutually interdependent. Prolonged peacekeeping is needed to create an environment in which development assistance can work. Peacekeeping is effective in radically reducing the risks of further conflict, but to date it has been conducted in a hit-and-miss manner. Postconflict aid for reconstruction can foster the economic growth that provides a workable exit strategy for peacekeepers. Even where postconflict aid is effective, however, often it is allowed to taper off too soon.

Decent governance, including the reform of bad economic policies imposed during wartime, is also necessary for rapid recovery. All too often, postconflict governance is weak, corrupt, or more dedicated to revenge and spoils-taking than rebuilding a damaged nation. The Peace-Building Commission of the United Nations, established in 2005, provides a possible forum in which these mutual responsibilities could be recognized. It established a form of compact analogous to the UN Global Compact founded by Secretary-General Kofi Annan in 2000, which links corporate behavior to 10 universally accepted principles of human rights, labor standards, environmental protection, and anticorruption measures. Together with some minimum standards and norms, the mutual recognition of responsibilities would provide a mechanism to improve the management of postconflict situations.

Guiding the Commodity Booms. The commodity booms taking place in some African countries present an opportunity to alleviate economic insecurity. Angola alone is getting more money in oil revenue than the entire stock of foreign aid flowing to the 60 or so poorest countries. The recent fall in prices shows that the large pulse of income was mainly temporary, and so it is vital to save and invest it rather than simply increasing consumption in an unsustainable way. Much of the recent revenues have yet to be

spent and so the decision as to how to use the revenue will be taken in the coming months. It is vital that the history of mismanagement not be repeated. Brave people in these societies are struggling for change and the key decisions are being taken now.

The developed democracies can help the forces pressing for reform by establishing voluntary international standards and codes that can be used to guide economic decisions. One such code, the 2002 Extractive Industries Transparency Initiative, has already prompted 23 governments to pledge adherence to a standard of revenue reporting. There is an urgent need to build on this success with new codes that focus on how revenues are used.

Harnessing Social Enterprise for the Delivery of Basic Services. In recent years, there has been a huge growth in social enterprise, especially in the United States. This kind of initiative has the potential to deliver basic social services in those environments where government provision has broken down beyond immediate repair, as in Liberia. Currently, there is no organizational model that connects publicly funded development assistance with social enterprise on a national scale, in a way that could transform the provision of basic services in such societies. Such aid tends either to remain channeled through traditional agencies of government or to be provided piecemeal and in an ad hoc fashion to particular initiatives. There is an urgent need to develop a 21st-century model of social funding acceptable to and inclusive of government. It should create genuine, measurable competition among different social entrepreneurs seeking funds. And it should be capable of pooling aid inflows from public *and* private donors and directing them on a sustainable basis to the purchase of services for ordinary citizens in the most difficult environments.

The developed world has a range of policies with which to tackle the problems of the bottom billion, yet to date they have not been coordinated. U.S. operations have often demonstrated how detached military policy was from the development instruments needed to rebuild a poor country's postconflict infrastructure. The same could be said of the other three instruments: foreign aid, trade, and codes of governance. Sometimes the United States has overrelied on the military, sometimes on aid. It has tended consistently to underplay trade and governance codes.

Coordinating all these instruments would not only promote poverty relief, but also reduce the likelihood of further civil wars and cross-border conflict. Usually, difficult situations require a package of policies. Only heads of state can bring about such a profound change in political and bureaucratic culture. A shared commitment to launch such a coordinated initiative has become increasingly urgent.

Protectionism

The promotion of protectionism in the U.S. Congress and in the public at large has reached the point where it seriously threatens America's strategic interests as well as its economic leadership. An immediate challenge facing the U.S. administration is to channel the political pressures fueling protectionism away from broadside attacks on trade expansion and other forms of international economic engagement and toward the enactment of meaningful measures to help U.S. workers and companies adjust to rapid globalization.

Why Protectionism Harms U.S. National Security

Protectionism is usually seen as a trade issue best left to trade negotiators and their counterpart committees on Capitol Hill. But protectionism should also be seen as a national security issue because it endangers U.S. domestic and global security interests in a variety of ways:

■ Protectionism undermines the image of the United States as a global leader. It belies the generosity, openness, and optimism once associated with postwar American leadership.

■ Protectionism damages U.S. relations with allies and friends. Since the United States preaches free trade and aggressively pursues the opening of markets for its own products and services, protectionism fuels charges of hypocrisy and double standards.

■ Protectionism deprives poor people in developing countries of the chance to compete. It stunts job creation in those countries, thus undermining the stability of governments still struggling to consolidate legitimacy. The prospect of long-term unemployment makes it more likely that frustrated young people, especially men, will take to the streets or join radical movements.

■ Protectionism gives other governments an excuse to delay opening their markets and provokes retaliation against U.S. exports, thus stifling U.S. job growth in the most competitive sectors of the economy. By shielding the weakest companies within a given sector, protectionism effectively punishes more competitive ones. By reducing competitive pressure, it slows the drive to improve productivity and develop more advanced technology.

■ Protectionism sets a poor example for governments striving to make a transition away from socialism and find a niche in the global economy. These governments face stiff resistance from vested interests, who seize on protectionism elsewhere in the world to shield themselves from competition.

■ Protectionism limits choices that would otherwise enhance U.S. military capability. "Buy American" and other protectionist laws and regulations impose costly procurement requirements on the U.S. Armed Forces and preclude purchase of the best products, technologies, and services.

■ Protectionism contributes to inflation and harms the poor because it makes imports more expensive and thus raises the price of basic items such as clothing and shoes.

■ Export protectionism (restricting certain exports on national security or other grounds) burdens U.S. high-tech companies, creates political tensions with other governments, and hampers military-to-military cooperation.

■ Investment protectionism discourages the inflow of foreign capital into key sectors and inspires or reinforces corresponding barriers to U.S. investment abroad.

■ Incoming-visitor protectionism (the denial of visas to would-be visitors and students) creates much ill will and reinforces the widespread view that Washington overreacted to 9/11.

Declining Political Support

Examples of protectionism in 2008–2009 include the insertion of "Buy American" language in President Obama's stimulus bill; congressional resistance to a major free trade agreement with South Korea; calls to postpone or reopen other free trade agreements negotiated in good faith, including the North American Free Trade Agreement (NAFTA), signed in 1993; efforts to halt or retard the offshoring of U.S. jobs by threatening to impose tax penalties on offending U.S. companies; opposition to certain incoming foreign investment bids; and alarm over the perceived threat posed by sovereign wealth funds (funds held by governments or government-affiliated entities). The combination of agricultural protectionism at home and aggressive market-opening demands on poor countries partially contributed to the 2008 collapse of the ongoing Doha Round of multilateral trade negotiations under the auspices of the WTO.

More damaging in the long run, perhaps, is that Congress has refused to renew the procedure, formerly known as "fast track" and now called Trade

Promotion Authority, which effectively permits the President to negotiate new trade agreements. In 2008, a dispute between Congress and the White House over the proposed U.S.-Colombia free trade agreement became so hostile that the White House submitted the agreement without the usual consultation, prompting the leadership of the House of Representatives to revoke Trade Promotion Authority's time-honored procedural rules.

Not all trade restrictions should be labeled protectionist. WTO rules permit the temporary imposition of import restrictions, known as safeguards, to cope with sudden import surges. Certain other agreements permit the use of trade limits in response to subsidies, violations of intellectual property, and other trade-distorting measures. Governments can invoke national security to block certain imports or to restrict foreign investments in militarily critical industries. New issues are arising that may justify expanding the scope of existing trade-limiting measures, such as disease control and climate change. Legislation calling for steep duties on imports from China to offset its determination to restrain the pace of currency appreciation is in a category by itself; some economists with impeccable free trade credentials support congressional action to impose a corresponding tariff on Chinese imports.

But leaving aside these exceptions, U.S. political support for engagement with the global economy in general has eroded so badly in the last 15 years or so that Congress has bottled up new agreements or passed them by a handful of votes after fierce and divisive debate. This hostility to deeper international economic engagement has spilled over into investment and finance.[11] Meanwhile, the list of technologies, systems, and components requiring U.S. export licenses remains too long despite decades of effort to narrow it down to truly critical items. U.S. military commanders complain that the unnecessary classification of entire systems impedes their ability to conduct joint exercises and training with other countries' forces.

The international scene is not promising either. As of 2009, the Doha Round was likely to fall far short of its original goals even if negotiators revived it. A trans-Pacific free trade area, originally adopted as a goal by the leaders of the Asia Pacific Economic Cooperation (APEC) forum in 1993–1994 and endorsed by President George W. Bush and others in 2005–2006, is still in the study phase. A few U.S. bilateral and regional trade agreements have been negotiated and ratified, but others have run aground.

The most important of those still awaiting congressional approval is the Korea-U.S. free trade agreement, which would be the largest single trade deal since NAFTA.

Causes of the Protectionist Upsurge

Growing doubts about the benefits of international economic engagement reflect a general loss of American faith in U.S. competitiveness. According to one series of polls, 10 years ago, 58 percent of Americans thought that growing engagement in the global economy was "good" (because of new markets and jobs associated with exports), as opposed to "bad" (because of unfair competition and cheap labor). By December 2007, that figure had dropped to 28 percent.

Current economic conditions contribute to the new pessimism. Prior to the current financial crisis, these included long-term wage stagnation and a decline in the number of manufacturing jobs, white-color layoffs, record U.S. trade and current account deficits, spikes in food and energy prices, soaring health care costs, and the huge income gap between the working class and the super-rich. Many blamed these trends on the globalization of production of goods and services and the spectacular rise of Asia, particularly China. Adding to the malaise are massive job losses, foreclosures, and business failures stemming from the severity and expected duration of the financial crisis.

Jobs. The most powerful driver of U.S. protectionism is the actual or feared loss of U.S. jobs, particularly in the manufacturing sector. It is a political fact of life that the jobs lost to import competition or outsourcing are far more visible than the jobs created either by imports (port services, retail, distribution, trucking, insurance, and so on) or by new export opportunities.

Like other industrialized countries, the United States has experienced a long-term increase in manufacturing productivity, and consequently a long-term decline in manufacturing employment. In the period 1940–2000, the proportion of workers employed in manufacturing declined from 32 percent to just below 13 percent, while manufacturing output increased elevenfold.[12] Wage stagnation, which began 10 to 15 years before NAFTA, has fed a widening income gap between blue-collar workers engaged in manufacturing and those in the higher end of the services sector.

Trade Deficit. In the last few years, the U.S. trade deficit has soared to record levels, cresting at over 6 percent of GDP in 2005. As long as Americans consume more than they produce, and invest more than they save, they will necessarily depend on imports to fill the gap. They pay for these imports by sending dollars abroad, putting huge piles of dollar-denominated assets into foreign pockets.

Much of the trade debate seems to rest on the obsolete assumption that goods are produced in one country alone. Most Americans, for example, would assume that a product bearing the label "Made in China" was wholly manufactured there. In reality, one-half to two-thirds of Chinese exports consist of imported materials and components. A similar proportion of China's exports are produced by foreign-invested enterprises investing in China, with or without a local Chinese partner. In 2007, for instance, almost half of what the United States imported from China flowed between parent companies and their subsidiaries. In other words, bilateral U.S.-China trade statistics disguise both the role of U.S.-based multinational companies and the region-based content of China's exports.

Even less well understood is the highly linked nature of trade and investment. Well over half of China's exports are produced by multinational companies, either alone or in joint ventures with Chinese partners. According to the U.S. Census Bureau, in 2007 trade between parent companies and subsidiaries accounted for 29.6 percent of U.S. exports (China was eighth on the list) and a whopping 47.4 percent of U.S. imports (China was fourth on the list).

In the year following the outbreak of the credit crisis in 2007, trade accounted for roughly three-quarters of U.S. growth.[13] The low value of the dollar stimulated a U.S. export boom and helped to keep an otherwise reeling economy growing. But this clear illustration of the value of trade evidently did little to dispel the appeal of protectionism.

Protectionist Rationale. The *-ism* in the world *protectionism* suggests an ideology of sorts, a systematic set of ideas and goals. But the people seeking protection from competition represent widely different interests; textile and apparel workers, for example, have little in common with sugar growers.

What unites protectionist forces is a sense of unfairness. It is only natural for people who lose their jobs to feel upset. But when lobbyists who represent them come to Washington, they tend to embed job losses in a broader narrative that runs something like this: Americans play by the rules, but foreigners do not. Americans are naive, but foreigners are sophisticated. Americans are willing to compete on a level playing field, but that field is tilted against them.

Americans believe in decent wages and working conditions, but foreign workers are willing to put up with exploitation. Because of this inherent unfairness, Americans have lost tens of thousands of jobs.

In some cases, the argument goes, national security is at stake. The United States is very vulnerable. We should not allow foreigners—even friendly ones—to acquire an influential role in any sector that is vital to America's military self-sufficiency. Whereas American companies are market-driven, foreign companies may become tools of their governments, whose hidden goal is to acquire and exercise political leverage. And if foreigners win a major defense contract, American military forces would become dangerously dependent on others and might not be able to operate freely in wartime.

When it comes to particular industries, this rationale attracts bipartisan sympathy. At a rhetorical level, one political party extols free trade and the other rallies around "fair trade," but that contrast quickly blurs when specific complaints arise. The Congressional Steel Caucus, for example, contains members of both parties. The result is a form of mercantilism: one-sided rhetoric that aggressively promotes exports abroad but justifies protection at home.

Priority Issues for the New Administration
Holistic Strategy versus Stovepipe Decisionmaking. The new administration needs to draw up a comprehensive, Government-wide strategy that integrates both military and economic components of U.S. foreign and domestic policy and deals with protectionism in that context. Such a holistic approach is particularly urgent in the case of U.S. policy toward Asia, where economic and security perspectives go hand in hand.

Implementation of such a strategy should be designed to overcome traditional stovepipe decisionmaking, which perpetuates turf battles and segregates decisions that ought to be made within a broad strategic framework. The new President should signal his intentions by revamping the staffing and organization of the National Security Council to fully reflect the intersection of political-economic and political-military issues. Decision memoranda brought to his desk should routinely incorporate both perspectives. He should also direct the relevant departments and agencies to ensure that trade policymaking is consistent with broad strategic concerns; narrow the scope of export controls and visa denials; and improve the review of incoming foreign investments by developing and applying key judgments consistently, such as degree of dependence, foreign availability, and industry concentration, among others.[14]

Embedding responses to protectionism in a broad domestic and strategic context means paying more attention to the legitimate political and economic needs of poor and middle-income countries. The result will be a negotiating posture that is a little less demanding, less fearful, and more generous.

Calibrating the new approach with the demands of good trade policy should not go too far. Many domestic reformers in other countries rely on American pressure to strengthen their case for carrying out needed changes in economic policy. Similarly, foreign entrepreneurs whose opportunities are currently blocked by domestic protectionist measures that favor vested interests would not support retaining the commercial status quo.

The main obstacle to such a shift in the tone and content of the U.S. negotiating posture is Congress. A new international economic policy will be dead on arrival unless the President and his top officials reach beyond trade subcommittees and appeal to a broad spectrum of members. They must justify the policy shift as a key element of a global national security strategy. They should point out, for instance, that a "kinder, gentler" trade policy would provide a constructive counterpoint to China's highly successful commercial diplomacy.[15] At the same time, they must bracket trade expansion with a far-reaching, comprehensive package of adjustment measures.

Comprehensive Domestic Adjustment. The long-term solution to protectionism lies in better education and domestic adjustment measures such as portable pensions, affordable health care, some form of wage insurance, and lifetime learning for all workers, not just those affected by trade. New legislation will require substantial efforts to overcome the current congressional gridlock. But since many Members of Congress are sympathetic to domestic adjustment measures and dislike having to cast trade votes, prospects are reasonably promising.

Ratification of Korean-U.S. Free Trade Agreement. The controversy surrounding the Korean-U.S. (KORUS) free trade agreement, and especially a dispute over the safety of eating American beef, has inflamed Korean public opinion and hobbled President Lee Myung-bak's ability to work constructively with Washington. The United States should not walk away from an agreement negotiated in good faith with an important ally. The President may have to include KORUS in some kind of package deal to get it rati-

fied. Passage of other trade agreements will probably depend on the vigor of the initiatives recommended above.

Revitalization of the Multilateral Trading System. Bilateral free trade agreements are no substitute for global and trans-Pacific trade liberalization. They effectively penalize countries that are left out. Complex rules of origin requirements are particularly burdensome for small countries. Wrapping up the Doha Round of multilateral trade negotiations should be the top priority, followed by trade and investment liberalization across the Pacific. Rather than spending political energy pushing for a trans-Pacific free trade agreement all at once, Washington has wisely decided to join the trade-liberalizing Transpacific Strategic Economic Partnership, initiated within APEC by Brunei, Chile, New Zealand, and Singapore.

Reducing protectionism to a politically manageable level is a strategic imperative. Telling people that "open markets are good for you" just does not work. Devising a multifaceted domestic adjustment policy, embedding trade and investment policy in a broader strategic policy framework, and explaining these vitally related initiatives to a skeptical Congress and the public are strategic imperatives. **gsa**

NOTES

[1] An efficient financial system can make up for a number of other strategic deficiencies. For instance, France, during the Napoleonic era, was more populous and had a far larger economy than Great Britain. Throughout the Napoleonic Wars, however, Britain consistently raised more capital than France—cash that William Pitt used to fight a global war, while also subsidizing most of Britain's continental allies. It stands to reason that the opposite—that weak financial institutions undermine a nation's strengths—is also true.

[2] With enactment of the Fiscal Year (FY) 2008 Supplemental and FY2009 Bridge Fund (H.R.2642/P.L. 110–252) on June 30, 2008, Congress approved about $859 billion for military operations, base security, reconstruction, foreign aid, Embassy costs, and veterans' health care for the three operations initiated since the 9/11 attacks: Operation *Enduring Freedom* (OEF), for counterterror operations in Afghanistan and elsewhere; Operation *Noble Eagle*, to provide enhanced security at military bases; and Operation *Iraqi Freedom* (OIF). This $859 billion total covers all war-related appropriations from FY2001 through part of FY2009 in supplemental appropriations, regular appropriations, and continuing resolutions. Of that total, the Congressional Research Service (CRS) estimates that Iraq will receive about $653 billion (76 percent), OEF about $172 billion (20 percent), and enhanced base security about $28 billion (3 percent), with about $5 billion

that CRS cannot allocate (1 percent). About 94 percent of the funds are for DOD, 6 percent for foreign aid programs and Embassy operations, and less than 1 percent for medical care for veterans. As of April 2008, DOD's monthly obligations for contracts and pay averaged about $12.1 billion, including $9.8 billion for Iraq and $2.3 billion for Afghanistan. See Amy Belasco, *The Cost of Iraq, Afghanistan, and Other Global War on Terror Operations Since 9/11*, CRS Report RL33110 (Washington, DC: CRS, July 14, 2008).

3 Barry Eichengreen, "Is the Dollar About to Lose its International Role?" April 14, 2005, available at <www.econ.berkeley.edu/~eichengr/reviews/handelsblatt5apr29-05.pdf>.

4 See Statistical Annex to Bank for International Settlements Quarterly Review, September 2008, 103, available at <www.bis.org/publ/qtrpdf/r_qa0809.pdf>.

5 Heather Landy, "Lehman Credit-Default Swap Payout Could Climb as High as $365 Billion," *Washington Post*, October 11, 2008, D3.

6 "The New Monetarism and the Credit Crunch," October 20, 2007, Independent Strategy, London.

7 Berkshire Hathaway, Inc., 2002 Annual Report, available at <www.berkshirehathaway.com/2002ar/2002ar.pdf>.

8 Charles Kindleberger, *World Economic Primacy, 1500–1900* (Oxford: Oxford University Press, 1996), 36.

9 The original purposes of the IMF, listed in Article I of the IMF's Articles of Agreement, include "to promote exchange stability," to provide fund resources to members "to correct maladjustments in their balance of payments," and "to shorten the duration and lessen the degree of disequilibrium in the international balances of payments of members." Today, private capital markets dwarf IMF resources.

10 Note that neither of these potentialities is currently being manifested by any sovereign wealth fund.

11 Agitation in Congress was mainly responsible for the withdrawal or cancellation of at least three major investments: the would-be purchase of Unocal by China's national offshore oil company in 2005; also in 2005, Dubai Port World's purchase of the U.S. portion of a London-based company that manages six major American ports; and Bain Capital's planned purchase of 3Com with a minority interest held by a Chinese company.

12 Kristin J. Forbes, "U.S. Manufacturing: Challenges and Recommendations," Council of Economic Advisers, March 25, 2004, 3.

13 Krishna Guha, "Revision Puts Focus on Global Conditions," *Financial Times*, August 29, 2008.

14 See, for example, Theodore H. Moran, "Three Threats: An Analytical Framework for the CFIUS Process: Identifying Genuine National Security Risks and Threats, Dismissing Implausible Allegations," July 8, 2008, unpublished paper originally prepared under the auspices of the International Business Advisory Panel, National Intelligence Council.

15 See Ellen L. Frost, James J. Przystup, and Phillip C. Saunders, *China's Rising Influence in Asia: Implications for U.S. Policy*, Strategic Forum No. 231 (Washington, DC: National Defense University Press, April 2008), 4.

Contributors

Dr. Ellen L. Frost (Chapter Editor) is a Visiting Fellow at the Peterson Institute for International Economics and an Adjunct Research Fellow in the Institute for Strategic Studies at the National Defense University. Her most recent book is *Asia's New Regionalism* (Lynne Rienner, 2008).

Dr. David L. Asher is a Washington, DC–based international affairs analyst specializing in finance and security. He has extensive experience both in financial markets and in government. Since 1990, he has worked in different capacities as policymaker and planner for the Department of State and Department of Defense, as well as a global strategist for three of the world's leading hedge funds.

Paul Collier is Professor of Economics and Director of the Centre for the Study of African Economies at Oxford University. He is the author of *The Bottom Billion: Why the Poorest Countries Are Failing and What Can Be Done About It* (Oxford University Press, 2007).

James G. Lacey is a Washington, DC–based defense analyst, who is widely published on international and economic affairs.

Robert Madsen is a Senior Fellow in the Center for International Studies at the Massachusetts Institute for Technology and a member of the Executive Council at Unison Capital. He previously advised the Robert M. Bass Group and served as Asia Strategist for Soros Private Funds Management.

William H. Overholt is Senior Research Fellow at the Harvard Kennedy School of Government and former Director of RAND's Center for Asia Pacific Policy. His most recent book is *Asia, America, and the Transformation of Geopolitics* (Cambridge University Press, 2008).

Chapter 2
Political Flux in a Nonpolar World

A Nonpolar World?

The gradual emergence of a multipolar world is likely to continue in the decade ahead. The age of Cold War bipolarity has ended even though serious tensions among the major powers remain. The myth of unipolarity was derived through a process of subtraction while the world succumbed to the sway of multiplication, which gave rise to aspiring and new centers of power. But the advent of a functioning multipolar world in all probability will take years to realize.

Today, the world is more nonpolar than multipolar, with no one power capable of mobilizing others around its agenda. The world also remains nonpolar in that most powers are reluctant to assume the role of global leader or security guarantor outside their borders. Even internationalist Europe is constrained by its lack of political consensus and its limited capacity to act decisively. Within these centers of power the general predilection, at least by default, is assigning the global security role to the United States, albeit in a

fashion that suits their common norms and interests. While political power has fragmented, emerging or re-surgent powers—China, Russia, India, and Brazil—do not possess the determination or capacity to take on the mantle of global leadership. Even though America is the strongest military power in the world, military power alone cannot be used outside of a political context. When considering the global, regional, and local political environment, military strength can become as much a liability as an asset. Moreover, the Nation does not have the capabilities to act as the principal security guarantor, at least on the level seen in past decades. Among other realities, the post–World War II security system is on its last legs, unable to keep astride of traditional threats as well as emerging threats of the 21st century.

While America will remain the single most important actor, especially militarily, its relative power has declined together with its political and moral influence. Thus, even though the Nation is

NATO foreign ministers meet to discuss enlargement and operations prior to Bucharest Summit, March 2008

unmatched in terms of military power projection, it has had difficulty translating its power into influence. The perception that the United States may contribute more to instability than to efforts to resolve it has eroded its claim on legitimacy and raised the transactional cost of action.

Some may regard U.S. military preponderance as inhibiting, but the fact is that America spends about 50 percent more on defense than China, Japan, India, Russia, France, Germany, Italy, and the United Kingdom combined. The global economic slowdown and looming world recession, however, may well start to reduce this asymmetry, but it is unlikely to change rapidly. Similarly, it is difficult to imagine any other nation or group of nations providing nearly the number of boots on the ground that the United States can mobilize in conflict and peacekeeping zones. No other country has provided even 10 percent of the deployed forces that America has in recent years. The next most significant troop contributor, the United Kingdom, labors under severe pressures and is hard pressed to honor its commitment in Afghanistan. Even if Europe contributes larger expeditionary forces, their impact will be qualitative and not quantitative. While China and other Asian powers maintain large armed forces, they are unlikely to commit large numbers of them far afield.

Europe is the obvious alternative center of power, with leaders in Paris, London, and Berlin proposing new ideas and in some cases making bold statements on the role that their nations, individually and as part of the European Union, can play in addressing traditional and nontraditional security challenges. France appears to be working in concert with rather than competing against U.S. power, and Britain remains focused on the long haul in Afghanistan even while it pursues a vital role in a global agenda centered on economics, energy, the environment, trade, and development. For all the concern expressed in recent years over the fact that Europe lacks a serious capability to intervene militarily outside its borders, the countries of Europe manage to deploy almost half the number of troops abroad as the United States, and with less than half the defense spending. Although European nations are well positioned to assume some of the security burdens that America is currently shouldering, the political will and popular consensus lag behind.

The resurgence of Russia has been focused on presenting a counter to American leadership, in particular through military posturing and leveraging energy supplies to reclaim authority in the so-called near abroad. While the conduct of Moscow can be explained, its willingness to resolve international security challenges outside its immediate sphere of influence is questionable given its ambivalence toward joining with Europe, the United States, and to a certain extent even China in cooperating on critical issues such as the disputed Iranian nuclear program. Defining a realistic, limited strategic partnership with Russia may prove to be as difficult as it is important.

Some consider the ascent of China as a global power to be an alternative to American influence in the world. Even if such a transfer occurred, and assuming that China embraced the values of the Enlightenment, Beijing definitely is not about to seek, accept, or be given chief responsibility for global security leadership in the foreseeable future. China's decision to help combat piracy by sending ships to the Gulf of Aden and Red Sea is a potential barometer of its willingness to contribute more to international security, as well as of the international community's willingness to make room for that role. As China's stake in the global economy has grown, so has its awareness that it has a common stake in protecting sea lines of communication that are vital for trade and energy supplies. But fathoming China's long-range intentions is difficult, and the direction of the People's Liberation Army may or may not be on the same trajectory as a cautious Communist Party or a more mercurial Chinese society. The meteoric rise of China since Deng Xiaoping opened the country in 1978 to impressive economic growth and created a challenging range of domestic environmental, social, and political concerns. The downturn in the global economy has deeply influenced the views of the Chinese leadership, which is hopeful but no longer supremely confident that tapping into huge cash reserves and pushing more competitive exports will circumvent systemic trouble.

Other emerging power centers such as India, Brazil, South Africa, Japan, Indonesia, and even Iran are flexing their muscles, but none is able to secure peace within its respective region on its own, and in the case of Iran, peace may not be the objective that some leaders have in mind—all of which underscores that the United States remains unique in its military prowess. But even though there is still no alternative to America as the leading enforcer of the world order, it would be risky to assume that it will take on international security missions simply because others will not or cannot. The United States has too many challenges to cope with and too few resources to apply to them. Redefining complex problems, exercising strategic restraint, mobilizing new power centers, and employing more leverage strategies will be crucial if the United States is to help balance its ambitious objectives with more constricted means.

In the decade ahead and most likely beyond, the United States will be the dominant military power on the international stage. But dominance is not what it used to be; the ability of military power to address modern security challenges is open to debate, and America has had difficulties in converting preponderance into influence. The change in Presidential administrations might turn the tide with regard to American legitimacy, but whether such a reversal of fortunes can be held together by a limited political consensus around the world remains to be seen. To the extent that the failure of the United States to achieve its security objectives has been the result of a breach of moral legitimacy among its closest allies, especially in Europe, there is an opportunity to mobilize international support around a common goal. As Sir Michael Howard opined:

American power is indispensable for the preservation of global order, and as such it must be recognized, accommodated, and where possible supported. But if it is to be effective, it needs to be seen and legitimized as such by the international community. If it is perceived rather as an instrument serving a unilateral conception of national security that amounts to a claim to world domination . . . that is unlikely to happen.

The evolving relationship among the major powers, the role of power centers and institutions in grappling with various traditional and global issues, the ability of nation-states to be effective political actors, shifting political norms, and the impact of religion and transnational forces are all salient issues that national security decisionmakers and military planners will be called upon to confront in the future. Some of the major questions that arise from a world in political flux are the following: how an expanding concept of responsible sovereignty may be useful in fashioning greater multilateral cooperation to tackle transnational challenges; the continuing relevance of shifting international norms; the evolving role of the nation-state and nationalism; the relationship between politics and religion, particularly Islam; and the complex political challenge posed by the fundamental problem of food security. The contributions that follow highlight these and other key issues.

International Cooperation in an Era of Transnational Threats

The greatest test of global leadership in the 21st century will be the way in which nations act in the face of threats that transcend international borders, from nuclear proliferation, armed conflict, and climate change to terrorism, biological hazards, and abject poverty. Today, national security is interdependent with international security. Globalization has led to unprecedented advances in every sector of the economy. The ability to use global markets for capital, technology, and labor has allowed the private sector to accumulate wealth unfathomable 50 years ago: it has helped lift hundreds of millions of people in emerging economies around the world out of poverty.

The forces of globalization that stitch the world together and drive prosperity could also tear it apart. In the face of new transnational threats and profound security interdependence, even the strongest countries rely on the cooperation of others to protect their national security. No nation, including the United States, is capable of successfully meeting the challenges, or capitalizing on the opportunities, of this changed world alone. But American foreign policy lags behind these realities. A new approach is required to revitalize alliances, diplomacy, and global institutions central to the inseparable relationship between national and international security. Leadership by the United States is indispensable in managing threats for the world. Yet that leadership must be focused on traditional partnerships with allies in Europe, Asia, and Latin America as well as on new relationships with ascendant powers such as China, India, Brazil, Russia, and South Africa. The attitudes, policies, and standards of major states will exert a disproportionate influence on whether the next 50 years move toward international order or entropy. Actions by the President, working in collaboration with the leaders of many traditional and rising powers, will profoundly influence the course of international security and fruits of prosperity in a global age.

Responsible Sovereignty

Spirited interdependence does not make international cooperation inevitable. Instead, shared interests must be turned into a common vision to revive an international security system that will profit everyone. Foresight, imagination, pragmatism, and political will, fueled by effective American leadership, established a new international era after World War II. Institutions such as the United Nations,

International Monetary Fund, World Bank, and General Agreement on Tariffs and Trade (now the World Trade Organization) contributed to economic growth with extraordinary results and prevented another conflict among major powers.

However, the vision for an international security system is clouded by the mismatch between post–World War II multilateral institutions premised on traditional sovereignty—a principle that says borders are sacrosanct and that insists on noninterference in domestic affairs—and the realities of a transnational world where capital, technology, labor, disease, pollution, and nonstate actors traverse national and regional boundaries irrespective of the intentions of sovereign states.

The domestic burdens inflicted by transnational threats such as poverty, civil war, disease, and environmental degradation point toward cooperating with global partners and strengthening international institutions. Entering into agreements or accepting help from other states does not weaken sovereignty—it is exercising sovereignty to protect it. The project on Managing Global Insecurity calls for building international cooperation on the principle of responsible sovereignty. This means taking responsibility for the external effects of one's domestic actions: sovereignty entails obligations toward other states as well as one's citizens. To protect national security, even sovereignty, states must have rules to guide actions that reverberate beyond their borders. Responsible sovereignty implies a positive interest by powerful states to provide weaker states with the capacity to exercise their sovereignty responsibly.

Sovereignty is emphasized because states are the primary units of the international system. As much as globalization has diminished the power of states, there is simply no alternative to the legally defined state as the primary actor in international affairs or substitute for state legitimacy in the use of force, provision of justice, and regulation of both public spheres and private action. Responsibility is raised because adhering to traditional sovereignty and deferring to individual state solutions have failed to produce peace and prosperity. In a transnational world, international cooperation is essential for the sovereignty of states: it protects people and advances interests. Responsible sovereignty is a guidepost to creating a better international system. Just as founding members of the United Nations and the Bretton Woods institutions had a vision of international cooperation based on a shared assessment of threat and a shared notion of sovereignty,

global powers today must chart a new course to meet greater challenges and opportunities.

Agenda for Action

Global realities have led to the convergence of international interests to build a security system for the 21st century. The case for action to defuse or prevent regional and global crises is not a soft-hearted appeal to the common good, but rather a realist call to action. If short-term crises crowd out lasting reforms, nations and policymakers will be denied the tools to address future disasters. If action languishes, nationalistic opportunism may provoke unilateral actions that undermine sustainable solutions. Then conflict, isolationism, and protectionism will be imminent threats to global security and prosperity. Climate change and nuclear proliferation, for example, could become existential challenges to the planet: the clock is ticking.

Member nation flags fly at United Nations Headquarters, New York

International cooperation requires power to underpin responsibility. This analysis identified five prerequisites: effective American policy and leadership, institutionalized cooperation among traditional and emerging powers, negotiated understandings of responsible sovereignty in threat areas, efficient and legitimate international institutions, and nations with the capacity to achieve their responsibilities toward their people and the international community. An action plan would embrace these prerequisites on parallel tracks to restore U.S. standing internationally, revitalize international institutions, respond to transnational threats, and manage future crises.

Track 1: Credible Leadership. No other nation in the world has the diplomatic, economic, and military capacity to rejuvenate international cooperation. But to lead, the United States must reestablish itself as a good-faith partner.

Unilateral action in Iraq, Guantanamo, and Abu Ghraib as well as the sanctioning of torture, use of rendition, and linkage of the Iraq War with democracy harmed American credibility. The Nation must demonstrate its commitment to a rule-based international system that rejects unilateralism and looks beyond exercising military power. In turn, major states will be more willing to share the burden in both resources and political capital to manage global threats. Toward that end, the United States should immediately undertake a number of initiatives that include:

■ sending top-level officials to consult with allies and rising powers on international priorities

■ delivering consistent messages on international cooperation, including in the lead-up to the Group of Eight (G–8) and United Nations (UN) General Assembly meetings by outlining a vision for a 21st-century security system

■ initiating the closure of Guantanamo and sustainable detainee policies, and committing to adhere to the Geneva Conventions, Convention Against Torture, and other traditional laws of war.

In time, the United States will need to dramatically upgrade its foreign policy apparatus, including doubling the number of Foreign Service Officers over the next 10 years and rewriting the Foreign Assistance Act to elevate development priorities and improve effectiveness.

Track 2: Power and Legitimacy. The status of international institutions must be enhanced by including representatives of emerging powers and refocusing their mandates on 21st-century challenges. Leaders and mandates of institutions from the G–8 to the UN Security Council have not kept pace with powerholders and dynamic threats in a changed world. Emerging powers are excluded from decisionmaking processes that affect their security and prosperity. The traditional powers cannot achieve sustainable solutions on issues from economic stability to climate change without new great powers at the negotiating table. Accordingly, global leaders should:

■ Create a Group of 16 (G–16) to engage with Brazil, China, India, South Africa, and Mexico (Outreach 5) and the Muslim-majority nations of Indonesia, Turkey, Egypt, and Nigeria. Replacing the outdated G–8 with the G–16 would serve as a prenegotiating

forum to forge agreements on key challenges.

■ Initiate voluntary veto reform of the UN Security Council as a confidence-building measure.

■ End the Euro-American monopoly of the International Monetary Fund and the World Bank, and refocus the International Monetary Fund to monitor exchange rate polices and facilitate unraveling of global imbalances.

■ Strengthen regional organizations, including a 10-year capacity-building effort of the African Union and support for a regional security mechanism for the Middle East.

Expansion of the UN Security Council would be a signal of the commitment to share the helm of the international system, but conditions for this reform are not likely to be propitious in 2009. However, the decisive expansion of the G–8 in 2009 would represent a credible foundation.

Track 3: Strategy and Capacity. It will be necessary to enhance international cooperation and institutions to manage the global agenda. A number of upcoming items will require action, including the UN Framework Convention on Climate Change, the Nuclear Non-Proliferation Treaty, and global trade issues. In the case of climate change, continuation of the current trends in using fossil fuels would be tantamount to a new era of mutually assured destruction. There is no doubt about the catastrophic effects if nuclear weapons are used. Global leaders should:

■ Negotiate a climate change agreement under the auspices of the framework convention that includes emission targets for 2015 and 2050 and investments in technology, rainforests, and mitigation.

■ Revitalize the core bargain of the nonproliferation regime of nuclear weapons states by reducing their arsenals, particularly those of the United States and Russia. Every nation should endorse the additional protocol and work to develop an international fuel bank.

■ Initiate G–16 prenegotiations on an open and inclusive trade regime to conclude a round of the World Trade Organization that benefits poor countries.

In addition, progress must be achieved on other global challenges—those threats associated with the use of biotechnology, regional and civil conflict, and global terrorism—in order to:

■ build local public health capacity to fully implement the International Health Regulations and develop an interagency panel to forge consensus on the dangers and benefits of biotechnology

■ increase international investments in conflict management with a goal of a reserve force of 50,000 peacekeepers and a $2 billion fund for peace-building

■ establish the post of UN High Commissioner for Counterterrorism to focus international efforts to build counterterrorism norms and capacity.

Track 4: Crisis Response. The diplomatic mechanisms for crisis response in the Middle East must be internationalized to address regional conflict and transnational threats. Global leaders must be confident that a 21st-century international security system will produce better outcomes for the crises at the top of their national security agendas. The Middle East is the most unstable region in the world and a vortex of transnational threats. The G–16, in cooperation with leading regional actors, can identify shared interests and catalyze more focused support to:

■ move the Annapolis Process forward to support an Israeli-Palestinian peace settlement

■ commit adequate forces and civilian capacity to create a stable peace in Afghanistan

■ focus U.S. and international efforts on a political settlement and civilian surge for Iraq

■ conclude successful regional diplomatic negotiations on the Iranian nuclear program

■ initiate efforts toward a regional security mechanism for the Middle East to provide a process to guarantee borders and protect stability as existing crises ease.

Sequencing and Targets of Opportunity

This agenda for action is sweeping but unavoidable. It will require immediate and sustained attention, political momentum, and parallel action to achieve results across diverse issues and pending crises facing global powers. The international community will look for signs that the United States is genuinely seeking global partnerships. Accordingly, Track 1 should begin in earnest to restore the standing of America as the basis for revitalizing the international security system. The world will not support Washington's lead to make reforms if the United States does not commit itself to cooperative efforts.

The convening power of the G–16 and the weight of its collective economic, diplomatic, and military strength as well as combined populations would create an unparalleled body to mobilize international

action: an entity to navigate the turbulence of diffuse power, transnational threats, and the changing distribution of power among key states. The formation of the G–16 in 2009 would help by revitalizing international institutions (Track 2), combating transnational threats (Track 3), and internationalizing crisis response (Track 4). G–8 leaders should make a concerted effort with their Italian host to shape the agenda for the meeting in 2009 to ensure G–16 formation. But if the G–16 is not created in 2009, the United States and other powers should act as if it does exist and convene informal meetings to achieve comparable effects. That may strain American diplomacy, but it will pay dividends in making the U.S. diplomatic efforts more effective.

The international agenda will impose a schedule of action on transnational threats, including the Conference of the Parties to the UN Framework Convention on Climate Change in 2009 and Nuclear Non-Proliferation Treaty review conference in 2010. These two events provide venues to sustain dialogue and take concrete steps on climate change and nuclear proliferation. Actions over the next 2 years will determine if the Doha Round of the World Trade Organization or another trade negotiation can produce an agreement that brings poor countries into global supply chains or undermines the organization's credibility as a rule-setting global institution.

Finally, crises will continue. They will remain at the top of domestic foreign policy priorities and thus require immediate attention. Yet powerful nations such as the United States will be more likely to reach a political settlement in Iraq, address the nuclear threat of Iran, and promote civil order in Afghanistan by working through stable global partnerships and effective international institutions. Progress on a larger agenda to revive the international security system and engage rising powers in cooperative arrangements must be accomplished in parallel. The success of this global agenda will not only address crises today but will also prevent disasters tomorrow.

Global leaders face a choice: they can either use this moment to shape an international rule-based regime that will protect their global interests or resign themselves to an ad hoc system in which they increasingly find themselves powerless to influence international events. An agenda for action will not be realized in 2 years or even 10. But the longer the delay in beginning to develop approaches to counter the threats of today, the more difficult it will become to meet the challenges of tomorrow. Leaders should chart a path that combines power and responsibility to achieve what cannot be achieved separately—peace and security in a transnational world.

The Normative Shift: Sovereignty versus Intervention

The modern world poses a set of realities for the international community that include terrorism, globalized markets, information technology, emerging powers, climate change, failing states, the changing nature of war, mass migration, proliferation, pandemics, and so forth. There is no shortage of challenges to the existing world of international law, and at the top of any list is sovereignty. For some observers, the issue for the international community is whether it can or should "recognize a responsibility to override sovereignty in emergency situations—to prevent ethnic cleansing or genocide, arrest war criminals, restore democracy or provide disaster relief when national governments were either unable or unwilling to do so."

Anti-American mural in Tehran, Iran

Courtesy Bertil Videt

The Cold War Consensus

It was fashionable to think of international law as creating norms that linked a three-tiered chessboard of interconnected power with overlapping integrated values. The top board featured military power. The West coalesced under collective agreements such as the North Atlantic Treaty Organization (NATO), and security was based on a mutual assistance pact. The Soviet Union and its satellites had the Warsaw Pact. Although proxy wars or crises punctuated 60-plus years of peace, a dreaded nuclear exchange was avoided. Liberation wars occurred from Korea and Cuba to Vietnam and Laos, and aborted revolutions in Hungary and Czechoslovakia embarrassed the Western powers, but still the international system held. All agreed that the Geneva Conventions governed the law of armed conflict, and violators expected worldwide opprobrium. Even though the expansion of the Geneva Conventions and the establishment of the International Criminal Court were not supported by the United States, compromises were found to preserve the international consensus. Developments such as the Non-Proliferation Treaty, the International Atomic Energy Agency, and the Nuclear Suppliers Group supported control of the number of nuclear powers and the production of nuclear bombs, which are the ultimate weapon.

The United Nations structured the middle board or international political power game where the post–World War II great powers navigated the tricky waters of containment, mutually assured destruction, and nuclear deterrence. When conflict strained the doctrines of nonintervention and self-determination, the Security Council promoted the international consensus on the balance of power. Issues such as the Palestinian question were deferred because they threatened to unhinge the board, but shifting coalitions held the pieces together. Although there were regional groups, such as the European Union or the Shanghai Cooperation Organization, international exchanges focused on the United Nations.

The bottom board, which supported the entire structure, was the economic game. In addition to the General Agreement on Tariffs and Trade, World Trade Organization, International Monetary Fund, and World Bank were international financial institutions and economic agreements that became legal underpinnings of the world market. The U.S. dollar replaced the British pound as the international reserve currency, and the Organization of the Petroleum Exporting Countries managed oil as a commodity. Markets became interconnected trading emporiums that gave rise to various industries, competitors, and globalization.

Cracks Become Chasms

The three-tiered game maintained the international status quo, and a great deal of effort was expended to ensure the top board never disabled the supporting boards. The West strove for consumer expansion without socialist influence while the East attempted to have growth without liberalism. Cracks in the boards appeared, with the rise of economic actors such as Brazil, Russia, India, and China. The Security Council gradually became impotent because of the veto exercised by the great powers, who protected special relationships with client states that began to implode. Although such behavior was anticipated in the case of China and Russia, the United States also began to consider any expansion of the board games as negative. America was reluctant to be constrained on any board, rejecting international treaties such as the expansion of the Geneva Conventions (that is, Protocols I and II), limitations on landmine use, the Non-Proliferation Treaty, the Kyoto Protocol, and the UN Convention on the Law of the Sea (UNCLOS).

The triple-tiered board game and international legal system were upended by the collapse of the Soviet Union, the attacks on September 11, 2001, and more recently the fall in the dollar and oil prices. The United States chose a three-tiered board strategy that was a radical departure or transformative approach to the game. On the political level, America and Europe outflanked the Security Council and the vetoes of Russia

and China by choosing NATO, a regional security organization, to legitimize involvement in Kosovo. Subsequently, on the military level, the United States ignored the Geneva Conventions and the protections for prisoners of war by using its new theory of unlawful combatants. The doctrine of self-defense was suspended to allow for preemption in an unusual expansion of the doctrine of prevention. Although the United Nations was approached on Afghanistan, the United States acted largely unilaterally in Iraq and ignored the protestations by the Security Council. In the face of a weakened Russia, and without a peer competitor on the horizon, the United States became a non–status quo power militarily.

The non–status quo power approach migrated to the political board based on military moves. Political unilateralism began to undermine the United Nations and European Union. Historic allies, members of regional alliances that once were thought to be counterweights to foes of nonliberal systems, now were seen as unwanted anchors to unfettered U.S. movement. Economically, domestic upheaval in the housing market combined with an external debt-driven growth model to devalue the dollar and spike oil prices. Although the World Trade Organization is strong and supported, it is clear the growth of globalism will entail a resource scramble to sustain economic powers that may upset the military board. These policies emboldened a rejuvenated, aggressive Russia, flush with increased oil revenues and profiting from economic and political uncertainty, to march into Georgia under the questionable justification of protecting its people from genocide. In August 2008,

Federal Republic of Germany (Bernd Kühler)

Leaders of Group of Eight leading industrialized nations gather during 2007 summit

as the world watched Russian tanks roll into Georgia and debated ways to react, some argued for sanctions on the economic board such as expulsion from G–8 economic summits while others contended that a new Marshall Plan for Georgia was needed. Although no response gelled, it was apparent that the global legal order was being tested and the international response would help define the future consensus over sovereignty versus global intervention.

Chasms and Bridges

At a conference on international law convened by Craig Allen at the Naval War College in 2006, a group of experts pondered a vision of the future global legal order. Allen boiled down the possibilities of the global legal order to six potential futures that may arise by 2020:

- no growth
- slow growth
- significant growth
- total disintegration
- fracturing the order into regional and bilateral arrangements
- no one single future—that is, constant flux.

American policies will be critical in determining which of the six futures will ascend. To some observers, the world has become a competition among three types of regimes: autocratic economies (Russia and China), Islamic traditional states (Iran and Saudi Arabia), and liberal democracies (the United States and European Union members). These groupings have internal rivalries but share certain values. Each will struggle on the three-tiered chessboard to expand power, gather satellites for alliances, and maneuver for comparative advantage.

The United States should adopt a fox bridge-building approach rather than a hedgehog go-it-alone strategy for each board. Board blending is the goal of the future whereby strategies must be understood in light of how they affect games on the other levels. On the political board, a call for a new multilateralism of both international actors and institutions is required. It should not be a council of democracies or a bloc comprised of the United States, European Union, and India versus the world. America should seek regional alliances with strategic local actors to establish agreed principles of regional intervention, which may require acceding to the International Criminal Court. More specifically, the Nation must forge coalitions to condemn

repressive actions by Sudan. The United States must work in concert with regional players in the event that national sovereignty is violated in the name of humanitarian rights.

Secondly, a number of conventions should be readopted, confirmed, and created. The Geneva Conventions and Convention Against Torture, Cruel, Inhuman and Degrading Behavior should be reaffirmed. Debate should be started on Protocols I and II, which have not been signed. The Senate should confirm UNCLOS and renew debate on the Kyoto Protocol and Land Mines Convention. Cyberspace has generated challenges that call for negotiating a convention on this new field, which can serve as an economic tool or potential weapon. Before Georgia was invaded by Russia, its infrastructure became a target of destabilizing cyber attacks. Moreover, the United States must reestablish its legitimacy through a process of reform. But the regional organization and Security Council tracks should be pursued simultaneously. Issues such as proliferation and international crime require shifting coalitions of like-minded states.

In sum, great powers and power blocs—old and emerging—must find ways to build bridges so sovereignty claims do not result in the projections of force that destroy the accomplishments of the post–World War era. Although the status quo did not help people under communism in the 20th century, it did succeed in allowing for a 21st century. The old saw that nation-states have become too small to handle global problems and too big to handle the new politics of identity has merit. Cold War institutions served their purpose but must be reformed to deal with current and emerging challenges. America will play a major role in determining the future bequeathed to the next generation, but it will not dictate its version to the world. The international community is watching to see if the United States can help build institutions for the next century.

The Fate of a Faith

Most great wars of the 19th and 20th centuries were waged in the name of nationalism. Moreover, they were fought by nations with large conventional forces and national liberation movements in league with insurgents. From the French Revolution and nation in arms to the anticolonial wars of the 1950s through the 1970s and beyond, nationalism and the nation-state remained front and center in the realm of international politics and the execution of military strategies.

Nationalism and the Nation-state

In the first half of the 20th century, both nationalism and the nation-state posed the greatest of all foreign challenges to the United States, culminating in two world wars. By 1910, the development of nationalism and the nation-state reached its most intense form in Wilhelmine Germany. Only the grand alliance of Britain, France, and America could marshal the forces to defeat and temporarily subdue the ferocious unity, determination, and ruthless efficiency of the German nation. And only two decades later, nationalism and the nation-state reached new heights in National Socialist Germany. Only the grander alliance of Britain, Russia, and America could assemble the means to defeat the German nation for a second time. Furthermore, almost as developed as Nazi Germany in terms of nationalism and the nation-state was Imperial Japan, which also posed an epic challenge to the United States. Indeed, in order to defeat the challenges from Germany and Japan, the United States itself developed a higher and more intense form of nationalism and the nation-state than it had in its past or has since then. It was overcoming these immense challenges that would lead to the American way of war.

The defeat of the United States in Vietnam was inflicted by a movement with international communist support that used nationalism to unify a nation by the force of arms. Unfortunately, by the 1960s, America possessed a much less vigorous nationalism and nation-state than it had only a generation before, which contributed to its ultimate defeat in Vietnam. For much of the 20th century, foreign threats to the United States came from some version of nationalism and the nation-state. But in the 21st century, transnational Islamist terrorist networks have replaced the once-central role of nationalism and the nation-state. Indeed, many political and military leaders and policy analysts have concluded that the era of nationalism and the nation-state has ended, or at least has abated with only the fading vestiges of those once-powerful forces still at play.

The ideology of nationalism and the nation-state was a product of a particular place and time. The place was Western Europe, initially Britain, then France and Germany, until all Europe was reshaped around nationalism and the efforts to institutionalize its manifestations in nation-states. The time was the high modern era from the French Revolution to World War II, which was the greatest conflict between nationalism and nation-states and was so destructive that it went far toward bringing an end to nationalism and independent nation-states in their homeland, Western Europe. That age also corresponded to the Industrial Revolution and the eventual development of mature industrial economies as well as mature industrial military organizations and warfare.

Postmodern Era

The current post-European, perhaps even post-Western, era is marked by the great and dynamic economic and political developments found beyond Europe, particularly in the rising great powers of China and India but also in the rising transnational religion of Islam. Moreover, in regard to the societies of Europe and more generally the West, this is also the postmodern age. Ironically, the most dynamic examples of nationalism and the nation-state today are China and, to a lesser but growing extent, India. Perhaps this is because these rising powers have entered their modern age, with rapid industrialization and burgeoning business and professional sectors, at the same moment that Europe and the West have been graduating from theirs.

The Middle East and Muslim world passed through a sort of modernizing and nationalist age of Arab nationalism in the 1950s to the 1980s, but in reality much of the Muslim world only resembled the Western originals. Modernization and nationalism never fit Muslim societies and, after a generation, ended in exhaustion and failure to be succeeded by the Islamic revival, or more accurately by the part-traditional, part-modern ideology of Islamism, which is postnational and transnational. The only real example of strong nationalism or the nation-state in the Muslim world has been Turkey, since Ataturk established the new republic in the 1920s. But today even Turkey is being transformed by a rising Islamism, albeit one that is less militant than the Arab, Iranian, and Pakistani versions, which in their most extreme manifestations threaten both the United States and Western Europe.

Since 2000, classical populism and anti-Americanism have been resurgent in Latin America, the form of traditional nationalism in that region. The waves of populism and anti-Americanism have come and gone before, normally about once every generation. The region has not been able to create widespread and well-grounded nationalist identities, such as Europe, or establish strong and legitimate nation-states. Finally, with regard to Sub-Saharan Africa, that vast and poor region is stuck in the era of tribalism and predator states, in which one tribe savagely preys upon the other. In Africa, nationalism and the European, modern-style nation-state remain divergent.

Overall, nationalism and the nation-state were once authentic, strong, and vigorous in Europe, but they are no longer so. Rather, they have been succeeded by a listless system composed of the supranational and spiritless European Union and by the subnational and self-centered individualism of postmodern Europeans. In the Muslim world, Latin America, and Sub-Saharan Africa, nationalism and the nation-state were, with rare exceptions, never truly authentic, strong, and vigorous, and have almost totally disappeared in both Muslim and African countries. The one place where nationalism and the nation-state still thrive is East Asia, particularly China.

Variations on European Themes

A century ago, the one dynamic society in East Asia was Japan, which was rapidly modernizing, industrializing, and nationalizing. Japan had developed nationalism and the nation-state to an almost perfect degree by brilliantly emulating nationalism and nation-states in Western Europe. The Japanese nationalism proceeded to terrorize the rest of East Asia, especially China, for about four decades until 1945 when the U.S. military devastated this exemplar of the nation-state. The Japanese reinvented nationalism and redirected their military prowess to economic prowess. This period also lasted for about four decades until the early 1990s. But today, Japanese society has become quite postmodern, and its nationalism and the nation-state are considerably weaker than during most of the 20th century.

China is moving along a path that is similar to but more sophisticated than the one that Japan took nearly a century ago. Indeed, China exhibits similarities to another modernizing, industrializing, and nationalizing state, Germany of a century ago. But China also resembles the United States in that era. America under Theodore Roosevelt was establishing an authentic, strong, and vigorous nationalism and nation-state, which the 26th President called the New Nationalism.

Of course in the examples of Japan, Germany, and the United States in the early 20th century, vigorous industrial expansion provided newly confident nations with modern armies and fleets. Today, nearly double-digit annual growth rates over most of the last two decades and confident nationalism are facilitating the modernization of Chinese ground, sea, and air forces. However, Beijing seems to be investing in the potential of cyberwar in the information age rather than in weapons systems of the industrial era. There is increasing evidence that China intends to trump the overwhelming American advantage in the most advanced warfighting systems by achieving an equality or even superiority in new technologies and cyberwar tactics of the information age as evidenced by attacks on Department of Defense computer systems. The increasing capacity of the Chinese to neutralize or contain traditional American military advantages within East Asia (including the U.S. Seventh Fleet in the Western Pacific) will pose a definite challenge.

The New Central Kingdom

How will nationalism and the nation-state unfold in China over the next decade, and what will it mean for the rest of the world and especially the United States? The Chinese path toward a fully developed nationalism and the nation-state may follow earlier Japanese, German, and American models, and it will make a great deal of difference to all parties concerned which of these modern countries China comes to resemble most closely.

However, China as a civilization and the Central Kingdom with its distinct way of ordering social relationships, including with its neighbors, had existed many centuries before the modern era of European-style nationalism and nation-states. For example, Imperial China traditionally ordered relations with eastern and southern neighbors (Korea, Okinawa, Taiwan, and Vietnam), not in a European-style colonial system of direct rule, but in a tributary system of indirect rule, in which local monarchs had a great deal of independence, as long as they deferred to the authority of the Emperor in Beijing and did not allow their territory to become a base for other powers to threaten China. The growing Chinese economic and cultural presence and soft-power offensive in Southeast Asia, and increasingly in Central Asia, bear similarities with this traditional manner of conducting foreign relations. In the event, both nationalism and the nation-state in China will have their own distinctive Chinese characteristics, to paraphrase the words of Mao Zedong.

In the fullness of time, China also may enter its own postmodern and postnational era, once again with its own distinctive characteristics. What China and the United States will look like at that time is almost impossible to tell. But one thing probably can be assumed. Just as China had existed as a distinct civilization long before nationalism and the nation-state came into existence, China will endure as a distinct civilization longer than nationalism and the nation-state.

Islamism and the Crisis of Governance

It is an undeniable fact that with the end of the Cold War and the eclipse of the Soviet Union, the political center of many if not all Muslim-majority nation-states has been occupied by those who see Islam not merely as a faith and value system, but also as a vehicle for political mobilization. Therefore, Islamism is a real phenomenon that cannot be discounted any longer, nor should it be regarded as an aberration, a quirk in the developmental process of the Muslim world.

For reasons that now have become clear, the ascendancy of political Islam is not accidental: Islamists were actively courted by their respective states as well as the United States as allies in the struggle against communism from the 1960s to the 1980s. In Indonesia, Islamist organizations were instrumental in checking the advance of the communists in 1965–1970. In Pakistan, Islamist parties such as the Jama'at-e Islami and Jamiat'ul Ulema-e Islam were influential in countering communists at home and in mobilizing Afghan jihadists against the Soviet occupation. It should come as no surprise that Islamists in countries such as Pakistan and Indonesia have achieved such preeminence, given their cozy relationship with the government in the recent past.

Muslim governments faced another crisis that came about as a result of the global economy. The impact of globalization has been manifold, opening up developing economies and societies faster than ever. But it has also meant that under the liberal market regimes favored by global capital, many developing states have experienced economic governance and protectionism, which reduce the role of the state as the determining factor in the national economy. From the 1960s to 1980s, it was the relative boom in many developing economies that allowed states to maintain their grip on the local Islamist movements through the combination of coercion and cooptation. Today, as globalization renders states weaker around the globe, the capacity to control, guide, and domesticate potential Islamist opposition in their own territories has been visibly weakened.

Because much of this globalization process has been driven by Western capital, globalization has come to be conflated with Westernization and more specifically Americanization—hence the constant attacks on the emblems of global consumerism that are equated rightly or wrongly with American culture, politics, and hegemony. The rejection of globalization-Americanization is not unique to the Muslim world, for similar campaigns have been waged against American popular culture in non-Muslim countries, such as predominantly Hindu India and predominantly Catholic Latin America.

The Othering of America

Another development that has impacted directly on relations between the West and Muslim states over the last three decades has been the gradual process of distancing or the *othering* of America, which resulted from many factors, chief among them U.S. foreign policy in the Muslim world. Research conducted over the last 7 years involving hundreds of interviews with Islamists in India, Pakistan, Malaysia, and Indonesia points to the conclusion that the United States is seen as a threat to Muslim interests and partisan in its approach to the global Muslim community. The factors accounting for this perception, which has become hegemonized and sedimented among Islamists, range from the American position on the Israel-Palestine peace settlement to interventionist policies in countries such as Iraq and Afghanistan and even Sudan.

It is important to note that this perception of the United States as a threat to Muslim identity and politics is relatively new. In the wake of World War II, America was seen in a positive light as the liberator that helped many Muslim countries remove the yoke of European imperialism or Japanese militarism. This is particularly true in the case of the biggest Muslim nation, Indonesia, where America is credited with challenging Dutch and British colonialism in the region.

America also was seen as the most important strategic ally to Muslim states and communities during the Cold War, when foreign aid and military assistance was sought by Muslim countries to fend off perceived communist threats. This was certainly the case in Indonesia and Malaysia in the 1950s and 1960s and Pakistan after the rise to power of Zia 'ul Haq. This spirit of mutual support and cooperation persisted throughout the Soviet occupation of Afghanistan and in many respects was seen as the model condition to emulate by Muslims the world over until the cessation of hostilities in Afghanistan. This also accounts for how and why so many Muslim governments turned to the United States for inspiration for their own development models, and why so many nations sent many of their students to American universities to continue their education.

The turning point came after the end of the Afghan conflict, and the period of relative neglect that followed. It was during this time that many Muslim governments began to feel the impact of their uneven development, with rising expectations that could not be satisfied because of weak political structures exacerbated by debilitating effects of a rapid globalization process.

Latent antigovernment resentment over unfair and uneven developmental policies coupled with the loss of patronage on the part of Muslim states meant that Islamists could mobilize and challenge the state. In the process, many populist, mass-based urban Islamist movements lashed out at comprador allies and patrons in their governments, and in sweeping generalizations made against their own elites condemned close associations with foreign governments, multinationals, and international agencies, many of which were either American or U.S.-based. Support of Muslim governments, many of which had assumed the role and stature of nonrepresentative or authoritarian regimes by the 1980s, meant that condemnation of Muslim leaders such as Suharto in Indonesia also included condemnation of their American allies and strategic partners.

The failure of American foreign policy outreach was ignoring mass-based populist Islamist currents and groups that were developing in countries such as Pakistan, Bangladesh, Indonesia, and Malaysia. It is important to note that much cooperation between America and its Muslim allies from the 1960s to the 1990s took the form of government-to-government ventures, and seldom focused on the ground-level developments that were taking place in emerging urban spaces such as universities. When new Islamist groups began to appear on Indonesian campuses in the late 1990s, many Western policymakers were caught by surprise, unaware of the fact that these groups had initially begun to organize and mobilize their efforts as early as the 1970s.

The New Voice of Islamism

The relative marginalization of the official discourse in many Muslim societies means that states no longer have exclusive monopolies on communication in their respective societies. In nations such as Pakistan, Bangladesh, and Indonesia, a new generation of Islamist leaders, orators, nongovernmental organizations, civic groups, political parties, and business networks contest dialogue of the public sector, and the state has become only one voice among many. Muslim governments, regardless of their relationship with the United States, are no longer in a position to moderate or determine the tone and tenor of popular Islamist discourse in their countries and cannot be depended on to balance the negative images of America.

For this reason, alternative modes of direct engagement must be considered in reaching out to Muslim societies today. In the 1970s, for instance, American and Western agencies could still cooperate with Muslim governments and civil society networks to jointly advance progressive social reforms such as family planning, for the simple reason that the

United States was regarded as a sympathetic ally to Muslim interests. But today, most attempts on the part of America and Europe to further agendas, such as gender equality, educating women, and democracy, is seen in a negative light as part of a plot to weaken the Muslim world. U.S. policymakers must realize that because of the popular reaction to the invasion of Afghanistan and Iraq, the American image in the Muslim world is at an all-time low. American foreign policy initiatives have been cast as unilateralist and detrimental to Muslim solidarity and welfare, and reform initiatives are regarded with suspicion. Top-down initiatives through courting and coopting Muslim elites, intellectuals, and spokespersons no longer work, as demonstrated by the failure to reform religious schools or *madrassas* in Pakistan and promote liberal Islam in Indonesia. In the latter instance, previously respected Indonesian scholars and activists who were identified as model progressive Muslims or Muslim democrats were labeled as traitors and American agents not only by hardline Islamists, but also by mainstream Muslim media. The hand of America can be costly for Muslim nations, and top-down modes of engagement may prove counterproductive in the short to long run.

Faced with the prospect of further alienation, American policymakers should consider means of engagement that are less controversial, direct, and restrictive. Engaging with the Islamists by listening to their grievances may be such an alternative. One example of this approach was the 2-week program for Islamists from Indonesia and Malaysia that was conducted in Berlin under the sponsorship of the Task Force for the Dialogue with the Muslim World with support from the German Ministry of Foreign Affairs. Equally needed is low-level, bottom-up engagement in the affected localities, rather than traditional inter-elite contact (often dubbed the Hilton Hotel inter-religious dialogue). Since many Muslim elites are themselves alienated from their societies and may have little credibility, the utility of such inter-elite dialogues has come into question.

Serious ground-level efforts should be undertaken in countries such as Pakistan, Bangladesh, and Indonesia to determine trends in Islamist mobilization, identify services these groups provide to meet local need, and find ways in which American agencies, nongovernmental organizations, and private groups can effectively cooperate with local Islamist movements to achieve common goals such as education and health care. These are areas where American and Western intervention is most in demand. Demonstrating a long-lasting commitment to addressing real needs instead of abstract issues such as theological debates will offset negative images of the United States and other Western nations as potential enemies of Muslim communal and social life.

Images of America were not always negative in the eyes of Muslims, and their shifting views are the indirect result of U.S. foreign policy. If the United States chooses to maintain, improve, and expand the communication with the Muslim world, it must go beyond inter-elite dialogue and cultivate mutually supporting initiatives on the local level. This in turn requires identifying new actors and groups on the ground with attachments to communities as well as determining the aspirations and material needs that motivate the politics of those communities.

Rapid Increases in Food Prices

Basic food commodities have risen 83 percent in price in the last 3 years. The price increases have not been driven by sharp reductions in agricultural production; rather, increases have been slow over the past decade compared to previous periods, which has contributed to the stress on prices. Studies by the World Bank, International Food Policy Research Institute, and Food and Agriculture Organization attribute increases to a dramatic rise in oil prices that drives up the cost of fertilizer, rapid increases in the production of biofuels that are heavily subsidized by

Western governments, speculators looking for shelter from the weak dollar and turbulent stock and bond markets in commodity markets, export quotas and trade restrictions imposed by 48 countries on food staples, and the hoarding of grain supplies in anticipation of further price increases.

Most analysts believe that pressures driving higher prices are unlikely to subside any time soon, although the level of future increases is a question of some debate with no obvious answer. Three factors will determine the impact of the increases: their steepness, their rapidity, and the level of poverty and destitution among the population prior to the food crisis. As a general rule, the steeper and more rapid the price increase and the poorer the people before the crisis, the more severe the nutritional, economic, political, and security implications.

This general rule applies only in states whose economies are integrated into the international food system. In developing countries depending on international food markets, price increases could have serious consequences. In rural areas engaged in subsistence agriculture and isolated from markets, rising food prices will have only minimal adverse effects because they grow and consume their own food. This is particularly true for Sub-Saharan Africa where 60 to 70 percent of the population live in rural areas, use minimal if any chemical fertilizer (the price of which had rapidly increased with the

Displaced people wait for food during distribution organized by UN and USAID, Mogadishu, Somalia

price of oil), and consume what they grow with only small surpluses, which they sell in urban centers. Increased food prices may raise the income of rural farmers in some parts of the world to the disadvantage of urban dwellers who pay higher prices.

Food is plentiful in Nairobi's many restaurants and supermarkets, but not all residents have access to it

Famines

Although pressure on agriculture commodity prices is unlikely to cause famines in all but three or four countries, they could occur if short-term prices spike. Thus, the dynamics of famine, which follow common patterns, could become relevant. Famines and food crises are not necessarily driven by reduced production. In one of the most celebrated formulations in famine literature, Amartya Sen, who won the Nobel Prize in economics for work on entitlement theory of famines, wrote: "Starvation is the characteristic of some people not having enough food to eat. It is not the characteristic of there being not enough to eat. While [the] latter can be a cause of the former, it is but one of many possible causes." His research indicated that famines have occurred in periods of increased food production when access by the most destitute people to food through purchase or trade collapses because of rapid decline in household income or massive increase in food prices over a short period of time, or both.

Poor families that are food-insecure even in good times have developed coping mechanisms to deal with

periodic shocks associated with famine. Typically, families under stress will reduce food consumption from two to one meal per day, then one meal every other day, or in extreme cases stop feeding the weakest family members, a survival technique to preserve enough food to keep everyone else alive. These families will sell household furniture, clothes, tools, and jewelry to buy food. Farmers and herders will sell domesticated animals, which are a form of savings in developing nations, creating gluts in the market as animal prices collapse. In extreme situations, some parents sell their children, or men sell their wives to get money to buy food and to reduce the number of mouths to feed. In the early stages of famine, men and teenage boys often migrate to urban areas in search of work. In later stages of a famine, the remaining people in a village or neighborhood will leave in mass population movements to urban areas in search of food.

The mass population movement has the most profound consequences. Coping mechanisms often result in economic havoc for families using them to survive, deepening their destitution, and making it difficult to recover from the loss of assets before another nutritional crisis occurs. But people who starve or suffer acute malnutrition in rural areas often suffer in silence because of their isolation. If mass population movements drive people to urban areas or food prices spike in urban markets where a sizeable population of poor people live, the risk of political upheaval increases exponentially as hungry and dying people become visible, demonstrate and congregate in displaced persons camps which become radicalized, and have access to media and government officials. It is also the case that disparities of wealth are more obvious in urban areas and may increase popular anger and frustration.

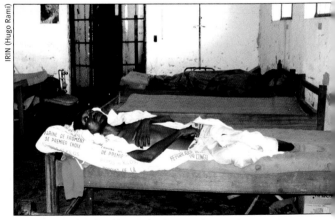

Inadequate public health care facilities in Kisangani, Democratic Republic of the Congo, offer little help to poor patients

Although most famines have occurred in rural areas, the nature of current price increases will likely create crisis in urban areas and spare the rural areas. The consequences of famine will be manifest in different ways depending on the political system in a given country. Indeed, rural areas that supply surplus food at market prices to urban areas could grow more prosperous as prices increase, which might redress the traditional disparity in developing nations between low incomes in rural areas and higher incomes in urban areas.

Democracy versus Totalitarianism

Some argue that famines do not occur in democracies because popular pressure on elected officials and media coverage of the crisis force governments to act. In addition, feedback in democratic systems, even when weak, gets messages to political leaders through multiple avenues about what is happening in society. Conversely, five famines occurred under totalitarian regimes in the 20th century: Russia during the forced collectivization in Ukraine in the early 1930s; China from 1958 to 1962 during the Great Leap Forward, which killed 29 million people (one of the worst famines in history); Cambodia under the Khmer Rouge in the 1970s; Ethiopia during the mid-1980s; and North Korea in the mid-1990s. These famines were prolonged, characterized by high mortality rates, and accompanied by repression designed to ensure the famine did not lead to political instability. Since totalitarian regimes exercise such extraordinary control over their populations and all sources of power and influence, none of them has been overthrown by popular unrest. Most famines, however, were followed by campaigns of terror waged by totalitarian leaders who exercise total control over the political apparatus of the state that may have been lost or declined to some extent because of the crisis.

While there remain four or five totalitarian states in the world, of these only North Korea is seriously at risk of famine. Between 1994 and 1998, it experienced the worst famine in the late 20th century, in which nearly 10 percent of the population died. The factors that led to that famine have not changed: the country has not abandoned its inefficient collectivized agriculture system that makes poor use of one of the lowest ratios of arable land to population in the world. Pyongyang continues to denude its mountains of ground cover, which causes extensive flooding that destroys crops, reducing already-meager harvests; and it refuses to move to a market economy, which might increase revenue to purchase food abroad. The precipitating factors that have led to this dramatic crisis in North Korea include China prohibiting grain exports because of increased

prices, South Korea abruptly ending food aid and fertilizer after the election of a new president, severe seasonal flooding that reduced production, depleting reserves for the military, and rising prices that restrict the amount of food that can be bought internationally with limited resources. The United States announced a 500,000-ton food contribution to the World Food Programme in 2008 after Pyongyang agreed to accept international standards for the monitoring and management of international food assistance. But assistance had been hampered by Pyongyang's policies in the first half of 2009, especially its restrictions on food distribution and its nuclear ambitions.

In fragile and failed states, famines often result in rebellions or coups because their political systems are too weak institutionally to respond to the crisis or repress popular outrage caused by crises. During the great West African Famine of 1968–1974, every government in the Sahel Belt with the exception of Senegal fell to a rebellion or coup, including the government of Emperor Haile Selassie of Ethiopia. African states are not well integrated into international food markets probably because they do not have the currency reserves or private capital to purchase food on international markets, and are less at risk than those fragile and poor states in other regions of the world that are dependent on these markets. Africa could be indirectly affected by food price increases because it receives 75 percent of all U.S. food aid, mostly for emergencies involving refugees and internally displaced people, and the total tonnage of assistance is declining again because of increased prices. This loss has caused major deficits in food within the international aid system that if not remedied could have serious nutritional consequences in Africa.

Productivity and Investment

Starting in the late 1980s, Western bilateral aid agencies and the World Bank began a precipitous drop in investments in agricultural development, particularly in Sub-Saharan Africa, which remains the most food-insecure region of the world. Although some of that insecurity is attributable to civil conflict, state failure, and regressive agricultural policies, it is obvious that reduced investment is also to blame. One striking example is Ethiopia, which is perhaps the most food-insecure country in Africa. Nonetheless, the U.S. Agency for International Development allocates 50 percent for the HIV/AIDS program, 28 percent for food aid, and only 1.5 percent for agricultural development because the White House and Congress have failed to fund the proposed agricultural programs in the annual budget for foreign assistance.

A major commitment by the United States to increased spending on agricultural development in Africa should advance a number of proposals for action, including the following:

■ Support large and small farms, research on genetically modified organisms, local scientific capacity-building in African governments, and rural roads, which are essential for development.

■ Provide scholarships for students from developing countries at U.S. colleges and universities to rebuild human capital in the agricultural sector, which has suffered from neglect for two decades.

■ Eliminate production subsidies, impediments to free global trade in agricultural products, and ethanol subsidies for corn, given that subsidies account for 30 percent of increases in corn prices.

■ Purchase up to 25 percent of American food aid locally in developing countries, which will increase the amount of aid that can be bought with a fixed appropriation given that 20 to 30 percent of the cost of U.S. food aid is for transportation.

■ Introduce market intervention plans developed by nongovernmental organizations, the World Food Programme, and the United States that auction food aid in local markets to stabilize prices and force hoarded food onto markets. **gsa**

Contributors

Ambassador Robert B. Oakley (Chapter Editor) is a Distinguished Research Fellow in the Institute for National Strategic Studies (INSS) at the National Defense University (NDU). During his career as a Foreign Service Officer, he served as U.S. Ambassador to Zaire, Somalia, and Pakistan, and later as a Special Envoy during the American involvement in Somalia in the early 1990s.

Dr. Farish Ahmad-Noor is a Senior Fellow in the S. Rajaratnam School of International Studies at Nanyang Technological University, Singapore, and one of the founders of the South/Southeast Asian Web site, <www.OtherMalaysia.org>.

The Honorable Dr. Patrick M. Cronin is Director of INSS at NDU, which was established by the Secretary of Defense and Chairman of the Joint Chiefs of Staff in 1984 to conduct strategic assessments for senior Department of Defense officials and decisionmakers. He took up the post at the beginning of 2008 after a 25-year career inside

government and academic research centers and spanning areas of defense, security, foreign policy, and foreign assistance. He is simultaneously Director of the Center for the Study of Chinese Military Affairs, which serves as a national focal point for multidisciplinary research and analytic exchanges regarding China.

Dr. James S. Kurth is Claude Smith Professor of Political Science at Swarthmore College. He received his A.B. in History from Stanford University, and his M.A. and Ph.D. in Political Science from Harvard University, where he was an assistant and associate professor of government. He has been a visiting member of the Institute for Advanced Study (Princeton University), visiting professor of political science at the University of California at San Diego, and visiting professor of strategy at the U.S. Naval War College.

Andrew S. Natsios is Distinguished Professor in the Practice of Diplomacy in the Walsh School of Foreign Service at Georgetown University. From May 2001 to January 2006, he served as Administrator of the U.S. Agency for International Development (USAID). During this period, he managed USAID's reconstruction programs in Afghanistan, Iraq, and Sudan, which totaled more than $14 billion over 4 years. President George W. Bush appointed him Special Coordinator for International Disaster Assistance and Special Humanitarian Coordinator for Sudan.

Carlos Pascual was nominated to become U.S. Ambassador to Mexico. He has served as Vice President and Director of Foreign Policy at the Brookings Institution. A former U.S. Ambassador to Ukraine and Senior Director on the National Security Council staff, Mr. Pascual is a specialist on international security policy, postconflict stabilization, nonproliferation, and economic development.

Harvey Rishikof is Professor of Law and National Security Studies in the National War College at NDU. He was Legal Counsel to the Deputy Director of the Federal Bureau of Investigation (1997–1999) and federal law clerk for the Honorable Leonard I. Garth. As Administrative Assistant to the Chief Justice of the Supreme Court (1994–1996), Mr. Rishikof served as Chief of Staff for the Chief Justice.

Chapter 3
The Impact of the Information Revolution

One of the most challenging issues for international security today is the information revolution. Although no single assessment can investigate every implication of this issue, this chapter highlights potential opportunities and dangers posed by the information revolution that will challenge the international security arena.

The chapter begins by focusing attention on the nexus of the information, technology, and defense sectors. It then explores ubiquitous cell phone connectivity, transparency, and cyber warfare—all trends in networked communications that indicate the information revolution is no longer limited to the West but involves every corner of the world. The next section looks at the threats posed by hackers. It suggests that the tendency toward overclassification actually intensifies these threats. The following section examines threats caused by the shift from hierarchical systems to networks and decentralized edge networks of hackers that operate beyond the reach of traditional control mechanisms. The responses to these threats will require standardizing international laws, sharing intelligence, and widening edge-to-edge contact at relatively low levels among nations, organizations, corporations, and individuals.

The use of the Internet by al Qaeda and its sympathizers is the topic of the next section, which offers a glimpse of the ways in which communications among people on the edge can turn into violence. Internet design precludes eliminating such conversations, and thus it is wiser to exploit them. The ensuing section considers space-based capabilities integral to the information revolution, including the global positioning system, video over the Internet, and global communications. Understanding the potential of space is essential in the development of a global information network. The final section, on the relationship of technology and the changing character of war, investigates how genetics, robotics, and nanotechnology have advanced through the information revolution. Technology, like information itself, will soon present both benefits and risks for public and private entities as well as corporate and individual actors using commercially available technology. And a peer competitor may arise from any of these areas.

The Information Environment

Thirty years ago, U.S. defense planners envisioned a military transformation in which war would be conducted by weapons infused with electronics and driven by information. Then, 15 years ago, graduate students created the first visual Web browser known as Mosaic that popularized Internet access. Today, the relationship between technology, information, and defense shapes the world and U.S. national security policy (see figure 3–1). Three trends in this information revolution are relevant to strategic concerns: ubiquitous cell phone connectivity, transparency, and cyber warfare.

Ubiquitous Connectivity

Just a few years ago, half of the world population had never heard a dial tone. In 2008, the number of people who own cell phones exceeded the number who did not. Places such as Africa and rural India, barely touched by the Industrial Revolution, are plunging headlong into the information revolution with the help of cell phones. Even where cell phone ownership is relatively expensive, many have found ways to enjoy its benefits through the work of institutions such as Bangladesh's Grameenphone that help micro-entrepreneurs lend phones on a per-call basis.

The full effect of ubiquitous person-to-person communications can only be guessed at, but some effects are already noticeable. Farmers and fishermen, for instance, are now plugged into local and even international markets on a nearly real-time basis—their incomes have risen 5 percent on average from simply being able to sell into the best markets. Rural parents are much better connected to their children who have moved to the city. Evanescent trading and employment opportunities can be communicated far more easily, lubricating the accommodation to the inevitable shifts wrought by globalization. Large political groups are capable of mobilizing their membership in protest (as they have done in Burma, Thailand, and the Philippines).

One would think that the ubiquity of cell phones—in 5 years Iraq (or at least that part controlled by Saddam Hussein) went from zero to 12 million cell phones—would be the insurgents' friend. With these devices, insurgents could acquire a command and control system that would rival U.S. and Iraqi government forces. Of late, the contrary has proven true. Indeed, insurgents have targeted cell phone towers and eliminated service in places such as Ramadi (Anbar Province), but motivated locals were using cell phones to provide intelligence on insurgent identities and whereabouts

Moreover, cell phones offer ways to combat terrorism by identifying dangerous individuals. The phones are hardware-dependent and need a handset and subscriber information module (SIM) that can be matched to cell towers and switches. Every time a cell phone is used, switches identify the phone and SIM card of the caller, the phone called, and the location of each phone through the global positioning system (GPS) and triangulation. Moreover, if it was possible to connect the identity of individuals with SIM chips, phone companies could learn more about customers. Although such knowledge can be used for nefarious purposes, it also could deliver government services, prevent illicit use of cell phones, inhibit insurgent use of cell phones, and provide forensic evidence and immediate intelligence to security forces. Influence over the cell phone screen and favorable billing policies can make it easier to establish neighborhood watch groups and provide feeds from approved sources. In more affluent countries, mobile communications are proliferating. Adolescents are more likely to use phones for texting than for talking. Phones with GPS capabilities can locate anything from the nearest Starbucks to the local hospital. Between the wired Ethernet, wireless short-range Bluetooth, medium-range WiFi, and long-range WiMax, it is hard to roam beyond Internet range. Social networking sites based on Web 2.0 such as Facebook, MySpace, LinkedIn, and Twitter make it possible to reach out and touch *everyone*.

Who will benefit more from this trend: we or our enemies? Once there were fears that terrorists would disrupt the Internet because it is a symbol of open societies. Instead, they have adopted it as a means of communication and recruitment. Tens of thousands of jihadist Web sites have sprung up to transmit messages, motivate sympathizers, and recruit new adherents. Many terrorists drawn to Iraq, and to a lesser extent Afghanistan, were attracted through these sites. However, the digital footprint left by jihadist use of the Internet has been a way of tracking would-be terrorists in the United States and Great Britain. Sunni jihadists and al Qaeda in Iraq among others use the Internet to influence supporters and threaten enemies. Fortunately, data can differentiate one group from another and provide intelligence on group dynamics.

Transparency

U.S. forces in Vietnam could enter and leave a village before anyone outside the area was aware of their presence. Given today's ubiquitous and instantaneous nature of communications systems, such opacity has disappeared. In fact, it is unclear if anything on a future urban battlefield can be kept secret for longer than it takes to establish a cell phone connection.

Global transparency is also increasing. The launch of several satellites with resolutions better than 1 meter makes quality imagery available to anyone with a credit card. Both Google and Microsoft supply the Internet with imagery via the Internet-based application, Google Earth. Although the U.S. Government has persuaded these companies to reduce the resolution of some pictures and established right of first refusal on real-time battlefield shots, the overall result is the same: no place on Earth can be hidden. Imagery has been used by nongovernmental organizations to monitor disaster sites and hold governments accountable for sins of omission and commission. The ability to get the word out with cell phones and the Internet makes official secrets difficult to maintain. In the case of Zimbabwe, where repression of political protesters and the press would have gone unnoticed, transparency and connectivity revealed the problems internationally. Nevertheless, determined authorities can resist the global transparency of the Internet. In the People's Republic of China, censorship remains effective despite the efforts of individual users to circumvent its restrictions.

Some believe that the Internet proliferates ideas, which in turn leads to greater openness and equality. Studies have indicated that when people have more freedom to choose among media outlets, they lean toward those that reinforce prior beliefs. As a result, established ideas are less often challenged or modified. Ironically, the openness of the Internet has permitted repression as well as justice to be voluntarily outsourced; witness the recent case of a Chinese student in America who protested repression in Tibet. She was identified by pro-Beijing peers over the Internet, and her family in China was harassed and threatened.

Cyber Warfare

Information technology and the Internet are increasingly vulnerable to cyber attack. Much of what once was controlled by hardware and physical infrastructure is now controlled by software, a medium that is infinitely malleable by other software, which makes cyber attack increasingly possible and harder to trace. Emblematic of this problem was the distributed denial-of-service attack that constricted access by

▼ *Continued on p. 57*

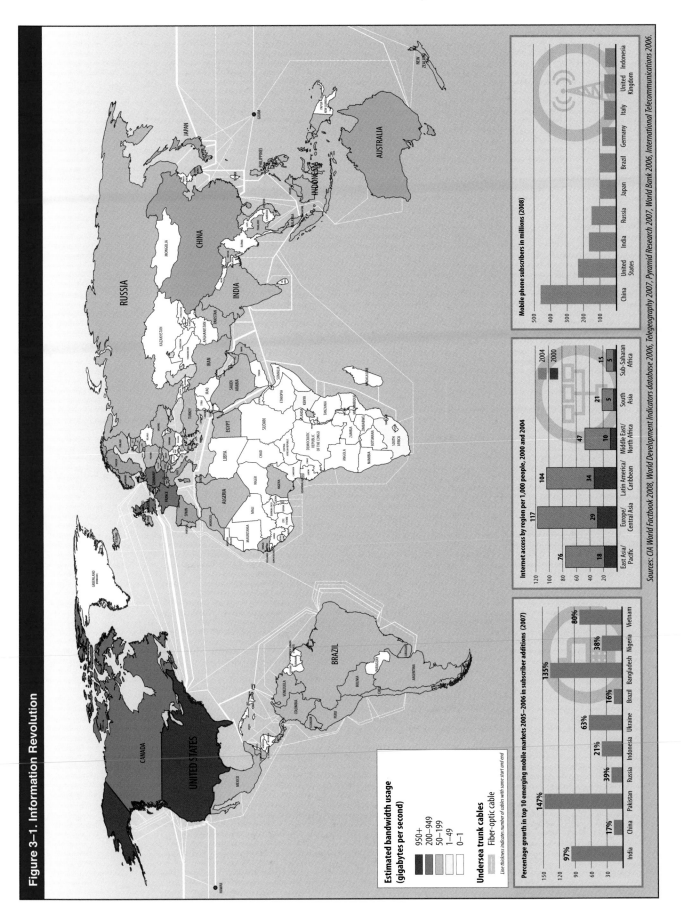

Figure 3–1. Information Revolution

Estimated bandwidth usage
(gigabytes per second)
- 950+
- 200–949
- 50–199
- 1–49
- 0–1

Undersea trunk cables
Fiber-optic cable
Line thickness indicates number of cables with same start and end

Percentage growth in top 10 emerging mobile markets 2005–2006 in subscriber additions (2007)

India 97% | Pakistan 147% | Russia 39% | Indonesia 21% | Ukraine 63% | Brazil 16% | Bangladesh 135% | Nigeria 38% | Vietnam 80% | China 17%

Internet access by region per 1,000 people, 2000 and 2004
2004 / 2000

East Asia/Pacific 76 / 18 | Europe/Central Asia 117 / 29 | Latin America/Caribbean 104 / 34 | Middle East/North Africa 47 / 10 | South Asia 21 / 5 | Sub-Saharan Africa 15 / 5

Mobile phone subscribers in millions (2008)

China | United States | India | Russia | Japan | Brazil | Germany | Italy | United Kingdom | Indonesia

Sources: CIA World Factbook 2008, World Development Indicators database 2006; Telegeography 2007, Pyramid Research 2007, World Bank 2006, International Telecommunications 2006.

Al Qaeda, Its Sympathizers, and the Internet

Al Qaeda, together with its affiliates and sympathizers, uses the Internet to spread its views on Salafi jihadism and reestablish the caliphate. The group regards attention by the media and *dawa*, or proselytizing, as indispensable to jihad, of equal or greater importance than violence. The Internet is central to its plans because it is the only medium to which it has unrestricted access.

Thousands of Web sites have content sympathetic to Salafi jihadists. For those people who seek information, these sites contain text, video, audio, graphics, chat rooms, bulletin boards, discussion groups, and even computer games. Discussions range from casual dialogue to highly sophisticated conversations about theology, politics, strategy, tactics, and weapons. Approaches range from the abstract to the practical expressed in styles from the polemical and exhortatory to the dispassionate and intellectual. The material is designed for a variety of functions, including planning, propaganda and radicalization, training, education, and social purposes.

Within the Salafi jihadist movement, there are two countervailing tendencies: one consciously prefers uniformity and another stands for individual action. Much Salafi jihadist activity is associated with one of several terrorist or insurgent groups that produce and disseminate branded material to the world. These groups are concerned with attribution and authority. Many have affiliated regional production centers that produce videos, magazines, information bulletins, and even poetry. For instance, as-Sahab Media is affiliated with al Qaeda central, while al-Furquan Media is associated with the Islamic State of Iraq. Their products are disseminated through Internet clearinghouses such as the al-Fajr Media Center or Global Islamic Media Front. Such clearinghouses typically serve as outlets for various production organizations. They also serve as guarantors of the authenticity of the material, which appears on elite, access-controlled Web sites such as al-Ekhlaas and al-Hesbah. Typically, about 90 percent of the products are text, about 9 percent video, and the balance is audio, graphic, and other forms. The majority of the text items can be classified as military reports and policy statements, while the rest are periodicals, books, and essays.

The balance of the material on the Web sites of Salafi jihadists is commentary and discussion springing from established as well as homegrown sources. The latter appear on many al Qaeda–affiliated and independent sites. Freelance self-styled intellectuals can draw significant followings on controlled access and quasi-official sites. Occasionally, original documents can gain substantial traction, as occurred with "Jihad in Iraq: Hopes and Dangers," which appeared in 2003 under the byline of an unknown group (never heard of again) and may have inspired the Madrid train bombings. This combination of controlled information and spontaneous contributions poses serious security dangers.

Effects

Young people are disproportionately likely to seek information, entertainment, and social contacts on the Internet. Moreover, an increasing amount of jihadist material is available. Thus, in the past few years the Internet, rather than physical locations, has become the venue for training young recruits who eventually commit acts of terrorism.

Radicalization on the Internet generally does not happen as a result of people reading official publications from as-Sahab, the Global Islamic Media Front, or some other organization. People are actually galvanized to radicalism and eventually action through the less formal aspects of the Internet, including discussion forums, chat rooms, email, and listserves.

In addition, ideas that could pass for military doctrine influence the global jihad. These ideas, such as the work of the Salafi jihadist strategic thinker Abu Musab al-Suri, strongly influence the actions of organized groups such as al Qaeda, but also reach informal parts of the Salafi jihadist world. They are particularly important in dealing with leaderless resistance.

Squelch or Exploit?

Individual extremist Web sites come and go. However, the prospect of impeding online Salafi jihadist discourse is minimal at best. Often the sites are hosted by nations with free speech protections. Furthermore, intelligence gain-loss calculations may suggest that it is preferable for some to operate. The prospects for making a serious dent in such Web sites with technical sabotage are low. The Internet was designed for almost endless growth, and it provides nearly anonymous communication. Indeed, some jihadist forums have been hosted on numerous uniform resource locators, but they continue to thrive. Historically, it was impossible to squelch the spread of subversive materials before the Internet came along. The experience of the Soviet Union with samizdat and extensive penetration of the speeches of Ayatollah Khomeini in Iran under the Shah by means of cassette tapes are two examples. Notwithstanding the success of taking down main Web sites that carried al Qaeda messages, at the end of the day exploiting communications may be more productive than trying to interrupt them.

▲ *Continued from p. 54*

major Web sites in Estonia. In reaction to Estonia's decision in 2007 to move a Russian World War II memorial, protestors mobilized thousands and possibly millions of computers to send packets to Web servers of government offices and national banks, knocking many offline. With few exceptions, these computer owners were unwitting participants in the attack. Unlike previous attacks using slow-moving "bots," these cyber tactics were organized and executed in hours. No one knows their origin: Estonia blamed Russia, Russia stonewalled Estonia, and the only person convicted was an Estonian of Russian descent.

State-sponsored cyber attacks are becoming increasingly commonplace. China is often cited as being in the vanguard of cyber espionage. Recently, state-sponsored hackers placed malicious code on computers when users downloaded material from suspect Web sites or opened email attachments from seemingly reliable parties. Once ingested in a targeted computer, the code opens data files from the inside, sending terabytes of information to the hackers. Victims of this tactic were users worldwide including military bases, defense contractors, and private businesses. Hackers look for technical information, but since malicious codes cannot tell one type of information from another, they must search many haystacks to find the needle.

In response to attacks, the U.S. Government added measures to tighten information security in late 2007. The National Security Agency was made responsible for protecting civilian as well as military networks. As a result, the number of government gateways to the open Internet will be drastically reduced. Other forms of counterespionage and cyber defense are being explored, but it is unclear if such activities can be deterred. Moreover, if cyber espionage is ever declared an act of war, it will have world-changing implications.

Network insecurity will remain problematic in the future. As computers become more secure, hacker tools will improve. The key to network security will reside in reducing vulnerabilities. In the meantime, governments should rely on primitive methods of security, including disconnecting critical systems from the outside world or refusing to use Web-based systems.

Understanding Cyber Attacks

Many people consider "computer network attacks" the domain of cyber-espionage and governments, with reviews restricted to highly classified environments. However, throughout the civilian arena, there are active, open source discussions about how to penetrate computer networks, and sophisticated penetration tools are available to anyone with Internet access. Nongovernmental actors have participated in real world attacks on governments, and unclassified laboratories exist to test new tools and train those responsible for Internet security.

A search on the term *computer network attack* generates some 17,600,000 references on Google[1] while *computer hacking* generates about 5,390,000.[2] Many of the sites generated by a search for *computer network attack* focus on policy, history, and concepts. In contrast, many of the sites generated by the term *computer hacking* display and teach specific tools for mischievous or malevolent activity. These malevolent sites run the gamut from "point and click" procedures that can be used by anyone with a computer mouse to powerful tools for experienced hackers.[3]

From a government perspective, classifying such tools and procedures is important to protecting sensitive activities and network vulnerabilities. Yet from the hacker's perspective, the information is readily available and thousands of users already know how to attack networks. For this reason, the government needs to be careful that it does not overclassify information about capabilities that already are available to opponents. Such knowledge is necessary for adequately defending networks from mal-intents.

Lessons from DEFCON

The DEFCON convention is held every summer in Las Vegas and bills itself as "the largest underground hacker convention in the world." This is a serious event—typically including more than 80 presentations in 4 or 5 parallel tracks, which often run well into the evening. It brings together talented people with

Team that developed first large-scale digital computer, the IBM automatic sequence controlled calculator, poses in front of the massive computer

diverse viewpoints. Topics discussed there can affect cyber security and information-sharing initiatives, so it is worth summarizing some points from recent years. Given the scope of each DEFCON, the observations that follow reflect only a part of the activities at the conferences, but they give some idea of the scope and sophistication of the subjects addressed.

In 2006, three of the focus areas were:

■ "Owning" an organization through the Black-Berry. (This was a physical access issue, reinforcing the point that all portable devices that can access networks need to be protected by passwords. BlackBerries are reasonably secure electronically.)

■ The dramatic increase in the *attack surface* (their term) afforded by the proliferation of wireless devices such as WiFi and WiMax. (Many security personnel do not understand the detailed data structures of these systems, and their spread contributes to increased use of wireless by people who do not pay much attention to security.)

■ The dramatic increase in the attack surface caused by the transition to Internet Protocol (IP) version (v) 6. (Once everything is native IP v6, it will be more secure than IP v4, but during the transition,

WiFi scanner in use at DEFCON, considered the world's largest underground hacker convention

many do not understand that there are vulnerabilities in the complex header structure and packets tunneling between IP v4, and v6 stacks are immune from "deep packet inspection.")

In 2007, the focus was more on identity theft and data manipulation. The first point was that the real objective of hacking is getting not only root access to a computer, but also the data itself—stealing it, corrupting it, hiding it, or manipulating it. The ways to get to the data are through the people (stealing identities), their applications, their operating systems, and only then the computer itself. In this context, presentations put special emphasis on programs that allow someone to scan an individual's total Web presence, cross-reference his email accounts and address books, look at cookies, identify frequent correspondents (who might not inspect attachments closely) and so forth. Identity theft poses special challenges since it can be used to circumvent many technical network defense measures and also is a key ingredient in online criminal activity.

In 2008, emphasis included:

■ Exploiting social software and social networks, primarily as a way of gathering information for identity theft and preparation for "custom-tailored, laser-focused attacks." Analytical programs such as "Satan" are particularly valuable for these purposes.[4] The point here is not to cast doubt on the value of social networks; they are an important feature of society, online and offline. In recognition of this, the Social Software for Security[5] initiative is looking for ways to encourage the government to take advantage of the energy and imagination being put into the development of social software by balancing functionality and security. "Risk management" (as opposed to "risk avoidance") in these environments is critical, but it is important to understand the tradeoffs.

■ Hacking opportunities provided by increasing use of wireless. "Always-on" connections mean "always-on" vulnerabilities. Talks at the conference discussed very imaginative attacks, especially focused on "men in the middle" operations to misdirect unwitting participants from what they think are secure Web sites to insecure ones. Most people still do not appreciate how much risk they are at in unsecured "wireless hotspots" at places such as airports.

■ Discussions of "Open Source Warfare": how to combine various tools to triangulate cell phone conversations with video coverage from low cost ($400), remote control helicopters to permit isolation, and potential targeting, of individuals.

■ Sophisticated social network attacks taking advantage of personal behaviors (for example, sending free iPhones to people in the mailroom and then using them to monitor an organization's network configurations).

Other DEFCON talks focused on things such as breaking into physical locks, compromising e-voting (seems distressingly simple in many cases), hacking the Boston subway system fare cards (good enough that the Metropolitan Boston Transit Authority sued to stop the presentation), compromising network data integrity, and hardware Trojans that showed low cost ways to make a "secure" router transmit data via largely undetectable infrared, radio frequency, or optical signals.

In sum, each annual DEFCON provides both interesting and troubling insights into a world of energetic, talented people devoted to getting at information and information systems that others try to protect. Though many of the techniques shown there may have been used by governments, all those discussed at the conference are available to anyone.

Georgia

In his research on the Russia-Georgia conflict, Evgeny Morozov, the Berlin-based founder of the news aggregator *Polymeme*, explored the possibility of launching an amateur cyber attack on the country of Georgia by setting out:

to test how much damage someone like me . . . could inflict upon Georgia's Web infrastructure, acting entirely on my own and using only a laptop and an Internet connection. If I succeeded, that would somewhat contradict the widely shared assumption—at least in most of the Western media—that the Kremlin is managing this cyber warfare in a centralized fashion. My mission, if successful, would show that the field is open to anyone with a grudge against Georgia.

With tools available online and a short program he wrote in a Microsoft Word document, Morozov developed programs to promote denial-of-service attacks. He then went to "Stop Georgia," a Web site that claimed to be linked to the hacker underground in Russia. This site offered target lists of sites that indicated disruption and also offered downloadable code to customize attack options that could be launched by clicking the button labeled "Start Flood." As Morozov discovered, "Within an hour I had become an Internet soldier. I didn't receive any calls from Kremlin operatives."[6]

The denial-of-service attacks explored by Morozov are less sophisticated and disruptive than would be possible with the kind of data manipulation, identity theft, or computer penetration described at DEFCON or available from hacker sites. However, the fact that the Russian campaign against Georgia included kinetic and cyber activities is likely to be typical of future military action. The ease with which Morozov launched attacks reflects the amount of malicious information on the Internet. It also points to the difficulty in distinguishing between *official* and *unofficial* activities. This ambiguity was evident in operations against Estonia in 2007.

Labs at IRMC

The Information Resources Management College (IRMC) at the National Defense University in Washington, DC, offers cutting-edge classes on a wide variety of cyber-related issues for chief information officers, chief financial officers, chief information security officers, and others. Its courses on information operations help dozens of leaders understand cyber-threats and prepare themselves for Service and joint assignments.

IRMC also has a set of laboratories covering areas such as information assurance, supervisory control and data acquisition systems, and virtual reality. These labs are built around internal networks,

U.S. Air Force (Adam M. Stump)

Vice Chairman of the Joint Chiefs of Staff General James Cartwright speaks at Air Force cyberspace symposium on importance of experimenting with cyber warfare implementation

isolated from the Internet but populated with Internet tools. As such, these labs are used for extensive experimentation. The information assurance lab, in particular, offers detailed opportunities for non-experts to implant malicious code in software applications and operating systems within these closed networks using openly available hacking tools. It emphasizes the importance of robust information assurance approaches and trains students how to implement them.

The supervisory control and data acquisition lab offers similar experiences regarding control systems for powerplants and other critical infrastructures. The virtual reality lab provides experience in the increasingly important area of avatars and virtual interactions. These are currently used in gaming but are expected to become integral to the command and control systems of the future. Not surprisingly, recent DEFCON conventions have included sessions on hacking avatars.

Any senior official associated with computer network operations, defense, exploitation, or attack should visit these laboratories. At a minimum, the capabilities developed in the labs and online should be synthesized into informational manuals that can be provided at unclassified levels to help train those who are operating and defending our networks.

A wise man recently asked: "What is more strategically threatening to the U.S. military than our inability to manage information in a contested environment?" Being able to operate and defend our networks is hard enough even when threats are well understood. Attack options available to opponents from open sources should be examined aggressively and disseminated with minimal caveats to strengthen our defensive posture on all networks, including the unclassified networks so important to personnel, medical, and logistic activities. More sophisticated tools may be available within classified channels, but this should not keep officials from knowing what is available to adversaries. Regular reviews to make sure that information is not over-classified could be a good way to avoid this danger.

The importance of cyber security also needs to be understood by senior officials across the new administration, not just those directly associated with the networks themselves. It should be taught as part of core courses in Department of Defense educational institutions, not only as electives. Cyber security is an issue of serious nationwide importance—it must be the concern of policymakers and commanders, not just communicators and technical specialists.

New Threats, New Responses

Enabled by modern network technologies, power is "shifting to the edge." This shift is allowing decentralized networked groups to vie with traditional hierarchical structures. Globalized communications and computing infrastructure combined with collaborative software permit hostile nonstate groups—terrorists, criminals, rogue corporations, antiglobalization movements, hackers, and others that act on behalf of nations or other entities—to threaten international security and stability. Increasingly, security arrangements based on geographic borders, sovereign control, and unilateral response to global threats by individual nations are inadequate to counter such groups. U.S. national security strategy must embrace a decentralized, multilateral public health model against unknown threats. This model should be based on local monitoring of emerging threats, swarming global response to counter manifest attacks, and developing resilient capabilities to withstand and recover in their wake.

Organizational Network

Emerging social and peer networking technology is enabling new organizational structures that afford opportunities for novel patterns of generative and degenerative activities. Such developments, which are popularly known as Web 2.0 or the Web as platform, underpin the decentralized networks as distinct organizational forms that have advantages over the traditional hierarchies in terms of flexibility, adaptability, and responsiveness.

As a result, the power to generate potentially catastrophic effects by organizing, coordinating, or sharing dispersed resources is shifting from the center to the periphery. Decentralized groups can synchronize activity globally without regard to political borders or local government control. If the groups are hostile, security arrangements that rely on the assumption that sovereign nations are responsible for activities in their territory and among their subjects are inadequate.

In the first stage of Internet development in Web 1.0, individuals, organizations, information, or devices at the edge of a network interacted with central servers, providers, or other authorities on an essentially one-to-one basis that mimicked hierarchical arrangements. In Web 2.0, the edges interact directly on a many-to-many basis. Although Web 1.0 enabled asynchronous mediated communication among edge elements, Web 2.0 enables synchronicity of effort without control or formal organizational structure. Although this greatly reduces the overhead associated with centralized management controls—and thus enhances the power

Figure 3–2. Satellite Technology

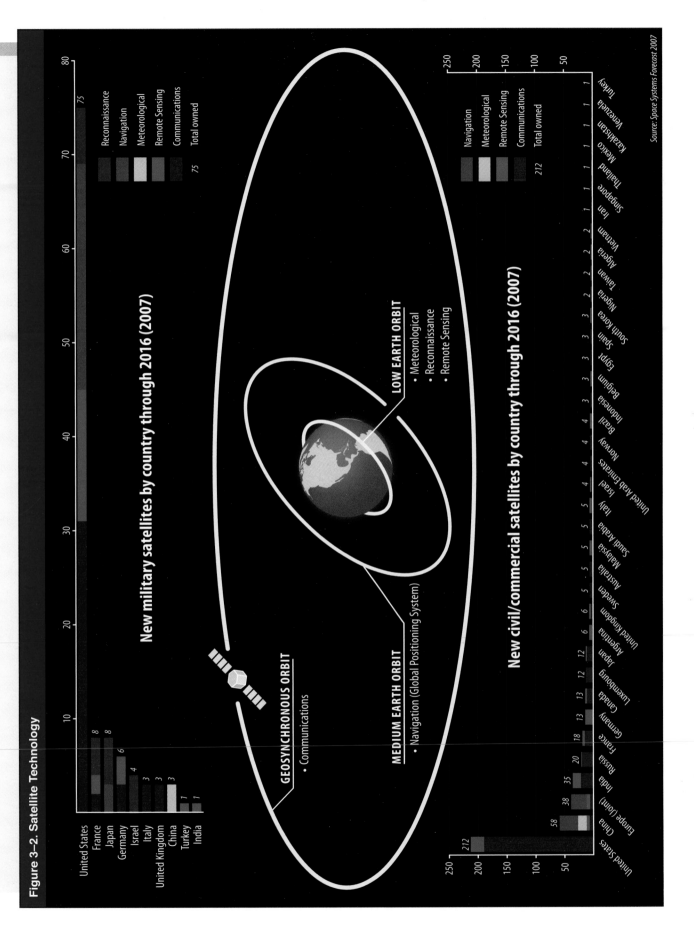

New military satellites by country through 2016 (2007)

Reconnaissance
Navigation
Meteorological
Remote Sensing
Communications

Total owned

75

United States 75
France 8
Japan 8
Germany 6
Israel 4
Italy 3
United Kingdom 3
China 3
Turkey 1
India 1

GEOSYNCHRONOUS ORBIT
· Communications

MEDIUM EARTH ORBIT
· Navigation (Global Positioning System)

LOW EARTH ORBIT
· Meteorological
· Reconnaissance
· Remote Sensing

New civil/commercial satellites by country through 2016 (2007)

Navigation
Meteorological
Remote Sensing
Communications

Total owned

212

United States 212
China 58
Europe (Joint) 38
India 35
Russia 20
France 18
Germany 13
Canada 13
Luxembourg 12
Japan 12
Argentina 6
United Kingdom 6
Sweden 6
Australia 5
Malaysia 5
Saudi Arabia 5
Italy 5
United Arab Emirates 4
Israel 4
Norway 4
Brazil 4
Indonesia 3
Belgium 3
Egypt 3
Spain 3
South Korea 3
Nigeria 2
Taiwan 2
Algeria 2
Vietnam 2
Iran 1
Singapore 1
Thailand 1
Mexico 1
Kazakhstan 1
Venezuela 1
Turkey 1

Source: Space Systems Forecast 2007

▲ *Continued from p. 63*

drove innovation at places such as Google. Amateur biologists and nanotechnology engineers are likely to do the same thing.

The defense implications go beyond biological threats. Dramatic performance enhancements would be a huge shock to warfare. Although large nations are likely to lead in the development of such enhancements, ruthless and unethical nations will have an advantage in this competition. GRIN research facilitates the modification of human beings for specific purposes. Initially, this manipulation was seen as a way of relieving illnesses such as tumors or discovering disease-causing genes. Now, however, it is also seen as a conduit to "improving" human beings.

There is substantial research being done on the posthuman future. Designer drugs produced in biotech labs interact with the brain in a genotype-specific manner either to improve memory or decrease the effects of sleep deprivation. Research on the brain-machine interface promises improvements in human senses such as hearing and vision. Exoskeleton suits allow soldiers to carry 200 pounds and bound long distances with little effort. Custom replacement organs will soon be generated from stem cells, and prosthetics with microprocessors will aid wounded soldiers.

Nanotechnology is a developing area, but it clearly links human biotechnology in various ways. A good deal of nanotechnology research is tied to biotechnology, which looks at the possible manipulation of the atom on the biomolecular level. It has even been posited that the robo-soldier of the future—rather than a human "cyborg"—may be a micro- or nano-robot that is versatile, inexpensive, impossible to detect, and able to penetrate nearly any space.

While it is clear that the trends previously discussed are fairly well understood among the scientific community, they are not well understood in the defense or civilian arena. We must develop a "first principle" understanding of what drives these trends and a method to assess the impact of these inevitabilities. We must understand the disruptive consequences that may result from the intersection of these technological trends. Only then can we leverage these advances to create risk management strategies. A sense of where these trends are headed is also an essential component of a robust strategy, which enables us to plan for and prevent potential disasters.

What is fueling these trends? Computing power is a relatively free global commodity, the net effect of which is that the barriers to competition in many areas are falling. Consequently, the concept of a peer competitor is taking on new meaning for defense planners. No longer can potential adversaries be limited to nations with large gross domestic products and large military arsenals. One example of lower barriers to competition is found in the world of information technology. Cyberspace has evolved into the most important global commons. Access to cyberspace is essential for national security, military competitiveness, and economic prosperity, and unfettered access to information is key to national power. Various actors are competing for dominance in this new commons, including adversarial nations as well as individuals, terrorist groups, and criminal hacktivists.

The 20th century was dominated by weapons systems based on advances in physics, engineering, computing, and mathematics, colloquially known as *big bang, big metal*. The future presents a range of new threats and increasingly inventive biological weapons that can cripple major bodily functions even as the same bioengineering advances offer great potential for medical science.

But defense planners must remain aware of the malicious use of engineered biological agents in combination with robotics, information technology, or nanotechnology for two reasons. First, there is the potential for nonstate actors and nations to conduct ambiguous aggression or subtle war. Such aggression is a situation in which a bioattack causes a deadly outbreak but is not seen as such. Instead, the outbreak may be blamed on either an influenza

U.S. Navy (John F. Williams)

Marine monitors virtual scenarios from control room of Gruntworks Research for Infantry Integration Testing facility

pandemic or abnormality in the food supply. This potential ambiguity makes defense planning and response highly complex. The second concern stems from the ease with which biological building blocks can be obtained. The widespread access to biological materials presents individual engineers with the capability to produce harmful agents that facilitate the creation of superempowered actors with the means to inflict large-scale global damage. The next generation of suicide bombers could be biobombers who infect themselves with bioengineered diseases and penetrate large population centers.

Nanotechnology is regarded as a major revolution in technology that enables structuring and restructuring of matter on a fundamental level. According to William Schneider, chair of the Defense Science Board, "Nanoscale sensors have the potential to dispel the fog of war. Richness in sensors allows commanders to have a complete picture of the tactical battlefield." Advances in nanotechnology could produce lighter, stronger, heat-resistant materials for new weaponry and make armor harder, camouflage better, military transport faster, and energy more efficient.

Nanotechnology is the key to distributed and configurable manufacturing, a model for goods produced locally near their point of use, which could have profound economic, social, and political impacts. Secure methods of obtaining electronic subcomponents are increasingly difficult in the globalized manufacturing economy. Distributed and configurable manufacturing could assure that production designs, manufacturing infrastructure, and even applications could be controlled securely.

There are significant advantages to manufacturing goods locally for defense, intelligence, and security applications rather than depending on a globally interconnected production chain. When manufacturing is done at the point of need, it is difficult to affect the national economy with a disaster or small number of attacks. The implications of local manufacturing might alter basic concepts of military operations, logistics, and sustainment. But strategically, planners must take account of the unintended consequences in destabilizing the interdependent globalized economy.

Defense planners have often anticipated new technologies to provide them with a competitive advantage, only to find their plans are flawed when viewed through the lens of moral principles. That debate continues today. In fact, some argue that the creation of autonomous soldier-robots with a conscience may be possible and that they may even be preferable to human soldiers.

Trends in ubiquitous computing, connectivity, and information-sharing will complicate future national security challenges. Some contend that this trend contributes to the decentralization or shift in power from nations to individuals or groups that are ill defined by political borders. The propagation of cutting-edge technologies that could harm national security interests are no longer reserved for elite, economically endowed nations. The result is much broader potential threats and increased uncertainty and ambiguity about the entities that may challenge the United States. This type of asymmetric attack, conducted by small groups in an ideological minority against a large group of potential victims, presents complex problems for defense planners.

Increased worldwide connectivity means people are more likely to encounter sympathetic co-conspirators, if only virtually. Social networks serve as recruiting mechanisms and offer added support for individuals who may want to launch such attacks. The social network of a potential attacker might create opportunities for simultaneous strikes across many locations.

New technologies are being developed at a fantastic pace and may intersect in unimaginable ways. Such advances potentially offer enormous benefits but create national security paradigms with challenges. Defense planners must be aware of the fact that new technology has unintended consequences as well as the potential for dangerous misuse in the hands of adversaries. **gsa**

NOTES

[1] GlobalSpec! offers a variety of products in response to the query "computer network attack." This is a good place to learn about network components, as opposed to attack tools, per se; see <www.globalspec.com/Industrial-Directory/Computer_Network_Attack>. Developer.net has a section on "measures of effectiveness" for computer network attack; see <www.developers.net/tsearch?searchkeys=measures+of+effectiveness+computer+network+attack>. There even are patent applications (for example, attack classification method for computer network security); see <www.freepatentsonline.com/y2008/0083034.htm>.

[2] See, for example, Hackers Home Page at <www.hackershomepage.com/>; How to Become a Hacker at <www.catb.org/~esr/faqs/hacker-howto.html?PHPSESSID=22f7378d0d1ea654962a22bf13166a5a>; and Secureroot at <www.secureroot.com/>.

[3] See also a range of attacks described by Ed Skoudis, "Information Security Issues in Cyberspace," in *Cyberpower and National Security*, ed. Franklin D. Kramer and Stuart Starr (Washington, DC: National Defense University Press, 2009).

[4] "Satan" is a software program that claims to "identify weaknesses in just about any network connected to the Internet."

[5] See Dr. Mark Drapeau's informative posts about Government 2.0 at <www.mashable.com>.

[6] Evgeny Morozov, "An Army of Zeros and Ones: How I became a soldier in the Georgia-Russia cyberwar," available at <www.slate.com/id/2197514/>.

Contributors

Dr. Thomas X. Hammes (Chapter Editor) served 30 years in the U.S. Marine Corps, including duty in Somalia and Iraq. He holds a Masters of Historical Research and Ph.D. in Modern History from Oxford University and has lectured widely at U.S. and international staff and war colleges. He is the author of *The Sling and the Stone: On War in the 21st Century* (Zenith Press, 2004) and over 80 articles and opinion pieces.

Evan Applegate contributed graphics support this chapter. He received his B.A. in international relations with a concentration in peace and security from the University of California at Davis in 2009. He is head print designer for the Center for Biophotonics Science and Technology.

Dr. Mark D. Drapeau is Associate Research Fellow in the Center for Technology and National Security Policy (CTNSP) at the National Defense University (NDU). He has a B.S. and Ph.D. in biology from the University of Rochester and University of California, respectively.

Dr. Peter L. Hays is a Senior Scientist with the Science Applications International Corporation supporting the Policy and Strategy Division of the National Security Space Office in the Pentagon and also serves as an Associate Director of the Eisenhower Center for Space and Defense Studies at the U.S. Air Force Academy.

Lieutenant Colonel Robert Klingseisen, USA, is Deputy Chief for Policy and Strategy in the National Security Space Office. He is the former Chief, Space Operations Division, U.S. Strategic Command and Assistant Professor of Geospatial Sciences at the U.S. Military Academy.

Dr. Martin C. Libicki is a Senior Policy Researcher at the RAND Corporation. He has written extensively on cyberspace, most notably *Conquest in Cyberspace: National Security and Information Warfare* (Cambridge University Press, 2007).

Terry J. Pudas is a Senior Research Fellow in CTNSP at NDU. Prior to joining the center, he served as the Deputy Assistant Secretary of Defense (Acting), Forces Transformation and Resources, in the Office of the Under Secretary of Defense for Policy. In September of 2001, he was appointed as the Deputy Director of the newly created Secretary of Defense Force Transformation Office. He served as the Acting Director from January 2005 to October 2006.

Mark E. Stout is a Research Staff Member at the Institute for Defense Analyses. He is the lead author of *The Terrorist Perspectives Project: Strategic and Operational Views of Al Qaida and Associated Movements* (Naval Institute Press, 2008).

Kim A. Taipale is the founder and Executive Director of the Center for Advanced Studies in Science and Technology Policy. He is also a Senior Fellow at the World Policy Institute and an adjunct professor of law at New York Law School.

Dr. Linton Wells II is a Distinguished Research Fellow in CTNSP at NDU, where he also serves as the Force Transformation Chair. Prior, he served in the Office of the Under Secretary of Defense (Policy) from 1991 to 1998, and finally as the Deputy Under Secretary of Defense (Policy Support).

Chapter 4
Energy and Environmental Insecurity

Energy security is now a commanding priority. The emerging energy system is far more complex and global than the industrial era system that it is slowly replacing. Today when security planners talk about energy security, they are as likely to be referring to carbon emissions and diminishing water supplies as energy self-reliance and affordable oil. Moreover, emerging energy and environmental security problems are increasingly beyond the ability of any single country to control. This chapter examines critical issues surrounding energy in the evolving security environment and proposes potential pathways for pursuing solutions.

The Emerging International Energy Security System

Energy has become one of the most pressing problems in national and global security. Significant increases in the price of oil have weakened the global economy, contributed to a sharp rise in global food prices, and transferred trillions of dollars to autocratic oil-exporting regimes. At the same time, rapid fluctuations in the price of oil—from around $25 per barrel in 2001 to as much as $150 in 2008 and back to below $50 in 2009—have increased risk and discouraged investment in energy technology and infrastructure ensuring that global markets will not be prepared for the next cycle of high prices. Internationally, energy diplomacy has become increasingly confrontational as states jockey for control of gas and oil markets and pipelines. Meanwhile, concerns about pollution and greenhouse gases have strained diplomatic relations with other nations and are forcing fundamental changes in energy policy.

The emerging crises are symptoms of a gradual transformation in the underlying geopolitical and economic system that has supplied the world with

Drivers in Kuwait use headlights to see through smoke from oil wells set afire by retreating Iraqi forces, Operation *Desert Storm*, 1991

cheap energy for over a century. Since the 1800s, cheap fossil fuels have powered the rise of industrialization and globalization. During this period, free-market mechanisms ensured that world markets had access to petroleum and other sources of energy. This system relied on market competition to drive the price of energy commodities toward the price of extraction and depended on a liberal trading order in which governments generally left energy transportation, supply, and demand to the market.

Over the life of the energy market, the fundamental threat to cheap and reliable energy commodities has been that government intervention in the supply, transport, and demand for energy would transform the global distribution system from one adjudicated mainly by markets to one based on politics and force. Threats to the market-based system have always been possible. States with diplomatic or military influence on the global lines of communication by which energy is transported have frequently been tempted to further their interests by charging rents for access. Supplying states have regularly attempted to band together to increase market prices. At least since the 1970s, environmental groups have put pressure on governments in rich states to look beyond the market and consider externalities when setting energy policy.

Despite these pressures, until recently, the world has generally maintained a global free-market energy economy in which the prices of energy commodities have hovered around the cost of extraction and supply has been dependable. Historically, this system has rested on three pillars: a reliance on freedom of the seas for most international energy trade; a multiplicity of energy-exporting nations and multinational corporations that made collusion and nationalization difficult; and the preference given by oil-importing nations to energy supply and price, over other considerations such as the environment. Each of these pillars, and hence the basic energy system, is increasingly uncertain.

Insecure Energy Lines of Communication

Unimpeded transportation of energy has never been assured. Throughout the history of the modern energy market, states attempted to influence transit routes for parochial reasons. During the World Wars, the Cold War, and the Iran-Iraq war, belligerents used diplomatic and military power to interdict opponents' energy supplies. However, because most global energy commodities traveled by sea, and because Great Britain and the United States were dominant sea powers, their opponents' efforts were generally frustrated in war and free-market distribution mechanics persisted in times of peace.

In recent years, however, a number of events have begun to undermine freedom of energy transportation. Over the last two decades, natural gas has become an increasingly important part of Europe's energy economy, and Russia and Central Asian states have begun to supply a large portion of that resource. Unlike petroleum exports, which mainly travel across oceans to final buyers, natural gas must generally travel by pipelines through sovereign territory. The main geopolitical implications of overland transport are that the United States cannot use its maritime power to secure energy sea lines of communication and that Russia can use its geographic proximity and influence on Central Asian and Eastern European states to seek economic and diplomatic rents from natural gas exports.

Russia has routinely made use of its influence over energy supply routes. In January 2006, Russia flexed its muscles by cutting off natural gas exports to Ukraine and did the same in 2007 to Georgia and Belarus. After Russia's intervention into Georgia in 2008, Russian leaders made it clear that opposition to Moscow could affect natural gas supplies. Russia's energy *realpolitik* has been effective. Major European states have regularly recoiled in the face of threats to their energy lifeline. Meanwhile, U.S. support for the free transport of gas in Central Asia and Eastern Europe has put it at odds with Russia.

Supply lines have also become less secure in the Persian Gulf's narrow Strait of Hormuz through which 40 percent of global oil exports flow. As Iran amasses modern antiair and antiship missiles and enhances its capacity for harassing tanker shipping, America's role as guarantor of the freedom of the seas assumes a riskier and costlier burden. In the longer term, China's growing dependence on Middle Eastern oil may heighten Beijing's concern about U.S. control of the sea lines of communication. These concerns have led China to expand its influence along the routes connecting the Arabian Gulf, Indian Ocean, Strait of Malacca, and South China Sea through a network of treaties, access to ports and airfields, and modernized military capabilities. If global petroleum demand continues to outpace supplies, the temptation for regional powers to seek diplomatic and financial rents by controlling sea lines and chokepoints is likely to increase.

From Free Market to Oligopoly

For more than a century, global energy supply has been dominated by international corporations competing to find and extract energy resources for profit. The result has been that known reserves have often expanded faster than demand and prices have usually remained low. Petroleum, in particular, has averaged around $20 per barrel in inflation-adjusted dollars for nearly a century. While energy-exporting nations have attempted to coordinate their export policies to reduce supplies and increase prices, the large number of exporting states and the critical role international corporations have played in providing technology and expertise have usually frustrated cartels.

The longstanding dynamics of the global energy market are changing. Known oil and gas reserves have become increasingly consolidated in the hands of a small clique of often politically unstable states. In four of the top eight reserve-holding nations—Iran, Iraq, Nigeria, and Venezuela—a combination of international sanctions, war, civil disorder, and corruption has reduced energy exploration and extraction below market expectations, diminishing supply and increasing prices. Over the same period, as extraction technology has spread from private companies to states, exporting countries have regularly nationalized their reserves and seized multinational oil and gas companies doing business within their territory. Whereas most reserves and nearly all major energy companies were once private, more than 80 percent of all reserves are now under state control and a progressively larger number of oil and gas companies are partly or wholly owned by exporting governments.

As this has happened, major importing powers have become keen to influence supplying nations through diplomatic and military instruments of state power. The system that allocates energy internationally has become more mercantilist. China has vigorously attempted to use its newfound financial muscle to bring autocratic African and Central Asian oil-exporting regimes within its sphere of influence to bypass market mechanisms. Russian attempts to control the flow of energy in Central Asia and Eastern Europe have regularly escalated to energy blackmail and threat of force. Similarly, at least since the early 1990s, the United States has used various diplomatic tools, including military-to-military contacts, with regimes in Central Asia and the Middle East to increase their connections with the West.

The net effect of these changes has been to reduce the amount of gas and oil on the international market and to move the market toward oligopoly. The emerging system is less stable and less predictable than the older market-driven system. In the old system, the large number of competing energy-supplying states and companies dampened the effects of actions by particular suppliers and inhibited the ability of suppliers to coordinate policy. In the new system, market supply is increasingly dependent on the nuances and preferences of individual states. Recently, even apparently trivial political events in exporting nations have been enough to cause dramatic fluctuations in prices, and the United States has, on occasion, been reduced to cajoling Saudi Arabia and other major exporters to increase energy supplies to reduce market prices. From the viewpoint of the emerging autocratic oil-exporting oligarchy, the system works. It is funneling trillions of dollars into their economies and increasing their political power at home and diplomatic power abroad. Even short term dips in prices help them in the long term by suppressing investment in conservation and alternative fuels. There is little reason to expect the current trend toward oligopoly to reverse itself or anticipate a return to the more stable energy environment of the 20th century.

Environment and the Diminishing Importance of Price

The third dynamic altering the current global energy market is the increasing importance of environmental concerns in determining importing states' energy policies. Whereas energy policies in rich states were once determined mainly with an eye to reducing price, price today is becoming decreasingly important vis-à-vis fears of pollution and particularly of global warming.

For several decades, the governments of rich countries have been under mounting pressure to modify energy policies to account for environmental factors. The success at influencing governments over the environment has varied across countries and time. But the contemporary era is particularly green, and the influence of environmental groups is growing rapidly. While clashes once mainly pitted naturalists against economic interests, as concerns about global climate change grow, the number and political influence of groups committed to environmental policies will expand. Today, many governments and nongovernmental organizations are lobbying the United States for more eco-friendly policies, and U.S. energy policy has become a major point of diplomatic, as well as domestic, friction.

It is difficult to predict the effect of environmental concerns on energy markets. In general, environmentalists argue for higher prices on carbon-based fuels to reduce demand. However, environmental science is too young and lobbying too disparate to make prediction easy. In the United States, conflicting interests sometimes pit one environmental interest against another. For instance, lobbies aimed at reducing radioactive waste and preserving natural ecosystems currently restrict the construction of U.S. nuclear and hydroelectric plants. In the process, however, they have caused the country to increase the number of dirty, carbon-producing coal plants. Also, some policies are self-defeating. To reduce greenhouse gases, the United States funds research on electric cars. However, since 50 percent of U.S. electricity is derived from coal, electric cars can produce more carbon and other pollutants per mile than cars running on regular gasoline. In addition, some policies have unintended consequences. Recent legislation that discourages the use of new fuels that emit more carbon across their lifecycle than petroleum appeared relatively benign when low oil prices made North America's vast reserves of unconventional fossil fuels unprofitable to extract and refine. However, should high prices make these reserves profitable—as they briefly did in 2008—the legislation will effectively limit access to most of America's oil reserves.

In the meantime, environmentalists and energy suppliers both hold out hope that new technology will eventually solve current problems.

Environmental concerns, and particularly global climate change, may prove to be this century's greatest security challenge. Whatever the eventual outcome, however, they are fundamentally changing the way the global system extracts, transports, and uses energy and injecting uncertainty into global markets. As concerns over climate change increase with time and governments search among myriad proposed solutions, the price and volatility of energy are likely to increase and incentives for privately funded research and infrastructure development are likely to be adversely affected.

As the global energy economy transitions toward a more statist and mercantilist system, policymakers are likely to find themselves operating in *terra incognita*. In the old system, private companies absorbed most of the risk; in the emerging system, states will bear a larger portion of the risk as they pioneer new policies. Many of the policies that will set the tenor for the next century will be developed and implemented in the next decade. Global leadership is needed, and difficult national choices will have to be made. The world is changing and the dynamics that facilitated a world powered by cheap fossil fuels are

▼ *Continued on p. 74*

Russian workers weld connection for new pipeline operated by state-run natural gas company Gazprom

European Energy: Security in Coordination

The states of the European Union (EU) face significant challenges to their energy security because of dependence on a limited number of oil and gas suppliers and serious concerns about Europe's contributions to global carbon emissions and climate change. Because EU members are mostly net energy importers, and because most energy-related policies are left to individual member states to negotiate, suppliers in the Organization of the Petroleum Exporting Countries (OPEC), and especially Russia with its nationalized oil and gas industries, hold a significant advantage in negotiations with European states. Europeans are well aware that energy security requires diversified suppliers and transit routes. However, this awareness has not yet resulted in the creation of a common energy policy enabling coordination of EU relations with international energy suppliers.

In 2007, the Council of the European Union proposed an energy policy for Europe to address the security of energy supply, climate change, and the creation of a single EU market for energy. The EU has done a better job of addressing climate change and its internal energy market than it has of solving the problem of supply diversity. As a cornerstone of a climate change policy, the EU introduced a "cap-and-trade system" for carbon dioxide (a concept also under consideration by the U.S. Congress). The EU is currently in a second round of cap-and-trade programs based on lessons learned from the initial round, which resulted in low emissions prices and little mitigation. The EU also introduced energy competition for electricity and natural gas by requiring member states to allow all residential, commercial, and industrial customers the right to choose energy suppliers. This competition policy came under pressure as consumers continued to see energy prices rise in spite of this liberalization.

The EU is aware of the growing problem of its energy security. A 2006 *Green Paper: A European Strategy for Sustainable, Competitive and Secure Energy*, for example, recommended the following trio of priorities: establish a functioning internal energy market; move energy conversion to low-carbon technologies, with renewable energy producing 20 percent of supply by 2020; and achieve end-use energy efficiency improvements, achieving a 20 percent reduction in energy consumption by 2020. These actions continue the EU's aggressive moves toward diversification in energy as a mechanism for creating competitive economies and mitigating climate change through programs fostering environmental sustainability.

The current European energy supply portfolio reflects a desultory track record of independent decisions made by the organization's 27 individual member states. These past decisions, involving the role of nuclear power, coal, and imported natural gas, have led to divergent energy portfolios. For instance, nuclear power accounts for 40 percent of France's energy needs, but it provides only 9 percent of the United Kingdom's power supply and none of Austria's. Similarly, coal has no role in electricity generation in France, but coal represents 92 percent of Poland's supply, 65 percent of the Czech Republic's supply, 62 percent of Greece's supply, and 50 percent of Germany's supply. The EU is moving ahead in some areas with EU-wide policies on energy supply using the issue of climate change as the policy driver. Thus, a January 2008 proposed directive on renewable energy requires that 20 percent of member state energy come from renewable sources by 2020, as recommended in the earlier Green Paper.

The EU is most vulnerable in the oil and gas sectors, with oil providing between 40 and 50 percent of primary energy needs for most EU members and natural gas sales dominated by Russia's Gazprom. More worrisome, forecasts suggest that the trend is toward greater EU foreign dependence, with the EU projected to import 90 percent of its oil and 80 percent of its natural gas by the year 2030. At present, 45 percent of EU oil imports are from the Middle East and 40 percent from OPEC members. Increased dependence on a small number of suppliers and supply routes will make the EU more susceptible to energy disruption.

Given the reluctance of individual EU member states to cede greater authority to the Union, members must rely on the hope that individual states will display solidarity in the event of a supply crisis. The EU is promoting the diversification of supply, analyzing stockpiling, and improving transparency through the establishment of an EU Energy Observatory to collect and verify energy data. The EU also plans to use its partnership mechanisms to enhance ties with energy suppliers in the Caspian Sea, Black Sea, and North Africa regions.

If the states of Europe were to relinquish more sovereignty to permit the European Union to make critical decisions on energy policy, the result might well provide greater energy security for the EU. In the near term, however, it appears that individual member states will continue to pursue their own national energy policies.

▲ *Continued from p. 72*

diminishing. Leaders face the question of whether they can overcome inertia and adapt and change with it.

Recent Trends in the Changing Energy Landscape

Recent trends in current energy markets suggest that the world is on an unsustainable and undesirable trajectory with regard to energy. These trends include tight supplies and the elimination of excess capacity, persistent and growing demand, infrastructure and capabilities limitations, heightened geopolitical and investment risk, higher prices, and growing concern over climate change. At the same time, absent a major strategic shift in policy, U.S. influence in global energy markets will continue to erode because of the emergence of new global players and trends that will play an increasingly larger role in shaping tomorrow's energy system.

The urgent need to address climate change presents both a challenge and a clear opportunity for the United States and other major states to shift energy priorities in favor of greater efficiency and low emission fuels. This shift will fundamentally alter the geopolitical, economic, and environmental dynamics. In so doing, however, caution must be taken to develop strategies that balance government policies and market practices, to deploy new technologies while maintaining existing infrastructure, and to facilitate the transition to a new and sustainable energy future without undermining the present system's relative stability.

Over the next 25 years, the world's population is projected to grow from some 6.7 billion to well over 8 billion people. With population, economic growth, and standards of living expected to increase in already densely populated areas, society will require greater resources (from water and food, to land, energy, and other basic materials) to fuel and sustain this expansion. As the world struggles to meet these energy needs, new trends and dynamics will shape our collective energy future.

Shifting Supply and Demand Dynamics

The first major trend shaping the energy future concerns the shift in who supplies energy and who demands it. Global energy demand is projected to increase approximately 55 percent by 2030, with nearly 74 percent of growth coming from developing economies, 45 percent from China and India alone. In fact, energy demand from developing economies (non–Organisation for Economic Co-operation and Development [OECD] countries) is expected to overtake energy consumption in the developed world within the next 2 years. Over the same time period, energy supplies are projected to come from approximately the same fuel mix, mainly fossil fuels, and many of the same resource holders that exist today.

While there is always a chance that energy demand will not achieve these projected levels of growth, either because of an economic slowdown or better than historic rates of energy productivity, the overall outlook nonetheless remains daunting. Slower economic growth, while temporarily forestalling the need for increased energy supplies, does nothing to alter the basic trend lines and carries with it adverse consequences. In addition, while higher energy prices have already slowed consumption growth in some areas of the world, notably in the United States and Europe, in other areas (such as the Middle East and Asia) demand growth has proven remarkably resilient. The emergence of the non-OECD world as a major energy consumer further accentuates the global economic shift already under way. In 1997, the Group of Eight (G–8) countries accounted for 65 percent of global gross domestic product (GDP). A decade later, that figure had dropped to 58 percent and projections indicate that by 2015, those nations will account for less than half of global economic activity. Non-OECD nations will then comprise both the majority of conventional resource holders as well as represent the bulk of new economic growth areas. Furthermore, as internal energy demand grows within producer nations, absent massive new investment in production capacities, export volumes will inevitably decline.

In addition, as oil demand continues to grow internationally, the inability of non–Organization of Petroleum Exporting Countries (OPEC) producers to keep pace has dramatically enhanced OPEC leverage. With Russian oil output reaching a plateau and production decreasing in the North Sea, the United States, and Mexico, the world is becoming more reliant on supplies from a handful of producer nations—many of which have different agendas, production policies, and internal political needs. The International Energy Agency (IEA) has projected that by the middle of the next decade, the "gap" between presumed oil demand and available global supply (after accounting for reservoir decline rates) could exceed 10 million barrels per day. While global inventories could help offset part of that deficit, at least temporarily, ultimately the allocator of scarce resources will be markedly higher prices.

The Changing Resource Base and Delivery Requirements

A second trend shaping the energy future is the changing resource base and the requirements for delivering it. The world is not running out of energy, but it is becoming more difficult to gain access to, produce, and convert the world's energy resources and deliver them to the people who want them. Energy resources are geographically, geologically, technologically, and financially more difficult to reach. Large supplies of conventional oil and natural gas remain located in the Middle East and Eurasia, while the Western Hemisphere is rich in unconventional fuels such as oil sands, oil shale, and extra-heavy oil deposits. Geographically, the presence of these non-conventional reserves should buttress security, but they also present sizeable environmental challenges, particularly in an age of carbon constraints.

Maintaining a robust, secure delivery infrastructure for long-distance transport of vast volumes of oil and gas through congested transit points is a salient concern. In the coming years, energy trade flows will be affected by a concentration of supply and demand centers not geographically collocated. Coal, natural gas, biomass, and other resources are being transported longer distances to reach demand centers. While alternative energy forms provide a welcome supplement to conventional energy resources, they are unable to serve as replacements at scale and require significant new infrastructure and investments of their own.

In a dramatic shift from previous decades, national ministries and national oil companies control more than 80 percent of conventional oil reserves and account for more than half of current crude oil and natural gas production. In contrast, international oil companies, which have been indispensable to the development of oil and natural gas resources throughout the world, are now in danger of marginalization. The new class of national oil companies is well funded, has access to advanced technology, is becoming involved in exploration and production activities in foreign markets, and is gaining experience and honing project management skills with each passing day. In places where foreign investment and international oil company involvement are politically unpalatable, bilateral energy agreements with other national companies are perceived to have

a competitive advantage over many international companies. Many of those companies are adjusting to this new operating environment, but the potential long-term implications are worrisome.

High Price Environment and Investment Challenges

A third trend shaping the energy future centers on the high price of energy and the risky nature of energy investments. Notwithstanding the drop in gas prices in late 2008, persistent demand and tight supplies, as well as escalating equipment and materials costs, have generally caused energy prices to rise across the board. While most analysts foresee some relief within the near term, the continued growth in demand will eventually lead to higher prices. Much of the world's economy was built on cheap energy. In the United States, homes, vehicles, transportation habits, and heating and cooling preferences are all geared toward

▼ *Continued on p. 80*

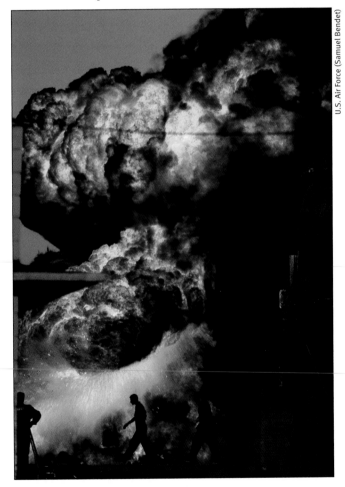

U.S. Air Force (Samuel Bendet)

Iraqi firefighters battle pipeline fire after rocket attack at Northern Oil Company in Kirkuk, November 2006

Major Contentious Oil and Natural Gas Pipelines

1 Cano Límon-Coveñas Frequent target of sabotage by guerrillas of the ELN and FARC; U.S. military advisers have worked with Colombian government forces to enhance security along the pipeline route.

2 East Siberia-Pacific Ocean (ESPO) Originally, Moscow agreed to terminate the ESPO pipeline at Kozmino Bay and deliver most of its oil to Japan, but persistent lobbying by Beijing has led to a plans for a spur from Skovorodino to Daqing in China, questioning the viability of completing phase two to the Pacific (though some oil will be delivered by rail cars). Major environmental hurdles also have to be overcome in completing the project.

3 Caspian Pipeline Consortium (CPC) The Russian state holds the largest share in CPC, but Chevron and other Western firms also hold significant portions. Kazakhstan seeks to expand capacity to 1.3 mb/d, but Moscow is balking over transit fees.

4 Kazakhstan-China Represents a calculated effort by China to reduce its dependence on Middle Eastern oil and enhance its energy security, in particular by reducing its vulnerability to a future trade blockade enforced by the U.S. Navy.

5 Baku-Tbilisi-Ceyhan (BTC) Built with strong U.S. backing to avoid reliance on pipelines transiting Russia or Iran. Russian hostility to the pipeline (and resulting U.S. support for the pro-Western government in Georgia) was a major factor in Moscow's August 2008 invasion of Georgia and its continuing support for the breakaway enclaves of Abkhazia and South Ossetia.

6 South Caucasus Pipeline (SCP) Like the BTC, viewed in Moscow as a challenge to its control over the flow of Caspian Sea energy to European markets and so a factor in its August 2008 invasion of Georgia.

7 Nabucco Designed to reduce heavy European reliance on Russian natural gas and so enjoys strong backing from the EU and the U.S. The Russian invasion of Georgia in August 2008 may have been intended to blunt enthusiasm for Nabucco as most of its gas would be obtained from Azerbaijan via the SCP.

8 Caspian Gas Pipeline Intended to transport Turkmen gas to Russia, Ukraine, and Europe via Gazprom's extensive pipeline network. The new conduit will connect to the existing Central Asia-Center gas pipeline network on the Kazakh-Russian border. Designed to frustrate EU and U.S. efforts to secure Turkmen gas for Nabucco via a proposed Trans-Caspian link to the SCP.

9 Chad-Cameroon Partly financed with a World Bank loan in the hope that increased international oversight would lead to a greater allocation of oil revenues to grassroots social and economic development in Chad. However, persistent intransigence by the Chadian government led the Bank to suspend loans to Chad in 2006; although a compromise was later reached, the government repaid the original pipeline loan in 2008 without satisfying the Bank's initial development objectives.

10 Trans-Saharan Gas Pipeline Intended to transport Nigerian gas to Europe. Could cost $21 billion or more and pass through extremely harsh and often embattled areas. Strongly backed by the EU as a way of reducing reliance on Russian natural gas.

Source: Country analysis briefs posted at Web site of U.S. Department of Energy's Energy Information Administration.
bcfd = billion cubic feet per day
bd = barrels per day
mbd = million barrels per day

RUSSIA

② ③ ④ ⑤ ⑥ ⑦ ⑧

Energy Use by Country

Energy consumption per capita in kilograms of oil equivalent per year (2005):

low (<1,000)

medium (1,000–3,499)

high (>3,500)

Disputed areas

- - - - **Internal borders in Russia**

→ = Oil Export Terminals

Atyraū to Samarra Pipeline

Caspian Pipeline Consortium

China Pipeline

Baku to Novorosslysk Pipeline

TENGIZ OILFIELD

Proposed Tengiz to Baku Pipeline

Russia Pipeline to proposed Caspian Gas Pipeline

Proposed Nabucca Gas Pipeline

South Caucasus Gas Pipeline

BTC Pipeline

SHAH DENIZ GAS FIELD

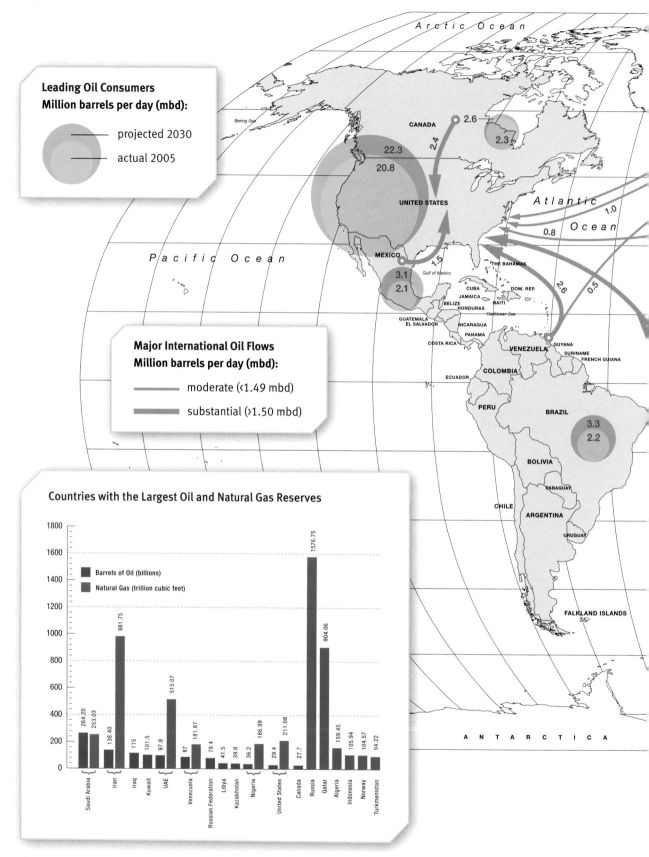

Leading Oil Consumers
Million barrels per day (mbd):

projected 2030

actual 2005

Major International Oil Flows
Million barrels per day (mbd):

moderate (<1.49 mbd)

substantial (>1.50 mbd)

Countries with the Largest Oil and Natural Gas Reserves

■ Barrels of Oil (billions)
■ Natural Gas (trillion cubic feet)

Source: BP, *Statistical Review of World Energy June 2008*.
Does not include unconventional products such as Canadian tar sands.

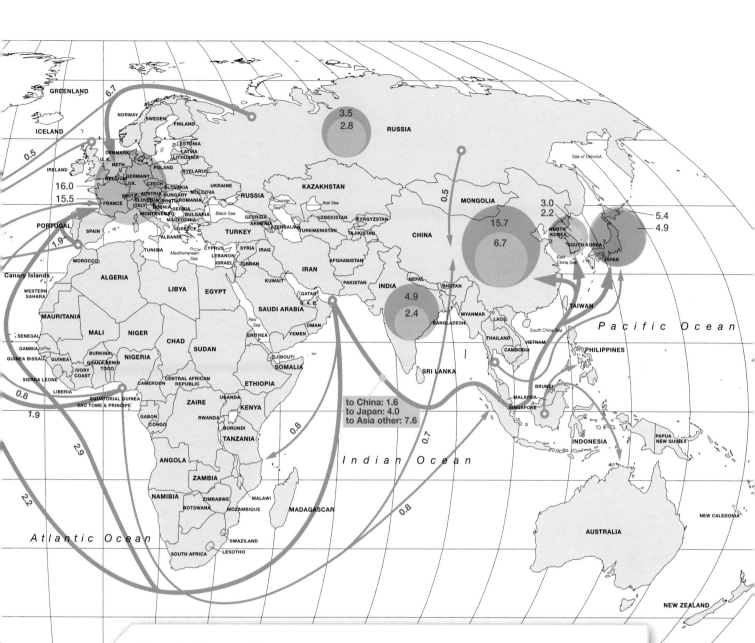

Vital World Oil Transit Chokepoints

Name	Location	Estimated 2006 Barrels per Day Oil Flow
Strait of Hormuz	between Iran and United Arab Emirates plus Oman; links Persian Gulf to Arabian Sea and Indian Ocean	16.5-17 million
Strait of Malacca	between Malaysia and Indonesia; links Indian Ocean to South China Sea and Pacific Ocean	15 million
Suez Canal and Suez-Mediterranean (SUMED) Pipeline	connects Red Sea and Gulf of Suez to Mediterranean Sea; approximately 3,000 tankers transit the canal annually; because of canal's narrow width oil is also transported via pipeline	4.5 million (3 million via SUMED)
Bab el-Mendab	between Yemen and Djibouti; links Gulf of Aden to Red Sea	3.3 million
Turkish Straits (Bosporus and Dardanelles)	between European and Asian Turkey; links Black Sea with Aegean and Mediterranean Seas	2.4 million
Panama Canal	connects Caribbean Sea with Pacific Ocean	.5 million

Source: U.S. Department of Energy, Energy Information Administration, "World of Oil Transit Chokepoints," January 2008

▲ *Continued from p. 75*

a world in which energy is relatively inexpensive. In places where energy prices are already unaffordable, governments often bear the burden of subsidizing the price of fuels and electricity. These subsidies dampen the demand response to price increases and place economic pressure on government budgets.

The IEA estimates that industry and governments will need to invest $22 trillion between now and 2030 to meet the forecast energy demand. That high figure does not take into consideration the investment necessary to shift the global energy system from its current state to a lower carbon alternative. The inability to access lowest cost reserves combined with new demands for materials and labor has substantially increased project development costs. New capacity, whether from conventional oil and natural gas, coal, nuclear power, pipeline and transmission facilities, or a new generation of renewable energy forms with its infrastructure, will require heavy and sustained investment over a long period.

Shifting Geopolitical Dynamics and Outmoded Institutions

Geopolitics constitutes a fourth trend shaping the energy future. Higher prices have caused a resurgence of resource nationalism and the tendency to exert greater state control over the resource base. The severity of restrictions on access to oil and natural gas resources ranges from a complete prohibition on foreign investment, to mandatory partnerships with national energy companies, to demands for a greater share of equity, control, and production-related revenues (sometimes retroactively) for the host government. While sovereign nations have always controlled their resources, the revision of legal and regulatory structures has created an atmosphere of investment uncertainty. Other factors—such as the changing role of geopolitical alliances in forming energy deals; poor governance and political stability issues; threats to facilities, infrastructure, and transit areas; and a greater focus on human rights, environmental degradation, poverty alleviation, and energy equity issues—have emerged as elements of the changing geopolitical landscape affecting energy production, delivery, and use. As a result of these factors and high prices, governments are increasingly concerned about their immediate and long-term energy security.

Global receptivity to U.S. alliances and Western-based institutions has declined in recent years—as a function of both the eroding legitimacy of the United States and the emergence of new global players with different cultures, business practices, foreign policy agendas, and clout. The rules of the road in today's more multipolar world have yet to be written; when they are, the writers will include a new group of global and regional powers.

These changing dynamics call into question the utility, relevance, and effectiveness of existing institutions, many of which are the result of a post–World War II order conceived in a decidedly different environment from the global dynamics we are currently experiencing. The existence and size of today's sovereign wealth funds are allowing strategic resource holders and burgeoning economic powers to self-finance new investments both at home and abroad without the involvement or structures of traditional lending institutions such as the World Bank, International Monetary Fund, and regional development banks; the emergence and desires of growing economic powers such as China, India, and Brazil are challenging traditional notions of free trade and globalization.

The capacities and leverage of existing institutions are also being challenged. Examples include IEA efforts to include major new consumers such as China and India that are not OECD members (a prerequisite for IEA membership), and United Nations (UN) attempts to fashion an equitable and effective climate change plan that incorporates the varied concerns of diverse nations. Similar challenges extend to regional and global treaty organizations now pressed to expand their traditional mandates to increasingly complex and expensive endeavors. The emergence of single focus, voluntary "coalitions of the willing" and nonstate actors, beyond traditional nongovernmental organizations, will further muddy the geopolitical and diplomatic landscape.

Urgent Environmental Concerns

Of all the trends listed so far, growing concern over climate change has the greatest potential to alter fundamentally the future of energy production and use. Fossil fuels have been identified as a major contributor of anthropogenic (human-generated) greenhouse gas emissions into the atmosphere—a key factor in global warming. Scientists state with increasing levels of certainty that atmospheric concentrations of greenhouse gases must be stabilized to avoid the most dangerous impacts of climate change. A key component of policies aimed at mitigating climate change is to slow, stop, and ultimately reverse the growth in greenhouse gas emissions from human activity. A prime target for action is the carbon dioxide emitted by the burning of fossil fuels.

The world relies on fossil fuels for nearly 85 percent of its energy needs. Reducing that dependence will require significant new investment, technology improvements, and massive-scale deployment. A recent IEA study confirmed that even halving global fossil fuel consumption (the goal being discussed among the G–8 leaders for whom the study was written) will require a titanic shift in public policy, changes in consumption behavior, and massive new investment, and will take decades to complete. Transitioning to a low-carbon energy future will require a complete transformation of the energy delivery system upon which the world has relied for a century and movement toward a new, more resilient and sustainable system, but one that is largely theoretical, untested at scale, and expensive. Given the unsustainability of the current system, however, such a transition must inevitably occur, and in many ways, the transformation is already under way.

These trends and challenges are not entirely new. Growing import reliance, increasing energy prices (albeit at lower levels), vulnerable infrastructure, diminishing access to resources, geopolitical tensions, and the environmental impact of energy production and use are phenomena the world has endured for years. Yet until recently, no one issue or combination of issues posed a serious enough concern to warrant sustained policy attention. In the future, this may no longer be the case. The fragility of the current system is akin to a house of cards. A significant shift in one or more of these trends or a precipitous action taken by one or more of the major or emerging players now

threatens the overall stability of the entire energy system, making the potential for serious consequences more likely on multiple fronts.

It is against this backdrop that future U.S. and global energy policy—and all of its various facets related to sustainable economic, environmental, and foreign/security policy—must be fashioned.

Energy and Central Asia

Central Asia and its energy are becoming increasingly important in international security. First, Central Asia contains large untapped reserves of oil and gas, located in countries that are not members of the OPEC cartel. Second, new oil and gas will be coming onto the market from these countries in the coming decade, and the routes of delivery are still in negotiation. These delivery routes are the focus of a competition for control over future resources that involves China, Russia, and Europe. Third, several Central Asian states are awash in oil revenues but still face serious governance challenges.

Kazakhstan has the largest share of Caspian oil and is home to Kashagan, the fifth largest oil field in the world—and the largest field outside the Middle East. Kazakhstan's current export output averages 1.2 million barrels per day (bbls/day) and is expected to more than double within the next 10 years. Export levels above 3 million bbls/day, which Kazakhstan envisions, would put it among the top five exporters in the world. In natural gas, Turkmenistan represents a similar opportunity. Under its previous leadership, full information about Turkmen natural gas riches was carefully

Table 1. Natural Gas Production and Proven Reserves, 2007

	Production (billion cubic feet)	Production Rank	Reserves (trillion cubic feet)	Reserves Rank
Central Asia				
Turkmenistan	2.432	11th	94.216	13th
Uzbekistan	2.302	12th	61.603	20th
Kazakhstan	0.985	23d	67.203	17th
Azerbaijan	0.345	‹25th	45.132	23d
Rest of the World				
Russia	23.064	1st	1,576.753	1st
United States	19.278	2d	211.085	6th
Canada	6.604	3d	57.550	21st
Iran	3.952	4th	981.748	2d
Norway	3.270	5th	104.567	12th

protected, but Turkmenistan may rank among the top 10 in world natural gas reserves. Kazakhstan, Uzbekistan, and Azerbaijan also have significant natural gas, with reserves ranking 17th, 20th, and 23d, respectively, in the world. Development of all these reserves depends on clear markets and delivery routes—and the latter pose particular challenges for these land-locked states.

Routes of Delivery

The challenge for Central Asia is to export its oil and gas through new routes, moving away from exclusive reliance on Russia. At present, only one gas and three oil pipelines offer export routes that do not cross Russian territory. Only one line has the added advantage of requiring no transit states: the small-capacity, relatively new Kazakhstan-China oil pipeline. The Baku-Supsa oil pipeline also has relatively small capacity, but has operated successfully for the longest period of time. The Baku-Tbilisi-Ceyhan (BTC) pipeline is longer and has a larger capacity (1 million bbls/day). To date, the oil is from Azerbaijan, but the pipeline may in the future include oil from Kazakhstan. The Baku-Tbilisi-Erzerum natural gas pipeline currently has a capacity of 8.8 billion cubic meters per year (bcm/year), expandable to 20 bcm/year. Continued successful operation of these lines

is critical to confidence of investors in oil and gas in the region, and Kazakhstan and Turkmenistan are seeking investors.

Kazakhstan's oil routes. Kazakhstan's President Nursultan Nazarbayev maintains that it is in his country's national interest to export energy resources in all four directions of the compass. Actual export patterns, however, demonstrate that Russia is a transit country for more than 80 percent of Kazakhstan's oil exports. In 2007, Kazakhstan exported 34 percent using Russian rail and pipelines, and another 52 percent using the Caspian Pipeline Consortium (CPC), a privately owned pipeline that runs across Russian territory (the Russian government is one of several owners). The likely doubling of Kazakhstan's exports within 10 years has caused great competition for future export routes. Kazakhstan is developing a system that will commit it to the BTC pipeline for the future. This project, the Kazakhstan Caspian Transportation System (KCTS), would connect onshore oil fields via pipeline to an Aktau port, from which 500,000 bbls/day would be barged to the BTC pipeline. KCTS would serve U.S. interests in keeping the BTC full even as Azerbaijan's oil declines, in strengthening Kazakhstan's economic ties to the West, and in giving Kazakhstan more independence from Moscow in transit.

U.S. Coast Guard (Michael Anderson)

Canadian ship *Louis S. St-Laurent* maneuvers to moor up with USCG *Healy* during cooperative science mission in Arctic Ocean

But the KCTS—which would rely on the security of Azerbaijan, Georgia, and Turkey as transit states—is not Kazakhstan's only option. For many years, Iran has accepted Kazakh oil shipments, used that oil in its northern cities, and then exported an equivalent amount of its own oil under the Kazakh flag into the Gulf. This is called an *oil swap* and helps Iran meet its domestic needs and circumvent embargoes of its oil. Approximately 6 percent of Kazakhstan's exports traveled through Iran in 2007. Iran's swap capacity was expanded in 2004 to 150,000 bbls/day. Iran could expand capacity to accommodate 500,000 bbls/day, but demand for that route—except during periods of regional conflict—has not been sufficient to justify expansion. A southern pipeline route through Iran would be direct and relatively inexpensive, but the United States maintains pressure on Kazakhstan and the oil companies working there to reject that possibility. China may be a more attractive recipient since demand in the Asian markets is expected to grow some 8 million bbls/day in the next 15 years. In 2007, only 7 percent of Kazakhstan's exports went to China. Plans to double the capacity of the Kazakhstan-China pipeline have been put on hold. For reasons both technical and political, the pipeline's current 200,000 bbls/day capacity is not yet fully used, even though Russian companies add almost one-quarter of the daily input.

The one route that seems to be well on its way toward expansion is the one planned by the CPC. Plans are under way to expand from its current 800,000 bbls/day to 1.34 million. Russia has not been an entirely satisfactory transit state—members of the CPC, though it is a private pipeline built for Kazakhstan oil exports, have often been subjected to pressure to include more Russian oil in the pipeline than specified in agreements. Russia has strongly favored expansion of the CPC. Kazakhstan's leadership assumes that it will continue a close energy relationship with Russia, but it remains unclear if Kazakhstan can expand its options without damaging that positive relationship.

Turkmenistan's natural gas routes. Turkmenistan is also being courted by the East and West to the possible detriment of the North. The Central Asia Center pipeline, which carries Turkmen gas to Russia and has been Turkmenistan's longstanding export route, is undergoing expansion to increase its capacity from 60 to 80 bcm by 2012. Two significant new routes that would not cross Russian territory are under consideration. The 1,100-mile Turkmenistan-China natural gas pipeline with a capacity of 30 bcm would originate on the Turkmen-Uzbek border. Crossing 325 miles of

Uzbekistan and Kazakhstan, the pipeline would end in northwestern Xinjiang. China is eagerly pursuing this route, and agreements necessary for construction have been signed. The reported timeline, however (coming on line by 2012), is probably unrealistically ambitious. Since actual amounts of natural gas available in Turkmenistan remain unclear, this pipeline is seen as competing with the European-favored Nabucco line. Europe and Azerbaijan have encouraged Turkmenistan to take part in this proposed pipeline, which would transport Azerbaijani and Central Asian gas to Europe. The proposed initial capacity is 13 bcm, expandable to 31 bcm. Success of this pipeline depends on Turkmenistan's participation and the construction of an undersea line across the southern Caspian. Russia has been working to keep Turkmenistan from committing to the Nabucco line.

Governance Challenges to the Region

Central Asian states face two key challenges: their current supply of oil and gas to outside markets can be interrupted by transit states, and the windfall profits in revenues from oil and gas make their weak states vulnerable to corruption, inflation, and increasingly authoritarian rule.

Security of supply. Typically, the United States frames security of supply in terms of the interests of importers. In this region, however, the ability to export freely is a key security concern. The United States throughout the 1990s promoted the idea among these states that *happiness is multiple pipelines*, but the August 2008 military incursions into Georgia have reminded the region that Russia's so-called near abroad remains significantly under Russian influence. The states must balance their economic desire for diversity with their political desire for harmony with Russia. This poses a challenge not only for western-bound supply, but also for eastern-bound supply. Although the Shanghai Cooperation Organization (SCO) has established energy as one of its platforms of cooperation, energy exports are more likely to drive a wedge into the organization than to strengthen it. Russia may attempt to use the SCO to manage China's efforts in Central Asia, but the Central Asian states' interests will be best served by using SCO as an additional access point to China, and an opportunity to involve China in moderating Russia's control over energy exports. In pursuing western routes, the Central Asian states must rely on market-motivated investors rather than states. Political events in the Caucasus have considerably increased the perceived political risk, which is likely to dampen investor enthusiasm for security-enhancing routes such as Nabucco. Such routes will require high-level political assistance in order to succeed, on a level with the political support received in years past by the BTC pipeline.

Petrostate governance. There is a tendency for governance in petrostates to become worse as revenues rise. In the Caspian area, governance has worsened in recent years. These already weak states are facing hyperinflation, increasing levels of corruption, and persistent lack of transparency in state affairs. States that depend on oil revenues often function as if it is safe to ignore the wishes of the population, since revenues come not from the people but from an industry to which the government has direct access. Central Asian states are energy rich and sparsely populated. Because these states have high reserves per capita, they have more of a cushion than densely populated petrostates. Even so, they are not immune to popular demands. However, the challenge of providing advice and assistance in improving governance will persist and will likely worsen in these states. States awash in revenues can easily resist offers from outside states to extend governance assistance. This makes the energy-rich states of Central Asia particularly vulnerable in the longer term.

Countries external to this region may define their key interest as securing access to the region's resources. More conservatively, they may define their key interest as ensuring that these states themselves are supported in their pursuit of open markets and the free flow of resources. Diversification in any direction helps Central Asia and reduces Russian influence there. However, routes toward China may have the unintended effect of making European countries even more reliant on Russia's energy resources.

Climate Change

Both greenhouse gases (GHGs) and climate change are important elements in global energy security. GHGs include a group that occurs naturally—carbon dioxide (CO_2), methane, nitrous oxide, and ozone—as well as compounds such as chlorofluorocarbons that do not occur in nature. All of these gases have become much more prevalent because of human activity.[1] Buildup of these gases has altered the composition of the Earth's atmosphere, with consequences for the Earth's climate. They are termed *greenhouse gases* because they trap heat in the atmosphere, reflecting that heat back to Earth.

The Threat and Its Estimations

The debate on climate change—whether it is happening, the extent to which it is anthropogenic (human-generated), and the extent to which it is a threat—has persisted in the United States much longer than in other developed nations. In spite of early U.S. leadership in climate science and climate policy negotiations, the United States now lags behind many other developed states in its policies and analysis. The Intergovernmental Panel on Climate Change (IPCC), a UN community of climate scientists who shared the Nobel Prize with Al Gore in 2007, has been united in explaining the risks for many years.

Why do the data—and the predictions—keep changing? Scientific uncertainty about the rate of warming persists because it is difficult to create predictive models about open environmental systems. As the atmosphere warms and nature responds, unanticipated effects continually appear. Early predictive models, for example, did not incorporate the impact of thawing permafrost tundra's release of methane into the atmosphere—a process that is accelerating GHG accumulation dramatically because methane is an especially potent GHG. Nor did the early models properly incorporate the increased growth rates of key tree populations that pull CO_2 out of the air—a process that is slowing upper atmosphere accumulation of greenhouse gases.

Evidence is compelling that nearly 1 degree Celsius warming has already occurred relative to pre-industrial times.[2] Continued acceleration of the rate of warming in recent years is the key source of concern. Many analysts identify 2 degrees as a critical threshold level—an environmental tipping point.[3] Two Washington area think tanks in 2007 collaborated on a careful comparison of available models of likely future climate change patterns and the potential security impacts.[4] Their analysis assumes a best-case scenario of a temperature increase of 1.3 degrees centigrade by 2040. Under such a scenario, they assert that key likely security impacts are increases in global prevalence of insect-borne diseases, coastal inundation (which will affect urban centers and agriculture), and migration caused by crop failure and loss of land. According to their analysis, changes above 2.6 degrees (their medium case scenario) would lead to devastating nonlinear events that may render areas ungovernable—events such as large-scale loss of potable water, spread of overwhelming pandemic disease, up to 15 million additional people being affected by inundation of coastal communities, and substantial changes in marine and ecosystems due to changes in undersea currents. Troublingly, the IPCC predicts that a warming of more than 4.5 degrees by midcentury is possible.

What we know with a high level of certainty is that the accelerated density of GHGs in the upper atmosphere is causing weather to behave less predictably. But the rate of temperature change and the security risks posed by such change remain uncertain. Even improved models cannot provide policymakers with certainty about the emerging interactive effects. The chances of catastrophic slowing of the thermohaline conveyor belt that warms the northern Atlantic remain unclear; increased threat of hurricanes is believed to be associated with global warming, but this cannot be definitively proven in the near term; and the number of degrees that ocean temperature is likely to rise in the 10-, 50-, and 100-year future is still intensely debated.

In a climate of uncertainty, when action is believed to be expensive and politically unattractive, it is tempting to do nothing. However, climate change belongs to a category of phenomena known as long-wave events: events in which, while the threat remains distant and not entirely understood, political will to act to reduce the threat is absent. Once the risk is evident enough to galvanize political will, the moment in which the risk could have been reduced is past and the task of nations becomes mitigation of consequences. (The unfolding of the HIV/AIDS epidemic in Africa is one example of such a long-wave event.)

The U.S. Role

The problem of climate change poses key security threats for the international political environment as well as for the natural environment. In spite of a lack of U.S. domestic consensus on the proximity of the threat, a clear fact remains. The United States is now and has historically been a lead contributor to the problem. The United States was the world's lead emitter of GHGs every year until 2007, when Chinese emissions surpassed U.S. emissions. Americans still produce more than four times as much carbon per capita as the Chinese, and have been producing high levels of carbon since the Industrial Revolution. Climate change is a key security concern for U.S. allies, so the United States fails to exercise leadership at its own peril. Strategists must consider not only the environmental risks of climate change, but also the international diplomatic risks of not doing enough about it.

The United States must move away from its recent role—internationally perceived as obstructionist—and seek to occupy a meaningful leadership role in international efforts to address the problem. The Kyoto Protocol, which entered force without U.S. signature, will expire in 2012. By that time, a new set of international mechanisms will be put into place for the future. It behooves the United States to be part of that process, preferably in a leadership role. As the United States contemplates its options, three issues should be foremost in the minds of policymakers: the key actors that must be involved in a meaningful solution, the key sectors that must be transformed as a matter of priority, and the key policies that could enable the United States to have the greatest impact on CO_2 abatement at the least cost.

Key State Actors

The key actors in treaty negotiation are states. States make policies and can bind their citizens to international commitments. Since high-altitude pollutants such as CO_2 have an impact globally, UN efforts have focused on involving as many nations as possible. The UN Framework Convention on Climate Change, which contained no binding limits on emissions, was ratified by 192 nations, including the United States, in 1992. It is on the basis of that treaty that all signatory nations use standardized measures of GHG emission and capture, and provide regular reports of energy consumption, emissions, and threats posed by climate change. This regime should be continued, regardless of the future of associated treaties, as it provides common language, a forum, and a useful information base.

However, since fewer than 20 countries are responsible for 80 percent of the world's emissions, it is often contended that including the other 150-plus countries as partners makes effective solutions more difficult to achieve. It is often argued that the number of nations truly needed to solve the problem of climate change is small. Since the current Kyoto Protocol is not signed by the United States and imposes no emissions targets on Brazil, India, and China, it does not touch key historical contributors or crucial rising emissions powers.

The earliest effort to create a new coalition was through the Gleneagles Dialogue on Climate Change, Clean Energy, and Sustainable Development initiated in 2005 under British leadership. The Gleneagles Dialogue has continued since then, and includes the G–8 countries plus China, India, Brazil, Australia, and a handful of other lead emitting states. It also includes international organizations such as the European Union, IEA, and World Bank. The United States has supported this forum, but it has also promoted a competing White House initiative called the Asia-Pacific Partnership on Clean Development, which includes Australia, China, India, Japan, and South Korea, focusing on voluntary measures to introduce more clean technologies relevant to greenhouse gas reduction. These projects to date have been partial fixes, ones that neither satisfy allies who believe the threat to be imminent, nor offer targets for reduction. There has also been substantial competition for who will be included, and how leadership and monitoring of progress will be achieved.

Key Actors within the States

Effective climate policy, domestic and international, will rely on the successful interaction of several communities. Domestic laws must lead: governments must be involved in setting policies and laws that regulate emissions and punish offenders within their territories. Since GHG emissions have historically been regarded as environmental externalities, their cost has not been incorporated into production of goods and services. Governments must create the incentives necessary to internalize these externalities. Industry must be closely involved to ensure that efforts to reduce emissions are undertaken in ways that encourage least-cost approaches and maximize innovation, the better to meet ambitious abatement goals. States, such as California, exercising leadership in state-based legislation on emissions should be encouraged, since their efforts provide laboratories to test potential future policies. However, at the present moment, the Federal Government is challenging the right of states to set such standards. Finally, the nongovernmental sector, including think tanks and foundations, must be involved to provide ongoing critique of the efforts and visions of the future in this area. Climate change is a highly complex phenomenon, not only in terms of open environmental systems, but also in terms of the economic, scientific, and policy interests and equities involved.

Key Sectors

In the same way that there are key nations, there are also key sectors that must be engaged if emissions reductions are to be meaningful. Analysis consistently suggests that these sectors are power, the building sector (often combined with power in analysis), industry (especially cement and steel), transport, and land use and agriculture. According to World Resources Institute, electricity and heat account for 24.6 percent of world GHG emissions, transporta-

tion constitutes 13.5 percent, industry 13.8 percent, deforestation 18.2 percent, and agricultural processes 13.5 percent. Complete GHG abatement policies will set clear guidelines and priorities for each of these sectors, which should be engaged in the development of least-cost policies. But the sectors must receive clear signals that regulation of carbon emissions is imminent and a serious policy priority.

Key Policies

The most widely recognized approach to reducing carbon emissions remains establishing a cap on them, combined with ensuring a functioning and regulated market for emissions permits. In 2008, both Presidential candidates endorsed such systems for the United States. Since these programs are mandated under the Kyoto Protocol, a number of signatory states have years of experience in creating and regulating such markets. The United States should learn from their best practices, complementing its own experience in other air quality cap-and-trade systems such as the United States Sulfur Dioxide program. The United States should also seek to retain its historic role as a leader in technological innovation, which can only occur if legislation presses for improved efficiency.

The Kyoto Protocol may represent a flawed international approach, but it has established important experience and precedents. The United States should not abandon the negotiations of a follow-on treaty. It may be effective to engage a smaller number of states in a separate agreement, but any "coalition of the willing" approach will be rightly criticized if it does not impose limits and does not offer resources for adaptation and mitigation for poorer nations. Such a separate agreement would ideally incorporate the group of countries responsible for 80 percent of emissions, rather than defaulting to countries with whom it is easiest to reach agreements.

Water Security

Water scarcity is the principal indicator of water security, and it includes both physical and economic water scarcity. *Physical water scarcity* is a situation in which water use for agriculture, industry, and domestic purposes is approaching or exceeding sustainable limits. *Economic water scarcity* is a situation where institutional, infrastructural, or financial limitations prevent populations from gaining access to water, even though there is enough available to meet human demands. Overall, the drivers of physical and economic water scarcity complicate sustainable management of water and create critical observable trends.

Table 2. Global Water Use by Sector (percent)

Region	Agriculture	Industry	Domestic and Residential	Ecosystems
Developing Countries	81	11	8	?
Developed Countries	46	41	13	?
World	70	20	10	?

Source: World Resources Institute, Earth Trends Environmental Database, 2007.

Quantity

Global. Researchers have calculated that, by the year 2025, water scarcity will affect more than 75 percent of the world's population. Currently, 2.8 billion people face some level of water scarcity.[5]

Globally, the United Nations Environment Programme (UNEP) points out that *excessive withdrawals from surface waters and aquifers, industrial pollution, inefficient use, climate change and variability, and natural disasters are major causes of water stress, threatening human well-being and ecological health.*[6]

The anthropogenic competition between agriculture, industry, and households for water is increasing (see table 2). Additionally, water required to sustain essential natural ecosystems is seldom included in global formulas for water usage. Moreover, the complex ecosystem services provided by functioning ecosystems, to include flood regulation, climate moderation, and water purification, are often underappreciated and unprotected.[7] In particular, global climate change is expected to create enormous stress on natural ecosystems and overall water quality and quantity.

Africa. Water security in Africa is tenuous. On the continent, more than 300 million people out of a total population of more than 800 million live with physical and economic water scarcity challenges. These water-scarce conditions exist even though Africa contains one-third of the world's major international river basins and its population uses less than 6 percent of its renewable water resources. The uneven spatial and temporal distribution of Africa's water resources exacerbates many complex regional water issues. On average, African governments spend less than 0.5 percent of their GDP on water resource development. The majority of African farmers depend on rainfall to supply water for crops. Water supplies in cities are comparatively better than in rural areas. In general, Africa needs more integrated approaches to water resource management.

Asia and Oceania. The water security situation in Asia and Oceania is also fragile. Similar to Africa,

Chinese contractor supervises Liberian workers building sewer system in Monrovia

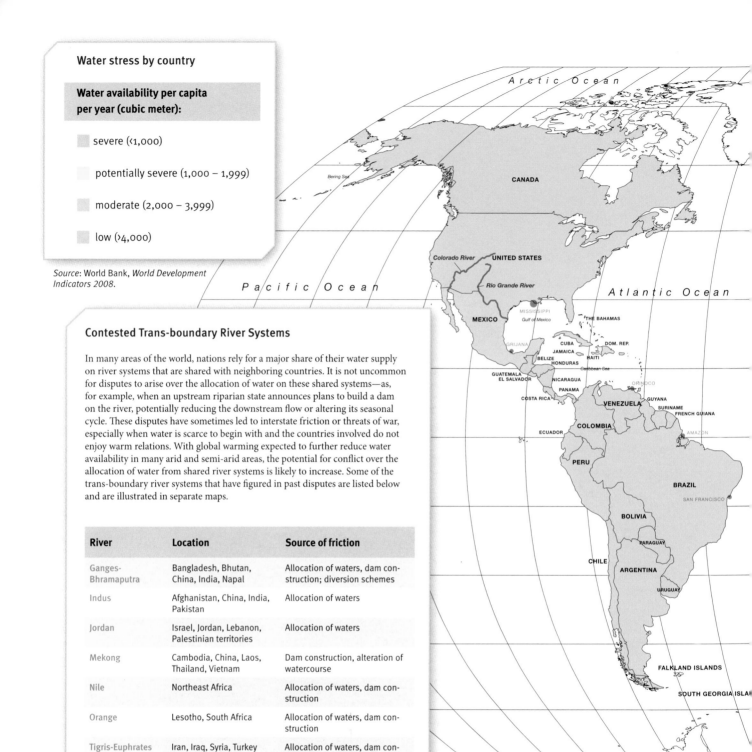

Water stress by country

Water availability per capita per year (cubic meter):

- severe (<1,000)
- potentially severe (1,000 – 1,999)
- moderate (2,000 – 3,999)
- low (>4,000)

Source: World Bank, *World Development Indicators 2008.*

Contested Trans-boundary River Systems

In many areas of the world, nations rely for a major share of their water supply on river systems that are shared with neighboring countries. It is not uncommon for disputes to arise over the allocation of water on these shared systems—as, for example, when an upstream riparian state announces plans to build a dam on the river, potentially reducing the downstream flow or altering its seasonal cycle. These disputes have sometimes led to interstate friction or threats of war, especially when water is scarce to begin with and the countries involved do not enjoy warm relations. With global warming expected to further reduce water availability in many arid and semi-arid areas, the potential for conflict over the allocation of water from shared river systems is likely to increase. Some of the trans-boundary river systems that have figured in past disputes are listed below and are illustrated in separate maps.

River	Location	Source of friction
Ganges-Bhramaputra	Bangladesh, Bhutan, China, India, Napal	Allocation of waters, dam construction; diversion schemes
Indus	Afghanistan, China, India, Pakistan	Allocation of waters
Jordan	Israel, Jordan, Lebanon, Palestinian territories	Allocation of waters
Mekong	Cambodia, China, Laos, Thailand, Vietnam	Dam construction, alteration of watercourse
Nile	Northeast Africa	Allocation of waters, dam construction
Orange	Lesotho, South Africa	Allocation of waters, dam construction
Tigris-Euphrates	Iran, Iraq, Syria, Turkey	Allocation of waters, dam construction, water quality

Source: International Rivers (Berkeley, California).

River Deltas and Megadeltas: Potential for Inundation and Social Disorder

Many scientists fear that some of the world's most highly populated river deltas are at risk of inundations due to sea-level rise as temperatures increase around the world, heating the oceans and causing them to expand. Global warming is also expected to increase the rate of glacier melt in Greenland and Antarctica, further adding to the rise in global sea levels. Many deltas are at risk due to natural subsidence and a loss of sediment buildup as a result of upstream dam construction. Added together, these risks pose a significant threat to the future habitability of various large deltas around the world. According to one study published in 2006, as many as 1 million people could face severe risk in the Nile, Mekong, and Ganges-Bhramaputra Deltas by 2050, and lesser numbers at some 21 other deltas. In many cases, these people will be forced to abandon homes and move to safer areas inland, often facing hostility of those already occupying these areas.

Degree of Risk   Extreme ●   High ●   Medium ·

Source: J.P. Ericson et al., "Effective Sea-Level rise and Deltas," *Global Planet Change*, 50 (February 2006), 63–82.

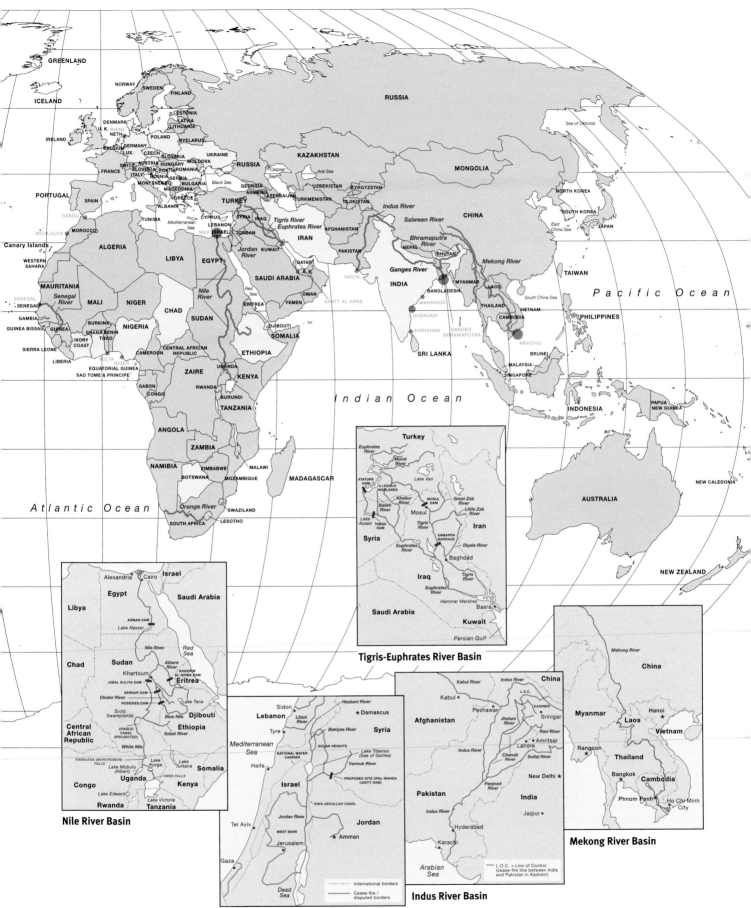

GREENLAND

ICELAND

NORWAY
SWEDEN
FINLAND

IRELAND
U.K. RHINE
DENMARK
ESTONIA
LATVIA
LITHUANIA

NETH.
GERMANY
POLAND
BYELARUS

BELGIUM
LUX.
CZECH
SLOVAKIA
UKRAINE

FRANCE
SWITZ.
AUSTRIA
HUNGARY
MOLDOVA

SLOVENIA
CROATIA
ROMANIA

PORTUGAL
SPAIN
ITALY
BOSNIA
SERBIA

MONTENEGRO
BULGARIA

ALBANIA
MACEDONIA
GREECE

RUSSIA

KAZAKHSTAN

MONGOLIA

NORTH KOREA

SOUTH KOREA
JAPAN

Sea of Okhotsk

Caspian
Sea
Aral Sea

Black Sea

GEORGIA
ARMENIA
AZERBAIJAN
UZBEKISTAN
KYRGYZSTAN

TURKEY
CYPRUS
SYRIA
IRAQ
Tigris River
Euphrates River

TUNISIA
Mediterranean
Sea
NILE
LEBANON
ISRAEL
JORDAN

TURKMENISTAN
TAJIKISTAN

Indus River
Salween River

CHINA

East
China Sea

TAIWAN

SEBOU

MOROCCO

MOULOUYA

Canary Islands

WESTERN
SAHARA

ALGERIA

LIBYA
EGYPT

IRAN
KUWAIT
QATAR
U.A.E.

SAUDI ARABIA

Nile
River

Red
Sea

OMAN

AFGHANISTAN

PAKISTAN

NEPAL

Bhramaputra
River

Ganges River
BHUTAN

Mekong River

MYANMAR

LAOS

THAILAND

Pacific Ocean

INDIA

BANGLADESH
MAHANADI

SENEGAL
Senegal
River

MAURITANIA

MALI
NIGER
CHAD

GODAVARI

KRISHNA
GANGES-
BHRAMAPUTRA

VIETNAM
CAMBODIA

PHILIPPINES

GAMBIA
GUINEA BISSAU
GUINEA

BURKINA
GHANA
BENIN
TOGO

NIGERIA

SUDAN

ERITREA
YEMEN

SHATT AL ARAB

MEKONG

SRI LANKA

BRUNEI

SIERRA LEONE
VOLTA
NIGER

IVORY
COAST
LIBERIA

EQUATORIAL GUINEA
SAO TOME & PRINCIPE

CAMEROON

CENTRAL AFRICAN
REPUBLIC

DJIBOUTI

SOMALIA

ETHIOPIA

UGANDA

MALAYSIA
SINGAPORE

GABON
CONGO

ZAIRE

RWANDA

KENYA

Indian   Ocean

INDONESIA

PAPUA
NEW GUINEA

BURUNDI

TANZANIA

NEW CALEDONIA

ANGOLA

ZAMBIA

AUSTRALIA

NAMIBIA

ZIMBABWE
BOTSWANA
MOZAMBIQUE

MALAWI

MADAGASCAR

Atlantic Ocean

Orange River

SWAZILAND

SOUTH AFRICA
LESOTHO

NEW ZEALAND

Tigris-Euphrates River Basin

Turkey

Euphrates
River
Murat
River

Lake Van

ATATURK
DAM
ILLEGIBLE
HIGHLANDS

Khabur
River

Great Zab
River

MOSUL
DAM

Little Zab
River

Balikh
River

Mosul

Iran

Lake
Assad
TABQA
DAM

Tigris
River

Syria

SAMARRA
BARRAGE

Diyala River

Euphrates
River

Baghdad

Iraq

Tigris
River

Saudi Arabia

Euphrates
River

Hammar Marshes

Basra

Kuwait

Persian Gulf

Nile River Basin

Alexandria
Cairo
Israel

Egypt

Saudi Arabia

Libya

ASWAN DAM
Lake Nasser

Red
Sea

Chad

Sudan

Nile River

Atbara
River

KHASHM
AL-GIRBA DAM

Khartoum

JABAL AULIYA DAM

Eritrea

SENNAR DAM

Dinder River
ROSEIRES DAM

Lake Tana

Djibouti

Sudd
Swamplands

JONGLEI
CANAL
(PROJECTED)

Sobat River

Ethiopia

Central
African
Republic

White Nile

KABALEGA (MURCHINSON)
FALLS

Lake Mobutu
(Albert)

Lake
Kyoga

Lake Turkana

Somalia

Congo

OWEN FALLS

Uganda

Kenya

Lake Edward

Lake Victoria

Rwanda

Tanzania

Jordan River Basin

Hasbani River

Sidon

Litani
River

Damascus

Lebanon

Tyre

Baniyas River

Syria

GOLAN HEIGHTS

Mediterranean
Sea

NATIONAL WATER
CARRIER

Lake Tiberias
(Sea of Galilee)

Haifa

Yarmuk River

PROPOSED SITE OFAL-WAHDA
(UNITY DAM)

Israel

KING ABDULLAH CANAL

Jordan River

Tel Aviv

WEST BANK

Jordan

Jerusalem

Amman

Gaza

Dead
Sea

- - - International borders
- - - Cease-fire /
disputed borders

Indus River Basin

Kabul River
Indus River
China

L.O.C.

Kabul

KASHMIR

Afghanistan

Peshawar

Jhelum
River

Srinigar

Ravi River

Lahore

Amritsar

Indus River

Chenab
River

Sutlej River

New Delhi

Pakistan

Panjnad
River

India

Indus River

Jaipur

Hyderabad

Karachi

Arabian
Sea

- - - L.O.C. = Line of Control
(cease-fire line between India
and Pakistan in Kashmir)

Mekong River Basin

Mekong River

China

Myanmar

Hanoi

Laos

Vietnam

Rangoon

Thailand

Bangkok

Cambodia

Phnom Penh

Ho Chi Minh
City

the irregular spatial and seasonal distribution of resources in Asia and Oceania complicates regional water security problems. China alone has over 22 percent of the world's population and only 8 percent of the world's fresh water. This fact has contributed to a shortage of drinking water for more than 12 million Chinese. Water shortages are causing rising food prices and forcing migrations in some areas of China. The UNEP points out that in India, *urban water demand is expected to double and industrial demand to triple by 2025.* In the Middle East, *between 1985 and 2005, overall per capita freshwater availability fell from 1,700 to 907 cubic meters/year and based on projected population increases, it is expected to decline to 420 cubic meters/year by the year 2050.*[8] Overall, population and economic growth will increase demands for water supply and irrigation services, and the fact that approximately 60 percent of the region's water flows across international borders further complicates demand challenges.

Europe. Europe's water quantity challenges are not as acute as Africa or Asia/Oceania but do exhibit state-centered problems. Cyprus, Bulgaria, Belgium, Spain, Malta, Republic of Macedonia, Italy, the United Kingdom, and Germany are showing signs of economic water scarcity, and Ukraine and Belarus are exhibiting indications of physical water scarcity. Salt-water intrusion into underground aquifers is

beginning to affect water resources in Italy, Spain, Malta, Cyprus, and Turkey. Overall, 14 percent of Europe's population is affected by water scarcity. However, many Europeans are moving to cities and the growing urban populations should have access to adequate water supplies for the near future. In addition, Russian and the Nordic countries have vast supplies of relatively untapped water and could supply fresh water to Europe, China, and Central Asia. In 2000, the European Union made water protection a priority with the implementation of the European Union Water Framework Directive.

North America. Americans and Canadians overall have ample water supplies. The United States and Canada possess approximately 13 percent of the world's renewable fresh water, but water users are not always close to water sources, and some consumers experience periodic shortages. In addition, over the last 20 years, North Americans have lowered their per capita water consumption yet remain the highest per capita water users in the world. However, sections of the western United States are beginning to experience physical water scarcity, and water rationing affects approximately 16 million Americans.[9] Global climate change is expected to exacerbate these and other water deficits. Agricultural irrigation, the major use for water, continues to increase and is competing with cities for limited supplies. In reaction,

UN (Martine Perret)

National park in Timor-Leste protects coral reefs and monsoon rainforest

■ Working with leaders in both the central government and the ungoverned area to regularize the area's status within the larger state. For example, in exchange for external economic development assistance or political concessions, local leaders may be open to limited but sufficient cooperation with government officials to curtail criminal or terrorist activity.

■ Pursuing deals with the de facto power structure in the ungoverned area independently of the de jure central authorities. The development of cooperative relations between U.S. forces and Sunni tribal sheikhs in Iraq's Anbar Province may provide a rudimentary model. In the long run, this course may lead to support for formal independence for the (formerly) ungoverned area.

■ Internationalizing the issue under the auspices of the United Nations (UN) or a regional security organization. Britain's Lord Robertson and Lord Ashdown specifically referred to the possibility of UN-mandated action to deal with ungoverned areas when they advocated the creation of more effective military forces under the auspices of the European Union in June 2008.

None of these courses is without peril. Past reliance upon locals to police themselves without effective incentives to do so effectively is, in some measure, the reason why areas such as Pakistan's FATA are practically ungoverned today. Choosing the wrong local power brokers to work with runs the risk of empowering warlords and creating what amounts to a giant protection racket. Clumsy attempts to buy off local populations by trading economic incentives for compromises on highly charged cultural or political issues can easily backfire by sparking moral outrage. Supporting independence for populations in formerly ungoverned areas will certainly create enemies in the rest of the country, probably provoke international condemnation on grounds of interference in the host country's internal affairs, and potentially lead to irredentist conflict in the future.

Ultimately, the degree of danger posed by the continuing lack of governance in the area in question will determine whether these risks are worth taking. If the area is being actively used by terrorist groups with global agendas and global reach, outside players may well judge that getting effective control in place is paramount to any other objective. If so, the choice may come down to which side to back: the official central authorities or the people in the region itself. If we truly believe, as our rhetoric would have it, that

governing people fairly and in a way consistent with their own desires and expectations is the surest path to preventing the use of their territory by terrorists or other illicit actors, then the choice will become that much clearer.

Pandemics: State Fragility's Most Telling Gap?

A nation-state's capacity to govern effectively faces no stiffer test than its ability to manage infectious disease crises. Pandemics require unprecedented multidisciplinary and multi-agency communication, expertise, and collaboration at the state, regional, and international levels, all of which are crucial for containment of the disease and mitigation of its consequences. Andrew Price-Smith has argued that

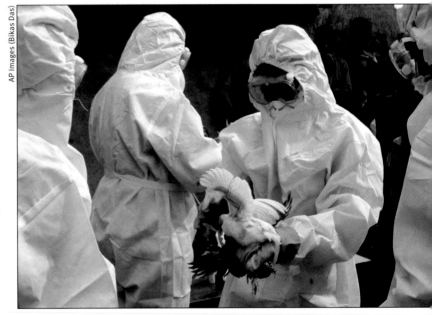

Indian health officials cull birds to curb spread of bird flu

"as disease intensity grows it will correspondingly reduce state capacity, increase economic deprivation, and deplete the reservoir of human capital within seriously affected states."[8] A strong correlation also exists between a population's health, as measured by life expectancy and infant mortality rates, and that state's capacity to govern. Disease management is a critical element in this equation.

Countries beset by poor governance and low levels of state capacity have failed in today's world to contain and manage the spread of a contagion and mitigate its economic and political toll. The data here are compelling: 75 percent of epidemics during the last three decades have occurred in countries where war, conflict, and prolonged political violence have crippled their capacity to respond, leaving their neighbors and the world vulnerable. Gaps in state capacity are defined as the protective public health infrastructure (water, sanitation, food, shelter, fuel, and health) and the systems that support and manage this infrastructure on a daily basis as being either insufficient, absent, not maintained, denied, or politically influenced, interfered with, or vulnerable to corruption.

Disease and State Weakness: A Vicious Cycle

Epidemics and pandemics are always public health emergencies. They easily elude a compromised health system and can rapidly cause confusion, fear, and chaos, and send populations fleeing across unprotected borders. An estimated 6.4 million people die each year from AIDS, tuberculosis, and malaria. An additional 1.3 million children die from diseases preventable by vaccine. AIDS, a pandemic whose spread and morbidity are directly fueled by (though by no means limited to) weak states and ungoverned spaces, has demonstrated how an infectious disease can "disrupt and destabilize" governance, becoming a major issue in national security debates. It has taught us how quickly an infectious disease can spread worldwide, and how poor and unrepresented populations are most affected.

In 2003, Severe Acute Respiratory Syndrome (SARS) highlighted the importance of broad outbreak control measures and information-sharing for mitigation and prevention efforts, when China's initial failure to disclose the epidemic resulted in its spread to over 40 countries around the globe. It required the World Health Organization (WHO) to aggressively expand advisories, real-time information-sharing, and broad outbreak control measures. This was an unprecedented measure, which in turn prompted a World Health Assembly resolution to revise old International Health Regulations (IHR) initially used to control smallpox, cholera, plague, and yellow fever decades before. The dated regulations had limitations such as a restricted surveillance capacity and inadequate mechanisms for swift assessment and investigation within sovereign countries that, if not revised, would fail to contain modern-day diseases across land borders and via air and sea travel and trade.

In 2005, WHO authority and surveillance capacity expanded when human rights principles were added

to the criteria for measuring public health interventions to stop pandemics. These changes represent a major development in the use of international law for public health purposes. The resulting international treaty of June 2007, which applies to "public health emergencies of international concern," ensures maximum security against the international spread of diseases, while addressing the need to minimize interference with trade and travel to mitigate the economic tragedy that prevails with any pandemic.

The management of the deadly avian influenza A virus (H5N1) outbreak that followed the SARS pandemic and that occupies our concerns today confirms that well-governed countries do have the capacity and will both to eliminate SARS and contain H5N1. Yet poorly governed countries remain endemically threatened by newly emergent and re-emergent bacteria and viruses. While the H5N1 virus is of global concern because it mutates incessantly and gains resistance the longer it remains unchecked, countries with poor governance tend to resent measures, even if designed by treaty to protect state and global populations, that appear to threaten their own national sovereignty. This can be a deadly combination: hidden repositories of disease may occur in any country, but fragile states and ungoverned spaces, with massive migration and displacement of human populations, represent an "ideal home" for any future viral mutation and propagation, and would elude the best intentions of the WHO and IHR. These diasporic populations are at risk for the transmission of disease and resistant organisms that are poorly identified and controlled, while they also jeopardize the global surveillance required under current international mandates. Finding a means to optimize global surveillance and to contain highly lethal and aggressive diseases remains a global priority.

AIDS, SARS, and H5N1 viruses and drug-resistant tuberculosis underscore how important it is to transcend conventional concepts of sovereignty if global pandemics are to be prevented or at least contained. The 2005 IHR is already under threat from trade, political, and social inequity concerns. In late 2006, Indonesia chose not to share with WHO live H5N1 virus samples from new cases; WHO hoped to carry out a genome study to determine whether a more lethal mutation had occurred, which is necessary for successful vaccine development. Fearing that expensive patented vaccines produced in rich countries would be less accessible to poorer countries, Indonesia suspended the transfer of live virus samples, claiming sovereign ownership of the virus itself. Other countries threatened the same action, challenging WHO authorities, the World Health Assembly, and the global health community to guarantee every country access to vaccines and equal protections and coverage.

Globalization, which has provided great economic gains in many Asian countries, has also increased discrepancies in health outcomes between the "have" and "have not" populations in the same country. A paradox of globalization is that state resources are often directed toward building private capacity resources at the expense of maintenance for public hospitals, health facilities, and systems, on the grounds that when the economic situation improves, health security will follow. Yet populations have increasingly seen their access to health care and medications diminish, and for many, health has become a major security concern. Megacity populations—most of whom are under age 25, poor, uneducated, and discontent—often occupy dense and disaster-prone areas in the developing world, devoid of public health infrastructure and protections, including surveillance capacity. Pandemics may prove to be the politically catalyzing event that exposes such vulnerabilities in otherwise promising economic globalization initiatives. The current crisis of insufficient health care workers in 57 poor African and Asian countries severely impairs their ability to provide even the most essential daily and lifesaving interventions. This crisis will make state sovereignty a moot point when an undetected epidemic in a fragile nation-state accelerates into a continent-wide pandemic.

Engaging the Problem

The existing 2005 IHR is not without legal disagreements and controversy, especially as it relates to fragile states and ungoverned spaces. David Fidler, who has led efforts to strengthen global capacity through international law, reminds us of more desperate legal limitations for fragile states and states with ungoverned spaces, beginning with the fact that neither the IHR nor other international legal instruments applicable to public health defines the terms *fragile state* or *ungoverned space*. International law does not recognize the right of a state, directly or indirectly, to infringe on another's sovereignty simply because it is "weak and experiencing difficulties effectively governing all parts of its territory." The fact that a state is weak or "fragile," or has less effective governance in some parts of its territory, does not dilute its rights as a sovereign state under international law.[9]

Rights and obligations under the 2005 IHR with respect to fragile and ungoverned spaces are unclear because the terms' lack of definition fails to inform such provisions under the existing law. The surveillance provisions in the 2005 IHR nevertheless are relevant:

■ First, they require all state parties to report to WHO all events within their respective territories that may constitute a public health emergency of international concern (Article 6.1). This includes governments of fragile states or those with ungoverned territories.

■ Second, the provision (Article 9.1) allows WHO to receive reports of disease events from sources other than governments, such as nongovernmental organizations (NGOs) or the media, and to seek verification of these reports. The expansion of WHO's ability to collect, analyze, and pursue epidemiologically significant information would allow WHO to raise surveillance awareness about disease events in fragile and ungoverned areas.

■ Third, the IHR (Article 9.2) requires a state party to report within 24 hours evidence that it receives of a disaster event occurring within the territory of another state party, which could produce reports of "a public health risk" occurrence in fragile and ungoverned areas.

Taken together, these three surveillance provisions in the IHR serve to increase transparency and the flow of information where governance has broken down. The IHR does not, however, grant any state party or WHO the right to intervene without the affected state's permission. Put bluntly, international law presently gives a state the right to let its people die even when help is at hand—a grim reality highlighted when Cyclone Nargis devastated Myanmar's Irrawaddy Delta area in May 2008, leaving more than 140,000 people dead or missing.

Short- and Long-term Solutions

Ultimately, the IHR is only as strong as its weakest link, and those weakest links worldwide clearly belong to infected populations from fragile states and ungoverned spaces. Peace-building that opens the door to improved governance requires sustained initiatives that move beyond rhetoric to strengthen nation-state institutions and modernize a country's political system.

A first step can come from building capacity in public health (surveillance and proven community containment and mitigation strategies) as an incentive for fragile states to accept improvements in basic governance. Such successes occurred through the "Health as a Bridge to Peace" initiatives that were implemented by WHO in conflict and postconflict zones, and are now being re-explored by WHO as possible models elsewhere. Another means is to link the guarantee of trade opportunities, security, surveillance, and public health infrastructure and systems development to values that speak to a common respect for global protection and security.

The IHR is far from perfect. In fact, from a clinical perspective, the IHR falls miserably short of what is responsibly required to control a pandemic, especially one that is aggressive and lethal to the human host. Additionally, decisionmakers rarely consider how indecision on health insecurity and the transmission of disease undermines their responsibility to global health. Fragile states and ungoverned spaces by definition have little or no public health protections.

U.S. Navy (Jason R. Zalasky)

Armed Somali pirates aboard MV *Faina* observed from U.S. Navy ship after they attacked, seized, and forced cargo ship to anchor off the Somalia coast, October 8, 2008

Strengthening the IHR would best come in incremental ways that ensure appropriate language, guarantees, and individual nation-state buy-in. The right to sovereignty does not come without the responsibility to protect one's population, a correlation that is currently being promoted under the "Responsibility to Protect (R2P)" initiative's guiding principles,

which hold that a state is entitled to full sovereignty so long as it abides by norms established by the international community. The R2P concept, however, is restricted to cases involving large-scale, violent atrocities, such as genocide and crimes against humanity.[10] In June 2008, the Indonesian health minister decided to restrict his office's reporting on avian influenza in humans to every 6 months, leading to concerns that such a delay could lead to a pandemic if important mutations are not detected in a timely manner. Indonesia's action challenges both the IHR and the R2P, leading experts to question whether the IHR can stand up to such pressure.

Yet a cognitive link can be made between a potential pandemic of global genocidal proportions and the R2P, especially if many of the worst outcomes are preventable. By incorporating emerging disease control as part of an international "right to health," the IHR can help ensure that infectious disease control becomes a human rights issue.

In the long term, the global community's disaster diplomacy must strengthen and leverage this unique opportunity in international law, as an initial step toward an expanded IHR, or as a model for further global health initiatives under existing United Nations Children's Fund (for example, vaccine initiatives) and other accepted health mandates (for example, U.S. International Partnership on Avian and Pandemic Influenza). A retooled globalization model must address the world's worsening health discrepancies and include a mandated health security requirement under future UN Charter reform. The worldwide health care worker crisis is arguably making all the good intentions of the IHR debatable. The protective shield begins with the global community, which has the responsibility to promote and support both short- and long-term nation-state and regional education and training infrastructure, and provide incentives for health care workers that emphasize public health, preventive medicine, and primary care.

State Failure: Devising Effective Responses

Since the 9/11 attacks, American policymakers have highlighted fragile and failed states as the central security challenge of our time. In fact, many Western countries have begun to address these situations, as it has become clear that some of the principal threats to their vital national interests—such as terrorist networks, illicit arms markets, counterfeiting, human trafficking, money laundering, and narcotics cartels— are drawn to failed states where these activities can operate with impunity, in the absence of state structures to control them. Many developed countries have begun to make structural and programmatic changes in their foreign policy apparatus to address the challenges they face from the consequences of these failed states. These changes are still in their infancy and appear to be inadequate to the task: poorly funded and staffed, with uncertain authority.

Within the United States, policy advocates frequently invoke the centrality of defense, development, and diplomacy as the primary instruments of power needed to address the challenge from marginal or failed states. Yet a profound discontinuity exists between the bureaucratic position, organizational strength, size, budget, and staffing of these three instruments of national power, and their relationship to the threat of fragile and failed states, which are principally caused by a failure of development. Sadly, it is the developmental instrument that is comparatively the weakest in the U.S. arsenal, and yet it is the one most needed to address the problem.

Setting aside these discontinuities of organizational power within the United States and other governments, what do we know about the nature of state fragility and state failure? While no two situations are precisely alike, failed states do tend to share five characteristics:

■ collapse of the authority of the central government, particularly outside the capital city, manifesting in a breakdown in the provision of public services, the efficacy of the criminal justice system, and the enforcement of law and order
■ macroeconomic collapse with double-digit unemployment, high rates of inflation, a deterioration in the value of the currency and its convertibility, and a decline in the gross domestic product
■ widespread civil conflict and human rights abuses
■ mass population movements into refugee or internally displaced camps, to escape the civil conflict
■ rising morbidity and mortality rates from malnutrition and sickness as food security and access to water break down and communicable disease spreads among the general population.

Devising effective responses to these interconnected problems is a daunting task for outside would-be interveners. The immediate temptation is to tackle all of these at once—an understandable reaction, but one that risks squandering scarce resources. Where, then, should priority be placed?

Emergency Response: The Humanitarian Imperative

The most visible and most immediate set of challenges these states face is humanitarian in nature: food insecurity, disease epidemics, and population displacement. During the 1990s, the humanitarian response systems through which the United States, other donor governments, and international institutions reacted to the crisis of state failure went through a profound evolution in doctrine, management, structure, and standard setting. Spending increased for emergency response to what aid agencies were calling complex humanitarian emergencies, their term for the crises that occur as a result of state failure. An extensive body of academic research and practitioner study has developed over the past two decades that analyzes the architecture of the humanitarian response system, its weaknesses, its strengths, what works well and what does not, and how it might be reformed or improved.

UN personnel help displaced persons return to homes in Pristina, Kosovo

To start with, authority in the international response system is very diffuse: clusters of institutions have developed with increasingly defined roles, but with no clear hierarchy for unified decision-making. Decisions tend to be made by consensus, a cumbersome and inefficient process. While the UN Office for the Coordination of Humanitarian Affairs, charged with the coordination function in the international system, has improved its leadership capacity and technical competence in providing a management framework since its creation in 1991, it neither controls funding, nor can it give orders to other actors even within the UN system, including the five specialized agencies where humanitarian resources are concentrated: the World Food Program, UN High Commissioner for Refugees, UN High Commissioner for Human Rights, UN Children's Fund, and the UN Development Program. The second institutional cluster is composed of international NGOs, of which perhaps two dozen dominate the system, in addition to three international organizations not formally part of the UN family: the International Committee of the Red Cross, International Federation of Red Cross and Red Crescent Societies, and International Organization for Migration. Finally, the bilateral response agencies of donor governments are also major actors in the system, since they provide over three-quarters of the total funding spent in humanitarian operations; these donor agencies usually have a field presence as well.

The response agencies have developed a set of principles or norms that are widely, but not universally, accepted: aid should be allocated by emergency based on need, separate from the political interests of donor and recipient governments and those of the contestants in the conflict; aid should be distributed to the population without respect to political ideology, position in the conflict, race, ethnicity, religion, or gender; aid should be used to encourage the rapid recovery of the population from the crisis and avoid the dependency syndrome; aid should be provided in a way that allows the population to have some control over its own recovery and that helps resolve

rather than exacerbate local conflicts; and aid is provided in a way that respects the culture and values of the people receiving it.

In the 1990s, a coalition of European and American NGOs and international organizations developed a set of technical standards in the major emergency disciplines (food and nutrition, water and sanitation, shelter, and public health and emergency medical care) called the Sphere Project standards, which the signing organizations agree to follow in their programming.[11] It is not clear to what degree NGOs in practice conform to these standards, as the enforcement mechanisms, which rely on peer pressure and self-reporting, are relatively weak. But the standards have existed now for more than a decade. While efforts have been made within aid agencies to bridge the operational and programmatic gap between emergency response and long-term development programs, known as the relief-to-development continuum, these efforts have achieved limited results at best. A greater focus on finding means to achieve success in this area would speed the recovery of failed states in the reconstruction phase.

The U.S. Government's humanitarian aid functions continue to be divided organizationally between the Department of State and the U.S. Agency for International Development (USAID). Within State, the Bureau of Population, Refugees, and Migration and the Bureau of International Organizations mainly provide block grants to multilateral bodies and have no operational capacity. Within USAID, the Democracy, Conflict, and Humanitarian Assistance Bureau's various units—including the Office of Foreign Disaster Assistance, the Office of Transition Initiatives, the

Pakistani trucks await security escort to deliver supplies to U.S. and NATO forces in Afghanistan

AP Images (Shah Khalid)

Office of Conflict Mitigation and Management, Food for Peace, and the Office of Military Affairs—possess the capability to deliver money, commodities, and programming into crisis areas that the international aid system sometimes avoids. Problems are compounded in the United States when Congress and the Office of Management and Budget (OMB) earmark humanitarian response funding by office, program, and sector. A consequence of conflicting approaches and earmarks is that frequently too much money is provided for some programs and emergencies, while others are underfunded.

Obstacles to Reconstruction and Development

As difficult as emergency response may be, in the United States it has traditionally been much better and more consistently funded over sustained periods of time than recovery and reconstruction, which are usually funded in supplemental budgets proposed by OMB and approved by Congress. The regular allocation for these emergency response accounts in the State Department and USAID budgets totals nearly $3 billion. By contrast, efforts to resource the follow-on phase through the regular budget of the State Department's Office of the Coordinator for Reconstruction and Stabilization (S/CRS) have been unsuccessful thus far, as Congress has refused to fund fully either the President's budget for S/CRS or the civilian reserve corps. Continuing tensions between S/CRS and the regional bureaus of the State Department, where policy and bureaucratic authority have traditionally been concentrated in the department, have exacerbated the difficulty.

Even with more resources, the conceptual issues are staggering. Oxford professor and former World Bank director Paul Collier, whose book *The Bottom Billion* has drawn much international acclaim, has identified four so-called traps that his empirical research suggests are all too common among the poorest performing states, complicating recovery and reducing the chances for success of international state-building efforts.[12] Collier proposes some remedies to these traps, and describes the results of his research on the efficacy of various interventions. His diagnosis and prescriptions are telling.

The conflict trap. Collier reports that 73 percent of the 1 billion people who live in fragile or failed states have "recently been through a civil war or are still in one." Conflict is more likely in the absence of economic growth, and it has a significant depressive effect on growth. Civil wars typically cut growth rates on average by 2.3 percent per year. Destitute, unem-

ployed young men can be recruited into criminal gangs or rebel groups. The more instability there is in a country, the less foreign or domestic investment it will attract, and the less investment, the less growth, which leads to more instability and conflict. According to Collier, "There is basically no relationship between political repression and civil war" or, for that matter, income inequality and war, based on a number of empirical studies. What does make a large difference in the risk of war and its duration is the country's income at the onset of conflict: the poorest countries have the highest risk. Additionally, much research has shown that countries that end civil wars through political settlements have a 50 percent chance for relapse, depending on how quickly economic conditions improve. The economy matters.

The natural resource trap. Dependence on primary commodity exports such as oil, diamonds, and timber "substantially increases the risk of civil war." Democracy and natural resource dependency do not mix well: resource rents undermine checks and balances because the influx of money increases the propensity for corruption. Only when there are powerful constraints on abuse (competitive bidding of public projects, for example) do the economies of resource-rich democracies grow. This does not mean, however, that autocracies flourish and democracies do not. Neither grows absent strong oversight, which is why natural resource wealth can be a serious impediment to growth in either case.

The location trap. Geography counts a great deal, in Collier's view. Being landlocked does not condemn a country to poverty, he reports, but 38 percent of the people in the bottom billion live in countries that are. If a landlocked country has good, unfettered access to a port that gives it an opening to international markets, the negative effects of being landlocked disappear. But without that access, and especially if hostile or uncooperative neighbors contribute to the problem, the economies of landlocked countries do not grow.

The bad governance/small size trap. Poor governance has long been recognized as a poverty trap in poor countries, but it is the most destructive, in the Collier analysis, in small countries. The three factors that increase the chances for a turnaround in a failed state are: if a country has a large population; if a large portion of the population has a secondary education; and, counterintuitively, whether the country has recently emerged from a civil war (after which entrenched vested interests are possibly broken up long enough to allow a reform process to take root).

How can countries break free of these disabling traps? Collier's prescriptions lay great stress on credible long-term commitments from external actors for a peace-building presence; aid in the form of technical assistance to build skills among the depleted ranks of government professionals and service providers; reconstruction of critical infrastructure such as roads and trade corridors that help landlocked countries connect to the outside world; and the negotiation of charters between a recovering country's government and its international backers to foster greater transparency and acceptable norms of behavior in everything from business investments to budgeting, and the disposition of revenues generated by oil or mineral wealth. Collier's recommendations are both ambitious and innovative. Unfortunately, the U.S. Government is poorly postured to step up to the task at hand.

Getting Our House in Order

Reforming U.S. Governmental structures and processes is never easy, but it is essential if the United States is to improve its capacity for responding to state failure and postconflict recovery. The overarching goal must be to better integrate the political, humanitarian, economic, military, and developmental instruments of national power in a fashion that increases the effectiveness of U.S. Government responses. Several priorities should guide this effort:

■ The initial emergency phase of humanitarian response should be structured in a way that facilitates economic reforms in the country at the grassroots level. At present, the response system does not rigorously, effectively, or consistently integrate economic interventions into its programming. A more systematic set of programs to stimulate economic activity and strengthen markets is a fundamental part of recovery.

■ Food aid, under the USAID Food Aid and Food Security Policy (Title II), makes up nearly half of the U.S. Government's budget for emergency response, but is the least flexible of all the sources of funding. One action the executive branch should consider is to urge congressional support for reform of U.S. food aid policies, most notably a provision that would allow up to 25 percent of Title II aid to be bought in developing countries. If used effectively, this new purchasing authority would be a powerful tool that aid officers could use to help stimulate local agricultural markets and increase economic activity.

■ More than any other element, economic growth, particularly early in reconstruction, appears one of the most important factors in a country's successful recovery. While growth can be stimulated by the careful investment of foreign aid resources, this avenue is not sufficient in itself. The reduction of trade barriers between a recovering state and developed economies can have a profound effect on growth rates if other factors are taken into account. A functional road and highway system, connection to ocean ports, and other infrastructure are important. Infrastructure and external aid must be combined with the lowering of trade barriers and the integration of a recovering state into the international economic order in the early stages of reconstruction. Finally, donors must contribute both funds and expertise to the creation of a favorable legal and regulatory framework for business development.

■ Reform must come from within; it cannot be successfully imposed by external actors if there is no local will or leadership to carry it through. International and bilateral efforts at state-building have limits. Consequently, international agencies should try to search for, embrace, and fund the indigenous change agents or reform-minded leadership in fragile or failed states on the road to recovery, as these are the people who will increase the chances for their states to succeed. This means making an active effort to identify and support the work of reform-minded ministers and community leaders.

Beyond these specific steps is the paramount need for sustained funding. While funding over a long period of time (10 to 15 years) may not ensure success, a 2007 RAND study demonstrated that the absence of sustained funding ensures the failure of state-building.[13] The creation of a permanent, predictable reconstruction and recovery account in the USAID budget for conflict countries would be a useful first step. Absent this reform, making the emergency response accounts of the State Department and USAID more flexible, so that funds can be used for reconstruction, might be a more politically realistic option. Either way, real improvement in U.S. performance will be hard to achieve without a resource base on which to build.

Complex Contingencies: Can They Restore Governance?

In contemporary parlance, armed interventions aimed at quelling conflict in fragile or failing states are often framed in remedial terms. The core objective, we are told, is to "export stability" into war-torn regions. But what does that really mean?

Past interventions have aimed variously at giving peace a chance by interposing peacekeepers between warring factions that begrudgingly consent to their intrusion, or at delivering emergency aid to desperate populations, or at toppling capricious dictators who threaten their fellow citizens or neighboring countries. If, however, durable stability is the real focus, even if only as part of the exit strategy, then an additional ingredient needs to be factored in: reconstituted governmental structures that people accept as legitimate.

Building or rebuilding governments amid the tumult of complex civil-military operations is an enormously difficult proposition. The operations themselves may involve elements of warfare, counterinsurgency, mediation, and capacity-building, all within the same venue. Often, as seen in places such as Sarajevo or Baghdad, the initial jolt of the intervention itself may trigger an onset of problems—looting, retributive violence, a spike in street crime—that need mitigation. Moreover, even when the governance issue is squarely on the table, practitioners will bring their own biases when the question of how best to proceed is raised.

Competing Strategies and Critical Tradeoffs

In their initial phases, many complex operations are afflicted by a dearth of basic information when it comes to daily patterns of local governance. The first and most obvious question is: who is really in charge? Even in a failed state, power abhors a vacuum; is it filled by tribal councils, family oligarchs, key religious leaders, warlords who extort others for a living, rebel leaders who fight for a cause, or figureheads sitting in some faraway national capital? Second, what keeps these leaders in charge: seniority, tribal loyalty, electoral sanction, a widely feared praetorian guard, wealthy outside patrons, or locally exploitable resources? And third, and most important, how are these leaders viewed by their constituencies: as revered masters, defenders of their rights, predators, or self-aggrandizers? It can be a great benefit when a recovering or transitional country has a national unifying figure in its midst, such as a Norodom Sihanouk, Nelson Mandela, or Xanana Gusmão, but these cases are very much the exception, not the rule.

The next challenge is to fit the strategy to the socio-political context. Broadly, outside interveners may favor either stability- or reformist-oriented strategies. The former tend to be ex ante–focused—that is, recovery of prewar stability—and attach over-

riding importance to achieving short-term priorities, such as reestablishing a modicum of security, restoring traditional elites, and providing vital services in whatever ways those were delivered previously. The latter strategies, by contrast, are more ambitious and forward looking. They aim at cultivating and empowering civil society in ways that promote human rights and build the rule of law, and thereby create greater demands for accountable government; not surprisingly, democracy promotion is often a key component of this approach.

Ideally, one would want a blend of the two, but achieving this mix is difficult. Stabilizers are often criticized for acting with excessive expediency and for accepting unfair status quos or corrupt leaders in the interests of pursuing other goals (for example, counterterrorism), thereby sacrificing longer term improvements in governance. Reformers, on the

AP Images (Bernat Armangue)

Missile explodes in northern Gaza Strip during assault by Israeli warplanes, December 2008

other hand, invite criticisms for purported indifference or hostility to the issue of cultural acceptance, while pursuing civic initiatives that can polarize local communities (such as schooling for women in patriarchal societies) or create the fact of political winners and losers (for example, through electoral processes), thereby introducing a new set of instabilities even as old ones are resolved. Controversy can also attach to each strategy's sectoral choices. Stabilizers typically concentrate on building capacity in the military or police organizations, primarily to ease the operational burdens on the outside interveners. Reformers tend to focus on civil governance reforms, but they worry the governance structures may not be able to control the empowered security apparatus they may someday inherit.

Finally, there is an important "vertical" dimension to choices about governance-building strategy. Outside interveners, not surprisingly, tend to focus on the national level initially, with the aim of finding ways to consolidate legitimate state authority and extend its writ into the country's hinterlands. In such diverse capital cities as Kabul, Baghdad, Port au Prince, Monrovia, or Phnom Penh, post–ColdWar era interveners have sought to strengthen or rebuild national ministries and to regularize their budgets, thus both cutting down on corruption and boosting the skills of their staff cohorts.

Even provincial level reconstruction activity, such as that carried out in Colombia, Afghanistan, or Iraq, has a writ-extending focus. Yet all these "top-down" approaches coexist uneasily with a "bottom-up" imperative in which the search for authority starts at the municipal level and may involve empowering local groups, such as Sunni militias in Iraq's Anbar Province, in the interests of countering or marginalizing locally based insurgents who feed upon the population's resentment of a national government whose legitimacy they contest.

Can't We All Just Get Along?

However the strategy is crafted, a basic question for any complex contingency is how well the interveners themselves can work together, not only at the inception of the operation but also through unit or personnel rotations that occur over long-duration missions. Especially in the governance arena, the civil-military character of these operations requires more than just the deconfliction or loose coordination of activity, but a full integration of effort between professionals from different institutional cultures with their own operating styles. Not surprisingly, stereotypes on each side abound; diversity within each community is often missed as a result. Just as civilians can be put off by the military's penchant for rigid operational routine, military

Afghan police destroy opium poppies during eradication operations

personnel are frequently frustrated by what they see as a haphazard or less-than-focused routine among their civilian colleagues. Somewhat ironically, it is in the more dangerous operating environments where civilians and military cadre tend to get along the best; there is no choice but to do so. As the setting becomes more permissive, internal coalition management becomes a more demanding task.

As the foregoing discussion on strategy suggests, the drama of capacity-building for governance usually unfolds on two levels. At the national level, the prime venue is found in the various ministries—interior, defense, trade, education, finance, and so forth—where policies are set, civil servants are recruited, and resources are matched to service delivery requirements across critical sectors (such as security, health, and commerce). For outside interveners, the key objective is to provide technical assistance and oversight, usually attained via the technique of embedding personnel directly into various ministries. These embedded personnel may have physical challenges such as getting to and from their ministries safely, but it is the cognitive domain that is the most difficult to penetrate. Learning how a given institution really works—its budgeting, personnel, and programmatic activities—and knowing how to be most effective in assisting positive growth in capacity, while challenging fraud, waste, and abuse, are daunting tasks, even for personnel who are already schooled in the local language and culture.

Generally, the civil-military dynamics at the national capital level are most likely to play out in terms of critical choices over security sector reform and its funding. The job of aligning policing and military tasks between the key ministries can be a contentious one, especially where the government faces an active insurgency and a huge demand for the protection of critical facilities (such as the energy grid). Beyond that, funding delays and program management shortfalls for civil police training, equipping, and advisory programs have been sore points for military commanders who find themselves hard pressed to staff their own training elements—a traditional arena for special operations forces pre-9/11—without the added complication of "mission creep" pressures they may find difficult to fend off. However, these challenges may pale in comparison to civil-military challenges at the second level of governance capacity-building, the provincial level.

Provincial governance challenges are often seen as the Achilles' heel of complex operations, and

not without reason. The political terrain can be rife with local power brokers and their armed loyalists, corrupt or unpaid civil servants, and dilapidated infrastructure, all amidst public expectations for improvement that the intervention itself has inflated to unrealistic levels. To meet these expectations, military commanders will seek to mobilize quick-impact programs with contingency funding explicitly intended for this purpose. What they have lacked, and chronically so, are rapidly employable technical experts who could advise them, say, on how best to fix a local irrigation system with longer term developmental priorities in mind, or what steps need to be taken to ensure that rebuilt community schools or health clinics will actually have teachers or doctors and nurses to staff them. The dearth of expertise and agile funding to bridge quick-impact programs and long-term recovery has been a huge challenge for complex operations.

Improving Field Performance

Without question, the array of challenges facing complex contingencies is enormous. Perhaps the biggest challenge, to embellish upon Reinhold Niebuhr's prayerful plea, is to somehow muster the courage to overcome those obstacles that can be surmounted, the skill to discern those that are impervious to remedy and work around them, and the wisdom to know one from the other.

Which obstacles can be overcome? In brief, it would be those that appear most responsive to infusions of greater knowledge, resources, or the right mix of skills. Four steps are critically important.

Fill information and analytic deficits. Despite recent improvements, U.S. agencies still have a long way to go in building a better knowledge base for likely operating venues. Improved situational awareness will help shape the terms of entry (for example, for forceful or negotiated entry) and generate better estimates of how interventions will reshape conflict dynamics within the country or region in question. That in turn will help to recapture the concept of ripeness as part of the U.S. Government's calculus for targeting expeditionary operations. Moreover, once they are deployed, information-sharing between military and civilian elements remains difficult. Procedures should be developed that enable the humanitarian and developmental data collected in stabilization missions to default into "common user space" unless affirmatively sorted into a classified channel for counterterrorism or counterinsurgency.

Enhance self-knowledge. Though it is often paid lip service, good analysis of lessons learned remains hard to do. Within the defense community, despite recent improvements in the joint arena, after-action reporting remains the preserve of specific commands and the military Services, while on the civilian side, the endeavor is still in its infancy. What is needed is a well-honed interagency lessons learned process that can cull out and review incoming assessments from a growing array of sources—blogs, commissioned studies, debriefings, and so forth—using an agreed methodology. Such a process could be a valuable corrective against the risk of "over-learning"—proffering up one experience in one venue as a best practice with broad applicability—as well as a good means to sort out instrumental from environmental explanations in determining the factors behind a given success or failure.

Improve capacity-building at the retail level. Since their unveiling in the early phases of the Afghan campaign, provincial reconstruction teams have proved their worth as useful vehicles for small-scale reconstruction projects, as well as for capacity-building for village- and district-level governance and police reform. They still remain constrained, however, by a lack of diversified expertise across all the areas—rule of law, engineering, agriculture, and police, among others—to which they could potentially contribute, and the task of identifying priorities across the sectors of governance, security,

and development remains idiosyncratic. A fourfold approach is needed: clearer interagency guidance for the planning and execution of projects; new funding streams for civilian-led stabilization comparable to those already available to military commanders; less reliance on contractors for key assignments where local engagement requires a U.S. Government presence on the expeditionary team; and more extensive team-building opportunities prior to deployment, so that the break-in time for newly arriving staff is as tightly compressed as possible.

Address equipment and service shortfalls. Meeting the equipment needs for expeditionary elements in nonpermissive field settings is an ongoing challenge, as is ensuring comparable support for the medical and other needs of civilian field personnel and contractors deployed by various agencies. Complex operations tend to draw heavily on areas where the United States has traditionally found it hard to match supply to requirements, most notably with respect to armored vehicles, nonlethal weapons, rapidly deployable explosive ordnance disposal, air defense countermeasures, and improvised explosive device countermeasures that work in multinational settings.

And for those obstacles that must be worked around? Broadly, they fall into an area characterized by differing institutional equities that drive predicable patterns of behavior and create friction along the way.

Resolve tensions between diplomatic mediators and expeditionary planners. Whenever the United States takes the lead role in negotiating the terms of entry for expeditionary forces into an operational arena, such as Bosnia (the Dayton process) or Afghanistan (the Bonn process), there is going to be an inherent tension between those who negotiate a settlement and those who plan and resource the subsequent operation. This is perfectly understandable. Mediators must zealously guard their talks from malign outside influence; they therefore tend to be exclusive. Planners by contrast need every available player with legal authority and funding at the table; they perforce must be inclusive. The problems are predictable: planning is delayed; the quick onset of an agreement produces pressures for near-instantaneous decisions on forces and resource commitments; and implementers then begin to pick apart the agreement at its weakest points. The best way to contain these tensions is to insist that the negotiation team be seeded with a few capable planners who can advise on the practicality of settlement provisions before the final deal is cut.

UN (Mario Rizzolio)

United Nations offered Burundian refugees in Tanzania cash grants and food packages as incentives to return home

Balance the stabilizers and reformers. When it comes to managing tensions between short-term and long-term priorities, complex operations planners have no choice: they need both perspectives. The question is how to ensure those tensions have a creative rather than a destructive result. Faced with initial stabilization imperatives, the operation's leadership should insist on capacity-building programs that keep pace with operational needs. For the reformist camp, that means some measure of compromise—that is, accepting programs that might not make the cut if long-term development were the only goal. By the same token, the leadership's injunction to the stabilizers should be that quick-impact projects that fail to achieve their promised results—for example, a schoolhouse with no teachers—are not a good investment, and that individual projects should be accompanied wherever possible by a transition plan that keeps long-term sustainment in sight. This is especially challenging in the governance arena, where the institutions that cushion the shocks of electoral alternation need to be put in place.

Tolerate differences between partisan and impartial actors. Certain civilian actors in the expeditionary environment, especially humanitarian relief providers, regard neutrality as a key to their operational effectiveness, so there is always going to be some level of tension between them and U.S. or coalition personnel whenever the latter are seen as partisans on the political landscape. The challenge here is to keep a good two-way dialogue, so that each knows what the other is doing and, where possible, to create agreed rules of the road. It remains the case, however, that the factors encroaching on NGO impartiality are numerous and are broader than simply guilt by association with the U.S. military. If NGOs cannot secure their protection by standing out as neutrals, as UN peacekeepers try to do, they must either blend in or armor up. Both options have their drawbacks in terms of gaining access to populations in need that are scattered across a dangerous landscape.

Manage competing lines of authority. In complex operations, it is a fact of life that the mission's leading civilian official and military commander will work up through their respective chains of command. Even in cases where the former has presidentially conveyed chief-of-mission authority, the latter can and will submit a reclama on decisions deemed risky, unwise, or wrong. This pattern has always been the case in multinational operations, where

assigned national units cross-check directives coming down the operation's chain of command against guidance from their own capital. There is no way around this fact of life; what we can reasonably aim to achieve is a greater unity of effort, if not a complete unity of command, forged by a shared view of core policy objectives, the strategies to achieve them, and the efforts of compatible personalities. This places an absolute premium on the need to build leadership teams.

In the end, policymakers have good reason to be wary of launching complex contingencies into weak or failing states, given how polarizing nation-building and counterinsurgency missions have been over the past half-century. Nevertheless, prevailing strategic conditions are not likely to let U.S. policymakers off the hook of tough decisions on whether to lead or support these kinds of missions in the future, given the mix of national security, political, diplomatic, and humanitarian interests that may be at stake. For this reason, the United States must do what it reasonably can to prepare for such missions. Greater preparedness in this area need not be seen as a license for wasteful, ill-advised interventions, but rather as a safeguard against them. **gsa**

NOTES

[1] Statistics Finland, "World in Figures," June 2008, available at <www.stat.fi/tup/maanum/index_en.html>.

[2] Francis Fukuyama, *State Building: Governance and World Order in the Twenty-first Century* (London: Profile Books, 2005).

[3] Robert Cooper, *The Breaking of Nations: Order and Chaos in the Twenty-first Century* (New York: Atlantic Monthly Press, 2003).

[4] For an informative review that compares and contrasts the various measures, see Susan E. Rice and Stewart Patrick, *Index of State Weakness in the Developing World* (Washington, DC: The Brookings Institution, 2008), 5–7.

[5] Stewart Patrick, "Weak States and Global Threats: Fact or Fiction?" *The Washington Quarterly* 29, no. 2 (Spring 2006), 27–53.

[6] Moisés Naím, "The Five Wars of Globalization," *Foreign Policy*, no. 134 (January-February 2003).

[7] George J. Tenet, "Written Statement for the Record," Joint Inquiry Committee, Senate Select Committee on Intelligence, October 17, 2002.

[8] Andrew Price-Smith, *The Health of Nations* (Cambridge: MIT Press, 2002).

[9] See the following publications by David P. Fidler: "Developments involving SARS, International Law, and Infectious Disease Control at the Sixth Meeting of the World Health Assembly," *The American Society of*

International Law Insights (June 2003), available at <www.asil.org/insigh108.cfm>; "Influenza Virus Samples, International Law, and Global Health Diplomacy," *Emerging Infectious Diseases* 14, no. 1 (January 2008), 88–94; and "Globalization, International law, and Emerging Infectious Diseases," *Emerging Infectious Diseases* 2, no. 2 (April-June 1996), available at <www.cdc.gov/ncidod/eid/vol2no2/fidler.htm>.

[10] United Nations General Assembly, "2005 World Summit Outcome," October 2005, available at <http://daccessdds.un.org/doc/UNDOC/GEN/N05/487/60/PDF/N0548760.pdf?OpenElement>.

[11] For background on Sphere standards and its collaborating organizations, see <www.sphereproject.org/>.

[12] Paul Collier, *The Bottom Billion: Why the Poorest Nations Are Failing and What Can Be Done about It* (Oxford: Oxford University Press, 2007).

[13] James Dobbins et al., *The Beginner's Guide to Nation-Building* (Santa Monica, CA: RAND, 2007), xxi.

Contributors

Dr. James A. Schear (Chapter Editor) is Deputy Assistant Secretary of Defense for Partnership Strategy and Stability Operations. Previously, he served as Director of Research in the Institute for National Strategic Studies (INSS) at National Defense University (NDU). Dr. Schear also served as an advisor to the United Nations on field missions in Cambodia and the Former Yugoslavia and held research appointments at Harvard University, Carnegie Endowment, Henry L. Stimson Center, Aspen Institute, and International Institute for Strategic Studies.

Dr. Frederick M. Burkle, Jr., is a Senior Public Policy Scholar at the Woodrow Wilson International Center for Scholars and a Senior Fellow in the Harvard Humanitarian Initiative at Harvard University. Dr. Burkle also holds academic appointments at Johns Hopkins University and the Uniformed Services University of the Health Sciences. He has served as a Deputy Assistant Administrator for the U.S. Agency for International Development (USAID) and has worked in numerous complex emergencies, including in northern Iraq, Somalia, Liberia, and the Former Yugoslavia.

Dr. Michael T. Klare is the Five College Professor of Peace and World Security Studies, a joint appointment at Amherst, Hampshire, Mount Holyoke, and Smith Colleges, and the University of Massachusetts at Amherst. He is the author of *Resource Wars* (Owl Books, 2001), *Blood and Oil* (Metropolitan Books, 2004), and *Rising Powers, Shrinking Planet: The New Geopolitics of Energy* (Henry Holt and Company, 2008).

Joseph McMillan is Principal Deputy Assistant Secretary of Defense for International Security Affairs. Previously, he served as Senior Research Fellow in INSS at NDU. A specialist on regional defense and security issues in the Middle East, South Asia, as well as transnational terrorism, Mr. McMillan has more than two decades of experience as a civilian official in the Department of Defense, and he also has served as academic chairman of the Near East South Asia Center for Strategic Studies.

Andrew S. Natsios is Distinguished Professor in the Practice of Diplomacy in the Walsh School of Foreign Service at Georgetown University. From May 2001 to January 2006, he served as Administrator of USAID. During this period, he managed USAID reconstruction programs in Afghanistan, Iraq, and Sudan, which totaled more than $14 billion over 4 years. President George W. Bush appointed him Special Coordinator for International Disaster Assistance and Special Humanitarian Coordinator for Sudan.

Chapter 6

Transnational Movements and Terrorism

National and international security now involves nonstate actors to an extent unprecedented in modern history. Transnational movements and substate groups have tremendous power both to contribute to the greater good and to bring about violence, death, and repression. The most prominent such threat arises from transnational Salafi jihadism, of which al Qaeda is the standard bearer. Al Qaeda and the larger movement that presently command America's attention remain serious threats for two primary reasons. First, this movement threatens the use of weapons of mass destruction (WMD), though its ability to do so in the near term is questionable. Second, the movement's ability to create humanitarian dystopias, as in Afghanistan and Iraq's Anbar Province, among other places, remains significant and should not be underestimated.

Nevertheless, the movement has substantial weaknesses and arguably is self-limiting.[1] It finds itself surrounded on all sides by opponents that include not only the Western democracies but also the media, the governments in majority Muslim countries, mainstream Muslims, and even other Islamists. Moreover, it is becoming clear that the Muslim community's familiarity with al Qaeda and its ilk is breeding contempt, not converts.

Recent poll results underscore some of these points. Gallup polls taken across the Muslim world make clear that many Muslims, justifiably or not, are extremely skeptical about U.S. actions and policies, but that these feelings do not translate into support for al Qaeda and its associates. In fact, only 7 percent of Muslims, some 91 million people, "fully support" the attacks of September 11, 2001, with another 7 percent leaning toward supporting it.

Clearly, then, the United States has some fence-mending to do among Muslims. The terrorism problem, however, is much smaller in extent than even

AP Images (Hatem Moussa)

Girl in Islamic Jihad headcovering rallies with Palestinian Islamic Jihad militants in Gaza City

Gallup's numbers indicate. Al Qaeda and likeminded groups boast as members only a fraction of 1 percent of the 91 million Muslims who may have celebrated September 11. Arguably, this suggests that increasing America's popularity among Muslims, while desirable in itself, is an inefficient way to shrink the number of Salafi jihadists. Indeed, some of America's staunchest allies against al Qaeda—such as Hamas, the Muslim Brotherhood, the Iranian regime, many radical preachers, even the much maligned Arab media—may be some of our staunchest foes on other issues. In short, an approach to the contest in which the United States remains active but does not insist on putting its actions (especially the military ones) at center stage may be most effective.

A look at the psychology of terrorists can also pay dividends. It turns out that terrorists of any stripe are mostly notable for their similarity to the rest of us (a point that the Gallup results make in a different way). What makes them different is not their individual psychology, but their group, organizational, and social psychologies. A comprehensive understanding of the social, historical, and political contexts in which terrorist groups arise suggests a typology of terrorism. Among the substate terrorists, there are five basic types: social revolutionary (left-wing), right-wing fascist, nationalist-separatist, religious extremist, and single-issue terrorists. The religious extremists divide into violent religious fundamentalists (such as al Qaeda) and those fighting for "new religions." Each of these types has a different group psychology, and thus different policy prescriptions are appropriate for each.

The next issue to consider is the nightmare scenario that terrorists will acquire and use WMD. The U.S. Government is not well prepared—intellectually, legally, organizationally, or in terms of capability—to respond to catastrophically disruptive incidents. Fortunately, few terrorist groups in recent decades have actually tried to use WMD, not least because there are more readily available conventional means of gaining attention. But al Qaeda does not fit that profile and has sought to acquire unconventional weapons.

Looking to the future, technology, notably biological technology, is in the process of "superempowering" not just small groups such as terrorist organizations, gangs, organized criminal networks, anarchists, and ultra-extreme environmentalists, but even Unabomber-style individuals. The successful response to this emerging threat will probably have to aspire to be an "all-of-society" response.

Assessing the Salafi Jihadist Movement

A particularly idiosyncratic understanding of the Sunni Islamic faith called "Salafi jihadism" by its practitioners underpins al Qaeda and inspires more than 100 kindred terrorist groups around the world, not to mention numerous isolated groups or even individuals.[2] Salafi jihadism is a minority, reactionary viewpoint within a wider acrimonious debate among Muslims about how to reconcile the progress and frustration unleashed across the Islamic world by modernization and globalization.[3] Though many Muslims (and, for that matter, non-Muslims) are concerned about the implications of globalization, only a tiny minority of Sunnis adhere to the stern tenets of this harsh and xenophobic worldview that calls for the formation of a caliphate—an Islamic superstate stretching from Spain to Indonesia—and the conversion of all other Muslims from their purportedly innovative, unfounded, and corrupt beliefs. (It is important to note that the destruction of the United States is not among the goals per se of Salafi jihadists, though many, perhaps most of them, would be happy to see it happen. Instead, they desire to see the United States quit the Muslim world as part of a process to topple corrupt regimes and hasten the beginning of the caliphate.)

Salafis seek a return to what they believe was the simple and pure truth of Islam as it was first practiced, hence, the Arabic word Salafi, which means "return to the forefathers." (Whether they are correct in their understanding of Islam's original nature is another question.) Even within the Salafi community, however, there are important divisions.[4] A large component of the community eschews engagement in politics, let alone violence, because they believe that such activities pit people against each other when they should, instead, be coming together in "true" (that is, Salafi) Islam. A second, probably larger component, which includes the Muslim Brotherhood, is willing to engage in politics—for instance, by standing for election—and to use violence when deemed necessary. The smallest component of the Salafi community is the actual Salafi jihadists themselves, who believe that violent jihad is presently an obligation incumbent on every true Muslim, and that democracy is un-Islamic. The Salafi jihadist theology was codified by Egyptian Sayyid Qutb (1906–1966) in the 1960s, proliferated via radical Egyptian and Saudi scholars during the 1960s and 1970s, oxygenated during the jihad against the Soviet Union in Afghanistan in the 1980s, and updated by al Qaeda's leadership in the 1990s. Today, al Qaeda remains its vanguard.

Salafi jihadism shares the major characteristics of the other great radical ideologies of the post–Industrial Revolution era:

- a social critique that resonates widely
- a call to violence as the only way to alter a corrupt social order
- a utopian vision of the future that will follow a violent uprising.

Like Karl Marx's critique of unconstrained capitalism, much of Salafi jihadism's social critique is powerful and resilient. It taps into widely accepted historic Arab and Sunni mythology about the manner in which Christian crusaders, Mongol hordes, and assorted Western colonizers have successively subjugated and oppressed Islam and Muslims for centuries. It further criticizes Muslims for being seduced by alien values such as nationalism, secularism, and democracy. It projects fault onto external forces: the Other. It dovetails with the blame that Arab and Islamic states have projected on the West for generations, but it extends fault to insufficiently pious Muslim government leaders, calling for their violent overthrow. Though parts of this critique are less well supported within the Sunni world, such as the opposition to nationalism and democracy, as a general proposition it has a strength, and a politico-cultural authenticity, that make it stubbornly resistant to counter-messaging from the outside.

Salafi jihadism's weakness is not in its social critique, but in its prescriptions. First, in its call for violent jihad, it is on shaky ground with the general Muslim population. Polling done by Gallup indicates that perhaps some 91 million Muslims worldwide see the September 11 attacks as fully justified. Yet only a minuscule fraction of even these most anti-American Muslims have been willing to join the Salafi jihadist movement, let alone al Qaeda itself. The fact is that most Muslims do not support violent jihad except (if at all) under very circumscribed conditions. They certainly do not welcome an "all jihad, all the time" approach. In fact, the polling compellingly points out that most Muslims who do support violence do so on political grounds, not, ultimately, on the religious grounds that are central to al Qaeda ideology. Indeed, the experience in such locations as Riyadh, Amman, and Iraq's Anbar Province, among many others, has shown that when the violence is no longer performed far away and out of sight against the "Zionist-Crusader" Other, but comes home to Islamic communities, it loses its appeal.[5]

Second, Salafi jihadism features the vision of a utopian future based upon historical fiction. This vision parallels an equally seductive ahistorical myth of socially ideal primitive communism espoused by Marx and Friedrich Engels. Much like its ideological forerunner, Salafi jihadism's vision of the future anchors on the myth of a near-perfect Sunni caliphate, under a single religious hub and sharia law, that stretched from modern-day Morocco to India during the 7th and 8th centuries. It aspires to "reestablish" this caliphate from Spain to Indonesia, arguing this will occur rapidly after the violent overthrow of corrupt Muslim autocracies and the elimination of all decadent Western influences throughout the region. Of course, as with human societies throughout history, there was less utopian bliss in the historic caliphate than Salafi jihadists advertise. The Taliban's real-life emirate established in Afghanistan from 1996–2001 displayed the many horrors for average Muslims that will come from the oppressive, misogynistic, and xenophobic caliphate that the Salafi jihadists desire.

Al Qaeda is the self-designated vanguard (another echo of Marxism) of Salafi jihadism. Its senior leadership cadre has worked since 1996 to communicate its social critique and vision of the future, while simultaneously recruiting, training, organizing, and inspiring the new generation of Sunni terrorists necessary to bring about that future. Nevertheless, Salafi jihadism existed for some two decades before al Qaeda established itself in the late 1980s, and there is every reason to believe that the far-flung, organizationally diffuse movement will outlast al Qaeda. Thus, the health of al Qaeda may be an important issue, but it is not necessarily the decisive issue. Rather, the United States and its allies must gauge the vigor of the broader movement.

Present Trends

American policymakers have recently been confronted with dramatically differing analyses of the health of and risk posed by al Qaeda and the rest of the Salafi jihadist community. One line of analysis argues that al Qaeda, operating from its safe haven along the Afghan-Pakistan border, remains the source of the gravest threat for catastrophic terror.[6] The contending perspective is that al Qaeda's operational decline renders it less salient to international security concerns than the growing threat from diffuse, low-level groups emerging out of local social networks and acting out of a shared belief in the Salafi jihadist mass media message.[7] What are global policymakers to think? Can both of these perspectives be correct? If not, which threat is more severe?

Ultimately, the question of whether al Qaeda itself or its relatively diffuse constellation of loosely affiliated co-religionists poses the greater threat may be moot. Both are substantial threats. Each requires a tailored response from its opponents. On the one hand, the al Qaeda–led globalized variant is more intellectually adaptable within its ideological commitment to nonstop jihad, but it faces major structural challenges. It has the greater ability to mount narrow but devastating attacks, as its track record makes clear. On the other hand, the surrounding movement with its violence-prone group of men poses a more widespread but less physically potent threat. There is growing evidence that the multifaceted approach to countering Sunni terrorism that has evolved in the past few years, with a concentration on denying al Qaeda its desired outcomes, is showing signs of success. While American strategy for countering terrorism can, of course, be improved, policymakers should use caution to avoid discarding methods that are known to work, in their zeal to get rid of what has not.

Responding to the Threat

In organizational and strategic terms, the Salafi jihadists have faced substantial setbacks over the last several years. The United States and its partners have continued regularly to kill or capture key leaders, such as a succession of operational chiefs of al Qaeda central, and a string of successive leaders of "al Qaeda in the Arabian Peninsula." There have been similar successes against Jamaah Islamiyah in Southeast Asia, and against other groups large and small across the globe. Important leaders of al Qaeda in Iraq, including Abu Musab al-Zarqawi, have been killed or captured. Moreover, the overall Salafi jihadist position in Iraq is, as of this writing, grim, under relentless American military pressure, and facing increasingly capable Iraqi services and the Sunni tribal "Awakening." In sum, because of the combined pressures of various national security services and the military, intelligence, and law enforcement services of the United States, al Qaeda and its allies find it hard to operate in most places in the globe.

At the same time, the movement has, arguably, made a grave strategic blunder. By allowing Zarqawi to reorient attention of the Salafi jihadists in Iraq and, indeed, in the entire Middle East, toward attacking the Shia, it took on an additional adversary, both ideological and physical, while it was still grappling with the formidable alliance of the "Jews, Crusaders, and [Sunni] apostates." This was not part of Osama bin Laden's or Ayman al-Zawahiri's master plan, for they always felt that the Shia would be quickly eliminated late in the process of forming a caliphate, when

Gunman takes position in Tripoli, birthplace of Lebanon's Salafi movement in the 1950s

the numbers of Sunni "true believers" would form an overwhelming weight to wield against Shia heretics.[8] As a result of these various developments, almost nowhere in the world is there a truly permissive environment for the operation of Salafi jihadists.

Nevertheless, al Qaeda and the broader movement have been adapting in a number of ways. First, al Qaeda has worked hard to reestablish a physical safe haven in Pakistan, and especially within the Federally Administered Tribal Areas (FATA). Al Qaeda requires a place of physical freedom to practice the management of a proto-caliphate, to congregate in an unfettered manner, and to plan and launch spectacular acts of terrorism against its opponents. Al Qaeda strategists are incessantly writing to each other about the good old days in Afghanistan (between the expulsion of the Soviet Union in 1989 and the post-9/11 invasion), and the need to generate a similar safe haven soon. They lament the loss of the once-promising safe haven in Iraq, particularly in Anbar Province, largely blaming Zarqawi's intemperance for this. Today, al Qaeda's strategists are trying to establish a permanent safe haven in Pakistan's border areas adjacent Afghanistan. Intense efforts since late 2005 have produced results. Al Qaeda gained a foothold in this area, which by 2009 had become a central battle ground. In alliance with young and highly militant Pakistani-Pashtun allies, al Qaeda has overthrown most of the tribal elder system in western Pakistan and embarrassed the Pakistani military. Many of the major attacks planned and executed against Western targets since 2002—including the London 7/7 bombings, the United Kingdom–U.S. airliner plot of 2006, and the Frankfurt airport plot of 2007—have common origins in western Pakistan and featured direct contact between key attackers and al Qaeda leaders.

Second, al Qaeda has expanded its formal franchisee arrangements with heretofore loosely affiliated Salafi jihadist groups. Al Qaeda's leadership has tried to formalize relationships and stamp the al Qaeda brand name on all forms of regional Salafi jihadist and insurgent activity. At the same time, these groups seek their share of the prestige, and often funding, that goes with the "al Qaeda" name and reach out to it. For instance, in 2004, Zarqawi's Iraqi group was assimilated into the movement as "al Qaeda of the Two Rivers," a reference not only to Iraq, but also to the wider territory extending toward southwestern Iran and Kuwait. Similarly, in early 2007, distinct references to "al Qaeda of Khoristan"

▼ *Continued on p. 127*

The View from the Muslim World

While military and economic strategies are of critical importance in capturing, killing, or containing terrorists, equally important is public diplomacy, the battle to win the hearts and minds of people who might be sources of recruitment or support for jihad. Although the United States and its allies have made progress in learning how both to understand and fight against global terrorism, the U.S. Achilles' heel has been a continued failure of public diplomacy, which lags far behind the military response. Too often, such diplomacy has simply taken the form of public relations, demonstrating how likeable the U.S. Government really is. Yet the most important factor, which is how the foreign policy of the United States and the rest of the developed world is perceived abroad, has been overlooked or downplayed.

Anti-Americanism is not based on who "we" are, but on what people believe "we" do—in other words, the perceived contrast between the way we walk and the way we talk. But neither of the two aspects of public diplomacy, public relations or public perceptions, can succeed without an understanding of what Muslims truly think. Getting an accurate fix on the Muslim world continues to be critical to limiting the feelings of alienation, powerlessness, and humiliation that foster radicalization and recruitment among Muslim populations.

The U.S. Government has been engaged in an ideological battle, a struggle it frames in terms of ideas, beliefs, and perceptions that tend to obscure its vision of the larger situation. Policymakers have had to rely on wildly differing "experts" who, however well credentialed, often lacked the global data to back up their reading of the Muslim world. Rather than seeing the Muslim world through the lens of a Western/American mindset, Washington needs new insights that come directly from what large numbers of Muslims across the Muslim world really think, not from outsiders or, especially, from the extremist terrorists who seized center stage and overshadowed the less demonstrative mainstream majority. Direct access to Muslim public opinion helps policymakers avoid the grand theories, individual political agendas, and ideologies that can blur important insights.

To respond effectively to global terrorism, U.S. foreign policymakers require a better understanding of how Muslim majorities see the world and, in particular, how they regard the United States. Major polling by a number of organizations, including Pew, Zogby, and Gallup, provide much needed insight into the minds and hearts of Muslims globally.

The Gallup World Poll, which has surveyed a Muslim population sampling representing more than 90 percent of the world's 1.3 billion Muslims, is the largest, most comprehensive study of contemporary Muslims ever done.[1] As such, it now enables us to answer such basic questions as: What do Muslims across the world have to say about their dreams, hopes, and fears? How many Muslims hold extremist views? What are their priorities? What do Muslims admire and what do they resent about the United States and the West?

Between 2001 and 2007, Gallup conducted more than 50,000 hour-long, face-to-face interviews with residents of more than 40 nations that are predominantly Muslim, and among significant Muslim populations in the West. Respondents represent the young and old, female and male, educated and illiterate, wealthy and poor, living in urban, suburban, and rural settings. With the random sampling method that Gallup used, results are statistically valid within a 3-point margin of error.

Extremism and Muslim Populations

Anger at the United States, a sense of not being accorded respect, and widespread religiosity seem an explosive combination. Muslims nevertheless are, in fact, at least as likely as the American public to reject attacks on civilians. While 6 percent of Americans think attacks in which civilians are targets are "completely justified," in Saudi Arabia, it is 4 percent; in both Lebanon and Iran, this figure is 2 percent. In Europe, Muslims in Paris and London were no more likely than their counterparts in the general public to believe attacks on civilians are ever justified, and were at least as likely to reject violence, even for a "noble cause."

Despite widespread disapproval of the U.S. leadership, only a minority sympathize with the attacks of September 11, 2001. Some 55 percent said it was completely unjustified (a 1 on a 1-to-5 scale from completely unjustified to completely justified); 12 percent gave this item a 2; 11 percent gave it a 3; 7 percent gave it a 4.[2]

To understand what drove public support for terrorism, however, Gallup looked at the outliers—the 7 percent of the population who saw the 9/11 attacks as completely justifiable (5 on the scale), and have an unfavorable view of the United States—and compared them to the rest. Where was terrorism finding a sympathetic ear?

Perhaps the most significant finding was the *lack* of a finding; there was no correlation between levels of religiosity and extremism among respondents. While 94 percent of the high-conflict group said religion is an important part of their daily lives, a statistically identical 90 percent of the nonviolent mainstream said the same thing. Similarly, no significant difference exists between the two groups in mosque attendance.

Gallup probed respondents further and asked both those who condoned and those who condemned

extremist acts why they answered as they did. The responses fly in the face of conventional wisdom, specifically the view held by many people that Islam, more than other faiths, encourages violence. Rather, it is politics, not piety, that drives 7 percent of Muslims to condone fully the attacks of September 11. Looking across majority-Muslim countries, Gallup found no statistical difference in self-reported religiosity between those who sympathized with the attackers and those who did not. Moreover, when respondents in selected countries were asked in an open-ended question to explain their views of 9/11, those who condemned it cited religious as well as humanitarian reasons. For example, 20 percent of Kuwaitis who called the attacks "completely unjustified" explained this position by saying that terrorism was against the teachings of Islam. In Indonesia, one woman said, "Killing one life is as sinful as killing the whole world," paraphrasing verse 5:32 in the Koran. In contrast, not a single respondent who condoned the attacks of 9/11 cited the Koran for justification. Instead, this group's responses were markedly secular and worldly—expressed in terms of revenge and revolution, not religion. For example, one respondent said, "The U.S. Government is too controlling toward other countries, seems like colonizing."

Limiting the growth of terrorism requires the United States not only to focus on and try to understand the politically radicalized few, but also to appreciate the mainstream majority. While not extremists today, a significant portion of the world's Muslim population, if further alienated and marginalized, represent the seed bed from which tomorrow's terrorists will grow. An analysis of the politically radicalized, the 7 percent (some 91 million) of Muslim respondents who believe that 9/11 was completely justified and who are convinced that the United States wishes to dominate the Middle East, can yield important insights.

Educated, Affluent, Optimistic Radicals

The politically radicalized are, on average, more educated and affluent than the mainstream majority, and they are also more internationally sophisticated. These individuals are surprisingly optimistic about their personal futures, but, as might be expected, when it comes to their political futures, they are more pessimistic.

The politically radicalized are not antidemocratic. A significantly higher percentage (50 percent of radicals versus 35 percent of the mainstream) say that moving toward democracy will foster progress in the Muslim world. In addition, they are even more likely than mainstream respondents (58 percent versus 44 percent) to believe that Arab/Muslim nations are eager for better relations with the West. They are more cynical, however, about whether improved relations will ever actually occur. While half (52 percent) of the mainstream disagree when asked whether the United States is serious about promoting democracy, that percentage is 72 percent among the radicalized.

The politically radicalized faction conveys a strong sense of being "dominated" or even "occupied" by the West. Responding to an open-ended question, they cite "occupation/U.S. domination" as their greatest fear. In contrast, while concerned about American influence, the mainstream respondents' top concern centers on economic problems.

"Why Do They Hate Us?"

A common answer to the question, "Why do they hate America?" has been, "They hate Americans for who they are and what they represent." While this response may accurately describe the terrorists, it does not adequately account for the widespread anti-Americanism among many in the Muslim world, and in other countries and regions of the world, who admire the principles and values the United States stands for but reject its conduct of foreign policy. Despite widespread anti-American and anti-British sentiment, Muslims around the world said that they do in fact admire much of what the West holds dear.

When Gallup asked all respondents in an open-ended question to describe what they admired most about the West, the most frequent response was technology, expertise, and knowledge; the second most frequent was the West's value system, hard work, and responsibility; and the third was its fair political systems and regard for human rights. When respondents were asked to describe their dreams for the future, they did not describe waging jihad, but instead cited the need for a better job, improved economic well-being and prosperity, and the possibility of a better future for their children. This was the most frequent response in Egypt, Jordan, Saudi Arabia, Iran, and Indonesia, among others.

A Question of Politics, Not Piety

Muslims do not see the West as monolithic; their perceptions of different nations fall along policy lines, not cultural or religious lines. For example, while unfavorable views of the United States (74 percent) and

the United Kingdom (69 percent) dominate, respondents view France and Germany as positively as they do other Muslim-majority countries. For example, only 21 percent of respondents have unfavorable views of France, while 30 percent view Pakistan unfavorably. This issue becomes especially clear when comparing the United States to its neighbor to the north: Canada. While 67 percent of Kuwaitis have unfavorable views of the United States, the number for Canada is 3 percent. Similarly, where 64 percent of Malaysians say the United States is "aggressive," only 1 in 10 associates this quality with France and Germany.

Although a significant number of Muslims admire and associate liberty with the West in general and the United States in particular, most do not believe Americans are serious about supporting democracy in the Muslim world, and seem to believe that U.S. policies deny Muslims the same rights of self-determination that they themselves enjoy. Doubting American intentions with regard to democracy is closely tied with the perception that America is an imperial power that controls the Middle Eastern region. More than 65 percent of Egyptians, Jordanians, and Iranians and 55 percent of Pakistanis believe that the United States will not allow people in their region to fashion their own political future the way they see fit, without direct U.S. influence. A perceived "democratic exceptionalism" when it comes to the Muslim world is also reflected in significant percentages who associate the adjective "hypocritical" with the United States.

The perceived deep gap between America's espoused values of self-determination, democracy promotion, and human rights on one hand, and its apparent "double standard" in failing to put these values first in the Muslim world on the other, lead many to believe that America and its allies must be hostile toward Islam and regard Muslims as inferior. Because the perception of how Muslims are treated is so antithetical to admired Western values, Muslims reason, these same Western powers must simply be singling Muslims out for disapproval. When Gallup asked Muslims around the world what the West can do to improve relations with the Muslim world, the most frequent responses were that the West should demonstrate more respect for Islam and regard Muslims as equals, not inferiors.

Religion and Terrorism: Challenging Assumptions

Understanding the relationship of religion to terrorism, both domestically and globally, remains critical in the 21st century. Religion remains an important factor in

mainstream Muslim politics, a source of national identity, and a factor in democratization movements and
electoral politics from Egypt and Morocco to Turkey,
Iraq, Bahrain, Kuwait, Afghanistan, Pakistan, Malaysia,
and Indonesia. At the same time, it is also a source
of identity and legitimacy for extremists and terrorist
organizations, domestic and global, which operate
from Spain to the southern Philippines.

The primary causes of global terrorism are often ob-
scured by the religious language and symbolism used
by extremists. In most cases, political and economic
grievances are primary causes or catalysts, and religion
becomes a way to legitimate the cause and to mobilize
popular support. Religiously legitimated violence and
terror add divine or ultimate authority, moral justification, religious obligation, and certitude of heavenly
reward that enhance commitment and sacrifice—a
willingness to fight and die in a sacred struggle. Yasser
Arafat, leader of a secular nationalist movement (the
Palestinian Liberation Organization [PLO] and then the
Palestinian National Authority), frequently used the
words *jihad* and *shahid* (martyrdom) to enhance his
influence. Similarly, the Palestinian militia (not just
the Islamist Hamas) appropriated religious symbolism, called itself the al Aqsa Brigade (a reference to
the mosque in East Jerusalem opposite the Dome of
the Rock), and used religious terms such as *jihad* and
martyrdom for recruitment, legitimacy, and support.

While a seemingly logical profile of terrorists assumes that they are psychological or social misfits,
poor, unemployed, and uneducated, this characterization, as in the above-mentioned profile of
the "politically radicalized" identified in the Gallup
World Poll, is often inaccurate. Like members, and
particularly leaders, of many social movements in the
Muslim world and the West, members of terrorist organizations are not solely the "have nots," but rather
bright, educated, motivated individuals responding to their perception of grave political or social
injustice. With some exceptions, the new breed of
militants and terrorists, from the 9/11 attackers to
the London bombers, are not the urban poor. Ayman al-Zawahiri, a pediatric surgeon, and other al
Qaeda leaders, as well as those responsible for the
World Trade Center and Pentagon attacks, such as
Mohammad Atta, were well-educated, middle-class
professionals. Many British Muslim militants, such
as Omar Sheikh, the convicted murderer of journalist
Daniel Pearl, have been products of the British public
school system.

Distinguishing between mainstream opposition and
extremists or terrorists can sometimes be difficult.
Drawing the line between national liberation movements and terrorist organizations often depends upon
one's political vantage point. Israel founders Menach-
em Begin and Yitzhak Shamir, the radical Zionist Irgun
and Stern Gangs, Nelson Mandela and the African
National Congress, and Yasser Arafat and the PLO,
to name only a few, were regarded by their opposition as terrorist leaders. Yesterday's terrorists may be
just that—terrorists; or they may become tomorrow's
statesmen. Even grayer and more difficult for some to
characterize are groups such as Lebanon's Hizballah,
which is a militia, a de facto local governing body, and
a major political party with seats in Lebanon's parliament, and Hamas, which has won electoral victories
not only in municipal but also in national elections in
Palestine.

Implications

Globally, majorities of Muslims clearly do not see
conflict with the West as primarily a religious war or
a "clash of civilizations." Instead, they distinguish
between specific Western powers in terms of policy,
and not principle. The clash-of-civilizations theory
provides no helpful answers and gains no support in
Muslim responses to the Gallup World Poll. It may be
helpful for policymakers to disaggregate "the West"
and the "Muslim World" into distinct countries, whose
conflicts and confrontations originate from the specific
policies of specific nations and their leaders, especially
the United States.[3]

When Muslims are asked what is the most important thing the United States could do to improve the
quality of life of people like them, the most common
responses after "reduce unemployment and improve
the economic infrastructure" are "stop interfering in
the internal affairs of Arab states," "stop imposing your
beliefs and policies," "respect our political rights and
stop controlling us," and "give us our own freedom."
Failure to respond effectively to the hopes and fears of
the mainstream, and especially those of the politically
radicalized, will make a bad situation worse.

The voices of majorities of populations should not
be ignored or overlooked because of the threat from
an extremist minority, or because Western countries
have established ties to authoritarian rulers in, for
example, Tunisia, Algeria, Egypt, Kazakhstan, or Saudi
Arabia. Acceding to and even supporting the growing
authoritarianism of some regimes because they are

allies in the so-called war on terror or because they warn that Islamists could come to power in elections would be seriously short-sighted. If it is to support self-determination in the Muslim world, the United States must make a crucial distinction, and separate violent extremists from the many mainstream Islamic activists and parties who have proven track records of participation in electoral politics and government. Perpetuating the culture and values of authoritarianism and repression will only contribute to the long-term instability and anti-Americanism that empower the terrorists.

The United States can counter its concerns about mainstream Islamists coming to power by supporting a strong civil society and rule of law. Multiple political parties and professional associations, an independent judiciary, and a free press and media offer Muslim populations broader political choices. If Islamists are the "only game in town," then their electoral support will come not only from their members, but also from those who want to cast the only vote they can against incumbent governments and for the critical changes needed to improve their future.

A wealth of data is available, from the polls cited here as well as from other sources, and it offers new insights that may point the way toward ending the ongoing conflict between the West and the Muslim world. It is about policy, not a clash of principles. The U.S. Government needs a greater understanding of the conflict's root causes; listening to the voices of a billion Muslims is a sound way to begin.

NOTES

[1] Gallup's self-funded Poll of the Muslim World is conducted in 40 predominantly Muslim nations and among significant Muslim populations in the West. It is the first data set of unified and scientifically representative views from Muslims globally. The Poll of the Muslim World is part of Gallup's larger World Poll, a self-funded effort aimed at consistently measuring the well-being of 6 billion world citizens (a sample representing 95 percent of the Earth's population) on a wide range of topics for the next 100 years.

[2] Based on a population-weighted average across Egypt, Indonesia, Jordan, Saudi Arabia, Turkey, Lebanon, Pakistan, Morocco, Iran, and Bangladesh, representing 800 million Muslims.

[3] David Kilcullen, "Countering Global Insurgency," *The Journal of Strategic Studies* 28, no. 4 (August 2005), 597–617.

▲ *Continued from p. 123*

(al Qaeda in Afghanistan, eastern Iran, and western Pakistan), and the announcement of its leader, Mustafa Abu al-Yazid, began to appear on the al Jazeera Web site, with reference to that jihadist group's evolving status as the Arab partner to the Taliban. Then, in September 2007, the longstanding Salafist Group for Call and Combat (GSPC) in Algeria announced formal affiliation with al Qaeda and changed its

American-born al Qaeda operative justifies future terrorist attacks against United States

name to the "al Qaeda Organization in the Islamic Maghreb (AQIM)." These moves extend al Qaeda's reach and reinforce the Salafi jihadist's narrative that a fundamentalist Sunni caliphate is borderless and destined to encompass the entire Islamic world (see map on p. 139). They also enhance previously informal communications and terror management conduits and potentially extend al Qaeda access to underdeveloped terror recruiting networks such as those affiliated with Algerian GSPC across France and in other parts of Western Europe.

By way of contrast, Salafi jihadists have only a limited ability to forge alliances with Muslims who are not Salafi jihadists, even those with whom they have very substantial theological similarities. For instance, Hamas and the Muslim Brotherhood on the one hand, and al Qaeda on the other, are constantly at daggers drawn, in particular over issues of the propriety of electoral politics and the relative value of violent and nonviolent aspects of the jihad.

If al Qaeda is unwilling to make common cause with non-Salafi jihadist groups, what of their blandishments toward individual Muslims? What is the health of the broader movement? Perhaps at the homegrown, grassroots level the movement has better prospects.

Of the three major features of the ideology's message, one remains resilient while the other two have demonstrated substantial weakness. The biggest asset the Salafi jihadist movement has is anti-American sentiment in the Muslim world. Much less helpful is the anti-Israel sentiment there because more and more voices are asking why Hamas and Hizballah have actively, and apparently successfully, fought Israel, while al Qaeda and other Salafi jihadist organizations have not even tried, despite their rhetoric and anti-Semitic stance. In other words, the Salafi jihadists are not viewed as being out in front on this issue. The preeminent Salafi jihadist Palestinian group, Fatah al-Islam, is a minor player in the region by comparison with Hamas, Hizballah, and even the Lebanese government.[9]

The credo of necessary violence is the Achilles' heel of the ideology, and its overexposure across the Islamic world in recent years has weakened the Salafi jihadist appeal. Since at least 2003, when a wave

of terrorism in Riyadh and Jeddah, Saudi Arabia, shocked many Muslim sensibilities about the killing of fellow Muslims, al Qaeda has struggled to retain a grip on message management regarding the use of violence and the desirability of a future Islamic caliphate. Al Qaeda has been forced to rebuke its Saudi Arabian arm and one of its few precious celebrities, the late Zarqawi, for excessive violence that was every bit as appalling to Muslims as to non-Muslims.

Since the summer of 2005, polling across the Muslim world has shown a dramatic drop in public support and admiration for Osama bin Laden and al Qaeda. Revulsion at violence has been the primary, though not the only, issue here.[10] To the extent that mainstream Muslim support for bin Laden as the figurehead of al Qaeda and the Salafi jihadist ideology remains, Muslims overwhelmingly link this support to his rhetorical stand on behalf of Islamic causes and his confrontation of the United States, while expressing little support for his violent methods of operation or his vision of a utopian Islamic state.[11]

The Salafi jihadists will have a hard time reversing the tendencies of many within the movement toward wanton violence. There are two obvious ways to control this problem. The first is through tough command and control; the second is to deny membership in the movement to those inclined to indiscriminate violence. For a series of interlocking reasons, neither of these seems probable. As previously discussed, the United States and its partners are busily impeding command and control functions within Salafi jihadist organizations. As a result, the ability of cooler heads at al Qaeda central (for instance) to prevail is inhibited. Indeed, some Salafi jihadist thinkers, notably Abu Musab al-Suri, have even started to argue that the movement should eliminate its bureaucracies and devolve to something more like "leaderless resistance" because the U.S. military and local security services are optimized to destroy terrorist or insurgent command and control structures.[12] Moreover, the Salafi jihadist movement claims to champion the only universally applicable version of Islam. Thus, while individual groups can control their own membership, the movement as a whole perforce is saddled with anyone who claims to be a Salafi jihadist, even if he is an incompetent or a bloodthirsty psychopath whose actions will discredit the movement in the vital Sunni Muslim audience. Ironically, the very growth of the Salafi jihadist movement will almost certainly undercut its popularity.

The vision of a utopian future brought about by violence has also worn poorly across the Sunni

AP Images (Manish Swarup)

Student members of India's ruling party protest terrorist attacks in Mumbai, December 2008

Muslim world among religious and revolutionary elites. Renowned Salafi jihadist and former ideological head of Egyptian Islamic Jihad, Dr. Sayyid Imam Sharif, also known as "Doctor Fadl," released a book in late 2007 formally renouncing violence, jihadism, and the path to social reform espoused by al Qaeda, largely on the grounds that it will not succeed.[13] Prominent Saudi clerics continue to issue decrees against violence and terrorism in the name of Islam. Finally, a growing network of non-Arab Islamic leaders has been condemning Salafi jihadism's violence and its inhumane treatment of Muslims in places such as Anbar Province, Iraq, and across western Pakistan.[14] Most recently, in late May 2008, the extremely conservative Deoband Muslim seminary in India issued an edict against terrorism as unjust and un-Islamic, while also criticizing the Taliban for going too far in their implementation of Islamic laws in Afghanistan and parts of western Pakistan.[15]

The growing criticism has put al Qaeda's leaders in an increasingly reactive mode. Deputy al Qaeda leader Ayman al-Zawahiri and media spokesmen, including the late Abu Laith al-Libi and Abu Yahya al-Libi, have been increasingly consumed in detailed ideological debates with these challengers within the Salafi jihadist movement and across wider Sunni Islam. For example, Zawahiri found it necessary to issue a 2-hour monologue in early 2008 to counter the impact of Dr. Sharif's renunciation of Salafi jihadism. Extensive and frequent public releases assert the necessity of violence, scold Islamic leaders and movements who are insufficiently activist, and defend the jihad and martyrdom as necessary for true believers.

Given these concerns, al Qaeda has expanded its efforts at mobilization and recruitment, simultaneously endeavoring to counter growing Muslim discontent with its aggressive methods and unpalatable goals. Much of this growth has come as a normal function of the ever-expanding Internet. Since 2004, al Qaeda has established its own media production company, As Sahab. It has also developed a new propaganda distribution network known as the Al Fajr Media Center, while widening its network of Web sites from fewer than 1,000 to more than 5,000.[16] Most of these operate overtly, while others have password protection and exhibit sophisticated access and message control. The network even features more than 100 sites operating in English. The content of these Web sites is increasingly aimed at the second- and third-generation Islamic diaspora across Europe.

For terrorism analysts who focus on measuring inputs, expanding Web sites would seem to indicate that a new form of self-radicalized, homegrown jihadist has become the greatest terrorist threat inspired by Salafi jihadism. In general, however, these efforts have not paid off in terms of recruits or converts. There is little evidence that they have played an important role in the increased anti-Americanism around the world or in any resurgence of "Islamic feeling" (if such indeed is under way at all). Rather, what has demonstrably contributed to America's bad poll numbers have been its overt acts in prosecuting the fight against terrorism, primarily the invasion of Iraq, and to a lesser extent Afghanistan, and the formal and informal media far beyond the jihadists' efforts, which convey inflammatory words and images from these conflicts.

Moving beyond mere empathy through affiliation and on to formal enfranchisement as a practitioner of Salafi jihadist terror would appear to require direct contact with the core of al Qaeda's trusted agents. Multiple reports over the past few years indicate that an increasing number of second- and third-generation European Muslims are being aggressively recruited to come to Pakistan for vetting, training, and incorporation into interchangeable terrorism operations within Pakistan, across the border in Afghanistan, and, most ominously, against targets in their countries of origin. Those who fail al Qaeda's litmus test or who cannot gain safe transit back to the West remain and conduct terror attacks in South Asia. Those whom the leadership trusts, and who can secure passage out to the West, will return there to conduct spectacular attacks. Consequently, the culmination of the process of radicalization to terrorism involves physical space. Today, that space is in western Pakistan (including the Federally Administered Tribal Areas, the Northwest Frontier Province, and Baluchistan).

At the same time, the Salafi jihadists have found that their media efforts are swamped by those of the globalized information and entertainment industry, not to mention the vast majority of the imams and Islamic scholars. The Salafi jihadists have found that these outlets and communicators are overwhelmingly hostile to them, even when they are virulently anti-American and anti-Israeli. Jihadist elites write lengthy denunciations of the news media while the rank and file threaten death to reporters from al Jazeera and al Arabiya.[17] The problem, however, from an al Qaeda perspective, is much worse than that. Popular media, music, and sports are all typically anti-Salafi jihadist in their orientation even when appearing, from a Western perspective, as nonpolitical. The movement is even plagued by the various September 11 conspiracy theories. For instance, it is difficult to attract new recruits if they believe that Osama bin Laden is a creation of the Central Intelligence Agency, or that the attacks were an inside job mounted by the Bush administration, or a plot by Israel's Mossad.[18]

Ultimately, then, the Salafi jihadist movement is failing to attract large numbers of people. Generous estimates put its total number at perhaps 250,000 worldwide. While even this possibly inflated estimate sounds like a large number, in fact it is not. It is roughly 0.03 percent of the 91 million Muslims worldwide who found the September 11 attacks "fully justified." Only some 0.02 percent of all Muslims in the world are Salafi jihadists.

These numbers underscore that there is no straight line from grievance to terrorism. In the words of one social movement theorist, "If we have learned anything from the last thirty years of social movement scholarship, it is of course that no such line exists. A huge analytic chasm separates grievances and specific strategies of collective action."[19] Another scholar put it more directly: "Making Arabs angry does not alone turn them into terrorists."[20] Given this, there is little reason to believe that burnishing America's image in the Middle East or among Muslims generally—even assuming such is possible, and recent scholarship on the many types of anti-Americanism suggests that perhaps it is not—will be an effective, let alone efficient, method of reducing the terrorism threat.[21]

Policy Considerations and Tradeoffs for the United States

The United States will continue carrying out defensive measures to protect itself and its allies against terrorist attacks. The difficult questions are what forms of offensive action should be undertaken, and by whom. Fortunately, the fundamental strategic situation is extremely grim for al Qaeda and the other Salafi jihadists. The movement is under tremendous stress and has failed to attract genuine adherents despite its media efforts, the once-high (but now declining) popularity of Osama bin Laden, and the fact that the U.S. prosecution of the wars in Iraq and Afghanistan is widely unpopular across the Islamic world.[22]

The problem, from the Salafi jihadist perspective, is the fact that experience has shown that, all other things being equal, the more Muslims are exposed to its indiscriminate violence, the less they support al Qaeda and the movement it represents. As many have argued—including those who still see al Qaeda as tremendously dangerous—the movement is inherently self-limiting.[23]

The United States, ironically, is the best friend that the Salafi jihadists have. The Salafi jihadists want the United States to use its military power extensively because they believe such actions help to mobilize Sunni Muslims to become Salafi jihadists. It is also worth remembering that what most contributes to anti-Americanism in the Islamic world is the perception that U.S. policies unfairly dictate how things must be. Reducing the visible American profile in the world would undercut Salafi jihadism at least to the extent that it can take the edge off of anti-Americanism. To this effect, the United States might wish to support regional programs that grow responsible local paramilitary and law enforcement capacity in Sunni Muslim states. Building local partner capacity, along with intelligence-sharing to help constrain the ability of organized Salafi jihadist terror groups to topple these regimes, might undercut the effectiveness of the terrorists while reducing America's military profile.

The United States must recognize that it is in a similar position to the terrorists. Not surprisingly, given its preponderance, the more it uses coercive force, the more it is likely to be seen as a threatening power. Arguably, the more visible the United States is, with the notable exception of manifestly humanitarian missions, the less it is liked. Indeed, al Qaeda usually wants the United States to act, believing that American actions will inevitably validate their narrative. Accordingly, the United States must avoid falling into a maximalist, activist, and interventionist approach. In addition, it must not make the mistake—too often committed by both sides of the political system—of believing that it alone has power and agency, and that the other peoples around the world have none. Furthermore, Washington must recognize the limits of its power, not only because America's intrinsic capabilities to deal with this (and any other) problem are finite, but also because Muslims themselves will always outnumber Americans in Muslim countries, and they have positional and cultural advantages over the United States. But the United States still enjoys numerous potential partners in fighting Salafi jihadist extremism and violence. These range all the way from the governments of Indonesia, Syria, and Iran, to Hamas and many other Islamist groups, to al Jazeera, to the United Nations (UN), to traditional allies such as the United

Kingdom, Canada, and Australia. Policymakers have a range of cooperative techniques available to them for dealing with these various countries and groups, ranging from unwitting to tacit to covert to overt.

The most important potential partners for the United States are Sunni Muslims, who have credible voices with other Muslims. Salafi jihadists' complaints suggest that most of those in the Islamic world are against them. If it is going to take full advantage of this fact, the United States might continue to quietly support Muslim voices opposing Salafi jihadism, while improving activities in areas where unacceptable al Qaeda strength remains, notably in the safe haven of western Pakistan.

Several other policy considerations stand out:

■ It may be helpful to measure proposed changes in U.S. counterterrorism policy against the possible harm from degrading what has already proved successful in the struggle against Salafi jihadism and al Qaeda. It is clear that an al Qaeda under pressure is less tactically and strategically effective. Similarly, the Salafi jihadist movement has, at various points in its 40-year history, apparently been contained or reduced to manageable levels. When the pressure was removed, the movement always rebounded.

■ While the United States wishes to be well liked in the Muslim world, it is clear that America's unpopularity is largely unrelated to the health of Salafi jihadism. Thus, policymakers may wish to carefully scrutinize calls for more and better strategic messaging campaigns to counter the social critique of Salafi jihadism. Reform of Islamic societies, under the leadership of mainstream Muslims, is most likely to render the Salafi jihadi social critique impotent. This reform will take time, but Western governments may be able to help indirectly by continuing to encourage temperate Muslim reformers and visionaries, while avoiding heavy-handed gestures and pompous demands for immediate change. To the extent that direct Western efforts can help, these need to be seen and not heard. By the same token, Western leaders may wish to take every opportunity to provide significant, visible assistance to Muslim victims of flooding, earthquakes, famine, and other natural disasters. As was the case with U.S. assistance to Pakistani Muslim victims of the October 2005 earthquake, and Indonesian Muslim victims of the December 2004 tsunami, such overt assistance to Muslims in need will slowly but surely erode general Muslim beliefs that the West is only about subjugating and exploiting Muslims.

■ The United States can provide additional indirect support for the growing number of Muslim critics of Salafi jihadism. Washington might encourage the natural tendency of Muslims who have been victims of the violence to speak out in front of fellow Muslims, for it is these voices that carry the most weight in discrediting the Salafi jihadist ideology.

■ Most importantly for 2009, American and allied leaders will have to face the major threat posed by al Qaeda and the Salafi jihadist ideology: namely, the terrorist safe haven in western Pakistan. A collaborative effort to fully and firmly engage the Pakistanis in order to eradicate al Qaeda may be indispensible to preventing another 9/11. The approach most likely to be successful will frame the al Qaeda safe haven in Pakistan as part of the more general problem with jihadism in terms of an ongoing Pakistani security strategy, and address this wider problem in the context of a reformulated South Asia security arrangement.

In short, Salafi jihadism remains dangerous. It is a threat that is irregular in nature but is easy to understand because it is an open mass movement with universal aspirations. It can be penetrated nearly at will, however, whether for the purpose of collecting information or for influencing its actions. This is a different problem from competing with closed societies such as the former Soviet Union. Salafi jihadists are remarkably open in discussing and debating their strategies, weaknesses, fears, and vulnerabilities. The United States might, then, profitably invest more in its ability as a nation to "know the enemy," which is the wider movement of Salafi jihadism. Washington can then tailor its strategies to exploit the movement's growing vulnerabilities in the Muslim world, while simultaneously taking only prudent offensive actions that inhibit catastrophic terrorism and supporting ongoing Muslim efforts to marginalize the Salafi jihadist ideology across the Islamic world.

The Mind of the Terrorist

What is inside the mind of the terrorist? The lay public widely assumes that terrorists driven to give their lives for their cause must be crazed fanatics. In fact, the consensus of scholars who have specialized in terrorist psychology holds that individual-level analyses fall far short of explaining terrorism.[24] As Martha Crenshaw has observed, "The outstanding common characteristic of terrorists is their normality."[25] Similarly, in a review of the "Social Psychology of Terrorist Groups," McCauley and Segal conclude that "the best documented generalization is negative;

terrorists do not show any striking psychopathology."[26] Indeed, terrorist groups and organizations screen out emotionally unstable individuals. They represent, after all, a security risk.

If it is not individual psychopathology, what is the major determinant of terrorist psychology? The Committee on the Psychological Roots of Terrorism concluded that:

group, organizational and social psychology . . . provides the greatest analytic power in understanding this complex phenomenon. Terrorists have subordinated their individual identity to the collective identity, so what serves the group, organization or network is of primary importance. For some groups, especially nationalist/ terrorist groups, this collective identity is established extremely early, so that "hatred is bred in the bone."[27]

AP Images (Franco Pagetti)

Crowds search rubble of U.S. Embassy, Nairobi, Kenya, after August 1998 car bombing

In considering psychological and behavioral bases of terrorism, it is important to consider each manifestation of terrorism in its own political, historical, and cultural context,[28] for terrorism is a product of its own place and time. It is an attractive strategy to a diverse array of groups that have little else in common. In considering the psychology of the broad spectrum of terrorist types—right-wing, nationalist-separatist, social revolutionary, single-issue, and religious fundamentalist terrorists—given how different their causes and their perspectives are, these types would be expected to differ markedly.[29] So the discussion should be about terrorisms—plural—and terrorist psychologies—plural—rather than searching for a unified general theory to explain all terrorist behavior.

After the attacks of September 11, 2001, President George W. Bush declared that this was "the first war of the 21st century." But in fact, the modern era of terrorism is usually dated back to the early 1970s, as represented by the radical Palestinian terrorist group Black September's seizure of the Israeli Olympic village at the 1972 Munich Olympics, an event that captured a global television audience and demonstrated powerfully the amplifying effect of the electronic media in the information age. In the early years of the modern era of terrorism, two terrorist types dominated the landscape. They were leftist social revolutionary terrorists, groups seeking to overthrow the capitalist economic and social order, and exemplified by the Red Army Faction in Germany and the Red Brigades in Italy; and nationalist-separatist terrorists, such as al-Fatah and other radical secular Palestinian terrorists, the Provisional Irish Republican Army of Northern Ireland, and the Basque separatist group Freedom for the Basque Homeland (Euskadi ta Askaratsuna, or ETA), which sought to establish a separate nation for their national minority. Both of these group types wished to call attention to their cause and would regularly claim responsibility for their acts. They were seeking to influence the West and the establishment. Often, there were multiple claims of responsibility for the same act.

Social-Revolutionary Terrorism

Social-revolutionary terrorists are rebelling against the generation of their parents who are loyal to the regime. They are disloyal to the generation of their families that is loyal to the regime. Their acts of terrorism are acts of revenge against the generation of their family that they hold responsible for their failures in this world. One of the Baader-Meinhof gang

Chapter 7
The Changing Character of War

One of the key challenges that strategists face is balancing the tension between the constantly changing character of war and its underlying, unchanging nature. During the early 1990s, technological enthusiasts suggested that information technology would eliminate the Clausewitzean fog and friction of war. Today, even its most stubborn proponents now admit that advanced technology cannot do so. It is equally important for traditionalists to admit that, although the underlying nature of war as described by Clausewitz has not changed, the character of warfare has and will continue to change along with society as a whole. This chapter addresses the changing character of modern warfare with an eye to both truths.

Combatants select from an entire range of tactics and technologies that are appropriate to their own societies; therefore, this chapter first explores how the concept of hybrid war has captured the latest incarnation of this trend and how it is affecting modern conflicts. After defining the challenges that hybrid war presents, the chapter moves on to explore specific manifestations of the phenomenon and how they challenge the United States. First, it discusses what has changed and what remained the same in insurgency and counterinsurgency. Then it explores the humanitarian issues that are an integral part of modern battlefields. Expanding the arena of conflict, the chapter next deals with the changing character of maritime and air power in the 21st century. The

U.S. Air Force (Aaron Allmon)

F–15E takes on fuel from KC–10 during combat mission over Afghanistan discussion of maritime conflict begins with the planned structure of the U.S. fleet and the trends that will impact that structure and closes with recommendations for how to deal with these trends in an era when maritime power is of increasing importance. Next, we examine the complex and flexible amalgam that is airpower and how it has adapted to the changing character of modern war. A final section provides a much longer term historical view of what constitutes asymmetry and the changing character of war.

The Challenge of Hybrid Warfare

The National Defense Strategy issued in 2005 was noteworthy for its expanded understanding of modern threats. Instead of historical emphasis on conventional state-based threats, the document identified traditional, irregular, terrorist, and disruptive threats, outlined their relative probabilities, and acknowledged increased vulnerabilities to more unconventional types of conflict. Moreover, the strategy even noted the overinvestment in traditional means of warfighting and the need for the United States to shift the focus and resources to other means.

Although intrastate wars and civil strife have occurred more frequently than interstate wars throughout history, their strategic implications and operational effects have had little impact on Western militaries, especially that of the United States. Instead, the U.S. Armed Forces have focused on state-based threats and high-intensity conflicts or conventional warfare.

The result has been overwhelming American military superiority, which has been measured in terms of conventional capabilities and global power projection. However, American force capabilities and investments must change as new enemies and altered conditions influence both the frequency and character of war.

After the National Defense Strategy appeared, a number of American and foreign observers complimented the Department of Defense for moving beyond a preoccupation with conventional warfighting. But they also cited an increased blurring of distinctions among various forms of warfare, rather than the clear-cut categories outlined in the strategy. The Pentagon itself suggested that most future complex challenges would involve synergy from the simultaneous application of multiple approaches. The National Defense Strategy explicitly stated that potential challenges could overlap and that "the most dangerous circumstances arise when we face a complex of challenges. . . . [T]he most capable opponents may seek to combine truly disruptive capacity with *traditional, irregular,* or *catastrophic* forms of warfare."[1]

Many defense analysts suggest that future conflict will be multimodal, combining various methods of warfare to increase both their frequency and potential lethality. This threat is frequently described as *hybrid warfare* where adversaries can employ unique combinations of *all* forms of warfare specifically targeted to U.S. vulnerabilities. Criminal activities can be considered part of this threat because they destabilize government authority and abet insurgents by providing resources. Such activities could involve smuggling, narcoterrorism, illicit transfers of advanced explosives and weaponry, or exploitation of urban gang networks.

Major challenges in the future will be posed not by a state that chooses a single approach but rather by states or groups that select an approach from a menu of tactics and technologies. Such potential enemies will blend diverse elements in innovative ways to suit their own strategy, culture, and geography. As Michael Evans of the Australian Defence Academy warned prior to the Quadrennial Defense Review: "The possibility of continuous sporadic armed conflict . . . means that war is likely to transcend neat divisions into distinct categories."[2] Still others point to the increasingly complex operating environment with large civilian populations, dense urban areas, and complex information activities that will abet the hybrid challenger. Colin Gray predicted that "there is going to be a blurring, a further blurring, of warfare categories."[3] The British and Australians are exploring the implications of this blurring and the desired countercapabilities

Soldier fires AT–4 rocket launcher during firefight near Asadabad, Afghanistan

required to effectively operate against hybrid threats. In fact, British thinking on the subject has surpassed American doctrine and incorporated hybrid threats within the construct for irregular warfare.

In many respects, Hizballah represented the rising tide of hybrid threats. The 34-day battle in Lebanon in 2006 revealed Israeli weaknesses, which had implications for American defense planners. Combining an organized political movement with decentralized cells that used adaptive tactics in areas outside Lebanese government control, Hizballah demonstrated that it could inflict as well as take punishment. Specifically, highly disciplined, well-trained, and distributed cells contested ground against modern conventional forces with a mixture of guerrilla tactics and technology in dense urban centers. Like the jihadist defenders of Fallujah during April and November of 2004, Hizballah skillfully exploited the urban terrain to lay ambushes, evade detection, and hold strong defensive positions in close proximity to noncombatants.

The Israelis grudgingly admitted that Hizballah resistance was several orders of magnitude more difficult to deal with than were counterterrorism operations on the West Bank or in Gaza. More importantly, the degree of training, fire discipline, and lethal technology wielded by Hizballah was far more advanced. The tactical combinations and technological innovations employed by Hizballah were particularly noteworthy. The antitank guided missile systems used against the defensive positions and armored vehicles of the Israel Defense Forces, coupled with decentralized tactics, were surprises. At the battle of Wadi Salouqi, for instance, a column of Israeli tanks was halted by these tactics. The antitank weapons in the Hizballah arsenal included the Russian-made RPG–29, AT–13 *Metis*, and AT–14 *Kornet*, with a range of 3 miles. The Israelis found that AT–13s and AT–14s were effective but not necessarily formidable against their own first-line Merkava tanks.

Hizballah even launched some armed unmanned aerial vehicles that challenged the Israelis to detect them, including Iranian Mirsad-1s or Ababil-3 Swallows. In addition, there is evidence that Hizballah invested in signals intelligence and monitored the cell phones of Israel Defense Forces as well as unconfirmed reports of de-encrypting Israeli radio traffic. Hizballah also appeared to use advanced surveillance systems and advanced night vision devices. The employment of C802 antiship cruise missiles also provided another side of hybrid warfare.

Perhaps the most unusual asset demonstrated by Hizballah was its stock of 14,000 rockets. Many were old and relatively inaccurate, but thanks to help from Iran or Syria, Hizballah also possessed newer missile systems that could reach deep into Israeli territory. These missiles were used to terrorize the civilian population as well as attack Israeli military infrastructure. The fact that Hizballah could launch as many rockets on the last day of the war as the first gave these old rockets a strategic impact far beyond their limited tactical value.

Hybrid wars represent more than traditional conflicts between states and other armed groups. They incorporate different modes of warfare including conventional capabilities, irregular tactics and formations, terrorist acts of indiscriminate violence, and criminal disorder. Hybrid wars can be conducted by states and various nonstate actors. Separate units or the same unit can conduct such multimodal activities that are operationally and tactically directed and coordinated within the main battlespace to achieve synergistic effects in the physical and psychological dimensions of conflict. Moreover, these effects can be achieved on all levels of war.

At the strategic level, many wars have had both regular and irregular components. However, in most conflicts the two occurred in different theaters or different formations. Examples include the Continental Army and militias in the Revolutionary War, the Army of Northern Virginia and Mosby's Rangers in the Civil War, British regulars and Spanish guerrillas in the Peninsula War, the British 8th Army and Bedouins under T.E. Lawrence in World War I, and

U.S. Army (Adam Mancini)

Soldier launches RQ–II Raven umanned aerial vehicle, Afghanistan

the North Vietnamese army and Viet Cong troops in the second Indochina War. But hybrid wars are different in that they blur capabilities or apply them in the same battlespace. The integration of irregular and conventional forces operationally and tactically is a new phenomenon.

The future does not portend separate threats relegated to distinct slices of a conflict spectrum. Traditional conflict will remain the most dangerous threat, but hybrid warfare will become more common. It will pose threats that blur and blend different methods and modes of warfare at the same time. Therefore, the most distinctive change in the character of war will involve combining various types of combat rather than a widening number of distinct challenges.

Hybrid wars blend the lethality of state military power with the irregular protracted conflict. Accordingly, potential adversaries such as states, state-sponsored groups, and self-funded actors will exploit advanced capabilities, including encrypted command systems, man-portable air-to-surface missiles, and other lethal systems. They will employ insurgent tactics such as ambushes, improvised explosives, and assassinations, and also combine high-tech capabilities such as antisatellite weapons with terrorism and cyberwarfare directed against financial targets.

Such challenges are not limited to nonstate actors. Conventional forces can be transformed into irregular units with new tactics similar to the Iraqi *fedayeen* in 2003. The evidence suggests that several Middle Eastern nations are modifying their militaries to exploit this mode of conflict. This development will make it increasingly difficult to characterize national forces as traditional and nonstate actors as irregulars. Future threats will present a more diverse array of effective countermeasures to Western capabilities as Hizballah clearly demonstrated.

Regardless of state sponsorship, the lethality and capacity of organized groups are growing as incentives to exploit nontraditional modes of war increase. This transformation will mean modifying current views about frequency and content of future conflicts. Irregular and protracted forms of conflict have been castigated as the tactics of the weak, employed by nonstate actors who lack the means to do anything else. That judgment is misleading since future adversaries may exploit such means precisely because they are militarily effective. In fact, such measures may come to be seen as tactics of the smart and nimble, rather than the weak and under-resourced.

The rise of hybrid warfare does not represent the end of traditional or conventional warfare, but it

introduces a complicating factor in the 21st century. Instead of thinking about conventional or irregular warfare, defense planning must be expanded to include hybrid combinations. Instead of conventional or irregular threats presenting an either/or situation, both types of warfare must be contemplated, perhaps simultaneously. The implications of added complexity are significant. As John Arquilla of the Naval Postgraduate School observed: "While history provides some useful examples to stimulate strategic thought about such problems, coping with networks that can fight in so many different ways . . . is going to require some innovative thinking."[4]

The Department of Defense recognized the need for exploring the nature of this complex challenge. Secretary of Defense Robert Gates discussed hybrid threats with the senior leadership as part of the broader issue of reprogramming the investment and capability mix. Consequently, the Pentagon has initiated research on the problem including large joint exercises.

Future conflicts will not be easily parsed in simple classes of conventional and irregular war. Many defense analysts acknowledge the blurred lines between them. Conventional and irregular forces, combatants and noncombatants, and physical or kinetic and virtual dimensions of conflict will be blended and blurred to pose complex challenges. Defense planners can no longer think in terms of conventional or irregular enemies. They must adapt to hybrid warfare.

Counterinsurgency Warfare

The United States has been slowly and painfully relearning the lessons of counterinsurgency. This process is reflected in efforts to develop a unified response to deal with insurgencies in both Afghanistan and Iraq. Of particular importance has been an understanding that insurgencies are no longer unified political movements such as those of Mao Tse-tung or Ho Chi Minh, but rather coalitions of the angry responding to perceived threats to their way of life. This evolution from single political actors to coalitions was evidenced in the anti-Somoza Nicaraguan movement, the anti-Soviet insurgencies in Afghanistan and Chechnya, the anti-Israeli organizations in Palestine, and the anti-American insurgencies in Iraq and Afghanistan. All of these movements can be best described as *anti* movements; they were not linked by any cause other than ejecting an outside power. Once that goal is accomplished, the insurgents know they will have to fight each other to resolve whose vision of the future will prevail in the contested area.

Inevitably, new insurgent coalitions have learned

from past counterinsurgency operations. Their most critical innovation is the understanding that against the outside power the message is the insurgency. They realize that they cannot inflict a military defeat on that outside power. There will be no Maoist third-phase conventional offensive that will crush the government forces. Instead, they plan to defeat the outside power by breaking its political will. They will accomplish this objective through effective strategic communications against that outside power while positioning themselves for the inevitable internal conflict that will follow the withdrawal of the outside forces. Thus, their strategic communications campaign will address both external and internal audiences by targeting the outside power while addressing potential supporters and neutral states.

Today, insurgencies arise spontaneously rather than under central planning and direction. For example, in the first Palestinian Intifada, Afghanistan, and Iraq, the insurgents launched effective strategic campaigns without unified leadership. They demonstrated emergent intelligence where independent actors following basic rules create strategic effects, and thus precluded any form of decapitation strategy. Of particular note was the bombing campaign in Iraq over the summer and early autumn of 2003. The insurgents attacked the Jordanian embassy, Red Cross, and United Nations. By doing so, they ensured that the U.S. coalition would get little or no help from Arab nations, nongovernmental organizations (NGOs), or international bodies. While this brilliant bombing campaign appeared to be planned, there is no indication the insurgents had a unified command. Thus, the intelligence behind the strategic campaign has the properties of emergence.

The development of coalitions of the angry that conduct aggressive strategic communications and that have links to emergent intelligence poses greater challenges to counterinsurgency operations than traditional Maoist movements. Nevertheless, the basics of counterinsurgency remain valid. Before any counterinsurgency effort can gain the support of the people, it must provide security. Moreover, that security cannot be transient and must protect all members of the society who have sided with the government against the insurgency. Just as some members of the public refuse to testify against drug pushers because of their fear of retaliation, most citizens in a country torn by insurgent violence avoid being associated with a government that cannot protect them.

Another basic element of counterinsurgency remains unchanged: the hope for a better future.

However, that concept of a better future must originate with the local people, not with outsiders. While the United States has promoted democracy in Iraq and Afghanistan, Islam stresses justice over democracy. The problem is compounded by a naïve belief that one form of democracy—national elections—is better than alternative local forms of democracy. This has led some to push national elections on societies which are not ready for complex powersharing arrangements. Remember, it took the English almost 450 years to advance from the Magna Carta to a parliamentary democracy. Yet some have planned to take a society with no experience in democracy from a dictatorship to a democracy in only a couple of years.

While the basics of counterinsurgency have not changed, the difficulty of achieving them has increased. Since the Nation no longer confronts a single, unified movement, it must understand the political, economic, social, and religious motives of various groups, which range from preserving a certain way of life to imposing a new type of government or a stricter form of religion and from protecting criminal enterprises to seeking revenge or personal gain. As noted, these coalitions are not committed to common beliefs but rather band together to fight outsiders. There is not even unity within major factions. Instead, each faction is networked together, often by preexisting political, social, or religious linkages. These simple networks allow insurgents to share information to attack outsiders, although they do not fully trust each other.

While not every counterinsurgent must be a state builder, efforts to establish security must be based on understanding players and intentions in any given area. There will not be a national-level solution but rather local responses to issues that motivate fighters in that area. Even when events are addressed, such as the Anbar Awakening, counterinsurgents must sustain powersharing compromises among the various groups to prevent the outbreak of civil war.

A final dangerous development in insurgencies is that nonstate actors in general and insurgents in particular have greater communications, technological capabilities, and arms than at any time in the past, which has made it possible to overmatch governments in many regions.

One key question is how often insurgencies will occur in the future. If the United States is convinced that it will never fight such enemies again, then it can ignore the problem and focus on other issues. But if defense planners accept that insurgents threaten strategic American interests, then they must be prepared to defeat them and develop a strategy for counterinsurgency operations. Since each insurgency has unique problems, each requires a unique approach. However, despite the fact they present unique challenges, each counterinsurgency effort will require an all-of-government approach.

And how does the United States achieve an all-of-government response? Does it require every component of the government to deploy trained personnel to respond to insurgencies, or does it task the military to provide the necessary personnel? If civilian agencies are forced to respond, what percentage of their personnel will be committed? How much will such operations cost and what laws must be enacted or amended to carry out these missions? Moreover, how extensive is the potential disruption to agency manpower policies in achieving a deployable force?

Similar obstacles are posed by all-military solutions. For example, if the Services must field the necessary response, can they recruit the necessary personnel? Should the military activate selected Reservists who have comparable jobs in the civil sector? Or should the military form units in either the Active or Reserve Components to accomplish these missions? And if so, how should the military revamp its force structure to gain such capabilities? What types of units are reduced or eliminated to free up personnel required to execute these new missions?

At the core of agency responsibility is the question of strategic communications. How can the United States engage in strategic communications to defeat insurgents while reinforcing its own political will? Given the centrality of strategic communications and

Future U.S. Naval Power

AIRCRAFT CARRIERS	11
MAJOR SURFACE COMBATANTS	
Arleigh Burke–Class Destroyer	62
DDX	7
CG[X]	19
LCS	55
TOTAL	**143**
SUBMARINES	
SSBN	14
SSGN	4
SSN	48
TOTAL	**66**
AMPHIBIOUS/ EXPEDITIONARY	
Amphibious Warfare	31
Command Support	30
Combat Logistics	20
MPFF Ships	12
TOTAL	**93**

Key: DDX=Next Generation Destroyer; CG[X]=Next Generation Cruiser; LCS=Littoral Combat Ship; SSBN=Ballistic Missile Submarine; SSGN=Guided Missile Submarine; SSN=Nuclear Attack Submarine; MPFF=Maritime Prepositioning Force (Future).

21st Century War

ASYMMETRY	TYPE
numbers of forces	degree
types of forces	kind
type/quality of leadership	kind/degree
type/amount of training	kind/degree
tactics and strategies	kind
geopolitical differences	kind/degree
economic differences	kind/degree

U.S. Air Force (Joe Laws)

Contractor monitors and maintains data link between Joint Terminal Attack Controllers on ground and tactical aircraft during exercise Bold Quest Plus

our notable failures in the recent past, an effective campaign is essential to counterinsurgency operations. However, the fragmented nature of insurgencies often increases the problem of developing that strategy. For example, a first-hand cultural understanding is essential to developing such a successful campaign. Unfortunately, American personnel systems do not support a career pattern that permits government employees to develop a sufficiently deep level of understanding. Thus, developing counterinsurgency strategy requires reconsidering the career paths for professionals in the field established by current personnel systems.

Once the civil and military roles are adequately delineated, the United States can build the requisite capabilities in the host government. Insurgencies are easiest to defeat at their inception and best defeated by indigenous forces. As such, they require a network of American specialists to advise on governance, economics, and local security. They should be a corps of professionals trained to support a cooperative security engagement strategy. In addition to these advisers, the military should provide training and equipment to assist indigenous security forces.

An additional challenge in developing a successful counterinsurgency strategy is the amount of manpower required. The ratio most often cited is 1 security officer for every 50 citizens. In Afghanistan alone, this guideline would demand nearly 600,000 personnel. Since this number is beyond the capabilities of the United States or its allies, the only solution is developing forces in the host nation. Even then, to meet this standard, 2 percent of the population would be needed in the security forces. Paying for this mobilization poses another challenge.

Advisory capacity will also be a major issue for the United States. Those nations threatened by insurgent movements typically lack the ability to provide key services. They require advisers in a range of ministries in addition to advisers for local security. In addition to building these capabilities, the statutory authorities and funding necessary to successfully achieve this strategy must be determined. Given the unpredictability and length of insurgencies, counterinsurgency strategies should be at least multi-year and perhaps even multi-decade in scope.

Even if the United States can successfully disengage from Iraq and Afghanistan, it must be prepared to meet other insurgent threats that are sure to arise. The Nation will require organizations, training, and skills to conduct effective counterinsurgency operations against coalitions of the angry.

Humanitarian Issues in Conflict Zones

The American military has dealt with humanitarian problems throughout its history, whether these involved victims of natural disasters or refugees in wartime. Since the 1990s, however, these problems have been constant in U.S. military operations, and the trend is likely to continue over the next decade. Sometimes humanitarian problems such as in Kosovo are the cause of military intervention and at other times they exist as a consequence of ongoing conflicts.

Military intervention involving humanitarian crisis may have one of two outcomes. First, an uncertain peace may follow the decisive end of fighting among warring parties. While various policies of the North Atlantic Treaty Organization (NATO) and the European Union on Kosovo and Bosnia remain open to criticism, the policies postintervention brought stability and allowed for relatively bloodless peacekeeping and nation-building. Second, conflicts may not end decisively, such as those in Iraq and Afghanistan.

To win against an insurgency, the host government must establish its legitimacy by providing its people with security, humanitarian assistance, basic public services, governance, and the start of postwar reconstruction. As a major force combating insurgents in Iraq and Afghanistan, the U.S. military has become deeply involved in the humanitarian and reconstruction efforts as a part of efforts to win the support of the people. Lack of security in many areas has further magnified military participation in humanitarian activities. The inability of underfunded and understaffed Department of State and U.S. Agency for International Development (USAID) activities also has drawn the military into the humanitarian sphere. American forces are now operating on the same playing field as civilian NGOs and international organizations. This inequality was exacerbated in the case of Iraq where the Department of Defense was initially placed in charge of postwar operations. In fact, the traditional humanitarian lines between civil and governmental entities generally tend to disappear in areas dominated by insurgency.

Various points of friction dominate humanitarian affairs. First, in both Afghanistan and Iraq, the enemy learned that attacking NGOs was a low-risk, high-reward strategy. For the insurgent, there is a payoff in attacking humanitarian organizations, particularly those that are unprotected, allied with the United States, or associated with unpopular religions. By attacking the military, the insurgent invites retribution. By attacking an element of either the United Nations or an NGO, the insurgent may strike a blow against the government's effort to create legitimacy at the local level, especially if the NGO subsequently chooses to cease operations in that area.

Second, colliding bureaucratic cultures also create problems. In Afghanistan, for example, special operations personnel initially fought in civilian clothes using concealed weapons, leading to objections from NGOs. This practice was changed by the military in 2002 but continued to be raised by NGOs into 2004. Meanwhile, well-intentioned military members advised NGO personnel that they were part of the same team and that civil affairs and other units were eager to coordinate humanitarian efforts, which is a poor choice of words. Most civilians resent being coordinated by military or governmental entities while the military regards coordination as simply a low-level activity that involves everyone. NGOs associate coordination with control, whereas the military associates it with interaction and communication.

Third, local reconstruction teams can become a point of friction. In late 2002, the Provincial Reconstruction Teams (PRTs) came into being in Afghanistan. These interagency teams of 50 to a few hundred personnel were designed to further security and reconstruction and promote host-government interests. There are 50 teams in both Iraq and Afghanistan, including 13 teams in Iraq that are non-regional and embedded with maneuver units and 14 in Afghanistan fielded by the coalition. While they have solved problems, they have created some as well.

PRTs initially heightened concerns of nongovernmental and international organizations as well as career diplomats over a military takeover of stabilization and reconstruction activities. Critics have also noted a lack of standardization, basic operational concepts, and doctrine among the various teams. On balance, however, PRTs have been a plus for coalition efforts and useful in resolving disputes between governmental and nongovernmental organizations. The teams have institutionalized American or coalition presence and also made it easier for NGOs to interact with both Department of State and USAID personnel.

As General David Petraeus stated to counterinsurgency military commanders in 2003, *money is ammunition.* This observation illustrates a fourth point of friction. Beginning in 2002, unit commanders who often could not wait for help from USAID or PRTs began to get Commander's Emergency Relief Program (CERP) funding for relief and reconstruction tasks. Since then, these funds have become a multibillion-dollar effort. As a result of this explosion in CERP funding, 20 percent of development assistance goes through the Pentagon. This form of humanitarian assistance has become a point of bureaucratic friction despite attempts by military commanders to work in close coordination with USAID and the PRTs.

U.S. Marine Corps (James A. Burks)

Marines conduct operation in Helmand Province, Afghanistan, April 2009

A fifth point of friction is the weakness of American instruments of power in the diplomatic and economic spheres. Despite a Presidential directive in 2005 making the Department of State the lead agency for stabilization and reconstruction, economic and security assistance amounts to only 5 percent of the Pentagon budget. The United States spends approximately $20 on defense for every $1 spent on Department of State and USAID programs combined. The last requested increase in defense budget equals the entire State-USAID budget. Moreover, the 8,000 Foreign Service Officers are simply inadequate to meet the requirements of 2 conflicts, 265 diplomatic and consular posts, and activities in over 120 countries. While Congress protects and expands defense funding, it barely supports the Foreign Service, which is roundly criticized for not solving problems that it is not adequately resourced to tackle.

The future promises more stability operations and humanitarian activities. U.S. participation in Iraq and Afghanistan will continue for some years to come. In short, the problem of failing and failed states will dominate international relations. While it is fair to believe that the Nation will be cautious of undertaking further commitments, it is easy to envision large-scale stability operations with or without conventional violence. Thus, the military role in humanitarian affairs will remain large in both conflict situations and natural disasters.

The United States must continue to build on recent progress in promoting stabilization and reconstruction activities. The Department of Defense has elevated stability operations as well as irregular warfare in doctrine and training. The Department of State has established an Office of the Coordinator for Reconstruction and Stabilization, which is supported by Secretary of Defense Robert Gates among others. USAID has also organized a military liaison office and, along with the Department of State, assigned senior advisers to combatant commands. The Departments of Defense and State, USAID, and U.S. Institute of Peace are working on *whole-of-government* and *whole-of-society* approaches to humanitarian problems. One promising initiative is the Consortium on Complex Operations, which is a virtual think tank for governmental agencies and other interested parties. Moreover, U.S. Africa Command and U.S. Southern Command function as interagency organizations in their areas of responsibility, a development that has brought praise as well as criticism. However, all of these organizational developments are still new and must be allowed to mature.

Despite some renewed interest, the U.S. military does not want to take the lead in stabilization and reconstruction activities. Although improving skills and programs for stability operations is important, nation-building is not a core military competency. It is an area for civilian leadership. In fact the last two Secretaries of Defense have been at the forefront in advocating substantially greater capabilities for stability operations in the Department of State and USAID. If the Nation fails to do this, then the military role in humanitarian operations will grow even larger—to the detriment of all concerned. Thus the Nation must consider ways to:

■ improve interagency planning for complex contingencies

■ dramatically increase the budget and manpower of the Department of State and USAID for stabilization and reconstruction activities, development assistance, and public diplomacy

■ broaden congressional understanding of the need for a multilevel civilian response corps

■ maintain current emphasis by the military on stability operations and irregular warfare

■ institutionalize and codify the military response to natural and other humanitarian disasters

■ disentangle the legislative authorities for humanitarian activities and stability operations

■ refine U.S. actions and programs to prevent deadly conflict and state failure.

The Changing Nature of Maritime Conflict

Like other maritime forces around the world, the U.S. Navy is engaged in a major fleet reconstruction program. Over the next three decades, its acquisition plan calls for reaching a fleet of 313 ships and submarines, with some 70 percent intended for major combat operations and the balance for other missions. This program offers long-term planning stability. Seven major projects already are approaching either lead-ship stage or full production. Moreover, a new-generation CVN–21 super-carrier, the CVN–78 *Gerald R. Ford*, will go into production this year. The resulting fleet will have 11 aircraft carriers, 143 major surface combatants, 66 submarines, and 93 amphibious, support, and expeditionary ships. This acquisition plan could transform the Navy into a force best suited to cope with the new conditions of the 21st century.

There are two problems with the plans for this fleet expansion. The first is that, in numerical terms, the naval force has declined since the Cold War to less than half of its size in the 1980s. This decline is alarming given the growing maritime capabilities of other nations such as China. Accordingly, the Chief of Naval Operations has warned that the present plan is insufficient and that the 313-ship Navy will not be adequate for missions in the coming years.[5]

The second problem with the planned expansion is the general view that the Navy will not be able to meet its target of 313 ships. Meeting this target would require constructing about 10 ships each year from now to 2037 at an estimated cost of $25 billion,[6] which is unlikely in the present fiscal environment. The problem is aggravated by the high operational tempo resulting from the conflicts in Iraq and Afghanistan. This tempo has shortened the anticipated life of both ships and aircraft while reducing the propensity for Sailors to reenlist and maintain existing force levels. For example, many observers were startled when two advanced *Aegis* ships recently failed their inspections and were declared unfit for service. These ships had deteriorated more quickly than expected largely because of operational tempo. Moreover, with the rate of technological change occurring today, it is increasingly difficult to have incremental modernization. Instead, the Navy is forced to identify transformational leaps in platform specification as evidenced by the Littoral Combat Ship, the DDG–1000 *Zumwalt*-class destroyer, and the CG (X) next generation cruiser programs. These are inherently riskier and costlier to fix when things go wrong. For all these reasons, alternate fleet structures as low as 220 ships have been predicted, which would clearly aggravate the resources-commitments gap still further.

The issues of fleet size and funding confronting the United States are part of a trend affecting all the navies of the world. Individual platforms, sensors, and weapons are simply getting more expensive relative to available resources for naval procurement. The result in Europe and much of the Asia-Pacific region has been substantial downsizing of naval forces. Although the capabilities of remaining platforms are greater, overall coverage and flexibility suffer.

U.S. planners are torn between the demands of major combat and those of stabilization operations. Combat operations require high-intensity sea-control capabilities for deepwater antisubmarine warfare, antiair warfare, and ballistic missile defense with seabased nuclear deterrence. Such operations are designed for combat with traditional symmetrical peer competitors. By contrast, stabilization operations are aimed at asymmetrical threats. These operations demand capabilities required for expeditionary warfare

such as projecting naval forces and supporting forces ashore. Stabilization also includes maritime domain awareness, small ship operations, and activities with coast guards. Finally, these operations are used for constructive naval engagement with other countries in areas such as surface ships and inclusive naval procedures. These types of operations are not cheap. Recent asymmetrical conflicts—such as the USS *Cole* incident in Aden, the ambush of a boarding party from the Royal Navy frigate HMS *Cornwall* by the Iranian Republican Guard, and the hit on the well-armed Israeli corvette *Hanit* by a C–802 missile fired by Hizballah forces in Lebanon—indicate the extent of the demands on maritime operations.

Balancing these demands against the requirements of hedging against a near-peer competitor is far from easy. *A Cooperative Strategy for 21st Century Seapower* is candid about the "tensions . . . between the requirements for continued peacetime engagement and maintaining proficiency in the critical skills necessary to fighting and winning in combat."[7] For example, while it is true that helicopters can deliver ordnance in a high-intensity war as well as humanitarian aid in a tsunami relief operation, it is also the case that a month spent learning Arabic is a month lost training for high-intensity operations. More specifically, the best ships for maritime security operations are often ocean and inshore patrol vessels, but these would be of limited utility in a conflict in the Taiwan Straits. Allocating scarce resources between competing sets of commitments is the most difficult conceptual issue facing naval planners.

In addition, the current focus on Iraq and Afghanistan aggravates planning. Priority is given to defense projects bearing on those conflicts and places others related to future contingencies on a back burner. This mindset affects the Navy and its allies in two ways. First, it jeopardizes or at least delays long-term projects that may be equally important as those projects associated with current operations. Second, it raises issues about the utility of naval power at a time when boots on the ground seem the main requirement. Despite an obvious shift in naval priorities from power *at* sea to power *from* the sea, the contribution that navies make remains both out of sight and out of mind. For example, in Great Britain over half the contingent deployed in Afghanistan was naval personnel, including marines, helicopter pilots, and medics. However, the Royal Navy got little credit because it operated more or less as army personnel. Some conclude that it might make sense to treat all naval personnel as such, a result of believing that navies do not matter as much

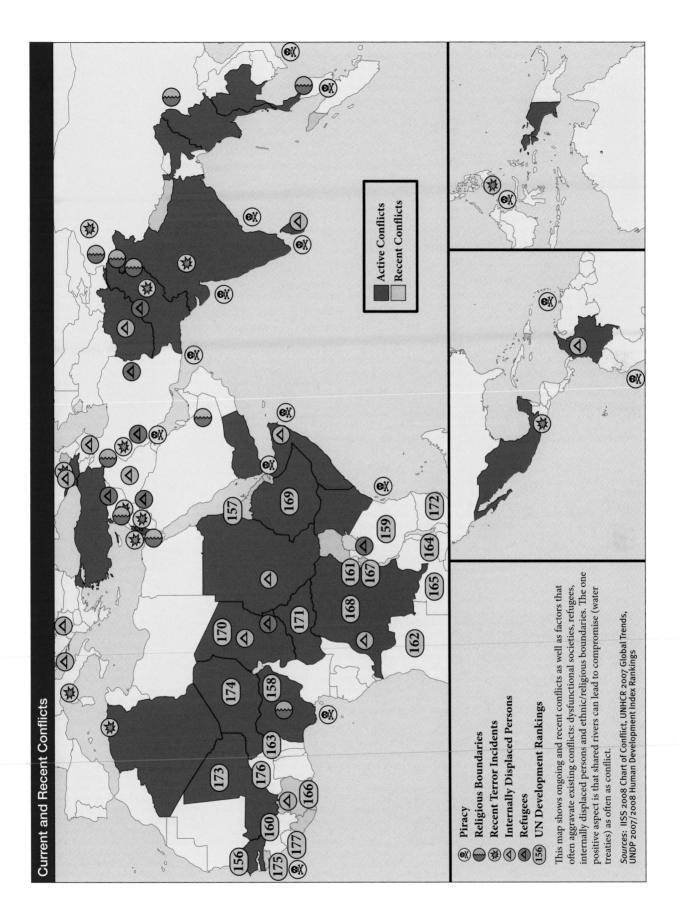

Current and Recent Conflicts

Active Conflicts
Recent Conflicts

- Piracy
- Religious Boundaries
- Recent Terror Incidents
- Internally Displaced Persons
- Refugees
- 156 UN Development Rankings

This map shows ongoing and recent conflicts as well as factors that often aggravate existing conflicts: dysfunctional societies, refugees, internally displaced persons and ethnic/religious boundaries. The one positive aspect is that shared rivers can lead to compromise (water treaties) as often as conflict.

Sources: IISS 2008 Chart of Conflict, UNHCR 2007 Global Trends, UNDP 2007/2008 Human Development Index Rankings

as they did in the past. This attitude negatively affects the debate whenever an expensive naval project is presented to the media or the political establishment.

The importance of seapower for the global economy is growing. Globalization in fact rests on the container and modern shipping industry. Low and decreasing seaborne freight rates mean that the cost of shipping $700 television sets from China to Europe is no more than about $10 per set. This helps keep American and European costs of living and rates of inflation down, encourages China to industrialize, and makes industrial relocation possible from both Europe and North America to the Far East. Lower costs also prompt the diversification of production lines in an increasing number of countries. Seaborne commerce produces mutual dependence among members of the international community in industrial production and consumption. The world is seen as an increasingly interconnected nexus of partners with high degrees of mutual economic as well as political interdependence in which the world's seas play a vital part.

Nevertheless, the system is under threat. Today, globalization relies on a supply-chain philosophy of just enough and just in time, which increases vulnerability to disruption. This situation is compounded by low stocks of life essentials such as oil and food that many states retain. The all-round maritime development of countries in the Asia-Pacific region,

especially China and India, suggests a sophisticated appreciation of the fact that the 21st century will prove the maritime century. There seems little doubt that by 2050 seapower will drive international events. But whose seapower will it be?

Solutions to these issues are likely to be sought in three ways. The first is making resources more cost-effective through better project management. This includes the establishment of a real partnership between the Navy and the defense industrial base that would prevent the kind of risk and blame-shifting characteristic of the Littoral Combat Ship while encouraging innovation such as the leasing by the Royal Navy of offshore patrol vessels from Vosper-Thorneycroft.

A second solution is making the best use of technology. While Iraq and Afghanistan indicate that superior technology is not the answer, it offers an important advantage. Networked naval forces can be dispersed and concentrated. Modularization provides design and operational flexibilities unheard of 20 years ago. Improved propulsion systems enable modern platforms to deliver more days at sea, allowing commanders to do more with less. But technological innovation presupposes an availability of manpower that many navies find difficult to achieve.

Finally, defense planners around the world must recognize that the range of risks and threats is wider

U.S. Marines investigate hole in earthen berm separating Iraq and Syria during Operation *Al Anbar Border Initiative* Phase II, north of Qaim, Iraq, to prevent smuggling between Syria and Iraq

than the resources available to even the most powerful individual nations. Furthermore, many risks and threats are challenges to all countries. This calls for the development of maritime partnerships, establishment of cooperation and coordination agreements, and recognition that operations may be best conducted through multilateral compromises on decisionmaking and standard operating procedures. The maritime consensus necessary to defend global trading must be seen as integral to operations rather than as unimportant peacetime activities.

The changing character of maritime conflict points to the importance of seapower in the future. Nonetheless, financial, industrial, and other trends may well impede the kind of ambitious fleet reconstruction plans discussed above. The Nation will be hard-pressed to balance the demands of the challenges maritime forces must address together with a greater reliance on international partnerships.

Airpower in a Nutshell

America has undergone a nonlinear growth in airpower over the past three decades. Its ability to contribute to combat operations at the high end of the conflict spectrum is exponentially greater because of the convergence of low observability or stealth, freedom to attack fixed and moving targets with high accuracy from relatively safe standoff ranges irrespective of weather or time of day, and expanded battlespace awareness made possible by developments in command, control, communications, and computers and in information, surveillance, and reconnaissance. As a result of such improvements, airpower has acquired capabilities to set the conditions of victory in joint warfare against organized opponents that field conventional forces.

Four important rules must be stipulated to clarify the meaning of the term *airpower*. First, airpower is a shorthand way of saying air, space, and cyberspace power. Second, airpower does not refer only to combat aircraft or the combined assets of an air arm. Rather, in its totality, airpower is a complex amalgam consisting of equipment and less tangible ingredients bearing on effectiveness, such as employment doctrine, concepts of operations, training, tactics, proficiency, leadership quality, adaptability, and practical experience. These soft factors vary among air arms around the world operating superficially similar kinds or even identical types of equipment. Yet they are given little heed in typical air capability analysis. Only through their combined effects can the success of raw hardware

▼ *Continued on p. 159*

Changing and Enduring Aspects of Conflict

Conventional wisdom holds that transformation, however defined, is necessary to compete in the current environment. Although that may be true, change that is strategically or operationally misinformed can lead to irrelevance or worse. To avoid that outcome, those responsible for the structure and implementation of any military or defense transformation would do well to arrive at a clear understanding of which aspects of warfare are new and changing as well as which are not. The task is not an easy one because a number of assumptions about contemporary warfare have been broadly accepted without the benefit of critical examination.

One assumption is that the wars of the 21st century will differ greatly from those of the past, in that future wars will be asymmetrical whereas previous conflicts were purportedly symmetrical. A second assumption is that the key to military success is knowledge of the enemy and greater situational awareness. Another assumption is that military transformation can deliver success irrespective of the political context in which the conflict occurs. But asymmetry is the rule rather than the exception in war. Moreover, *asymmetry* itself is not a particularly useful term since knowledge is dependent on the time available to obtain it, and real-world time constraints mean militaries must be able to function in an atmosphere of uncertainty. The political context plays a decisive role in whether transformed militaries can deliver victory.

The term *asymmetric* has become enormously popular in defense literature. Its current usage falls into two categories. The first suggests that asymmetrical warfare is a newer and cleverer way of fighting, and thus the exception rather than the rule. The second category uses the term to describe any conflict that appears to differ from conventional or traditional ways of fighting. Examples of asymmetrical conflicts include the war on terror or any guerrilla war, insurgency, irregular, or small war, even stabilization and reconstruction operations.

Both usages of asymmetric are flawed and misleading. The first presumes that belligerents have been and in most cases are symmetrical. Yet this presumption is not supported by historical analysis. In fact, in reviewing the historical record, the opposite is true. Symmetry between or among opposing forces is less common than asymmetry. Every enemy is asymmetric relative to its opponent in important ways. Likewise, every conflict is asymmetric. Asymmetry results from the interplay of political, cultural, economic, and geographic factors that cause communities to evolve differently. It is unavoidable and exists even when protagonists are not consciously using it to their advantage. It is also the state of nature—the rule rather than the exception.

The second usage of asymmetric requires accepting that irregular wars are less frequent than conventional conflicts. However, as Max Boot points out in *Savage Wars of Peace*, America has fought more so-called small or irregular wars in its history than conventional ones. Moreover, the Nation has forces designed for such wars and has developed them over decades. One can argue over whether there are enough forces for this purpose or whether they are properly deployed, but the point remains that asymmetrical conflicts are natural events, and fighting them has hardly posed an unfamiliar challenge for the United States.

Asymmetries are common in warfare and fall into two categories: kind or degree. Disparities in numbers, training, and leadership are asymmetries of degree. Basic differences in strategy, weapons, or sources of strength—Sparta, for instance, was clearly a land power and Athens a naval power—are examples of asymmetries of kind. Distinguishing between asymmetries demystifies the term by providing a framework for understanding them. This categorization underscores the point that asymmetric wars are the rule and the types of asymmetry may vary over time.

Because asymmetry is the rule, describing enemies or types of conflicts as asymmetrical adds little to strategic analyses. In confronting asymmetrical adversaries, those adversaries are also, by definition, facing asymmetrical adversaries. Thus, it is important to grasp the particulars. Simply put, how does the adversary differ from you and how should you alter your thinking to meet the challenge? And in a counterinsurgency, the adversary should be called *insurgents*. Second- and third-order questions, such as political objectives, weapons, and others, should be brought to the forefront.

Asymmetry is a natural state of affairs while symmetry is the exception to the rule. Military operations involve multiple asymmetries of both kind and degree, and it is impossible to predict which particular difference or combination of differences will prove decisive. Consequently, the term *asymmetric* offers little value. It does not matter whether the next adversary or conflict is asymmetric. Rather, what matters are the second- and third-order questions that, in turn, ought to reveal how to maximize strengths and minimize weaknesses of a military force.

A debate has raged for over a decade over whether information-age technology will result in a revolution in military affairs. At the risk of oversimplification, the argument is focused on how much confidence should be placed in technology versus human judgment. Certainly, knowledge is more desirable than

ignorance, particularly in war. In addition, new technology is making more information, if not knowledge, available to operating forces. But knowledge is not an independent variable, separate from the actors, objectives, and actions in a given contest. When information is regarded as a dependent variable, the argument for making it a fundamental premise, as is the case for U.S. defense transformation, weakens considerably. This premise is based on the flawed assumption that decisions can usually be delayed until sufficient knowledge becomes available. While that may be true in some cases, it is by no means universal. It is certainly not true in a war where political circumstances and other factors may force the timing of decisions.

Decisions on implementing the surge depended to some extent on information gained from strategic assessments from across Iraq. However, timing the surge was driven more by political concerns, both domestic and international. While knowledge gained by means of the assessment was the key variable to decisionmaking, it was dependent on timing. The required knowledge had to be gained within a certain timeframe. Knowledge not gained during that period was simply not available to decisionmakers at the time of the decision. Accordingly, decisions were made based on the best information available at the time.

Knowledge is largely a function of the time required to gain it. It is not infinite, and therefore decisions must be made before all the information is available. This implies that many decisions entail some degree of uncertainty and is particularly true in war where both sides are actively engaged in denying information to each other. Acquiring knowledge in war is a continuous, often violent activity, and requires intrusion into many different domains. Furthermore, it is likely that legal and ethical constraints will limit such intrusions, despite advances in enabling technologies. Accordingly, leaders will not have the luxury of making decisions with complete knowledge. Rather, they will have to operate in an environment characterized by some degree of uncertainty. Thus, the development of the ability to make decisions in ambiguous environments must remain an integral part of any transformation process.

It is generally accepted that military transformation is critical to strategic success. However, this judgment assumes that transformation will proceed in the right direction and that political context—the constellation of power relationships that exists among key players whether states or nonstates—is unimportant. Unfortunately, history demonstrates that even a transformed military is not enough to overcome bad strategic decisions. To be sure, all parties involved in an armed conflict will make mistakes. Misperceptions and misjudgments occur more often than thought. Although many mistakes can be corrected during the course of a war, one of the most difficult to overcome is the failure to appreciate the political context surrounding a conflict.

The rebuilding of the German *Wehrmacht* between World War I and II has long been touted as a textbook case of successful transformation. It involved creating a new air arm, an expanded navy, and notably land forces organized and trained for mobile warfare. However, that machine could not compensate for a flawed strategy, which failed to appreciate the political context, and particularly the position of the European powers and, ultimately, the United States.

The British, French, and Soviet militaries also transformed during the 1920s and 1930s, each shaped by political and cultural influences that made them unique. The British placed emphasis on preserving their maritime power, the French invested in static defenses, and the Russians moved toward reliance on tanks and heavy artillery. Nonetheless, strategic and political decisions made within the existing political context set the course for success or failure.

A cautionary note is found in ongoing defense transformation—established on the principles of speed, precision, knowledge, and jointness—that may yield a truly exquisite military machine. However, that machine will not necessarily be able to overcome strategic mistakes and generate success. In other words, transformation of the U.S. military cannot replace strategy.

Contemporary defense policymakers must challenge the conventional wisdom regarding war. A fixation on irregular or asymmetric warfare must not obscure either the enduring or changing character of warfare. At a minimum, we must avoid oversimplified labels such as asymmetric, which tell us little about the similarities and differences between adversaries. Similarly, the talk about transformation, change, and reform must not obscure fundamental aspects of warfare, not least the crucial issue of strategy.

▲ *Continued from p. 157*

in producing desired combat results be determined.

Third, airpower is inseparable from battlespace information and intelligence. Thanks to the dramatic growth in the lethality and effectiveness of American airpower in recent years, it has become fashionable to speak increasingly not of numbers of sorties per target killed, but rather of number of kills per combat sortie. Nevertheless, airpower involves more than merely attacking and destroying enemy targets. It involves knowing what to hit and where to find it. On one hand, it is almost a cliché to say that airpower can kill anything it can see, identify, and engage. On the other hand, it is less widely appreciated that it can kill only what it can see, identify, and engage. Airpower and intelligence are opposite sides of the same coin. If the latter fails, the former is likely to fail as well. For that reason, accurate, timely, and comprehensive information on enemy assets is not only a crucial enabler but also an indispensable precondition for success.

Fourth, properly understood, airpower is not the province of one Service alone. It embraces not just aircraft and other combat capabilities of the Air Force, but also the aviation assets of the Navy and Marine Corps, along with Army attack helicopters and surveillance aircraft. Although the Air Force is the only Service that can provide full-spectrum airpower in all mission areas, recognition and acceptance of the fact that air warfare is an activity in which all four Services have important roles to play is a necessary first step toward a proper understanding and assimilation of the changed role of airpower in modern warfare.

As evidenced by successful U.S. combat operations against conventionally equipped forces since the Gulf War of 1991, airpower has become a strategic force. The effectiveness of earlier air offensives was limited on the operational and strategic levels because it simply took too many aircraft and too high a loss rate to achieve too few results. Today, airpower can make its presence felt quickly. Its superior power can affect an enemy from the outset of battle and the subsequent course of a joint campaign. Of course, all military force elements have gained the opportunity in principle to achieve such outcomes with new technologies and concepts of operations. American airpower is distinctive in that it has pulled well ahead of surface forces, both land and maritime, in its capacity relative to our enemies. This progress is attributable not only to stealth, precision, and information dominance, but also to the abiding characteristics of speed, range, and flexibility. Current and emerging air employment options offer theater commanders the possibility of engaging and neutralizing enemy forces from standoff ranges with virtual impunity, thereby reducing the threat to U.S. troops who otherwise might have to directly engage the enemy and risk sustaining high casualties.

It is fundamentally wrong to assume that airpower can win conflicts without ground and naval involvement. Yet although success in major wars will continue to require integrated participation by all forces, current air warfare capabilities promise to allow joint force commanders to conduct operations more quickly and efficiently than ever before. One can argue that air assets of all the Services have the potential to seriously degrade fielded enemy forces of all kinds, thus enabling other force elements to achieve objectives in combat with a minimum of pain, effort, and cost.

Perhaps the greatest payoff in transforming American airpower since the mid-1980s has been the increase in situational awareness of friendly forces while denying that capacity to the enemy. That information advantage entails breakthroughs in targeting capabilities and creates a powerful force multiplier in concert with high-accuracy attack systems. Indeed, the area of sensor fusion is arguably more pivotal than any other technology development in the air warfare arena because it is the precondition for extracting the fullest value from new imposition options.

A second major payoff afforded by recent improvements in airpower is the potential that it holds for situational control from the outset of combat, such that the first blow can often predetermine the subsequent course and outcome of a major war. Airpower, at least in principle, permits the attainment of strategic objectives through simultaneous rather than sequential means of plodding from tactical through operational to strategic levels with an exorbitant cost in lives and national treasure. This differs from what airpower classicists such as Giulio Douhet and his followers envisaged. America today has the ability with airpower to cause early destruction or neutralization of enemy war-making potential. However, critical targets are no longer leadership, infrastructure, economic potential, and other objectives listed by the proponents of strategic bombardment. Instead, targets embrace key assets that enable enemy forces in the field to organize their actions. With the recent advent of offensive cyberspace warfare, the initial attack may even be surreptitious.

Finally, the transformation of airpower has enabled U.S. forces to maintain constant pressure on the enemy from a safe distance, increase the number of kills per sortie, selectively target with near-zero unintended damage, substantially reduce reaction

time, and cause a complete shutdown of the ability of the enemy to control its forces. While these and other payoffs are not all-purpose substitutes for a balanced force able to operate effectively in all mediums of warfare, they allow joint force commanders to rely on airpower to conduct deep battle for the greater extent of a joint campaign. This foreshadows an end to the need for friendly armies to plan on conducting early close-maneuver ground combat as standard practice.

In addition to its effective performance in higher intensity combat involvements since 1991, the airpower of all the Services has been increasingly critical for counterinsurgency operations in Iraq and Afghanistan. Although kinetic capabilities in irregular conflicts have proven less applicable than conventional warfare such as Operation *Desert Storm* or the 3-week high intensity fighting that ended the Iraqi regime, the achievements by coalition assets in Southwest Asia have disabused those people of the notion that airpower in counterinsurgencies is rarely presented with lucrative targets. On the contrary, experience bears out the proposition in the Air Force counterinsurgency manual that airpower can be effectively leveraged in irregular warfare, notwithstanding the fact that such conflicts are overwhelmingly ground-centric in nature.

Airpower has several advantages in counterinsurgency warfare. First, it offers mobility and air dominance without which nothing else is possible. Moreover, its unique advantages in speed and range enable it to span large areas with a rapid-response capability while allowing coalition and indigenous ground forces to focus their efforts wherever needed. In addition, with theater-wide situational awareness, the air and space assets of joint force commanders can monitor ground operations for emerging threats in one region, bring firepower to bear in another, and provide critical border security in yet another. As for other advantages, air and space assets can disrupt insurgent's freedom of movement and ability to mass forces, and also prevent an irregular conflict from spreading to conventional fighting. They also can geolocate, fix, and target insurgents and terrorists as well as provide prompt on-call medical evacuation of wounded to rear-area facilities. In addition, airpower affords minimal intrusiveness and makes a small footprint in other nations. Much activity of airpower occurs outside the range of combatants on the ground. Yet it proves increasingly pivotal in shaping the outcome of joint counterinsurgency operations.

Perhaps the most innovative use of airpower in counterinsurgencies involves nontraditional intelligence, surveillance, and reconnaissance (NTISR), which currently is being performed by coalition fighters over Iraq and Afghanistan. NTISR assets are combat aircraft equipped with electro-optical and infrared sensors in their onboard targeting pods, the main purpose of which is not intelligence collection but strike support. Such aircraft are being increasingly and routinely used to fill the gaps in existing ISR coverage. Their targeting pods allow fighter pilots to provide real-time situational updates to friendly troops in contact with enemy forces, often in conjunction with Predator unmanned surveillance aircraft operations. This development has greatly improved the ability of coalition ground forces to locate and engage nearby insurgents.

Despite airpower enhancements in developed countries, including potential competitors such as Russia and China, America remains indisputably on the cutting-edge of technological innovations in the field of military aviation. Only the United States possesses high-end stealth capabilities such as found in B–2 and F–22 aircraft. Moreover, there is a substantial gap between U.S. aerial combat assets and those of other nations in size, technical capability, extent of reach, sustainability, and breadth of operational and support services. Among the air forces of the world, only the United States maintains full-spectrum land- and seabased strike assets, intercontinental-range bombers, and supporting tanker, airlift, and space surveillance and targeting adjuncts, which offer the ability to engage in global power projection and all-weather precision attack. This description in no way demeans the air arms of allied and friendly nations around the world. Rather, it merely acknowledges the advantages that American airpower offers theater commanders. Most countries are likely to use their air arms only as partners in a U.S.-led coalition. With the exception of the Israeli use but inconclusive effect of airpower against Hizballah in 2006, only America has demonstrated the capacity to organize and conduct a full-scale air campaign in support of joint and combined operations. **gsa**

NOTES

[1] *The National Defense Strategy of the United States of America* (Washington, DC: Department of Defense, March 2005), 4.

[2] Michael Evans, "From Kadesh to Kandahar: Military Theory and the Future of War," *Naval War College Review*, Summer 2003, 136.

[3] Colin S. Gray, *Another Bloody Century: Future Warfare* (London: Weidenfeld and Nicolson, 2006).

[4] John Arquilla, "The End of War as We Knew It: Insurgency, Counterinsurgency and Lessons from the Forgotten History of Early Terror Networks," *Third World Quarterly*, March 2007, 369.

[5] David Sharp, "CNO: 313-ship fleet represents a minimum," Associated Press, January 8, 2008.

[6] Eric J. Labs, "Current and Projected Navy Shipbuilding Programs," testimony before the Subcommittee on Seapower and Expeditionary Forces, Committee on Armed Services, U.S. House of Representatives, March 14, 2008.

[7] James T. Conway, Gary Roughead, and Thad W. Allen, *A Cooperative Strategy for 21st Century Seapower*, October 2007.

Contributors

Dr. Thomas X. Hammes (Chapter Editor) served 30 years in the U.S. Marine Corps, including duty in Somalia and Iraq. He is the author of *The Sling and the Stone* (Zenith Press, 2004).

Colonel Joseph J. Collins, USA (Ret.), teaches strategy at the National War College. From 2001 to 2004, he was Deputy Assistant Secretary of Defense for Stability Operations.

Dr. Antulio J. Echevarria II is Director of Research at the U.S. Army War College. He is author of *After Clausewitz* (University Press of Kansas, 2000), *Imagining Future War* (Praeger, 2006), and *Clausewitz and Contemporary War* (Oxford University, 2007).

Lieutenant Colonel Frank G. Hoffman, USMCR (Ret.), is a Research Fellow in the Center for Emerging Threats and Opportunities at the Marine Corps Combat Development Command.

Dr. Benjamin S. Lambeth is a Senior Research Associate at the RAND Corporation. A long-time specialist in air power and international security, who earned his doctorate at Harvard University, he has flown or flown in more than 40 different types of combat aircraft with the U.S. Air Force, Navy, Marine Corps, and eight foreign air arms. He is author of *The Transformation of American Air Power* (Cornell University Press, 2000).

Professor Geoffrey Till is Director of the Corbett Centre for Maritime Policy Studies at King's College London but is based at the United Kingdom Defence Academy. His latest work on maritime strategy is *Seapower: A Guide for the 21st Century* (Routledge, 2009).

Chapter 8

The Proliferation of Weapons of Mass Destruction

Problems of WMD Proliferation

Our worst fears regarding the proliferation and use of weapons of mass destruction (WMD) have not been realized to date, but important trends bearing on nuclear, biological, and chemical weapons have made it increasingly possible that they will be.

WMD Use

The absence of catastrophic WMD use is the most positive WMD trend of the last decade. No nuclear weapons were detonated except for test purposes. As disruptive and costly as the 2001 anthrax letters incident proved, only 5 people are known to have died and 22 to have sustained injury as a result of those letters. Terrorist use of chlorine gas in conjunction with high explosive attacks in Iraq in 2006 had little impact. A radioactive isotope, polonium, was used to assassinate Alexander Litvinenko in 2007.

Why there has not been catastrophic (or much of any) WMD use is unclear, particularly given how easy it would be for terrorist entities that have expressed interest in acquiring and utilizing such weapons to obtain some forms of WMD. The reasons probably reflect some combination of deterrence, offense, defense and interdiction, and technical obstacles. Sources of deterrence include the threat of retaliation, particularly against states, given the explicit U.S. threat of an "overwhelming response" to WMD use against it and its allies; fear of failure, given strengthened homeland security and force

Iranian Shahab-3 missile, allegedly capable of carrying a nuclear warhead and reaching Europe, Israel, and U.S. forces in the Middle East, displayed in Tehran

protection measures; and fear of alienating core constituencies, given the criticism increasingly directed against al Qaeda within the Islamic world for its violence against Muslims. The U.S.-led war on terror likely has denied al Qaeda and its co-travelers the time and space they need to develop WMD. And while some forms of WMD currently are accessible to terrorists, they may consider more familiar and more easily acquired high explosives sufficient or preferable for their purposes.

Nuclear Proliferation

WMD proliferation developments over the last decade have been mixed. There is little information available about actual terrorist development or acquisition of WMD. On the state side, Iraq and Libya shed their WMD programs or legacies as well as their rogue state status. India and Pakistan emerged from U.S. sanctions imposed after their 1998 nuclear tests. This reflected in part those states' geopolitical importance in the post-9/11 international security environment, and in part efforts or assurances they made to contain their nuclear rivalry with one another and secure their nuclear capabilities. The recent U.S.-India agreement on civil nuclear cooperation[1] was approved by the U.S. Senate in October 2008 and signed into law by President George W. Bush. The agreement, signed by Indian External Affairs Minister Pranab Mukherjee and his counterpart Secretary of State Condoleezza Rice, represents an important effort to bring into the broader nuclear nonproliferation regime a nuclear weapons state not recognized as such under the Nuclear Nonproliferation Treaty (NPT).

In April 2003, North Korea became the first state ever to withdraw from the NPT (joining at least India and Pakistan as nonmembers), asserted its possession of nuclear weapons in early 2005, and tested a nuclear device in October 2006. More recently, North Korea took significant initial steps toward implementing an agreement under the auspices of the Six Party Talks to abandon its nuclear weapons program in return for specified economic and political concessions. In September 2008, however, North Korea moved to restart its Yongbyon nuclear facilities in protest over the Bush administration's failure to remove North Korea from its terrorism blacklist, as was promised in the earlier agreement. While the Bush administration subsequently fulfilled that promise in October 2008, Pyongyang moved ahead with a test launch of a ballistic missile on April 5, 2009, subsequently declared that it had restarted

its nuclear weapons development program, asked International Atomic Energy Agency inspectors to leave the country in mid-April, and exploded another nuclear device in May. Thus, the path ahead for North Korea's denuclearization remains long and the outcome more uncertain than ever.

Iran's covert development of uranium enrichment and other nuclear weapons–relevant capabilities was exposed, at least to the general public, in 2003. Iran has defied international efforts, including sanctions imposed through United Nations Security Council resolutions, to halt its uranium enrichment activities and demonstrated the peaceful nature of its nuclear program. Although a November 2007 U.S. National Intelligence Estimate assessed that Iran had, in 2003, suspended those aspects of its nuclear program directly related to weaponization,[2] the United States and its major European allies, among others, remain concerned that the continuing expansion of Iran's uranium enrichment capability is removing the greatest obstacle to its ability to develop nuclear weapons.

Syria more recently appeared on the nuclear stage. In September 2007, Israel bombed a site in Syria that U.S. Government officials and outside analysts contend was a nuclear reactor nearing completion, built covertly and with North Korean assistance. Syria denies the nuclear nature of the site, but it moved quickly after the Israeli bombing to eliminate traces of the bombed structure.[3]

North Korea's and Iran's demonstrated or suspected pursuit of nuclear weapons, and perhaps also Syria's, could set the stage for another round of nuclear proliferation. Following North Korea's 2006 nuclear test, prominent individuals in Japan and South Korea called for their nations to reconsider their non-nuclear weapon status,[4] although both nations' governments reaffirmed their longstanding policy of not pursuing such weapons, and the United States reiterated its extended nuclear deterrence commitments to these allies.[5] While any additional defections from the nuclear nonproliferation regime could cause more states to reconsider their nuclear status, Japan's defection would be disproportionately significant as it is one of the most prominent proponents of that regime and claims exceptional moral authority as the only country to have suffered nuclear attack.

Iran's apparent pursuit of a nuclear weapons capability likely is a significant factor in the recent dramatic expansion in the number of nations in its region expressing interest in establishing civilian nuclear programs. Of the nearly 30 nations currently interested in joining the more than 30 that already operate nuclear reactors, 13 are Arab or border Iran.[6] Some of these 14 nations perceive Iran as a security threat that is exacerbated by its nuclear program. Others may feel less directly threatened by Iran, but could feel their security threatened or their regional leadership positions challenged if other regional states acquired nuclear weapons in response to Iran's nuclear program.

By expressing interest in establishing civilian nuclear programs, at least some of these states are signaling to Iran, their neighbors, and the United States that they are not prepared to cede the nuclear option to Iran or others in their region. They thereby may hope to dissuade Iran or other regional states from pursuing nuclear weapons programs and/or to motivate the United States and other international actors to do more to stop Iran's program or otherwise address their security concerns. To the extent that they act on their interest in civilian nuclear energy, they can acquire expertise and infrastructure useful to a potential nuclear weapons development effort. While technologies exist that would allow these countries access to nuclear power without leading to a weapons capability, if any of these countries decide to develop their own capacity to enrich uranium and/or reprocess spent reactor fuel, they could pose a serious proliferation risk.[7]

The prospects for a new round of nuclear weapons proliferation will be significantly influenced by the extent to which the United States and the larger international community can contain the regional proliferation impulses fueled by North Korea's, Iran's, and Syria's demonstrated or suspected nuclear weapons programs.

Chemical and Biological Proliferation

In contrast to the nuclear efforts of North Korea, Iran, and Syria, no states are newly pursuing, or suspected of pursuing, in an overt or exposed manner, chemical or biological weapons. This probably reflects in part the fact that chemical and biological weapons programs are comprehensively prohibited by international conventions, to which almost all nations are signatories.[8] Membership, of course, does not necessarily constitute compliance. The United States has expressed concerns about a number of parties' compliance with these conventions, among them Russia and China.[9] Noncompliance is hard to detect and harder to prove, however, because chemical and biological weapons programs can be concealed within dual-use facilities and activities. Moreover, the Biological and Toxin Weapons Convention has no enforcement mechanism, and no challenge inspections have been conducted

Army Chief of Staff General George W. Casey, Jr., speaks during CBRNE incidents consequence management response force exercise

under the Chemical Weapons Convention's enforcement mechanism.

Most concerns about chemical and biological weapons proliferation center on the spread of scientific/technological and industrial capacity. Chemical manufacturing has globalized. Production no longer is dominated by a few, mainly Western, multinational companies, but now occurs in many more facilities spread over many more countries. This means that more people will be involved in chemical technology and manufacture. Growth has been particularly pronounced in Asia. Production facilities also are getting smaller and utilizing new technology: individual plants used to focus on the bulk production of just a few chemicals, while modern plants can economically produce a wide range. Furthermore, it may be harder to detect illicit activity in smaller plants that are utilizing new technology.[10] Such developments could facilitate chemical weapons proliferation.

New tools, including robotics, micro reactors, and ever more powerful computing capabilities, have dramatically increased the number of new compounds that can be synthesized, and the rate at which they can be synthesized and screened. Commercial entities are creating large libraries of new chemical compounds, some of which may be highly toxic and useful for weapons.[11] Nanotechnology is another rapidly developing area that could have important implications for chemical warfare, particularly for the identification and development of new or improved dissemination techniques. Ongoing work to use nanotechnology to improve the delivery of drugs for therapeutic purposes is one possible pathway.[12] There is an increasing convergence of chemistry and biology as biological and other scientific disciplines are increasingly being applied to the search for new chemical compounds with particular effects on biological systems.[13]

The rapid pace of development in the biological sciences and biotechnology is making the expertise and technology to produce biological weapons more accessible, and also may be enabling new types of such weapons. Organisms are available throughout the world. Most of the requisite expertise and equipment for biological weapons is dual-use, and much dual-use equipment is available for the production, processing, and dissemination of biological agents. The commercialization of bioreactors has made it easier to produce agents. Commercial technologies like agricultural sprayers, dry agent production techniques, and, more recently, microencapsulation, could facilitate agent dissemination, which had always been one of the chief obstacles in weaponization.

Revolutionary insights in biology are lowering the educational threshold needed to produce a pathogen. The diffusion of advanced techniques in the biological sciences has made routine what was once advanced science, just as the commercialization of advanced biotechnology has made common what was once a sophisticated capability. The number of recorded genetic sequences has increased dramatically. New classes of infectious agents have emerged, including prions, viroids, and satellite viruses/nucleic acids. The relatively new fields of synthetic biology and bioengineering already have enabled scientists to create the polio virus from scratch, and perhaps, in the not-so-distant future, will enable the "from-scratch" creation of more pathogenic viruses, like smallpox (which no longer exists in nature), as well as the engineering of new organisms, some of which may prove conducive to weaponization.

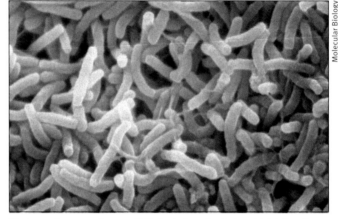
Molecular Biology

Electron microscope image of *Vibrio cholerae* bacteria, which infect the digestive system

Conclusions Regarding Proliferation

We still do not fully understand how the rapid advances in biological and chemical science and technology will change the landscape for biological and chemical weapons. These emerging developments are commercially driven and promise to yield many beneficial products for mankind. Yet like almost all scientific and technological progress, the potential to do good carries with it the potential to do harm, and where such potential exists, bad actors will endeavor to exploit it. The bad actors able to exploit the most technologically sophisticated developments first most likely will be states with offensive biological and/or chemical weapons programs, but commercialization and globalization already have made the catastrophic use of biological and chemical weapons potentially accessible to terrorists. Rapid advances in science and technology likely will accord a continuing advantage to offense over defense, as defensive responses lag behind the development of new forms of attack. As technical barriers decline, adversary intent will become an ever more important part of the biological and chemical threat equation.

These trends toward a more WMD-capable world represent a serious threat to the United States and the international community because they give a much broader range of actors, state and nonstate, a capacity to inflict destruction and disruption that historically was available only to a few large and powerful states. As dangerous as powerful states have proven over the ages, they at least constituted a narrower focus for intelligence, diplomacy, and defense. Even the effectiveness of a Cold War–type nuclear deterrence becomes less certain as the number and nature of WMD-capable adversaries and rivals multiply, and particularly as terrorists acquire such catastrophic weapons.

International Net Assessment for the Second Nuclear Age

Strategic nuclear deterrence is becoming far more complex than in the "first" age. During the Cold War, the United States and its allies developed elaborate nuclear deterrence doctrines against a Soviet regime that turned out to be essentially conservative, stable, and unlikely to disrupt the status quo. After a short interlude in the 1990s, however, the world entered what Colin Gray has called "the second nuclear age," characterized by the original nuclear powers plus emerging states that either now have, or likely soon will have, nuclear weapons. Not all of them are stable, which poses serious questions for allied policymakers regarding how they will respond to proliferated nuclear threats, particularly with regard to deterrence strategies.

In addition to the increasing number of nuclear powers, technological developments have added unprecedented wrinkles to deterrence strategies. Offensive systems are more accurate, harder to find, and more mobile; some, including missiles that can reach from Esfahan to Berlin, are also more available on the global weapons market. Longer range missiles are able to span half the globe or more. Antimissile defenses at the mid- and long-range level did not exist in the past, and now add complexity to deterrence calculations on both sides of the Atlantic and the Pacific. Japan, for instance, is adding modern-

AP Images (Joerg Sarbach)

Federal Agency for Radiation Protection investigator removes computer disk from home in Haselau, Germany, where traces of radiation were found linked to poisoning of former Russian spy Alexander Litvinenko

ized antimissile-capable Aegis systems to its fleet. Additionally, the prospect that nonstate entities like terrorist groups could obtain nuclear weaponry casts doubt on the future reliability of deterrence strategies as they are presently understood.

The U.S. Department of Defense (DOD) defines deterrence as "the prevention from action by fear of the consequences. Deterrence is a state of mind brought about by a credible threat of unacceptable counteraction."[14] Fundamentally, though, "deterrence" is a difficult concept to prove, based as it is on causing something not to happen. Used against a more traditional nation-state with all the equities and responsibilities of statehood, strategies of dissuasion and deterrence are interwoven with traditional mechanisms used to maintain international stability, such as negotiations, treaties, arms control agreements, and other diplomatic tools. The same is not necessarily the case, though, when opaque outlier states like North Korea gain nuclear weapons. States with authoritarian governments and tendencies toward bellicose behavior may be less likely to enter into stable relationships than states with a history of more responsible behavior. Along with arms control agreements, international inspection regimes, and other diplomatic and military strategies designed to maintain a stable international system, deterrence may have little appeal to the leaders of North Korea, Iran, or a state-sponsored terrorist group with access to nuclear weapons. The nuclear world has changed to such an extent that creating credible "second age" nuclear strategies of deterrence and use is not simply the extension of previous experiences in statecraft, but a new challenge entirely.

Net Assessment

If nations are to work together to maintain stable nuclear weapons strategies in a proliferating world, they must establish some mechanism to understand and react appropriately to potentially hostile nuclear powers whose cultural and operational frames of reference for nuclear weapons may be far different from those in the West.[15] The predominant view that nuclear weapons are not "just a bigger bullet" is based on decades of increasingly sophisticated theorizing on the effects of nuclear persuasion, coercion, or deterrence. As a consequence, policy planners have long believed that nuclear forces serve primarily political functions. The United States and allies like the North Atlantic Treaty Organization (NATO), Japan, South Korea, and perhaps Israel are mostly concerned with the prevention of nuclear use,

or wielding successfully the influence of the nuclear threat, rather than actual employment.

From that point of view, transparency concerning nuclear arsenals, aims, and capabilities is a major step toward deterring nuclear use by unstable regimes, just as clarity regarding capabilities and intentions is fundamental to the two-way dialogue necessary for deterrence policies. At present, though, the United States and its allies have no mechanism to measure accurately the nuclear balance between their own capabilities and those of potential opponents, a fundamental requirement for clarity on both sides of a deterrence dialogue. Given the growing complexity of the strategic environment, the need for a process that pulls together allies in this most complicated arena, and the vital necessity for universal transparency regarding nuclear deterrent policies, the United States should propose and lead the development of a common method to assess the net strengths of allies against potential threats as they relate to nuclear deterrent policies.

Of course this would not be the first time the United States has led in the formulation of nuclear deterrent policies. During the Cold War, U.S.-led nuclear policy development was the centerpiece of NATO defense planning. To develop valid deterrence strategies, in the early 1970s, DOD established the Office of Net Assessment, whose purpose was to make an accurate assessment of the capabilities and intentions of the Soviet threat as it measured up against NATO. Since net assessment is fundamentally the business of power balances, the term came to mean a process by which "Blue" (U.S. and NATO) and "Red" (Soviet and Warsaw Pact) forces could be weighed, wargamed, and studied, so policymakers could come to appropriate conclusions about their relative strengths. In the words of Paul Bracken, "Net assessment emphasizes that strategic interactions are shaped by the complex sprawling organizations that break complex problems into smaller ones. . . . Net assessment, thus, had its origins in the need to integrate Blue and Red strategy in a single place. This is where the term 'net' came from.[16]

So long as net assessment dealt with the roughly symmetrical balance between two peer adversaries, it could at least rely on roughly understood boundaries and the experience that came from decades of focusing on a single threat. Using this tool, over time the United States and its allies built a highly proficient nuclear deterrent subculture within the military and certain civilian agencies that culminated in the Single Integrated Operations Plan (SIOP), a combined nuclear war plan that took priority over all other allied military operational planning; when SIOP was invoked, the bottom line was nuclear war and the survival of the West. Of course, everything else took a back seat.

With the collapse of the Soviet Union in 1991, the United States and its allies no longer focused on nuclear strategies with the same determination that had produced NATO nuclear strategy and the SIOP during the Cold War.[17] U.S. "strategic" intelligence was reoriented from nuclear threats to the support of operational forces, particularly during Operation *Desert Storm* in 1991 and, after 9/11, in Afghanistan and Iraq. Strategic intelligence staffs overall were cut; many of the intelligence analysts who spent their careers focused on Soviet nuclear missile sites were reassigned to other missions or retired. But with the emergence of potentially hostile nuclear capable states that are secretive by nature and often antagonistic to the West, there is a renewed need for expert strategic analysis and a realistic understanding of nuclear power balances. (Whether resources have followed the need remains an open question.) Shifts in allied policies and intra-alliance balances since the 1990s indicate a need to refocus and reenergize allied nuclear policy development; in particular, this means agreeing on common net assessments of potentially hostile nuclear powers. Common net assessments are essential for a unified approach to deterring nuclear capable rogue states.

Since "deterrence" works best when accurately focused on the motives and objectives of potential foes, the re-invention and internationalization of net assessment requires the development of new methods of analysis to take into account the more varied cultural and political motives of newly nuclear states. All states, not only our friends but also potentially hostile closed states like North Korea or Iran, have unique decisionmaking traditions and processes. Discerning the motives and common ground among friends is tough enough; understanding the hidden political and military milieu of potential adversaries is far harder. Future nuclear deterrent strategies must be developed in a cooperative, transparent, and joint environment, with broad political and military engagement among allies and partners. By the same token, each potential nuclear opponent will likewise require nuanced, tailored strategies appropriate to the specific circumstances. This is a call for highly detailed and accurate intelligence and analysis. As nuclear threats proliferate, allied intelligence agencies must return to Cold War levels of intensity to find

out what makes certain ruling cliques or cadres tick, because what dissuades or deters one may be a spur to action for another.

Not all actors in international politics calculate utility in making decisions in the same way. Differences in values, culture, attitudes toward risk-taking, and so on vary greatly. There is no substitute for knowledge of the adversary's mindset and behavioral style, and this is often difficult to obtain or apply correctly in assessing intentions or predicting responses.[18]

Developing the ability to lead international second-age net assessments of emerging and existing nuclear threats should be a top priority for the United States, as a method to underpin successful future strategies of deterrence, as a way to reconcentrate U.S. intelligence and operational expertise on serious threats, and as a process to foster cooperative and sustainable international responses to nuclear proliferation.

Building the Structure

Any net assessment process requires focus and boundaries to keep it manageable. Commonly, these boundaries are set by mutually agreed conflict scenarios that include both military and political analyses. During the Cold War, the well-understood nuclear arsenals of the West on one hand and the Soviet Union on the other set the boundaries of Cold War nuclear net assessment. There were only two viable scenarios: one in which war began by miscalculation, and one in which the Soviet Union attacked Western Europe and the United States. Though our knowledge of Soviet motives and intentions was never as good as we wished, certain assumptions and conclusions could be drawn by U.S. and allied policymakers.[19] In either case, the overarching scenario became all-out nuclear exchange, in which first- and second-strike capabilities could be analyzed and described to senior policymakers.

Second-age nuclear net assessment, though, must deal with more complex possibilities. A three-tiered system can be developed to group systematically the weapons, command and control, and policymaking structures of potential adversaries. The first, of course, comprises the "traditional" nuclear powers of Russia and China, the former of which maintains a substantial nuclear arsenal. Both potential adversaries are signatories to the Nuclear Nonproliferation Treaty, and both are veterans of the decades-long series of negotiations and agreements to limit the spread of nuclear weapons and discourage their use.

Although neither state can be taken for granted, tensions between the two and the United States do not now rise to the level of concern about potential nuclear war.

The second tier may be more worrisome. India tested in 1974, but Pakistan and North Korea are more recently declared nuclear states, and Iran may well become a nuclear power within a decade. While Israel, India, and Pakistan are aligned with the United States, North Korea is a decidedly less friendly state with an opaque if uncertain leadership that periodically threatens Japan and South Korea. Additionally, North Korea is suspected of exporting nuclear weapons technology, most recently to Syria.[20] Iran could become a nuclear power within the decade.[21] Its leadership varies from the pragmatic to the zealous, though over decades it has been hostile to the West in general and the United States in particular.

Since the industrial capacity required to produce nuclear weapons can be built only by nation-states, access by nonstate groups to nuclear weapons can come either through sponsorship by a nuclear state or by the theft of sufficient fissile materiel to build a crude weapon. Tier three is therefore occupied by nonstate terror groups that either have potential nuclear state sponsors, and thus would be susceptible to pressure or control from their sponsor, or can manage on their own to obtain sufficient nuclear materials to produce their own weapon. Hizballah is potentially an example of the former, because it receives support from Iran. Al Qaeda is the unassociated terror group that is most likely to be seeking stolen nuclear materials.

Net assessment of these third-tier threats differs from those of state actors because the weapons balance between the United States and the threat—the net in net assessment—is stated in different terms, and nuclear net assessment of nonstate entities relies more on highly discriminating intelligence regarding specific groups than generalized assumptions about terrorists. Each terrorist group and splinter group has distinguishing characteristics that might provide some leverage for dissuasion or deterrence. In his book, *On Nuclear Terrorism*, Michael Levi says:

Nuclear experts often hold intuitive assumptions about terrorism that are not borne out in the study of actual terrorist groups. At the same time, it is impossible to adopt traditional counterterrorism strategies to the nuclear program without accounting for the special properties of nuclear weapons. Thus, any assessment should interweave expertise on nuclear weapons with expertise on terrorism, something that has not always occurred in past analysis.[22]

Scenarios play a vital role in "bounding" a nuclear net assessment, which is not simply a catalog of the other side's nuclear arsenals and governing systems, but a comparative analysis of the two sides' total capabilities with regard to potential nuclear conflict. An initial key consideration is what scenario the assessment should use, since scenarios provide the essential context for any analysis. Just as the East-West standoff was couched in terms of aggression by the Soviet Union against NATO, assessment of other potential nuclear threats must be undertaken within a scenario of the most likely nuclear conflict—for example, a North Korean attack on the South. Military experts then must spin away portions of the conflict that do not affect nuclear outcomes.[23] Assumptions on Red nuclear doctrine and a thorough knowledge of Red's arsenals and the backgrounds and predilections of Red's leadership are prerequisites, since some battlefield reverses might trigger Red nuclear responses.

Wargame results of nuclear effects—missile attacks and defenses, weapons effects, and the like—provide "hard" data based on both sides' weapons characteristics, missile flight data and dispositions, and so on. "Soft" data on policy, leadership, and intentions, derived from intelligence sources, is also critical—and in some ways more critical than the outcomes of weapons use. The data are arrayed in a four-way analysis that examines the scenario from four perspectives:

Blue against Red and Red against Blue can be standard gaming that pits the opposing sides against one another in the chosen scenario. For realism, all participants in a Blue-Red conflict must participate at some level; for example, in a North Korean scenario, major Blue players would be the United States, Japan, and South Korea, but a host of other Blue actors would have equities in the conflict and should be represented; other Asian states, U.S. allies, and the United Nations come to mind. Within the U.S. Blue team will be players representing the appropriate U.S. combatant and allied commands. Red would be a tougher challenge, because although North Korea has no formal allies, other states might be presumed to be friendly and provide intelligence or other aid. Games are conducted in order to determine likely outcomes should deterrence fail, and are assessed from both the Blue and the Red perspective. Both "hard" and "soft" assessments are made during the game, and planners may find it necessary to execute more than one game.[24]

Blue against Blue and Red against Red are seminar and conference-style debates conducted after the wargames, and are designed to examine fundamental assumptions or reservations that Blue or Red hold about themselves but that may not be true. For example, how strongly does the North Korean government control its army? Would it actually devolve to ground commanders the authority needed to fight a modern war? What likely fissures would the threat of nuclear war open within the North Korean leadership? Are Blue missile defenses, based both in the immediate theater and around the world, really able to defeat certain modern missiles? Are allies sufficiently confident in joint defensive systems that they would risk the security of their countries?

Following conclusions taken from the Blue and Red analyses, an inclusive assessment should be possible to address the balance of nuclear forces between Blue and Red in a specific theater—in this case, Northeast Asia—and those consequential variables that might tip a balance decisively one way or another. The nuclear net assessment does not set policy, but rather offers up a picture of the balance of forces and possible outcomes, and most important, an understanding of Red's leadership, its motives and perspectives on nuclear use, and how it potentially would react in the most likely conflict scenario. An internationally derived nuclear net assessment would also encourage dialogue and intelligence-sharing among allies, and substantially support the development of common views on specific nuclear states and issues.

This process applies as well to a net assessment of nuclear terrorism, though some distinctions must be made between third-tier terrorists. Nuclear forensics, a process that makes possible the identification of the origins of nuclear material, could play a powerful role in detecting and thus deterring those states willing to turn over nuclear materials to nonstate groups. In any case, all terrorist organizations have motives, hierarchies, cultures, and internal fissures that can be discerned in a "Red against Red" analysis, and thus can be balanced against Blue capabilities and doctrines. The purpose of nuclear net assessment is to find power balances; therefore, any splits and contradictions in terrorist leadership or organizational failures that are highlighted—all logical outcomes of the assessment process—and a raised consensus among members of the Blue team would be advantageous to the development of common goals for countering nuclear terrorism. Michael Levi points out that states can play a role in discouraging nuclear terrorism:

U.S. Coast Guard (Cory J. Mendenhall)

Border Enforcement Security Task Force boarding team conducts security boarding on tanker off Long Beach, California, to enforce maritime laws and combat smuggling in ports

If states can play an important role in facilitating nuclear terrorism beyond directly transferring nuclear materials to terrorists, targeting such relationships could undermine nuclear terrorism in a variety of ways. In the face of potential cooperation between states and terrorists, diplomacy might be used to break state-terrorist relationships, or at least to convince states that supporting nuclear plots might be unwise.[25]

An allied program to develop shared nuclear net assessments would be most likely to succeed initially if it were begun within a standing treaty organization like NATO, where defense staffs and officials have over time forged the intelligence-sharing and bureaucratic ties necessary for a robust assessment process. The United States should lead, principally because it commands many of the new technologies, such as missile defenses. This project would require the development of consensus positions on intelligence, likely Red motives and alliance responses, as well as a vetting process at lower levels to ensure that military scenario development—the excruciatingly detailed description of missile sites, intelligence systems, and command and control systems—precedes and supports the more difficult identification and recruitment of experts in the softer fields of policy and political intelligence, both for Blue and Red. Older hands in the policy and weapons business will find considerable similarity between the present reorientation and deliberation on nuclear threats and SIOP planning decades ago. The primary difference is that the SIOP signified the failure of deterrence, the execution of the unthinkable, while nuclear net assessment will be a building block for a more nuanced nuclear deterrent policy.

An international net assessment program would focus policymakers, intelligence specialists, and military planners on allied nuclear objectives at a time when nuclear weapons appear likely to spread to irresponsible and potentially hostile states. Even if the United States, with its greater resources, agrees to lead an international net assessment program, getting consensus, assembling the right people, and doing the analysis is years away; begun soon, the first net assessment would probably be available about the time Iran fields its first nuclear weapon. But the alternative is worse: deterrent policies developed independently by leading states; little or no inclusive dialogue to develop agreement among allies; and the proliferation of nuclear weapons with no commonly held strategies, or even agreements on what the strategy should be. It is time to begin building the first international nuclear net assessment.

Homeland Security and Defense

The capacity to launch attacks with catastrophic effects, particularly those involving WMD, are no longer marshaled only by states or state-sponsored groups, but also by small, organized terror cells or even lone individuals (such as the 1995 Oklahoma City bombing). From advances in biotechnology and pharmaceuticals to the prevalence of chemical manufacturing and the widespread availability of radiological materials such as Cesium, the threat is increasingly global and dynamic and blurs criminal intent with national security consequences. This makes fashioning an effective response to protect the homeland highly complex.

While new actors and capabilities emerge to pose a different kind of challenge to the homeland, they augment rather than replace more traditional dangers, which did not disappear when new challenges appeared. State-based missile or nuclear weapons development and proliferation continue to menace U.S. and international security. Today's threat continuum ranges from homegrown extremists to global opportunists to criminal networks to pariah states.

This dynamic security environment requires an equally dynamic and vigorous response. Much conceptual confusion, however, continues to plague efforts to effectively combat the danger of catastrophic terrorism. Greater attention must be paid to the development of appropriate responses to a different type of enemy—one that blurs the distinction between crime and terror, and one that can easily exploit traditional divisions between Federal, state, and local governments.

Al Qaeda is one such adversary: its attacks come with little or no warning, entail potentially catastrophic consequences, and have the potential to overwhelm the capabilities of first responders. The 2007 National Intelligence Estimate makes this clear:

We judge the U.S. homeland will face a persistent and evolving terrorist threat over the next three years. . . . Al-Qa'ida is and will remain the most serious terrorist threat to the homeland. . . . . Al-Qa'ida's homeland plotting is likely to continue to focus on prominent political, economic and infrastructure targets, with the goal of producing mass casualties. We assess that Al Qa'ida will continue to try to acquire and employ chemical, biological, radiological or nuclear material in attacks and would not hesitate to use them if it develops what it deems is sufficient capability. The ability to detect broader and more diverse terrorist plotting in this environment will challenge current US defensive efforts and the tools we use to detect and disrupt plots.[26]

Combating this threat requires coordinated procedures and synchronized efforts across the state, local, and Federal levels of U.S. Government. And at each level, particularly the Federal level, departments and agencies charged with law enforcement and national defense must be organized and equipped to act in an integrated and mutually reinforcing manner. Homeland security, conceptually and organizationally, brings together responsibilities and organizations that are spread out across the Federal Government. It attempts, through plans and strategies such as the National Response Framework, to link protection, detection, and response across the state, local, and Federal divide. The objective is to harmonize policies, develop effective capabilities, and deter adversaries. Four homeland security goals identified in the 2007 National Strategy for Homeland Security are to prevent and disrupt terrorist attacks; protect the American people, critical infrastructure, and key resources; respond to and recover from incidents that do occur; and, continue to strengthen the foundation of security to ensure our long-term success.

Who Does What?

In the United States, homeland security is a concerted national effort to prevent terrorist attacks, reduce the vulnerability to terrorism, and minimize the damage of and assist in the recovery from terrorist attacks.[27] The Department of Homeland Security (DHS) has the primary responsibility. Beyond the prevention of terrorism, DHS also has the responsibility to prepare for, respond to, and aid in the recovery from natural and manmade disasters, attacks that involve weapons of mass destruction, and other emergencies.

The Department of Justice enforces the law and defends the interests of the United States according to the law. The Attorney General, as chief law enforcement officer, leads the Nation's law enforcement efforts to detect, prevent, and investigate terrorist activity within the United States.

The Federal Bureau of Investigation (FBI) is the investigative arm of the Justice Department. The FBI protects and defends the United States against terrorist and foreign intelligence threats, upholds and enforces the criminal laws of the country, and provides leadership and criminal justice services to Federal, state, municipal, and international agencies and partners. The FBI is also responsible for crisis management of a terrorist event if it occurs in the homeland.

While homeland security is a national effort that involves various interagency actors such as Homeland Security, Justice, and the FBI, homeland defense is a critical subset of homeland security. Homeland defense is the protection of U.S. sovereignty, territory, the populace, and critical defense infrastructure from external threats and aggression or other threats as directed by the President. DOD serves as the Federal agency with lead responsibility for homeland defense; DOD may execute homeland defense missions alone or with support from other agencies such as DHS.[28]

DOD also supports homeland security by assisting U.S. civil authorities. Homeland defense and civil support operations may occur in parallel and require extensive integration and synchronization. Civil support operations may also shift between missions—for instance, from homeland defense to civil support to homeland security, with the lead depending on the particular circumstances of the situation and desired outcome or mission objectives. In areas of overlapping responsibility, the designation of a Federal agency with lead responsibility may not be predetermined. In time-critical situations, on-scene leaders are empowered to conduct appropriate operations in response to a particular threat.[29] As a result, the role of DOD may not be a fixed one during any particular crisis. Whether leading homeland defense operations against external threats, or supporting homeland security missions and tasks led by the Department of Homeland Security or other designated Federal lead agency, DOD's uniquely trained force and capabilities (including WMD detection, protection, and decontamination assets), coupled with command and control capacity from the tactical to the strategic level, make it an important component in homeland security.

DOD Homeland Defense

Defense of the homeland is DOD's highest priority, with the goal to defeat threats at a safe distance from American soil.[30] Therefore, while the U.S. military's primary focus is on overseas combat operations in furtherance of national defense, DOD does have a role, albeit a primarily supporting one, in domestic homeland security. The traditional limits on DOD's domestic role arise from deep skepticism after the Civil War over military forces acting in a domestic law enforcement capacity, embodied in the Posse Comitatus Act of 1878. In today's threat environment, where surprise is likely and the effects potentially catastrophic, the tradeoff against this prohibition is based on the premise that DOD may have the most ready and effective capabilities, personnel, and command and control for the homeland security mission. These capabilities, some argue, can save time during a response, and saving time may save lives. For example, DOD has a range of unique resources, from chemical, biological, radiological, and nuclear (CBRN) expertise to large-scale logistics execution and management capabilities. The question then becomes how to effectively integrate those unique DOD capabilities with the civilian homeland security response, while respecting the principle of posse comitatus, which says that defense personnel should engage in law enforcement activities only as a last resort.

The Defense Department's concept or philosophy for civil support in any particular case is based on the understanding that civil resources and capabilities will be exhausted before DOD plays a major role in a response. For example, the response to Hurricane Katrina brought into question fundamental assumptions of the role of the Federal Government and the specific role of DOD in supporting civil authorities as they respond to a catastrophic natural disaster. With the Federal response predicated on augmenting state and local civil authorities, it is justifiable to question whether this framework is reasonable and even workable where local and state capacity to respond to an event no longer exists and the social fabric of a large urban area is no longer functioning. Large natural disasters such as hurricanes, pandemics such as an avian influenza outbreak, and CBRN attacks on, say, a state capital, certainly present the prospect of a situation where there was little, if any, remaining civil authority for a Federal response effort to augment. DOD plans call for civil support missions to be limited in duration and scope, and terminate as the crisis abates and civil authority is able to manage the situation effectively. While defense support to civil authorities will be a Total Force effort that utilizes both Active and Reserve elements as needed, the primary reliance for civil support will fall on the Reserve Component. Over time, "the goal is that the capacity of other agencies and state and local governments to respond to domestic incidents will be sufficient to perform their assigned responsibilities with minimal reliance on U.S. military support."[31]

To satisfy the broader homeland defense requirement, DOD established joint doctrine to provide guidance on this role. This doctrine calls for securing the United States from attack through layered "defense-in-depth" that integrates capabilities in the forward regions, the geographic approaches to U.S. territory, and within national borders. For the forward regions, or those areas far outside U.S. territory, the objective is to detect, deter, prevent, and defeat threats to the United States before they can mature to pose a threat to the homeland. For the approaches, the areas reaching from U.S. borders to the forward regions, the objective is to identify, characterize, and defeat threats as far away as possible. And for threats on U.S. soil, DOD must be able to take immediate, decisive action to defend against and defeat threats as they arise.

U.S. Northern Command (USNORTHCOM) has the operational responsibility for the conduct of military operations within the United States, utilizing forces to deter, detect, or defeat an incursion into sovereign territory. The command also maintains the responsibility for civil support activities for most of the United States.[32] USNORTHCOM carries out civil support missions with forces assigned as required from all the armed Services, typically through the creation of a joint task force.

Conclusion Regarding Homeland Security and Defense

Threats to the United States are not static, and responding to them requires flexibility. As traditional threats evolve and new ones emerge, DOD's homeland defense requirements will change and may require new approaches and tools, such as developing a joint command and control element for homeland defense and civil support missions, or a similar capability to manage the consequences of major catastrophic events, be they manmade or natural. Recognizing DOD's unique role in protecting the United States and capitalizing on its unique capabilities will assure U.S. security as the Nation adapts and responds to the emerging threat environment.

Proliferation and the Militarization of Space

Many concerns about WMD proliferation intersect issues related to the increasingly contested domain of space. Security through space and security in space are increasingly important issues. The proliferation of technology to disrupt or destroy satellites and other space assets is proceeding, even as reliance on these systems is growing. Not only are nuclear weapons and deterrent strategies interwoven with space systems, but also asymmetric attacks in space could pose potentially devastating security consequences and create major social and economic disruption.

Background

Since the launch of Sputnik by the Soviet Union in 1957, the uses of space—for economic, military, scientific, mass media, and other socio-cultural purposes—have grown dramatically, as has the number of actors involved with space. Globalization, arguably the defining dynamic of the 21st cen-

tury, is dependent on the space-enabled information networks that have transformed the nature of human and technological interaction. Use of space is no longer just for superpowers. If one includes all parties that use at least some product or service created by activities conducted in space, then space activities directly benefit most people in the developed world and many in the developing world. From mobile telephones, Internet communications, and television to money transfers and automatic teller withdrawals, space-based technologies and services permit people to communicate, companies to do business, civic groups to serve the public, and scientists to conduct research. Much like highways and airways, water lines and electric grids, global utilities such as precision navigation and timing data (provided via satellite free of charge) form an increasingly important part of the global information infrastructures. A truly international space industry has developed and has witnessed the emergence of several international consortia with no readily ascertainable national identity. Revenues for the commercial space sector now exceed $100 billion per year. Today, commercial and even individual customers worldwide can purchase launch services or global imagery and other remote sensing data that were once available only to governments.

As critical as the space-enabled information infrastructure is to continued global economic growth and vitality, the full extent of this dependency on space is not widely understood. And with this dependency comes vulnerability, even if that vulnerability is often shared. Conflict involving threats to space-related assets would have serious effects on information flows vital to the global economy.

The military and national security uses of space have also grown. Intelligence information collected from space platforms has been an essential part of maintaining transparency in the international system, dating back to the "open skies" policy created by the space systems of the United States and the Soviet Union during the Cold War, to verify treaties through "national technical means" and be warned of missile attacks. Today, states use satellites for national security purposes to provide global communications capabilities; conduct photoreconnaissance; collect mapping, charting, geodetic, scientific, and environmental data; and gather information on natural or manmade disasters. This intelligence is essential to all aspects of national defense, from the formulation of policy to the management of crises and conflicts, the conduct of military operations, and the development of needed

Rocket simulating speed and trajectory of North Korean rocket launched from Alaska as target for ground-based interceptor from Vandenberg Air Force Base, California

AP Images (Missile Defense Agency)

capabilities. Space-based capabilities allow military forces to communicate instantaneously, obtain near-real-time information that can be transmitted rapidly from satellite to attack platform, navigate to a conflict area while avoiding hostile defenses along the way, and identify and strike targets from air, land, or sea with precise and devastating effect.

At the beginning of the space age, many space systems and capabilities were specialized to perform one specific function for a single user. Today, many space systems have become dual-use in that they simultaneously support both military and civilian applications. For example, commercial imagery companies now provide a major portion of space imagery used by the U.S. Government, and commercial systems carried over 80 percent of satellite communications traffic during the combat phase of Operation *Iraqi Freedom.*

Moreover, while space may have been perceived as a strategic sanctuary in the past, today it is becoming an increasingly contested military domain like land, sea, or air, where satellites face a variety of threats such as space debris, crowding, jamming, and the diffusion of countersatellite technology to a larger number of actors via dual-use capabilities and dedicated development.

Such capabilities are not just theoretical. China launched a direct-ascent antisatellite (ASAT) weapon on January 11, 2007, which struck a Chinese weather satellite in low Earth orbit. The successful test demonstrates China's ability to threaten a number of satellites in low orbit, which may include those used for reconnaissance, remote sensing, surveillance, electronic surveillance, and meteorology, as well as some civilian satellites with military applications. These satellites and the International Space Station are also at increased, although not significant, risk from the debris cloud created by the Chinese ASAT test. The direct-ascent ASAT appears to be part of a larger Chinese ASAT program that includes ground-based lasers and jamming of satellite signals.[33]

The United States has also demonstrated the ability to destroy satellites. On September 13, 1985, an F–15 fighter aircraft launched a miniature vehicle to destroy a defunct U.S. satellite. On February 21, 2008, the United States used a modified Navy missile (the Standard Missile 3) to shoot down a crippled reconnaissance satellite that was falling out of orbit and threatening to spill its toxic rocket fuel upon reentry.

The "Militarization" of Space

The "militarization" of space is an imprecise phrase. Some would note that space has been militarized for decades, with satellites used for intelligence and ballistic missiles that fly through space. Others think of militarization of space as involving kinetic weapons in space that could destroy either satellites or targets on Earth. Neither is a very enlightening or satisfactory way of looking at the issue.

There are two important military and security aspects for spacefaring nations or other actors to consider: security through space, and security in space.

Security through space implies the use of space assets to enhance the security posture of an actor or set of actors on Earth. Space capabilities may be used by an actor to prevent conflict and ensure stability through either transparency or deterrence. Transparency refers to the ability to "see" capabilities as they develop and events as they unfold. Deterrence could be holstered because space-based reconnaissance provides warning as well as command and control for nuclear forces. Conversely, a nation may use its space assets to enhance its terrestrial combat capability through either force enhancement or force application. Forces could be enhanced by the precision and capability of air, land, and sea forces through positioning, navigation, and timing; command and control; and intelligence, surveillance, and reconnaissance. Force application would result from actors developing ways to apply force directly from space to generate combat effects on the terrestrial battlefield, and from defenses that might be deployed in space to deter and protect against ballistic missile attacks.

Security in space concerns the protection of space assets themselves, whether used for military or civilian purposes. Nations, particularly those that already possess a strategic advantage, will seek to maximize their freedom of action in space. To do so, an actor may seek capabilities in four areas. The first area concerns transparency. Situational awareness is essential to identify potential threats in space. Equally important is the ability to track potential adversaries' ground-based activities as they relate to space. Second, security in space also involves protection. The fragile and vulnerable nature of space assets, particularly commercial and civil devices, suggests that protection measures be considered early in the design cycle of space systems. Military forces may be called upon to protect critical civilian assets. Denial is a third issue, because of the ability to negate an adversary's space capabilities, through such means as

▼ *Continued on p. 179*

Preventing Nuclear Proliferation: An Overview

There is a deep and longstanding worldwide recognition that the proliferation of nuclear weapons is dangerous and must be prevented. The ideal path to nonproliferation is to eliminate the reasons why countries may feel that they need nuclear weapons. Since, amid the world's political complexities, that cannot always be swiftly or dependably achieved, the countries of the world have assembled a substantial structure of more specific instruments. The record of achievement by this structure since the 1968 conclusion of the Nuclear Nonproliferation Treaty (NPT) is, in the round, not discouraging, and claims that the prevention regime now stands on the edge of an abyss are neither well founded nor helpful. There are, however, risks and dangers to be addressed in at least four areas:

- the problems of particular countries
- general weaknesses in the nonproliferation regime itself
- the danger of material diversion and terrorism
- the call for further disarmament by the nuclear-armed states.

Country Problems

The nonproliferation regime faces one definite new breakout (by North Korea) and one potential breakout (by Iran). The United States and others with a stake in the outcome must maintain pressure on North Korea to live up to its agreements and also must keep a close watch on Pyongyang's propensity for pernicious export activity. As long as Japan, in particular, sustains its mature refusal to let this beleaguered minor state provoke it into reversing its nonnuclear policy, a move that would be gravely unsettling region-wide, the North Korea problem is less troubling than that of Iran.

The size, resources, and location of Iran make it a much more important state. There may be no clear agreement among its leadership about ultimate goals, but present actions seem plainly to head toward creating at least a "threshold" capability, from which breakout to a deliverable nuclear weapon (with delivery vehicles already available) could be relatively swift. Even if progress went no further, that would be deeply damaging to the global regime and disruptive to Iran's region. Efforts to avert this outcome, through a combination of incentives and penalties, must continue to command a high priority in the international community. Policy—and public

utterances about it—must, however, recognize an awkward tension. The hard truth is that if Iran is determined to continue down its current path, whatever the cost, it cannot permanently and dependably be prevented, whether by military intervention (which would, at best, carry massive costs for the interveners and their allies) or otherwise. Efforts at prevention must resolutely continue, with no hints of ultimate willingness to acquiesce. But prudent planning should also consider what could be done, if prevention does eventually fail, to ensure both that Iran suffers a lasting penalty and that regional neighbors do not feel compelled to traverse the same road.

A third country-specific issue, albeit one of a very different character, concerns India, a massive democratic state of increasingly positive global weight. Other states must balance their desire to assist in its nuclear energy program to ensure the program's safety and security with the maintenance of an objectively even-handed approach to the operation of the nonproliferation system. This issue interacts with more general questions about the future working of the regime.

General Weaknesses in the Nonproliferation Regime

An array of instruments and institutions that amount to a strong structure of constraint on proliferation has grown up around the cornerstone of the NPT itself—including, for example, the International Atomic Energy Agency (IAEA), the Nuclear Suppliers Group, and the U.S.-led Proliferation Security Initiative. But participation in some of them remains less widespread or energetic than it should be, and at least three specific weaknesses need to be tackled if the regime is going to be more effective.

The first concerns verification of the NPT's constraints. After the 1990–1991 Gulf War unmasked sweeping concealment and evasions by Iraq, a valuable Additional Protocol was given to the IAEA to apply; it would extend safeguards to help detect undeclared nuclear activity. But not enough states parties to the treaty have been willing to accept and implement the protocol, or to allocate adequate resources to the IAEA for its enforcement.

The second weakness is that Article X of the NPT allows states parties to withdraw from it—as North Korea has intermittently done—simply by giving 3 months' notice and some account (not subject to any evaluation) of its reasons for doing so. An entitlement of this

NOTES

[1] The United States-India Nuclear Cooperation Approval and Non-proliferation Enhancement Act was signed into law on October 8, 2008.

[2] National Intelligence Council, *Iran: Nuclear Intentions and Capabilities, National Intelligence Estimate*, November 2007, available at <www.dni.gov/press/releases/20071203_release.pdf >.

[3] The transcript of the U.S. intelligence briefing on the Syrian nuclear site is available at <www.dni.gov/interviews/20080424_interview.pdf>. The outside analysis referred to is that of David Albright and Paul Brannan at the Institute for Science and International Security, in particular to their April 24, 2008, and May 12, 2008, publications; available at <www.isis-online.org/publications/syria/SyriaUpdate_24April2008.pdf> and <www.isis-online.org/publications/syria/SyriaReactorReport_12May2008.pdf>.

[4] For example, on October 13, 2006, South Korean parliament member Kho Jo-heung remarked, "We have to make the U.S. military bring back tactical nuclear weapons or possess our own nuclear weapons." See "S. Korea Divided over Redeployment of U.S. Tactical Nuclear Weapons," Yonhap, October 19, 2006. On October 15, 2006, Shoichi Nakagawa, chairman of the Japanese Liberal Democratic Party's policy research council, stated that Japan needed "to find a way to prevent Japan from coming under attack" and that "nuclear weapons are one such option." See Reuters, "Japan Should Reexamine Its Nuclear Weapons Ban, Ruling Party Official Says," *The Washington Post*, October 16, 2006, 16, available at <www.washingtonpost.com/wp-dyn/content/article/2006/10/15/AR2006101500657.html>.

[5] For example, "Japan 'is absolutely not considering' building a nuclear arsenal in response to the North Korean nuclear test, Japanese Foreign Minister Taro Aso said Wednesday, moments after Secretary of State Condoleezza Rice reiterated that Japan was protected by the American nuclear umbrella." See Glenn Kessler, "Japan, Acting to Calm U.S. Worries, Rules Out Building Nuclear Arms," *The Washington Post*, October 19, 2006, A24. Regarding U.S. extended deterrence guarantees, Secretary Rice stated, "First, we are strengthening our strategic relationships in Northeast Asia. I made it clear last week that the United States has both the will and the capability to meet the full range, and here I stress, the full range, of our security and deterrent commitments to allies like South Korea and Japan." Condoleezza Rice, Annual B.C. Lee Lecture, The Heritage Foundation, Washington, DC, October 25, 2006.

[6] These 13 nations are Algeria, Azerbaijan, Bahrain, Egypt, Jordan, Kuwait, Morocco, Oman, Qatar, Saudi Arabia, Turkey, United Arab Emirates, and Yemen.

[7] The United States and the International Atomic Energy Agency Director both advocate, albeit by different means, changes to the current nuclear nonproliferation regulation to end the proliferation of enrichment and reprocessing capabilities to countries that do not already possess such capabilities, regardless of the purposes for which they seek it. Such efforts have met considerable resistance from some states that do not yet have such capabilities.

[8] Only seven nations—Angola, Egypt, Iraq, Lebanon, North Korea, Somalia, and Syria—are not signatories to the Chemical Weapons Convention, and Iraq has indicated its intent to accede. Syria and North Korea long have been assessed to maintain major chemical weapons stocks for offensive purposes. Twenty states remain outside the Biological and Toxin Weapons Convention, most of which are small countries in Africa or the Pacific; Israel is the only major nonsignatory state.

[9] For example, see U.S. Department of State, "Adherence to and Compliance with Arms Control, Nonproliferation, and Disarmament Agreements and Commitments," August 2005, available at <www.state.gov/documents/organization/52113.pdf>.

[10] As the director general of the Organization for the Prohibition of Chemical Weapons noted in his opening statement to the Second Special Session of the Conference of the States Parties to Review the Operation of the Chemical Weapons Convention:

Important changes are taking place. The layout, design, and characteristics of plant sites are under continued review by industry. Very importantly, globalization is bringing about a massive redistribution and regional migration of chemical production and trade in the world. In parallel with these movements, there has been an exponential growth in the number of declared Other Chemical Production Facilities (OCPFs). ...Due to their technological features ... a number of [these facilities] could easily and quickly be reconfigured for the production of chemical weapons. ...This is all the more pertinent in view of the evolving threat posed by terrorism.

See <www.opcw.org/index.php?eID=dam_frontend_download&fileID=1874>.

[11] The February 2008 Report of the Scientific Advisory Board on Developments in Science and Technology for the Second Special Session of the Conference of the States Parties to Review the Operation of the Chemical Weapons Convention, available at <www.opcw.org/index.php?eID=dam_frontend_download&fileID=1871>, noted, "New biologically active molecules are being discovered at an unprecedented rate. The tools for such techniques are becoming widely available and could be selectively target at toxic materials."

[12] Ibid., 11.

[13] Alexander Kelle noted, "The chemistry of the 21st century is a far cry from the one of the 1980s. . . . The new chemistry is utilizing other scientific disciplines and technologies to a much higher degree in its quest for new chemical compounds. Alexander Kelle, ed., "Introduction," *The Changing Scientific and Technological Basis of the CBW Proliferation Problem*, report of the workshop on Preventing the Misuse of 21st Century Chemistry: State of the Art of Drug Development and Delivery, and Selected Enabling Technologies, Belfast, Ireland, January 13–14, 2006, 7,

available at <www.brad.ac.uk/acad/sbtwc/ST_Reports/ST_Report_No_7.pdf >.

[14] Department of Defense, Joint Publication 1–02, *Dictionary of Military and Associated Terms*, April 12, 2001 (as amended through October 17, 2008), available at <www.dtic.mil/doctrine/jel/new_pubs/jp1_02.pdf>.

[15] "The West" is used here to signify Western-oriented states; the term includes South Korea, Japan, Israel, and other states aligned with the United States and other allies.

[16] Paul Bracken, "Net Assessment; a Practical Guide," *Parameters* (Spring 2006), 92, 93.

[17] The investigation carried out by Admiral Kirkland Donald for Defense Secretary Robert Gates in spring 2008 found, among other problems, a decline in nuclear expertise through the Air Force. Other studies have come to similar conclusions regarding the status and expertise of nuclear forces.

[18] Gordon Craig and Alexander George, "Force and Statecraft," in *Deterrence in the Second Nuclear Age*, ed. Keith Payne (Louisville: University Press of Kentucky, 1996), 45–46.

[19] As Soviet archives are opened to historians, we are discovering that many of our basic understandings of Soviet intentions were badly flawed.

[20] For example, the *Boston Globe* discussed classified briefings for U.S. policymakers on North Korean assistance to Syria on April 24, 2008 ("U.S. Says North Korea Gave Syria Nuclear Assistance.")

[21] An example is "A Tantalizing Look at Iran's Nuclear Program," *International Herald Tribune*, April 29, 2008.

[22] Michael Levi, *On Nuclear Terrorism* (Cambridge: Harvard University Press, 2007), 144.

[23] Tricky, but it can be done. Mononuclear combat may affect the nuclear equation if both sides withhold and one side starts to lose. If Red can be predictably assumed to withhold until the tide becomes adverse, then that becomes fodder for assessment. A thorough knowledge of Red's nuclear and conventional doctrines and policy is required, which is intrinsic to the assessment process.

[24] If experience is any guide, more than one game will be necessary to explore possible Red and Blue options.

[25] Levi, 35.

[26] National Intelligence Council, *The Terrorist Threat to the U.S. Homeland*, National Intelligence Estimate, July 2007.

[27] The White House, *National Strategy for Homeland Security*, October 2007, 3.

[28] Joint Publication 3–27, *Homeland Defense*, July 12, 2007, A–3.

[29] Department of Defense, *Strategy for Homeland Defense and Civil Support*, June 2005. This strategy provides guidance, objectives, and direction for Defense's role in the civil support component of homeland defense.

[30] *Homeland Defense*.

[31] *Strategy for Homeland Defense and Civil Support* reinforces the "Lead, Support, Enable" organizing construct.

[32] U.S. Pacific Command has responsibility for civil support for incidents in Hawaii and the Pacific territories.

[33] Phillip C. Saunders and Charles D. Lutes, *China's ASAT Test: Motivations and Implications*, Institute for National Strategic Studies Special Report (Washington, DC: National Defense University Press, June 2007).

[34] See <http://history.nasa.gov/1967treaty.html>.

[35] Bhupendra Jasani, ed., *Outer Space: A Source of Conflict or Co-operation?* (Tokyo: United Nations University Press, 1991), published in cooperation with the Stockholm International Peace Research Institute, quoted in David Webb, "On the Definition of a Space Weapon (When is a Space Weapon Not a Space Weapon?)" The Praxis Centre, Leeds Metropolitan University, available at <praxis.leeds-met.ac.uk/praxis/documents/space_weapons.pd>.

Contributors

M. Elaine Bunn (Chapter Editor) is Distinguished Research Fellow in the Institute for National Strategic Studies at National Defense University (NDU).

Dr. W. Seth Carus is Deputy Director of the Center for the Study of Weapons of Mass Destruction (CSWMD) at NDU. He is author of numerous publications on bioterrorism.

John P. Caves, Jr., is Senior Research Fellow in CSWMD at NDU. He previously served in the Office of the Secretary of Defense (Policy), most recently as Deputy Director for Counterproliferation Policy.

M. Creighton Hottinger is Research Associate in CSWMD at NDU.

Colonel Robert B. Killebrew, USA (Ret.), served 30 years in a variety of assignments that include Special Forces, tours in the 82d and 101st Airborne Divisions, XVIII Airborne Corps, high-level war planning assignments, and instructor duty at the U.S. Army War College.

Richard A. Love is Senior Research Fellow and Professor in CSWMD at NDU. His current projects involve weapons of mass destruction (WMD) interdiction, foreign consequence management, and combating WMD strategy and operations.

Sir Michael Quinlan (1930–2009) was a United Kingdom (UK) civil servant from 1954 to 1992.

Most of his career was spent in the defense field, including a tour of duty at the North Atlantic Treaty Organization Headquarters in Brussels. At the UK Ministry of Defence, he was Deputy Under-Secretary (Policy) from 1977 to 1981, and Permanent Under-Secretary from 1988 to 1992. After retirement from the UK Civil Service, he was Director of the Ditchley Foundation from 1992 to 1999.

Heather L. Villena is Research Assistant in CSWMD at NDU.

Section II
Assessing Complex Regional Trends

During Operation *Tornado*, joint Afghan and ISAF troops meet with local leaders in Uruzgan Province, Afghanistan, October 2008

In a globalized world, every region is important. When viewed through a regional prism, some international challenges are magnified while others appear more manageable. This section posits some of the more likely challenges that may arise in major regions over the next decade.

The Greater Middle East is the epicenter of conflict today. Iraq's stability and Iran's appetite for power could top the global security agenda within the next 5 to 10 years. Declining U.S. support for Iraq may unleash divisive forces that lead to civil war and strengthen a nuclear-armed Iran under its Revolutionary Guard Corps. But if Iraq can increasingly stand on its own while the United States reduces its presence, and if a clash with Iran can be averted, then the region could become more stable before 2020. In particular, there may be scope for a renewed peace process by Israel and its neighbors. It is obvious that negotiations, with or without preconditions, will be mulled in many capitals. The United States will be pressed by its allies and partners—such as Israel, Jordan, Egypt, and the Gulf Arab states—who will look for reassurance in the face of a real and present danger as adversaries and spoilers remain suspicious of American motives. The United States might revive support for freedom and democracy, based on a recognition that reform comes from within societies, that effective governance takes decades to achieve, and that American values do not constitute a formula for regime change. Whether the Greater Middle East is more or less peaceful a decade from now may hinge on the capacity of Washington to work with a growing number of countries. But in a region noted for taking hesitant steps toward peace, any success will require significant investments of American prestige and largesse.

A growing insurgency in Afghanistan and along the Afghan-Pakistan border, which serves as an incubator for the Taliban, al Qaeda, and other extremist groups, ensures that South Asia will rival the Middle East as

the most dangerous security challenge in the next 10 years. The lesson of September 11, 2001, appeared to be that developed nations would not allow remote, almost ungovernable areas of the world to provide safe havens for terrorists—not when globalization has facilitated the destructiveness of ideologically motivated zealots who murder people of all faiths around the globe. But the antidote—stabilization, reconstruction, and state-building—is far more costly and takes more patience than originally contemplated. An international effort is needed to strengthen the fledgling government in Kabul against political violence and extremism, build local security forces and institutions, and provide alternatives to an economy fueled by the trade in illicit narcotics. Both the United States and the North Atlantic Treaty Organization (NATO) will have to find effective ways to deliver nonmilitary assistance to the contested areas of Afghanistan, where Provincial Reconstruction Teams have been useful in recovery and state-building projects during stability operations. Meanwhile, finding the means to check violence emanating from Pakistan without undermining the new civilian government in Islamabad will require considerable finesse. Some may expect an increasingly powerful India to address regional problems, and no doubt it can help in reducing the risk of conflict with Pakistan, including nuclear escalation. But the role of India in solving the Afghanistan question is necessarily circumscribed, as even positive acts on its part are likely to be misperceived by Islamabad. Instead, a long-term solution would involve helping the more than 40 million Pashtuns in Afghanistan and Pakistan attain a better standard of living. While India will become increasingly active on the regional and global level, it is likely to seek greater latitude in its external affairs than it enjoyed as the leader of the Non-Aligned Movement. Consequently, building a strategic partnership with Delhi will be a gradual process. In addition, India will primarily focus on managing its economic

Left to right: Israeli soldiers provide security in Jerusalem; Afghan villagers meet with joint team investigating allegations of civilian casualties in Tagab; Georgian defense officials meet Vice Chairman of the Joint Chiefs of Staff in Tbilisi

development in the foreseeable future while retaining a cautious role abroad, which is inseparable from its democratic coalitions.

If the Middle East and South Asia are likely to dominate the security agenda in the near term, East Asia continues as the most promising region in which to promote international security. An ascendant China, while encouraging hedging by neighbors, is more likely to be regarded as a responsible stakeholder or frontline state in meeting 21st-century transnational challenges, be it energy security, water supplies, or the environment than as a spoiler. The Korean Peninsula will remain a flashpoint as long as the closed society in the North clings to nuclear weapons for its survival. Developing a serious diplomatic framework to achieve tangible progress in reversing that trend could be the springboard for a new level of multilateral cooperation, including with respect to the Six-Party Talks that have been crucial in the nonproliferation effort. Although the region has overlapping agreements and forums, U.S. bilateral alliances, especially in the case of Japan, the Republic of Korea, and Australia, underpin regional security interests; maintaining alliances and transforming them into effective mechanisms for security cooperation will require sustained American leadership and involvement with the countries of the region. Moreover, the combination of problems facing the countries of Southeast Asia cannot be ignored. In all, East and Southeast Asia will continue to generate hope in a world seeking effective leadership and institutions to forge genuine solutions to current as well as future strategic challenges.

The conflict between Russia and Georgia in August 2008 seemingly ended two decades of imagining Europe as a whole and free region. The price of hydrocarbons served as a catalyst for Russia's startling economic revolution. Trade in energy resources, in turn, emboldened Moscow to assert itself, especially on the periphery of the old Soviet empire. While many

observers were bewildered by the first intervention by Russia outside its borders since the Cold War, frustration had been mounting in the Kremlin because of real and perceived slights to its national prestige and interests. Yet a new Cold War is not looming on the horizon, if only because few predict that Russia can manage its own enormous challenges, including diversifying an economy addicted to energy, achieving ethnic and religious integration in the face of demographic trends that sharply reduce the number of ethnic Russians, and maintaining control and legitimacy within a semi-authoritarian state. But cooperating with Moscow in the next decade will be problematic, not least because of its neighbors. How Europe and the United States work with the countries on Russia's periphery, from the Baltic to Ukraine and Georgia and energy-rich Central Asia, will be a major challenge in the short and medium term. Even cooperation among major powers over shared interests such as nuclear nonproliferation may be difficult, since Russia seems prone to take issue over its differences with the West rather than to seek areas of agreement. Whether the relationship between Russia and China deepens may turn on the ability of the United States to overcome its popular depiction as a unilateral military power and whether Beijing can convince Moscow that its ascendancy does not pose a challenge to Russia's centrality in Eurasia.

A strong and prosperous united Europe will ensure that the transatlantic community performs its vital security role while dealing with emerging problems of the 21st century. Increasingly, the European Union and NATO seem more synergistic and less competitive than once feared. Yet Europe is divided on how much to focus on its own security versus that of the other regions of the world. Clearly, the challenges in the Balkans will continue, as future stability pivots on Kosovo and Serbia. Turkey, which apparently has passed the high water mark of secular Kemalism, is torn by questions about its identity with regard to religion and

Left to right: High-rise buildings in Beijing; Leaders from Germany, France, and Great Britain discuss financial crisis during EU summit, October 2008

civil-military relations, demands by ethnic Kurds, and integration into Europe. Meanwhile, many European nations are increasingly concerned about terrorism on their soil, whether imported or homegrown, and seeking ways to promote internal security and multicultural assimilation. In the aftermath of U.S. intervention in Iraq, some European governments implied a normative if not moral superiority to America, which they thought had slipped from its ethical moorings; a new administration in Washington provides an opportune moment to broach the Atlantic divide on issues of institutional values that have arisen in Europe and elsewhere in the recent past.

The myriad problems of Africa warrant greater attention than the international community has mustered until now. The continent is more accurately perceived as a series of subregions and not as a vast homogeneous land mass, with North Africa, the Sahel Belt, West Africa, Central Africa, the Great Lakes, East Africa, and Southern Africa presenting far more differences than similarities. The Horn of Africa—Somalia, Sudan and Darfur, Ethiopia, and Eritrea—is the most dangerous area, both on land and offshore. Although weak states explain some of the risks, including piracy and communal strife in Somalia, ethnic cleansing in Darfur can be attributed to Sudan, which could descend into civil war. Ineffective multilateral institutions and mechanisms for resolving conflicts point to the need for external assistance, but it remains unclear whether U.S. Africa Command can become a credible source of whole-of-government approaches to the problems of the region, only some of which are related to terrorism and military threats. While the United States and other developed nations agree on the need for increased cooperation with African states and organizations, the global financial crisis may curtail or delay integrated plans for assistance and collaboration with a new generation of enlightened African leaders.

Both positive trends and latent risks in the Americas pose a dilemma for Washington: while the region eschews a hegemon, it does not benefit from U.S. neglect or retrenchment. Brazil has emerged on the regional and international scene in an impressive fashion, though how it forges closer relations with the United States will define the region for the next decade. Meanwhile, the establishment of subregional communities and trading blocs offers the potential for dealing with problems through multilateral dialogues on the local level, provided an actor such as Venezuela does not succeed in destabilizing them. Regional security challenges will increasingly center on global and transnational issues such as development, energy dependence, and the environment. The succession of Raul Castro in Havana does not necessarily imply that the future transition of Cuban society will be a crisis-free process. Moreover, despite enormous progress in the period since September 11, 2001, cooperation by the United States, Canada, Mexico, and The Bahamas on border security is a daunting task. Washington will have to cooperate with many states in the region to tackle basic problems rather than their symptoms, including poverty, governance, and narcotics. Indeed, the last of these challenges underscores a wider problem—that of drug cartels and their associated criminal networks—which will only proliferate in the years ahead.

In the decade ahead, every region has the potential to contribute to international order and stability. But as nations attempt to enhance their own security and prosperity, new challenges will require innovative approaches and institutions. Moreover, some regional troubles may demand greater effort on the part of the international community as a whole. The combination of enduring threats and emerging global and transnational issues will tax the most influential and fastest rising individual states and the most affluent regions, even while they deal with traditional concerns. **gsa**

Left to right: Djiboutians gather for opening of new well; Skyline of Sao Paulo, Brazil, overlooking Favela Morumbi slum

Chapter 9
The Greater Middle East

The Greater Middle East: Strategic Change

From the 1970s, when the United States first assumed responsibility for the security of the Persian Gulf, through the mid 1990s, the region called the Greater Middle East was relatively stable. Regime change occurred within families, parties, or tribes, was usually orchestrated, and was rarely challenged. Hafiz al-Assad ruled Syria for nearly 30 years, Saddam Hussein ruled Iraq for 35 years, the late King Hussein of Jordan held power for nearly 50 years, and Sultan Qaboos has ruled Oman for almost 40 years. Where leaders died suddenly, as with the assassinations of Egyptian President Anwar Sadat in 1981 or Israeli Prime Minister Yitzhak Rabin in 1995, the political system did not change. There were two exceptions to this political passivity: the 1979 revolution in Iran that replaced the shah and the monarchy with clerics and an Islamic republic, and the military takeover in Sudan that brought General Omar Bashir to power in 1989.

The region's wars occurred primarily in the Gulf: Iraq invaded Iran in 1980 and Kuwait in 1990; Iraq was defeated by a U.S.-led coalition in 1991. (The second U.S. invasion of Iraq, in 2003, was unusual in that the American military force liberated Iraq from Saddam's grip and destroyed the existing political system, only to begin a long occupation while it tried to reinvent the government, politics, and the civic structure of the devastated country.) The main interests of the United States in this 25-year period primarily were ensuring access to oil and safe passage for shipping, containing the influence of the Soviet Union, supporting Israel, and maintaining a balance of power, especially in the Persian Gulf region. Washington preferred not to engage in the region's wars, including the four Arab-Israeli wars, and used surrogates, such as the shah of Iran and the king of Saudi Arabia, when instability threatened U.S. interests in the Persian Gulf.

Two events propelled the United States to take a much more active and visible role in the region:

U.S. Air Force (D. Myles Cullen)

U.S. convoy passes triumphal arch built by Saddam Hussein to commemorate Iran-Iraq War

Iraq's occupation of Kuwait in 1990, and the terrorist attacks on the World Trade Center and Pentagon on September 11, 2001. In the 1990s, the key security issues driving U.S. policy in the Greater Middle East were to maintain a secure and reasonably priced oil supply, support Israel, limit the spread of weapons of mass destruction (WMD), and keep Iraq and Iran—labeled pariah states for their wars, support for international terrorism, and efforts to acquire and use WMD—contained. The events of September 11 moved international terrorism to the top of the list.

Today, U.S. interests remain focused on maintaining access to oil, curbing nuclear weapons proliferation, eliminating terrorism, protecting Israel, and isolating those governments and parties, including Iran, Syria, Hamas in Gaza, and Hizballah in Lebanon, that are deemed pariahs. The region of the Greater Middle East faces many problems, but four stand out as critical issues for U.S. strategic planning and security policy in the decade ahead: the future of Iraq, Iran's regional ambitions and nuclear policy, the lack of an Arab-Israeli and Palestinian-Israeli peace process, and the impact of reform—or lack thereof—in the Arab world.

Iraq and Iran: Risks and Opportunities

Iraq and Iran present a complicated and interwoven series of policy dilemmas for the United States. Not a failed state, Iraq's government—the first freely elected in its history—is struggling with sectarian militias at war with each other, and politicians fighting for personal power, wealth, and national independence. Provinces and tribes are not fighting each other, nor are they fighting on the same side as each other. Most seek independence from the United States and from central authority concentrated in Baghdad, which most Iraqis have always opposed. The Shia-dominated government must work out the modalities of political and economic control in a government deliberately designed to be weak, decentralized, and dysfunctional. Comparative suffering is still a measure of citizenship and prevents meaningful moves toward national reconciliation. Yet the political process appears to be working, oil is flowing, the insurgencies have abated, and the central government under Prime Minister Nuri al-Maliki is trying to assert its authority while it balances the needs and demands of its powerful patrons, the United States and Iran.

Iran, for its part, is also in the midst of political confusion and economic stress, and faces the prospect of tougher sanctions if it does not change its nuclear policy. Unanticipated oil profits not only eased economic burdens in many oil-producing countries, but they also raised popular expectations in an unstable market. The government in Tehran has not provided promised economic benefits, adequate housing, or jobs sufficient to meet the needs of many Iranians, and Mahmoud Ahmadinejad won a disputed election in June 2009. The strategic interests of Washington and Iran intersect in Iraq.

Decisionmaking in Iran: Deliberate, Consensual, Ambiguous. The Islamic Republic of Iran is a contradiction in terms to many observers and analysts. It is a republic and the only example of a modern, clerically dominated regime. It is a participatory democracy, yet resembles a totalitarian system in that it proclaims the absolute supremacy of a religion (Islam), as interpreted by a clerical elite, over public and private life. Islam provides the moral compass for political governance and social behavior in Iran. It holds elections in which the people sometimes have a genuine choice, yet all candidates must be screened for ideological correctness. It has multiple sources of power and checks and balances, yet in the end one person, not elected by the people, is the ultimate decisionmaker.[1] The result is confusion. It is difficult to know where real power lies in Iran, how decisions are made, and how informal networks of relationships interact with formal structures of power.

Several trends shape decisionmaking on security issues and foreign affairs under Supreme Leader Ali Khamenei and the 8th parliament that was elected in March 2008.

First, decisionmaking is institutionalized and state-centered. Ayatollah Khamenei is a powerful and influential force in security policymaking. Unlike his predecessor, Ayatollah Ruhollah Khomeini, who was not a nationalist and avoided identification with political factions, Khamenei is centered in the conservative camp. At times, he appears uncomfortable with policies and pronouncements made by President Ahmadinejad, whose outspoken views on foreign and security issues far exceed his constitutional limitations. Khamenei uses his authority to discreetly offset decisions and appointments made by the president and his more extreme conservative faction. Multiple centers advise the Supreme Leader on security issues and policy options; some are traditional, such as the Ministry of Foreign Affairs, while others are appointed by the Supreme Leader to advise him from a perspective other than that of the "official" institutions. Khamenei, for example, created the Supreme

▼ *Continued on p. 194*

The World as Seen from Tehran

Iran's ambitions as the preeminent power in the Greater Middle East are longstanding. The quest for regional hegemony began under the shahs and has been continued by the clerics of the Islamic Republic. Iranian foreign policy has always been designed to protect a nation and empire that was long coveted by more powerful neighbors (Ottoman Turkey and Tsarist Russia), and divided into spheres of influence by the Great Powers of the 20th century (the Soviet Union, Great Britain, and the United States). Viewed through this historical prism, these ambitions have little to do with exporting its Islamic revolution or expanding its borders, although occasional reminders to the Sunni Arab–led Gulf Arab states of Iran's territorial claims, and of the Shia and Persian-origin communities within their borders, serve to warn those states of their vulnerability.

Several factors shape Iran's strategic and military priorities:

■ The need to secure Iran's territorial and political integrity and recognition of the regime's legitimacy. Iranians under both shahs and ayatollahs are proud of their long history as an empire and nation-state and of the role of Islam in shaping religious and political values. Like their Arab neighbor states, which were created and divided by 19th- and 20th-century European imperialism, they reject all foreign efforts to guide or deny their political, economic, or security aspirations.

■ The need to reassert Iran's traditional role of regional hegemon in the Gulf and beyond. Iran's leaders see their country as encircled by real and potential enemies: Iraq, which used chemical weapons against Iranian troops and missiles against Tehran in their 8-year war; the Gulf Arab states, which host the U.S. military presence and are seen as repressing their Shia communities; Pakistan, which is occasionally involved in hostile skirmishes with Iran on their common border and has encouraged anti-Iranian activity in Afghanistan; and Central Asia, once pro-Soviet, now a source of economic opportunity, sectarian risk, and occasional basing for U.S. military forces. Above all, the United States, a virtual neighbor since the occupation of Iraq in April 2003, and Israel are viewed as enemies. Both threaten Iran's nuclear achievements and deplore Iran's efforts to derail any peace process between Israel and the Palestinians or Israel and Syria.

Washington, in particular, is seen as keen to keep the Persian Gulf as its militarized zone, maintain pro-U.S. regimes in Baghdad and Kabul, and marginalize Iran.

■ The need for an enhanced capability to defend Iran against any threat of military aggression. Tehran wants independence and self-sufficiency in strategic and tactical terms. It believes that it must build its own military industries, reconstitute a modern military force, and have minimal reliance on foreign suppliers. At the same time, Tehran is seeking to acquire nuclear technology and the capability to produce nuclear weapons, probably as a cost-effective way to compensate for military weakness and relative strategic isolation.[1]

Iran's leaders, whether moderate Persian nationalist or conservative Islamist, view the world with a mix of confidence and trepidation. Regardless of where they stand on the political spectrum, they likely share a common view of the threats to the security of the Iranian homeland and regime, and the measures necessary to protect Iranian interests. This consensus includes an assumption that at some point they will fight again and alone, just as they did from 1980 to 1988, and that Iran must be able to defend itself by itself.

NOTE

[1] For further discussion of Iranian ambitions and regional reactions, see Judith S. Yaphe and Charles D. Lutes, *Reassessing the Implications of a Nuclear-Armed Iran*, McNair Paper 69 (Washington, DC: National Defense University Press, 2005).

▲ *Continued from p. 192*

Council on Foreign Relations after Ahmadinejad issued some of his more outrageous policy statements. Issues once negotiated by the Foreign Ministry, such as the nuclear enrichment issue, are now under the control of the president's security establishment. Ahmadinejad did not take power away from the Supreme Leader. The Supreme Leader exercises authority behind an opaque screen. Governance in Iran is a push-back system—Ahmadinejad has a strong sense of what authority the president should exercise and has pushed the envelope to see how far he can go before the Supreme Leader pushes back.

Second, strategic decisions are shaped by military security perceptions, not by diplomats or clerics. Policies once fashioned around ideological correctness or export of the revolution have become more purposeful and pragmatic, intended to end Iran's strategic isolation and establish its authority in the region. Discussions on key issues are held in the National Security Council (NSC), with recommendations to the Supreme Leader based on group consensus. No Iranian official would oppose a decision recommended by the NSC and confirmed by the Supreme Leader, especially one citing the need for a strong national defense as the primary reason for developing nuclear power and new weapons systems.[2]

Third, veterans from the Iranian Revolutionary Guard Corps (IRGC), military, and security services probably have a greater role in decisionmaking than clerics. Once a central feature of the Islamic state, the number of clerics in the parliament has dropped from 140 in the early 1980s to 32 in the latest parliament. Two non-clerics have served as speakers in parliament, and the current president, while religious, is not a cleric. The IRGC was created after the 1979 revolution to be a praetorian guard for the new regime. It reports directly to the Supreme Leader, but over the past decade, it has expanded its role in security issues and provincial government, as well as the government bureaucracy.[3] In addition, it has become an economic engine through its investment, job creation, and import-export activities.

The shift in power from the clerics in government to the IRGC began in July 1999, when local conservative militias orchestrated by the IRGC savagely beat students at the University of Tehran. In what is seen by many Iranians as the most serious internal threat to the regime to date, students protesting conditions at the university publicly demanded the ouster of the Supreme Leader. In response, 24 senior IRGC officers published a letter in a leading conservative newspaper, warning that the IRGC "cannot tolerate the situation anymore" and threatening action against the reformist government of then–President Mohammad Khatami. The student riots provided the government the opportunity to further centralize power and limit dissent. The Guard Corps was able to expand its power and influence inside the regime, while the government signaled that it would tolerate what it called a "democratic game," provided the basic foundation of the Islamic Republic was not challenged.

Despite growing opposition to Ahmadinejad, his contested victory in the June 2009 presidential election dampens immediate hopes for reform in Iran or a more moderate tone in foreign policy. Opposition to Ahmadinejad dates back at least to the parliamentary elections in March 2008.[4] In that election, his supporters won 70 percent of the 290 seats, but one of his most vocal critics, Ali Larijani, became speaker of the parliament and remains one of the competing centers of power in Iran. Moreover, in the 2009 presidential election defeat of Mir-Hussein Moussavi, many Iranians took to the streets to protest potential election fraud, suggesting an unprecedented degree of disgruntlement over Ahmadinejad. Although Moussavi is by no means a liberal reformer, his apparently softer stance on nuclear issues and concern about Iran's isolation would no doubt have made it easier for outside powers to engage Tehran.

U.S.-Iran: The Legacy of Missed Opportunities. The list of possible opportunities for reconciliation between the United States and Iran is long and often recited as if all the opportunities were real ones. Some were meant seriously by one side and dismissed offhandedly by the other. Most were interpreted as indicating weakness in the other. Few were pursued, and the limited results they achieved were satisfactory to both sides. When Iran offered to cooperate during operations in Afghanistan following the events of September 11 and during the U.S. war on Iraq in 2003, Washington's response was to quietly accept both of Iran's offers and, in the latter case, declare Iran part of the reviled "axis of evil." When then–Secretary of State Madeleine Albright offered Iran security discussions in 1997, Iran heard the Clinton administration deny it legitimacy and recognition by rejecting any dealings with Iran's "unelected" leaders. When the last American held hostage in Lebanon was released in 1991 after 7 years of captivity by Hizballah, Iran asked why the United States was not grateful to then–President Ali Akbar Hashemi-Rafsanjani.

Both Tehran and Washington were delighted with the collapse of the Taliban and Ba'athist regimes, but neither saw a need to prevent the slide from cooperation, however limited, to confrontation. Iran certainly agreed with short-term U.S. goals in Iraq—a quick war followed by an equally rapid withdrawal of forces and the institutionalization of democratic practices, especially elections. The differences were over longer term issues: a secular democratic state or an Islamic republic; simple and majoritarian, and therefore sectarian, rule, or the protection and participation of minorities in governance. Underlying the differences was a basic shift in how national priorities would be identified: would Iraq remain as the eastern front of the Arab world, as defender of Sunni Arab nationalism against the Persian Shia threat, or would it become part of the western wall of the Iranian Islamic Republic, provider of strategic depth to Iran against threats from the Arabs and Israel? If both sides hoped the new Iraq would serve as a model for emulation and change in the region, what was the model?

In 2003, Iran was in a weakened position, seemingly encircled by the United States, which had pro-American governments and military forces in Afghanistan, Iraq, Turkey, the Gulf states, and the Central Asian republics bordering Iran. Some Iranians talked of the "Iraqification" of Iran—meaning the takeover of important posts, such as the Justice Ministry, by officials born in Iraq. Others predicted that Iran's most respected Shia scholars and clerics, many of whom oppose Khomeini-style theocratic rule, would flee to Najaf, where they could freely question the religious legitimacy of the Islamic Republic. Worry about being the next target for American efforts at regime change, and the apparent U.S. rejection of an opening for talks, heightened the paranoia in the Iranian political establishment.

Six years after the U.S. invasion of Iraq, the tide has turned. The Iranian regime is stronger and more certain of its ability to shape events in the region, while the United States and its allies are perceived as weakened by years of insurgency and terrorism in Iraq. The regime in Tehran has become more stable, more repressive, and less amenable to foreign pressure than in its earlier decades. Iraq's new political elite has established close ties with the Iranian regime, and Ahmadinejad used the first visit by an Iranian leader to Baghdad in February 2008 to offer political and economic assistance to Baghdad and advertise their close ties.

What Does Iran Want in Iraq? Iran has key strategic interests in Iraq, many of which are similar to those of the United States. The 8-year war with Iraq in the 1980s left both countries with high casualties and extensive damage to their economic and military infrastructure. Iraq had used chemical weapons on Iranian territory and was working on acquiring nuclear weapons; Iran had none. Iraq had managed to both heavily subsidize the war and meet civilian needs with $80 billion in "loans" from the oil-rich Gulf countries of Saudi Arabia, Kuwait, the United Arab Emirates (UAE), and Qatar, and arms sales from the United States, Russia, and most European countries; Iran had no loans, no debt, and a badly damaged military. For the next 15 years, as Iraq faced war and crippling sanctions for its invasion and occupation of Kuwait, Iran began carefully reconstructing its image and its regional role.

Iraqi oil minister tours K3 oil refinery, a main source of income for Al Anbar Province and jobs for Iraqi citizens

The Islamic Republic wants an Iraq that is stable, united, and nonthreatening, and one that is an economic, political, and strategic ally facing common enemies—Israel, the United States, anachronistic Arab monarchies, and obstreperous minorities, such as the Kurds. Iran assumes it is by right the preeminent power in the Persian Gulf and the Greater Middle East region. It has the largest population, largest land mass, largest military, and oldest culture and civilization. It believes it is the economic engine of the region, the most innovative in the application of science and technology, and the leader of the world's Muslims. Iran would prefer Iraq to be an Islamic state under shariah law similar to its own theocratic façade, but if forced to choose between a precarious Islamic state and a stable unitary state, would almost certainly choose the latter.

Iran's "region" is more than the Gulf or Central Asia. It extends from Afghanistan through the Gulf, Iraq, and Turkey to Syria, Lebanon, Palestine, and Israel. As the preeminent power, it expects to be consulted on all issues affecting the region, in much the same sense that Syrian President Hafiz al-Assad interpreted his and Syria's role. Iran believes that the roads to a U.S. exit strategy from Iraq, to a peace settlement in the Arab-Israeli conflict, and to stability in the Gulf run through Tehran. Without Iran, the country's leaders believe, there can be no peace, no resolution of conflict, and no "justice."

Iran wants to expand its influence and authority in the region, but it is not interested in territorial expansion. Rather, it seeks to build its clout through a policy of aggressive outreach short of war— by building and supporting surrogate networks throughout the region, providing political support and economic assistance to key actors, bolstering trade and commercial ties with neighboring countries, and signing security and defense agreements. In implementing its strategies, Iran operates on two intertwined principles to build its networks of surrogates, intimidate opponents and critics, and make foreign policy: the first is *plausible deniability*, and the second is *deliberate ambiguity*.

How successful has Iran been in this effort? The question resonates today as it did 25 years ago, when Iran began constructing its Lebanon policy and building Hizballah. How much control does Iran exert over surrogates such as Hizballah and Hamas? Are extremist leaders, such as Lebanese Hizballah's Hassan Nasrallah or Iraqi Mahdi Army head Muqtada al-Sadr, totally subservient to the wishes of Iran's Supreme Leader and the doctrine of clerical rule? Would Hamas do more than pray for Iran if the latter was threatened with imminent attack? Or do they act independently of Iran, as do Lebanese and Palestinian nationalists willing to work within their respective systems of government so long as they can shape them? The answer probably remains the same today as it was in the 1980s: there is great personal loyalty and devotion to the ideals of the Islamic Revolution and to its clerical leaders, but a tendency to pursue self-interest, with or without Iran's approval. Iran may not be consulted on all operations, or if it is, may not approve, but it would not openly oppose actions by Hizballah or Hamas, or risk a breach with its most successful surrogates.

Iraq as Risk and Opportunity. In their 8-year-long war, both Saddam Hussein and Ayatollah Khomeini made certain judgments about the other's country.

Khomeini assumed Iraq's Shia would join the Shia Islamic Republic to defeat the secular, Sunni Arab–dominated regime in Baghdad; Saddam assumed the Arabs of Iran's Khuzistan Province would join Arab Iraq to defeat the mullahs. Both were wrong. Iraq's Shia Arabs fought to defend the state of Iraq from defeat by Persians and were rewarded by Saddam for their loyalty; Iran's Arabs remained loyal to the republic.

The collapse of Saddam's regime in April 2003 gave Iran an unanticipated opportunity. Its primary regional enemy was gone. Iraqi Shia militants who had spent two decades in Iranian exile could now return and demand a role in the post-Saddam government. Iran had created the major exile group—the Supreme Council for the Islamic Revolution in Iraq (SCIRI)— as an umbrella organization for Iraqi exiles; it was led by members of a prominent pro-Iranian clerical family, Ayatollah Muhammad Baqr al-Hakim and his brother Abd al-Aziz al-Hakim.[5] Iranian pilgrims could now visit the Shia shrine cities of Najaf and Karbala while traders, businessmen, diplomats, investors, security personnel, and intelligence operatives could easily cross the virtually unguarded 900-mile border. Iran called for free elections and democratic institutions in the new Iraq, correctly assuming that the majority Shia population would win any election and, for the first time in history, govern Iraq.

With opportunity, however, comes risk. Iran is pouring money into Iraq in the form of business investment and community reconstruction. It is refurbishing the mosques and shrines of Najaf and Karbala, building community infrastructure, and providing various forms of support—including money, advisors, training, and intelligence—to many of the political factions and government ministries, especially the Interior Ministry, according to accounts told by Iraqis and reported in the press. In early 2008, President Ahmadinejad, on the first visit made by an Iranian leader to Iraq, offered Iraq development assistance, including joint projects for oil, pipeline and refinery construction, and a billion-dollar loan. Iraq turned down the loan offer but signed economic and trade agreements, and issued tenders for construction of a pipeline to Iran. Iran has funded virtually every Shia candidate standing for election to the National Assembly. Some Iraqis claim that the IRGC supports Sunni extremist factions in the center and north of Iraq as well in order to expand its influence and assets there. It expects, in return, a compliant government in Baghdad willing to accede to its vision of the New Iraq. By contrast, some of the oil-rich Gulf states—

once the source of more than $80 billion in loans to help Iraq defeat Iran—are only now beginning to approve debt relief (Saudi Arabia and the UAE) and nominate ambassadors to Baghdad. They still oppose additional assistance to Iraq.

Economists disagree over the impact Iranian promises of development assistance will have on Iraq. While the assistance may help in the very short term, Iran, they say, cannot give Iraq what it needs most: the advanced technology and capital for industrial, oil, and gas-field development. Iran needs the same help, most of which is unavailable to it under sanctions. Iran's influence in Iraq is probably at its highest point now. Over time, that influence will lessen. Iraq will no longer need the goods and services that Iran now supplies, trade will diminish, and Iraq could become an investor in Iran.

According to interviews with Iraqis, a growing number of Iraq's Shia, Sunni Arab, and Kurdish populations are uneasy with the extent of influence Iran and the IRGC wield in Iraq. They raise several important questions: How extensive is Iranian influence in Iraqi ministries (especially Defense, Interior, and Intelligence)? Have Iranians been involved in targeting Iraqi intellectuals, academics, or military officers for assassination? Are the Iranians, through the IRGC, communicating with or assisting al Qaeda or other extremists in Iraq? Are the Iranian religious scholars in the seminaries of Qom trying to displace those of Najaf from the intellectual and spiritual leadership of Shia Islam, or to join them?

Whether Iran is engaged in all, some, or none of these activities, an increasing number of Iraqis are growing uncomfortable with the pattern of Iranian involvement in their affairs. Iraq's Sunni Arabs have long warned about the influence of the turbans (clerics) in politics, and many label Iraq's Shia Arabs as Persians or Safavids (meant as an insult referring to the 16th-century Persian dynasty that waged and lost several wars with the Sunni Ottoman Empire in Iraq's provinces). More importantly, Iraqi Shia Arabs in greater number reject Iran's efforts to control their country's politics, economics, and security. This includes Iraqis—clerics and government officials—who belonged to clandestine Shia movements under Saddam and did not seek exile and safe haven outside Iraq. These sentiments are expressed discreetly to avoid raising Iranian ire and do not reflect consensus among Iraq's many political elements.

Iraq's government must balance American complaints that Iran is supporting anti-U.S. acts of terrorism in Iraq with Iranian demands that the United States leave Iraq and the Gulf. Support from both Washington and Tehran is critical to the survival of any government in Baghdad. Thus far, the Nuri al-Maliki government has managed to bring Americans and Iranians together for several meetings in Baghdad, and Tehran appears to have reined in Muqtada al-Sadr by insisting he abide by his ceasefire and draw down his militia. Muqtada is not an Iranian loyalist. That role is reserved for SCIRI (now called the Islamic Supreme Council in Iraq), which has proven itself a much more witting tool and ally of Iran. The negotiations between Baghdad and Washington over a treaty defining relations and a status of forces agreement were made more difficult because of Iran's concern that Iraq would agree to allow the United States access to military facilities that could be used to monitor and attack Iran.

The Gulf Cooperation Council: Avoiding Risk, Seeking Opportunity

Since the early 1960s, Saudi Arabia, Kuwait, Bahrain, Qatar, the UAE, and Oman have preferred to have governments outside the region defend them, define their security policies, and provide for their needs. New to acting like states rather than tribes, not yet wealthy from oil, and accustomed to letting tradition determine the governance and institutions of civil society, the smaller Arab states of the Persian Gulf initially followed their colonial protector, Great Britain, to shelter themselves from the Arab and Persian nationalist storms that periodically swept through the neighborhood. The exception was Saudi Arabia, which enjoyed better relations with the United States than with the United Kingdom. When the British decided they could no longer afford to protect the Gulf Arabs and withdrew in 1971, the small and fragile Gulf states turned to the United States to assume the British mantle.[6] Concerned about possible Soviet encroachments in the Gulf, President Richard Nixon created the Twin Pillars policy, which designated Iran and Saudi Arabia as proxies for a U.S. military presence in the region.[7] This was followed by the Carter Doctrine on U.S. military engagement in the Gulf and the expansion of the American force presence and operations during the 1980–1988 Iran-Iraq war.

Through the 1970s and 1980s, the Arab states of the Gulf faced the hegemonic ambitions of Iran, first under the secular and intensely nationalistic regime of the shah and then under the revolutionary Islamic Republic of Iran, also nationalistic and determined to export its revolution across the Gulf. In between Iranian challenges came Iraqi feints at territorial acquisition, as well as attempts to gain influence in decisionmaking on Gulf and wider Arab political, economic, and strategic affairs. In 1981, as the Iraq-Iran war continued and Iran broadened its efforts to export its Islamic revolution, the six states formed the Gulf Cooperation Council (GCC).[8] It was not intended to be a political or security organization similar to the European Union (EU) or the North Atlantic Treaty Organization (NATO); instead, its members focused on common economic interests, such as forming a common customs union and trade zone and cooperating in local police and security matters.

U.S. Navy Inshore Boat awaits permission to dock at Khawr Al Amaya oil terminal as part of security mission in Persian Gulf

Despite a prohibition by Ayatollah Khomeini against relations with the Saudis, today's Iranian government values its expanding ties to Saudi Arabia and the other Gulf Arab regimes. Even the UAE maintains links to Iran, despite their seemingly intractable dispute over ownership of three small islands in the Gulf, the Tunbs and Abu Musa. Iran's outreach extends to Shia communities in Iraq (approximately 55 to 60 percent of the population), Saudi Arabia (10 to 15 percent of the population, concentrated primarily in the oil-rich Eastern Province), Kuwait (approximately 20 percent), and Bahrain (about 75 percent). Iran's approach to neighboring Arab states and their Shia communities has changed over the years. Initially, it consisted of efforts to organize antiregime movements through the local mosques and prayer houses, led by local Shia clerics or Iran-based activists. Since

Khomeini died in 1989, however, Iranian efforts have focused on diplomatic overtures to restore relations with its Gulf neighbors, primarily Saudi Arabia.

The Gulf Arabs' Security Vision

Gulf Arab security policies have traditionally been based on risk avoidance, collective reaction, and reliance on nonregional powers to ensure security and survival. The strategy is to avoid provoking either of the dominant and powerful governments in Baghdad and Tehran, pay for protection, use arms sales as an extension of foreign policy, and above all, maintain a balance of power in the Gulf. Iraq's invasion and occupation of Kuwait in 1990 should have exposed the weakness in this form of strategic thinking, but the Gulf governments still prefer to maintain the kind of balance of power under which they once felt comfortable—a balance maintained by cordial relations with regional powers and backed up by a more distant U.S. presence.

Several developments in the past few years have produced a significant shift in the strategic thinking of the Gulf states. The first was the spread of religious-based terrorist attacks following the al Qaeda attacks of 9/11. Al Qaeda and other extremist elements accuse the Al Sa'ud and other ruling families of being un-Islamic puppets of the United States and have conducted terrorist operations on Saudi and American targets in Saudi Arabia. Saudi youth have been recruited for operations in Iraq, and press reports indicate Gulf nationals have been caught both in Iraq and on their return to the Peninsula states.

The second major development is the rise of political and sectarian movements demanding reform. All of the Gulf states are witnessing the growing political influence of ultraconservative religious, ethnic, and tribal factions. These factions demand a greater role in decisionmaking, constitutional limitations on ruling family power, adherence to a strict version of Islamic law, and an end to corruption in government. In Kuwait, for example, elections for the national assembly in May 2008 saw Islamists and tribal conservatives win nearly half of the seats. These conservative elements are now challenging the ruling Al Sabah family for the right to appoint cabinet ministers and for limitations on the power of the amir.

The collapse of Saddam Hussein's regime and the installation of a non-Sunni government in Baghdad has also had a major impact on the Gulf states, which see risk whether Iraq fails or succeeds. A failed Iraq means more cross-border terrorists entering or returning to the Gulf intent on overthrowing the traditional ruling elites. It also raises the risk of sectarian or ethnic unrest in countries where significant minority populations have long been discriminated against by Sunni Wahhabi prejudices and Arab nationalist sentiment. If Iraq succeeds in stabilizing under a democratic-leaning, elective form of governance, especially one with a weak central government and strong semi-independent provincial authorities, then the Gulf states worry about the export of "advanced" political ideas, which they say their countries do not need or are not prepared to adopt. Either strategically or tactically, Iraq will no longer be the eastern flank of the Arab world and protector of the Sunni world against the Persian Shia crescent; rather, it will provide strategic depth for a hegemonic-minded Iran.

The Gulf Arab states have only recently begun to express unease with a nuclear-empowered Iran. Loath to provoke Iran by denying its right to nuclear energy capability, the Gulf Arabs now speak openly of their concerns about Iran developing nuclear weapons, its insistence on full-cycle control of uranium enrichment, and its plans for as many as 20 more nuclear powerplants strung out along the northern shore of the Gulf. They deny that Iran would use a nuclear weapon against them, but their fears of weaponization appear at this point to rival their fear of environmental damage from a Chernobyl-style accident or natural disaster (such as an earthquake at a nuclear plant built on or near a fault), and Iran's lack of responsible planning or preparation for consequence management in the event of a nuclear accident.

Finally, the Gulf Arabs worry that the United States will launch a war against Iran or negotiate security issues with Iran without consulting Gulf friends and allies. Should the United States launch military operations against Iran, it would be the fourth Gulf war in one generation. Gulf rulers would like Washington to consult them before making any overtures—hostile or friendly—toward Iran. Privately, many admit that they would feel compelled to support America, but are uncertain about the willingness of the United States to honor its commitments to their stability and security (meaning their survival).

Response to Risks

The GCC states are consumers and not producers of security. They publicly urge the United States to get out of Iraq—but only after establishing a secure and stable government there. For them, Iraq is the litmus test. If the United States does not stay the course in Iraq, then how strong will its commitments be to the Gulf governments? Their response to

these new risks has been to reconsider their strategic options. The most important shift has been to seek stronger commitments to their security from the U.S. and European governments and from new friends and customers in Asia (China, India, and Japan) who may be willing to extend security guarantees in exchange for assured access to oil, investments, and arms sales. The extent of their discussions with European and Asian governments is unclear, but France, Spain, and Germany have been talking with individual members of the GCC about security issues (France will deploy a 500-man contingent to the UAE). Although China, India, and Japan are increasingly dependent on Gulf oil and gas, none appears interested in contributing to Gulf security or protecting sea lanes and access to those commodities.

In response to Iran's nuclear aspirations and threat, the Gulf Arab states have announced their interest in acquiring nuclear facilities similar to Iran's civilian nuclear energy program. Together, the GCC states control nearly half the world's known oil reserves, but mostly in response to Iran's nuclear programs, several states have expressed interest in nuclear energy for domestic consumption. The International Atomic Energy Agency (IAEA) sent a team of experts to Riyadh in 2007 to discuss building nuclear energy plants. Saudi Arabia, Bahrain, and the UAE seem especially interested, but all declare that any nuclear energy facilities built would be placed under IAEA and Nonproliferation Treaty safeguards.[9]

Underlying these options is the desire to keep the diplomatic door open and maintain correct relations with Iran. In keeping with tradition, the GCC allowed Ahmadinejad to speak at its annual summit in December 2007. Saudi Arabia then welcomed him to make his first hajj, the annual pilgrimage to Mecca and Medina required of all Muslims. This was the first appearance by an Iranian at a GCC meeting and the first hajj visit by a sitting Iranian president.[10]

Israel and the Arabs: The Price of Peace

Hopes for change in Israel's relations with the Palestinians and its Arab neighbors rose in 2008. Where once everyone predicted the conflict would stagnate at best or Palestinian society would completely break down at worst, Israel and Palestinians engaged in extensive negotiations, Israel and Syria started indirect talks, and Israel permitted U.S.-led train-and-equip measures to upgrade Palestinian security capabilities.

Syrian President Assad will make no decision until and unless the new leadership in Israel proves strong enough to deliver on any promises and unless the United States engages actively in the coming months. Indeed, it is widely believed that Assad's motivation for peace talks is to enhance relations with the United States and the West. At the same time, Damascus remains in close contact with Iran, Hizballah, and Hamas, unwilling to risk the certainty of these alliances for the sake of uncertain concessions from Jerusalem. What seems certain is Israel's inability to take any decisive steps soon because of its prolonged domestic political crisis, Syria's reluctance to reenter direct negotiations with Israel without U.S. involvement, and continued infighting among Palestinians for control of a failed state and process. None of the leaders appears able

Israeli soldiers provide security in Jerusalem

to gain popular or official support for the far-reaching compromises under consideration.

Resolution of the Arab-Israeli conflict is a vital national security interest of the United States. American attention—or lack thereof—to advancing the peace process by resolving conflicts between Israel and the Palestinians and Israel and its Arab neighbors affects regional perceptions of, and willingness to support, U.S. policies and actions. American approaches to the Palestinian dilemma and Washington's tendency to apply different standards to Israel have been used, in particular, to undercut regional support for the U.S. war against terror and efforts to promote regional security. Governments that have supported U.S. regional security policies in the past have come under increasingly heavy domestic criticism for their pro-American ties. Some may now be focused more on their own internal security issues and new threats from religious extremists and political reformers. For them, the Palestinian issue may be of lesser importance, but the fate of the Palestinians resonates with Arab and Iranian popular opinion and cannot be safely ignored.

The Options

Several plans to restart the peace process are on the table. Their outlines have been discussed since 2000, when President Bill Clinton made an effort to reach a settlement before he left office. At that time, the talks hinted at ways to resolve the most pressing issues, with both sides apparently considering concessions. The Palestinian right-of-return could possibly be settled by limiting the returnees to refugees from the 1948 war, or by allowing Palestinians to "return" not to their previous homes in Israel but to the new Palestinian state. Israel's borders with the new Palestinian state might resemble, but would not be restricted to, the pre-1967 borders, and, as promised in the Oslo Agreement, no new settlements would be established. There also could be agreement that land could be swapped to allow Israel to keep some settlements around Jerusalem and two other areas in exchange for land elsewhere in the West Bank. There was even a hint that the Palestinians might gain control over Palestinian-inhabited areas of East Jerusalem, minus the Old City and the non-Muslim religious sites, which would remain under Israeli control. The talks failed.

Variations have surfaced since then, but the failure of the George W. Bush administration to pursue peace between the Arabs and Israel until its last

Israeli Settlements and Palestinian Refugee Camps on the West Bank

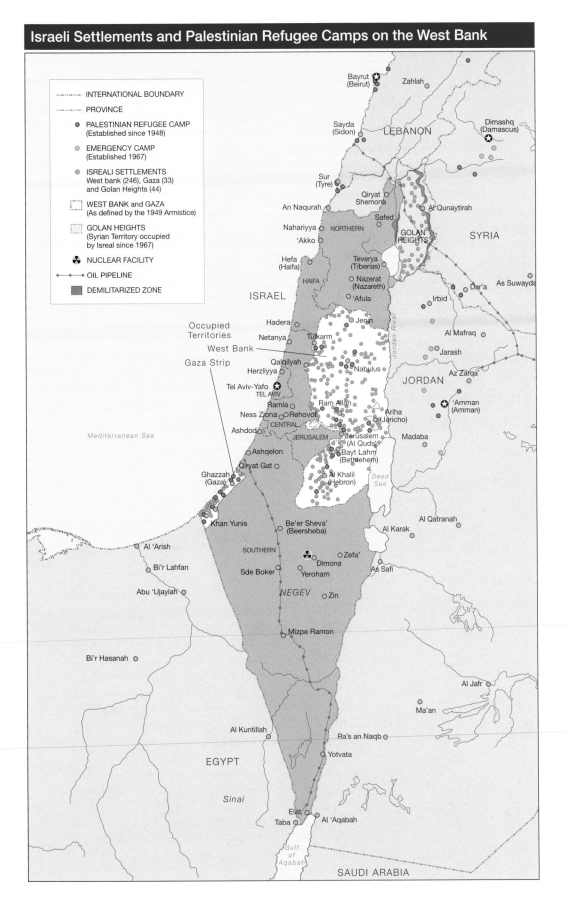

INTERNATIONAL BOUNDARY

PROVINCE

● PALESTINIAN REFUGEE CAMP
(Established since 1948)

○ EMERGENCY CAMP
(Established 1967)

○ ISREALI SETTLEMENTS
West bank (246), Gaza (33)
and Golan Heights (44)

WEST BANK and GAZA
(As defined by the 1949 Armistice)

GOLAN HEIGHTS
(Syrian Territory occupied
by Isreal since 1967)

☢ NUCLEAR FACILITY

OIL PIPELINE

DEMILITARIZED ZONE

year in office, or to adequately support President Mahmud Abbas, has made resolution nearly impossible. No direct talks were held between 2001 and 2008, and no draft agreement has been presented to either the Arab or Israeli governments or their publics. As in 2000, too much pressure was brought to bear for a quick resolution to the six-decade-old conflict on leaders who lacked the support of their governments and publics for these compromises. Indeed, little has been done to prepare Israelis or Palestinians for the kinds of concessions under discussion since 2000, and both the Israelis and Pales-

tinians are probably waiting to see what a new U.S. administration will offer. Several choices remain:

■ Israel appears ready for discussions about the key issues, but will seek assurances of American support for Israel's positions. Israel may be unwilling to freeze settlements or dismantle unauthorized outposts, and may continue to expand existing settlements around East Jerusalem, while also completing the security wall.

■ The Palestinians need immediate progress toward a settlement—including an Israeli settlements

Syria: Stabilizer or Spoiler?

Can Syria be a force for stability in the Middle East, or will it always be a spoiler? Since the advent of the Hafez al-Assad regime in 1970, Syria's external actions have been characterized by two mutually exclusive dynamics: on some occasions, Syria cooperated with the American order—the so-called *Pax Americana*—in the Middle East; at other times, Syria was at the forefront of those challenging that order. Despite the appearance of a dichotomy, however, Syrian foreign policy *is* consistent. The tension between Syria's contradictory modes of behavior is explained by its quest to recover the Golan Heights, occupied by Israel in 1967.

Syria functions as a stabilizing force when its leaders' focus on Syrian interests (that is, the recovery of the Golan Heights) is taken into account. There are multiple examples of Syria's stabilizing actions: its acceptance of the U.S.-brokered 1974 disengagement of forces agreement with Israel following the October 1973 war; its intervention in Lebanon in 1975 to tame the Palestinian Resistance Movement; and its alliance with the U.S.-led coalition against Iraq in 1990. In 1991, Syria accepted Washington's invitation to the Madrid Conference (in fact, Hafez al-Assad was the first Middle East leader to accept that invitation); this conference opened the way to the Oslo Agreement between Israel and the Palestinians, and to the Jordanian-Israeli peace treaty. More recently, Syria agreed to attend the Annapolis Conference in November 2007, thereby endowing it with greater legitimacy among the Arabs. The Bashar al-Assad regime agreed to attend on condition that the issue of the Golan Heights was added to the agenda of the conference.

Despite this positive record, however, Syria has also played the spoiler role when its interests were not taken into account. For example, Syria, along with Iraq, mobilized the Arab world against Egyptian President Anwar Sadat's separate peace with Israel; torpedoed the May 17, 1983, agreement that would have established a separate peace between Israel and Lebanon; and, along with Iran, tried to destabilize Lebanon prior to the 2007 Annapolis Conference. Nevertheless, when offered a seat at the table, along with the promise that the Golan would be discussed, Syria joined the negotiations, much to Iran's displeasure.

As evident from this pattern of behavior, the recovery of the Golan is the hinge upon which Syrian foreign policy swings. By extension, Syria's external actions reflect Washington's efforts to help Syria recover the Golan: when the United States actively pursues that goal, Syria cooperates. Conversely, when Washington excludes Damascus from a potential deal between Israel and other Arabs, Syria does what it can to sabotage it, including the use of terrorism. From a Syrian perspective, how Washington acts with regard to the Syrian-Israeli conflict will determine whether Syria is a spoiler or a stabilizer in the Middle East.

This has significant implications for U.S. policy in the region. Peace between Syria and Israel, based on the United Nations land-for-peace formula, is among the requisites for regional stability. Hence, if Syria's grievance is addressed, namely Israel's withdrawal from the Golan Heights (in return for Syria's recognition of Israel within secure boundaries free from the threat of war), Syria will have no more use for militant anti-Israel groups. Peace between Syria and Israel would then marginalize Hizballah and Hamas. It would also isolate Iran. The onus is thus on Washington.

freeze—if the government of President Abbas is to retain control of the West Bank and counter rival Hamas' hold over Gaza. Abbas needs something tangible to demonstrate his skills at negotiating with the Israelis, and his ability to create and maintain a stable, secure Palestine.

■ Hamas wants to consolidate its hold on Gaza and obtain international assistance. It and Israel may have been preparing for contact in July 2008 when a prisoner swap was arranged; some high-value Hamas prisoners held in Israel were to be exchanged for the bodies of two Israeli soldiers and kidnapped soldier Gilad Shalit abducted in the 2006 war. Hamas has offered Israel a truce (*hudna*) rather than a permanent negotiated settlement several times. Israel rejected these offers and any dealing with Hamas so long as rocket attacks on Israel continue. They may, however, find it convenient to renew the current ceasefire.

■ Saudi Arabia's King Abdullah tabled an Arab peace proposal in 2002 and again in 2007 that offered Israel official recognition, normalization of relations, and secure borders in exchange for its withdrawal to the pre-1967 borders.[11] Gulf Arabs have permitted some openings to Israeli business interests and hosted Israeli Foreign Minister Tzipi Livni at a trade conference in Qatar in 2008. Abdullah also invited a prominent Israeli Orthodox rabbi to an interfaith religious conference held in Spain in July 2008. The Arab states hope that by no longer questioning Israel's existence and focusing instead on Israeli withdrawal to the pre-1967 boundaries, all issues can be resolved, thereby allowing the focus to shift to the threat posed by Iran to Saudi and Arab interests.

■ Syria has held indirect discussions with Israel through Turkish mediators. As it was in the 1990s, Syria's price for peace is return of the Golan on its terms (pre-1967 lines). At issue is more than the Golan; it is control of the sources of water for most of northern Israel and Jordan. This was one of the reasons for the failure of Hafiz al-Assad's negotiations with Israel in the 1990s.[12]

Will opportunities exist for active U.S. peacemaking in the Arab-Israeli context? If not, can the United States do anything to help create such opportunities? The issues that need addressing are well known—the right of return for Palestinians, secure borders for Israel and Palestine, no new or expanded settlements, divided versus undivided Jerusalem—but the proposed solutions have yet to be officially presented or publicly debated. The Arab initiative can help the peace process by giving Palestinians the confidence

to take hard but necessary decisions to reach a settlement, but it will not be enough for the Palestinians that the Arab states will pay for those decisions. This could present an extraordinary opportunity for U.S. diplomacy to build on this foundation and bring the parties toward the historic tradeoffs and the detailed plans necessary to construct a two-state solution.

The Obstacles

Serious obstacles need to be removed before progress can be made. The trend toward political and religious radicalization is growing not only among Palestinians, but also among some Israelis and their hardline American supporters. A two-state solution has been at the core of Middle East peace efforts, but there are indications that support for it is waning. Hamas' victory in the 2006 Palestinian legislative elections was attributable as much to a failure of the peace process as it was to a rejection of the failed Fatah–Palestine Liberation Organization leadership style, growing disenchantment with secular solutions, growing religiosity, corruption, and mismanagement. Hamas' appeal in 2008–2009 is feeding off similar discontent within Middle Eastern society, especially the conviction that peace with Israel is not possible and thus "Islam is the solution."

Completion of the security fence separating Israelis from Palestinians may also carry a subtle warning of a shift in Israeli thinking about the viability of a two-state solution. Long before the establishment of the Jewish state, Zionist pioneers, immigrants, and those Jews born in *Eretz Yisrael* (the land of Israel) assumed Israel would fit into and be a part of the Middle East physically and psychologically. Some Israeli strategic thinkers now look more toward Europe for succor.[13] They and others in the United States talk of Israel as part of a democratic alliance of states that share the same political values and institutions. Israel is one of the six Mediterranean states considered junior partners of the EU and conducts joint training exercises with NATO. Is membership in the EU and NATO in Israel's future? More importantly, do Israelis see a strengthened connection to both organizations as a new security check that would possibly undercut European support for the Palestinians and wean Israel from its long-time dependence on its "special relationship" with the United States?

Several other obstacles could intrude on restarting Palestinian-Israeli and Arab-Israeli talks:

■ A failed Palestinian state will leave Israel with no partner for negotiations. The authority of the Palestinian Authority and its scope of control have been circumscribed since Hamas' 2007 election victory and takeover of Gaza. Palestinian Authority President Abbas and the PLO-Fatah are losing credibility both among their own people and on the international scene. One of the most critical aspects of a successful peace process is to ensure that the Palestinian Authority does not collapse and remains a partner in negotiations with Israel.

■ The weakness of Israel's governing coalition will stall progress. Israeli governments are almost always drawn from quarrelsome parties with deep divisions and a taste for high-risk political gambling. Israeli leaders often dangle promises of settlement and fears of an existential threat to rally support in an election. The campaign and elections of February 2009 were no different.

■ Isolating Syria would slow but probably not prevent limited progress on Israeli-Palestinian discussions. At issue is Syria's willingness to end its ties to Hizballah, Hamas, and ultimately Iran, in exchange for concessions on the Golan. Engaging Syria would limit its capacity to derail progress on Palestinian-Israeli talks.

■ Another Israel-Hizballah war would almost certainly disrupt if not break down any peace process. Lebanon's internal stability, which in 2008 had not been a priority for Washington, needs attention from the United States and its allies.

What Is to Be Done?

Most U.S. administrations begin their terms expecting to focus on domestic economic issues and stabilizing the Gulf region. Few have relished tackling the Gordian knot of the Palestinian-Israeli peace process, but none ultimately has been able to ignore it. Some suggestions for the new U.S. administration, drawn from past experiences, include:

■ Avoid focusing on short-term fixes and delaying discussion of the main issues of Palestinian return, settlements, and borders. All are difficult issues, especially Jerusalem, but baby steps will no longer buy time or ease tensions. Interim or partial agreements usually fail to build confidence on either side and will only breed more distrust.

■ Isolating Syria will not encourage a change in behavior. Damascus will need to succeed in its goal of regaining the Golan if it is to risk altering its ties with Iran and Hizballah.

The Challenge of Political Reform

The period since 2001 has seen the rise and fall of international interest in political reform in the Arab world. Where there once was heady optimism and enthusiasm, there is now increasing pessimism and despair. The current struggle for political reform began

▼ Continued on p. 206

DOD (Robert Reeve)

U.S. M1A1 tanks move across desert in Kuwait, Operation *Desert Storm*

Kuwait: Democratic Vanguard or the Next Islamic Republic?

In the years since 1991 and Kuwait's liberation from Iraqi occupation, many states in the Middle East region have instituted political reforms. Some of the changes have been significant, others minimal, intended more as window dressing to impress domestic populations and foreign critics than as real change. Most regional governments now hold elections for a tame parliament or municipal councils. Some monarchies have broadened political participation for nonroyal elites and women. Progress has been uneven at best, with many governments unwilling to move at a faster pace than conservative tribal and religious elements.

Kuwait in many respects has been the vanguard of change in the Gulf. The first state to have an elected parliament (1963) and to dissolve it when it refused to follow government guidance, Kuwait today has the most independent and transparent system in the region. Kuwait also illustrates the limitations of political reform. Twice since 1961, the ruling Al Sabah family suspended parliament indefinitely. After liberation in 1992, however, the family bowed to heavy domestic and American pressure, agreeing to reinstate the National Assembly and call for new elections if it were dissolved.

Kuwait's parliamentarians have ventured into areas of power and politics where few in the Arab world have dared go. They have been encouraged in this by dysfunctional factionalism within the ruling family. Liberals, nationalists, Islamists, and tribal deputies compete with each other and the government for public attention. The result has been a parliament that can block reform when it wishes but cannot take positive action on its own. Moreover, tribal deputies, who are anxious to secure economic benefits for their followers, frequently clash with Islamist deputies who have a different social and economic outlook. Both have a far more conservative social vision than the Al Sabah government, and favor rolling back government decisions, especially on postwar reconstruction and investment issues and educational reform (which they regard as too secular, insufficiently religious, and too permissive of mixed sexes). They oppose votes for women, demand that women wear the *hijab* (headscarf), and oppose women cabinet ministers. They seek the right to question members of the government, including Al Sabah family members, veto laws approved by the government, form political parties, name cabinet members, and approve the prime minister, who they believe could be a commoner. In response, the government dissolved the parliament in 2008, rejected calls to dismiss officials, and reduced the number of voting districts from 25 to 5 to weaken the conservative Islamist-tribal bloc. The ploy failed. No women have been elected to the National Assembly and the conservative alliance now holds nearly half the seats in parliament, a significant increase over its numbers in the previous parliament.

Elsewhere in the region, democratic reform has taken place, but it has rarely changed the fundamental nature of politics. Bahrain had a parliament briefly from 1973 to 1975. It was not restored until 2002. Shia make up approximately 75 percent of the population but only 17 of its 40-member parliament. The king and tribes from its Sunni Arab minority rule this small, oil-poor state, and the government is criticized for trying to shift the population balance by granting citizenship to foreign Sunnis. Bahrain's Shia parliamentarians demand an end to political, employment, and religious discrimination; all parliamentarians would like the right to question cabinet members. Oman, Qatar, and Saudi Arabia have experimented with municipal elections. Only the United Arab Emirates (UAE) has had no elections, though it has adopted an odd step by designating a small number of citizens who may vote when elections are held—in short reversing the normal democratic arrangement by having the rulers pick the voters rather than the other way around. Kuwait, the UAE, and Oman have women in their cabinets, but Bahrain took an even more unusual step in 2008 when it named a Jewish woman as its ambassador to the United States.

The political deadlock in Kuwait has led its citizens to speculate that the ruling family will once again abandon democracy by suspending parliament. Once seen as a positive model for other Gulf states, Kuwait's democratic experiment is currently at an impasse, which critics can now cite as a reason to avoid adopting democratic reforms in their own country.

▲ *Continued from p. 204*

decades ago, and not just when its lack was identified as a possible contributing factor to the rising popularity of religious extremism. Popular demand for reform is unlikely to disappear, especially as deep political problems related to governance in the Middle East show little sign of abating. Even if the United States scales back on its commitment to regional political reform, as it seems now to be doing, and security concerns appear more pressing for most regional regimes, demands for change in governance will continue and are likely to complicate U.S. security efforts.

Regional Reform Trends . . .

Middle Eastern societies have changed in some fundamental ways over recent decades, and the pace of change is not likely to slow. Political conflicts and the vicissitudes of high oil prices in consumer states have shifted power and influence in the region. The rapidly growing population in many Middle East societies has created a "youth bulge," and even though growth rates show signs of slowing, the ripple effects of that bulge will be felt for years to come. The rapid expansion of education has created a literate population in many states, but the quality of that education has left the labor force poorly prepared for a globalized economy. The era after independence saw most regimes make strong commitments to provide for the material needs of their population. Whether socialist or capitalist, republic or monarchy, the state assumed responsibility for providing food, health care, employment, and education to the entire citizenry. In recent years, however, governments have worked hard to

jettison many of these commitments, with uncertain success (even oil-rich states with small populations, such as Kuwait, have shown some discomfort with the level of material benefits they are expected to provide). But with an uneven record at best of participation in a globalized economy, the decline of the welfare state leaves behind social, economic, and political tensions that will be difficult to resolve.

Interstate conflicts will also likely show little sign of abatement. The Israeli-Palestinian conflict may be moving away from settlement, regardless of the signs of possible truce between Israel and Gaza, Syria, and Lebanon. This and the possibility that Iraq could disintegrate has set off a new round of regional rivalries and tensions. Such conflicts have domestic repercussions because they undermine the legitimacy of existing regimes that seem unable to pursue a clear policy toward, much less address, such conflicts.

In short, regional regimes are likely to appear increasingly unable to meet popular needs and respond to regional challenges. Widespread political cynicism has set in, with existing political elites widely regarded as corrupt, ineffective, and unaccountable. Such cynicism has rarely taken revolutionary form—the stability of existing regimes is remarkable in light of their poor policy performance—and that is unlikely to change because rulers have become adept at suppressing, dividing, and coopting opposition movements. Instead of dramatic upheaval, the region is likely to pass through a period in which rulers are weak but not unstable, continuously fending off pressure to reform but unable to respond effectively to economic and political challenges.

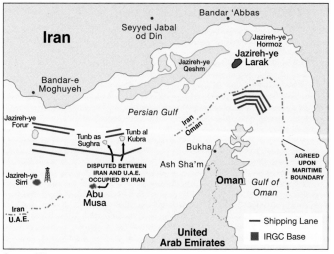

Source: CIA

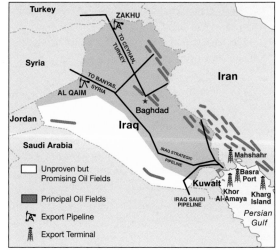

Source: CIA

. . . and U.S. National Security Interests

At first glance, domestic debates over the kind and quality of political reform would seem to have little relevance for the security presence and strategic regional interests of the United States, or its relations with friendly governments. If regimes believe that they are not likely to face revolutionary challenges, then it would seem possible for Washington to maintain longstanding stable government-to-government relations. The United States has been careful to mute its rhetoric on the necessity of political reform and the virtues of Western-style democracy, and most rulers appear willing to continue their cooperation with the United States despite popular criticism. If a replay of the 1979 Iranian revolution occurs, however, and a regime hostile to the United States replaces a critical security partner, then U.S. arrangements and relationships will be at serious risk.

If domestic political difficulties are unlikely to pose a dramatic challenge to U.S. security interests, there are some important exceptions. Support for al Qaeda and other extremist movements among dissidents in the Arab world grew with the conviction that the United States was a more important target than their own governments. This popularity reflects an Arab "street" frustrated with the U.S. stance on the Palestinian issue, support for Israel, and protection of rulers seen as corrupt and un-Islamic. Al Qaeda's leaders argue that the best way to confront domestic political shortcomings is to expel the United States from the region. Al Qaeda was spectacularly successful in 2001, but it has been far less successful in shifting the debate within regional societies. Most Islamist movements remain focused on domestic agendas.

The pressure for political reform will likely confront the United States with more subtle challenges. In a region of unpopular regimes that lack domestic legitimacy, Washington will continue to find that good government-to-government relations aggravate rather than undermine its unpopularity. Moreover, blame for the persistence of regional crises—most notably if the Israeli-Palestinian conflict continues and should Iraq fail—will be linked directly to U.S. policies. Demands for political reform and the unresolved nature of regional conflicts will not disrupt U.S. business relations with governments in the region, but the United States will continue to be identified with unpopular policies and regimes and unjust regional realities.

Complicating the U.S. Mission

Given these realities, pursuit of U.S. national security interests in the Greater Middle East is likely to be complicated in three ways:

■ Long-term government-to-government security relationships can be pursued, but they could be unpopular and embarrassing to regional governments. Jordan, for example, is one of America's closest and oldest security partners in the region. Yet Amman strives to obscure the depth of its cooperation from its public. This is likely to be a continuing pattern in the region. It will make bilateral relations sometimes rocky, especially if weak regimes feel compelled to scale back on security ties.

■ The United States will become—whether it likes it or not—an unwitting player in domestic politics in the region. Because it has built its security posture on good government-to-government relations, the United States is seen as "propping up" regional autocracies. In some ways, this perception overstates its capabilities; autocracy is very much a home-grown phenomenon, and America's ability to sustain unpopular regimes, while real, is greatly exaggerated. At a minimum, Washington will find itself a political football; at a maximum, it will be called upon to help support regimes that have lost the confidence of their own people.

■ The United States may become involved in governance missions. The wall between security interests and governance issues characteristic of past decades of U.S. regional policy has collapsed. Governance issues, when they were raised in Washington,

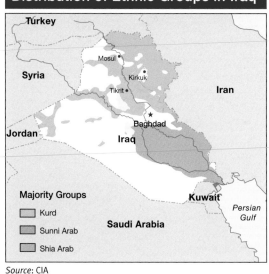

Distribution of Ethnic Groups in Iraq

Turkey

Mosul

Syria

Kirkuk

Tikrit

Iran

★ Baghdad

Jordan

Iraq

Majority Groups

Kuwait

Persian Gulf

☐ Kurd

☐ Sunni Arab

Saudi Arabia

☐ Shia Arab

Source: CIA

Islamists: Why They Won't Go Away

The challenge of political Islam is often viewed through a security prism, an unsurprising perspective after the attacks of September 11, 2001. But from a regional perspective, Islamist movements are better seen as a long-term political challenge than as a short-term security threat.

Islamist movements are broadly based social movements that encompass a wide variety of activities—social, educational, charitable, missionary, and political. In the second half of the 20th century, the authoritarian political environment in the Arab world actually led many to deemphasize politics: those who wished to build more Islamic societies found opportunities to do so through quieter paths, such as building kindergartens or encouraging students to form religious study groups.

In a paradoxical fashion, this led Islamist movements to become more powerful political actors. No longer are Islamists organized in tightly formed, hierarchical ways that are easier to control or suppress. Instead, they tend to be loosely organized social movements with deep roots and broad constituencies; these are very difficult for governments to contain or root out.

In the 1970s and 1980s, some Islamist movements began to reenter politics. The most radical groups insisted that any regime failing to implement Islamic law was illegitimate and should be overthrown. Such radical movements challenged regimes in Egypt, Syria, Algeria, Saudi Arabia, and other places. But in all cases, they were defeated. Al Qaeda is attempting to unite the remaining fragments of these groups into an international network that turns its attention from overthrowing regional regimes to combating the Western forces that it holds responsible for propping up regional dictators.

But while the radicals have captured the headlines in recent years, they hardly represent the mainstream. Other, far larger groups embarked on a very different path. They continued their efforts to reform society in other realms while taking advantage of whatever political openings occurred to organize more freely, develop political programs, and even run for office. For these groups, the political struggle is only one part of a broader mission of social progress, and they see their role as reformist rather than revolutionary. They aim not to replace the regime but to transform it.

These groups, best exemplified by the Muslim Brotherhood and its offshoots in various countries, can shift between calls for far-reaching change and more soothing, conservative, and modest reform proposals. The fact that they are Islamist, that they have broad constituencies, and that they share some common origin with the radicals leads many regimes to treat them as security threats. The problem is that such an approach leads to short-term repressive measures that do little over the long term to confront the challenge posed by this strain of political Islam. Regimes find over time that Islamists, because of their deep social roots, cannot easily be suppressed, which has led a few to experiment with political strategies of incorporation by seeking to pull such groups into the system rather than stamp them out. The deep authoritarian streak that characterizes most regimes in the region, however, militates against such a political approach.

were generally addressed through diplomacy and foreign assistance, not through defense and security relationships. That began to change with the 2003 Iraq War and the U.S. military's uncharacteristic role in post-Saddam governance and operations against the endemic insurgencies. On a more modest level, greater attention will be paid by political leaders to the governance implications of security arrangements. U.S. security assistance, for instance, may need to be designed in such a way as to bring issues of civilian control of the military and security forces, political accountability, and respect for human rights to the attention of the recipients.

A general implication of these challenges is an increased likelihood that when regional tensions are highest, and the United States needs security cooperation the most, regional partners will be the least reliable. Even regional actors with a long history of security cooperation with the United States, such as Saudi Arabia, are clearly coming to view the relationship as a problem to be managed as much as it is a source of support. It is increasingly common to hear once-close U.S. allies in the region indicate that they regard the United States much more warily than previously. Many say they now see it more as a source of political instability in the region than a security guarantor.

Coping with Change

After 2003, the United States embarked on an ambitious project of regional transformation. The new administration will be forced to deal with the consequences of that project's shortcomings. This will encompass two related challenges:

■ How can we pursue political reform in a less messianic fashion? It is clear that the nature of regional governance will complicate the U.S. posture in the region and that political reform must be part of a long-term strategy. But the tools the United States has used to promote political reform were developed for use in the former Soviet bloc and Latin America—very different places, whose governments (in the 1990s) welcomed U.S. assistance in bringing reform. When the United States turned its attention to the Middle East, it found such tools ineffective, and the attempt to add a new tool (Iraq-style forced regime change) is hardly one that is likely to be used repeatedly. Washington will need to find tools for pursuing political reform that are effective but gradual.

■ How can we balance short-term crisis management with long-term reform? The turn away from political reform since 2006 is marked, but it is not absolute. And the reasons are clear: the press of political crises in the region has made political reform seem like a long-term luxury rather than a short-term need—and indeed, with the strong showing of Islamists in regional politics, it has come to be seen as a long-term luxury that complicates short-term problems. The United States will have to find a way to promote political reform in a manner that balances long-term strategies with short-term crisis management.

Elements of a New U.S. Strategy

When oil sold for $20 a barrel and Asia was not a major consumer of the world's energy resources, the United States had greater leverage on the Gulf states. And when the United States first entered Iraq in 2003, its influence was at its highest point. Neither lasted long. What, then, are U.S. options for the issues outlined here?

Engagement or Isolation for Iran and Syria?

American administrations since the 1979 Islamic revolution and hostage crisis have believed that the Iranian regime's most important goal was recognition of its legitimacy and that talking to Iranian leaders would be tantamount to recognition and a reward for bad behavior. The tactic may have been effective in the 1980s, when Iran was at war with Iraq and considered a rogue state intent on exporting its extreme version of Islamic revolution to Iraq, Lebanon, and the Gulf. But denial of recognition may no longer be the sole trump card for Washington. Neither Ahmadinejad nor Supreme Leader Khamenei seems intimidated by U.S. refusal to recognize the Islamic Republic. Equally important to Ahmadinejad and most Iranians are recognition and acceptance of Iran's claims as the dominant power in the Gulf region, and a participant to be consulted in matters dealing with the Greater Middle East, including Israeli-Palestinian and Lebanese issues, and the Islamic world in general.

Similarly, offering to hold talks with Iran or Syria does not imply recognition of or approval for bad behavior. It would, however, signal Iran's neighbors and the Greater Middle East region that the United States is willing to revitalize diplomacy and seek areas of common ground. Washington and Tehran have some key interests in common; for example, both have a huge stake in Iraq's survival as a unified state that functions within acceptable parameters and quells its sectarian unrest. Washington's refusal to talk to Iran has placed the burden of responsibility for failed negotiations on the United States. An offer to enter talks, however, would shift the onus of obstructionism onto Iran.

Other steps the United States could take include an end to the vilification of Iran or Syria as rogue states. Frequent public condemnation of Iran and outraged responses to Ahmadinejad's vituperative statements only serve to enhance his stature among Iranians and the Arab street. Conversely, recognizing Iran's security perceptions and giving it a voice in a regional forum would allow Iran the political, economic, and strategic interaction it seeks, but would also set the agenda and terms of engagement on the basis of Iran's behavior before it tries to make demands based on its nuclear status. Washington could offer to end or eliminate some of the sanctions that preclude economic development in Iran. The sanctions clearly hinder Iran's efforts to develop its economic infrastructure; in July 2008, the French oil company Total pulled out of plans to develop some Iranian oil projects because of political pressure and economic risk. Acquiescence to a pipeline project to carry Central Asian gas and oil through Iran would be an important signal that the United States is aware of Iran's economic needs. It could also defuse potential Iranian dependence on Chinese investment in the energy sector of its economy.

Promote Cooperation or Isolation between Iraq, Iran, and Their Gulf Neighbors?

For the next 10 to 15 years, Iraqis will need to concentrate on reinventing themselves, their identity, their political institutions, and their economic infrastructure. To do so, they will need cooperation from their neighbors to stabilize trade and development plans and maintain secure borders. The United States needs to encourage Iraq's neighbors—especially Turkey, Saudi Arabia, Kuwait, and Syria—to assist Iraq in border security and to end arms, narcotics, and human trafficking. In the long term, Iraq could return to challenge Iran for the coveted position of paramount leader of the Gulf region. It could also resume efforts to build up its new military into more than a defensive force and, if Iran has crossed the nuclear weapons threshold, try to acquire WMD again.

Iraq and U.S. friends in the Gulf will continue to move cautiously in developing ties to Iran. Those ties, for now and the foreseeable future, will probably

▼ *Continued on p. 211*

The Strait of Hormuz, Iran, and the Risk: A Fact Box

The sea channel that abuts Iran's coastline at the entrance to the Persian Gulf is often described as the world's most important waterway because of the huge volume of oil exported through it daily. The Strait of Hormuz is located at a narrow bend of water separating Oman and Iran, and connects the biggest Gulf oil producers, such as Saudi Arabia, with the Gulf of Oman and the Arabian Sea. At its narrowest point, the strait is only 34 miles (55 kilometers) across. It consists of 2-mile (3.2-kilometer)-wide navigable channels for inbound and outbound tanker traffic as well as a 2-mile-wide buffer zone.

Some additional facts about the Strait of Hormuz:

■ Oil flowing through the strait accounts for roughly 40 percent of all globally traded oil supply, according to the U.S. Energy Information Administration. The figure fluctuates with changing output from the Organization of the Petroleum Exporting Countries. In May 2007, the International Energy Agency estimated 13.4 million barrels per day (bpd) of crude passed through the narrow channel on tankers. An additional 2 million barrels of oil products, including fuel oil, are exported through the passage daily, as well as liquefied natural gas.

■ Exports from the world's largest liquefied natural gas exporter, Qatar, also pass through the strait en route to Asia and Europe, totaling some 31 million tons a year.

■ Ninety percent of oil exported from Gulf producers is carried on oil tankers through the strait.

■ Japanese officials say 90 percent of their oil imports come from the Gulf. Industry sources report that more than 75 percent of Japan's oil passes through the strait.

■ One of U.S. Central Command's key missions in the Gulf is to ensure the free flow of oil and energy supplies. Between 1984 and 1987, a "tanker war" took place between Iran and Iraq, in which each nation fired on the other's oil tankers bound for their respective ports. Foreign-flagged vessels were caught in the crossfire. Shipping in the Gulf dropped by 25 percent because of the exchange, forcing the intervention of the United States to secure the shipping lanes.

■ Iran has admitted to deploying antiaircraft and antiship missiles on Abu Musa, an island strategically located near the strait's shipping lanes and claimed by the United Arab Emirates. In 2008, Iran announced the Iranian Revolutionary Guard Corps naval force would establish a post at the point where shipping enters the Gulf.

■ The Energy Information Administration predicts oil exports passing through the strait will double to between 30 million and 34 million bpd by 2020.

■ Merchant ships carrying grains, iron ore, sugar, perishables, and containers full of finished goods also pass through the strategic sea corridor en route to Gulf countries and major ports such as Dubai.

■ Heavy armor and military supplies for the U.S. Armed Forces in Iraq and other Gulf countries pass through the channel aboard U.S. Navy–owned, U.S.-flagged, and foreign-flagged ships.

Published by Reuters, July 1, 2008.

Sources: International Energy Agency, U.S. Energy Information Administration, United Nations Conference on Trade and Development, GlobalSecurity.org, U.S. Navy Military Sealift Command, and Clarkson shipping consultancy.

▲ *Continued from p. 209*

remain limited to cooperation on trade, commerce, police matters, and sharing of intelligence on drugs and narcotics trafficking. They are not likely to include any significant security pact whose terms express a demand for the immediate withdrawal of U.S. military forces from the region. Gulf governments may prefer to avoid antagonizing their larger and dangerous neighbors, but they also realize that the U.S. presence and commitments to their security allow them the freedom to negotiate with former enemies Iran and Iraq.

Pursue Effective Deterrence and Collective Defense Options at the Same Time?

Continued arms sales to the region are no panacea for countering a nuclear-armed Iran, but two alternatives are frequently mentioned. Both have drawbacks. The first is a regional nuclear-free zone, but neither Israel nor Iran seems interested. The second is to turn the GCC into a regional defense and security organization that would include Iraq, Yemen, and, eventually, Iran. Unfortunately, the GCC would be hard pressed to become the Persian Gulf's or Middle East's equivalent of NATO, the Organisation for Security and Co-operation in Europe, or the EU. Moreover, pan-regional solutions will not work; they are too broad in scope, and too vague in purpose.

The United States could cooperate with its European partners and those Asian states dependent on the region's energy resources to support the establishment of a subregional security organization as a venue for threat reduction talks, confidence-building measures, and cooperative political, economic, and security unions. This could be a venue to discuss security measures to keep sea lanes in the Persian Gulf open and protect access to and shipment of oil. China, Japan, and India are becoming increasingly dependent on the Gulf states for their energy needs (Japan receives 90 percent of its oil from the Gulf, and China and India meet probably half of their energy needs with Gulf oil). Yet all depend on the United States, and the United Kingdom to a lesser extent, to protect the Strait of Hormuz. A regionwide security venue could encourage them to participate in regional measures to protect the strait and Gulf shipping. Their participation would encourage Iran, Iraq, and the Gulf states to join.

Similarly, Washington should engage Europe, non-Gulf Arabs (Egypt and Jordan), and Asian powers with influence in the region to address security issues that are not specifically military. Most states in this region share transnational problems: terrorism, religious and nationalist extremism, organized crime, arms smuggling, illegal immigration, environmental pollution, drug and human trafficking, disease, poverty, lack of water resources, and desertification. Turkey, for example, under the Islamist AK Party (*Adalet ve Kalkınma Partisi*, or Justice and Development Party) has been looking east to the Arab world and Iran for a new role in regional developments and cooperation against common enemies. It has a significant investment in Iraqi reconstruction and trade with Iran, and Ankara cooperates with Iran to contain anti-Turkish PKK (*Partiya Karkerên Kurdistan*, or Kurdistan Workers' Party) terrorists sheltered in Iraqi Kurdistan.

Offer the GCC Expanded Security Guarantees and a Smaller Military Presence?

In the face of a nuclear-capable Iran or a rearmed Iraq, the Gulf Arabs are likely to seek expanded U.S. guarantees of enhanced protection and promises to defend them if a confrontation is imminent. This could include advanced missile defense systems or even inclusion under the American nuclear umbrella. They are not likely, however, to support an American policy of preemptive strikes to lessen their Iran problem or to welcome the presence of a substantial U.S. military force on bases or with access to base facilities. Nor will they join Iran in a security arrangement that would preclude a U.S. presence in the Gulf, reflecting in part their understanding that the U.S. military presence allows them to improve relations with Tehran now and Baghdad some day. At the same time, the Gulf regimes are wary of closer ties to the United States, fearing popular protest against the costs of the U.S. presence and dependence on its military for protection that their own governments should be able to provide.

Push Hard on American-style Political Reform or Insist on Timetables for Change?

Even without U.S. pressure, the governments of the Greater Middle East will face daunting challenges over the next decade, including rising demands for an end to authoritarian rule (whether monarchies, ruling families, single parties, or tribes), and greater restrictions on or opportunities for women. There may be problems of overdevelopment and a risk to the fragile Gulf ecosystem from increased tanker traffic, lack of potable water, or a nuclear accident or

Turkey Faces East

After decades of passivity and neglect toward the Middle East, Turkey is once again becoming an active player in that region. For most of its republican history, Ankara did not consider the Middle East a foreign policy priority. The official ideology of the republic, Kemalism, turned its back on the Islamic world and pursued an exclusively Western path. This one-sided orientation began to change with the end of the Cold War. It reflected Turkey's new geostrategic horizons, cooling ties between Europe and Turkey, and perceived threats and opportunities in regions surrounding Turkey. As a result, first under the late Turgut Ozal (prime minister from 1983–1989 and president from 1989–1993), and more recently under the Justice and Development Party (*Adalet ve Kalkınma Partisi*, or AKP) from 2002 to the present, Turkey became more involved in the Greater Middle East. In recent years, Ankara adopted a more active approach toward the Israeli-Palestinian issue, sent troops to support the North Atlantic Treaty Organization mission in Afghanistan, contributed to the United Nations forces in Lebanon, assumed a leadership position in the Organization of the Islamic Conference, attended Arab League conferences, established closer ties with Iran, Iraq, and Syria, and improved its economic, political, and diplomatic relations with most Arab and Muslim states.

Turkey is deeply polarized over its Muslim, secular, and national identities, and Turkish foreign policy is certainly not immune from such divisions. In one camp, secularist critics of the AKP government maintain that Turkey's activism in the Middle East abandons the republic's Western vocation and orientation. These skeptics usually focus on AKP's Muslim political pedigree and tend to see a hidden Islamic agenda behind openings to the Arab world. In the opposing camp are those who argue that such an Islamic agenda simply does not exist, mainly on the grounds that the AKP is the most pro–European Union (EU) political party in the Turkish domestic political scene. Despite its Islamic roots, the AKP has indeed worked much harder than previous Turkish governments to improve Ankara's chances of EU membership. Such efforts were eventually rewarded with the opening of accession negotiations between Turkey and the EU in December 2005. Since neither of the camps is able to convince the other, this polarized debate continues. Ankara's Middle East policy also presents a dilemma for policymakers in Washington, who are often puzzled by Turkey's rapprochement with countries such as Syria and Iran.

What is the rationale behind Ankara's new interest in the Middle East? There are two conflicting drivers of Turkish policy, namely the Kurdish challenge and neo-Ottomanism. Turkey's Middle East policy is increasingly driven by the tension between these two alternative visions and priorities. Neo-Ottomanism seeks to transcend the Kemalist norms of the republic, which define Turkey's preoccupation with its Kurdish challenge. Kemalism considers Kurdish ethnicity and nationalism as existential threats to the national and territorial integrity of the Turkish Republic. Even the Kurdish language and cultural rights for Kurds are deemed dangerous, on the grounds that they make Kurdish assimilation—the official policy of the republic since 1923—much more difficult. The nationalist aspirations of Kurds in Iran, Iraq, and Syria pose a similar challenge for Turkish foreign policy. As a result, when the Kurdish question dominates Ankara's agenda, Turkish foreign policy becomes apprehensive, reactive, and insecure.

Neo-Ottomanism, by contrast, seeks to rise above this Kemalist myopia. Compared to Kemalism, neo-Ottoman instincts are more self-confident and less focused on the Kurdish threat. Neo-Ottomanism embraces a grand geostrategic vision in which Turkey is an effective and engaging regional actor, working to solve regional problems as a bridge between East and West. Rather than pursue a neoimperialist policy aimed at resurrecting the Ottoman Empire, however, neo-Ottomanism is essentially about projecting Turkey's "soft power" as a Muslim, secular, democratic, capitalist force. Similar to French Gaullism, it seeks Turkish "grandeur" and an influential foreign policy. Today, Turkey appears torn between these two alternative visions of foreign relations. While the Kurdish challenge forces Ankara to be reactive, cautious, and sometimes overly insecure, neo-Ottomanism motivates Turkish policymakers to be more audacious, imaginative, and proactive. Needless to say, the secularist Kemalist mindset is uncomfortable with the neo-Ottoman vision, which it perceives as unrealistic, adventurist, and pro-Islamic.

In dealing with the Middle East, the challenge for Ankara will be to balance its Kemalist and neo-Ottoman instincts. The challenge posed by the Kurdistan Workers' Party (known as the PKK) movement plays into the hands of Kemalist hardliners in the military, which means that in the short term, the Kurdish question is likely to remain a central factor in the formulation of Turkey's national security policy. Although Turkey has legitimate concerns about terrorism, military means alone will not solve the Kurdish question. Much hinges on Turkey's success in becoming a more liberal democracy, where cultural and political rights for Kurds are not perceived as a national security threat. Ultimately, whether Turkey can positively engage the Middle East and solve its Kurdish dilemma will require reconciliation between the neo-Ottoman and Kemalist visions, both at home and in foreign policy.

oil fire. The region also faces a challenge to keep its small, rich populations happy and expatriate labor unorganized and isolated (more than 85 percent of the population of Qatar and the UAE is foreign labor, for example). Washington will need to choose its issues carefully, especially since a strong public stance on domestic political reform often triggers local cynicism that the United States does not live by its ideals and that its security is heavily reliant on dysfunctional or unpopular regimes in the region.

The United States has key national security interests and objectives in the Greater Middle East. The U.S. military is likely to be present in the Gulf for some time. The desire to reduce the U.S. military footprint in Iraq and the vulnerability of forward-deployed forces need to be balanced against the diplomatic and deterrent value of a visible U.S. military presence in the Gulf. If friends and enemies no longer see U.S. forces and operations, they may conclude that the Gulf governments are once again vulnerable to intimidation or outright threat and that the United States is less likely to defend its interests and honor its security commitments in the region. As U.S. policymakers approach decisions on the future forward presence posture for the Gulf, several political realities need to be taken into account:

Iraq, Iran, and Syria are not perceived by the Arab states as major and imminent threats to regional security, and most believe the United States needs to shape strategies to engage them positively.

Palestine is important. The fact or perception of Israeli intransigence, as well as divisions within the Palestinian Authority and U.S. reluctance to take the lead in finding a solution, shapes public attitudes and damages U.S. influence in the Greater Middle East to a significant degree.

Political change in Iran may come smoothly or violently, but it will not alter a defense strategy based on the acquisition of a nuclear capability and is unlikely to lead to major reversals in Tehran's foreign and security policies. The 2005 presidential election was fought between conservatives and reformists, but the 2009 battle was waged mainly between the "strict" conservatives loyal to Ahmadinejad and the "pragmatic" conservatives around Mir-Hussein Mossavi.

Is there a Sunni-Shia confrontation ahead? Probably not, although some scholars and leaders in the region predict it, or at least feign concern about it.[14] The Shia-Sunni tensions that wrack the region are, if not unprecedented, certainly impressive in their intensity. They are a consequence of the 2003 war and pose security problems for the region. Iran's ultimate goal in Iraq is to prevent Iraq from reemerging as a threat, whether of a military, political, or ideological nature. Iraq's failure, its collapse into civil war, or the emergence of independent ethnic or sectarian-defined ministates would have huge implications for disaffected minorities in Syria, Turkey, Iran, and the Gulf states.

Convincing Iran that the United States is not set on regime change there will be very difficult. A major factor in Iran's policymaking calculus is a desire to maintain "strategic depth" in Iraq. Iranian leaders will remain convinced that the United States and Israel will continue to plan on the use of force to stop Iran's nuclear program. The ability to retaliate against U.S. troops in Iraq, as well as against Israel via Hizballah in Lebanon, is seen by Iranian officials as leverage that diminishes the chances of an American attack on Iran. **gsa**

NOTES

[1] Supreme Leader Khamenei was chosen by the circle around Ayatollah Khomeini and serves for life; he is subject only to a yearly approval by the elected Council of Guardians. The president of Iran, however, can serve two terms successively, and then must stand down before he can run again in a general election.

[2] In a speech before the 2008 Majles election, Supreme Leader Khamenei declared that "Allah would reprimand those voters who failed to support the controversial nuclear power program."

[3] IRGC leaders must have favored the election of one of their own as president. Ahmadinejad joined the paramilitary basij as a youth and fought in the Iran-Iraq war as a member of the IRGC.

[4] In the March 2008 parliamentary elections, 4,500 of 7,200 registered candidates ran for office. Most of those disqualified by the Council of Guardians were reformists, but a grandson of Ayatollah Khomeini was also rejected on the ground that "he lacked loyalty to Islam and the constitution."

[5] Muhammad Baqr al-Hakim was the spiritual leader of the movement; he was assassinated in August 2004 outside the Imam Ali Mosque in Najaf. Abd al-Aziz was in charge of the SCIRI militia, the Badr Brigade, and fought with Iranian forces against Iraq in the Iran-Iraq war. He currently heads the organization. Apparently at the suggestion of the Iranians, SCIRI changed its name to the Islamic Supreme Council of Iraq in 2007.

[6] For a short history of the U.S. military engagement in the Persian Gulf, see Richard Sokolsky, ed., *The United States and the Persian Gulf: Reshaping Security Strategy for the Post-Containment Era* (Washington, DC: National Defense University Press, 2003).

[7] The United States first entered the Gulf with a small naval presence—the U.S. 5th Fleet—in 1947 in Bahrain and a U.S. Air Force presence in Dhahran, Saudi Arabia, from the 1940s through the early 1960s.

[8] In 2001, the GCC extended a special status to Yemen but is reluctant to extend full membership to Yemen, Iraq, or Iran.

[9] Other nations that have said they plan to construct civilian nuclear reactors or have sought technical assistance and advice from the IAEA, the Vienna-based United Nations nuclear watchdog agency, in the last year include Egypt, Jordan, Syria, Turkey, and Yemen, as well as several North African nations. See Bob Drogin and Borzou Daraghi, "Arabs make plans for nuclear power," *Los Angeles Times*, May 26, 2007.

[10] Iranian sources claim the GCC invited Ahmadinejad to speak, but Gulf officials say the Iranian invited himself to Doha for the summit. He reportedly spoke about a 12-point plan for regional security, but no further information has been made available.

[11] See <www.al-bab.com/arab/docs/league/peace02.htm>.

[12] Details on these and other meetings are available at the following Web sites: for Clinton 2000, see <www.prospectsforpeace.com/Resources/Plans/Clintonpeace.doc>; for the 2001 negotiations between Israelis and Palestinians in Taba, see <www.peacelobby.org/moratinos_document.htm>; for the nonofficial Israeli-Palestinian Geneva Initiative in 2003, see <www.geneva-accord.org/mainmenu/english>; and for the Ayalon-Nusseibeh principles agreed in 2003, see <www.7th-day.co.il/mehumot/ayalon.htm>.

[13] See Ronald D. Asmus and Bruce P. Jackson, "Does Israel Belong in the EU and NATO?" *Policy Review* (February and March 2005), 47–56; and Uzi Eilam, *Israeli Membership in NATO: A Preliminary Assessment*, Tel Aviv Notes No. 99 (February 11, 2004).

[14] See Vali Nasr, *The Shia Revival: How Conflicts within Islam Will Shape the Future* (New York: Norton, 2006); and statements by King Abdullah of Saudi Arabia and King Abdallah II of Jordan warning of the danger from a resurgent Iran and Shia community.

Contributors

Dr. Judith S. Yaphe (Chapter Editor) is Distinguished Research Fellow in the Institute for National Strategic Studies at the National Defense University (NDU).

Dr. Bahman Baktiari is Director of the School of Policy and International Affairs at the University of Maine. Effective July 2009, he will be the Director of the Middle East Center at the University of Utah.

Dr. Nathan J. Brown is Professor of Political Science and International Affairs at The George Washington University, where he also directs the Institute for Middle East Studies. He serves as Nonresident Senior Associate at the Carnegie Endowment for International Peace.

Dr. Murhaf Jouejati is Professor of Middle East Studies in the Near East South Asia Center for Strategic Studies at NDU. He is also Professorial Lecturer in Political Science and International Affairs at The George Washington University and an adjunct scholar at the Middle East Institute.

Dr. Daniel C. Kurtzer is S. David Abraham Visiting Professor in Middle East Policy Studies at the Woodrow Wilson School of Public and International Affairs at Princeton University. Formerly, he served as Ambassador to Israel and Egypt under Presidents William Clinton and George W. Bush.

Dr. Omer Taspinar is Professor of National Security Studies at the National War College and Director of the Turkey Program at the Brookings Institution. He is the co-author of *Winning Turkey: How America, Europe and Turkey Can Revive a Fading Partnership* (The Brookings Institution Press, 2008) and *Kurdish Nationalism and Political Islam in Turkey: Kemalist Identity in Transition* (Routledge, 2004).

Chapter 10
South Asia

South Asia is a region of startling strategic contradictions, at once the locus of booming high-tech economies and crushing poverty, of vibrant multireligious, multiethnic democracy and bitter insurgencies fueled by ethnic, economic, tribal, and sectarian grievances. The most daunting transnational threats converge in the South Asian zone: narcotics trafficking, human trafficking, proliferation of weapons of mass destruction, and terrorism. With the populations of China and Russia combined in an area the size of the contiguous United States west of the Mississippi, South Asia presents strategic challenges of unparalleled diversity, ranging from the preservation of a stable balance between nuclear- and missile-armed rivals to the conduct of irregular mountain warfare. In one part of South Asia, the principal policy challenge is how to create the most rudimentary capacity for effective governance, while elsewhere it is managing the process by which an emerging India takes its place among the leading powers of the world.

Afghanistan: The Quest for Stability and Legitimacy

In the months following the 9/11 terrorist attacks, the international community seemed to have learned not to underestimate the stake it had in Afghanistan. Chronically too poor to afford to govern itself or meet the basic needs of its scattered and ethnically diverse population, the Afghan state has always been vulnerable to conflicts exacerbated or triggered by foreign powers. The most recent of these conflicts, which began with the 1978 coup d'état by Soviet-trained army officers, had finally left most of the country under the rule of the Taliban. This movement of rural clergy imposed a harsh version of Islamic sharia law on a society badly damaged by uncontrolled violence. The Taliban's parochial

U.S. Navy (John Gay)

Afghan villagers meet with joint team investigating allegations of civilian casualties in Tagab

leadership, which lacked all experience with the international system, became increasingly dependent upon both the Pakistani intelligence agency, the Directorate for Inter-Services Intelligence (ISI), and Osama bin Laden, who reestablished his global terrorist operation on Afghan soil when he was expelled from Sudan in May 1996.

Once the United States and the Afghan forces it armed and funded ousted the Taliban regime in late 2001, the international community set out under the framework of the Bonn Agreement (December 2001) and later of the Afghanistan Compact (January 2006) to rebuild the institutions of governance that seemed to hold the key to preventing yet another violent cycle of Afghan history. Since the adoption of the compact, however, the limited progress it symbolized has badly unraveled. Both the leadership of al Qaeda and a diverse, locally rooted insurgency have exploited the strategic mistakes of the United States, the weakness of Afghanistan's shattered institutions, and the contested and loosely governed status of the areas in Pakistan's frontier with Afghanistan to reconstitute their leadership infrastructure and carry out insurgencies in both countries.

Creating a stable and peaceful Afghanistan requires an integrated strategy that incorporates political and developmental, counterterrorist, and counterinsurgency components. Moreover, it requires recognition that the Afghan government's ability to prevent its own territory from being used as a base for international terrorism depends on the integrity and democratic development not only of Afghanistan itself but of Pakistan as well.

Background

The problem of Afghanistan ultimately goes back to the power vacuum left by the collapse of Safavid and Moghul power in the area between Persia and India in the 18th century. Unable to extract sufficient resources from the barren terrain to govern the area's diverse and fractious population, the newly formed Afghan empire turned to conquering its wealthier and more fertile neighbors as its main source of revenue. It was partly to stop such depredations against its Indian empire and partly to prevent Russia from advancing toward India from central Asia that Britain created the multi-tiered security structure whose lines continue to define the geopolitics of Afghanistan and Pakistan to this day.

The independence and partition of India in 1947 altered the strategic stakes in the region. Afghanistan promptly repudiated the validity of the line separating itself from the tribal areas of the former Indian empire. When the United States refused the government's request for aid, it turned to Moscow to build its national army. An April 1978 coup by communist

Afghan National Army commandos return to base after air assault mission to capture suspected insurgents in Khowst Province, March 2009

military officers led to a massive Soviet invasion in 1979; in response, the United States, Pakistan, Saudi Arabia, and others began spending billions of dollars to back the anticommunist Afghan mujahideen and their Arab auxiliaries—and thereby laid the foundations for an infrastructure of regional and global jihad. The result has been some 30 years of almost uninterrupted fighting that has left Afghanistan devastated.

The United States treated Afghanistan's collapse into warring chiefdoms—many of them allied with neighboring states or other external forces—as a matter of little concern once Soviet forces departed in 1988. Washington saw no potential benefit from involvement in Afghanistan's politics; Afghans and Pakistanis saw that the United States had no permanent interest in and took no consistent responsibility for the region. It took 9/11 to force Washington to recognize that a global terrorist opposition had created a base for itself among the ruins of Afghanistan, using the very human and physical capital that the United States and its allies had armed and supplied, through Pakistan's intelligence services, in pursuit of a Cold War agenda over a decade before. It was this recognition, not the immense humanitarian emergency in Afghanistan, that led the United States and others to send tens of thousands of troops and spend billions of dollars to establish internationally recognized institutions in the country.

The Afghan Environment Today

The United States had a doctrine and capacity for overthrowing hostile regimes; neither it nor international institutions has adequate doctrine or capacity to rebuild states and societies. The U.S. administration originally declined to finance reconstruction or to participate in any part of the security sector except for training the army, which it saw chiefly as a partner in counterterrorism. The Afghan National Army has been a relative success. As of June 2009 some 86,000 recruits were on the books and it was set to expand to 134,000. It depends heavily, however, on embedded U.S. trainers as well as on U.S. financial, logistical, airlift, and medical support. It cannot undertake independent operations. The police are in far worse condition than the army, as the United States did not become involved in their rebuilding until 2006. The justice system, necessary for the police to do their job, is so corrupt as to be nonfunctional.

Failures in security have undermined gains in political legitimacy. Under the process outlined in the Bonn Agreement of December 2001, an interim government chosen at the Bonn talks presided over a transition that gradually restored the institutions of the Afghan state, but in a more democratic framework. A constitution adopted in January 2004 provided for a presidential system and a bicameral

Indian Border Security Forces man western sector of India-Pakistan international border after November 2008 attack in Mumbai

legislature, as well as provincial and district councils in accord with Afghanistan's system of centralized, unitary government. The process culminated in the inauguration of both houses of the National Assembly in December 2005.

The Bonn Agreement was then followed by the Afghanistan Compact, adopted in London in January 2006, which provided for a program of state-building (security, governance, and development) to enable the government to meet its obligations. The combination of a rising security threat and the departure of some senior reformist ministers from the cabinet, however, meant that institution-building has largely stalled. Instead, corruption fed by currency inflows from drug exports and foreign aid threatens to engulf the government, which Washington estimates controls fewer than 20 percent of Afghanistan's 365 districts. The insurgents control slightly fewer districts, while most are contested or ungoverned by any organized entity.

Economic development has led to some successes, notably the enrollment of half of all school-age children in school, and a decrease in infant and child mortality. Nevertheless, while the total licit gross domestic product has grown robustly, the living standards of much of the population have declined in the face of increasing prices of food and fuel. Unemployment is estimated at about 60 percent. While poppy cultivation is restricted to the most conflict-affected provinces for now, the drug industry, accounting for one-quarter to one-third of the total licit plus illicit economy, continues to expand throughout the country, as discussed in greater detail in the next section.

After the expulsion of the Taliban and al Qaeda leadership from Afghanistan in 2002, U.S. counterterrorism policy impeded reintegration of the many former Taliban who would have stayed in Afghanistan, as the Afghan government could not guarantee they would not be detained. Consequently, the Taliban regime shifted wholesale to Pakistan, as did al Qaeda. While Pakistan captured hundreds of al Qaeda members, losing many troops in the process, it quietly welcomed the Afghan Taliban. The U.S. administration, focused on the upcoming conflict in Iraq, moved intelligence and military assets to the Persian Gulf, devoting few to surveillance of the Taliban's activities.

As a result, since the fall of 2005 there has been a steady annual increase in the tempo, sophistication, and effectiveness of attacks by insurgents and terrorists in Afghanistan. Increasingly sophisticated tactics have included suicide bombing, modeled on techniques used in Iraq. The timing of the escalation of the insurgency may be due to the time required to reorganize; it may also be due to a political decision made by Pakistan in response to the handover of military command from the U.S.-led coalition to the North Atlantic Treaty Organization (NATO) and the increasing Indian presence in Afghanistan. U.S. intelligence finds continuing links between the Pakistani ISI and the Afghan Taliban and other insurgents; the Afghan and Indian governments charge that Pakistan directs their activities.

The link between Pakistan and the insurgency in Afghanistan has now become the most serious obstacle to the stabilization of Afghanistan. The al Qaeda safe haven in Pakistan is protected by the umbrella organization *Tehrik-i Taliban-i Pakistan* (TTP, Taliban Movement of Pakistan). The TTP collaborates with militant groups that have fought in Kashmir, as well as with Uzbeks and Chechens. It has built a support base among the local population using a combination of money (funds from al Qaeda, Persian Gulf donors, and drug and other trafficking), force (death threats against tribal elders), and the provision of public services such as justice. The Afghan Taliban's *Shura* (council), located in Quetta, capital of Pakistan's Balochistan Province, directs insurgent operations in southern Afghanistan and loosely oversees the rest of the movement. An officially subordinate but largely autonomous center of Afghan Taliban leadership based in Pakistan's North Waziristan Agency is the network commanded by Jalaluddin Haqqani and his son, Sirajuddin. The Haqqanis collaborate closely with al Qaeda and the TTP. Another center of Afghan insurgency is Gulbuddin Hikmatyar's faction of *Hezb-i Islami*, based in northwest Pakistan and northeast Afghanistan.

All of these Afghan groups were closely supported and monitored by Pakistan's ISI and had bases and logistical structures in Pakistan for many years before 9/11. Afghan and Indian intelligence have long charged that ISI directly organizes the most spectacular attacks and acts through these groups—charges that gained credence when U.S. intelligence sources claimed to have evidence of an ISI role in the July 7, 2008, suicide bombing of the Indian embassy in Kabul.

Strategic Imperatives

The core challenge now faced collectively by the United States, NATO, other troop contributors and donors, and the Afghan government is the existence of a transnational movement of terrorists and insurgents, spanning the Durand line (the tenuous border established by the British between Pakistan and Afghanistan in 1893) and providing a safe haven from which al Qaeda and its allies can plan, train for, and potentially carry out renewed terrorist attacks comparable to 9/11. This movement is fueled by the lack of legitimacy and capacity of the Afghan state, the Pakistan military's perception of the post-9/11 political arrangement there as a security threat, the political conflict between the two states over the status and management of the border region, and turmoil in the governance of Pakistan itself.

In the coming months, the U.S. administration will confront an urgent task affecting the political legitimacy of the Afghan government: the presidential elections of August 2009. Hamid Karzai remained the frontrunner, though much of Afghan and international opinion has concluded that he had serious shortcomings as a leader. Furthermore, under current security conditions, it was going to hold a contested election in all parts of the country whose results would be accepted as legitimate. Failure to elect a legitimate president will undermine the foundational legitimacy of the government. Whatever the process, the maintenance of some degree of stability will require urgent political, financial, and security assistance from the Obama administration and global community.

Legitimacy will also require a thorough cleansing of the Afghan administrative apparatus of criminal elements. As many of those who will have to be dismissed lead armed groups, the Afghan president will require strong backing from the international community. Making the government work better with less corruption requires an urgent effort to establish a nationwide computerized payments system for the government payroll, which still does not exist after 7 years.

The Afghan government and its international partners are discussing the possibility of a negotiated political solution with insurgents. The international coalition's current red lines are no participation by al Qaeda or those associated with it; no sharing of control over the territory or government; and no safe areas or ceasefires before reaching a political agreement.

There is currently no adequate plan to sustain the Afghan National Security Forces. The current cost structure requires foreign funding for the foreseeable future, and that funding is largely dependent on supplemental appropriations from the U.S. Congress. One proposal is to put the security forces on the U.S.

recurring budget; another is to finance them through an international trust fund. The creation of well-armed but unsustainable security forces could pose a threat to the future of the country.

Counternarcotics and economic development have to be considered together, as narcotics production is the largest industry in the country. Afghanistan has become a monetized economy, and farmers will not return to subsistence agriculture. As discussed in greater detail elsewhere in this volume, the economic alternative to the drug industry is not another "crop," but jobs. Such jobs need not be in rural areas or even in Afghanistan. Rural communities need money, not plants.

No amount of reform in Afghanistan can resolve the insurgency and the terrorist safe haven that it provides, however, unless cross-border support from Pakistan is also addressed. The festering problems of transnational insurgency and al Qaeda's presence in the tribal agencies are so closely related to the deterioration of security and governance throughout Pakistan, the strategic posture of Pakistan's security establishment (including its nuclear deterrent), and the weakness of civilian institutions in Pakistan that they cannot be addressed without a comprehensive strategy that deals with both Afghanistan and Pakistan in their entirety, as well as with the broader region beyond. For example, unilateral military action by the United States may, in exceptional cases, target the top leadership of al Qaeda in Pakistan or TTP support to insurgents in Afghanistan, but such action cannot address the expansion of Taliban control in Pakistan itself and may trigger a backlash that aggravates rather than mitigates the strategic challenge. A sustainable political solution in Afghanistan depends on a sustainable political solution in Pakistan, one that makes cross-border cooperation and the operation of international forces there much more feasible.

A regional strategic perspective on Afghanistan, however, must go beyond Pakistan. For one thing, it must address Pakistan's concerns about Indian paramilitary and intelligence activities in Afghanistan. The new U.S. administration might also do well to reconsider engaging Iran on cooperation in Afghanistan, as well as the Shanghai Cooperation Organization.

Afghanistan: The Challenge of Narcotics

According to a recent United Nations Office on Drugs and Crime (UNODC) report, 157,000 hectares of opium poppies were cultivated in Afghanistan in 2008, a reduction of nearly 19 percent from the previous year and slightly below the 165,000 hectares cultivated in 2006. Thanks to higher crop yields, however, at 7,700 metric tons, the amount of opium produced from this crop remains more than one-third higher than in 2006. Despite recent progress, Afghanistan still supplies some 90 percent of the global opiate market; as the UNODC stated in 2007, "No other country in the world has ever produced narcotics on such a deadly scale." The explosion of illicit drug production makes defeating the insurgency and building a viable state in Afghanistan more difficult. The drug trade finances illegal armed groups, empowers nonstatutory power holders, sustains criminal networks, and corrupts government, all of which undermine the establishment of stability, good governance, and rule of law in the country.

The weak Afghan state, together with endemic violence and poverty, contributes to the growth of the country's illicit drug industry. Therefore, all of Afghanistan's stakeholders must cooperate to find a solution that brings together the development of security, governance, rule of law, and the economy—the same elements that must comprise a comprehensive strategy for defeating the insurgency that afflicts the country. Massive eradication of opium poppies alone will help in neither reducing the illicit drug industry nor defeating the insurgency.

Background

Afghanistan has a relatively short history of opium production. Before 1978, the country produced only 100 tons of opium a year, though production had increased tenfold by 1992. The growth of the illicit drug industry was caused by decades of continuing violent conflict and a long drought cycle that destroyed the rural economy. The country, according to journalist Pierre-Arnaud Chouvy, was on the verge of attaining food self-sufficiency at the time of the Soviet invasion but has since seen its irrigated farmland halved. During the 1990s, the amount of arable land—only 12 percent of the total territory to begin with—declined by more than a third. As a result, farmers began to view the production of a high-value, easily marketable commodity such as opium as the only way to survive in an unpredictable and dangerous environment. Opium is nearly 10 times more lucrative to produce than any practicable alternative crop, such as wheat ($5,200 per hectare versus $545 per hectare). Even factoring in bribes and rake-offs by traffickers, Afghans see opium as sufficiently profitable that 14 percent of the population grows the crop. Many farmers claim that they

would prefer a licit income but see no alternative to growing opium in order to support their families.

The market incentives to grow opium poppies were established as part of a drug-based political economy that developed during the 1992–2001 civil war and the fighting that followed the 2001 U.S.-led intervention. Western support to the various Afghan factions dried up in the early 1990s in the aftermath of the communist regime's collapse, and as a result some groups turned to the illicit drug industry to mobilize new sources of financing to fuel their continuing power struggle. This reliance on drug revenue created not only a ready number of poppy producers but also a vast supporting network of financiers, protectors, traffickers, and political patrons who became vested in the industry. The situation persisted during the post-Taliban period, as the U.S.-led coalition co-opted the local militias and warlords, who controlled the drug trade, into ousting the Taliban and fighting terrorism. The absence of an international peacekeeping force or a viable central authority allowed these powerbrokers to dominate local administrations and resist counternarcotic efforts. Militia leaders, warlords, insurgents, and drug traffickers flourished in such an environment.

Current Challenges

The struggle against Afghanistan's illicit drug industry exhibits three key characteristics: the prevailing insecurity in the area where opium production is concentrated; the consolidation of the drug trade by a network of politicians and traffickers; and disagreements over counternarcotics strategy among members of the international community.

Opium cultivation in Afghanistan is concentrated in areas of the country where security is poor, access is difficult, and economic development is sluggish. In 2007, 70 percent of Afghan opium was produced in the five southern provinces where the insurgency is strongest. In contrast, a significant reduction in poppy cultivation was seen in more stable and accessible areas in the north. It is thus clear that the suppression of the drug trade is intimately linked to the provision of security.

The consolidation of the drug trade by a network of traffickers and politicians has spawned a parallel polity that provides financial and marketing services, security, and conflict resolution more effectively than the Afghan government. Filling a void created by poverty, violence, and lawlessness, the network influences every aspect of political,

Pakistan's Troubled Borders

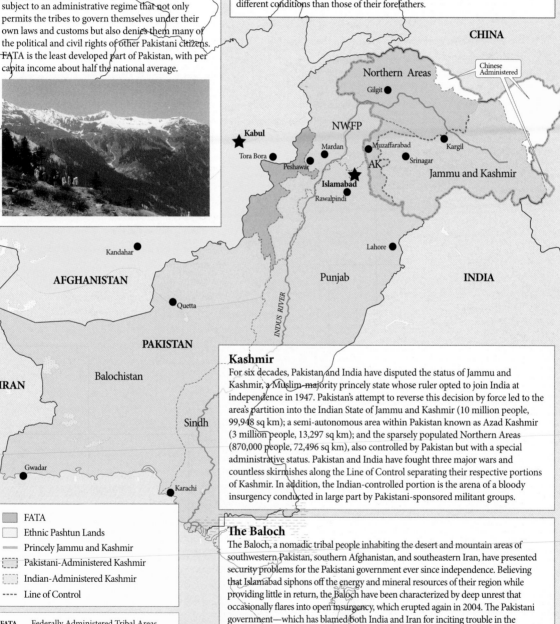

FATA
Pakistan's Federally Administered Tribal Areas (FATA) comprise a quasi-autonomous mountain region along the Afghan border in which lack of central government control has permitted the development of a safe haven for terrorists and insurgents. Established during the 19th century as one of several tiers of progressively diminishing British control along the northwest frontier of India, the seven agencies of FATA are subject to an administrative regime that not only permits the tribes to govern themselves under their own laws and customs but also denies them many of the political and civil rights of other Pakistani citizens. FATA is the least developed part of Pakistan, with per capita income about half the national average.

The Pashtuns
Some 45 million Pashtuns live in Afghanistan and Pakistan, divided by the so-called Durand Line that was drawn by the British in 1893 to separate their Indian Empire from the Kingdom of Afghanistan. Of these, fewer than 20 percent reside in the remote mountain areas of FATA and the adjacent Afghan provinces. Pashtun culture is heavily influenced by the tribal social norms known as *Pashtunwali*, which emphasize such traditional values as honor, hospitality, and reciprocity. However, Pashtun life has not been immune from the effects of war, migration, and globalization, and millions of Pashtuns today live and work in quite different conditions than those of their forefathers.

Kashmir
For six decades, Pakistan and India have disputed the status of Jammu and Kashmir, a Muslim-majority princely state whose ruler opted to join India at independence in 1947. Pakistan's attempt to reverse this decision by force led to the area's partition into the Indian State of Jammu and Kashmir (10 million people, 99,948 sq km); a semi-autonomous area within Pakistan known as Azad Kashmir (3 million people, 13,297 sq km); and the sparsely populated Northern Areas (870,000 people, 72,496 sq km), also controlled by Pakistan but with a special administrative status. Pakistan and India have fought three major wars and countless skirmishes along the Line of Control separating their respective portions of Kashmir. In addition, the Indian-controlled portion is the arena of a bloody insurgency conducted in large part by Pakistani-sponsored militant groups.

The Baloch
The Baloch, a nomadic tribal people inhabiting the desert and mountain areas of southwestern Pakistan, southern Afghanistan, and southeastern Iran, have presented security problems for the Pakistani government ever since independence. Believing that Islamabad siphons off the energy and mineral resources of their region while providing little in return, the Baloch have been characterized by deep unrest that occasionally flares into open insurgency, which erupted again in 2004. The Pakistani government—which has blamed both India and Iran for inciting trouble in the region—has a substantial economic interest in sustained peace with the Baloch given the importance of the area as a prospective energy transit route.

FATA	Federally Administered Tribal Areas
AK	Azad Kashmir
NWFP	North-West Frontier Province

- FATA
- Ethnic Pashtun Lands
- Princely Jammu and Kashmir
- Pakistani-Administered Kashmir
- Indian-Administered Kashmir
- Line of Control

Twenty-first Century Pashtuns: Change amid Continuity

At least 40 million and perhaps as many as 50 million Pashtuns live in Afghanistan and Pakistan. They constitute 40 to 50 percent of Afghanistan's people and in Pakistan are the largest minority group, making up 15 to 20 percent of the population. Although their original homeland is situated between the Hindu Kush in central Afghanistan and the Indus River bisecting Pakistan, Pashtun communities are now scattered over a vast territory, from the Amu Darya River on Afghanistan's northern border with Central Asia, to the southern Pakistani port city of Karachi on the Arabian Sea, which has one of the largest urban Pashtun populations.

With war, invasion, and endemic civil violence as constant features of Pashtun history, the group has never been fully integrated into a single empire, state, or political system. This historic pattern of political instability also preserved and reinforced the tribal nature of Pashtun society. While some writers have tried to understand Pashtun society by tracing the genealogies of tribes, clans, and lineages, it is best understood by looking not only at its internal structure but at its wider environment as well.

Today, the Pashtun live under various political arrangements and engage in a wide variety of economic activities, some involving a high degree of globalization. The social makeup of Pashtun communities varies according to whether they are rural or urban, the degree of their inclusion or seclusion from the surrounding societies, and the extent of their absorption by modernity and development. All of them, however, are characterized by the prevalence of what anthropologists call "segmentary lineages." Such a system conceives of societies in hereditary tree-like hierarchies. In the Pashtun case, the smaller lineages, or *zai*s and *khel*s—male descent groups—merge into larger tribes and tribal confederations.

Most Pashtuns speak Pashto, an Indo-European language related to Persian, as their mother tongue. But bilingualism is now common in urban areas and regions with mixed ethnic populations. Some small groups still identify themselves as Pashtuns despite speaking a different first language because of their ethnic heritage; the former ruling family of Afghanistan is a case in point. Nevertheless, Pashto still remains a key identity marker of Pashtuns because use of the language is closely tied to the notion of observing the code of *Pashtunwali*.

Rooted in the tribal organization of the society, *Pashtunwali* embraces a number of values that it shares with surrounding Muslim societies, but it also includes a set of fundamental ideals of individual and collective behavior seen as specific to Pashtuns. *Pashtunwali* includes the handful of norms to which it is frequently reduced by Western writers—honor, hospitality, and reciprocity (often confused with revenge)—but the whole is much more complex than that. *Pashtunwali* also includes the values of forgiveness, equality, egalitarianism, and chivalry, as well as the institution of the *jirga* or council of elders, which is summoned for the resolution of disputes and to deliberate on new threats and challenges. Over centuries, some Pashtun tribes have developed their own peculiar *narkh*, or sets of unwritten customary laws to implement the principles of *Pashtunwali*.

The overwhelming majority of Pashtuns are Sunni Muslims of the Hanafi school, although the Turi tribe in the Kurram Valley of Pakistan, some clans of the neighboring Bangash tribe, and small communities in Afghanistan are Twelver Shia. Some sufi orders, too, have a considerable following among Pashtun tribes. Over the past three decades, however, the Pashtun regions in Afghanistan and Pakistan have become home to a brand of political Islam that now manifests itself primarily in the form of global jihadism.

Pashtuns were not the chief actors in bringing this change to their society. The transformations began when the Cold War boiled into a hot war after the 1979 Soviet invasion of Afghanistan. What began as an indigenous nationalist resistance to the communist occupation of Afghanistan was swiftly transformed into a religious struggle, partly because of Pakistani fears that the perpetuation of Afghan nationalism might lead to the strengthening of Afghan irredentist claims to Pakistani territory and boost domestic Pashtun ethno-nationalism within Pakistan itself.

Three decades of war in the Pashtun borderlands created new classes, alliances, and leaderships at the expense of the old ones. For the first time in history, networks of puritanical Sunni clerics and Islamist militant commanders became more powerful than the traditional secular tribal and political leadership. This transformation of the Pashtun social fabric, accomplished over the course of years through external patronage and billions of dollars of covert and overt funding from outside for armed factions, culminated in the rise of the Taliban in both Afghanistan and Pakistan. By default, this enabled al Qaeda (the lead-

▲ *Continued from p. 231*

with neighbors, and internal ethnic, social, and environmental cleavages and challenges also constrain it. Even if in absolute terms and by a range of conventional indices India today remains a limited power, its trends, scale, and comparative potential raise questions about its structural role in the emerging international system.

Too often, debate over whether India is a rising global power obscures the implications of the *simultaneous* strengths and weaknesses of the country's power as they are manifested in its external interests. This combination of strengths and weaknesses, combined with India's own perceptions of its interests and the instruments of power available to it, will shape its actions in the world. It is with this combination that the international community must contend.

From Independence through the Cold War

During the 60 years of its independence, India has had diffuse and diverse relations with the international community. India's closest security ties were for a long time with the Soviet Union; its economic ties were relatively evenly spread among the West (North America and Europe), the former communist bloc, and the Middle East; and its principal political links have been with the "South" or lesser developed countries. Meanwhile, India's closest educational, cultural, and personal ties have been with the West, especially the United States and Britain.

Notwithstanding this rich diversity of interactions, however, India was less thoroughly integrated into the broad international system than it might have seemed, to its own disadvantage. It was overly dependent upon one country, the Soviet Union, for military hardware and political support on key issues. Conversely, it was estranged from the United States and isolated from other key countries and regions of increasing importance to the post–World War II international order, including China, Japan, and much of Asia. It was unable to exert a "pull of attraction" as a partner for trade, investment, or other commercial opportunities, and by the end of the Cold War found itself remarkably isolated from international relations considering its geographical position, large size, and ambitions of its political and diplomatic elite.

Since the end of the Cold War, India's international role has steadily evolved. With the disappearance of its main Cold War partner, economic reforms were launched and policy decisions taken that shifted India's place in the world. These ranged from the detonation of nuclear weapons to the initiation of a "Look East" policy that sought enhanced ties with the rest of Asia as a way to compensate for the loss

AP Images (Rafiq Maqbool)

Soldier destroys opium poppies while on patrol with Afghan police of political, economic, and military support from the former Soviet Union and Eastern Bloc countries, and to escape isolation and marginalization in a U.S.-led "new world order." Some two decades later, India's policy adjustments have created new interactions between it and the international community and potentially augur further change in the years ahead.

Exercising Indian Power

India's external power and interests can essentially be divided into two categories, economic and politico-security, with the latter encompassing India's involvement in multilateralism.

Economics is a growing factor in India's international strength and interests, an important shift from the last six decades during which India had an essentially closed economy. This shift in orientation is the main factor accounting for predictions of India's rise in the international system. Its increasing integration into the international economy has been primarily in the areas of trade (especially service exports and energy imports), borrowing, and remittances from the Indian diaspora. Of lesser but growing importance are investment (both inward and outward) and outward foreign aid.

There are two broad constraints on the impact these elements will have on India's external interests and power. The first is a set of domestic consider-

ations, particularly the need for equitable growth that will both reduce overall poverty levels and provide employment for India's large population of underemployed young people. The second is the low base, relative to the size of its population, from which India's economic rise is starting. For example, India accounts for only about 1 percent of global trade and worldwide foreign direct investment. Moreover, while economic interaction with certain countries such as the United States and China and regions such as the European Union (EU) is critical to India, the opposite is not true. Hence, India accounts for only about 1 percent of U.S. two-way trade, while the United States accounts for more than 10 percent of India's. Similarly, India accounts for only about 1.4 percent of China's, 0.6 percent of Japan's, and 1.7 percent of the European Union's trade.

This mixed and asymmetrical profile of Indian economic power and interests suggests that India's international role and behavior will likely follow certain consistent patterns.

First, the United States will remain critical to India's economic interests because it is India's largest export market (though China is catching up fast), its largest source of private commercial borrowing, and the key to its access to multilateral aid, and because it hosts a large Indian diaspora that not only accounts for an estimated 50 percent of remittances but also creates nonmonetary wealth such as networks and influence useful to India's global engagement. The United States is also emerging as the largest destination of *India's* own foreign direct investment (FDI).

Second, in terms of regions, Europe and the Persian Gulf are critical to India in different ways. The EU accounts for the largest share of India's trade, excluding petroleum. Including petroleum, the Persian Gulf is India's largest regional trade partner. The EU, however, remains the largest regional source of FDI, though Gulf and Middle East investments in India are increasing. Other regions have risen or declined in importance. Eastern Europe and Russia (the one-time members of the Soviet-era Council for Mutual Economic Assistance) no longer account for much of India's trade or other economic interactions. On the other hand, East and Southeast Asia's increasing importance to India is especially notable, and the growth rates of Indian economic interaction with Africa and Latin America are higher than other regions, albeit from a considerably lower base. Africa is emerging as an important source of Indian energy supplies and as a destination for Indian aid and proj-

AP Images (Rahmat Gul)

Afghan security guard stands watch as opium is destroyed outside Kabul

ect exports—which partly explains India's hosting of the first India-Africa summit this year. A third feature of India's external economic power and interest profile is the degree of its diversification; roughly 50 percent of trade (both exports and imports) is with countries other than its top 10 partners.

The implications of the above contours of India's external economic power and interests for India's international engagement more generally are as follows:

Given that no single region is overwhelmingly important to India's external economy, and that nearly 50 percent of its trade is with non–top 10 bilateral partners, India must pursue overlapping global, bilateral, and regional efforts to achieve its trade objectives. India will be active everywhere, from Latin America to Africa, because marginal gains matter when the absolute amounts of its trade are so low. (India's total world exports in 2007 were only $100 billion, less than half the value of the U.S. trade deficit with China alone.)

The diversity and diffusion of countries and regions that contribute to its economic interests will complicate India's ability to maintain coherence in its external economic strategy. It will seek to shape the outcome of global trade talks on the one hand (not least because of the need to address domestic agricultural interests), while pursuing free trade–type agreements (for example, with the Gulf Cooperation Council [GCC] and the Association of Southeast Asian Nations) and new multilateral arrangements (for example, India–Brazil–South Africa [IBSA]) on the other, to garner absolute and incremental trade gains as well as to leverage its negotiating power with competing partners. Bilateral deals will be especially important, and so will engaging the Indian diaspora, which is strongly present in five of the eight "nodal" countries that account for almost half of India's trade.

Finally, nothing India can do economically vis-à-vis a foreign country or region matters more than what it must do at home to reform and develop its economy to attract the world. Moreover, the social and political, not to mention economic, demands for poverty alleviation, equitable growth, and more employment mean that India's external economic engagement and negotiations will reflect a carefully considered calibration of what is possible in domestic terms for an elected government to sustain and stay in power.

As with economics, India's political and security interests and the power it has available to pursue them are diverse and diffuse across regions and countries. India's main international diplomatic and security interests revolve around the following objectives:

■ strategic autonomy, attained through a combination of multipolarity and national strength
■ international acceptance of the status quo in Kashmir, or at least reduced pressure to change it
■ wider and deeper access to defense and high-tech imports
■ de facto and de jure recognition as a nuclear weapons state
■ a permanent seat on the United Nations (UN) Security Council
■ a leading role in international and regional organizations.

Because of the limits of Indian power and the nature of the objectives themselves, pursuing them requires wide-ranging, overlapping, and often inconsistent engagement on diverse bilateral and multilateral tracks. For example:

■ The quest for strategic autonomy under conditions of limited national capacity requires persistent efforts to broaden options by fostering multipolar relationships, from IBSA to the recently formed BRIC (Brazil-Russia-India-China) nexus.

AP Images (Mohammad Sajjad)

Pakistani paramilitary soldiers protect supply route to U.S. and NATO troops in Afghanistan from militant attack

■ Realizing the benefits of a far-flung Indian diaspora requires engagement with countries from North America through Australasia.

■ Attaining a permanent UN Security Council seat mandates coordination with other countries also seeking reform of the council's structure, such as Japan, Brazil, and Germany. Gaining other memberships, such as in the Asia-Pacific Economic Cooperation (APEC), requires even wider outreach.

■ Gaining support for policies regarding Kashmir and Pakistan requires cultivating interlocutors such as the United States, Russia, Japan, and key members of the EU and GCC.

India's evolving power profile and interests also indicate a likely shift in its approach to multilateral institutions. It is noteworthy that, for the most part, India is either not a member or at most an observer in the multilateral groupings, such as the Group of Eight, that are most important to achieving its economic and political objectives, while it is a full or even founding member of organizations that are either underfunctioning (such the South Asia Association for Regional Cooperation and the Bay of Bengal Initiative for Multisectoral Technical and Economic Cooperation) or have outlived their usefulness and relevance (such as the Non-aligned Movement and G–77). While domestic political pressures will continue to require a certain level of commitment to groups symbolizing the solidarity of the global "South," economic and security realities are increasingly leading India to pursue its own version of ad hoc multilateralism. Such an approach is leading India to promote new multilateral arrangements in which it is a full member (such as IBSA and BRIC), to seek an increased role in others (for example, the Shanghai Cooperation Organization and APEC), and to participate actively in the debates of those groupings such as the World Trade Organization that can provide (or deny) benefits to Indian interests.

Future Prospects for Indian Strategy

This complex picture of India's power is unlikely to change in the next 4 to 8 years. By most indices and analyses, India will continue to increase its economic and politico-security profile incrementally and steadily, but certainly at a much faster pace than during the first half-century of independence. Only an unlikely major disruption such as war or domestic crisis is liable to interfere with this prognosis.

Therefore, the combination of weaknesses and strengths in India's power and consequent interests suggests an international approach that will be characterized by:

■ An increasing emphasis on key bilateral relationships, in contrast to India's traditional focus on region-wide and multilateral organizations. Apart from pursuing a concrete set of calculated interests, this approach is consistent with India's own self-image and ambitions as a major power. The specific countries to be engaged will vary according to the interest affected, but Russia will remain important for weapons and spare parts, China for trade, Saudi Arabia and the United Arab Emirates for oil, and the United States for everything.

■ To the extent that it continues to follow regional approaches, India's future focus is likely to remain on Asia and the Persian Gulf. The relative importance of the EU will ebb while Africa probably will continue to grow in importance.

■ India will be active everywhere, using a mixed kit of diplomatic and economic tools, because the strengths and weaknesses of its power profile dictate a search for marginal and incremental gains at every opportunity. As a result, India cannot be "assigned" by other countries to a region where cooperation is to be pursued.

In essence, India will persist in a revised version of its post-independence policies that seek to make the best of its strengths and weaknesses by being active everywhere and through varying mechanisms. What is perhaps the most fundamental difference between now and the past is that India will go forward from a base of new strengths, including its attractiveness as an economic partner, as a cash-paying arms purchaser, as a high-demand energy consumer, and as a diplomatic partner whose decisions—whether on trade talks or climate change—will have increasingly important implications for the international community. **gsa**

NOTES

[1] Larry Thompson and Michelle Brown, *Security on the Cheap: PRTs in Afghanistan* (Washington, DC: Refugees International, July 8, 2003), available at <www.interaction.org/newswire/detail.php?id=1816>.

[2] Steve Coll, *Ghost Wars: The Secret History of the CIA, Afghanistan, and bin Laden, from the Soviet Invasion to September 10, 2001* (New York: Penguin, 2004), 100.

Contributors

Joseph McMillan (Chapter Editor) is Principal Deputy Assistant Secretary of Defense for International Security Affairs. Previously, he served as Senior Research Fellow in the Institute for National Strategic Studies (INSS) at National Defense University (NDU). A specialist on regional defense and security issues in the Middle East, South Asia, as well as transnational terrorism, Mr. McMillan has more than two decades of experience as a civilian official in the Department of Defense, and he also has served as academic chairman of the Near East South Asia Center for Strategic Studies.

Dr. Stephen P. Cohen is Senior Fellow in Foreign Policy at the Brookings Institution. He is author, co-author, or editor of more than a dozen books, the most recent of which are *Four Crises and a Peace Process: American Engagement in South Asia* (The Brookings Institution Press, 2007) and *The Idea of Pakistan* (The Brookings Institution Press, 2006).

Dr. Timothy D. Hoyt is Professor of Strategy and Policy at the U.S. Naval War College and co-chair of the Indian Ocean Regional Studies Group. He specializes in the challenges of contemporary conflict, including irregular warfare and terrorism, and issues related to the diffusion of military technologies in the developing world, including the proliferation of strategic weapons.

Ali A. Jalali served as Interior Minister of Afghanistan from 2003 to 2005 and is now Distinguished Professor in the Near East South Asia Center for Strategic Studies at National Defense University. Mr. Jalali began his career as an officer in the Afghan army and served as a top military planner with the resistance following the 1979 Soviet invasion.

Dr. David J. Kilcullen, currently a senior fellow at the Center for a New American Security, is a noted expert on counterinsurgency. He previously served as a Senior Advisor to the Secretary of State and to the Commanding General of U.S. and coalition forces in Iraq. Dr. Kilcullen is a former Australian infantry officer with 22 years of service, including operational deployments in East Timor, Bougainville, and the Middle East.

Dr. Satu P. Limaye is Director of the Washington office of the East-West Center. Dr. Limaye previously served as Director of Research and Publications for the Asia-Pacific Center for Security Studies, and has written, edited, and co-edited numerous books, monographs, and studies on Asian security affairs.

Dr. Barnett R. Rubin, an internationally recognized authority on Afghanistan, is Director of Studies in the Center on International Cooperation at New York University, where he directs the program on Afghan reconstruction. He is author of *The Fragmentation of Afghanistan: State Formation and Collapse in the International System* (Yale University Press, 2002).

Abubakar Siddique is a correspondent with Radio Free Europe/Radio Liberty based in Prague, where he reports and comments on Afghanistan and Pakistan. He has covered the South-Central Asia region as a reporter and an anthropologist for more than 10 years, focusing primarily on Pashtun culture and politics.

Chapter 11
Russia/Eurasia

Paradigm Shift: Dealing with Russia after 08/08/08

The Russian-Georgian war in August 2008 put an end to nearly two decades of Western attempts to design and build a new transatlantic security architecture with Russia as its easternmost pillar. Three successive U.S. administrations—those of George H.W. Bush, William J. Clinton, and George W. Bush—and their European Allies sought to integrate Russia into Western security and political structures as a partner that, with the passage of time and progress of internal reforms, would fully embrace Western values and interests. Russia's inte-gration into the Group of 8 (G–8), special relation-ship with the North Atlantic Treaty Organization (NATO), and partnership with the European Union (EU) were supported and actively promoted by the United States based on the premise that Russia would transform and that, as a result, its values and interests would coincide with those of the United States. The war in Georgia put an end to that vision and signaled to the United States and its European Allies that modern-day Russia requires a new and different approach.

Then–Russian Federation President Vladimir Putin delivers remarks at 2007 Munich Security Conference

A Promising Start

Russia's integration into Western security and political structures, which was pursued by the United States and its Allies in tandem with the steady expansion of their security sphere from its Cold War–era boundaries eastward, was part and parcel of an American policy guided by a vision of Europe whole, free, and at peace with itself and its neighbors. It was a vision of the continent without dividing lines, without spheres of influence, and without competing political-military blocs.

That Russia did not embrace this vision from the outset is well known. Moscow opposed the expansion of NATO as the centerpiece of the new European security framework, and it resented the European Union's absorption of former Soviet satellites, motivated by the belief that the West was expanding its sphere of influence at Russia's expense while Russia was weak. For a long time, however, the EU and NATO Allies viewed Russia's intransigence as a legacy of the Cold War that Russia would eventually shed as it regained domestic stability and prosperity and realized that its true interests would be best served by partnership with the West.

U.S. and European leaders were not ignoring Russia's opposition to Western security policies. NATO and EU expansion projects moved along despite Russian complaints, because they were viewed then as the best way to put an end to the continent's division while integrating Russia at the same time. Western Allies were under strong pressure from Moscow's former satellites to open NATO and EU doors to them. The Allies had two options: to devise a wholly new security system for Europe to replace both NATO and the defunct Warsaw Pact, or to build on the foundation of the Cold War–era institutions and adapt them to the new times. Russia, limping from one economic or political crisis to the next and focused on its domestic problems, was in no position to play a constructive role in either of these two pursuits. The rest of Europe could not wait, and the Allies moved on, building the post–Cold War security structure on Cold War–era foundations, but reserving for Russia a seat at the table once it recovered from its time of troubles.

An Unexpected Recovery

Russia's domestic recovery has been followed by its gradual return to the international arena as a major actor, especially around its periphery, where Moscow has felt its interests were concentrated. What is noteworthy is that Russia's recovery and return to prominence in the international arena were not accompanied by a shift in Russian attitudes toward the Western-designed and -built security architecture. More than a decade after NATO and the European Union embarked on the path of expansion in Central and Eastern Europe, Russian resentment

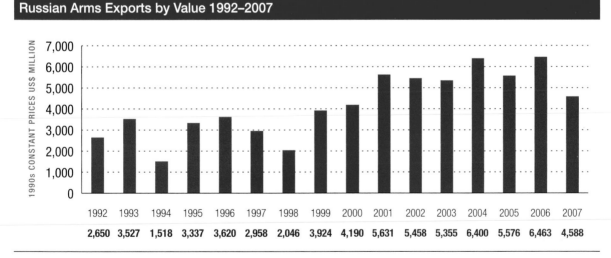

Russian Arms Exports by Value 1992–2007

	1992	1993	1994	1995	1996	1997	1998	1999	2000	2001	2002	2003	2004	2005	2006	2007
	2,650	3,527	1,518	3,337	3,620	2,958	2,046	3,924	4,190	5,631	5,458	5,355	6,400	5,576	6,463	4,588

(y-axis: 1990s CONSTANT PRICES US$ MILLION)

Russian arms sales have been steadily increasing since 1998, but saw a decline in 2007 due to a sharp cut in purchases from China, the largest importer of Russian weapons. Sales have suffered other setbacks, such as the return of a MiG–29 delivery by Angola due to the poor quality of the aircraft and suspension of a tanker contract with China. Russia continues to be one of the top arms exporters in the world, ranking second after the United States and accounting for 25 percent of all arms exports during the period of 2003–2007. Recent figures show that Russia had a record year for sales in 2008, totaling $8.35 billion in arms exports.

Source: SIPRI online database on arms transfers, available at ‹www.sipri.org/contents/armstrad/at_db.html›.

of their moves remained palpable. The notion that with domestic political stability and a measure of prosperity Russia would move closer to Western values and embrace the new, non–zero-sum approach to international relations stipulating that NATO and EU gains would be also Russia's gain, was apparently mistaken.

Moreover, not only was Moscow resentful of NATO and, to a lesser degree, EU moves farther east and closer to Russia's border, it felt aggrieved by the new European security system's actions; the conflict in Kosovo and its settlement, both of which Russian authorities viewed as illegitimate, left a deep impression on their attitudes toward NATO and the EU. NATO's military action in Serbia, they complained,

was undertaken in spite of Russian objections, and Russia was too weak to intervene and stop it.

As Russia regained its strength, it took steps beyond mere protestations and complaints against NATO actions. Ukraine and Georgia, whose leaders have been among the most eager advocates of their countries' membership in NATO, have seen their energy prices rise dramatically, and both experience occasional disruptions in their fuel deliveries from Russia. The three Baltic states, Latvia, Estonia, and Lithuania, formerly occupied by the Soviet Union and newly admitted into NATO and the EU, experienced disruptions in fuel shipments from Russia and occasional trade sanctions as well. In 2007, Russia suspended its participation in the Conventional

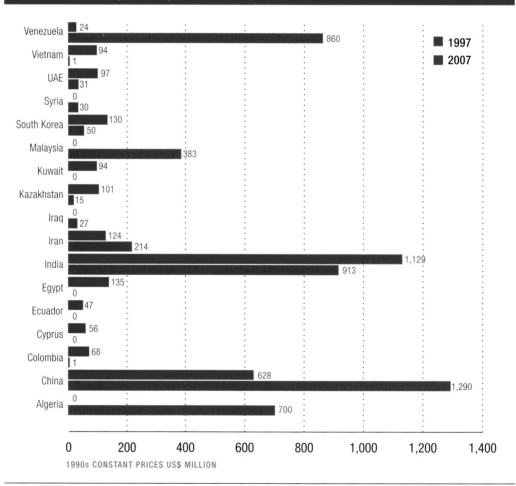

Russian Exports by Country 1997/2007

1990s CONSTANT PRICES US$ MILLION

Russia has continued to be the primary supplier of arms to Syria, Iran, India, and China, and has recently signed large arms agreements with Venezuela. While some customers have changed since the 1990s, India and China in particular remain the primary purchasers of Russian arms and equipment.

Source: SIPRI online database on arms transfers, available at ‹www.sipri.org/contents/armstrad/at_db.html›.

Forces in Europe (CFE) Treaty to protest NATO expansion, U.S. plans to deploy missile defense components in Europe, and the NATO Allies' decision to hold treaty ratification hostage to the withdrawal of Russia's remaining troops from Georgia and Moldova.

Speaking in Munich at a major security conference in February 2007, then-President Vladimir Putin delivered a warning to the West that NATO's course of expansion and disregard for Russian interests would lead it into a new Cold War with Russia. Georgia and Ukraine—NATO's presumed next targets for expansion—in a sense represented a new frontier for

NATO, which to date had not admitted a bona fide ex-Soviet state (the three Baltic states had never been formally ceded to the Soviet Union by the West). Georgia and Ukraine emerged as battleground states between the West and Russia, which has drawn a red line around them, insisting that NATO should stay out of Russia's traditional sphere of influence and interests.

Russia has reemerged from a period of introspection and reconstitution forced upon it by the breakup of the Soviet Union and the ensuing economic and political calamities, but it has reemerged with a very different outlook on the world, its place in it, and the

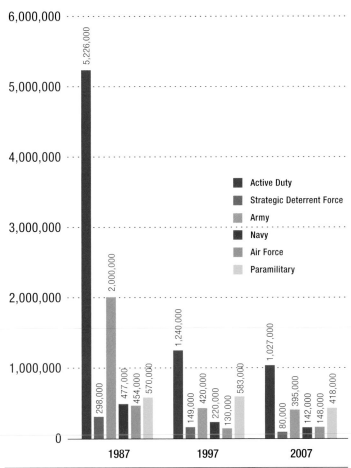

Armed Forces Sizes (USSR/Russian Federation)

Legend:
- Active Duty
- Strategic Deterrent Force
- Army
- Navy
- Air Force
- Paramilitary

1987:
- 5,226,000
- 298,000
- 2,000,000
- 477,000
- 454,000
- 570,000

1997:
- 1,240,000
- 149,000
- 420,000
- 220,000
- 130,000
- 583,000

2007:
- 1,027,000
- 80,000
- 395,000
- 142,000
- 148,000
- 418,000

The size of the Russian armed forces has continued a steady decline from its Soviet heights with drastic reductions visible in active personnel and combat readiness. Russian armed forces suffer from a broad range of endemic problems ranging from a lack of housing for personnel to shortages in serviceable equipment and funding for upgrading aging arsenals with new technology. However, Russia's plans remain ambitious, working to maintain a military with one million personnel while modernizing and reforming the component services.

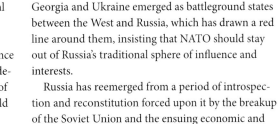

South Ossetian separatist fighters in breakaway Georgian province of South Ossetia, August 2008

AP Images (Musa Sadulayev)

nature of relationships with key partners, than had been expected by both internal and external observers at the outset of the post-Soviet era. The international system, in this world view, is organized around a series of major powers that balance their interests against each other and act as gravitational poles for a collection of smaller and lesser countries that follow them as satellites in orbit. Russia's first foreign policy priority is to be recognized as a major, "system-forming" power, responsible—along with the United States, Europe, China, and perhaps a handful of other regional actors—for maintaining the international system in a state of equilibrium, achieved by balancing among the major powers. The second

priority, related to the first, is to secure an exclusive sphere of influence around Russia's periphery, where Russian interests would not be challenged by other major powers. This notion had gradually emerged in Russian foreign policy discussions over the course of several years, but was most clearly articulated by President Dmitry Medvedev following the 2008 Georgian war as a sphere of Russia's "privileged" interests, not to be tampered with by outsiders.

Notwithstanding the formal pretext for the war in Georgia, it would be difficult to mistake Russian military action in Georgia for anything other than a clear message to Georgia and arguably to Ukraine, as well as to Moscow's Western interlocutors, that its red lines should be respected, that its warnings are to be taken seriously, and that it is no longer to be treated as a transitional entity without a clear sense of its own place in the international system. It was, furthermore, an indication from Moscow that it had not embraced the "non–zero-sum, win-win" approach to European security that the architects of NATO and EU enlargement had banked on, and that Russia has always viewed as an opportunistic expansion of the Western sphere of interests at the expense of its own. Having reemerged from its domestic troubles, Russia was signaling that it would not be a joiner in a Western-designed European security system, but would instead insist on having a hand in shaping one.

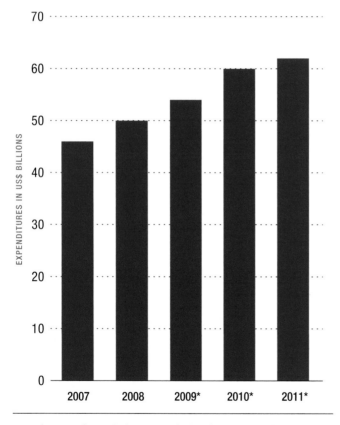

Russian Defense-Related Security Expenditure (2007–2011 Projected)

Russia has recently switched to a 3-year budget framework and has made considerable changes to the presentation of budgetary data, much of which has become classified again. However, projections suggest that defense expenditure will continue to increase in the near future as military spending has become a priority for the Russian government.

*Estimated numbers, based on an average exchange rate of 1USD:34Rbl and expenditure estimates
Source: International Institute for Strategic Studies, *The Military Balance* 2007–2009 editions.

Different Values, Different Interests

At the center of disagreements between Russia on the one hand and the United States and Europe on the other is the question of values and their role in international relations. Values, particularly democratic values, occupy a prominent place on U.S. and European foreign policy agendas. In those—not infrequent—instances when tensions develop between them, finding a compromise is rarely an easy task. The search for balance between values and interests has proven to be one of the most enduring challenges for makers of U.S. foreign policy from the earliest days of the republic.

In post-Soviet Russia, the tradeoff between values and interests has been settled—at least for the foreseeable future—unequivocally in favor of interests. According to leading Russian policymakers, interests should play by far the dominant role in foreign policy formulation, and relations between countries should be based on the balance of their interests. Speaking in Berlin in June 2008, President Medvedev proposed to European leaders to develop a new

on political freedoms in exchange for stability and prosperity—is threatened by the economic crisis as well. Despite the leadership's assurances that Russia was immune to global economic turbulence, Russian citizens have experienced the country's difficulties first-hand—falling currency, rising prices, and unemployment. The government's efforts to support the falling ruble and the vast sums of money it has spent on that task suggest that it is extremely sensitive to the social and political consequences of the country's economic difficulties. The Russian government's worries about the impact of the crisis on domestic stability are grounded in Russian realities.

Russian domestic politics is not the picture of tranquility that Putin's and Medvedev's strong approval ratings might lead one to believe. Russia in the early 21st century is not the Soviet Union of the late 20th century. Millions of Russians have now travelled abroad. They have largely unimpeded access to the Internet; they are free to read Western literature and news reports about developments in Russia and elsewhere in the world. They enjoy a significant measure of freedom to express themselves, as indicated by the lively Russian-language blogosphere. Public opinion data describe a population that is alienated from the ruling elite but that has accepted certain restrictions on personal freedoms in exchange for the stability and economic security of the new era, which stands in stark contrast with the despair and turmoil of the previous decade. It is, however, a population that, absent the promise of further economic growth, could prove difficult for the ruling elite to control.

Challenges Abroad

As if these domestic problems were not enough, Russia is facing major new challenges in the international arena. It is surrounded by weak states in Central Asia and the South Caucasus that in turn border on the world's most turbulent area—the greater Middle East. Should one or more states on Russia's doorstep stumble, others could fall like dominoes along and across its southern frontier. This would not be a new phenomenon for Russia, which saw its security threatened during the previous decade when the Taliban declared their plans for an Islamic caliphate in Central Asia. Few Russian policymakers are likely to have illusions about their ability to control Russia's borders, something that the Russian security services were unable to do during the 1990s, when the war in Chechnya became a rallying cause for foreign volunteers eager to support their Chechen Muslim brethren in their struggle for independence from Russian occupiers.

The recent war in Georgia has not made Russia more popular in its immediate neighborhood. Support for Russia has been lukewarm at best among its closest neighbors, all of whom had to one degree or another been looking to build and expand ties with NATO and the EU, and all of whom have been taught the lesson of not sticking their necks too far out for fear of Russian punishment. All of Russia's neighbors are bound to proceed from this point with great caution in forging ties with NATO or the EU, but none is likely to abandon these efforts. Moreover, the EU's lead role in the settlement of the Georgian war is drawing the organization into a region in which, until recently, it had been reluctant to involve itself. Despite Moscow's insistence on an exclusive sphere of influence around its periphery, its neighborhood has long been open to new partners besides NATO and the EU, most notably Turkey in the Caucasus and China in Central Asia. It appears highly improbable that in the aftermath of the Georgian war, this trend will be reversed and Russia's neighborhood will revert to its exclusive sphere of influence. To the contrary: Russia's neighbors are more likely now to hedge against its attempts to reassert itself at their expense by pursuing quiet, cautious engagement with other powers.

What Next?

Triumphant in the aftermath of its victory over Georgia, Russia is confronting a combination of challenges at home and abroad that suggests that despite

AP Images (Dmitry Lovetsky)

Russian armored vehicles moving toward the border with North Ossetia, 70 km (43 miles) north of Tskhinvali, South Ossetia, August 2008

its assertiveness and insistence on revising some key aspects of the post–Cold War order in Europe, Russia is hardly in a position to disrupt the international system. Considering the multitude and nature of the challenges facing Russia, common sense would suggest that it has a compelling interest in preserving and strengthening that system.

Russia wants to be recognized as a major power with its own sphere of influence, but it is unable to secure that position and stand up to other major powers. Russia wants to challenge U.S. dominance in international affairs, but it has a stake in a special relationship with the United States because of the special, unique status that relationship confers on Russia. Russia needs foreign investment and know-how, but it does not want outside interference in its internal affairs and wants to limit foreign investors' access to key sectors of its economy. In sum, Russia wants a bigger stake in the international system, but is not prepared to pay the full price for it.

Russia is also a country that, despite all the difficulties associated with forging a productive relationship with it, will remain very important to the United States as either a partner or an adversary. The task of managing this relationship will remain one of the leading concerns of U.S. policymakers for a long time to come.

Enduring Aims

The United States and its Allies will remain committed to the same four essential objectives with respect to Russia as before the Georgian war:

- the security of Russia's nuclear arsenal and support for global nonproliferation efforts
- a secure and stable Europe, with regional conflicts resolved through negotiations
- a secure and sustainable energy flow from Russia to international markets
- the independence and sovereignty of Russia's neighbors.

This is not an exhaustive list of Western interests in Russia, but merely a list of the essential ones. Some of these interests, such as the flow of energy from Russia to world markets, parallel Russia's own interests. Others, such as the independence and sovereignty of Russia's neighbors, will be areas of tensions and competition.

Different Means

To achieve their objectives, the United States and its Allies will need to devise a new approach to Russia and its neighbors. It will require coordination, patience, and communication on the part of

▼ Continued on p. 251

Russian atomic agency chief and head of Iran's Atomic Energy Organization at joint press conference at Iran's Bushehr nuclear powerplant as officials began test-run of Iran's first nuclear plant, February 2009

AP Images (Hasan Sarbakhshian)

Russia and Arms Control[1]

As U.S.-Russian relations evolve from an unfulfilled partnership toward an association based on balance of interests and power, arms control has regained a measure of importance by comparison with the previous decade, when it was considered largely a relic of the Cold War. Both the United States and Russia still maintain nuclear arsenals that can be justified only in the Cold War terms of mutually assured destruction. Arms control agreements and their attendant verification regimes provide a measure of transparency and predictability to both sides' nuclear postures that otherwise would be difficult to achieve. Russian interest in arms control can be explained by an overall preference for traditional diplomacy and concerns about the unconstrained nature of U.S. defensive and offensive strategic programs and the long-term impact of these programs on the U.S.-Russian strategic balance. A return to a more traditional, formal arms control agenda could serve U.S. interests as well. It would contribute to a stronger overall global nonproliferation regime as a sign of U.S. and Russian adherence to their Nuclear Non-Proliferation Treaty commitments to reduce their arsenals and would provide the United States with additional leverage to press Moscow for greater cooperation on issues that are more important to Washington, such as Iran's nuclear program or Russian theater nuclear forces.

Strategic Arms Reduction Treaty

The United States and Soviet Union signed the first Strategic Arms Reduction Treaty (START) on July 31, 1991. START officially entered into force on December 5, 1994, limiting long-range nuclear forces—land-based intercontinental ballistic missiles (ICBMs), submarine-launched ballistic missiles (SLBMs), and heavy bombers—in the United States and the newly independent states of the former Soviet Union. Each side can deploy up to 6,000 *attributed* warheads on 1,600 ballistic missiles and bombers. (Some weapons carried on bombers do not count against the treaty's limits, so each side could deploy 8,000 or 9,000 actual weapons.) Each side can deploy up to 4,900 warheads on ICBMs and SLBMs. START also limits each side to 1,540 warheads on "heavy" ICBMs, a 50 percent reduction in the number of warheads deployed on the SS–18 ICBMs in the former Soviet republics.

START contains a complex verification regime. Both sides collect most of the information needed to verify compliance with their own satellites and remote sensing equipment—the National Technical Means of Verification. But the parties also use data exchanges, notifications, and on-site inspections to gather information about forces and activities limited by the treaty. The United States and Russia completed the reductions in their forces by the designated date of December 5, 2001.

START expires in December 2009. The United States and Russia have held discussions about the treaty's future, but the two sides have sharply different views on what that future should look like. Neither side wishes to continue the treaty as is and there are a number of potential stumbling blocks for agreement. Differences are likely to emerge on the establishment of new rules for counting deployed nuclear weapons, stockpiles, and means of delivery. Other issues could include any further reductions in the number of deployed warheads, the regulation of multiple warhead missiles (MIRV), development and testing of new nuclear weapons, and means of delivery. If no agreement can be reached within the year, it is likely the two sides will seek an extension of the existing treaty but only under the condition and expectation that it will be replaced by 2010.

Intermediate-range Nuclear Forces Treaty

The United States and the Soviet Union signed the Treaty on Intermediate-range Nuclear Forces (INF Treaty) on December 8, 1987. The United States and Soviet Union agreed to destroy all intermediate- and shorter range nuclear-armed ballistic missiles and ground-launched cruise missiles, which are those missiles with a range between 300 and 3,400 miles. The launchers associated with the controlled missiles were also to be destroyed. The signatories agreed that the warheads and guidance systems of the missiles need not be destroyed; they could be used or reconfigured for other systems not controlled by the treaty. The Soviets agreed to destroy approximately 1,750 missiles, and the United States agreed to destroy 846 missiles, establishing a principle that asymmetrical reductions were acceptable in order to achieve a goal of greater stability. The parties had eliminated all their weapons by May 1991.

The INF Treaty returned to the news in 2007. Russia, partly in response to U.S. plans to deploy a missile defense radar in the Czech Republic and interceptor missiles in Poland, has stated that it might withdraw from the INF Treaty. Some Russian officials have claimed this would allow Russia to deploy missiles with the range needed to threaten the missile defense system, in case it were capable of threatening Russia's strategic nuclear forces. Analysts outside Russia have also noted that the Russians might be responding to concerns about the growing capabilities of China's missiles or those of other countries surrounding Russia.

Strategic Offensive Reductions Treaty

The United States and Russia signed the Strategic Offensive Reductions Treaty, or Moscow Treaty, on May 24, 2002. The treaty entered into force on June 1, 2003, and is due to remain in force until December 31, 2012, after which it could be extended or replaced by another agreement. In theory, the parties might be able to increase their warheads above the 2,200 limit as soon as the treaty expires. The treaty also states that either party may withdraw on 3 months' notice. This provision differs from the withdrawal clause in previous treaties, which required 6 months' notice and a statement of "extraordinary events" that led to the nation's withdrawal.

Article I contains the only limit in the treaty, stating that the United States and Russia will reduce their "strategic nuclear warheads" to between 1,700 and 2,200 by December 31, 2012. The text does not define "strategic nuclear warheads" and, therefore, does not indicate whether the parties will count only those warheads that are "operationally deployed," all warheads that would count under the START counting rules, or some other quantity of nuclear warheads.

It does not contain any monitoring or verification provisions, and there are no restrictions on nonstrategic nuclear weapons. During hearings before the Senate Foreign Relations Committee in 2002, Secretary of Defense Donald Rumsfeld and Secretary of State Colin Powell agreed that the disposition of nonstrategic nuclear weapons should be on the agenda for future meetings between the United States and Russia, although neither supported a formal arms control regime to limit or contain these weapons.

Conventional Forces in Europe Treaty

In late 1990, 22 members of the North Atlantic Treaty Organization (NATO) and the Warsaw Pact signed the Conventional Armed Forces in Europe (CFE) Treaty, agreeing to limit NATO and Warsaw Pact nonnuclear forces in an area from the Atlantic Ocean to the Ural Mountains. The participants signed the so-called Tashkent Agreement in May 1992, allocating responsibility for the Soviet Union's treaty-limited items of equipment (TLEs) among Azerbaijan, Armenia, Belarus, Kazakhstan, Moldova, Russia, Ukraine, and Georgia. It also established equipment ceilings for each nation and the implied responsibility for the destruction/transfer of equipment necessary to meet these national ceilings.

The CFE parties negotiated a Flank Agreement in early 1996. This agreement removed several Russian (and one Ukrainian) administrative districts from the old "flank zone," thus permitting existing flank equipment ceilings to apply to a smaller area. CFE placed alliance-wide, regional (zonal), and national ceilings on specific major items of military equipment. It sought to promote stability not only by reducing armaments, but also by reducing the possibility of surprise attack by preventing large concentrations of forces. The CFE Treaty also provides for detailed data exchanges on equipment, force structure, and training maneuvers; specific procedures for the destruction or redistribution of excess equipment; and verification of compliance through on-site inspections. Its implementation has resulted in an unprecedented reduction of conventional arms in Europe, with over 50,000 TLEs removed or destroyed; almost all agree it has achieved most of its initial objectives.

On April 26, 2007, in his last state of the union speech, President Putin announced a "moratorium" on Russian CFE compliance, pointing to, among other things, the fact that the NATO nations had not ratified the treaty as adapted. A Russian request to the Organisation for Security and Co-operation in Europe for a special conference of CFE signatories in June was granted. The conference failed to resolve any of the outstanding issues, and the state parties were unable to find sufficient common ground to issue a final joint statement.

NOTE

[1] This text is based on Amy F. Woolf, *Arms Control and Nonproliferation: A Catalog of Treaties and Agreements, Congressional Research Service Report for Congress* (Washington, DC: Congressional Research Service, April 9, 2008).

▲ *Continued from p. 248*

both the United States and Europe. It will require a much keener sense of priorities with respect to U.S. objectives vis-à-vis Russia than what was implicit in the old, non–zero-sum-game approach, whereby U.S. interests were presumed to be the same and of equal urgency as Russia's and therefore did not require tradeoffs by the United States. In the future, the United States may have to choose between Russian support for U.S. nonproliferation objectives and NATO membership for some of Russia's neighbors.

Coordinating actions between the two sides of the Atlantic and among the Group of 7 partners will be essential, considering the asymmetrical but uniquely important relationships the United States and Europe have with Russia. The United States and Russia have the special relationship that is rooted in the Cold War and the legacy of their nuclear competition. Europe and Russia have geographic proximity, trade, and human ties that bind them together. Together, Europe and the United States are in a unique position to influence Moscow. Their failure to agree on a common vision and set their priorities accordingly could be fatal to the entire enterprise of developing a new approach to Russia.

The Allies should tackle the challenge of a new Russia policy with alacrity, but with patience that does not count on quick results. Considering the breadth, depth, and longevity of popular support for the Kremlin's policies, elite, middle class, and rank-and-file attitudes will not change quickly. The United States and its Allies should allow themselves ample time to demonstrate to Russia the benefits of cooperation, as well as the costs of competition.

Communication will be essential, for the Allies will need to reach their critical target audience—the Russian people. Western dialogue with Russia should make clear that the goal of the United States and Europe is not to isolate Russia, but rather to encourage its greater openness to Western contacts and cooperation.

To that end, the Allies should weigh carefully any steps they might be tempted to take as retribution for Russia's war in Georgia. For example, does it make sense to hold up Russian membership in the World Trade Organization (WTO) if membership carries with it the possibility of greater Russian openness to international pressures, and a greater Western ability to influence Russia through WTO institutional arrangements?

By contrast, the G–8 could be an appropriate venue for letting Russia know that its actions in Georgia are not without consequences. The group lacks formal institutional structure and responsibilities, but has an established parallel format, the G–7, that allows the United States and its key Allies to address major issues of the day *without* Russia.

Which Way NATO after the War in Georgia?

The assumption that Russia will accept—eventually—NATO enlargement and see it as beneficial to its interests has proven unrealistic, at least for the foreseeable future. The notion that NATO enlargement has been accompanied by its transformation into a 'new' organization, different from its Cold War-era predecessor, has faded in the wake of the Georgian war, threatening Russian statements aimed at Poland and the Czech Republic, and the cyber attack on Estonia in 2007. NATO's Article V guarantee, always viewed as the cornerstone of the Alliance, had nonetheless lost some of its saliency when the Cold War ended, and a new confrontation in the heart of Europe seemed unthinkable. Renewed concerns about Russia and its direction have once again underscored the importance of 'old' NATO with its Article V guarantee, especially to NATO's newest members, who continue to treat the Article V guarantee no less seriously than they did during the Cold War.

Moreover, the Georgian war has demonstrated that extending NATO membership, or holding out the possibility thereof, to countries that the Alliance is not fully committed to defend makes them potentially more vulnerable to Russian pressures. NATO's Bucharest promise to eventually admit Georgia arguably left that country more vulnerable to Russian actions than if the Allies had said nothing about its membership prospects.

With Georgian and Ukrainian NATO prospects on hold, the United States and its European allies need to develop a new formula for integrating these two countries, whose Euro-Atlantic aspirations are not in doubt, into European political and security architecture. The approach adopted by the United States and Europe after the Cold War—NATO membership first, EU second—has worked well elsewhere in Eastern Europe, but is unlikely to work in Ukraine and Georgia. Many European allies of the United States are opposed to Ukrainian and Georgian membership in NATO, even if some of NATO's newest members are strongly in favor of it. The debate surrounding this issue promises to be deeply divisive for the alliance and—ultimately—probably inconclusive, and is therefore likely to do more harm than good.

▼ *Continued on p. 253*

The Russian Far Eastern Energy Complex and Russia's Reemergence in East Asia

In recent years, the Russian government has emphasized the urgency of socioeconomic development in the Russian Far East, a region mired in economic and social stagnation. The Russian Far East (or the Far Eastern Federal District) has always lagged behind European Russia economically. Russia has long felt strategically vulnerable in the region due to its remoteness from the center of Russian power in Europe and its proximity to rival powers China and Japan. Today, the region is facing yet another threat: a demographic decline of unprecedented proportions. The region's population has declined by almost 15 percent since 1989 and is projected to continue falling over the next decade, giving China's ponderous proximity and vibrant economic growth a highly sinister aspect in the eyes of many Russians. The Russian government has stated on numerous occasions its commitment to reverse the situation in the region, though its chances of accomplishing that task appear in doubt.

At the heart of the Kremlin's vision for the Russian Far East is a plan for a massive development project known as the Far Eastern energy complex, which will include pipelines, regional gasification efforts, electrical grids, rail lines, and even tunnels to Sakhalin Island's oil and gas fields. The government has also drawn up a blueprint for a socioeconomic development plan, wherein it would invest as much as $300 billion in the infrastructure of the region. The accomplishment of such a plan would definitively mark Russia's strategic reemergence in northeast Asia after almost two decades of marginalization.

The centerpiece for the energy complex is the East Siberian–Pacific Ocean (ESPO) oil pipeline. The pipeline is under construction and will travel roughly 3,000 miles from the town of Taishet in an oil-producing region northwest of Lake Baikal to a terminus on Kozmino Bay, near Vladivostok on the Pacific Ocean. The cost for the first stage of the pipeline is expected to exceed $12 billion. The second stage would likely cost more than $15 billion. The primary partners in the project are Transneft, a state-owned pipeline monopoly, which would be responsible for constructing the pipeline, and Rosneft, a state-controlled oil company.

The ESPO pipeline captured the attention of many observers beginning in 2002, as the Chinese and Japanese governments became engaged in a diplomatic tug-of-war over the route of the still-uncompleted pipeline. The Chinese government thought that it

had reached an agreement for the construction of a pipeline to the refining center of Daqing in northeastern China in 2002. But the Japanese government intervened at the eleventh hour and put forth an attractive proposal for a Pacific-bound pipeline, which the Russian government tentatively agreed to in 2004. As of 2008, however, there is still no firm commitment from the Kremlin as to which branch will have priority, though it appears that the pipeline eventually will go to both places.

As part of a national energy strategy published in early 2006, the Kremlin announced that it plans to increase gas and oil exports to the Asia-Pacific region from their current level of 3 percent of total Russian energy exports to 30 percent. The ESPO pipeline would be expected to export 80 million metric tons of oil annually by the year 2020 (or roughly 1.6 million barrels of oil per day). As of the end of 2006, however, East Siberian fields were producing only 1 million tons per year. Thus, the commercial viability of the project is still in doubt, unless new discoveries are made in Eastern Siberia.

Nevertheless, the Russian leadership sees the issue of Russian Far Eastern economic development in terms of national security; therefore, economic viability is not an overriding factor. In a speech several years ago, Vladimir Putin warned that if the economic and social conditions in the Russian Far East were not improved, residents of the region would be speaking Chinese, Japanese, or Korean in future generations. Later, he warned that the crumbling socioeconomic situation in the region was a "threat to national security." Ironically, in order to complete these massive Far Eastern development projects, the Russian government will probably need to import—at least temporarily—foreign labor.

Aside from the ESPO pipeline's commercial feasibility, and doubts surrounding the overall viability of the ambitious $300-billion government-sponsored development project in the Far East, there is the larger question of whether Moscow's plans for the Far East are likely to restore Russia's position as a major power in northeast Asia or to further marginalize it by increasing its dependence on Chinese labor, Chinese markets, and Chinese imports of industrial equipment, consumer goods, and the like. If, as some Russians fear, economic development of the Far East comes at the price of its de facto colonization by China, then what is Russia's interest in it?

▲ *Continued from p. 251*

Instead, the United States and Europe should launch a new trans-Atlantic project to help Ukraine and Georgia launch firmly toward their goal of EU membership. The project would entail a U.S.-EU commitment to support Ukrainian and Georgian reforms necessary for the two countries to undertake in order to become viable candidates for EU membership, as well as a commitment from the EU to consider them eligible for membership once they implement those reforms. Ukraine, much like Georgia, should be focused on domestic consolida-

Nor are U.S. interests in this situation easily identified. On the surface, more oil pumped into the global marketplace from anywhere would appear to serve U.S. interests as an energy consumer. Given China's thirst for oil, quenching it with the help of Russian producers appears overall to benefit the economic interests of the United States.

The question is whether Moscow's attempts to reassert itself in northeast Asia will prove to be a factor for increased regional stability or tension. What if its current plans lead to more, not less, Russian dependence on China as a trade and investment partner? What if the result of this development is that Russia emerges as Beijing's junior partner in the region? It is highly improbable that in the next decade Russia could, through its "pipeline diplomacy," gain a position of influence in northeast Asia remotely comparable to its current clout in Europe thanks to its energy role there. The most optimistic forecasts predict that East Siberian oil would only account for 15 percent of Chinese and Japanese oil imports. Therefore, the completion of the ESPO pipeline is unlikely to drastically change the strategic balance in northeast Asia, and despite its ambitions, Russia's options are likely to remain constrained in the Far East.

How would Russia try to avoid or cope with this predicament? Would it lead to renewed Russian-Chinese tensions? Or would Moscow simply accept the inevitable and agree to ride China's economic coattails in the region? Would that in turn lead to Russia falling in as China's junior partner? None of these scenarios has obvious implications for U.S. interests in northeast Asia, beyond further complicating the situation in the region. All of them, however, call attention to the evolving situation in northeast Asia, including Russia—a region where the United States has much at stake, and where fading Cold War memories are likely to produce more, not fewer, tensions.

tion and a lengthy reform agenda whose purpose should be to move them ever closer to the goal of EU membership. This approach should make it possible for the United States and Europe to continue working toward their goal of Europe whole and free, while avoiding new divisions within the Alliance and new tensions with Russia, whose cooperation both Europe and the United States need in the Middle East, the Far East, and Afghanistan.

Frozen Conflicts

The war in Georgia has demonstrated that the so-called frozen conflicts on the territory of the former Soviet Union can thaw in unpredictable and dangerous ways. Moreover, the explicit connection made by Russia (and prior to that, ironically, by Georgia) between Kosovo on the one hand and South Ossetia and Abkhazia on the other suggests that the argument put forth by U.S. and other European officials that there is no similarity between the two types of conflict, and that therefore the former is not a precedent for the latter, lacks credibility. There can be little doubt that the Kosovo settlement—leading up to its independence from Serbia—was seen as a precedent-setting event in Georgia with its breakaway territories, as well as in Russia. With the map of Georgia de facto redrawn as a result of Russian military actions, the premise of a return to status quo ante through negotiations to restore Georgian sovereignty within its Soviet-era borders appears highly unrealistic. What, then, is the way ahead and out of the impasse that these frozen conflicts have reached?

There appear to be few alternatives to deadlock other than for the United States and its EU partners to acknowledge that the Kosovo settlement *could* serve as a precedent for settling frozen or separatist conflicts. This approach calls for considerable compromise on the part of the United States and Europe, premised on the strength of their systemic advantages, as well as a long-term and profound commitment to the well-being and security of the Caucasus region. This course of action would recognize, in principle, that the Kosovo experience *could* constitute a precedent for settling frozen conflicts in the Caucasus, provided that certain critical conditions are met. These conditions should be patterned after those established for Kosovo but adapted to the specific circumstances of each conflict situation.

This course of action would require a full and impartial examination of the successes, failures, shortcomings, and missed opportunities of the Kosovo experience, so as to draw the correct lessons.

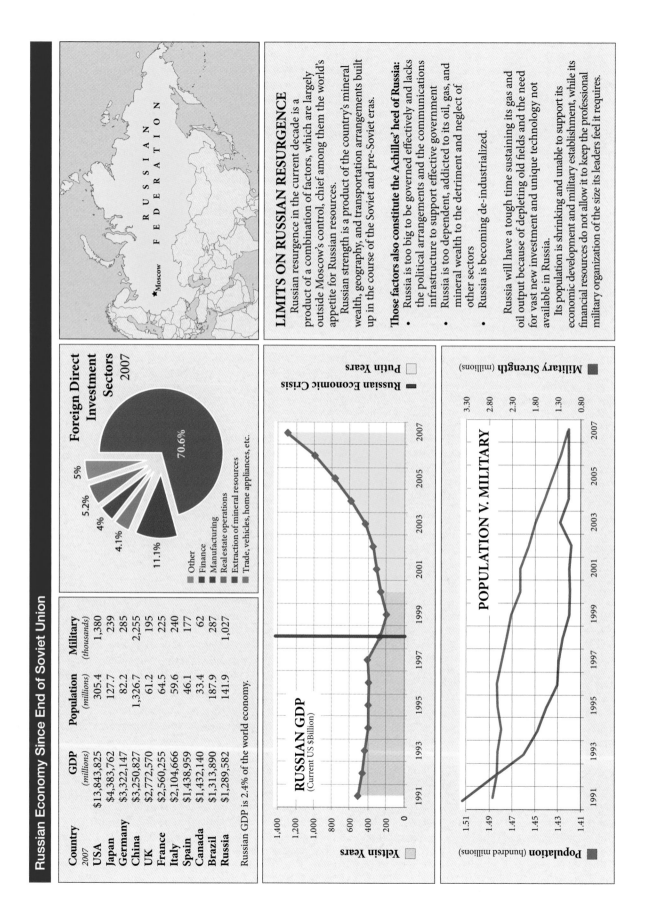

Russian Economy Since End of Soviet Union

Country 2007	GDP (millions)	Population (millions)	Military (thousands)
USA	$13,843,825	305.4	1,380
Japan	$4,383,762	127.7	239
Germany	$3,322,147	82.2	285
China	$3,250,827	1,326.7	2,255
UK	$2,772,570	61.2	195
France	$2,560,255	64.5	225
Italy	$2,104,666	59.6	240
Spain	$1,438,959	46.1	177
Canada	$1,432,140	33.4	62
Brazil	$1,313,890	187.9	287
Russia	$1,289,582	141.9	1,027

Russian GDP is 2.4% of the world economy.

Foreign Direct Investment Sectors 2007

- 70.6%
- 11.1%
- 4.1%
- 4%
- 5.2%
- 5%

Other
Finance
Manufacturing
Real estate operations
Extraction of mineral resources
Trade, vehicles, home appliances, etc.

RUSSIAN GDP (Current US $Billion)

Yeltsin Years
Russian Economic Crisis
Putin Years

POPULATION V. MILITARY

Population (hundred millions)
Military Strength (millions)

LIMITS ON RUSSIAN RESURGENCE

Russian resurgence in the current decade is a product of a combination of factors, which are largely outside Moscow's control, chief among them the world's appetite for Russian resources.

Russian strength is a product of the country's mineral wealth, geography, and transportation arrangements built up in the course of the Soviet and pre-Soviet eras.

Those factors also constitute the Achilles' heel of Russia:

- Russia is too big to be governed effectively and lacks the political arrangements and the communications infrastructure to support effective government
- Russia is too dependent, addicted to its oil, gas, and mineral wealth to the detriment and neglect of other sectors
- Russia is becoming de-industrialized.

Russia will have a tough time sustaining its gas and oil output because of depleting old fields and the need for vast new investment and unique technology not available in Russia.

Its population is shrinking and unable to support its economic development and military establishment, while its financial resources do not allow it to keep the professional military organization of the size its leaders feel it requires.

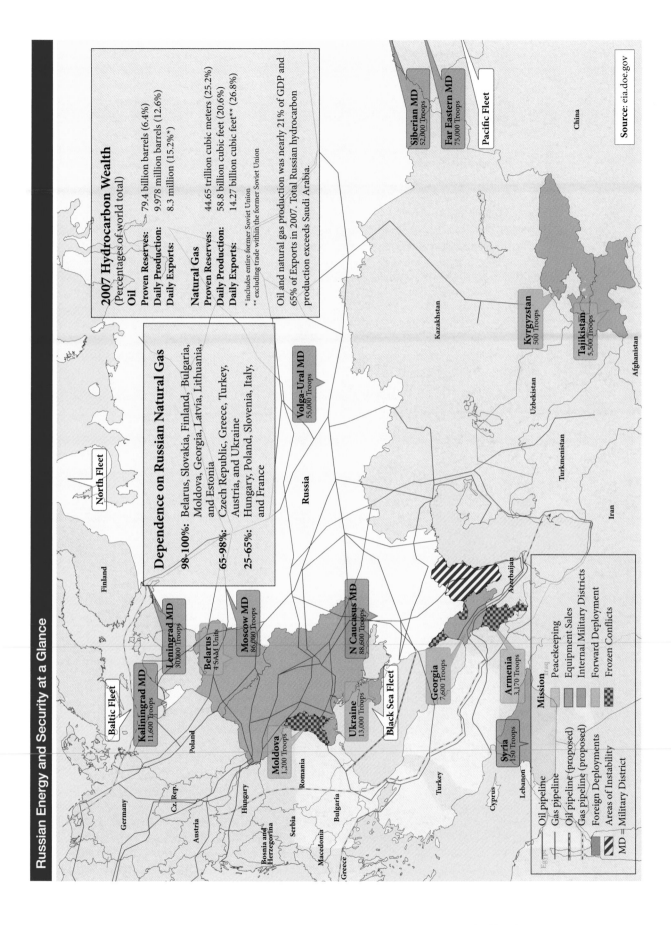

Russian Energy and Security at a Glance

2007 Hydrocarbon Wealth
(Percentages of world total)
Oil
Proven Reserves: 79.4 billion barrels (6.4%)
Daily Production: 9.978 million barrels (12.6%)
Daily Exports: 8.3 million (15.2%*)

Natural Gas
Proven Reserves: 44.65 trillion cubic meters (25.2%)
Daily Production: 58.8 billion cubic feet (20.6%)
Daily Exports: 14.27 billion cubic feet** (26.8%)

* includes entire former Soviet Union
** excluding trade within the former Soviet Union

Oil and natural gas production was nearly 21% of GDP and 65% of Exports in 2007. Total Russian hydrocarbon production exceeds Saudi Arabia.

Dependence on Russian Natural Gas

98–100%: Belarus, Slovakia, Finland, Bulgaria, Moldova, Georgia, Latvia, Lithuania, and Estonia

65–98%: Czech Republic, Greece, Turkey, Austria, and Ukraine

25–65%: Hungary, Poland, Slovenia, Italy, and France

Source: eia.doe.gov

Before embarking on this course, the international community—under the auspices of major international organizations—would have to fully record, analyze, and assess the Kosovo experience to produce an impartial lessons learned document, including recommendations on what and what not to do in future crisis situations, that could provide a road map for the future.

A shift of this magnitude in U.S. policy does not need to come without preconditions set by the United States and Europe. In exchange for conceding that Kosovo could serve as a precedent for resolving separatist conflicts in the South Caucasus, the United States and the European Union could and should insist that international recognition be accorded the de facto states only as a result of their own domes-

tic transformation and their ability to fulfill commitments in the areas of civil society, rule of law, political reforms, return of refugees, minority rights, and willingness to negotiate peaceful settlement with their former metropoles. The United States and Europe would thus take an impartial approach to the issue of frozen conflicts, but would offer a path toward their eventual resolution rather than stay on the open-ended course of attempting to negotiate settlements that have little or no chance of acceptance by either party to the conflicts.

Taking Russia at Its Word

In recent months, Russian leaders have issued several appeals to the West to devise a new security architecture for Europe. Lacking specificity, these proposals have been viewed with suspicion in the West, where some have interpreted them as an attempt to weaken NATO and the transatlantic ties. This proposal is worth exploring, however, as an opening to a new dialogue about European security and its underlying principles. With skillful diplomacy, patience, and a firm commitment to their core principles, the United States and its European Allies, as well as quite a few other countries around Russia's periphery, would have a strong hand to negotiate a new arrangement with Russia that, just like the Commission on Security and Cooperation in Europe a generation ago, will not replace NATO, but will provide a new venue for Russia and the West to address their differences.

The Shanghai Cooperation Organization: The Lowest Common Denominator

The establishment of the Shanghai Cooperation Organization (SCO) in 2001 has been referred to as the emergence of a new anti-Western alliance in the heart of Eurasia; as a Russian-Chinese condominium in Central Asia; and as the start of a new, powerful regional bloc that could rise to dominance in Eurasia if it were to admit to its ranks India and Iran. These descriptions seem to ignore, or at the very least underestimate, some of the fundamental trends in Eurasia, particularly as they pertain to the changing fortunes of Russia and China, as well as the outlook for the four Central Asian states that make up the rest of the organization (Kazakhstan, Kyrgyzstan, Tajikistan, and Uzbekistan).

After 7 years, the SCO remains much less than the sum of its parts. The fact that it brings together the two biggest countries in the world and more than 2 billion people (counting the observer states of Mongolia, Pakistan, India, and Iran) is likely to

AP Images (Mikhail Metzel)

Man changes figures on exchange rate display as Russian ruble dropped against U.S. dollar and Euro, February 2009

foster an inflated notion of the organization's cohesion and capabilities. The number and size of SCO member-states say nothing about its vision, interests, differences, and ability to act. A closer look at the organization reveals that it is, paradoxically, held together to a large degree by its differences. To be sure, organizations that are established to manage their members' differences can make a valuable contribution to the security of both their members and the international community. But when considering their capabilities and potential, it is important to keep in mind their inherent limitations.

Not an Alliance

Unlike NATO, the SCO is not an alliance. It does not have a binding set of agreements among its members about joint action or mutual assistance in case of need. The SCO does not have committed military capabilities or command arrangements. It is an organization that, far from promulgating internal cohesion in its ranks, has held respect for each member's differences as one of its key founding principles.

Far from being an alliance, the SCO resembles a loose association of countries with diverse interests, where the balance between cooperation and competition is shifting gradually toward the latter. The shared interests of the organization's biggest and most important members, China and Russia, are outweighed by their competing interests. Although both play a very important role in Central Asia and in the SCO, Russia and China are going in very different directions and face different strategic predicaments, which in turn shape their respective interests in Central Asia and the SCO.

China's Gain

China's interests in Central Asia, which presently manifest most clearly in the economic sphere, in the future are unlikely to be limited to trade, investment, and energy flows. Central Asia borders on China's western provinces, where separatist Uyghur movements have long challenged Chinese control. The breakup of the Soviet Union and the resulting destabilization of Central Asia must have been a worrisome development for Chinese leaders, one that they certainly are not prepared to accept as precedent-setting.

From China's point of view, Central Asia represents an opportunity for a long-term investment in an important area, which nonetheless is secondary to the premier strategic arena for Beijing: the Pacific Rim. Chinese interests in Central Asia pale in comparison to Chinese interests in the East: Taiwan, and relations with North Korea, Japan, the United States, and a whole host of neighbors in Southeast Asia. With its strategy for securing its Western provinces resting on the domestic pillars of economic development and ethnic assimilation, Beijing appeared content to leave Central Asian security to Russia and the United States, while expanding its economic ties in the region. The fruits of that expansion have begun to ripen in recent years, as China emerged as a major player with regard to Central Asian energy resources.

Thus, membership in the SCO has served China well, giving it a major voice in Central Asian affairs without antagonizing Russia or alarming regional leaders, and while keeping the United States at bay.

Russia's Loss

Russia, despite its economic rebound and international resurgence during Vladimir Putin's tenure as president, is a country in a state of long-term decline. Demography, geography, and globalization, the factors that will define its glide path and strategic direction, are largely outside its leaders' ability to manage in the short and medium term. China looms large on the agenda of Russian policymakers in all three of these areas.

There are fewer Russians than there were a decade ago, and likely to be fewer still as time goes by. With a total population projected at 128 million by 2025, Russia will need to import labor to sustain economic growth, develop new mineral resources, and man its military.

Russia's geography does not leave the country's leaders much room for maneuver. The country shares a 3,600-kilometer border with China in the Far East. This is a situation that many Russian analysts view with growing unease, considering the demographic imbalance between the two neighbors and China's latent territorial claims against Russia, as well as a Chinese economic dynamism that acts like a magnet for nearby regions of Russia, which are experiencing a much weaker gravitational pull from the rest of their country.

Russia shares an even longer border—6,800 kilometers—with Kazakhstan, which also shares a 1,500-kilometer border with China. Once the dominant power in Central Asia, Russia is having to adjust to the fact that since the breakup of the Soviet Union, the region's geographic proximity to China has enabled the latter to expand its presence and influence in Central Asia.

This combination of geography and politics has resulted in a new and complex challenge for Russia: it has to keep a wary eye on the unstable Central Asian region, which borders on Afghanistan and Iran, and it has to contend with growing Chinese economic and political influence there. The benefits that Russia has long derived from its proximity to Central Asia, particularly the ability to exploit the region's mineral wealth and control its exports, are being eroded by Chinese economic expansion and pursuit of Central Asian resources, in particular oil and gas, just as Russia is becoming more dependent on Central Asian gas to make up its own shortfall in production from existing fields.

The unfavorable picture for Russia is further clouded by the effects of globalization, including rapid technological change and the emergence of new manufacturing powerhouses in Asia, coupled with abundant and cheap labor, also in Asia. These developments render Russia—with its crumbling infrastructure, limited and comparatively expensive labor supply, and obsolete industrial base—unable to compete, especially with China.

A Tough Neighborhood

There is no doubt that Russian-Chinese relations have improved immeasurably since the era of Sino-Soviet confrontation. But Russia remains deeply suspicious of its giant neighbor and shares only a limited agenda with China in Central Asia, for which the SCO provides a useful vehicle.

One of the key items on that agenda is to limit the U.S. presence in the region. This has long been a key objective of Russia, given the priority it has assigned to the task of securing an exclusive sphere of influence in the territories of the former Soviet states. Russian zeal for containing U.S. influence in Central Asia subsided somewhat in the aftermath of September 11, and Moscow most likely saw an added benefit to its security interests from the demise of the Taliban regime in Afghanistan. The long-term U.S. military presence on Central Asian bases, however, has been an irritant for Russian policymakers, as demonstrated by Russia's reported push to expel the United States from the Manas airbase in Kyrgyzstan in 2009.

Moscow's and Beijing's positions were pushed closer together as the United States embarked on a course of democracy promotion in the second George W. Bush administration. Both saw the U.S. initiative as fraught with dangerous destabilizing consequences that would not necessarily be contained in one Central Asian country, or even in the entire region,

and that could spill across their borders to endanger their own domestic stability. United in their opposition to U.S. influence, Moscow and Beijing have used the SCO to declare their region-wide opposition to Washington's pursuit of democracy.

This Russian-Chinese united front has served the interests of the Central Asian countries as well. Their leaders, ranging from mildly authoritarian to kleptocratic, were eager to enlist the support of the two giant neighbors in opposition to U.S. policy.

The Central Asian states' interests are also well served by the SCO. For these relatively small countries, long isolated from the outside world and forced to navigate an independent course in what one of them described as a "tough neighborhood" with little advance warning when the Soviet Union broke up, the SCO has served as a vital forum for engaging two giant and important neighbors.

Wary of the two giants, however, and fearful of domination by them, the Central Asian countries have pursued their own careful balancing act intended to offset growing Chinese and Russian influence in the region with ties to other powers. Key among them has been the United States, whose presence in Central Asia has served as a useful check on Russian influence and could play a similar role vis-à-vis China in the future. But for the Central Asian countries, any rapprochement with the United States has to be balanced with ties to China and Russia for fear of provoking their negative responses. There is also the danger of getting too close to the United States and in the process exposing the region to too much destabilizing U.S. influence. For all of these pursuits, the SCO has proved a reliable and useful vehicle.

No Greater than the Sum of Its Parts

Despite its utility to all of its participants, the SCO as an organization is hampered by limitations that stem first and foremost from members' diverging interests. Russia and China are competing for influence in the region. The Central Asian countries want to have a common forum for engaging Russia and China but, fearing their domination, do not want to endow the organization with too much power and authority. At the same time, they would like to maintain ties to the United States, Europe, and other powers that are taking more and more interest in Central Asia. However, they do not want to be too closely associated with the United States, fearing its disruptive influence on the region's politics.

Russia's military campaign against Georgia, and its subsequent recognition of the two breakaway territories of Abkhazia and South Ossetia, have introduced new tensions into the SCO. Russia's neighbors and erstwhile colonies, some of which still have sizeable Russian populations, no doubt feel vulnerable and fear that Russia will intervene in their domestic affairs or, worse, use force against them under the same pretext that Russia used in Georgia, namely, protecting its citizens abroad. For China, Moscow's decision to recognize South Ossetia and Abkhazia was an unwelcome surprise, considering Beijing's own problems in Tibet and Sinkiang and of course with Taiwan. This lack of support for Russia's move was evident in the lukewarm reaction from the SCO summit participants in August 2008, in Dushanbe, Tajikistan.

Amidst all this discord and competition, one pattern appears to emerge as the critical long-term trend in the region: China's continuing economic expansion, and with it, growing influence in Central Asia, most likely at the expense of Russian influence. The SCO is almost an ideal vehicle for Beijing's interest in the region: it provides China with a major voice in regional affairs but is in no way binding and leaves it full freedom to pursue its bilateral initiatives in Central Asia and elsewhere. As China is pursuing its economic and ultimately political agenda in the region, Russia and the United States provide for the region's security. It is an arrangement that in the short and medium term serves its stakeholders well. **gsa**

Contributors

Dr. Eugene Rumer (Chapter Editor) is Director of Research in the Institute for National Strategic Studies (INSS) at National Defense University (NDU). Previously, he served at the Department of State, on the staff of the National Security Council, and with the RAND Corporation. He has written extensively on Russia and the former Soviet states. He holds degrees from Boston University (B.A.), Georgetown (M.A.), and the Massachusetts Institute of Technology (Ph.D.).

Joseph P. Ferguson is a consultant for LMI, a nonprofit strategic organization. He also teaches courses on International Relations at the University of Washington. He is the author of *Japanese-Russian Relations, 1907–2007* (Routledge, 2008).

Michael Kofman is a Program Manager in INSS at NDU and a Contributing Editor for *The Diplomatic Courier*. He previously conducted research on international security issues at the U.S. Institute of Peace and worked on education programs at the National Aeronautics and Space Administration. Mr. Kofman holds a Master's degree in Security Studies from the School of Foreign Service at Georgetown University.

Dr. Simon Serfaty holds the Zbigniew Brzezinski Chair in Global Security and Geostrategy at the Center for Strategic and International Studies, where he previously served as Director of the Europe Program. He is also Professor and Eminent Scholar in U.S. foreign policy at Old Dominion University. His most recent book is *Architects of Delusion: Europe, America, and the Iraq War* (University of Pennsylvania Press, 2007).

Dr. Jeffrey Simon analyzed Eastern and Central Europe for more than a quarter of a century as an INSS Senior Research Fellow at NDU. The author of numerous books and monographs on the region, Dr. Simon remains an Adjunct INSS Senior Research Fellow.

Chapter 12
East and Southeast Asia

Today, East Asia's vitality and connectedness are astounding. Economic, political, and social developments in the region have created new linkages and opportunities. Northeast and Southeast Asia are connecting with each other through trade, investment, and cooperation across a spectrum of goods and services.

Yet within this same dynamic East Asia, three trends and concerns play a key role in the security considerations of countries in the region: a rising China and how the United States manages that key relationship; a potentially fragile North Korea with nuclear weapons and how the region grapples with that country's nuclear program and potential succession crises; and the preservation of and relationship between traditional bilateral alliances and multilateral and regional approaches to security.

One obvious dilemma is that of managing U.S.-China strategic competition within a broader U.S. China strategy. While China is restrained in its international behavior, seeking to reassure neighbors of its peaceful intentions as it continues to expand its regional and global influence, it also has launched an ambitious military modernization program that complicates the U.S. ability to pursue a multifaceted relationship with it.

In this context, both U.S. allies in Northeast Asia—Japan and the Republic of Korea (ROK)—confront a complex strategic environment characterized by the uncertainty posed by North Korea's pursuit of nuclear weapons. They also are challenged by a fragile global economy, concerns about how the region will be transformed by China's resurgence, and the implications of that resurgence for their own security and relationship with the United States. This highlights the need for managing expectations and building mature partnerships as the strategic landscape evolves.

The current pattern of interaction among Association of Southeast Asian Nations (ASEAN) member states is very different from the environment of conflict and confrontation in which ASEAN was established in 1967. The present-day vitality and connectedness of Southeast Asia do not imply that ASEAN states have overcome their internal and external challenges, however. In fact, all face a diverse set of problems, some of which are an outgrowth of the issues that brought ASEAN together in the first place.

Just how important is Asia? Carefully weighting Asia's potential provides an integrating thread, giving context to Asia's economic emergence and exploring the centrality of the United States in Asia's rise.

Managing Strategic Competition with China

One critical foreign policy challenge for the Obama administration will be dealing with a more powerful China that generally behaves in a restrained manner and seeks to reassure its neighbors of its good intentions, while simultaneously developing advanced military capabilities and expanding its regional and global influence. The United States should welcome restrained and responsible Chinese behavior, but must also recognize and prepare for the more complex policy challenges a strong China will pose. A more powerful China will have a major impact on Asia-Pacific security and create new challenges for U.S.-China relations.

U.S. Strategy toward China

China has defied the predictions of those who expected its communist system to fail in the aftermath of the 1989 Tiananmen crackdown and the collapse of the Soviet Union. Instead, a brief period of political retrenchment was followed by continuing economic reforms that have produced rapid and sustained economic growth, albeit with only limited political reforms.

In 1995 and 1996, Beijing's seizure of Mischief Reef in the South China Sea and its use of missiles to intimidate Taiwan stoked regional fears of a hostile and expansionist China. Worried that the United States and other countries might seek to contain it, China's leaders sought to allay regional concerns through a combination of military restraint, friendly diplomacy, active participation in multilateral and

Imaginechina via AP Images (Yu guiyou)

Beijing

regional organizations, and offers to allow others the chance to benefit from China's rapid growth. Simultaneously, Beijing launched an ambitious military modernization program (with double-digit real defense budget increases) and worked to expand its influence within Asia and beyond. China's restrained behavior over the last decade has limited the willingness of its neighbors to balance against its rising power, but has not eliminated concerns about how a stronger China might behave in the future.

Awareness of China's power potential and uncertainty about its long-term evolution have been key considerations in U.S. strategy. Instead of defining China as a partner or adversary, the United States has sought to reap the benefits of cooperation while hedging against China's potential emergence as a future threat. The first element of U.S. strategy emphasizes cooperation and integration into global institutions as a means to influence Chinese behavior and shape China's future evolution in positive directions. The second emphasizes maintenance of U.S. military capabilities and alliances as a hedge against a potentially aggressive future China. Ideally, U.S. alliances and military capabilities should discourage aggressive actions and encourage Beijing to pursue its goals through peaceful means. The challenge is to keep the elements in balance, so that overemphasis on cooperation does not leave the United States in an unfavorable strategic position, while overemphasis on the military hedge does not push China toward confrontation.

Within this strategic context, the Bush administration increased cooperation with China on a range of important economic and security issues including energy security, nonproliferation, and counterterrorism. It also tried to influence Chinese thinking about its own long-term interests by proposing a vision of China as a "responsible stakeholder" that both benefits from and plays an important role in maintenance of the current international system. This concept, elaborated in a 2005 speech by then–Deputy Secretary of State Robert Zoellick, recognizes China's increasing influence on the international system and seeks to obtain Chinese support to sustain the global institutions and norms that have helped enable its remarkable economic success. It aims to expand the scope of U.S. and Chinese common interests and to place potential conflicts of interests within a larger framework of cooperation.

The responsible stakeholder concept is fundamentally sound but has ambiguities that deserve attention. First, there is no clear definition of what constitutes "responsible behavior" in many areas of international relations. China is unlikely to accept a definition of responsibility based on what is most helpful for American interests or most congruent with American policy. The United States will have difficulty holding China accountable to international rules and norms that Washington itself does not always respect. Second, Zoellick's speech acknowledges the reality of increasing Chinese influence in

Asia but avoids specifying which Chinese interests are legitimate and must be respected by the United States; it also does not clarify the extent to which the United States is willing to consider changes in existing rules and institutions to accommodate Chinese concerns and interests. Finally, the concept assumes China will have influence within an international system where the United States plays the leading role. If U.S. power wanes, this assumption may eventually come into question.

The China Challenge

A strategy of engaging and hedging that seeks to integrate China into the international system as a responsible stakeholder makes sense in light of uncertainty about China's future. But U.S. policymakers have not fully grappled with the challenges posed by a China that behaves in a restrained and generally responsible manner while simultaneously developing strategic capabilities that may threaten U.S. interests. Chinese military planners—like those in other advanced militaries—are interested in developing new technologies and capabilities that can increase military effectiveness. This does not make China uniquely aggressive, but it does raise questions about how a stronger China might use these capabilities in the future.

China is modernizing its forces and developing new capabilities to deal with a range of internal and external contingencies. Concerns about the possibility of Taiwan independence have been the key driver of Chinese military modernization since the mid-1990s, but China is now laying the foundations for military capabilities that can perform other missions, such as protecting its territorial claims and sea lines of communication. China is reshaping its military to take advantage of opportunities provided by advanced command, control, communications, computers, intelligence, surveillance, and reconnaissance and precision strike. Areas of particular concern include China's modernization of its nuclear arsenal and efforts to develop advanced space and counterspace, cyber warfare, and conventional force capabilities that may limit U.S. military access to the western Pacific. These capabilities represent a nascent antiaccess capability designed to limit U.S. strategic mobility in the western Pacific, limiting the U.S. military's ability to fulfill its security commitments.

Beijing's near- to midterm objective is not to match U.S. military capabilities across the board, but rather to create sufficient U.S. vulnerability to ensure that Washington behaves cautiously when core Chinese interests, such as preventing Taiwan from attaining de jure independence, are at stake. China's investments in advanced strategic capabilities eventually are likely to challenge current U.S. dominance in some key areas. The United States should and will

Vietnam's first oil refinery, opened February 2009, will meet one-third of nation's petroleum needs

make investments to improve its own capabilities. China nevertheless will reap some operational advantages from its own investments and develop some ways to limit American ability to apply its military capabilities in a conflict. Continued U.S. dominance in key strategic areas is preferable but may be technologically impossible (due to the offense-dominant nature of some strategic domains) or unaffordable (due to high costs and competing demands).

One potential U.S. response might involve efforts to dissuade China from acquiring advanced military capabilities. Dissuasion was a prominent theme in Bush administration strategic documents such as the 2001 and 2006 Quadrennial Defense Reviews and the 2005 National Defense Strategy. U.S. strategic documents do not single out China as an object of dissuasion, but several academic analysts have examined dissuasion's potential applicability to the China case. Successful dissuasion requires persuading the other state that it will not derive the hoped-for benefits from investments in strategic capabilities or that the direct and indirect costs of pursuing advanced capabilities will outweigh the potential benefits. Three main avenues have been explored in the academic literature: pursuing competitive strategies that invite China to engage in costly arms competitions that it cannot win; raising the political and economic costs of Chinese efforts to develop and deploy advanced strategic capabilities; and linking U.S. economic and strategic cooperation with China to restraint in its strategic development programs.

All three approaches are problematic when applied to China. Although it may be possible to raise the costs of Chinese behavior that violates established international rules and norms, the utility of advanced military technologies means that dissuasion is unlikely to prevent China from developing additional advanced nuclear, space, conventional, and cyber capabilities.

Managing U.S.-China Strategic Competition

An all-out arms race is not inevitable, but the United States will have to think more seriously about how to deal with China if it no longer enjoys unquestioned dominance in key areas. Washington will need to be willing either to accept greater costs and risks in the pursuit of its interests or to scale back its objectives. The U.S. military has operated successfully in high-risk situations in the past, but the expectation that the U.S. military will be dominant and able to carry out major operations with few casualties will need to be revised. Some degree of vulnerability

is inevitable, but the United States should seek to maintain a balance that makes the use of force more costly for China than for the United States and thus maintains some U.S. freedom of action.

Given ongoing military operations and competing demands, many in the nuclear, ballistic missile defense, space, and cyber communities are likely to be frustrated at resource, technology, and policy limitations that restrict the development of advanced U.S. capabilities. These strategic communities will focus intently on Chinese efforts in their areas, and seek to draw leadership attention and resources to their missions. Their Chinese counterparts will do the same. If U.S. efforts do not sustain dominance, some members of these communities are likely to appeal to the broader political system to attract more attention to their concerns. The structure of U.S.-China strategic competition suggests that nuclear, missile defense, space, and cyber issues will be at least irritants—and potentially major destabilizing factors—in bilateral relations for some time to come.

The ultimate effect will depend on whether these strategic issues can be compartmentalized or whether they come to dominate the broader relationship. Those Americans with responsibilities for specific strategic domains are likely to urge that their concerns be linked with wider bilateral issues as a way to increase U.S. leverage. Such a move, however, may undercut broader U.S. efforts to integrate China fully into the international system as a responsible stakeholder. Because different elements of the government have different responsibilities and perspectives, the effort to strike the right balance between cooperation with China and strategic competition in particular domains is likely to be an enduring tension in U.S. China policy.

The Road Ahead

The U.S.-China relationship will remain ambiguous, with substantial areas of cooperation coexisting with strategic tensions and mutual suspicions. The United States and China are not inevitable enemies, but managing the competitive aspects of the relationship will require wise leadership on both sides of the Pacific. Even though the United States is likely to maintain its technological edge, China will develop some advanced strategic capabilities that will allow it to inflict significant damage on U.S. forces in the event of a military conflict. If the countries manage their relations carefully, the negative effects of strategic competition on the broader relationship may remain modest. If strategic conflicts of interest become prominent—most likely over Taiwan—then competition may intensify and poison other aspects of the relationship. Conversely, if the Taiwan issue appears on a path toward peaceful resolution, strategic competition will likely be more muted. In any case, Sino-American strategic competition has begun to move beyond Taiwan to include concerns about respective future military capabilities and relative influence. Even as the two militaries explore potential areas of security cooperation, each appears increasingly concerned about the other.

The United States will need to improve its ability to pursue a multifaceted relationship with China within the context of its overall strategy. This should involve cooperation where American and Chinese interests are compatible, combined with active efforts to engage China to influence how it defines and pursues its interests. Given U.S. security commitments and the importance of U.S. alliances for Asia-Pacific security, the maintenance of robust military capabilities will remain an important part of U.S. strategy. Because of the difficulty of dissuading China from acquiring additional advanced strategic capabilities, the United States must be prepared to compete vigorously with it in important strategic domains while simultaneously seeking to limit the impact of this competition on the broader bilateral relationship.

How can U.S.-China strategic competition be managed effectively? One way is to try to place some limits on any competition that might make both sides worse off. For example, unrestrained nuclear competition or all-out efforts to weaponize space would require huge investments that might ultimately produce no strategic advantages once the other side's response is factored in. Mutual restraint, strategic understandings, and informal limits on the development or deployment of particular capabilities may be valuable to reduce or manage competition. The United States is using its strategic dialogue and military-to-military contacts with China to try to address its strategic concerns and to correct misperceptions about U.S. strategic intentions. Official and unofficial dialogues on nuclear issues and ballistic missile defense over the last decade have played a useful role in making each side aware of the other's concerns and have had modest success in reducing mutual suspicions. These efforts are continuing, and can be enhanced (including a dialogue on space issues), albeit with modest expectations about their ultimate impact.

A second approach is to keep the competitive dimensions of U.S.-China relations within the context of a broader, generally cooperative relationship that is of huge importance to both countries. By placing narrow areas of strategic competition in proper proportion, leaders can make informed decisions about how important these areas are, what investments are appropriate, and what damage to the broader relationship is justified in terms of strategic benefits. Clearly, the specifics of the U.S.-China balance in particular strategic domains would become very important in a military crisis. Both sides should be careful not to let concerns about worst-case scenarios and unlikely contingencies steer the broader relationship. Handled properly, these concerns can remain remote contingencies rather than the primary drivers of policy.

A third way is to recognize that integrating China into the international system as a responsible stakeholder requires showing Beijing a path by which it can pursue its legitimate aspirations through peaceful means. As John Ikenberry has written, the current liberal international order is remarkably flexible and has done a good job so far of accommodating China's rising power. The United States will have to recognize that if China is to make greater contributions to maintaining the international system, it will expect a greater voice within that system. The original formulation of the "responsible stakeholder" concept was silent on the question of which Chinese interests were legitimate and deserving of respect. The United

Kyodo via AP

Chinese President Hu Jintao (left) with Japanese Prime Minister Yasuo Fukuda during Hu's visit to Tokyo, May 2008

States will not be able to ignore this question forever; answering it will likely require some adjustments in both the international system and U.S. foreign policy goals. Just as markets provide ways to reconcile competing economic interests, however, an open international system can provide ways to reconcile competing strategic interests without war.

A final point is that the division of labor implicit in a strategy of engaging and hedging—with the State Department and economic policymakers concentrating on engagement and military policymakers concentrating on the hedge—can potentially result in a lack of focus and increase the difficulty of making appropriate tradeoffs between U.S. economic and security interests. The issues involved are complex, and reasonable people can disagree about the answers. An enduring consensus is likely to be elusive. Strong political leadership and effective use of the National Security Council as a coordination mechanism will be essential to the successful implementation of an effective strategy for dealing with a stronger China.

The U.S.-Japan Alliance: Managing Expectations

In Northeast Asia, Japan is faced with both immediate and long-term security challenges. A nuclear North Korea, armed with ballistic missiles capable of reaching Japan, represents Tokyo's immediate challenge. China represents the long-term strategic challenge. Despite guarded optimism about recent trends in the Japan-China relationship and their accelerating economic engagement, Japan is at the same time cognizant of China's growing military power. Beijing's 20-year run of double-digit increases in defense spending and its lack of transparency are matters for growing concern in Japan. In Southeast Asia, China's diplomatic standing as well as its political and commercial influence are perceived as rising across the region, adding to Japan's strategic uneasiness.

Domestic Situation

The 2008 Economic Survey of Japan by the Organization for Economic Co-operation and Development (OECD) projected the economic expansion that began in 2002 to continue through 2009, with growth rates in the range of 1.5 to 2 percent. By mid-2008, however, rising energy and commodity prices, declining consumer spending, and a fall-off in industrial production and housing construction combined to temper growth forecasts. To revive the economy, the government of Prime Minister Taro Aso proposed a stimulus package of tax cuts and increases in government spending, likely to increase government debt which in 2007 amounted to 180 percent of gross domestic product (GDP). At the same time, a rapidly aging population will increase claims on the government's financial resources for health and social welfare spending.

Building on its historic victory in the 2007 Upper House elections, the opposition Democratic Party of Japan (DPJ) is actively seeking to displace the Liberal Democratic Party (LDP)–New Komeito Party ruling coalition. An intensification of politics, including foreign policy and national security issues, will mark Diet deliberations as each side maneuvers for electoral advantage. This political logjam, coupled with the stultifying internal effects of bureaucratic scandals, has brought policy decisionmaking in Japan to a standstill.

From 2001 to 2006, under successive LDP-Komeito governments headed by Prime Minister Junichiro Koizumi, Japan moved to support Operation *Enduring Freedom* and Operation *Iraqi Freedom* by deploying the Maritime Self-Defense Force (MSDF) to assist refueling operations in the Indian Ocean, the Air Self-Defense Force to Kuwait to provide airlift supply, and the Ground Self-Defense Force to Iraq to assist in postwar reconstruction. Although he deployed the Self-Defense Forces under United Nations (UN) Resolution 1368, Koizumi anchored his decision to authorize the deployments as a function of the U.S.-Japan alliance, in support of Japan's sole alliance partner. In a March 23, 2003, convocation address to the National Defense Academy, Koizumi defined the alliance as "absolutely invaluable" to Japan. The prime minister explained that Japan could not count on U.S. support on North Korea if Japan did not support the United States in Afghanistan and Iraq.

Koizumi's term as prime minister provided unusual political continuity to Japanese policy. His successor, Shinzo Abe, however, failed to last 1 year, resigning after the LDP lost control of the Upper House of the Diet to the DPJ in the July 2007 election. Abe's successor as prime minister, Yasuo Fukuda, who also resigned unexpectedly in September 2008, had to deal with the consequences of the election defeat, an opposition aimed at forcing dissolution of the Diet and a Lower House election, and the resulting legislative and policy gridlock. Fukuda's LDP successor, Taro Aso, faced Diet elections shortly after his own elevation to the LDP leadership position. In the short term, Japan's governments are not likely to experience the continuity of the Koizumi years.

In the present political context, alliance-related issues—such as implementing the Defense Policy Review Initiative (DPRI), relocating the U.S. Marine Corps' Futenma Air Station to northern Okinawa and troop relocation to Guam, and maintaining present levels of host nation support (HNS)—have become matters of active policy and political debate. Should the DPJ form the core of a successor government, the new government will seek adjustments in the HNS budget as well as amendments to the Status of Forces Agreement. Moreover, former DPJ president Ichiro Ozawa has long held that Japan can only deploy the Self-Defense Forces overseas under UN auspices, a position he underscored in his opposition to the 2007 reauthorization of Japan's Anti-Terrorist Special Measures Law, which authorized the MSDF refueling operations in support of Operation *Enduring Freedom*.

Looking Outward

Japan's difficult fiscal environment will continue to affect defense and foreign policy budgets. For political reasons, defense budgets have been maintained at 1 percent of gross national product; the 2008 defense budget, however, lowered spending to 0.89 percent. Fiscal constraints are similarly apparent in Japan's declining Overseas Development Assistance (ODA) budget. For 2007, the Development Assistance Committee of the OECD reported that Japan's ODA disbursements totaled $7.7 billion, a reduction of 30 percent from the previous year. As a result of the 2007 reduction, Japan—formerly the leader in ODA— has dropped from third to fifth place among ODA donors. Concerned with Japan's drop in international standing, the Fukuda government made an effort to increase ODA spending in Africa and Southeast Asia. This effort toward greater diplomatic and ODA activism was driven in part by concerns with China's growing presence and influence in both regions.

At the time of the 1991 Persian Gulf War, Japan's security responsibilities under the U.S.-Japan alliance, in addition to the defense of the home islands, extended 1,000 nautical miles out from Japan for sea lane defense. Despite strong financial and diplomatic backing for the coalition forces, Japan was criticized in the United States for its risk-averse "checkbook diplomacy." Moved in part by such criticism, as well as a growing recognition that Japan should be more actively engaged in efforts to support international stability and security, the Diet in 1993 adopted legislation to allow Japan to participate in UN peacekeeping operations.

Meanwhile, a series of events during the 1990s— the 1993–1994 North Korean nuclear crisis, the 1996 Taiwan Strait crisis, and North Korea's launch of a Taepo Dong missile over Japan in 1998—underscored the tenuous nature of the security environment in which Japan existed. These developments prompted efforts by Tokyo to strengthen its alliance with the United States, culminating in the Tokyo Declaration of April 1996 and Japan's subsequent commitment to provide rear-area support to U.S. forces for contingencies in the areas surrounding Japan.

In the Diet debate over legislation to implement Japan's rear-area support commitment, members tried to get some clarification from the Foreign Ministry concerning the geographic reach of "areas surrounding Japan." The Foreign Ministry, in an effort to maintain flexibility with regard to the applicability of the concept, retreated to diplomatic ambiguity and defined it as functional rather than geographic. Following the attacks on the World Trade Center, the MSDF deployed to the Indian Ocean in support of *Enduring Freedom*.

Reauthorization of the MSDF mission, however, eventually fell victim to politics. Once in control of the Upper House, the DPJ, in a possible preview of its national security policies should it gain control of the government, refused to reauthorize the mission because it lacked a specific UN mandate. In January 2008, Japan passed the New Anti-Terrorism Special Measures Law, which reauthorized the MSDF mission through January 15, 2009. The law was again extended through January 2010. The Iraq Special Measures Law, which authorized the Air Self-Defense Force to transport personnel and goods for the UN and Multinational Force between Kuwait and Iraq, terminated December 12, 2008. Japanese ground and air units were withdrawn shortly thereafter.

Looking back to 1991, the record of the past 17 years points to growing Japanese involvement in support of international stability and security. It is in the national interest of the United States that Japan continues to focus outward.

The Road Ahead

The major challenge facing the new administration is to continue to strengthen the U.S.-Japan alliance and to sustain and encourage Japan's slowly evolving engagement in support of international stability and security.

At the strategic level, there is a firm consensus on the central importance of the U.S.-Japan alliance. There is, however, a gap between strategic consensus and performance on "nuts and bolts" issues. The relocation of the Futenma Air Station and the 8,000 Okinawa-based Marines to Guam are issues the new administration will inherit. Implementation will require careful and continuing attention.

The realignment issues are operational in nature but are strategic in consequence, and will be central to the health of the alliance over the next decade. For the United States, the alliance is the cornerstone of its strategy toward the Asia-Pacific region and a central element of U.S. global strategy.

The new administration has inherited an active program in missile defense cooperation, the enhancement of which—including encouraging the Japanese government to adopt comprehensive legislation to protect classified information—will lead to greater integration of defense capabilities and strengthen Japan's defenses against the ballistic missile threat posed by North Korea. Missile defense cooperation will serve to reassure Japan of Washington's commitment to its security over the next decade and beyond, as would a U.S.-Japan dialogue on extended deterrence, should the nuclear challenge posed by North Korea remain unresolved.

The new administration has an opportunity to put its own historic stamp on the alliance and the U.S.-Japan relationship. The year 2010 will mark the 50th anniversary of the U.S.-Japan Treaty for Mutual Cooperation and Security. A new joint vision statement along the lines of the 1996 Tokyo Declaration, which carried the alliance into the post–Cold War world, and the 2005 Joint Statement of Common Strategic Objectives, which globalized alliance cooperation, could reaffirm mutual commitments to the alliance and shape its direction toward midcentury. Without progress on DPRI implementation, however, a new vision statement would lack a firm operational foundation.

Japan will also host the 2010 meeting of the Asia-Pacific Economic Cooperation (APEC) forum. This will provide another opportunity for the United States and Japan to cooperate to promote the vision of an Asia-Pacific free trade area (FTA). A trans-Pacific FTA comports with historic U.S. interests of being "included" in East Asia.

As for broader cooperation among U.S. allies in Northeast Asia, both Japan and the Republic of Korea have expressed interest in reestablishing trilateral coordination with the United States on issues that go beyond North Korea to shared regional and global concerns. Since the initiation of the Six-Party Talks, thought has been given to seeing the structure evolve into a successor Northeast Asia Peace and Se-

The U.S.-Japan Alliance: Key Documents

A series of documents issued by the U.S.-Japan Security Consultative Committee constitute a framework and work program for the alliance. These include the February 2005 Joint Statement; the October 29, 2005, "Joint Statement on the U.S.-Japan Alliance, Transformation and Realignment for the Future"; the May 1, 2006, joint statement, "United States–Japan Roadmap for Realignment Implementation"; and the May 1, 2007, statement on "Alliance Transformation: Advancing United States–Japan Security and Defense Cooperation."

The February 2005 Joint Statement marked the convergence of a common strategic vision and a shared understanding that the alliance enhances the security of the two partners, the Asia-Pacific region, and the cause of "global peace and stability." The document set out a number of common strategic objectives toward the region and beyond and judged the consolidation of the U.S.-Japan partnership to be in the interest of "peace, stability, prosperity worldwide."

The October 2005 Joint Statement identified specific areas for improved security and defense cooperation, and provided for a realignment of the U.S. force posture in Japan as well as a joint study on roles, missions, and capabilities. Realignment centered on the relocation of U.S. Marine forces from Okinawa to Guam and the return of the Marine Corps Air Station at Futenma to the Okinawa prefectural government.

Subsequent joint statements reaffirmed the common strategic objectives, provided a detailed roadmap for realignment, and strengthened missile defense and operational cooperation.

Japanese and U.S. lawmakers hold first meeting under newly created official Japan-U.S. parliamentarian exchange organization, Washington, DC, June 2008

curity Mechanism. Absent the complete denuclear-ization of North Korea, however, such a mechanism remains a distant possibility.

Nevertheless, the new administration will find that multilateral cooperation has built outward from our alliance-rooted strength in the region. The concept has not been exclusionary, but one that stems from our shared values and complementary interests, and allows the alliance partners collectively to engage others with greater confidence.

The U.S.–ROK Alliance: Building a Mature Partnership

The Republic of Korea confronts a complex strategic environment. To its north, across the Demilitarized Zone (DMZ), the Democratic People's Republic of Korea (DPRK) remains a closed, unpredictable society. The DPRK's conventional military, although degraded, remains formidable in terms of numbers, but it is North Korea's attempted development of nuclear weapons and ballistic missile delivery systems that defines the major security challenge. At the same time, North Korea's totalitarian political system, its aging and ill political leadership, and its fragile and failing economy combine to raise the specter of unrest, instability, and regime collapse. Well aware that the financial cost of reunification to the government of South Korea is generally expected

to dwarf the sum involved in German unification at the end of the Cold War, ROK governments have cautiously addressed the issue.

Beyond the peninsula, South Korea's booming economic relations with its immediate neighbors, China and Japan, are balanced by longstanding territorial disputes, intense political nationalism, and the unhappy legacy of conflict and colonialism.

China is South Korea's top trading partner, with two-way trade amounting to $145 billion in 2007, nearly one-quarter of the ROK's total trade. This gives Beijing considerable leverage in Seoul. China's diplomatic leadership in the Six-Party Talks, aimed at resolving North Korea's nuclear challenge, also is well appreciated in Seoul. Yet China's growing economic influence in North Korea and its claim to the ancient territory of Koguryo, which includes large areas of ancient Korean kingdoms, have raised concerns that China's long-term interests and objectives toward the peninsula may not correspond to those of South Korea. Keeping the past alive, South Korea's history textbooks record China's numerous military advances into the peninsula and the subservience of Korea's tributary status.

Japan is South Korea's third leading trading partner, with two-way trade in 2007 totaling $63.6 billion. Yet memories of the Japanese empire's annexation and harsh occupation of Korea from 1905

Imaginechina via AP Images (Feng lei sd)

Chinese bank clerk counts foreign exchange banknotes at branch of Agricultural Bank of China, Liaocheng

to 1945 remain intense and volatile in South Korea's body politic, and complicate management of the bilateral relationship between Seoul and Tokyo. Visits to the controversial Yasukuni Shrine by Japan's political leaders to honor their country's war dead, which include 14 Japanese Class A war criminals, and the sovereignty dispute over the Liancourt Rocks have the potential to reignite still-smoldering resentments.

The Advent of the Lee Administration

On December 19, 2007, Lee Myung-bak of the right-center Grand National Party (GNP) was elected president of the Republic of Korea. Lee's victory marked the end of a decade of left-center governments under Presidents Kim Dae Jung and Roh Moo-hyun. Lee, a former president of Hyundai Construction Company and mayor of Seoul, campaigned on a platform of economic revitalization, a policy toward North Korea that demands reciprocity, and a commitment to strengthen the ROK–U.S. alliance.

In contrast to the income redistribution policies of the previous government, Lee's economic policies highlight deregulation, investment incentives, tax cuts, and pro-growth and *chaebol*-friendly initiatives (*chaebol* are large family-controlled firms with strong government ties), all aimed at making South Korea the world's seventh largest economy, raising per capita GDP to $40,000 and achieving a 7 percent economic growth rate. Early in 2008, however, in light of rising oil prices and a slowdown in the U.S. economy, Lee's economic team lowered projected growth figures to 6 percent, while the Bank of Korea forecast a 4.7 percent growth rate. Both the Samsung Economic Research Institute and the state-run Korea Development Institute estimated growth at 5 percent for 2008 despite unfavorable external economic conditions. By mid-year, slowing growth, combined with the rising prices of oil and agricultural commodities, combined to raise concerns of stagflation.

With regard to North Korea, the Lee government announced plans to assist the DPRK's economic development, proposing to raise per capita income to $3,000 over 10 years, helping to create over 100 export companies, and creating over 300,000 industrial jobs—conditioned on North Korea's cooperation in denuclearization. The new government also made clear that it would review the large-scale economic infrastructure projects announced at the October 4, 2007, South-North Summit between former President Roh and North Korea's Kim Jong Il to ensure that the projects served the economic interests of South Korea. The Lee government also announced that it would not refrain from criticizing North Korea's human rights violations. Seoul's new willingness to criticize North Korea and its emphasis on reciprocity in its dealing with Pyongyang marked a departure from the policies of leftist governments since the June 2000 summit in Pyongyang.

U.S.–ROK Alliance Relations

Improving relations with the United States is at the center of Lee's foreign policy. As a presidential candidate, Lee made clear his intent to strengthen the ROK–U.S. alliance; as president, he proposed the development of a "Strategic Alliance for the 21st Century" that would expand alliance cooperation from the peninsula to East Asia and beyond. Lee also stressed the importance of the U.S. ratification of the Korea–United States (KORUS) Free Trade Agreement signed by his predecessor in 2007. Legislation to implement the FTA is pending in the U.S. Congress and the ROK national assembly.

For over 50 years, South Korea has been allied with the United States. Since its inception, the alliance has served to deter the outbreak of a second Korean War, while allowing South Korea to devote its resources to the development of a world-class economy and a vibrant democracy. Over the years, however, South Korea's prosperity, growing national confidence, and emergence as a stable democracy have combined to build political pressures to restructure and transform the alliance.

Officials of the Lee government characterize alliance management under Presidents Kim and Roh as "ten lost years." While it is true that ROK–U.S. relations experienced political turbulence in South Korea from 2000 to 2008, it is also true that significant steps were taken to transform the alliance into a more equal military and political structure.

Strategic dissonance in policies toward North Korea marked relations between Seoul and Washington in the years following the June 2000 South-North Summit, which served to foster more benign views of North Korea in the ROK. Subsequently, large numbers of South Korean citizens came to see North Korea as a poor, weak, and highly insecure neighbor, whose intractable, belligerent behavior was often attributed to U.S. policies, which were perceived as isolating or pressuring the regime in Pyongyang. Indicative of this trend, the ROK's Ministry of Defense 2005 White Paper ceased to identify North Korea as an enemy, and, in a 2004 South Korean public opinion poll, the United States was viewed as a greater threat to peace than was North Korea.

Roh came into office in 2003 with a highly nation-alistic agenda, determined to redress long-perceived inequities in the ROK–U.S. relationship. With regard to the alliance, Roh made the transfer of wartime operational control of ROK forces back to South Korean command the touchstone of his efforts to transform the alliance into a more equal structure.

At the same time, the Bush administration, in re-sponse to the 9/11 terrorist attacks, initiated a global transformation of U.S. forces aimed at making them lighter and more readily deployable. On the Korean Peninsula, this imposed a new security requirement on U.S. forces—in addition to being prepared to defend South Korea, they were also to be prepared to deploy off the peninsula to deal with the threat posed by international terrorism.

This combination of U.S. and ROK imperatives to meet the security challenges of the post-9/11 world and the demands for greater equality within the al-liance resulted in consecutive bilateral negotiations: the Future of the Alliance Talks (FOTA) and the Strategic Policy Initiative (SPI). The talks resulted in the redeployment of U.S. forces from bases at the DMZ to the Osan-Pyongtaek area and the Taegu-Pusan area; the return of approximately 60 camps and installations to the ROK; the relocation of the Yongsan Garrison in downtown Seoul to Pyongtaek; and the transfer of wartime operational control to the ROK by April 17, 2012. South Korea's "Defense Reform 2020" provides for the acquisition of es-sential upgrades in command and control, commu-nications, computers, and intelligence capabilities to support transfer of operational control. At the same time, the United States agreed to provide necessary bridging capabilities through 2020. While some in South Korea continue to express uneasiness with the readiness of the ROK military to assume wartime op-erational control, the initiative continues on track.

The Road Ahead

The ability of the United States and the Republic of Korea to advance their bilateral relationship and strengthen the alliance will depend on the interplay of a number of factors: the capacity of the Lee gov-ernment to overcome its initial stumbles and govern effectively in the face of vocal and determined oppo-sition; the implementation of FOTA and SPI agree-ments; the success of the ROK's Defense Reform 2020; the maintenance of coordination on policies toward North Korea; and the fate of KORUS.

Less than 2 months after its inauguration, the Lee administration met with an unexpected reversal when his Grand National Party escaped with a narrow ma-jority victory in the National Assembly elections. The narrowness of the victory, 153 out of 299 seats, was in part due to the defection of 26 GNP members to an alliance led by Park Geun-Hye, Lee's unsuccessful rival for the GNP presidential nomination.

In advance of his summit visit to Washington, Lee announced his decision to implement the commit-ment, made by the Roh government, to re-open the Korean market for U.S. beef (U.S. beef imports had been banned since 2003, following the outbreak of mad cow disease in the United States). Many South Koreans saw the announcement as an arbitrary exercise of power, one that put Lee's relationship with Washington ahead of the health of the Korean people. Massive demonstrations, first by students and civil society organizations, later supported by opposi-tion parties, resulted in plummeting public approval ratings for the president, the reorganization of the president's staff, strikes by the Korean Confederation of Trade Unions, opposition parties' refusal to allow the opening of the National Assembly, and finally, a presidential apology.

Lee's emphasis on reciprocity in South-North relations—demanding denuclearization as a condi-tion for economic assistance—meant that for many months in 2008 South Korea had refused to send food and fertilizer to North Korea. With public pressures building for a response to reports of an intensifying famine in North Korea, however, Lee reversed his position. In his address to the open-ing of the National Assembly, he called for renewed dialogue with North Korea "to alleviate the pain of the North Korean people." In reply, an editorial in North Korea's *Rodong Sinmun* newspaper blasted the president for his responsibility for the aggravated state of North-South relations.

Challenges and Opportunities

In the midst of transforming the bilateral U.S.–ROK alliance, President Lee is facing determined opposition on defense budget issues, including appropriations for Defense Reform 2020, for the Special Measures Agreement (Host Nation Support), and for implementation of the FOTA and SPI agree-ments on the redeployment of U.S. forces on the peninsula. Also, the opposition is determined to raise issues related to the environmental cleanup of U.S. bases returned to the ROK.

The Lee government has repeatedly emphasized the strategic importance of the alliance with the United States, and Lee has made clear his interest in turning the Cold War–origin alliance into a "Strategic Alliance for the 21st Century," expanding its scope from the peninsula to East Asia and beyond. Korean officials frequently point to the Tokyo Declaration of April 1996, which defined a post–Cold War role for the U.S.-Japan alliance, as a model. Cooperating with the ROK in defining such an alliance would allow the administration the opportunity to put its mark on a new initiative in Asian security.

Efforts to develop a new vision of the alliance, however, have diverted attention from implementation of the FOTA/SPI agreements. Despite a shared understanding on the importance of the alliance, a gap exists between strategic consensus and actual performance on nuts-and-bolts issues. Funding and implementation of FOTA/SPI—operational issues with strategic consequences—will require the careful and continuing attention of the new administration in Washington.

The Obama administration has inherited the KORUS Free Trade Agreement. Senior ROK officials have privately communicated that a U.S. failure to ratify the agreement would be "a major blow" to the Lee government. Furthermore, such an outcome would negatively affect the U.S.–ROK relationship and mark a significant retreat from the commitment of past administrations, Democratic and Republican alike, to free trade.

North Korea: Choices for the New Administration

The challenge of halting North Korea's pursuit of a nuclear weapons program has now bedeviled American Presidents for over two decades. The George H.W. Bush administration attempted to bring North Korea under International Atomic Energy Agency (IAEA) inspections after becoming concerned about North Korea's Yongbyon gas-graphite power reactor in the late 1980s. When discrepancies arose between North Korea's declaration and evidence gathered by IAEA inspectors during 1992, the ensuing dispute sparked the first North Korean nuclear crisis and led to bilateral negotiations under the Clinton administration that resulted in the Geneva Agreed Framework. By the terms of this deal, North Korea froze construction and promised to eventually dismantle its plutonium-based nuclear program upon delivery of two light-water reactors for electricity production by a U.S.-led multinational consortium.

Lack of political will among the parties to the agreement, the withholding of funding by the newly elected U.S. Republican Congress, and delays in the timetable for provision of the two light-water reactors as promised in the Agreed Framework caused relations between North Korea and the United States to deteriorate over the next several years, and sowed the seeds for the next North Korean nuclear crisis.

Background

In 2002, the U.S. Intelligence Community concluded that the DPRK had pursued a covert uranium enrichment path to achieving nuclear weapons capability in contravention of the Clinton-era agreement, spawning a second crisis over North Korea's nuclear ambitions. U.S. allegations to this effect during an October 2002 visit to Pyongyang by President Bush's special envoy, Assistant Secretary James Kelly, sparked an angry response from the North Koreans and the unraveling of the Agreed Framework. In retaliation for a U.S. decision to halt deliveries of heavy fuel oil that had been promised under the framework agreement, North Korea expelled IAEA nuclear inspectors and reinstalled fuel rods that had been put in storage near Yongbyon since the mid-1990s. Following on-again, off-again six-party negotiations established in 2003 that included China, Russia, Japan, South Korea, North Korea, and the United States, North Korea's apparent October 2006 test of a nuclear device dramatically illustrated the policy failures of successive administrations. The test catalyzed a uniformly negative international response, including rapid passage of UN Security Council Resolution 1718, which placed severe economic sanctions on the DPRK. The implementation of those sanctions was suspended, however, when the Bush administration pursued bilateral U.S.–DPRK negotiations in the context of the six-party negotiations.

The outcome of those negotiations was a February 13, 2007, implementing agreement and a more specific October 3 agreement in which the DPRK was to shut down, disable, and dismantle its Yongbyon nuclear facilities. These agreements would allow IAEA monitors to return to the complex, and offer a "complete and correct declaration" of its nuclear facilities, programs, and materials. In return, the United States would remove North Korea from the list of state sponsors of terrorism from the Trading with the Enemy Act; Japan-DPRK relations would improve; and North Korea would receive one million tons of heavy fuel oil or its equivalent from the other parties (with the exception of Japan). The agreement was built on a Six-Party Joint Statement of Principles for addressing the North Korean nuclear issue that had been completed on September 19, 2005, a year prior to North Korea's nuclear test. The "grand bargain" that had been envisaged in the joint statement traded North Korea's denuclearization for multilateral economic support and the political benefits of diplomatic normalization with the United States, under agreed-upon principles of "action for action."

The February 13, 2007, agreement covered only the first steps that would have to be taken toward North Korea's full denuclearization. They were to be completed within 90 days, but it took until summer to complete only the first phase of the agreement. North Korea also missed a December 31, 2007, deadline for submitting a "complete and correct" declaration of its nuclear program, materials, and facilities; it was finally submitted in June 2008. With this, President Bush notified Congress that he would remove North Korea from the list of state sponsors of terrorism within 45 days. However, North Korea refused to agree to the verification measures requested by the United States, ROK, and Japan, and took initial steps to refurbish nuclear facilities at Yongbyon. Following what is believed to be a verification protocol, the Bush administration announced that it had delisted North Korea on October 10, 2008.

On April 5, 2009, North Korea, in the face of international opposition, conducted a missile test over

Japan into the Pacific Ocean. On May 25, Pyongyang tested its second nuclear device. In response the United Nations Security Council, on June 13, adopted UNSC 1874, sanctioning North Korea for its action.

The Obama administration faces multiple challenges with respect to North Korea: reinitiating nuclear talks, verifying any accords, and managing a possible regime transition. This task may have been made more difficult by the fact that there remain ambiguities in the agreement regarding some components of the verification regime. These issues are complicated by the fact that Kim Jong Il experienced a "medical event"—a possible stroke—that may have temporarily incapacitated him in mid-August 2008. Although the continuity of his leadership within North Korea apparently has not been challenged, this event has highlighted the possibility of internal political instability in the North, with uncertain implications for both regional stability and nonproliferation.

The first issue is Kim Jong Il's health. Although reported to have recovered from the August 2008 medical event, the uncertainty regarding his physical condition appears to have accelerated the process of structuring a succession. Judging from recent pronouncements from Pyongyang, Kim appears to have settled on his youngest son, Kim Jong Un, as his successor. The medical event and Kim Jong Il's subsequent recovery also may constitute a de facto test of loyalty among those closest to him. How North Korean powerholders have responded to Kim's ill health could affect their subsequent standing in North Korea's leadership hierarchy. Kim's vulnerability also may influence North Korean bureaucratic organs in their willingness to carry out orders. A top priority for the United States is to assess the impact of the political situation inside North Korea for Pyongyang's external priorities, especially as they relate to the task of denuclearization.

Kim Jong Il's health situation also has exposed the need for greater coordination and more active sharing of contingency plans among the United States and North Korea's neighbors. Once such planning has occurred in the context of the U.S.–South Korea and U.S.-Japan alliances, there might be an opportunity to initiate a deeper discussion of such issues with China, especially as it relates to coordination of humanitarian assistance to North Korea and best practices for responding to refugees in the event of a political vacuum inside North Korea.

Uncertainty regarding the future direction of North Korea's political leadership may also influence

North Korean leader Kim Jong Il (second from right) talks with Wang Jiarui (left), head of Chinese Communist Party's International Department, Pyongyang, February 2009

North Korea's tactical and strategic approaches to the Six-Party Talks. In response to the international outcry that followed the April 5 missile test and the May 25 nuclear test, Pyongyang announced that it would no longer participate in the Six-Party Talks, restart the Yongbyon reactor, and pursue a uranium enrichment program. While the United States, China, Japan, the ROK, and Russia have called on Pyongyang to return to the Six-Party Talks, it is not likely that the talks will resume in the near future. North Korea's actions may suggest that Pyongyang is attempting to maximize leverage in dealing directly with the United States on a bilateral basis or, conversely, that it has no intention of surrendering its nuclear ambitions.

A major challenge that has beset past administrations when they tried to determine an effective policy strategy toward North Korea has been the need to reconcile the constraints imposed by America's regional policy objectives with the parameters of America's global nonproliferation objectives. A successful approach has not yet been forged that can meld the objectives of nonproliferation while also strengthening America's regional role and credibility. The Bush administration sought to manage this dilemma by increasing both the stakes and the level of responsibility felt by North Korea's neighbors through the six-party negotiations process. But in the course of pursuing such a policy, differences have persisted between those who believe that U.S. objectives are best served by preventing North Korea from engaging in proliferation of nuclear technologies or weapons to other countries, and those who believe that it is necessary to roll back North Korea's program as a means of supporting nonproliferation as an enforceable norm. This debate is likely to continue in the new administration.

North Korea's immediate neighbors should be most concerned about a nuclear North Korea. The six-party process brought together those neighbors as the main actors, but has been relatively ineffectual in achieving concrete results. The priorities of regional powers such as China (and even South Korea) place stability above North Korea's denuclearization, despite a rhetorical consensus in favor of a nuclear-free Korean Peninsula. As a result, there are limits both to regional support for U.S.-led coercive approaches and to the degree of pressure that North Korea's neighbors are willing to apply even in the context of support for diplomacy. In fact, China and South Korea have been more interested in pressing the United States to avoid coercive options than in pressuring North Korea to give up all components

of its nuclear program. This approach has enabled the North Koreans to engage in careful tactics that permit them to retain ambiguity about their overall nuclear status while reaping maximum rewards for limited cooperation.

The Road Ahead

As the Obama administration determines the priority of issues and the means by which it pursues North Korea's full denuclearization, it will be important not to imply in word or deed that a new status quo that includes a North Korea with a limited nuclear arsenal would be acceptable. The administration also will have to weigh various coercive options against continued negotiations in some bilateral or multilateral form as alternatives to achieve North Korea's denuclearization. The depth of this ongoing policy dilemma over North Korea's program is compounded by the contradiction between the widespread perception that North Korea's denuclearization may be impossible without regime change, and the priority that North Korea's immediate neighbors place on maintaining regional stability. This underscores the need for more active pursuit of coordinated contingency planning to deal with the effects of political instability in North Korea.

The Bush administration's approach to negotiations fell short of achieving North Korean denuclearization. The new U.S. administration may be in a stronger position to negotiate effectively with North Korea. Possible policy approaches include continuing six-party negotiations by offering North Korea a last chance to pursue political normalization in exchange for North Korea's denuclearization, while promoting more active compellance efforts among other participants in the Six-Party Talks; setting aside the six-party process and bolstering a common resolve among the other parties, thereby convincing regional partners to push North Korea toward denuclearization; pursuing a bilateral "dealmaking" approach in which the United States quietly offers concrete economic and political incentives in return for the removal of North Korea's plutonium from the country (along the lines of the "preventive defense" efforts led by Defense Secretary William Perry in the mid-1990s); and quietly beginning a policy dialogue with South Korea, and subsequently with China, on how various parties might respond to contingencies should North Korea face future political instability. As a practical matter, any solution to the North Korean nuclear crisis will require regional acquiescence and support if it is to be effective. But the top priority of China and South Korea has been to prioritize regional stability over destabilizing regime change or nonproliferation. For this reason, the first step for the Obama administration is likely to be negotiations, preferably by affirming the U.S. commitment to the principles enshrined in the 2005 joint statement and requiring North Korea to do the same. At the same time, there is much more that the other participants in the Six-Party Talks can and should do to encourage North Korea that it is essential to regional stability to fully implement the joint statement. If negotiations fail, there will be expectations in the United States that the other five parties will take concrete actions to address the North Korean threat, but it is still not clear at this stage that the other parties will perform according to U.S. expectations. The United States will have to devise a strategy that strengthens political will in Northeast Asia in support of a denuclearized Korean Peninsula.

The new U.S. administration should reaffirm commitments to nonproliferation by reenergizing strategic nuclear arms reduction negotiations and providing continued leadership to address the difficult cases of North Korea and Iran. But such statements will be taken seriously only if the United States also implements a policy that continues to insist that a nuclear North Korea will not be accepted as part of a new status quo on the peninsula and in the region. Effective U.S. leadership in managing the North Korean nuclear issue can demonstrate that the United States remains an essential actor in dealing with pressing regional security issues, in ways that no other single party is able to do. Strengthened cooperation with other parties in the six-party process will limit North Korea's scope to play off of the respective strategic dilemmas of the other parties and will foreclose North Korean alternatives to cooperation.

A prerequisite for strengthening cooperation among the other five parties is more effective coordination with allies in South Korea and Japan. An approach that begins with allies and builds out to other parties would ensure that multilateral coordination within the Six-Party Talks does not contradict American alliances, and emphasize that U.S.-led diplomacy can make important contributions to stability as a supplement to U.S. military alliance commitments in the region.

President Obama has inherited the task of achieving North Korea's denuclearization, following two decades of repeated failures. His administration is in a better position than any of its predecessors to join hands in promoting the kind of regional solidarity necessary for a breakthrough with North Korea. Nevertheless, the perils are great. The administration could also stumble if it fails to align nonproliferation and regional security.

Reengaging with Southeast Asia and ASEAN

The Obama administration likely will be responding to criticism by U.S. allies and friends in Southeast Asia[1] that Washington has not been sufficiently engaged in Asia-Pacific regional affairs in recent years. This perceived neglect has been attributed in part to the Bush administration's preoccupation with other issues around the globe (Iraq, Afghanistan, terrorism, North Korea, and Iran). The fact is that when the United States does reengage more fully in Southeast Asia, it will find that China's resurgence has transformed the region.

Challenges Confronting ASEAN States

From its initial boom in the 1960s, Southeast Asia has been an extraordinarily dynamic region driven by high rates of economic growth and modernization. In little more than a generation, real per capita incomes in Thailand, Malaysia, Singapore, and Brunei—and in many urban areas elsewhere—have quintupled. The sea lanes that traverse the Malacca Straits and the South China Sea have become the world's busiest, in terms of both volume and value. Most societies of the region have changed almost beyond recognition. Never in history had so many people had their lives transformed for the better—that is, until China launched on the same trajectory about 15 years later. Economic development has been accompanied by less dramatic, but nevertheless substantial, political development.

Change of this speed and scope creates inevitable strains and tensions throughout most of ASEAN. Economic growth in the region is uneven, both within countries and particularly among them. In the same archipelago with Singapore, which has living standards higher than Great Britain, for example, lies East Timor, one of the poorest and least developed countries on the planet. Sharing a border with booming Thailand is remote, isolated, dependent Laos, where modernization remains an idea, not a fact. Economic change often produces political fragility, as existing institutions and authorities are challenged by newly empowered, or aggrieved, groups. Southeast Asia has more than its share of still-developing democracies. A country as sophisticated and modernized as Thailand has been unable to break the cycle of recurrent military coups. The Philippines seems locked in a perpetual state of political incapacity, aggravated by frail leadership, endemic corruption, and weak government institutions. Indonesia, by contrast, has effected a democratic transition that has amazed even the most knowledgeable (and sympathetic) observers. Meanwhile, Vietnam, not unlike China, maneuvers uncertainly between a Marxist authoritarian order and a free-enterprise, open society.

The most graphic evidence of systemic political weakness in ASEAN is the persistence of secessionist movements that challenge the legitimacy of the state itself in Thailand, the Philippines, Burma, and, to a lesser degree, Indonesia. Many of these are the legacy of past empires (European and indigenous) that left significant groups disenfranchised, isolated, and disaffected.

The emergence of Islamist terrorist networks has been one manifestation of societal change and stress. When young Southeast Asian militants returned home from fighting in Afghanistan in the 1980s, they found societies vulnerable to their newly absorbed, violent dreams of an Islamic renaissance. Ethnic divisions, particularly between the Chinese urban minorities that are ubiquitous throughout the region and the majority indigenous non-Chinese, can also reflect the strains of modernization as one group (usually the Chinese) fares better economically than the others. Even the piracy that bedevils regional sea lanes (the crowded Malacca Straits has the highest rate of piracy in the world) reflects economic disparities: it is no surprise when some boatmen from poor seafaring villages on the east coast of Sumatra, watching great wealth pass by in the Malacca Straits with no hope of benefit, try to seize what they can. Inevitably, breakneck economic growth has also produced widespread environmental despoliation—for which nature exacts a price. Recurrent floods in the Philippines, massive uncontrolled fires in Indonesia, and the virtual disappearance of traditional fishing grounds are all of a piece.

Significant interstate tensions exist as well. Unresolved territorial disputes complicate relations between Vietnam and China and among multiple claimants to the Spratly Archipelago and the South China Sea itself. Lesser maritime disputes have impaired relations among Singapore, Malaysia, and Indonesia. Very recently, an old boundary dispute between Cambodia and Thailand has rekindled, with troop movements and bellicose statements by national leaders. Burma represents a special, difficult case: not only is it geographically part of the region and a member of ASEAN, but it is also a political pariah and economic recluse that remains unintegrated into regional institutions, spurns widely held political and economic values, and resists efforts to foster greater regional cohesion. The Thai-Burma border remains perpetually neuralgic. Vietnam's relationship with China is a complex amalgam of communist fraternity and geopolitical rivalry. For Vietnam's military and security officials, the great strategic challenge is to carve out greater freedom of action under the suspicious gaze of the increasingly powerful and ambitious behemoth to the north. Meanwhile, as these various forces work with and against one another, growing economies have permitted growing support for military budgets in much of the region.

Collective Efforts of ASEAN Members

Despite these challenges, the efforts of ASEAN states to work collectively have translated into a number of economic cooperation and integration initiatives, which include China's positive engagement in the region and the spurring of regional security dialogues. ASEAN has attracted attention and partnerships both inside and outside the region. Its external relationships today are based on its 1997 strategic paper, ASEAN Vision 2020. They range from extended relationships with China, Japan, and the ROK in a forum called ASEAN Plus Three, to bilateral trading arrangements between its member countries and China, Japan, and the ROK, to cooperative relations with Dialogue Partners (Australia, Canada, China, the European Union, India, Japan, the ROK, New Zealand, the Russian Federation, and the United States) and the United Nations Development Program. ASEAN also maintains relations with a number of intergovernmental organizations and actively participates in the APEC forum, the Asia-Europe Meeting, and the East Asia–Latin America Forum.

The ASEAN Plus Three relationship is an outgrowth of the Asian financial crisis of 1997. China, Japan, and South Korea, together with ASEAN, initially sought a mechanism that would support regional efforts to prevent, or at least mitigate, the effects of such a crisis in the future. This relationship has since expanded beyond finance and economics. During the 2002–2003 Severe Acute Respiratory Syndrome crisis, and in the midst of severe avian influenza outbreaks, for instance, ASEAN Plus Three engaged ministers of health and other senior officials in multiple levels of dialogue to explore prevention and mitigation strategies. Since then, other nontraditional security challenges have found their way into the ASEAN Plus Three agenda, as well as throughout other broader ASEAN venues.

Southeast Asian views of China have changed dramatically since the mid-1990s. China's embrace of multilateral diplomacy, its efforts to reassure Southeast Asian countries of its benign intentions, and its booming economy have led countries in the region to see China more as an economic opportunity than as a strategic threat. This view stems in part from the reality that China is a neighbor and its economic, political, and military resurgence will have an impact on the region. China's growing influence is especially evident in poorer countries such as Burma, Laos, and Cambodia. Others in the region have endeavored, bilaterally and through ASEAN, to benefit from the opportunities afforded by China's boom, while at the same time seeking to create an environment conducive to China's peaceful integration in regional and global affairs. ASEAN nevertheless remains wary of China's overtures and has sought to use the United States as a balancing force within the region. In particular, ASEAN has rejected Chinese attempts to propose greater cooperation on "hard" security matters in favor of "soft" or non-traditional security matters such as terrorism and human and drug trafficking.

The explosion of opportunities for closer engagement in the region, however, also has given rise to questions concerning relations between ASEAN and other countries and the sustainability of regional architectures. Questions about regional architectures remain a complex issue. ASEAN does not appear wedded to a single organizational architecture; instead, it tends to see value in overlapping circles of cooperation. The East Asian Summit brought in India, New Zealand, and Australia; APEC involved the United States and some Latin American countries. In principle, ASEAN appears content to work within its own and other existing regional mechanisms (including APEC, the ASEAN Regional Forum, ASEAN Plus Three, and the East Asian Summit) in the belief that a community must be based on a sense of common destiny and the ability to cooperate in the pursuit of common interests, and that the goals and principles of a Southeast Asian community will eventually emerge as a natural evolution of interaction and consensus-building in the region.

Prospects for ASEAN Cooperation

Any political portrayal of Southeast Asia must acknowledge the remarkable effort over four decades to build institutions that seek to integrate the region

economically, politically, and psychologically. ASEAN is the centerpiece of this effort. Although it is easy to disparage the organization as being far more talk than action, ASEAN nevertheless has succeeded in its core purpose, which is to create processes and a mindset that can prevent the myriad strains within the region from becoming flashpoints for military conflict. Moreover, ASEAN has, to a remarkable degree, given Southeast Asia a central role in much of the multilateral diplomacy of Asia. Whether this achievement can be sustained into the future as larger players become more active on the Southeast Asian stage is an open question.

The diversity of the region and its geography, containing both maritime and continental states, creates economic competition and differences of interests among the member states. Domestic concerns— economic growth, political and regime stability— are often key drivers. Obstacles to collective action come to the surface in disputes over intra-ASEAN sovereignty, the intransigence of the Burma problem, and China's ability to win over weaker ASEAN states through economic influence. While sovereignty and the principle of noninterference provide a common face to ASEAN identity (often referred to as the "ASEAN way"), internal political development and economics dictate national interest for these countries, often producing obstacles to intra-ASEAN cooperation.

The ASEAN leadership has recognized that the changing geopolitical landscape (and the rise of China and India in particular) means ASEAN cannot be complacent about its success. ASEAN concerns were reinforced by a McKinsey competitiveness study, which warned that the association may be in danger of losing its competitiveness and had only a few years to respond or be marginalized.[2] ASEAN commissioned the Eminent Persons Group to provide practical recommendations on the organization's future direction and the development of an ASEAN Charter (which was signed on November 20, 2007). ASEAN sees two broad challenges for its organization: first, shaping community-building efforts among its members and second, maintaining ASEAN's centrality as it deals with its dialogue partners. In connection with this second challenge, ASEAN leaders express concern about the telling relative absence of the United States in Southeast Asia.

The inability of ASEAN states to work collectively is clearly reflected in its institutional weakness. ASEAN's response to the humanitarian crisis in Burma that resulted from Cyclone Nargis in May 2008

The World's Assembly Line

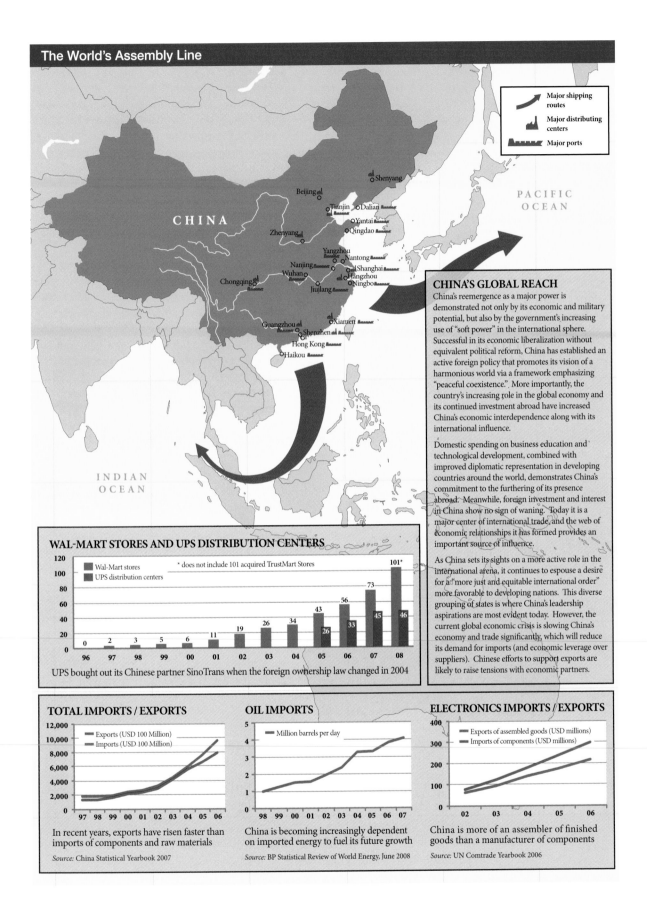

Legend:
- Major shipping routes
- Major distributing centers
- Major ports

CHINA

PACIFIC OCEAN

INDIAN OCEAN

Cities labeled: Shenyang, Beijing, Tianjin, Dalian, Yantai, Qingdao, Zhenyang, Yangzhou, Nantong, Nanjing, Shanghai, Wuhan, Hangzhou, Chongqing, Ningbo, Jiujiang, Guangzhou, Xiamen, Shenzhen, Hong Kong, Haikou

CHINA'S GLOBAL REACH

China's reemergence as a major power is demonstrated not only by its economic and military potential, but also by the government's increasing use of "soft power" in the international sphere. Successful in its economic liberalization without equivalent political reform, China has established an active foreign policy that promotes its vision of a harmonious world via a framework emphasizing "peaceful coexistence." More importantly, the country's increasing role in the global economy and its continued investment abroad have increased China's economic interdependence along with its international influence.

Domestic spending on business education and technological development, combined with improved diplomatic representation in developing countries around the world, demonstrates China's commitment to the furthering of its presence abroad. Meanwhile, foreign investment and interest in China show no sign of waning. Today it is a major center of international trade, and the web of economic relationships it has formed provides an important source of influence.

As China sets its sights on a more active role in the international arena, it continues to espouse a desire for a "more just and equitable international order" more favorable to developing nations. This diverse grouping of states is where China's leadership aspirations are most evident today. However, the current global economic crisis is slowing China's economy and trade significantly, which will reduce its demand for imports (and economic leverage over suppliers). Chinese efforts to support exports are likely to raise tensions with economic partners.

WAL-MART STORES AND UPS DISTRIBUTION CENTERS

Legend:
- Wal-Mart stores
- UPS distribution centers

* does not include 101 acquired TrustMart Stores

Year	Wal-Mart stores	UPS distribution centers
96	0	
97	2	
98	3	
99	5	
00	6	
01	11	
02	19	
03	26	
04	34	
05	43	26
06	56	33
07	73	45
08	101*	46

UPS bought out its Chinese partner SinoTrans when the foreign ownership law changed in 2004

TOTAL IMPORTS / EXPORTS

Legend:
- Exports (USD 100 Million)
- Imports (USD 100 Million)

(Chart y-axis: 0 to 12,000; x-axis years: 97 98 99 00 01 02 03 04 05 06)

In recent years, exports have risen faster than imports of components and raw materials

Source: China Statistical Yearbook 2007

OIL IMPORTS

Legend:
- Million barrels per day

(Chart y-axis: 0 to 5; x-axis years: 98 99 00 01 02 03 04 05 06 07)

China is becoming increasingly dependent on imported energy to fuel its future growth

Source: BP Statistical Review of World Energy, June 2008

ELECTRONICS IMPORTS / EXPORTS

Legend:
- Exports of assembled goods (USD millions)
- Imports of components (USD millions)

(Chart y-axis: 0 to 400; x-axis years: 02 03 04 05 06)

China is more of an assembler of finished goods than a manufacturer of components

Source: UN Comtrade Yearbook 2006

demonstrated its potential to act as a mechanism for regional cooperation. Yet such optimism concerning ASEAN's effectiveness rapidly evaporated as internal disagreements over Burma's lack of human rights progress dragged on. ASEAN also remained uninvolved in the Thai-Cambodia border issue, despite Cambodia's plea for it to intervene and help end the dispute. ASEAN's reflexive noninterference has been attributed to its design and function as an institution. Some suggest that while the principle of noninterference facilitates consensus-building among members on some issues (such as nontraditional security challenges and economics), in the long term, it may pose other problems for the organization. Following ASEAN's refusal to become involved in the Thai-Cambodia dispute, Cambodia appealed directly to the United Nations. Such action has the potential to weaken ASEAN's authority within the region in the absence of an effective dispute settlement mechanism, and brings into question the contradiction between the principle of noninterference and ASEAN's desire to establish a political and security community by 2015.

Despite its strong economic partnership with many Southeast Asian states, a sustained military presence, cooperation on counterterrorism, and,

more recently, its response to Southeast Asian concerns about nontraditional security challenges, the United States is perceived as lacking a comprehensive strategy and sustained commitment toward the region. Some assert that the United States exercises its strategic presence primarily through its bilateral and multilateral security relationships, and believe that military and other security assistance in today's strategic environment are insufficient for the United States to maintain its presence.[3] But the majority laments its lack of diplomatic engagement, most notably with ASEAN, whose desire for greater regional integration and vision of an East Asian community has placed it at the center of "some very creative diplomacy."[4] The new administration's level of attention to the region will go a long way toward either reassuring ASEAN that Washington's commitment is undiminished, or convincing the region that Washington's attention is indeed diverted. Signaling the U.S. Government's intention to sign the Treaty of Amity and Commerce, placing the newly created U.S. Ambassador to ASEAN in the region, and participating consistently and at a high level in ASEAN meetings would go a long way toward telegraphing the message that our future is still tied up with the prosperity and well-being of the region.

Antigovernment protesters and supporters of ousted Thai Prime Minister Thaksin Shinawatra attack prime minister's car, Bangkok, April 12, 2009

AP Images

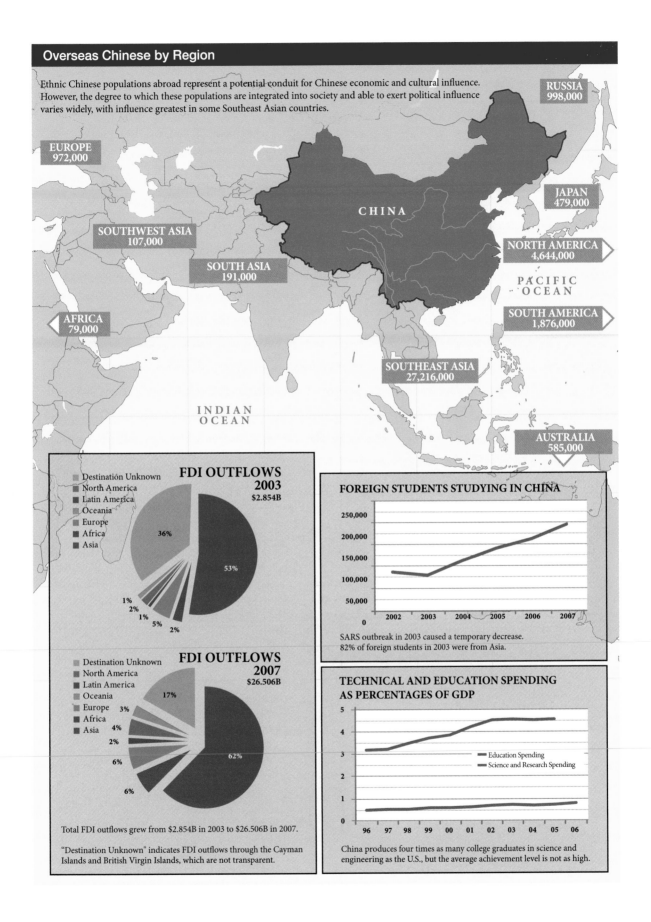

Overseas Chinese by Region

Ethnic Chinese populations abroad represent a potential conduit for Chinese economic and cultural influence. However, the degree to which these populations are integrated into society and able to exert political influence varies widely, with influence greatest in some Southeast Asian countries.

RUSSIA
998,000

EUROPE
972,000

CHINA

JAPAN
479,000

SOUTHWEST ASIA
107,000

SOUTH ASIA
191,000

NORTH AMERICA
4,644,000

PACIFIC
OCEAN

AFRICA
79,000

SOUTH AMERICA
1,876,000

SOUTHEAST ASIA
27,216,000

INDIAN
OCEAN

AUSTRALIA
585,000

FDI OUTFLOWS 2003
$2.854B

- Destination Unknown
- North America
- Latin America
- Oceania
- Europe
- Africa
- Asia

53%
36%
1%
2%
1%
5%
2%

FDI OUTFLOWS 2007
$26.506B

- Destination Unknown
- North America
- Latin America
- Oceania
- Europe
- Africa
- Asia

62%
17%
3%
4%
2%
6%
6%

Total FDI outflows grew from $2.854B in 2003 to $26.506B in 2007.

"Destination Unknown" indicates FDI outflows through the Cayman Islands and British Virgin Islands, which are not transparent.

FOREIGN STUDENTS STUDYING IN CHINA

250,000
200,000
150,000
100,000
50,000
0

2002 2003 2004 2005 2006 2007

SARS outbreak in 2003 caused a temporary decrease. 82% of foreign students in 2003 were from Asia.

TECHNICAL AND EDUCATION SPENDING AS PERCENTAGES OF GDP

5
4
3
2
1
0

96 97 98 99 00 01 02 03 04 05 06

— Education Spending
— Science and Research Spending

China produces four times as many college graduates in science and engineering as the U.S., but the average achievement level is not as high.

Weighting for Asia

Just how important is Asia? As eminent experts and indisputable data tell us, Asia's economic weight and consequent importance to the United States and the world are increasing at an awesome pace. Asia has 6 of the world's 20 largest economies,[5] 9 of the world's 20 largest foreign exchange reserves,[6] and many of the world's fastest growing economies over a sustained period of time. As a corollary, Asia's significance to the United States continues to grow. A new initiative of the East-West Center entitled *Asia Matters for America* demonstrates that Asia is a rising source of exports, employment, investment, and student revenue, not only nationally but also disaggregated across U.S. states and congressional districts.[7] No longer is Asia's importance confined to or concentrated on a handful of states, especially those on the coasts of the Pacific and Atlantic oceans. Led by the renewal of Chinese power, the anchor of Japanese strength (still the second largest economy in the world), the progress of South Korea, Taiwan, Malaysia, and Thailand, and the stirrings of India, Vietnam, and Indonesia, Asia's economic gravity and dynamism are facts of international life unseen in centuries. Recent books have transformed reality into zeitgeist, declaring the arrival of "three billion new capitalists" based on the "great shift of wealth and power to the east" and a "power shift" based on "China and Asia's new dynamics."

Prognostications of Asia's arrival to power have animated American discourse for over a century. Waves of anticipation (and anxiety) have crashed on the shores of reality; Japan's aggressive rise was staunched by World War II, Japan's economic boom in the 1980s burst on its own, while the 1997 financial crisis interrupted a decade of fast growth across Asia. Today, however, conventional sense holds that Asia has crossed the Rubicon, not as an act of war, but as a sign of arrival to power and prosperity without a chance of return. This may turn out to be true, but there are caveats and enigmas about Asia's arrival—and its future path.

Both absolutely and relatively, Asia's macroeconomic weaknesses are surprising. For example, Indonesia's GDP is slightly less than Sweden's. Accounting for population differences (230 million versus 9 million, respectively), it is much less. Alternatively, India's and South Korea's economies combined are about equal to California's. The reasonable retort is that the potential of Asian economies exceeds that of many countries, primarily from Europe, who occupy the top tier. Perhaps this is true. Largely for demographic reasons, Europe's economies are alleged to have lower ceilings than most of Asia's. But Asia is not immune from such constraints, particularly in its two largest economies, Japan and China, whose populations are aging relatively rapidly. Moreover, large-scale immigration as a means to address demographic constraints and labor needs may not be an option in Asia as it has been in the past in Europe, given Asia's different notions of society, nationality, and citizenry.

More importantly, a second caveat about Asia is its still-provisional nature, as a region where internal and external upsets could derail economic progress. Of Asia's five biggest economies (Japan, China, India, South Korea, and Australia), the prospect of a domestic crisis sufficient to imperil, not simply slow or temporarily interrupt, economic growth is likely only in China and possibly India. Nevertheless, even if Asia does not confront an acute threat of economic collapse, its massive unfinished nation- and state-building challenges keep the future conditional. Indeed, one of the striking contrasts in the analytical expectations of Asia is the gap between the positive portrayal of the whole region and the mixed reviews of its constituent countries. Hence, while region-wide assessments portend "power shifts," "new dynamics," and even "new hemispheres," and proclaim phenomena signaling vitality such as "thunder" and "fire" from the east, country-based appraisals offer more contradictory conclusions. Countering the many studies of

AP Images (Han Jae-ho)

North Korean and South Korean officials meet for inter-Korean prime ministerial talks, Seoul, November 2007

China's achievements are those predicting its collapse. Considerations of Japan's economic future veer between expectations of revival and terminal decline. For every study anticipating India's emergence is another acknowledging its "strange" or "turbulent" rise. In addition, a host of possible external shocks, from a cross-strait or Korean conflict, to North Korean rogue actions, to a major power clash, could damage the *entire* region's economy. It is difficult to envision such shocks in Europe, Latin America, or Africa (though not so difficult in the Middle East). In short, Asia's macroeconomic achievements are evident but mixed, and their future uncertain.

Asia's rising economic weight in America's economy is full of surprises, too. While U.S. exports of goods and services to the Asia-Pacific region exceed those to the European Union, and four Asian countries have consistently been among the top 10 U.S. trading partners, U.S. exports to all of Asia are marginally more than its exports to Canada alone. Certainly the growth rates of exports to Asia in general and to specific Asian countries are high, but not so high as to come close to dislodging Canada and Mexico from their spots as first and second U.S. trade partners. On investments to and from Asia, the asymmetries are more striking. The direct investment position abroad on a historical cost basis shows that by the end of 2005, U.S. investments in Asia were about a third of investments in Europe, just $20 billion or so more than in Latin America, and $50 billion less than in Great Britain alone. Of the $376 billion in U.S. investment in Asia, nearly a third, or $113 billion, was in Australia, with the other $263 billion spread over China (the smallest at $16 billion), Hong Kong ($37 billion), Singapore ($48 billion), Japan ($75 billion), and other Asian countries.

Asia's investments in the United States are similarly skewed. They are less than a third of Europe's, though much higher than Latin America's U.S. investments. But it is Australia and Japan that together account for over 90 percent of Asian investment in the United States, while the rest of Asia combined accounts for just 8 percent. Again, however, trends are changing. For example, India's investments in the United States are now approaching the level of U.S. investments in India. Other considerations of Asia's importance to the United States are even more complex and nuanced. American imports from Asia are massive (hence big trade deficits), but they keep inflation down and provide consumers choice and value. A significant share of these imports, particularly from China, comes from U.S. companies operating there. This fact qualifies the strength of these national economies, but also raises their importance to the United States.

A final consideration is the continuing centrality of the United States for Asia's economic emergence, both globally and vis-à-vis the United States. For all of America's current difficulties, the sinews of its structural strengths (for example, demography, education, stable political system, geographical location, and strong civil society) are profound. America's relative power will ebb in this century as other countries rise—especially in Asia. But the rise of others cannot happen without a vibrant United States, and the United States will in turn gain opportunities from them. Hence, the United States and Asia will continue to be increasingly interlinked, and declarations that America and Asia are "de-coupling" economically are premature.

The bottom line is that the world, including the United States, is increasingly, and correctly, "weighting" for Asia economically. But Asia's journey is incomplete and enigmatic. Thus, the world also is still waiting for Asia.

East Asia is increasingly important for American prosperity and security. It houses 29 percent of the world's population and produces about 19 percent of global GDP. Asia accounts for 30 percent of total U.S. trade and includes 8 of the top 15 destinations for U.S. exports. One of the biggest stories is China's remarkable economic reforms, which have produced a sustained growth rate of more than 8 percent for almost 30 years. China's economic success, supported by sophisticated regional diplomacy, has turned Beijing into a key economic partner for most countries in Asia (including U.S. allies) and underpinned a dramatic expansion of Chinese regional influence. But Asia is also home to Japan's huge economy, a dynamic South Korea, a rising India, and successful Southeast Asian economies. It is the most economically dynamic region of the world, and Asian countries now hold about two-thirds of global foreign exchange reserves. This shift in economic power as Asia and Asian countries gain greater weight in the world economy is producing parallel changes in the political and security spheres. Asians feel that they deserve a greater voice in global economic and governance institutions, and the economic and increasing military power of China (and to a lesser degree India) has already begun to reshape regional politics.

The United States still holds a strong position within a changing region. Unmatched U.S. military power, enabled and supported by its regional alliances, provides hard security in Asia that no other country or set of security institutions can replace. Countries in Asia look to the United States to provide balance against a rising China whose regional ambitions remain unclear and which has maritime and territorial disputes with many countries in the region. This is seen nowhere more clearly than from Tokyo, where close integration into a bilateral ballistic missile defense network is emblematic of effective practical cooperation under difficult political restraints.

The U.S. market is a key factor for regional economic growth with many of the goods produced by regional production networks throughout Asia ultimately winding up in the United States. The negative impact of the severe worldwide financial crisis and the ongoing U.S. economic slowdown on Asian economies and stock markets illustrates the continuing importance of the U.S. economy. In the face of persistent complaints about the Bush administration's distraction from Asian issues due to the Middle East and overemphasis on a narrow counterterrorism agenda, there is considerable appetite among Asian governments for a more active U.S. regional role.

Despite these strengths, the U.S. position is beginning to be challenged in both the traditional and nontraditional security domains. Rapid growth has allowed China to make substantial investments in military modernization, many of which are focused on antiaccess capabilities that may eventually challenge the U.S. ability to operate in the western Pacific and to fulfill its traditional security responsibilities. China also is developing increased power projection capabilities, including both nuclear-armed missiles and more accurate and longer range conventional ballistic missiles, which can threaten Taiwan and Japan. Intense diplomatic efforts to constrain and eliminate North Korea's nuclear weapons ambitions and potential so far have failed to prevent North Korea from testing a nuclear device, heightening regional concerns about nuclear proliferation. The ability of the Six-Party Talk process to produce verifiable denuclearization of the Korean Peninsula remains in doubt, and will be an important policy challenge for the new administration.

At the same time, countries in the Asia-Pacific are grappling with an increasingly important nontraditional security agenda that requires cooperative solutions and has a direct impact on the day-to-day lives of the people. Issues such as energy security, terrorism, infectious disease, disaster relief, and maritime security have the potential to affect the regional stability and security necessary for continued economic development. Asia-Pacific countries have begun to address these issues through a variety of political and security organizations including the ASEAN regional forum, the East Asian Summit, the unofficial Council on Security and Cooperation in the Asia-Pacific, the Shangri-La Dialogue, and a series of bilateral efforts. Although some Asian experts see these organizations as a foundation for a new cooperative security approach, they remained limited in both their practical accomplishments and their ability to address contentious traditional security issues such as territorial disputes and potential conflicts on the Korean Peninsula and in the Taiwan Strait. Nevertheless, these organizations are becoming focal points for regional cooperation as well as venues for great power competition. Major powers such as China, Japan, and India see nontraditional security issues as a means of justifying new military capabilities and expanding their regional influence in a nonthreatening way. The United States is an active player on both traditional and nontraditional security issues in the Asia-Pacific, but it will need a more consistent and comprehensive approach if it is to maximize its positive influence in the region.

U.S. alliances continue to provide the foundation for the U.S. hard and soft security presence in the region. Indeed, the Bush administration made concerted efforts to repair and strengthen the political and security foundations of the key U.S. alliances with Japan and South Korea. Alliance transformation is deepening security cooperation and leading to shifts in responsibilities within each alliance. With political foundations strengthened, the new administration will be able to follow through on planned relocations of U.S. forces, and on efforts to build the capabilities of its alliance partners. This will require consistent political engagement, close attention to detail, and patience during consequential negotiations over burdensharing and roles and missions.

A "business as usual" attitude toward U.S. alliances will be insufficient. Japanese security experts are concerned about potential threats from China and North Korea and are raising concerns about the credibility of extended deterrence that must be addressed. The issue of Kim Jong Il's poor health is a reminder that collapse or crisis in North Korea are real possibilities, and could involve the U.S.–ROK alliance in both new military tasks and delicate, short-fused diplomacy with other regional powers. China has become a key economic partner for Australia, making inroads "down under."

There are, of course, many opportunities for enhanced relations available to the United States.

The interoperability and combined capabilities developed with U.S. allies (including Australia, Thailand, the Philippines, and Japan) can be applied outside alliance structures to deal with regional challenges in cooperation with other countries. The 2004 Indian Ocean tsunami and 2005 Pakistan earthquake relief efforts show the strong potential for regional security cooperation and the attractiveness of combining soft power with military capabilities. The challenge for the United States is to develop new models of open security cooperation and work with allies, partners, and other interested countries to address a broader range of security issues. In some cases the United States may take the lead, and in other cases we may be more effective in supporting regional initiatives.

The Obama administration has inherited a reasonably sound foundation for U.S. power in Asia, along with new and growing challenges. It will need to articulate a clear regional vision and policy priorities in order to reassure Asian countries that the United States will adopt a strategic approach and devote sufficient high-level attention to implement its proposals. Doing so will require more effective integration of U.S. economic and security policies to convert U.S. power potential into actual regional influence, especially in the face of increasing Chinese influence.

Asia-Pacific nations will watch U.S. statements about China with particular care, and track closely the outcomes of Sino-American relations. They not only support U.S. efforts to encourage positive Chinese behavior through active engagement under the "responsible stakeholder" framework, but also want an active U.S. role that maintains regional balance and limits their vulnerability to Chinese pressure. The regional nightmare scenario is a U.S.-China conflict that destroys regional stability and forces the nations of the Asia-Pacific to choose sides. The most difficult challenges the new administration faces in Asia involve positioning China properly within the framework of a broader U.S. regional strategy, and striking the right balance between the cooperative and competitive elements of the U.S.-China relationship.

The potential of the Asia-Pacific cannot be overstated, both for stable economic growth and political cooperation as well as for disruption and instability. America's own potential, in the region and for the region, is equally profound, clearly appreciated, and closely tracked throughout Asia. East Asia's challenges are its opportunities as well for the United States, for which expectations remain very high throughout the region. **gsa**

NOTES

[1] *Southeast Asia* here is defined as the 10 countries comprising the Association of Southeast Asian Nations: Brunei Darussalam, Cambodia, Indonesia, Lao People's Democratic Republic, Malaysia, Myanmar/Burma, the Philippines, Singapore, Thailand, and Vietnam.

U.S. Marine Corps (Kamran Sadaghiani)

Marine Corps Air Station Futenma, Okinawa

[2] Adam Schwarz and Roland Villinger, "Integrating Southeast Asia's Economies," *The McKinsey Quarterly*, February 2004.

[3] Surin Pitsuwan, "U.S.–ASEAN Cooperation," Center for Strategic and International Studies *Southeast Asia Bulletin* (February 2008), 1.

[4] Ellen L. Frost, *Asia's New Regionalism* (Boulder, CO: Lynne Rienner Publishers, 2008), 3.

[5] See <http://siteresources.worldbank.org/DATASTATISTICS/Resources/GDP.pdf>.

[6] See <www.cia.gov/library/publications/the-world-factbook/rankorder/2188rank.html>.

[7] See <http://www.asiamattersforamerica.org>.

Contributors

Captain Renata Louie, USN (Chapter Editor), is a Senior Military Research Fellow in the Institute for National Strategic Studies (INSS) at National Defense University (NDU), specializing in Asian security issues, nontraditional security, and conflict management and resolution. She is co-author of *Cooperative Crisis Management and Avian Influenza: A Risk Assessment Guide for International Contagious Disease Prevention and Mitigation* (Center for Technology and National Security Policy, 2006).

Dr. Thomas Bowditch is a Senior Research Analyst and Director of the Strategy Initiatives Group at the Center for Naval Analyses. He recently returned from Camp Smith, Hawaii, where he was a special assistant for the Commander of U.S. Pacific Command. Dr. Bowditch received his Ph.D. in International Relations from the University of Virginia (UVA), holds two master's degrees from UVA and the Naval War College, and received his B.A. from Bates College.

Dr. Satu P. Limaye is Director of the Washington office of the East-West Center. Dr. Limaye previously served as Director of Research and Publications for the Asia-Pacific Center for Security Studies, and has written, edited, and co-edited numerous books, monographs, and studies on Asian security affairs.

Dr. Marvin C. Ott is Professor of National Security Policy at the National War College. He is the author of numerous articles and monographs on Southeast Asia with previous positions as a Senior Associate at the Carnegie Endowment, Senior Analyst at the Central Intelligence Agency, and Deputy Staff Director of the Senate Select Committee on Intelligence.

Dr. James J. Przystup is Senior Research Fellow in INSS at NDU, specializing in Asian security issues, particularly those involving Japan and Korea. He has worked on Asia-related issues for more than 20 years in both the public and private sectors, including assignments with the Policy Planning Staff at the Department of State, Office of the Secretary of Defense, and Subcommittee on Asian and Pacific Affairs of the House Foreign Affairs Committee.

Dr. Phillip C. Saunders is Senior Research Fellow in INSS at NDU. He previously served as Director of the East Asia Nonproliferation Program at the Monterey Institute's Center for Nonproliferation Studies and as a staff officer in the U.S. Air Force. He has written on a wide range of China and Asian security topics for INSS, academic, and policy publications.

Scott Snyder is Director of the Center for U.S.-Korea Policy at The Asia Foundation and a Senior Associate at The Asia Foundation and Pacific Forum Center for Strategic and International Studies. He is also an Adjunct Senior Fellow for Korean Studies and Director of the Independent Task Force on Policy Toward the Korean Peninsula at the Council on Foreign Relations. His latest book is *China's Rise and the Two Koreas: Politics, Economics, Security* (Lynne Rienner, 2009).

Chapter 13
Europe

Rethinking Euroatlantic Security Structures

The North Atlantic Treaty Organization (NATO), backed by strong U.S. military and political commitments to the Alliance, has been the primary guarantor of Europe's defense from armed attack since 1949. With the end of the Cold War, NATO assumed new roles: building defense and security partnerships with new democracies in Central and Eastern Europe that prepared many for Alliance membership; extending dialogue and cooperation on political-military issues to Russia, Ukraine, and other states of the former Soviet Union; and leading complex military and stabilization operations in the Balkans and Afghanistan. Throughout its existence, NATO also has performed the vital job of promoting intra-European as well as transatlantic collaboration regarding threat assessments, political-military strategy, defense planning, equip-ment standards and interoperability, and training and exercises.

Yet NATO's "unipolar moment" has passed. Most Europeans want to preserve robust transatlantic links through NATO that are reinforced, in many cases, by basing, information-sharing, and other bilateral ties to the United States. Russia's behavior in Georgia in the summer and fall of 2008 and its muscular statements of intent to "protect the life and dignity of [Russian] citizens wherever they are" have renewed interest in NATO's collective defense role, particularly among Eastern and Northern Europeans. Many Europeans, however, no longer view the most pressing threats to their security, or the tools needed to address them, as predominantly military. And while public opinion polls indicate a modest recovery in positive European views of the United States since the Iraq-related nadir of 2003–2004, European publics remain less confident than a decade ago that

NATO members discuss expanding ISAF operations and missions in Afghanistan, June 2006

U.S. interests, strategy, and policies will closely match their own. Hence, Europeans increasingly endorse the notion that, to protect and advance their common interests and values in defense- and security-related matters, NATO must share the stage with the European Union (EU).

Defining how this shared responsibility should be carried out in practice will prove difficult for Europeans, notwithstanding the fact that 21 of 27 EU member states belong to NATO and 5 others work with NATO, sometimes quite intensively, through the Partnership for Peace (PFP). This task is complicated by profound differences between NATO and the EU in terms of their respective functions, structures, and procedures, as well as internal tensions over strategy, capabilities, and the uneven political will of their members.

NATO under Pressure

NATO's solidarity and effectiveness are being tested in the caldron of Afghanistan, where European Allies and PFP members are contributing some 27,500 of nearly 56,500 troops that make up the International Security Assistance Force (ISAF).[1] European leaders broadly agree that if Afghanistan were to become a "failed state" rather than a fragile one, terrorist networks would again be able to operate there with relative impunity, posing a direct threat to an unstable and nuclear-armed Pakistan and, eventually, the European and North American homeland. At the same time, many European officials fear the trends in Afghanistan are unfavorable, and public support in Europe for the ISAF effort is wavering. Despite Allied and PFP member troop increases in Afghanistan since NATO's April 2008 Bucharest Summit, there is little prospect that Europe will provide significantly larger forces in 2009 and beyond. Indeed, over the next 2 years, some Allies plan to scale down or terminate their presence in southern Afghanistan where, contrary to initial expectations, their involvement in combat missions frequently has overshadowed peacekeeping and reconstruction tasks.

NATO's difficulty in meeting force requirements for ISAF extends beyond troop levels. Some Allies continue to invoke so-called caveats that restrict how and where their nation's forces can be employed by the ISAF commander. European leaders understand the inherent dangers of a two-tier NATO, in which some members are more fully committed than others. Still, certain important ISAF contributors would face serious domestic opposition were they to shift their focus from the relatively stable northern

and western regions to higher risk operations in the south and east. None of the European Allies is prepared to contemplate military involvement inside Pakistan, despite the acknowledged problems posed by virtual sanctuaries for Taliban, al Qaeda, and other opposition militant forces along the Afghanistan-Pakistan border.

In addition, the costs associated with ISAF are taking a heavy toll on some troop contributor nations. Under standard NATO practice, nations must absorb the lion's share of costs associated with their participation in operations. This is a particular disincentive to Allies who have the political will to sustain or increase troop contributions in the most demanding missions but lack sufficient resources to do so. Several Allies nevertheless resist suggestions to increase NATO's common funding for operations or collective assets; faced with low and relatively stagnant defense budgets, they fear greater NATO common funding would come at the expense of national programs and priorities.

Afghanistan also raises hard questions regarding NATO's role in long-term stabilization missions. The "Comprehensive Approach" agreed at the Bucharest Summit aims to integrate international civilian and military assistance to support the Afghan government's efforts to build capable security forces; develop the economy; improve governance and rule of law; and tackle the narcotics problem. Europeans, however, have not taken a common approach regarding their militaries' engagement in such nontraditional roles. And some European officials worry that the United States might try to have NATO build its own civilian capabilities for use alongside the military in stabilization operations—a move that, in their view, would duplicate and undermine efforts by the United Nations (UN), EU, and other international actors.

Finally, NATO's deepening engagement in Afghanistan has raised doubts in several European capitals regarding overall strategy and priorities. None of those governments openly contests the need for NATO's commitment and success in expeditionary operations or advocates a return to Cold War models of territorial defense. But their officials increasingly fret that NATO might lose its raison d'être of collective defense—and vital parliamentary and public support—by focusing too heavily on out-of-area missions that seem disconnected from threats closer to home. For some Allies, the scaling back of the 25,000-strong NATO Response Force after its failure, in 2007, to maintain full operational capability—due, in part, to troop and capability shortfalls that many Allies attributed to their commitments in Afghanistan, the Balkans, and Iraq—exemplifies tensions between the requirements of ongoing missions and those that might be needed for Article 5 contingencies. This sentiment is reinforced by a widespread European perception that U.S. strategic priorities have shifted, perhaps permanently, from Europe to the greater Middle East and northeast Asia.

Russia, for example, is a growing security concern for several European Allies. Even before long-simmering tensions between Russia and Georgia exploded into violent combat in August 2008, Moscow had taken a series of moves—suspending its compliance with the Conventional Armed Forces in Europe Treaty, opposing Kosovo independence, warning of military countermeasures to the planned deployment of U.S. missile defense assets in Poland and the Czech Republic, and (according to some European officials) abetting the 2007 cyber attack against Estonian public and private institutions—that signaled a more assertive posture vis-à-vis NATO. Some, especially Poland and the Baltic states, have argued for additional signs of NATO's preparedness to meet its collective defense commitment, along the lines of increased NATO contingency planning and exercises to deter and, if necessary, respond to any direct military intimidation by Russia. Meanwhile, other Europeans question whether the Alliance is doing enough to prevent or, if necessary, respond to the proliferation of dangerous weapons technologies and delivery systems in the greater Middle East, potential large-scale terrorist attacks against NATO countries, or the threat of energy supply interruptions.

Faced with such questions, many Europeans foresee difficult debates during preparation of a new strategic concept for the Alliance, a process launched at the NATO 60th anniversary summit in April 2009. The purpose of this public document is to help reestablish a solid transatlantic consensus on, and renewed commitment to, Alliance goals, strategy, and capabilities. This presupposes, of course, that NATO successfully manages its most pressing challenges—notably in Afghanistan—in the meantime.

EU Seeking to Define Its Role

Nearly a decade after its formal launch, the EU's European Security and Defense Policy (ESDP) is firmly rooted within the EU's legal and institutional frameworks. ESDP is supported by civilian and military decisionmaking structures that roughly parallel NATO's (albeit with much smaller staffs),

and the 2003 European Security Strategy document (updated in late 2008) that underlies ESDP sets out a broad vision of EU policy goals and approaches. The record of some 20 ESDP military and civilian operations undertaken to date is generally positive, although most of these have been modest in size, of limited duration, and relatively low risk. The notion once floated by a few European officials that ESDP would develop into a "counterweight" to American influence in Europe and beyond has been largely discredited. But while EU governments frequently differ over the priorities and resources they are prepared to assign to ESDP, even the most "Atlanticist" among them have come to accept ESDP as a legitimate and important pillar of the EU's global influence.

Leaders from Germany, France, and Great Britain discuss financial crisis during EU summit, October 2008

Within the EU, debate regarding ESDP largely revolves around the balance between military and civilian tools for crisis management and how best to generate additional military and civilian capabilities. ESDP's initial focus was largely military, very ambitious, and heavily influenced by European lessons learned from the Balkan conflicts of the 1990s. For example, in 1999 the EU pledged to develop, by 2003, the ability to deploy, within 60 days, some 50,000 to 60,000 military personnel to crisis spots thousands of miles from Europe, and to sustain them for at least 1 year for tasks ranging from humanitarian operations to peacekeeping and separating warring parties. Faced with substantial capabilities shortfalls, however, the EU shifted its attention in 2004 to creating some 15 battle groups, each comprised of approximately 1,500 troops; two such formations serve in alert status for 6-month periods and, in theory, would be able to deploy within 10 days of an EU decision and sustain operations for up to 120 days. (To date, the EU has not operationally deployed a battle group, but EU officials cite Africa as the most likely venue for any future use.)

Some EU governments continue to place priority on the development of military capabilities within ESDP. They favor the periodic conduct of "autonomous" military operations—that is, operations without NATO assistance available through the "Berlin Plus" arrangements agreed between NATO and the

Turkish president and first lady attend memorial ceremony in Japan

EU in 2003—to demonstrate ESDP's practical value, encourage higher defense spending, and build habits of intra-European cooperation in increasingly challenging missions.[2] They also favor expanded joint research, development, asset pooling, and acquisition programs managed by the EU's European Defense Agency (EDA). That said, in recent years the limits of such efforts have become clearer. For example, the 2008–2009 ESDP operation in Chad and the Central

African Republic proved more difficult and expensive than anticipated. In addition, European defense budgets remain stubbornly low and in many cases excessively weighted toward personnel expenditures, limiting the possibilities of significant new investments in EDA programs, especially if such programs are seen by some members as duplicative of NATO efforts or biased to give advantage to another member's defense industry.

Increasingly, EU members look toward their civilian capabilities—including police mentors and experts in justice, corrections, customs, and public administration—as key tools to be deployed in crisis prevention or crisis management operations. These capabilities can be used in conjunction with EU financial and developmental assistance and, depending on the circumstances, alongside an ESDP or NATO military component. Recruiting, training, and deploying qualified civilians for these purposes have not been easy in some cases; the EU finds itself, in effect, competing with its member governments. Still, the EU is accumulating valuable experience through several ongoing civilian ESDP missions, notably in Kosovo and Afghanistan.

European governments will remain careful to protect national prerogatives in the conduct of foreign, defense, and security policies. As a former EDA chief executive has pointed out, no EU member "will allow itself to be forced to enter conflict, or to change how it spends its defense budget, by 'Brussels'—whether an EU institution, or a majority of its partners."[3] The past decade's trend toward greater coordination within the EU, however, is unlikely to be reversed, despite the setback to ratification of the Lisbon Treaty occasioned by its defeat in the June 2008 Irish referendum.

This will not be an easy transition for the EU. It will need time to overcome its institutional impasse. Depending on the issue at hand, the EU might sometimes appear more assertive with its transatlantic partners and, at other times, more hesitant. A deep and enduring transatlantic rift is not preordained, since most Europeans favor continued engagement with, not estrangement from, the United States. But as their "European" sense of identity continues to deepen, their past deference to U.S. "leadership" will continue to erode.

A New Security Triangle?

For most Europeans, the need for a close, cooperative, and pragmatic relationship between NATO

▼ *Continued on p. 291*

Europe: A Normative Superpower?

The real power of a postmodern, post–Cold War state, some scholars allege, lies not in military or economic or other coercive power but in *normative power.* States exhibit normative power by successfully promoting principles such as democracy, rule of law, or human rights across the international arena through processes based on legitimacy, leading by example, and suasion rather than use of material or physical force and threats. By resting on legitimacy, normative power is independent of force and possibly undermined by its use. In this dimension, the argument continues, Europe is a superpower, outstripping the United States and other major or emerging powers in flexing a new kind of muscle on the world stage.

Normative power has resonance among both those who fret that Europe has a limited autonomous security capacity and those who disapprove of it possessing one. Neither the concept of normative power nor the assessment of its ascendance in Europe finds much empirical validity, however. This sidebar briefly notes the areas in which Europe has allegedly demonstrated normative power, reviews the concept of norms, and suggests some ways (albeit ones not diametrically opposed to security power) in which Europe has indeed done influential things with them.

The normative power approach argues that through dialogue and example, Europe, and especially the European Union (EU), has raised the salience of some issues and has promoted changes in domestic and international practices and understandings, thus acting as a "civilizing power."[1] A core set of EU actions and priorities is usually associated with the normative power approach. The most cited example is its role in spreading international human rights in the form of promoting the abolition of the death penalty, first within the EU and then abroad. But supporters of this view also claim Europe has spread values such as civil activism, transnational collective action, and support of peace by promoting development rather than intervention, making "sustainable peace" initiatives a central part of policy in the Balkans and Afghanistan, and championing other policies that emphasize crisis prevention rather than military intervention.[2] In truth, however, the EU has not significantly shaped domestic opinion regarding the death penalty in the state that has been the biggest target of its rhetorical action: the United States. And norms that explicitly favor crisis prevention and eschew intervention have not taken hold, even among Europe's leadership. Normative authority,

then, does not seem to be a significant source of power and certainly not one that Europe can easily harden to meet specific policy objectives.

Moreover, the emergence of an EU defense and security dimension, from rapid reaction forces to the European Defense Agency (EDA), is often construed by "normative power Europe" proponents as a further challenge to the idea. They mournfully note an EU "march towards military potency"[3] that undermines the concept of a normative actor. Normative power, thus, seems a fragile thing: difficult to leverage where it does exist and easy to erode, if it is part of a zero-sum game juxtaposed with the use of force. This is ironic, as the EU has been one of the most innovative international organizations in history with respect to the creation of more formal international law and rule-based commitments. It is also unclear that EU influence in either security affairs or the creation of international rules has shrunk over time, making it worth reconsidering what we mean by "norm" and what the EU has done with norms.

It is generally accepted that one of the most innate human social behaviors is rulemaking—and rules or norms, whether constitutions, contracts, or table manners, underpin social interaction over groups and time. They allow people to make all kinds of social transactions from building communities to doing business where the delivery of goods or services is separated by long distances or periods of time. Far from being a special and exclusive concept, international human

ISAF French task force commander and district governor inaugurate new bridge in Kalakan, Afghanistan, May 2008

rights norms are simply one kind of rule that fall on a spectrum of what scholars such as Douglass North have identified as "institutions."[4]

Broadly construed, institutions can be said to vary along two dimensions: specificity and "bindingness." At one end of this spectrum fall something like commercial contracts—binding, specific, and detailing what parties will do and the consequences for failing to do so—so that everyone shares a fairly clear understanding of what it looks like if they are out of compliance with those rules.

International law, which is typically only applicable to broadly aggregated actors such as states, tends to reside at the more distant end of the binding spectrum. However, detailed charters of human rights, for example, can be influential in that the more specific they are, the more precise and concrete grounds they provide for negotiating behavior and discussing whether, at a minimum, actions are consistent or not with those rules. General norms like democracy, civic activism, and rule of law—the various alleged examples of the EU's normative power by cultural example—reside at the extreme far end of the binding *and* specific spectra, however, which is why they are rather dubious levers in international arenas. A focus on general concepts also overlooks some interesting things the EU has done with rules.

At its inception in the 1950s, what is today called the EU—comprising weak supranational bodies, using procedures strongly favoring unanimous decisionmaking by member states, and governed by treaties that established an international law that was binding only on states rather than individuals—did not look particularly different from other international organizations. Over time, however, it dramatically transformed how rules are created and used within Europe and, as it became more of an international actor, across the world. Through a series of activist rulings in the 1960s, the EU's high court, the European Court of Justice (ECJ), used a set of technical, concrete cases dealing with the details of trade law to announce some principles of broad importance. In these rulings, it established the supremacy of EU law over national law and the principle that EU law is applicable to citizens as well as member-states and is "intended to confer upon them rights." This "constitutionalization" of the treaties and turn to precedent-based decisionmaking by the ECJ was the first step toward the dramatic "institutionalization of European space," a trend that continued as the European Parliament and Commission grew in power, yielding a vast legislative output that significantly structures what can and cannot be done within and by Europe.

This body of law has had consequences for both European security policy and EU interlocutors. Detailed, binding, and technically specific EU rules have diffused across the EU and beyond. The most sweeping example of this has been the adoption of the *acquis communautaire*—the body of EU law accumulated thus far—by its new member states, which has in the matter of a decade transformed the business, tax, and contracting landscape and inserted a modern legal code into former communist countries. EU antitrust laws now significantly affect international firms, and its new regulations on defense procurement and the creation of a European defense market will have an impact on non-European as well as European technology research and development. Detailed EU provisions on passenger screening and data privacy have direct implications for U.S. homeland security and immigration practices.

Thus, the EU has constructed a densely institutionalized space in which binding and specific—indeed, notoriously technocratic—norms are promulgated with great consequence for actors, whether they are individuals, governments, or international firms. When these norms have security implications and are coupled with Europe's economic weight, they are increasingly significant for non-Europeans in ways that have real implications in international space. It is also an instructive case study in the conditions under which norms *can* come to matter internationally—as they move further down the dimensions of "bindingness" and specificity, driven by motivated, activist international actors. Therefore, although Europe as a normative superpower—in the sense depicted by academics—has not and is unlikely to ever come to pass, it is perhaps the most compelling example extant of the growing importance and dynamics of rules and institutions in the international setting.

NOTES

[1] See Ian Manners, "Normative Power Europe: A contradiction in terms?" *Journal of Common Market Studies* 40, no. 2 (2002), 235–258; Ian Manners, "Normative power Europe reconsidered: beyond the crossroads," *Journal of European Public Policy* 13, no. 2 (2006), 182–199; François Duchêne, "Europe's role in world peace," in *Europe Tomorrow: Sixteen Europeans Look Ahead*, ed. R. Mayne (London: Fontana/Collins, 1972).

[2] Manners, "Normative Power Europe."

[3] Ibid.

[4] Douglass North, *Institutions, Institutional Change and Economic Performance* (Cambridge: Cambridge University Press, 1990). See also Martin Shapiro and Alec Stone Sweet, eds., *On Law, Politics and Judicialization* (Oxford: Oxford University Press, 2002).

▲ *Continued from p. 288*

and the EU is no longer seriously contested. The operational strains on Europe's pool of forces caused by commitments in the Balkans, Afghanistan, Lebanon, and Africa, combined with projected low levels of European defense spending, serve as a powerful brake on efforts within either organization to expand existing missions or create new and potentially duplicative structures. And when it comes to doctrine, training, and equipment interoperability, European military commanders understand that inconsistent practices within NATO and the EU could increase the inherent risk of military operations.

A formal "division of labor" between the two organizations, advocated by some European security experts, is unlikely for the foreseeable future. EU governments would find it as difficult to agree on a fixed ceiling for ESDP military operations—in terms of force size, capabilities, and deployment regions—as NATO would find it difficult to set a bottom limit for its involvement. And neither organization is prepared to subordinate its decisionmaking autonomy to the other. In practice, however, certain notional differences in each organization's level of ambition already are taking shape. On the one hand, for example, none of the EU members is prepared to engage in large-scale combat operations without the United States, although only the United Kingdom (UK) has been willing to state this publicly. On the other hand, many Europeans believe that the EU has a comparative advantage, thanks to its array of developmental and civil-military tools, in crisis prevention and management in Africa.

Moreover, some initial assumptions on the nature of NATO and EU cooperation have proved too narrow. For example, many European defense and military planners believed during the period from 1999 to 2002 that NATO and the EU would not be involved simultaneously in the same country. The transitions from NATO-led to EU-led security operations in Macedonia in 2003 and Bosnia-Herzegovina in 2004, followed by continued partnerships between the organizations in both instances, demonstrated otherwise. More recently, civilian ESDP missions, focused on rule of law and police training, have taken hold alongside NATO operations in Kosovo and Afghanistan. Although formal NATO-EU linkages are hampered by continuing political blockages— largely due to disputes involving NATO ally Turkey and EU member Cyprus—the precedents set by practical cooperation in Kosovo and Afghanistan are promising indicators of improved collaboration between the two organizations on a "comprehensive" civil-military approach.

From a European perspective, however, Euroatlantic security cooperation cannot be limited to the NATO–EU relationship. Globalization has blurred the dividing lines between external and internal (or homeland) security. Many problems of greatest concern to European publics fall under the purview of EU structures that have little or no connection to ESDP instruments; among these are illegal immigration, so-called homegrown extremism, transnational crime, critical infrastructure protection, and environmental security. And while such problems can have a serious impact on transatlantic relations, many have limited, if any, direct connection to NATO's core competencies.

An important and growing bilateral U.S.–EU relationship already exists in areas such as counterterrorism, transportation security, nonproliferation, and combating transnational crime. Moreover, pragmatic approaches can open the way for expanded operational cooperation, as demonstrated by the 2008 U.S.–EU agreement to place some 100 American civilian trainers and mentors within the EU civilian ESDP mission in Kosovo. But as the EU increasingly serves as the Europeans' venue for strategic discussions and decisionmaking on these and other interrelated security issues, the United States will want to ensure that its views are taken into account before EU policies are set in stone. This, in turn, will pose an increasingly difficult policy question for Washington: where does it draw the line between discussing strategic questions at NATO, where there is a U.S. seat at the table alongside its European Allies, and at the EU, where the United States and "Europe" sit at opposite sides of the table?

There are inherent limits to bilateral U.S.–EU relations insofar as defense matters are concerned. One is the obvious mismatch of memberships: the United States is more loath to put at risk its military and political relationships with the non-EU Allies (Canada, Turkey, Norway, and Iceland) by circumventing NATO councils to consult, plan, and operate with the 21 other Allies who are EU members. Another, albeit less obvious, factor is equally important: NATO's strength and effectiveness derive, in large part, from the multinational nature of its civilian and military structures, where Americans, Canadians, and Europeans sit side by side to discuss, plan, decide, and implement a broad range of political and military functions. A bilateral U.S.–EU relationship would not include those structures, and duplicating them makes little sense. Similarly, letting them atrophy is a recipe for "decoupling" the United States from Europe in a manner that would put both at risk.

One point seems clear: the transatlantic community is unlikely to come to grips with today's wider, more complex security agenda absent a continued transformation of both NATO and the EU, much improved cooperation between them, and a demonstrated willingness by the United States and Europe to work flexibly and pragmatically with both organizations to advance common interests and values.

European Strength in an Unpredictable World

September 11 came late to Europe, but more than 7 years after 2001, it is in the European consciousness. Among Europe's larger countries, the analysis of the changing security environment is converging with that of the United States. Germany's *Weissbuch* ("White Book") of October 2006 and France's *livre blanc* ("White Paper") of June 2008 overlap with the most recent national strategy papers released by Britain (March 2008) and the United States (March 2006). These are all compatible, too, with the NATO Comprehensive Policy Guidelines of November 2007. In a world that is described in the French White Paper as "neither better nor more dangerous" than two decades ago but "more unpredictable" and "exposed to new vulnerabilities," the transatlantic partnership is no longer divided along Robert Kagan's celestial lines of Mars and Venus. A healthier understanding of Europe's capabilities and a sobering appreciation of America's limits now define the

transatlantic partnership as a more balanced relationship between relative strengths and weaknesses.

Following sharp clashes over Iraq, Europe's newest political leaders are generally pragmatists who can work well together and with their main partner across the Atlantic. So it is, most visibly, with French president Nicolas Sarkozy, whose warm embrace of the United States parallels his interest in closer relations with the UK and support for an enhanced ESDP that would complement rather than compete with NATO. "We need both," said Sarkozy in June 2008, adding, "A NATO and European defense that oppose each other makes no sense." This apparent willingness to end the so-called French exception is welcome in the UK, whose most important bilateral relationship is with the United States, and Germany, which traditionally has been torn between its two central but estranged partners and institutions of choice. As a result of these shifts in perspective, the four main Euroatlantic powers can at last agree on the main precondition of Euroatlantic solidarity: *there can be a distinctive "European" way only to the extent that it is framed as a cooperative Euroatlantic endeavor, but conversely, there can be no cohesive "Atlanticist" way unless it acknowledges specific European preferences and needs, even when these seem distinct from U.S. preferences and needs.*

Learning to Say "Yes"

The French "return" to NATO in 2009 is significant not only in terms of added value for NATO, but also because of the opportunity it provides for a broader rethinking of U.S.-European and intra-

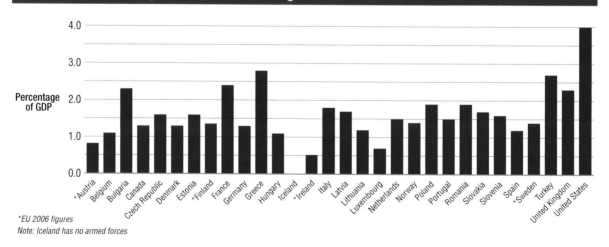

EU/NATO Defense Expenditures as Percentage of GDP 2007

*EU 2006 figures
Note: Iceland has no armed forces

Source: International Institute for Strategic Studies, *The Military Balance 2008*.

European relations: the EU with the United States, and NATO with the EU. Admittedly, current French expectations echo those of former president Jacques Chirac, who in December 1995 called for America to share leadership responsibilities (including high NATO command assignments for Paris), and for Europe to build up its defense policy (with an indispensable assist from the UK). At the same time, the French government does not want to abandon its "freedom to commit [its] armed forces" by having them "permanently placed under NATO command in peacetime." Yet changed political circumstances should now make it easier for both France and the United States to voice and manage these expectations more effectively. The United States must help the UK to say "yes" to France in Europe, now that the French government is willing to say "yes" to NATO. France in turn should help Germany say "yes" to a more vigorous ESDP, based on a more consistent security strategy than was put in place by Javier Solana in 2003. Finally, the United States, Britain, France, and Germany have to be willing to say "yes" to each other, so that the 32 members of the EU and NATO (including the 21 common European members) can achieve a much-needed strategic unity along national and institutional lines.

The past 5 years have shown that the states of Europe cannot play an effective role in the world, in analytical or in policy terms, when only one or two national capitals collaborate at a time. To be effective and credible in that role, the EU must mitigate its internal divisions, which can lead any of its 27 members to block the will of the 26 others, as hap-

pened with the June 2008 Irish referendum on the 2007 Lisbon Treaty. Thus, ESDP is an intra-European debate that begins with two participants (France and Britain). Germany then joins in before the debate is enlarged to six or seven (with Italy, Poland, Spain, and even Sweden). Eventually, it is extended to all EU members.

Although better aware of their own limits, the French remain torn between their traditional passion for autonomy and their newly found need for interdependence. The French military's current equipment and capabilities are the product of a Gaullist orthodoxy that prevailed some 30 years ago and still assumes a state-based, symmetric enemy (that is, the Soviet Union). But the rise of asymmetrical threats and operations that are smaller and of greater frequency is compelling France's strategic planners to make changes that were not part of France's previous White Book released in 1994. The goal of France's forces now is to be the first to enter a major theater of operations—apparently on the principle that security concerns convey a right of interference (*droit d'ingérence sécuritaire*). Paris, however, does not wish to do so alone, nor with only a few poorly prepared EU partners. The new tests for the French military are tests of efficacy and synergy: with a shrunken army said to be inadequately equipped and resourced, France needs to do more with less. It can only hope to do so by working with its Allies. The questions remain: if not with the United States and thus with NATO, with whom; if not with the UK and through the EU, how; if not now, with Sarkozy, when?[4]

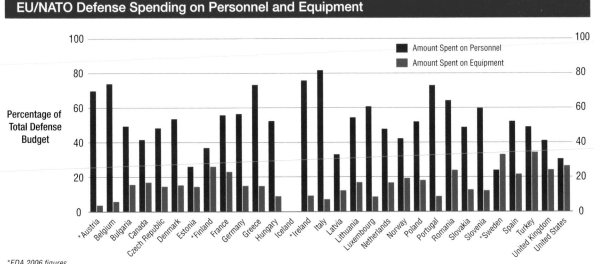

EU/NATO Defense Spending on Personnel and Equipment

Percentage of Total Defense Budget

■ Amount Spent on Personnel
■ Amount Spent on Equipment

*EDA 2006 figures

Source: European Defence Agency, *NATO 2007*.

The French approach to ESDP is not yet compelling for Prime Minister Gordon Brown or for the UK in general, where France's longstanding interest in a fully operational EU military headquarters to plan and manage EU military operations remains especially contentious. Some fear such an EU headquarters will partially duplicate NATO capabilities without bringing added value. Over the years, British skepticism regarding an EU operational headquarters has been shared by the United States. The UK's opposition to such a move, however, is less a vote for NATO, where France is poised to increase its participation, than it is a vote against the EU, which the UK always appears about to depart. The United States can now encourage the UK to join France in an effort to build new capabilities for a Euroatlantic West that combines NATO and the EU. At the very least, and to facilitate the next steps of the European security debate, the EU needs to constitute a new mechanism to help coordinate the work of the EU's civilian staff with NATO's military personnel.

Besides the importance of Anglo-French unity, Germany holds the key to the future of ESDP, and the key to Germany is its leadership. That a German commitment has been missing since the EU established ambitious new headline goals in 2004 is all too clear. For the past two decades, German defense expenditures have fallen steadily—from 2.8 percent in 1989 to 2.2 percent in 1991, to 1.5 percent in

2001, to 1.3 percent in 2006. Yet the goals of the 2006 *Weissbuch* are compatible with ESDP and NATO targets (Headline 2010 and Comprehensive Political Guidance), especially as they relate to threat assessment, force transformation, and *Bundeswehr* reform. In the new political context created by closer bilateral and multilateral relations (between France and the United States within NATO; Britain and France within the EU; and the United States, the EU, and NATO within an expanding Euroatlantic community), a second Angela Merkel–led governing coalition after the autumn 2009 elections in Germany could exert, by 2010, the leadership needed to resume an evolution in German security thinking that began in 1994, when a constitutional court ruling enabled the deployment of German troops abroad during the waning years of Helmut Kohl and the contentious chancellorship of Gerhard Schroeder.

Converging Views

Without a doubt, the states of Europe and the United States faced one of their most difficult crises ever over the use of force in Iraq. Before the war, a more united Europe might have better influenced the Bush administration's decisions for war or provided, within a more cohesive alliance, the additional capabilities needed for the nonmilitary missions that followed the decision to go to war. Aside from Iraq, however, the United States and the states of Europe,

Members of NATO and the European Union

European Members of NATO

European Members of the EU

Albania
Croatia
Iceland
Norway
Turkey

Belgium
Bulgaria
Czech Republic
Denmark
Estonia
France
Germany
Greece
Hungary
Italy

Latvia
Lithuania
Luxembourg
Netherlands
Poland
Portugal
United Kingdom
Romania
Slovakia
Slovenia
Spain

Austria
Cyprus
Finland
Ireland
Malta
Sweden

as well as the institutions to which they belong, do or can now agree on many endogenous factors (political and economic interests, ambitions, values) and exogenous realities (threats, risks, and partnerships that are all in turn nurtured by historic experiences and geographic location). Thus, it is mostly agreed that:

■ A diverse and interconnected array of issues— military (including the proliferation of weapons of mass destruction), political (good governance), economic (access to and manipulation of vital resources), social (pandemics and even poverty), environmental (climate change), and human (demographic curves)—creates an increasingly complex, unpredictable, and unfamiliar security situation. The members of the Euroatlantic defense community and their institutions are neither adequately prepared nor properly equipped to address many of these, whether in terms of capabilities and know-how, organization, or policies. Nor can many, if any, of these threats be addressed exclusively with any single tool, military or otherwise. Most of them require a mixture of military and civilian capabilities, as well as a combination of national and institutional tools. Thus, the new goal of an emerging strategic vision is for a "more integrated" or "comprehensive" approach that can "bring together the objectives and plans of all departments, agencies, and forces involved in protecting our [Britain's] national security"—a view also articulated in the new French strategy, which is designed to combine, "without confusing them, defense policy, homeland security policy, foreign policy, and economic policy."

■ Such multifaceted security concerns require a major overhaul of national and institutional capabilities, including national capabilities for the exercise of hard power, nonmilitary capabilities for the use of soft power, and joint capabilities that will enable the use of both hard and soft power. Admittedly, the United States (and NATO) has pursued this path for some time, though not as effectively with regard to the nonmilitary dimensions of security policy: in 2002, the United States Government still spent a mere $13 billion in external assistance versus the EU's $36 billion. For the countries of Europe and their Union, it is especially difficult to upgrade military power because of budget pressures that leave national governments with little more than cost-cutting options. The intensity of this pressure varies from country to country, however; it is less in France than in Germany, but more than in the UK, for various reasons. The UK, for instance, is not sensitive to the EU pressures exerted on euro-zone members. The resulting emphasis on "capability over quantity" may sound more like a political alibi than strategic thinking or raw necessity, but even in the UK, where defense spending has had its longest period of sustained growth since the 1980s (with the 2010 budget projected to be 11 percent higher in real terms than in 1997), it is recognized that the armed forces are stretched to the point of exhaustion, and the defense industry is approaching panic levels over the thinness of its order books.

■ Relative to such a community, the notion of exclusive security "neighborhoods" for either side of the Atlantic is too limiting. In a globalized world, everywhere "over there" can intrude anywhere "over here." Seemingly eager to cure the EU of its "parochial myopia," the states of Europe should be willing to strive for a strategy that goes global—along the strategic arc sketched by the French and stretching from the Atlantic via the Mediterranean to the Persian Gulf and the Horn of Africa, and on to South Asia. For the French, this means a commitment of scarce

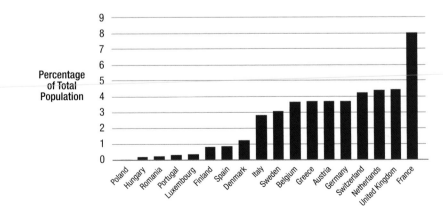

Estimated Proportion of Muslims in Selected European Countries, c. 2000

funds in areas that would enable them to know early (intelligence) and thus, like the UK, engage promptly (carriers), strike visibly (Rafale fighters), and stay late (gendarmerie, which represents a sizable share of the French defense budget). Germany's goal is to contribute quickly with smaller, more mobile crisis intervention forces for high-intensity, short-durability conflicts, or to field longer duration, low-intensity operations for postconflict stabilization. But no strategic paper and no declaratory policy can make up for the limits of national capabilities and will: the French White Paper anticipates 377 billion euros in military spending from 2009 to 2020, which, even at the current favorable exchange rate ($581 billion), would barely exceed the current annual U.S. defense budget. Hence an emphasis, again, on the virtues of efficacy: while French defense spending remains relatively high (2.5 percent of gross national product, about the same as in 2001), it falls to 1.7 percent if pensions and gendarmerie are excluded; more tellingly, 40 percent of that budget is for combat personnel and operational duties, as opposed to about 60 percent for administration and supporting roles (the reverse of the British budget, which the French government aims to emulate).

■ Spurred by its members, the EU now agrees that international terrorism is a "significant threat"—though not "the decisive ideological struggle of the 21st century" postulated by the United States—whose global reach and potential access to weapons of mass destruction make it fundamentally different from previous expressions of local terrorism in postwar Europe. Even Germany agrees on the "need to expand the constitutional framework for the deployment of armed forces," including on home soil, as "a result of the growing threat that terrorist attacks pose to German territory," and in order "to secure access to energy resources" as a primary security interest potentially threatened by nonstate aggressors. Yet while every EU country has been making significant efforts in all areas singled out in the EU's counterterrorism strategy—"prevention, protection, pursuit, and response"—Europe offers nothing comparable to a homeland strategy à l'américaine, still makes little room for the use of military instruments abroad, even in the areas of "pursuit" and "response," and continues to show a deep national reluctance to share intelligence widely within the EU.

■ NATO and EU member expectations that Russia might emerge quickly as a strategic partner have dampened. In August 2008, the war between Russia and Georgia confirmed that traditional threats, in the form of massive territorial invasion by large military forces, remain real and can demand the sort of collective response mandated by Article 5 of the North Atlantic treaty, but now over a much larger geographic area than was envisioned in April 1949. This means that while NATO must keep the membership door open to Georgia and Ukraine, no date for such enlargement can be set until NATO's current members reach a consensus over the most effective ways to discourage Russia from trying to reestablish a commanding influence at its periphery. Outside Europe and beyond Russia, emerging poles of power in Asia (especially China, but also India and Japan) will need to be brought in as stakeholders in a new multilateral order. The members of the EU and NATO will also need to engage, reform, and strengthen other institutions—including the Group of Eight, UN Security Council, International Monetary Fund, and World Bank—a goal that is especially emphasized in the British national strategy paper. In this context, former Secretary of State Condoleezza Rice's renewed emphasis on "transformational diplomacy" as a display of "realistic idealism" restores the old-fashioned imperatives of stability and order, and suits Europe's predilection for a new multilateralism that insists on good governance, civil society, social and political reforms, rule of law, and so forth.

Learning to Act Together

As the Obama administration prepares for the difficult agenda that looms ahead, in and beyond Europe, it is comforting to find that in recent years, the views of at least the 32 states of the EU and NATO have become more compatible regarding their total security environment; the logic of unity can at last prevail over that of division. Nevertheless, in a reversal of Cold War conditions, even as Europeans and Americans are growing closer in spirit, the risk is that they might remain distant in practice. This is especially true with regard to the use and usefulness of military force, and it is especially significant with regard to Iran, a key priority outside the Euroatlantic area. Relations with Iran will be a driver of future policy decisions involving the expected but gradual withdrawal of American and coalition forces from Iraq, improved stabilization and reconstruction efforts in Afghanistan, the instability of Pakistan, and some resolution of the Arab-Israeli conflict.

Over the past few years, EU unity, U.S.–EU cooperation, and Alliance solidarity on Iran have been impressive—but only thus far. As is to be expected from the members of an alliance, as distinct from a single-mission coalition, some Allies have agreed at least to delay what they might otherwise have done sooner (a military strike), while others have agreed to what they otherwise are reluctant to do (impose more economic sanctions). Throughout, consultation has been a prerequisite to consensus, although it was originally by and for a few (the United States and the so-called EU–3—Britain, France, and Germany) before it was extended to the EU and NATO. Yet there should be no illusion: however united the Alliance may seem to be on the goal—to deny Iran access to nuclear weapons—its members are still divided over the means, whether it is the use of military force by members or an Israeli decision to make use of its forces, with or without U.S. consent. Notwithstanding vague references to "preemptive engagement [that] can void serious problems in the future" written into the EU strategy paper after its endorsement by member states at the Thessaloniki Summit of June 2003, there is little place for preemption in the national strategy of the leading European states and their Union. In 2009, or possibly a bit later, that distinction will be tested as Americans and Europeans are called upon to debate what is to be feared more, a nuclear Iran or a war with Iran. The question will be how and when best to deter Iran—with military threats before Iran achieves, or approaches, nuclear status, or afterward with threats of instant "obliteration," as then-president Jacques Chirac warned. The United States and Europe do not always share the same priorities regarding other problems in the Greater Middle East. "Why are we in Afghanistan?" or "Why should we be involved with Pakistan?" are questions raised in Europe with a different sense of urgency than in the United States. Nor is there much discussion on either side of the Atlantic of the "years after" in Iraq, when the withdrawal of most coalition forces will have been completed, likely ahead of the next U.S. Presidential election in 2012. Nor, finally, is there a solid consensus on the terms of diplomatic engagement in the Middle East, for instance, on whether Syria or Hamas or Hizballah can be legitimate interlocutors for some even when they are dismissed by others, or even between Israel on the one hand, and the United States and the states of Europe on the other.

On these and many other issues, one of Chirac's earlier questions lingers unanswered: "Who does what?" he asked in 2000, during the EU's so-called finality debate. It is an equally valid question for an emerging Euroatlantic finality debate. The question raises three distinctive but overlapping sets of national and institutional issues: what degree of autonomy can or should the EU and its members have relative to NATO and to each other; what degree of autonomy can or should NATO and its members have relative to the EU and to each other; and what degree of autonomy can or should the United States have relative to NATO? Admittedly, these questions cannot be answered convincingly on paper until they have been tested empirically, over time. Still, the appeal of recent strategic documents—the recent British, German, and French White Papers, as well as the past EU Strategy Security Paper, the White House national security paper, and even the NATO Comprehensive Political Guidance—lies not only in what they and their state sponsors want to do about the world and its problems, but also in what they say, directly or by implication, about the Alliance or the EU, and their members.

For Europe, the EU, the United States, and NATO, in all their various relationships, asserting a will to act in common on the basis of compatible values, overlapping interests, and common goals may go a long way toward recasting an alliance that has seemed to be adrift in recent years. At this moment, there is an unusual opportunity for the Obama administration, as it reviews its National Security Strategy in 2009, to rely on the areas of convergence discussed here to define a compatible, if not identical, Euroatlantic strategic approach (EU–U.S., U.S.–NATO, and NATO–EU–U.S.) to the daunting challenges of the post–Cold War, post-9/11, post-Iraq world ahead.

Balkan Challenges

Since the end of the Cold War, the Balkan region has presented major security challenges to the United States, NATO, and the EU. Several Balkan wars erupted from the disintegration of the former Yugoslavia in 1991, leaving a powerful legacy of distrust among the region's governments and populations.

After a slow initial response from Europe (and hesitation by the United States) to wars involving Croatia, the former Republic of Yugoslavia (dominated by Serbia), and Bosnia-Herzegovina, the NATO-led Operation *Joint Endeavor*, backed by a 60,000-troop Implementation Force, began its deployment in December 1995 to enforce the Dayton Peace Agreement. In March 1999, in an effort to halt a humanitarian catastrophe involving Serbian-led ethnic cleansing in Kosovo, NATO launched an air campaign, Operation *Allied Force*, against Serbia. Three months later, when Serbian forces began to withdraw from Kosovo,

NATO established Operation *Joint Guardian* with the 50,000-troop Kosovo Force (KFOR). In December 2004, NATO transferred its military security tasks in Bosnia-Herzegovina to an EU force (EUFOR-Althea), but some 16,000 KFOR troops remain in Kosovo.

In February 2001, interethnic tensions flared into armed conflict between Macedonian government security forces and Albanian extremists. NATO and the EU responded by coordinating negotiations that led to the August 2001 Ohrid Framework Agreement, opening the door to numerous amendments to the Macedonian constitution and far-reaching legislative changes. NATO also launched successive operations to disarm ethnic Albanian groups, destroy their weapons, and protect international monitors overseeing the implementation of the Ohrid settlement. Operating under the Berlin Plus arrangements, NATO transferred its military security role in Macedonia to the EU's Operation *Concordia* in March 2003, which was followed in December by an EU civilian police mission, Operation *Proxima*, through December 2005. By July 2006, Macedonia was able to conduct parliamentary elections that, while marked by confrontations within ethnic Albanian and ethnic Slav political parties, were assessed to meet EU and NATO standards.

Despite the qualified successes of NATO- and EU-led stabilization efforts, regional conflicts and the risk of state failure have reemerged as looming challenges in the Balkans. These have become even more pronounced since the declaration of Kosovo's independence in February 2008.

The Future of Kosovo and Serbia

Kosovo and Serbia will determine future Balkan stability and security. The Serbian parliament unanimously approved a new constitution in September 2006, declaring its independence and reaffirming its position that Kosovo—with its overwhelmingly ethnic Albanian population—remained an integral part of Serbia. Two international efforts—led first by a UN special envoy and later by a "troika" of the United States, the EU, and Russia—failed to broker an agreement between Belgrade and Pristina during 2006–2007. After Kosovo declared independence in February 2008, the United States and more than 40 EU and non-EU countries extended recognition to the new Kosovo state, while Serbia, Russia, China, and some Balkan neighbors opposed it. This ambiguous situation has resulted in a hardening of nationalist positions and increased political instability.

Limited international recognition of Kosovo's independence has serious consequences. Kosovo's ethnic Serbian population, which constitutes the majority of the population north of the Ibar River, wants nothing to do with Pristina. They consider themselves part of Serbia and enjoy support from Belgrade, backed by Russia. Under its continuing UN mandate, KFOR protects both ethnic Serbs and ethnic Albanians in Kosovo. After the Kosovo constitution came into force in June 2008, full powers devolved from the UN Mission in Kosovo to Kosovo's state institutions, except in the areas of justice and policing, which remain, for a transition period, under the jurisdiction of a new EU rule of law mission.

Since Serbia and Russia do not recognize the legitimacy of an independent Kosovo, the EU mission could come into conflict with Belgrade's efforts to create a separate Kosovo Serb parliament and to protect ethnic Serbs (which Belgrade considers as Serbian citizens) in northern Kosovo. With tensions seething just below the surface, KFOR will be needed for some time to protect the ethnic Serbs who remain in small enclaves south of the Ibar River and those ethnic Albanians still living north of the river. The longer the existing standoff continues, the more regional tensions will increase, possibly creating a new "frozen" conflict that will undermine long-term prospects for Balkan stability.

However the Kosovo question is resolved, the integration of Serbia and Kosovo into the Euroatlantic mainstream will be a major challenge. Serbia's politics are still roiled by bitterness and resentment over the wars of secession that split apart Yugoslavia. NATO invited Serbia to join PFP in November 2006 and has encouraged its cooperation with other partners and Allies in the region. In April 2008, the EU and Serbia signed a Stabilization and Association Agreement (SAA).[5] NATO and the EU will need to reach out to Serbia to help democratic reform there and coordinate its PFP and SAA activities, while working with its Balkan neighbors to create a secure and stable surrounding environment. At the same time, KFOR will need to continue to protect both ethnic communities while the EU mission in Kosovo facilitates the institutional development of judicial and police authorities.

Bosnia-Herzegovina: Unresolved Issues

In many respects, the transition in 2004 from a NATO-led stabilization force to EUFOR-Althea has become, after a bumpy start, a positive example of cooperation through the Berlin Plus arrangements. Some 2,200 EUFOR-Althea troops remain in Bosnia-Herzegovina under a UN mandate, coordinating closely with a small NATO headquarters in Sarajevo, which assists Bosnia-Herzegovina in defense reform, counterterrorism, and intelligence-gathering. Meanwhile, the EU has shifted its overall emphasis from stabilization to support for Bosnia-Herzegovina's "integration" into Euroatlantic structures. For example, the EU Police Mission has mentored the fledgling multiethnic police service, which is struggling to cope with exploding organized crime and human, drug, and arms trafficking.

More needs to be done. NATO and the EU will need to better focus and coordinate their programs and activities to combat organized crime and to counter terrorism. Areas needing priority attention include police reforms and amendments to the Bosnia-Herzegovina constitution that would strengthen the powers of the central government relative to the ethnic entities.

For example, although Bosnia-Herzegovina created a new state-level defense ministry in January 2006 and joined PFP later that year, it faces obstacles, largely explained by ethnic mistrust, to moving other institutions from the entity level to the state level. The prime minister of Republika Srpska (the ethnic Serbian region of the country) continues to resist police reform under a state-level ministry of the interior. In 2006, proposed amendments to the Bosnia-Herzegovina constitution, which would

have accomplished such reform, failed to acquire the necessary two-thirds majority in both houses of parliament. The Bosniak (Muslim) leadership wants to eliminate the separate ethnic entities and build a stronger centralized state, while ethnic Croats want constitutional reforms to guarantee their security and equality. For their part, Republika Srpska leaders want, at most, a loose federation of two entities; some have threatened to use the Kosovo "precedent" to hold a referendum on its constitutional status within Bosnia-Herzegovina.

EUFOR-Althea's mission will be accomplished when Bosnia-Herzegovina's state-level institutions have been consolidated and are functioning adequately. No one can predict when this will happen, however. Recognizing that local politicians must ultimately accept responsibility for the result, the EU Office of the High Representative believes it is still premature to shift to state-level institutions, preferring that the EU Special Representative remain in the country for at least another year. The issue of a new constitution is now coming to the fore as well. Since 70 percent of the population wants to join the EU, the EU agreed to sign an SAA in June 2008 not as a reward for merit, but as an incentive for administrative reforms.

▼   *Continued on p. 301*

Italian ISAF troops search for weapons cache in Musahi Valley, south of Kabul

Turkey at a Crossroads

Turkey faces a defining moment in its history as it tries to handle the twin challenges of deteriorating civil-military relations and maturing demands from its ethnic Kurdish population. How it manages these challenges will significantly affect its relations with the United States, the EU, and NATO.

Relations between the civilian government—led by the Justice and Development Party (*Adalet ve Kalkınma Partisi*, or AKP) and its popular prime minster, Recep Tayyip Erdogan—and military leaders have taken a turn for the worse since April 2007, when the military attempted to counter AKP's nomination of foreign minister Abdullah Gul to become Turkey's president. (Gul's wife wears a headscarf, which the military, in particular, sees as a threat to secularism.) The AKP picked up the challenge by calling for early elections in July 2007, which handed Erdogan an unprecedented victory. Turkey, it seemed, had once again narrowly averted the abyss of a coup d'état.

Another showdown, however, developed a year later, when the constitutional court—at the instigation of the judiciary, military, and other elements of the arch-secularist establishment—agreed to consider charges that the government had violated constitutional provisions guaranteeing a secular state. A ruling against the government would have closed down the AKP and effectively banned its members from holding office and other political activity. In July 2008, faced with domestic and international pressure, the court by a narrow margin decided not to close the AKP, but to punish it by imposing a fine.

These developments have alarmed EU members who have generally been sympathetic to the AKP's efforts—however erratic—to substantially reform Turkey's judicial and political system in line with the EU's Copenhagen Criteria. Had the constitutional court banned the AKP, the EU likely would have suspended its accession negotiations with Turkey, further distancing the Turks from Europe and, more broadly, from Western institutions. At a minimum, EU consideration of Turkey's membership would have been pushed down the road for several years. The court case demonstrated the fragility of Turkish-EU ties. Those Europeans who have second thoughts about Turkish accession will be scrutinizing the evolution of the civil-military divide.

The court's decision was a setback for hard-line secularists, but this does not mean that the Turkish political system is out of the woods. The decision clears the way for the consideration of a badly needed new and liberal constitution. By recalibrating the role of the military in society and politics, such an effort could reignite the divisions in Turkey between the vast bulk of the population and elites, between civil society and the state apparatus, and between democrats and those who believe that the state trumps individual liberties and rights. A more turbulent political picture could also have economic reverberations.

Similarly, continued political uncertainty will affect the other challenge facing Turkey: the Kurdish question. Turkish Kurds are far more politically mobilized than ever before. They have drawn inspiration from the Kurdish experiment in autonomy in northern Iraq and, while unwilling to secede from Turkey, are adamant in their demands for certain cultural and basic rights from Ankara. The two issues intersect in another way: the main Kurdish political party (which, like the AKP, has been threatened with closure) and the AKP account for the totality of Kurdish votes in Turkey. Kurds expect that these parties will deliver new solutions to their problems and likely will rally behind the party that best meets their aspirations for greater autonomy. The Kurdish question is another arena of civil-military discord and is the single most important determinant of Turkey's policy toward Iraq.

The AKP closure case distracted the Turkish body politic from more pertinent and important issues of foreign and domestic policy. Turkish-American relations improved with Washington's decision to support limited Turkish cross-border operations in Iraq's Kurdish area. Yet those relations continue to face an important test in Iraq—in particular, over northern Iraq. The United States expects that Turkey will engage with the Kurdistan Regional Government to resolve outstanding disputes. The AKP government has indicated that it is interested in greater dialogue with Iraqi Kurds and Baghdad, but it will need U.S. support. The question of relations with the Iraqi Kurds is an explosive issue because of their ties to Turkey's Kurds. How the AKP government manages the competing pressures coming from Turkey's disparate influential sectors will help determine the future character of Turkey. The danger is that a Turkish government that just muddles through may alienate Europe and Turkey from each other. Such an outcome will mean that Ankara will be less likely to cooperate on issues such as Iran or human and drug smuggling. Alternatively, Ankara may seek to invoke Turkish "exceptionalism" to win American support, thereby placing Washington in a quandary with regard to its European Allies.

▲ *Continued from p. 299*

Macedonia: Renewed Tensions

Though Macedonia passed the elections test in 2006, recent Kosovo events have renewed interethnic tensions. Skopje has so far refused to recognize Kosovo's independence. Ethnic Albanians want to do so, but Macedonian Slavs remain hesitant to upset Belgrade and feel threatened by growing Albanian nationalism. Immediately before NATO's April 2008 Summit, the Democratic Party of Albania left the ruling coalition because the government did not meet its demands, which included recognizing Kosovo. It only returned to the coalition because of its desire to see Macedonia invited to join NATO. When Greece blocked Macedonia's invitation (due to a longstanding dispute over the formal name of the Macedonian state), this shock also heightened interethnic relations and contributed to violent incidents surrounding the June 2008 parliamentary elections, further clouding Macedonia's international image.

A near-term solution to the name dispute appears unlikely. Meanwhile, Macedonia's frayed interethnic relations, heightened by differences over Kosovo, will bedevil the government and cast an additional shadow over regional stability.

Avoiding a Wider Crisis

Issues surrounding Kosovo's independence have helped to stoke renewed Balkan tensions. If left unattended, these could well provoke a series of uncontrolled and enormously damaging events. Considering NATO's post–Cold War investment in the Balkans, the Alliance's prestige would experience a considerable setback if its Balkan missions unraveled. The EU, which has made enormous strides since the early 1990s, more than ever needs to coordinate its efforts with NATO. If the EU and NATO fail in the Balkans, transatlantic ties could be weakened at the time of greatest need.

European Counter-radicalization Strategy

Europe's security challenge is as much focused internally as externally. Preventing terrorism is a high priority across Europe, and that objective is being pursued by major European nations through various counter-radicalization policies. The UK may well be the bellwether for countering terrorism in Europe. Although there have been terrorist attacks in the UK since September 11, it has also successfully thwarted prospective attacks. The UK counterterrorism plan,

called Operation *Contest*, was developed in 2003 (but was made public only in 2006). The UK plan differs from the approach taken by France, the European country with the largest Muslim population.[6]

The UK Experience

The UK has suffered repeated terror attacks or attempted attacks in the past few years, beginning with the Dhiren Bharot radiation plot in the summer of 2004, the July 2005 London underground/bus bombings (known as the 7/7 bombing), the Heathrow airline plot in August 2006, and the Haymarket/Glasgow airport episodes in June 2007.

The Heathrow plot, in particular, might have been a watershed for the UK government, which had been largely focused on managing the threat through the criminal law system. Shocked to find that the majority of the perpetrators in the 7/7 bombing and Heathrow plot were born and raised in the UK, authorities realized that they had a homegrown terrorism problem, albeit one with a pervasive link

Australian soldiers patrol in Tarin Kowt, Afghanistan, as part of ISAF mission

to Pakistan and Kashmir, the original homelands of the majority of British Muslims. The radicalization of British Muslim youths begins at home, often with advanced training in violent extremism at al Qaeda training camps in Pakistan's Federally Administered Tribal Areas over which the government of Pakistan has minimal control.

In addition to building up its security and police departments, the UK government in late 2006 made a strategic decision to focus on prevention by reaching out to British Muslim youths before they were at risk of becoming violent extremists. Significant funds were allocated over several years to the Department of Communities and Local Government to deepen contacts between municipalities and local Muslim communities. The government is also funding counter-radicalization projects through the Foreign and Commonwealth Office to assist cities and villages in Kashmir and Pakistan where the extended families of many British Muslims still reside. Finally, a nerve center for counter-radicalization efforts, the Office of Security and Counter Terrorism, has been set up in the Home Office. Part of the government's goal is to build up resilience within the wider community while encouraging moderate Muslims to stand up, as some did following the Glasgow attack, and say, "Not in my name."

The government also created a strategic communications unit to ensure that all government departments and civil servants are giving a consistent message, which is to emphasize the "shared values" of all Britons and to avoid language or labels that demonize the Muslim community.[7] The key to successful prevention, in the government's view, is the ability to mobilize its own Muslim community to isolate and identify those who are espousing violent extremism and plotting attacks in Britain.

The French System

At the heart of traditional British and wider European multiculturalism is a reluctance to assert the superiority of any value system and an attitude of tolerance toward the diverse immigrant communities. The traditional French approach, by contrast, is to impose its state-derived value system: the republican ideal that subordinates ethnic or religious identity to a universal secular citizenship based on *Liberté, Egalité, Fraternité*. Those who reject republican ideals face a system defined by *laïcité*, or secularism, which sets limits on expressions of religion in the public sphere. In short, the French approach relies on assimilation.

When it comes to combating extremism, the French system of assimilation is buttressed by a tougher legal regime than is found in the UK and other European countries. French law prohibits hate speech and authorizes the preventive detention of those who incite violence, more or less indefinitely. These measures make it easier to deport extremists, even if they hold French passports. French law also permits the security apparatus to engage in more

extensive surveillance techniques. A specialized judiciary branch for terrorism has evolved, with judges who act in some ways as prosecutors.

The French do not devote nearly as many resources to counter-radicalization as the British because, in their view, Muslims in France have not become nearly as radicalized. The French challenge is more socioeconomic. "Angry young men" in the depressed, largely North African and African areas outside Paris and other major cities suffer from joblessness and social exclusion, and the solutions may lie less in UK-style counter-radicalization than in affirmative action–type outreach programs, not unlike those adopted in the United States in the 1960s, following race riots in several American inner cities.

While France has been spared much of the extremist Islamist rhetoric and pressure for cultural "shariaization" that appears elsewhere in Europe, the UK model is perhaps more relevant to the rest of Europe than France's assimilation policy. This is because most other countries, like the UK, have had a "live and let live" policy of multiculturalism toward their Muslim communities until Islamist terrorism came to their cities. They will be watching closely to see whether the UK's counter-radicalization program is successful.

Where Europe May Be Heading

Certain assumptions are made by European counterterrorism strategists about the causes of violent extremism. The very use of the term *violent extremists* in the title of the UK Home Office's 2008 "Prevent Strategy" report appears to suggest that nonviolent extremists—or extremism in and of itself—are not the primary concern. British politicians are debating whether it makes sense in the long term to engage and empower political Islamists, including supporters of the Muslim Brotherhood, who espouse nonviolence, as a way of isolating and diminishing the violent extremists from the Takfiri/jihadi/Salafist schools. Some argue that the government should reach out beyond the so-called gatekeepers, such as the Muslim Council of Britain, whose agenda promotes primarily grievance politics and "victimhood," in which criticism of Islamist radicalism is often branded "Islamophobia."

Rather than adopting a simplistic binary view of European Muslims as either violent or moderate, it may be useful to adopt a three-tier differentiation comprising:

■ extremists who blend Takfiri/jihadism with Salafism and who justify violence against fellow Muslims for apostasy and against non-Muslims deemed infidels;

■ political Islamists who advocate cultural separatism and sharia, Muslim issues in foreign policy, and a politics of victimhood and grievances, and who put their British, Dutch, or Danish national identity and civic responsibilities second to their obligations to fellow Muslims at home and transnationally; and

■ the majority of Muslims who view Islam as a faith, not a political ideology, and who identify primarily as citizens of the European country where they live, not as members of a transnational political community.

Some contend that the Muslims who should be empowered by governments are those who reject the ideological underpinnings of jihad, which postulates a possible religious-based war in the near term or long term between Muslims and non-Muslims. They argue that it is shortsighted to empower political Islamists who are ideologically committed to long-term jihad and the establishment of Islamic governments, such as the Muslim Brotherhood, in the hope of weakening violent extremist al Qaedists, who advocate the immediate political decapitation of Western and moderate Muslim leaders.

While tactically it may make sense for police and security officials to engage with nonviolent political Islamists in order to thwart imminent terrorism from homegrown violent extremists, there is a seemingly well-placed concern that violent extremists come from and are nurtured by communities where political Islamism is the prevalent ideology.[8] If so, the crucial task of governments would be to empower those Muslims who are willing to debate the ideological Islamists over their respective visions for Muslim life in Europe. In short, some experts argue that the visions of Islamist and counter-Islamist Muslims are vastly more different than the visions of violent extremists and political Islamists.

By recognizing the full implications of the Islamist challenge as a war of ideas, governments might avoid the trap of empowering one group of Islamists to outflank another. Currently, the UK government is promoting Islamic studies as a way of countering the narrative of violent extremists who prey on Muslim youth with only a superficial understanding of the Koran and Islam. While the idea of teaching the benevolent and tolerant aspects of the Koran is laudable, the actual funding for new Islamic studies initiatives in British universities, typically starved of state funding, comes from Persian Gulf countries

that often are interested in promoting a rigid Wahhabist perspective of Islam. Once again, some worry that it is shortsighted for the government and British universities to promote Islamic studies and scholarship that dilute rather than reinforce identity with British national interests.

Cold War Analogy

While historical analogies can be as misleading as they are illuminating, the Cold War provides useful lessons on how—or how not—to conduct battles for ideas. During the Cold War, the United States sought ways to buck up Western Europe against the inroads of communism. While some Cold Warriors such as Sidney Hook railed against socialists and other leftists together with communists, the Central Intelligence Agency took a different tack by funding *Encounter*, a European cultural and political magazine dominated by socialists who opposed communism. Just as the West embraced the Stephen Spenders of British cultural life to win the hearts and minds of Europeans in the propaganda war with the Soviet Union, today European governments are reaching out to moderate Muslims to engage in the battle of ideas with anti-Western Islamists. Again, the question of which so-called moderate Muslims to engage is critical.

The European socialists who received support from others in the Western community fundamentally supported, and were loyal to, their respective governments, though they clashed over certain of their policies. Similarly, the Muslims who might be empowered in the current battle for hearts and minds are those who feel they are citizens in their countries, with affirmative responsibilities as well as rights, and who support European values notwithstanding sharp disagreement over specific domestic and foreign policies. Some groups, however, may simply be pursuing long-term goals that are inconsistent with the future of the liberal democratic state system in Europe.

Non-Muslim Elites Begin to React

There is a new phenomenon in British intellectual life. Among the majority, non-Muslim community, there appears to be an increasing willingness to assert and promote "Britishness," a British version of the national aspirations associated with the "American dream." A more coherent British identity would make it easier for immigrants to become British and understand their obligations as British citizens. *Standpoint* magazine was launched in 2008 to celebrate, debate, and articulate Western values, albeit in an inclusive way intended to engage non-Western British citizens. Such measures appear to be early signs of pushback against assertive Islamism. Some Europeans are beginning to question the reflexive moral relativism of a hyper-secularized society where people are reluctant to assert that some values are better than others. There is, arguably, a general, increasing recognition that the liberal values of toleration, equal opportunity, and gender equality are superior to those value systems that promote intolerance and the subordination of women to men.

KFOR (Armend Aqifi)

Portuguese KFOR soldiers patrol in Mitrovica, April 2008

Convergence between Multiculturalism and Assimilation

Countries such as Britain, Germany, and the Netherlands were steeped in multiculturalism and respect for cultural autonomy among ethnic and religious groups. They are, however, slowly moving in the general direction of a French-style state-derived identity. Meanwhile, under President Nicolas Sarkozy, the French are backing off from a rigid assimilation model by recognizing distinctions among their religious and ethnic communities, albeit as a means of targeting deprived ethnic communities in order to further their upward mobility and integration into the French system.

Europe is likely to pursue a multipronged, sometimes contradictory policy of reaching out to the moderate elements in Muslim communities, beefing up community policing and counterterrorist

surveillance, clamping down on immigration from countries outside the EU with large Muslim populations (for example, ones in South Asia, the Middle East, North Africa, and perhaps Southeast Asia), and thinking harder about what it means to be British, Danish, or Dutch, so that immigrants can have a better idea of what social norms they are expected to accept.

Meanwhile, long-term demographic trends loom over the entire integration and social cohesion and radicalization issue. As indigenous European birthrates plunge and Muslim families remain larger than non-Muslim families among the second and third generations, it may be crucial for societies to find a way to encourage Muslim women to avail themselves of educational opportunities and join the workforce. Statistics show that the birthrates of educated working Muslim women will converge with the lower birthrates of indigenous Europeans. The rates for stay-at-home Muslim mothers without higher education will not.[9]

A vocal minority of political Islamists in a Europe that is 5 percent Muslim would seem a manageable challenge.[10] Presently, the offspring of non-Muslim immigrants tend to intermarry, become secular, and have fewer children than the offspring of Muslim immigrants, who tend to marry within their own ethnic group, remain religious, and have several children.[11] If demographic trends continue, we are looking at a Europe in 2050 where one out of every three children under the age of 15 is Muslim.[12] Security officials worry that the demographic preponderance of Muslims in cities and towns across Europe would make it far more difficult to counter the separatist agendas of Islamists and the cultural penetration of sharia law. The long-term prognosis for terrorism in Europe would seem to depend on the ability of governments to empower Muslim counter-Islamists with a narrative that is convincing for the next and much larger generation of European Muslims. **gsa**

NOTES

[1] "International Security Assistance Force Fact Sheet," available at <www.nato.int/isaf/docu/epub/pdf/isaf_place-mat.pdf>. NATO figures are current as of February 13, 2009. NATO Ally Canada and non-NATO member Australia provide an additional 2,830 and 1,090 troops, respectively, to ISAF. The United States contributes approximately 25,000 military personnel to ISAF and 13,000 to Operation *Enduring Freedom*. In February 2009, President Obama

authorized the deployment of an additional 17,000 U.S. military personnel to Afghanistan.

[2] For an explanation of "Berlin Plus" arrangements, see NATO Web site at <www.nato.int/issues/nato-eu/evolution.html>.

[3] Nick Witney, "Re-energizing Europe's Security and Defence Policy," European Council of Foreign Relations, July 29, 2008, available at < www.ecfr.eu/content/entry/european_security_and_defence_policy>.

[4] For a survey of current French defense issues, see Leo G. Michel, *Defense Transformation* à la française *and U.S. Interests*, Strategic Forum No. 233 (Washington, DC: National Defense University Press, September 2008).

[5] The Stabilization and Association Agreement process establishes special political and trade relations between the EU and Western Balkans countries with a view toward promoting democratic reform and economic development in those countries and their eventual accession to the European Union.

[6] UK Home Office Guide, "The Prevent Strategy: A Guide for Local Partners in England: Stopping People becoming or supporting terrorists and violent extremists," and a shorter companion guide, "Preventing Violent Extremism: A Strategy for Delivery," both issued in May 2008.

[7] The Research, Information, and Communications Unit is a cross-governmental strategic communications resource on counterterrorism set up in 2007 and located within the Home Office.

[8] Some argue that engaging political Islamists even on a tactical basis does not make sense. See Melanie Phillips, "This country is so pro-Muslim it is giving succor to the extremists who would destroy us," *Daily Mail*, July 8, 2008, available at <www.dailymail.co.uk/news/article-1033189/This-country-pro-Muslim-giving-succour-extremists-destroy-us.html>.

[9] Kirk Scott and Maria Stanfors, "Fertility of the Second Generation: Do children of immigrants adjust fertility to host country norms?" Lund University, Sweden, 3, available at <http://epc2008.princeton.edu/download.aspx?submissionId=80047>.

[10] Currently, the number of Muslims in Western European countries ranges from 1 percent in Spain to several countries in the 3 to 5 percent range to over 8 percent in France. See B. Marechal, *A Guidebook on Islam and Muslims in the Wide Contemporary Europe* (Louvain-la-Neuve: Academia Bruylant, 2002).

[11] Eric Kaufmann, "Eurabia? The Foreign Policy Implications of West Europe's Religious Composition in 2025 and Beyond," paper presented at the International Studies Association Conference, San Francisco, CA, March 26, 2008, 13, 16.

[12] Anne Goujon et al., "New Times, Old Beliefs: Projecting the Future Size of Religions in Austria," in *Vienna Yearbook of Population Research 2007*, available at <www.oeaw.ac.at/vid/publications/VYPR2007/Yearbook2007_Goujon-et-al_pp237-270.pdf>.

Contributors

Leo G. Michel (Chapter Editor) is a Senior Research Fellow in the Institute for National Strategic Studies (INSS) at National Defense University (NDU). Mr. Michel's work focuses on transatlantic defense and security issues. Before joining INSS in July 2002, he was Director for North Atlantic Treaty Organization Policy in the Office of the Secretary of Defense.

Dr. Henri J. Barkey is the Bernard L. and Bertha F. Cohen Professor and Chair of the International Relations Department at Lehigh University. He is also a nonresident senior associate in the Carnegie Endowment for International Peace Middle East Program. He has authored, co-authored, and edited five books, among them *Reluctant Neighbor: Turkey's Role in the Middle East* (U.S. Institute of Peace Press, 1997), *Turkey's Kurdish Question* (Rowman and Littlefield, 1998), and *European Responses to Globalization: Resistance, Adaptation and Alternatives* (JAI Press, 2006).

Dr. Margaret McCown is Associate Research Fellow in the Center for Applied Strategic Learning at NDU. She was previously a Fellow at the Max Planck Institute for Research in Collective Goods. Dr. McCown writes on European law and politics and on policy simulations.

Jonathan S. Paris is a London-based political analyst and former Fellow at the Council on Foreign Relations. He is currently an Adjunct Fellow at the Hudson Institute, a Fellow at the University of Buckingham Centre for Security and Intelligence Studies, and an Associate Fellow in the International Centre for the Study of Radicalization at King's College London.

Dr. Simon Serfaty holds the Zbigniew Brzezinski Chair in Global Security and Geostrategy at the Center for Strategic and International Studies, where he previously served as Director of the Europe Program. He is also Professor and Eminent Scholar in U.S. foreign policy at Old Dominion University. His most recent book is *Architects of Delusion: Europe, America, and the Iraq War* (University of Pennsylvania Press, 2007).

Chapter 14
Africa

The Seven Africas

Africa's challenges and opportunities are as diverse as the continent itself. Africa is perhaps better considered as a series of subregions, including the following seven: North Africa, the Sahel, West Africa, Central Africa, the Great Lakes region, East Africa, and Southern Africa. Africa's many conflicts tend to be local and entrenched, but the Horn of Africa and Sudan pose particular security challenges in the next 5 to 10 years. For the United States, a clear understanding of history may help to overcome the temptation to react to superficial events rather than to deal with underlying problems and long-term solutions. Enduring challenges such as fragile institutions and poverty have rich but different histories, geography, and identities. Both conflict and opportunities abound, but the United States is only one of the external actors and not equally active or welcome in all areas.

North Africa

North Africa's five countries have similarities, but each is also distinct. The three countries classically referred to as the Maghreb (Morocco, Algeria, and Tunisia)[1] retain a French orientation. In this region, the United States is mostly seen as a potential market (or, in the case of Algeria, a real market) for raw materials and primary industries and, in the case of Morocco, as an ally.[2] The governments of all three Francophone Maghrebi states—but particularly Algeria—are challenged by radical Islamist movements of differing intensity; the so-called al Qaeda Orga-

Djiboutians gather for opening of new well

nization in the Land of the Berbers (established in 2005 by the now-deceased Abu Mussab al-Zarqawi) attempts to address them all, working through and with a variety of front or allied extremist groups. Nonetheless, there is a range of homegrown Islamist movements, some political and nonviolent, and some radical, that challenge the countries' leaders.

Algeria has promoted the removal of Western Sahara from Moroccan sovereignty since the Spanish colonial occupiers ceded it back to Morocco in February 1976. Algeria's sponsorship of the armed movement known as POLISARIO (*Frente Popular para la Liberación de Saguia El-Hamra y Rio de Oro*, or Popular Front for the Liberation of Saguia el-Hamra and Río de Oro), which has claimed the right to self-determination of the territory, continues to be a flashpoint between Algeria and Morocco. Despite the size difference between Algeria and Morocco, the latter has historically fared well in military engagements with Algeria. As a result, an ongoing military buildup by Algeria must be viewed with concern.

Libya is closer than ever to change. Its leader, Muammar Qadhafi, is aging and Libyan institutions remain frail. The country's export wealth from oil has risen, and foreign investment in new oilfields has been offset to some degree by failure to sufficiently maintain older infrastructure. In recent years, Libya has opened up considerably, especially as the international isolation that followed the bombing of Pan Am flight 103 over Lockerbie, Scotland, in 1988 is coming to an end. But the urgent reality is the growing immobility of Qadhafi and the belief that his reign may be drawing to a close, without adequate provision for succession. Qadhafi has said that one of his sons, Saif al-Islam, would succeed him. However, neither Qadhafi nor his immediate entourage will give Saif al-Islam visible support, leading to speculation that the immediate post-Qadhafi era could be marked by a strenuous power struggle.

Several groups oppose Qadhafi, including the moderate Senussi Muslim movement—the *Sanussiyyah*—centered on the Cyrenaica region of Eastern Libya, and generally supportive of a restoration of the Senussi monarchy. The Senussi movement is the diametric opposite of the Wahhabist movement in that the Senussi is tolerant, liberal, and modernizing. However, there are also radical Islamists in the Wahhabist or Salafist mold functioning as an active opposition in Libya. Stability in Libya will be a key element in ensuring the modernization of North Africa and its incorporation into the Mediterranean trading basin.

Egypt, Libya's neighbor, also faces the question of leadership succession. President Hosni Mubarak turned 80 in May 2008. One of the President's son's, Gamal, appears to be in line for succession, as suggested by his movement through the ranks of the National Democratic Party. But it is not clear whether such a succession would be challenged and, indeed, whether Gamal Mubarak would have the public, military, and political support necessary to address the challenges that could come from a presently constrained opposition movement. Certainly, there is a vibrant opposition, much of it radical and religious.

Egypt's political and cultural dominance of much of the Middle East, North Africa, and to a lesser degree of Africa as a whole means that the Egyptian succession process is of strategic importance, especially with the added weight given by Egypt's control of the Suez Canal and the Red Sea. Egypt, so dependent on U.S. military and civil support since the Camp David Accords of 1978, has been under a formal state of emergency since the assassination of President Mubarak's predecessor, Anwar Sadat, in 1981. In recent years, however, Egypt has become less politically involved with the United States, and it is possible that the next generation of Egyptian leadership may decide to move still further from a tacit alliance unless the United States undertakes initiatives that prepare for, and preempt, such a shift in Egyptian attitudes.

Sahelian Africa

Extending from Mauritania to Chad (but encroaching culturally on the eastern parts of West Africa and the northern part of Central Africa), the Sahel is an area of transition. Its very name, Sahel, in Arabic means *the shore*, reached after crossing the Sahara. The main foreign influences on the Sahelian states remain France and Morocco, even if the Sahel's most troubled areas (Darfur in western Sudan and northern Nigeria) are now increasingly Muslim in outlook, albeit of African Islamic moderation.

There is a growing concern about potential radicalization in this area because this part of the continent is home to some of the poorest people, institutions are brittle, and the United States has a low profile. The Sahara plays an overriding role, not least because of the southern drift of the Algerian radical Islamist movement and the growing interest of the Wahhabist al Qaeda Organization in the Land of the Berbers movement. Stemming radical Islamist movements is delicate but feasible because they are culturally heterogeneous and generally not welcomed by the African populations to the south. Significantly, Wahhabist and Salafist Islamic groups have contended for influence in this area along with groups sponsored (until 2003) by Saddam Hussein and Qadhafi. Iraqi-sponsored Ba'athists, for example, were behind coup attempts in Mauritania, culminating with the defeat of Ba'athists in the Mauritanian army in 2003, the same year that the prime minister moved to suppress al Qaeda elements that had been trying to establish a base of operation.

U.S. Navy (Jesse B. Awalt)

Muammar Qadhafi was elected chairman of the 12th African Union Summit in Addis Ababa, February 2009

West Africa

West Africa is an area of extreme cultural diversity, where European—specifically, French, Portuguese, and British—influences overlap. It is also an area of extreme economic disparity, where the various economies range from poor (Burkina Faso) to nationally wealthy (Nigeria) with a number of countries (Cam-

eroon, Ghana) aspiring to middle-income status. Nigeria is the natural regional power, but it is a dangerously splintered one, with its northern Sahelian region aspiring to retain the national domination inherited from colonial times and the Biafra War, while the Niger Delta states have been torn apart by a mounting low-intensity conflict. The conflict has its roots in a growing distortion of state-federal relations that have seen the central government take what the Delta states feel is a disproportionately large share of oil and gas export revenues, while neglecting infrastructural and human needs.

The Niger Delta crisis emerged through 2008 as perhaps the single greatest threat to the supply of foreign energy to the United States, Europe, and China. Nigeria's federal government was constrained in dealing effectively with the crisis because legal challenges to the legitimacy of the presidential elections of April 2007 were still being considered by the nation's supreme court. Some analysts estimated that the disruptions and threats to Niger Delta oil and gas production contributed at least 20 percent to the significant rise in oil prices in mid-2008.

Nigeria's leadership in creating the Gulf of Guinea Commission in recent years has attempted to weld some cohesion among the countries along the Western African coast, almost all of which were, or potentially were, energy-producing states. This organization and the Economic Community of West African States (ECOWAS) are key to building effective indigenous institutions that can address the rich diversity represented by the region's states and populations. At the same time, a growing network of energy pipelines is extending through the region, with the vision of ultimately linking South African west coast energy resources with other energy production up the entire Western African coast, and ultimately by undersea pipeline across the Mediterranean to southwestern Europe. In the meantime, the pipeline network is a building block for regional modernization and economic growth.

Central Africa

The heart of the continent, Central Africa, hinges on the Democratic Republic of the Congo (DRC), a country still rebuilding from more than three decades of rule by President Mobuto Sese Seko. This was followed by "Africa's First World War" (1998–2003), the deadliest conflict in the world since World War II that left almost 4 million dead. Beyond the DRC, the region includes parts of West Africa (the Gabon, most of the Republic of

Congo–Brazzaville), as well as northern Angola and western Zambia.

This is a totally underdeveloped area of immense potential wealth. Blessed with a low population-to-resources ratio, Central Africa is perhaps the richest part of the whole continent and, if well governed, could aspire to middle-income status. The DRC, which was once approaching this level of development, has today the lowest per capita income on the continent.

Significantly, the linkage between the DRC with the neighboring Great Lakes state, Rwanda, is largely through ethnic and clan relationships, which is why substantial numbers of Hutu Rwandans—and much of the Hutu *Interahamwe* militia—fled to the DRC following the Rwandan civil war of 1994. This linkage also accounts for the profound influence that Rwandan President Paul Kagame has over the DRC government—and much of the territory of the DRC. It is not coincidental that both the DRC and Rwanda were controlled as a colony (the Belgian Congo) and League of Nations mandate protectorate (Rwanda) by Belgium. Both territories shared not only some ethnic and cultural overlap, but also a common, and searing, experience under Belgian control until less than a half-century ago.

The Great Lakes

The Great Lakes region is made up of only two full-fledged countries—Rwanda and Burundi—but also comprises regions of others (eastern DRC, western Uganda, and western Tanzania). This is a densely populated mountainous region (approximate to those of the Netherlands or the Asian great river deltas), and overpopulation is perhaps the main problem. The genocidal cycles that the region has periodically suffered since 1959 have been attributed in many ways to an intensive but traditional agriculture, which finds it difficult to support a rapidly expanding population. This theory, however, has been strongly contested, with other theorists pointing to the Belgian occupiers' predilection for favoring the promotion of the Hutu people over the traditionally ruling Tutsi. Although sharing a common language (Kinyarwanda), religion (Roman Catholicism), and culture, the Tutsi have Nilotic ethnic origins (from the Hamitic regions around southern Ethiopia) while the Hutu have Bantu origins (from southern Africa). The whole region remains extremely explosive, and the war provoked by the flight of Hutu militia from Rwanda into the DRC is still simmering in the Eastern Congo, with or without Rwandan involvement.

The "peace agreement" that began to take effect in

Burundi with elections in 2005 remains extremely fragile because it rests on the capacity of a stagnant agricultural economy to integrate thousands of disenfranchised Hutu who expect miracles from the new dispensation. Rwanda itself remains delicately balanced, despite recent economic growth, given the Tutsi-led government of President Kagame's successful presentation of itself to the international community as inclusive, balanced, and democratic. Kagame, however, retains a strong grip on the internal security

U.S. Air Force (Nathan Lipscomb)

Nigerian air force brigadier general, chairman of Africa Endeavor 2008 planning committee, explains objectives of U.S. European Command–sponsored exercise to U.S. Embassy Nigeria Chief of Mission

situation, especially in light of the 1994 genocide that failed to stop the Tutsi from seizing back the power the Belgians had taken from them and given to the Hutu. The spillover potential of the as-yet-unresolved conflict—particularly the eastern DRC component of it—remains significant. In spite of its small area, the Great Lakes region has roughly 40 million inhabitants, vastly more than the 14 million affected by the Chad/Darfur conflict in North Africa. The United States has barely begun to understand and address the Great Lakes region, although the appointment of an experienced Africa-oriented U.S. Ambassador to Rwanda in late 2008 upgraded Washington's focus on the region.

East Africa

East Africa is one the most culturally coherent areas of the continent, both because of the relative closeness of the precolonial cultures and because the whole region received a strong British imprint during the colonial period. The core area is constituted by the three countries of the former British East Africa—Uganda, Kenya, and Tanzania—but the socioeconomic coherence of the region extends to Malawi and to large parts of Zambia. This is an area of relative political equilibrium since Uganda grew out of civil war 20 years ago. The residual violence in northern Uganda is now more Sudan-related than homegrown.

The whole region is slowly moving toward a middle-income position, provided it can avoid political backsliding (as in Kenya recently, or in Uganda potentially the day President Yoweri Museveni departs). But there are no structural causes making political strife probable, other than the ethnic differences, such as those that rose to the surface during the 2008 Kenyan elections. Ethnic and religious differences remain the subtext for politics in Kenya, in particular.

This is an area of relative democratic governance, with a strong potential for more given the importance of the civil society. This is also the part of the continent that has perhaps the most positive view of the United States.

Southern Africa

Southern Africa comprises two former Portuguese colonies, Angola and Mozambique, along with the former British colonies—Botswana, Zambia, Zimbabwe, Namibia, Lesotho, and the Republic of South Africa—and the former British Protectorate, the Kingdom of Swaziland.

Southern Africa is in many respects the most economically developed part of the continent, with additional vital geographic significance, given its domination of the Cape of Good Hope. South Africa's gross national product equals that of the whole of the other sub-Saharan Africa states. In South Africa, the key may be managing economic growth among the black population without disenfranchising the whites. This will require sustaining relative stability and strong economic discipline—and therefore foreign investor confidence—following the country's second leadership transition since the end of apartheid rule in 1994.

In Angola, the challenge is how to distribute nationally the growing oil wealth presently concentrated in the hands of a culturally marginal minority of coastal white, half-caste, and black *assimilados*, whose victory in 2002 over the National Union for the Total Independence of Angola—after three decades of civil war—gave unchecked power to the

Popular Movement for the Liberation of Angola government of President José Eduardo dos Santos.

The political, economic, and social outlook for Zimbabwe remained unpredictable at the end of 2008, given the reluctance of Zimbabwe African National Union–Patriotic Front leader and President Robert Mugabe to relinquish real power in the face of national elections. As of late 2008, Mugabe was continuing to flout a power-sharing agreement that kept him in the presidency, but which brought Morgan Tsvangarai to the Prime Ministership; Mugabe's unilateral appointments, including of a second vice president, met no immediate, effective opposition.

Quite apart from poor governance and human misery, the problems of Zimbabwe are not restricted to that country alone. The country's prevalence of HIV/AIDS, unchecked through years of national isolation, has spawned a virulent and (as yet) incurable form of tuberculosis that has the potential for broad international transmission. With some 2 million Zimbabwean refugees already living in difficult conditions in South Africa, many just outside Cape Town, the trouble has already begun to spread and can only get worse if stability in Zimbabwe is not created to avert further outflows of refugees.

Unaddressed, and pointedly ignored by the great power of the region, South Africa, has been the protracted issue of the restoration of Swaziland's stolen territories. A significant part of Swaziland's territories were apportioned out to Mozambique (then a Portuguese colony) and South Africa (then a British colony) by the United Kingdom, acting in its capacity as the invited Protector of the Kingdom of Swaziland.

America's Security Role: The Horn of Africa

The Horn of Africa, stretching from North to East Africa, is arguably the area of greatest security engagement for the United States. There are at least three broad, interlocking sets of problems in the Horn:

■ security and economic growth in Ethiopia, Eritrea, Somalia, Somaliland, and Kenya

■ political, ethnic, and religious developments, which are critical for stability and moderation in the greater Middle East

■ maritime security in the Red Sea and Suez sealanes, which increasingly link the affairs of Horn states with those of the Middle East (Yemen, Saudi Arabia, Israel, and Iran) and Indian Ocean area (India, Pakistan, Malaysia, and Australia).

While U.S. engagement in the complex affairs of the Horn of Africa has deepened in recent years, it is far from new. During the 1970s, authoritarian socialist governments with close links to the Soviet Union ruled Ethiopia and Somalia. Previously close relations with the West, including the United States, had largely dissipated. Human rights abuses were flagrant, and the economies, plagued by Soviet-state socialism and civil war, fell into disarray. Both countries concluded military cooperation agreements with the Soviet Union, including hundreds of Soviet and Soviet bloc advisors and massive amounts of Soviet weapons. Particularly in Somalia, as did the United States before, Soviet aircraft and naval vessels had virtual sovereign use of vital airfields and port facilities. Operating out of Somalia, the Soviet Union posed a serious threat to U.S. alliances—and shipping—in the Persian Gulf, Indian Ocean, and Red Sea, including the southern approach to the Suez Canal. The Horn of Africa thus had become a significant zone of East-West confrontation.

Somalia

Suddenly, in October 1977, Somalia leader Siad Barre sent his army to "liberate" the large ethnic Somali Ogaden region of Ethiopia. Moscow swiftly stopped all military assistance to Somalia, withdrew its advisors, and poured weapons and advisors into Ethiopia. What became a major Soviet presence in Ethiopia began when the Carter administration withdrew its support for Emperor Haile Selassie I, who was overthrown by army major Mengistu Haile Mariam; when denied U.S. support, Mengistu allied himself with the Soviet Union. Soviet help for Mengistu included several well-trained, heavily armed brigades of the Cuban army. The Somalis were quickly routed by the Soviet-backed Ethiopian forces, and Siad Barre turned to America for help. Only too happy to counter growing Soviet influence in the Indian Ocean region, the United States provided considerable military and economic assistance. The U.S. Navy began using Somali airfields and ports, particularly at Berbera in the former area of British Somaliland, which, with the collapse of the Siad Barre government, withdrew from the Somalia union of 1960 and later reasserted its independence as the Republic of Somaliland in 1991. Despite U.S. assistance, Siad Barre's autocratic rule had led by 1990 to widespread dissatisfaction and civil war, resulting in his ouster in 1991. A prolonged drought in the late 1980s plus the depredation of the continuing war resulted in famine. Some 500,000 people had died by

mid-1991, generating pressure for outside intervention when the feuding Somali warlords disrupted food deliveries by the United Nations (UN) and the International Committee of the Red Cross.

Civil war among Somali-based militants was accompanied by a drought that caused some 400,000 deaths by the summer of 1992. UN efforts to end the civil war so that humanitarian assistance could be delivered had failed. President George H.W. Bush, with the approval of the UN Security Council, organized an international coalition of some 30,000 troops in a unified task force under the command and control of the United States. It began operations in December 1992. By March 1993, humanitarian assistance was flowing freely, and the country was stable enough for a new force (United Nations Operation in Somalia II or UNOSOM II) to replace the unified task force. But, once again, the UN effort failed. It became embroiled in a renewed Somali civil war and suffered serious casualties. In an effort to support UNOSOM II—and the prestige of the United Nations—President Bill Clinton dispatched Task Force Ranger, a unit of special operations forces, to neutralize the most powerful of the militias involved in the conflict led by Mohamed Farrah Aidid. However, U.S. forces were taken by surprise and lost 18 men in the first Battle of Mogadishu. Pakistani and Nigerian units lost substantially more troops in the engagement, and the Pakistani forces were vital in helping recover U.S. personnel. Under pressure from an enraged Congress, President Clinton ordered the withdrawal of all U.S. forces. Without U.S. support on the ground, an attempt by UNOSOM II to continue operations came to an end by March of 1994. The Somali civil war continued and, over time, an Islamist movement emerged as the most probable actor for ending the violence.

After the September 11, 2001, terrorist attacks, the United States feared that al Qaeda and Taliban remnants could find sanctuary in Somalia following their defeat in Afghanistan. It established multinational naval and air patrols to prevent such an incursion and created Combined Joint Task Force–Horn of Africa (CJTF–HOA). Based in Djibouti, CJTF-HOA was designed to carry out political, military, and economic activities—particularly in Ethiopia and Kenya—aimed at combating terrorism and strengthening the capacity of regional governments and the well-being of their populations.

In Somalia, by late 2005, the United States had become afraid that an indigenous politico-religious movement—the Islamic Courts Union (ICU)—was gaining strength and could pose a serious terrorist threat, collaborating with al Qaeda. Like the Taliban in Afghanistan, its initial apparent success in ending widespread clan-based violence and crime, buttressed by its religious zeal, garnered substantial popular support. By the fall of 2006, ICU militias were threatening to overrun the Somali Transitional Federal Government (TFG). Although recognized by the UN, the TFG was too weak to enter Mogadishu. The ICU was also threatening to move into the Ogaden region of Ethiopia where ethnic Somali guerrillas were already active. This caused the Ethiopian army—supported with considerable U.S. assistance including two airstrikes—to move into Somalia. Once it had done so, it quickly routed the ICU militias whose remnants were pushed into the region near the Kenyan border. The TFG was reestablished in Mogadishu but had almost no authority and was dependent on the Ethiopian army, which was itself under almost daily harassment by ICU remnants and other disgruntled Somalis.

U.S. Air Force (Stan Parker)

General William Ward, USA, Commander, U.S. Africa Command, speaks at change of command ceremony for Combined Joint Task Force–Horn of Africa at Camp Lemonier, Djibouti, February 2009

Although weakened by the actions of some 40,000 Ethiopian military forces, Somali Islamist radicals, strengthened by a growing upsurge of an anti-Ethiopian insurgency, retained a capability to regroup and rearm should Ethiopian forces withdraw, or should they be able to circumvent efforts to prevent them from receiving external assistance.

Attempts by the international community to resolve the serious problems of Somalia came to naught. Following a United Nations-brokered peace, Ethiopian forces withdrew from Somalia in January 2009. In the same month a moderate Islamist, Sheik Sharif Sheik Ahmed, was installed as President. As of June 2009, fierce fighting continued between the government and Islamist groups opposed to it, which has resulted in a significant number of casualties and displaced persons especially in and around Mogadishu.

In late 2008, towns outside the capital were still falling to the ICU. Significantly, the ICU has received significant financial and weapons support from the Eritrean government in a bid to weaken Ethiopia, and various Somali officials, particularly the president, have benefited financially and in other terms from support from Yemen. Given the president's background as the former warlord of Puntland, this has boosted armed attacks on the pro–Western Republic of Somaliland, which has worked closely with the United States and United Kingdom on counter-terrorism issues.

Ethiopia

Ethiopia has been wracked by civil war. In 1990, two allied secessionist movements rapidly gained strength, one band in Eritrea, and one in the Tigray Province of Ethiopia. By May 1991, Ethiopia leader Mengistu Haile Mariam had fled the country, and the Tigray People's Liberation Front leader, Meles Zenawi, found himself, with significant Eritrean People's Liberation Front (EPLF) military support, in the Ethiopian capital, Addis Ababa. The United States, at this time preoccupied with the collapse of the Soviet Union, essentially sanctioned Meles' seizing control of Ethiopia, even though his secessionist war had been fought to wrest Tigray away from Amhara-dominated Ethiopia. Meles, however, had been allied with the EPLF leader, Isaias Afwerki, and, with the support of the former, as a result of a 1993 UN-monitored referendum, Eritrea split from Ethiopia to become an independent state.

Following Eritrea's independence, the two countries, led by erstwhile allies, enjoyed an amicable relationship. However, relations began to sour, bilateral attempts at policy coordination and economic cooperation faltered, and border incidents recurred in 1997. The failure of the two governments to bridge their policy differences, defuse their simmering tensions, and resolve the underlying causes of their deteriorating bilateral relations led to full-scale war by June 1998. Demanding a return to the status quo ante, Ethiopia declared war on May 13, 1998, and abandoned its use of Eritrea's ports. A joint U.S.-Rwandan initiative and an Organization of African Unity (OAU) attempt failed to prevent further escalation. The war was joined and unfolded in three intermittent rounds: June-July 1998, February 1999, and May-June 2000.

Persistent efforts by the United States, the OAU, and the United Nations succeeded in brokering the Algiers Agreements, namely the Agreement on Cessation of Hostilities of June 18, 2000, and the Comprehensive Peace Agreement of December 12, 2000. The war ended. The peace accord provided, among other things, the establishment of a neutral body, the Eritrea-Ethiopia Boundary Commission (EEBC), with the mandate to delimit and demarcate the colonial treaty border based on the pertinent colonial treaties (1900, 1902, and 1908) and applicable international law.

The two governments agreed that the decision was to be final and binding. The peace agreement was guaranteed by the United Nations and the OAU. The Boundary Commission issued its delimitation decision on April 13, 2002. Contravening the terms of the agreement, Ethiopia refused to unconditionally accept the boundary commission's decision and withdraw its forces from territories awarded to Eritrea. Ethiopia obstructed the physical demarcation of the boundary, thereby impeding the full implementation of the Algiers Agreements and causing the long impasse of neither peace nor war between the two countries.

After 4 years of fruitless effort (from April 2002 to November 2006, during which attempts to demarcate a land boundary floundered over Ethiopia's refusal to cooperate and scant support from the UN Security Council), the Boundary Commission issued a deadline. In November 2006, the EEBC gave the parties 1 year in which to erect or allow it to erect the pillars on the boundary, failing which it would demarcate by coordinates. At the end of the deadline, November 26, 2007, the EEBC declared that the boundary stood demarcated in accordance with the coordinates and reaffirmed that the delimitation decision of April 2002 and the demarcation by coordinates were legally binding on the parties per the Algiers treaty.

Subsequently, the mandate of the United Nations Mission in Ethiopia and Eritrea was terminated July 31, 2008, and the Boundary Commission has ended its operations, as stated in its 27th and final report submitted by the UN Secretary General to the UN Security Council on October 2, 2008. It remains for the Security Council to endorse the EEBC's virtual demarcation, catalyze physical demarcation, and facilitate reconciliation between Eritrea and Ethiopia.

The war caused enormous destruction of property, huge loss of human life, and hundreds of thousands of internally displaced people, and entailed a significant lost opportunity for development on both sides. The Eritrean and Ethiopian economies and peoples have suffered as their governments pursue the politics of a zero-sum game in futile efforts to undo each other, prolong their authoritarian rules, and postpone a durable solution. Furthermore, the unresolved Eritrea-Ethiopia conflict has a pervasive spillover effect; it exerts a negative impact on the internal stability of both countries as well as on regional peace and security in the strategic Horn of Africa, in general, and on the Somali and Sudanese crises, in particular, as both governments operate to undermine each other by supporting each other's domestic and regional opponents.

The resolution of the conflict and the ensuing normalization of bilateral relations and restoration of political and economic cooperation between Eritrea and Ethiopia would not only serve the interests of the two countries and their peoples but also contribute to regional peace and security in the volatile Horn of Africa. The United States must thus consider the benefits of a nuanced regional stance and a balanced policy in the Horn that promotes conflict resolution and peacemaking in accordance with international law; enables it to use its considerable assets to influence events; and promotes democracy, rule of law, and good governance conducive to sustainable development in the region. If stability can be maintained, then there is reason to believe that Ethiopia can increase its role as the great heartland power of the Horn, with some 70 million people, and capacity to increasingly influence the security of the Red Sea and Suez sea lines of communication.

Sudan

In 1989, General Omar Bashir seized power in Khartoum in partnership with radical Islamist leader Hassan al-Turabi. They opened Sudan's doors to Islamist radicals from other countries: Hamas, Abu Nidal, Black September, Hizballah, and the Egyptian organizations, the Islamic Group and Al Jihad (led by Ayman al-Zawahri). In 1992, the Sudanese government gave safe haven with freedom to train, equip, and operate to Osama bin Laden and his al Qaeda organization, which had been expelled from Saudi Arabia. The government also provided large tracts of the best farmland and major construction contracts. In the early

1990s, Al Jihad conducted suicide attacks on senior Egyptian officials in Egypt and other countries. This culminated in an unsuccessful attempt to assassinate Mubarak during his 1994 visit to Ethiopia (Al Jihad later became part of al Qaeda). In December 1992, an al Qaeda *fatwa* was issued in Khartoum calling for worldwide Islamist terrorist activities directed against the United States as well as Saudi Arabia. In January 1993, al Qaeda blew up a hotel in Yemen, which was being used by U.S. forces en route to Somalia. In October 1993, bin Laden claimed responsibility for the "Black Hawk Down" attacks upon U.S. forces in Mogadishu. This was a false claim but it greatly enhanced al Qaeda's stature in some Muslim communities.

In the early years of the 21st century, Ethiopia was no longer supporting oppositionists to the government in Khartoum. However, Eritrea was harboring ethnic separatists from eastern Sudan and a northern Sudanese political organization at odds with President Bashir's Islamist administration in Khartoum. U.S.-backed peace talks between John Garang's Sudanese People's Liberation Army (SPLA) and the Bashir government got under way in 2002, in which the Intergovernmental Authority on Development (IGAD) played an important role. Its members included both Ethiopia and Eritrea. The Comprehensive Peace Agreement between North and South Sudan was completed in January 2005.

The continued confrontation between Ethiopia and Eritrea has had a deleterious impact on developments in Darfur. As a means of pressure to prevent the Khartoum government from establishing closer relations with Ethiopia, Eritrea has provided financial support and weapons to some of the Darfur rebel groups fighting the Sudanese army in collaboration with Libya (and the government of Chad). This is another example of the interlinked web of issues confronting countries in the Horn. At the same time, however, Sudan and Eritrea have worked together on anti-Ethiopian issues, while currently Ethiopia and Sudan are working harmoniously on defining their collective border, which had been unresolved since the British/Egyptian occupation of Sudan ended in the 20th century.

Djibouti

Despite a small, ethnically divided population and threatening neighbors, Djibouti has made surprising progress over the past decade. The longstanding military presence of the French, and more recently of the United States, has provided security and political stability. Other countries have also provided economic

assistance. More importantly, Djibouti's strategic location near the oil-rich countries of the Gulf has provided an economic boom for investors from the Gulf and other countries. The Djibouti government wishes to expand shipping and other facilities connecting the Gulf and the rest of the world. The huge economic benefits have been such that the entire population has benefited, further enhancing stability and attracting more investment.

The presence of CJTF–HOA in Djibouti has succeeded in preventing al Qaeda and other terrorist networks from gaining a major foothold in the Horn as had been feared. Civic action programs and other assistance from the United States, and assistance from other countries such as the United Kingdom and France, has effectively neutralized them. However, all the countries of the Horn—not only the worst case of Somalia—have major internal problems that provide ready kindling for Islamist radicals to start future fires. Obviously, the negative view of the United States in some Islamic communities creates problems, as does the sizeable U.S. assistance to and support for the authoritarian government in Ethiopia, which is all too widely misperceived as a junior partner to a putative anti-Islamist war.

Underlying Trends and Concerns

The United States has historically looked at the Horn of Africa primarily through a strategic lens (for example, the Cold War and the global fight against extremism), with periodic responses to humanitarian crises. Underlying long-term problems of ethnic and religious tensions, tribal and clan differences, governance, and poverty have not been given the same priority. When they have, no nostrums have been discovered. This is also the case for other outside actors that are more concerned with economic and social issues (such as the World Bank and the African Development Bank), as well as regional political organizations such as the African Union and IGAD.

There are also immense and growing problems associated with demography, climate, and water. This is especially true for Ethiopia, because of its large and rapidly growing population, as well as Somalia. The climate is prone to periods of drought and famine. This has combined with efforts—largely ineffectual despite foreign assistance—to modernize agricultural development and with internal conflict to keep domestic food production far below the minimum needs of the population. International food prices have been rising speedily. The United States and other traditional suppliers are no longer able to supply the large amounts of subsidized food needed for the Horn. The major long-term political impact of this situation is self-evident.

In light of the recent past, close attention should be paid to several potentially serious security problems in the Horn of Africa:

■ a renewal of major conflict between Ethiopia and Eritrea, nominally over unresolved territorial issues

■ the continued upsurge of Islamist radicalism in Somalia and potential sanctuary for terrorist networks such as al Qaeda

■ the collapse of the Comprehensive Peace Accord in Sudan (see the essay on Sudan in this chapter), which would have far-reaching consequences on economic development, energy, migratory flows and refugees, and external interference.

Persistent Conflicts

The media perception of Africa is as a continent in conflict, and yet most of Africa is at peace. Where there is insecurity, it is often related to poverty-driven crime, but it is important to note that most external perceptions of Africa are stereotypes that, if they were ever accurate for even parts of the continent, are usually years or even decades out of date.

The reality of Africa is that it has many areas of calm and many areas of real economic and social promise.

This does not mean that the legacies of colonialism, tribalism and ethnicity, language barriers, and the like have been entirely overcome, but African states are moving at different rates toward national identities beyond the postcolonial era. Even so, substantial intrastate and interstate conflicts continue. But there are also mechanisms and institutions for conflict resolution that may support greater stability and peace in the years ahead.

Active or simmering armed conflicts in Africa include the following:

■ the unresolved conflict over the future of the former Spanish Western Sahara, which is now legally part of Morocco

■ the Touareg rebellion on the Algeria/Mali Sahara confines

■ the rebellion in Chad

■ the northern Central African Republic rebellion

■ the Sudanese civil war in Darfur

■ various low-intensity regional guerrilla conflicts in Eritrea, with some directed toward Djibouti

■ the ongoing Eritrean-supported Oromo Liberation Front rebellion in Ethiopia and a number of other ethnic-based insurrections in Ethiopia, including the simmering Ogaden rebellion

U.S. Air Force (Joe Zuccaro)

Villagers wait to see U.S. medical personnel from Combined Joint Task Force–Horn of Africa in Milo, Ethiopia

■ the unresolved border war between Eritrea and Ethiopia, which has substantial potential for resurrection into a major conventional war

■ clan warfare in Somalia (the former Italian Somaliland) internally, and the separate confrontations between Somalia and Somaliland, particularly originating from Puntland

■ the Lord's Resistance Army remnants hovering between southeastern Central African Republic, northeastern Democratic Republic of Congo, southern Sudan, and northern Uganda

■ the Nkunda rebellion in North Kivu (DRC)

■ *Frente de Libertação do Enclave de Cabinda* (Liberation Front of the Enclave of Cabinda) remnants in the Cabinda enclave (Angola)

■ a presently dormant conflict in Côte d'Ivoire, where part of the national territory escapes government control

■ the escalating armed conflict between various groups and the Nigerian federal government in the country's oil- and gas-producing Niger Delta over states' rights and revenue-sharing.

There are of course many other regions where social, cultural, or ethnic unrest lies semi-dormant and could reignite under appropriate conditions. Within this context, at the intersection of the Uganda/Ethiopia/Sudan/Kenya quadri-borders, a cluster of pastoral tribes (mainly the Karimojong, Dessanech, Nyangatom, Toposa, and Turkana) are engaged in recurrent cross-border cattle raiding. In the Lower Congo, the Bundu dia Kongo ethno-religious sect lives in a state of semipermanent political secession from the DRC. And in the Caprivi Strip, the Lozi tribe hopes to (re) create a country (Barotseland) out of various pieces of Zambia, Namibia, and Botswana. All of this unrest matters, but none of it seriously threatens the security of any established state, however weak.

Other areas of political tension exist, but in most of these cases—including, for example, the refusal of the people of the Bakassi Peninsula to allow themselves to be recategorized as Cameroonian citizens while claiming to remain part of Nigeria—armed conflict may well be avoided. In addition, Swaziland's claims to recover territories expropriated during the British Protectorate era and placed under South African and Mozambican control could generate military reactions from the states now controlling former Swazi lands and people.

In some African states, issues of leadership succession remain areas of security concern, although Africa has moved strongly toward democratic processes which have, as their principal value, the orderly transition from one government or leader to the next without causing major disruptions to the processes of building national institutions and economic progress. If it continues, this significant move toward orderly succession of governments—with the support of armed forces, which are becoming increasingly committed to civilian control—will move much of Africa toward greater stability. There remain areas, even beyond North Africa, however, where this process has not yet taken root, and those countries where no plan for constitutional succession processes are in place are states that run the risk of both instability and economic dislocation.

Quite apart from outdated external perceptions of stability and security in Africa, the challenges and conflicts that do arise there are not, in general terms, the same. Each situation has distinct characteristics that require external assistance to be carefully tailored to the local historical and cultural context.

Even so, the overriding problem is that of how modern African states were created and how they have developed. In many instances, African states are both too strong (vis-à-vis their civil society) and too weak (when considering the developmental needs they should tackle). Even Somalia, where the state, having disappeared, cannot be said to be at the heart of the present anarchy, fits within this theory: one of the reasons the state disappeared in Somalia was that the excesses of the Siad Barre administration (1969–1991) contributed not only to its own demise but also to discrediting the very notion of the state in a nomadic, ultra-democratic society that was highly suspicious of the state concept from the outset. There are few African states in which the economy has the significant degree of independence from the state that is evident in most highly developed industrial societies, but a number of African societies are diversifying, becoming more complex and less state-centric.

Weak civil societies, where they continue to exist in Africa, cannot stand up to delinquent and often rogue states. Countries such as Rwanda or Angola had no civil society worth the name, and the state (or the rebels) was enabled to create significant levels of disorder. However, the December 2007 Kenya election resulted in the killing of about 1,500 people, but a powerful civil society was one of the factors that then brought under control a potentially deadly civil conflict. Similarly, whether the situation resulting from the 2008 parliamentary and presidential elections in Zimbabwe will end up in civil war largely depends on the confrontation between the fairly developed Zimbabwean civil society and the Zimbabwe African National Union–Patriotic Front political structures and leaders that continue to retain significant authority, despite the powersharing agreement achieved on September 15, 2008, with Morgan Tsvangirai (as prime minister) of the Movement for Democratic Change. Any dislocation within Zimbabwe is likely to exacerbate the flow of refugees from the country, and particularly into neighboring South Africa.

Borders and Interstate Conflict in Africa

Porous artificial borders, stemming from colonial occupation, are a source of criminal activity and other security challenges. At its creation in 1962, the OAU, seeking to avoid a series of territorial wars in postcolonial Africa, laid down, as a principle, that national borders set by colonial powers should become fixed and agreed upon among the independent states of Africa. This minimized interstate conflict—certainly over borders—for the next half century, but did not eliminate all problems. The AU, which succeeded the OAU as the collective forum for African states in 2002, continued its predecessor's stricture on the maintenance of the former colonial boundaries, but this did not eliminate a series of attempts to redraw the African map.[3]

Conflict Resolution and Stabilization Mechanisms

Although the African Union lacks adequate resources, it has helped to foster a gradual transformation of acceptable norms and good governance in Africa.

Other regional bodies include ECOWAS, founded in 1975, and headquartered in Abuja, Nigeria. ECOWAS functions through a commission, in some respects similar to the European Union (EU).[4] Also like the EU, ECOWAS has a parliament, in which the 15 member states are represented, and which gives the body some executive authority over the region.

There are a range of other regional bodies, such as the Southern Africa Customs Union (SACU), the world's oldest customs union (created in 1889). Since 2002, SACU has had an independent secretariat and a headquarters established in Windhoek, Namibia. Other regional governance bodies include the Gulf of Guinea Commission, which brings together the energy-producing states of the gulf on Africa's west coast. Others include the Community of Sahel-Saharan States (CSSS), formed in 1998; the IGAD in eastern

Africa, created in 1996 to supersede the Intergovernmental Authority on Drought and Development, founded in 1986; the Southern African Development Community, established in 1980; the East African Community, originally founded in 1967 and revived in 2000; the Arab Maghreb Union, formally joined in 1989; the Economic Community of Central African States, established in 1983; the Common Market for Eastern and Southern Africa, formed in 1994; and a range of other specialist cooperative organizations, including one dealing with the interstate sharing of criminal intelligence, for example, and others, such as the West African Monetary Union, which was created in 1994 to promote a common currency.

There are, then, a significant array of mechanisms that enable interstate dialogue and cooperation, and these have led to an effective pattern of cooperation minimizing major conflict on the continent in recent decades.

The growing move by the United States to focus attention on Africa, which gained momentum with the end of the Cold War in 1990, has led to the creation of U.S. Africa Command (USAFRICOM), which effectively stood up as an independent military command in October 2008 and is headquartered in Stuttgart, Germany. USAFRICOM clearly supports the projection and protection of U.S. interests in Africa, but it is unique as a military command in that it works closely with nonmilitary elements of the U.S. Government to project "soft power" approaches[5] designed to help stabilize and build Africa, on which the United States is becoming increasingly dependent for energy.

By 2005, Africa—particularly the Gulf of Guinea states, such as Nigeria—was providing more oil to the United States than the Middle East.[6] America was expected to import as much as 25 percent of its oil and gas from the Gulf of Guinea states by 2015, not only making U.S. interest in the stability of the region of paramount importance, but also adding wealth to the region. What has been significant has been the low percentage of the gross domestic product, which African states, on average, commit to defense spending. In 2007, when global military spending reached an estimated $1.34 trillion, the entire African continent spent only $18.5 billion on defense, with South Africa having the highest defense budget in sub-Saharan Africa.

The role of USAFRICOM is to assist in conflict resolution in Africa, in concert with local governments, and to assist in humanitarian actions, while at the same time helping to improve the professional development of African armed forces. Aside from direct security benefits for the region, this also contributes to continuing the process whereby African militaries gain an increasingly respected place in supporting the framework of democratic governance.

African states have turned more to legal mechanisms than to conflict to resolve interstate differences. A major example was the case in the International Court of Justice in The Hague, which in October 2002 decided the ownership of the disputed 700-square-kilometer oil-rich Bakassi Peninsula between Nigeria, which had run the area historically, and Cameroon. The court decided, after a 10-year court case, in favor of Cameroon. The area was reincorporated into Cameroon on August 14, 2008.

The Bakassi Peninsula example may be one that is followed by Swaziland in pursuing its claims against South Africa for the restoration of Swazi territory occupied by South Africa since that country was a British colony. But there is a difference, in terms of conflict resolution, between African states deciding themselves to pursue internationally binding arbitration and external powers forcing international legal settlements. A case in point was the distortion of the African solution to resolving the Liberian civil war.

Nigeria had lost many of its youth fighting to bring an end to the Liberian civil war and there-fore had no love for Liberian leader Charles Taylor, whose forces had opposed them. Nonetheless, as a means of resolving the conflict, Nigeria offered asylum to Taylor as a means of letting him voluntarily depart Liberia. Taylor accepted, but the United States—having initially urged the asylum option on Nigeria—had now begun to press Nigeria to extradite the infamous Taylor to face International Criminal Court charges. In forcing Nigeria to accept extradition, the option of providing asylum as a means of removing embattled leaders was discredited. It is possible that this affected the decision by Mugabe to fight to retain power in that country, despite having lost the 2008 elections. An African solution had worked in several other cases, including removing the Ethiopian Dergue leader, Mengistu Haile Mariam, in order to minimize the damage caused by civil war. From the vantage point of some in Africa, external interference in a successful mechanism for conflict reduction was unhelpful.

Global Attention to Africa at a Critical Time

Africa's mineral and energy resources have become a major focus for foreign investors during the first decade of the 21st century, a trend likely to continue to expand in importance. The People's Republic of China (PRC) has turned to Africa to meet its rap-

U.S. Navy (Chad R. Erdmann)

USS *Iwo Jima* passes under Mubarak Peace Bridge transiting the Suez Canal, March 2009

idly growing energy needs, and this has contributed significantly to competition for Africa's products. There is little doubt, then, that this competition will place increased pressure on U.S. and European administrations to commit more political, diplomatic, and other resources to ensure the stability—and the friendship—of African states.

High resources prices, not only for oil and gas but also for iron ore and a range of other minerals, gems, and gold, mean that some African states will prosper. Of special importance, however, is the question of whether this will help or hinder balanced national growth, bearing in mind that the oil boom of the 1960s and later in Nigeria effectively took the workforce away from agriculture to seek some of the energy wealth in the cities. This caused the rapid and unplanned growth of cities—with commensurate increases in poverty and violence—while at the same time reducing Nigeria from a net food exporter to an import-dependent nation. A number of African leaders have begun stressing the need for a return to agriculture as a core of national economic success and have begun moves to encourage investment and political and infrastructural support for the primary sector.

The United Nations in 2000 adopted the Millennium Development Goals as a means of creating a focus for reducing poverty by 2015. Critics of this approach, however, have said that these goals risk labeling some African states as "failures," even though they have made strides in achieving, for example, improvements in education in a timeframe that was far shorter than one in which the United States made comparable progress.

Nonetheless, Africa's new centrality as an energy and mineral resource for the world has concentrated a growing level of policy interest in the continent from the industrialized world, which has seen the merit in fighting HIV/AIDS. This attention is likely to increase, with benefits for African economies, particularly as competition for resources grows among the United States, Europe, and China. The PRC has already displaced a number of Western companies for priority in minerals development and in energy projects in Africa, and this competition will become politically significant, both in Africa and in the industrial societies, over the coming decade.

This, in turn, will factor into the costs of energy and raw materials to U.S. and global consumers. The sharp spike in world oil prices in 2008 was partially attributable to unrest in the Niger Delta region, suggesting an urgent need for international support for

conflict resolution and good governance in Africa.

USAFRICOM could well become a critical element in helping to galvanize U.S.-African relations, given that the command is more an instrument for military-led diplomacy than one for power projection. USAFRICOM, in fact, represents a milestone in the American employment of soft power and gives the United States a range of tools between pure diplomacy and force projection, especially given the reality that USAFRICOM can be used to assist African nations in resolving security, emergency response, and national development projects.

Toward Possible Incremental Solutions

The impatience of the international community with Africa has been a major impediment toward progress. Three more long-term approaches that the United States and other countries could take to advance progress would focus on education and diplomacy.

A first step toward a long-term investment in Africa would be to revitalize Africa Studies in universities. The level of knowledge about Africa in the Western world is much lower than it was during colonial times.

A second step toward advancing African development would reverse the current "brain drain" by providing more economic opportunities for African students to work in Africa. Building further African capacity in higher education, including through international partnerships with universities throughout the world, could contribute to this effort.

Thirdly, expanding diplomatic interaction with Africa would upgrade the level of attention paid to Africa and Africa's many problems and opportunities. Clearly diplomacy must avoid reducing Africa to single issues, whether terrorism or energy, and instead help to deal with Africa with all of its diversity.

Sudan and the Threat of Civil War

The forces pulling Sudan apart since its independence from Great Britain in 1956 accelerated over a 3-year period from 2006 to 2008. These trends combined with the growing weakness of central authority have significantly increased the potential for the disintegration of the Sudanese state, which would cause a humanitarian, human rights, political, and security crisis for the Horn of Africa greater than any it has witnessed in the past. Of key importance in this are the Darfur conflict and the deteriorating North-South relationship that are driving the current crisis.

The Darfur Crisis

Three ethnically African Darfur tribes—the Fur, Zaghawa, and Massalit—launched a rebellion against the Sudanese government in early 2003. These tribes rebelled over their brutal treatment by the Arabs who have long dominated the regional government in the province and the poor conditions caused by the underdevelopment of the region by successive central governments. In 2003–2004, the Sudanese government engaged in an "ethnic cleansing" campaign designed to eliminate the base of support for the rebellious tribes, in which they destroyed 2,700 villages, systematically executed any young men who might be potential recruits to the rebellion, and engaged in a campaign of intimidation that degenerated, either deliberately or accidentally, into the systematic mass rape of women and girls.

The ethnic cleansing campaign was carried out by the Sudanese air force (with the help of the Syrian air force) and the Janjaweed militia, a decades-old Arab supremacist movement (known previously as the Arab Gathering) whose aim has been the reclaiming of nomadic grazing areas encroached on by farmers from African tribes. The Arab Gathering was reorganized by the Sudanese government in 2003 after its regular military forces were repeatedly defeated in battles with the rebels. It was the third tribal war Darfur was to suffer in 20 years.

An estimated 250,000 people, most civilian, have died in the civil war that has driven more than 2 million people into internally displaced camps now supported by a massive international humanitarian aid effort run by UN aid agencies and international nongovernmental organizations. Sixty percent of the cost is funded by the U.S. Government. The vast majority of deaths—about 96 percent—occurred during the first 2 years of the rebellion. In 2007 and the first half of 2008, the death rate fell to an average of 100 per month, with the huge drop associated with the influx of international assistance to provide relatively secure camps for the internally displaced.

The Darfur peace agreement signed by one of the two main rebel factions in April 2006 in Abuja, Nigeria, has not brought peace to Darfur as it has not been implemented by the Sudanese government and has not had broad public support. One of the major rebel leaders—Abdul Wahid Nur—did not sign the agreement, has continued to mobilize public opposition to it, and has threatened to kill his own followers who support the agreement or participate in any negotiated peace settlement with the Sudanese government. The peace talks sponsored by the UN and AU in Sirte, Libya, in October 2007 failed because Abdul Wahid Nur, along with other minor rebel leaders, refused to attend, arguing that there needed to be peace and security on the ground before negotiating any peace settlement.

The two original Darfur rebel factions have now atomized into, by some counts, as many as 50 smaller groups with no central command and control, a very tenuous connection between the armed rebel groups and the rebel political leaders, no supply system for provisioning the troops (which means they live off what they steal), and no clear political agenda. Negotiating a political settlement with 50 armed groups with no clear leader would be virtually impossible.

Four neighboring countries—Libya, Chad, Eritrea, and Egypt—along with some others have interests in Darfur, many of which are in conflict with each other. Egypt wishes peace and stability at nearly any price, as they fear the breakup of the Sudanese state or its takeover by radical Islamist forces. Chad is locked in an undeclared war with the Sudanese government driven by internal Zaghawa tribal politics, as President Idriss Deby of Chad is a Zaghawa and is a blood relation of one of the rebel leaders. The Zaghawa provide most of the strongest and most effective rebel military commanders and are most feared by the Sudanese government. Eritrea and Libya have both attempted unsuccessfully to broker (each separately outside the UN or AU negotiations) unification efforts among the rebels and a peace agreement between the Sudanese government and the rebels, as they see their regional prestige and political influence affected by their ability to bring peace. Both have more influence on the ground among the rebel factions than any Western country, the AU, or UN.

Unless the interests of the four regional powers are aligned with each other and with the contestants in the conflict, and the rebel groups have been unified into one chain of command bringing the military and political leadership together, no peace agreement will be possible. It is unlikely the Darfur crisis will be settled in the near or medium term; the best that can be hoped for is to prevent further deaths, stabilize the economic and social systems, and get UN/AU troops approved by the Security Council to increase security.

The authorized strength of the hybrid UN/AU force in Sudan, as set out by the Security Council

▼ Continued on p. 322

Counterterrorism in Africa

Combating terrorism in Africa did not begin on September 11, 2001. It began in the 1990s in Sudan, where Osama bin Laden operated and where an attack against Egyptian President Mubarak was organized.[1] Three years later, in 1998, al Qaeda cells blew up the U.S. Embassies in Nairobi and Dar es Salaam. In retaliation for these attacks, the United States, in addition to an attack in Afghanistan, bombed a chemical plant in Sudan, claiming that it was producing elements for chemical weapons for al Qaeda. From the time of these attacks, moreover, U.S. policy in Somalia became preoccupied with searching out, capturing, and killing the perpetrators of those attacks who were believed to have taken refuge there. More recently, terrorist acts in Europe, particularly the train attack in Spain, have been linked to cells in Morocco, Bosnia, and Algeria, which interact with North African residents in Europe, and both Morocco and Algeria have been victims of recent terrorist bombing attacks. Jihadists returning to these and other African countries from Iraq are considered a serious threat.

Since the September 11 terrorist attacks, the U.S. focus on terrorism in Africa has become much more pronounced. For the first time since 1993, the United States has deployed a sizeable contingent of U.S. troops on the continent, with the establishment in late 2002 of CJTF–HOA. In addition, President Bush announced a $100 million counterterrorism initiative for East Africa and the Horn in 2003. Counterterrorism efforts became even more pronounced in U.S. Africa policy after the Islamic Courts Union took power in Mogadishu in 2006, leading to the Ethiopian invasion of Somalia, with tacit U.S. support, and the current fighting that now consumes that country.

At the same time, U.S. European Command spearheaded a series of training and military support operations in the Sahel, aimed at the Algeria-based Great Lakes Policy Forum; the program later blossomed into the much larger Trans-Sahara Counterterrorism Initiative that now involves both North African and Sahelian states. Most importantly, the Pentagon established USAFRICOM to bring together its varied programs on the continent, a sign of increasing U.S. focus on security in Africa. USAFRICOM will focus on two threats: terrorism and the security of energy supplies primarily from West Africa. As noted below, it also may well have to focus on the drug cartels gaining headway in Africa.

It is clear that Africa is no more immune to the threats from terrorism than any other continent. Its combination of relatively weak states, ethnic and religious diversity and sometimes discrimination, its poverty, and in many places its "ungoverned spaces" all lend Africa a significant susceptibility to the growth of radical and sometimes internationally connected movements that employ terrorism. Some of these are aimed specifically at African governments (for example, the radical Islamic Maitatsine and "Taliban" in Nigeria, or the pseudo-Christian Lord's Resistance Army in northern Uganda); others clearly have a more international agenda (for example, the al Qaeda cells along the east coast of Africa and presumably the North Africans and Sudanese who have returned to their home countries from training and participating in the insurgency in Iraq).

However, while the war on terror usually relates to internationally linked terrorists, Africans face other security threats of equal or greater significance, posing a question of focus for U.S. as well as African counterterrorism efforts. There are several organized rebellions or insurgencies in Africa, while not always classified as terrorists, which wreak terrible havoc on African people and threaten national stability. These include various militias in eastern Congo, who have been the target of the International Criminal Court for their crimes against humanity, the insurgents in the Niger Delta of Nigeria, who have shut down more than 10 percent of Nigeria's oil production, and the Janjaweed militia in the Darfur region of Sudan. It is notable that USAFRICOM lists the Lord's Resistance Army, the Democratic Forces for the Liberation of Rwanda, and the obscure Afrikaner Boeremag in South Africa along with a host of Islamic groups as among the "Terror Groups in Africa."[2] Another problem is the growing use of African countries for transit of drugs to Europe. Guinea-Bissau, a severely poor country in that region, has become a major operational site for Colombian cartels. The link of narcotics and terrorism has been demonstrated in Latin America and could easily take hold in Africa.

African states have responded to this threat in different ways. In West Africa, Sahelian states have welcomed U.S. help in gaining control over their ungoverned spaces but still face unrest from within those territories. Counterterrorism programs in these countries in fact often run counter to efforts to pacify historically restive groups, such as the Taureg, who trade across boundaries and resent increased government security presence. Other countries, such as Kenya and South Africa, facing the growth of Islamic terrorist groups, have struggled to balance the need for new security legislation with the preservation of newly gained civil rights. Some, like Chad and the previous government of Mauritania, have used the terrorist threat to solidify policies of suppression and antidemocratic practices, while solidifying U.S. support for their antiterrorist policies. And at least one, Zimbabwe, has turned the issue on its head, countering U.S. and other international criticism of its antidemocratic practices by labeling its domestic opponents as "terrorists." At the same time, operating in isolation, Zimbabwe has become a major host to terrorist-related Islamist organizations, laundering funds and narcotics.

Two major challenges now loom in the African and U.S. responses to terrorism. Many Africans and some U.S. critics are concerned that USAFRICOM and other U.S. antiterrorism programs signal an increased militarization of U.S. policy in Africa. These critics argue that only a continual intensive attack on the root causes of terrorism and violence—that is, poverty, authoritarianism, discrimination, weak states, and similar conditions—will effectively combat such threats. They contend that a focus that relies too heavily on security will encourage authoritarian practices and undermine Africa's move toward more democratic governance.

A second challenge relates to the continued ability of the Africa Union to provide leadership in conflict resolution and the timely provision of peacekeepers as it has done in recent years in Burundi, Darfur, and Côte d'Ivoire. Following the difficulties that the AU force in Darfur has encountered, the current security crisis in Somalia may have dragged the AU into an untenable situation that could fundamentally undermine the promise of that organization as a force for peacemaking. After promising a force of 8,000 to replace the Ethiopians in Somalia, the AU has mobilized only 2,000 from Uganda and Burundi, a force which has become caught up in the violence. This occurred at the same time that the AU may experience diminishing support from Nigeria—which has historically provided the bulk of African peacekeeping forces—and perhaps South Africa (both distracted by domestic security

U.S. Ambassador to Egypt Margaret Scobey and Admiral Mullen meet with Egyptian minister of defense, Field Marshal Mohammed Hussein Tantawi, in Cairo, April 2009

and political issues), the most influential countries in Africa, as leaders change in those countries.

Fortunately for the United States, most African states share the concern over terrorism and are prepared to cooperate in fighting it for their own safety and security. They are also beset, however, with other priorities and limitations. The United States has the tools to respond broadly, with recent initiatives such as the President's Emergency Plan for AIDS Relief (PEPFAR), the Millennium Challenge Account, and generally rising aid levels. It has skillful diplomats and the ability to call on the United Nations and others to advance complex political solutions, as will surely be needed in the Horn. Keeping these fully engaged along with direct security programs, the partnership with Africa in this area can be advanced and deepened.

NOTES

[1] Arguably, it began much earlier with such incidents as the terrorist assassination—ascribed to Islamists—of Sadat in October 1981, and the uprising of Islamist *Maitatsine* movement from Northern Nigeria, in Lagos in the early 1980s.

[2] Brigadier General Jeffrey Marshall, ARNG, "EUCOM Engagement in Africa," briefing presented to the Conference on AFRICOM at Airlie House, VA, September 23, 2007, 16.

▲ *Continued from p. 320*

in July 2007, is 19,555 military personnel and 6,432 police. The difficulties faced by the force in providing security are underscored by the fact that even by the end of March 2009 the total strength of the force numbered only 15,351 uniformed personnel.

The Current Crisis

The carnage in Darfur has diverted international attention from the revived crisis between the north and the south, which could result in the dissolution of the Sudanese state, bringing with it much worse bloodshed than what Darfur has experienced. Sudan is no longer simply a humanitarian and human rights crisis. Any disintegration of Sudan would open its neighbors to instability, prompt mass population movements across borders, and would likely draw destabilizing forces, which feed off state weakness, or worse, chaos, to the region. At one point in 2007, al Qaeda added Darfur to one of its usual web sites, portraying it as its new battleground with the West, and threatened that if Western troops disguised as UN peacekeeping troops were sent to Darfur, their holy warriors would follow them to do battle.

Comprehensive Peace Agreement

The United States played a central role in initiating the peace process that ended the civil war in 2002, facilitating the negotiations and acting as a guarantor of the agreement along with other countries. The Comprehensive Peace Agreement signed in 2005 ended, albeit temporarily, 22 years of civil war between the north and the south, which claimed the lives of 2.5 million southerners. Many of the easiest provisions of the agreement have been implemented: new governments have been formed in the south and north, nearly $4 billion in oil revenues have been transferred to the southern government's treasury, the northern army has been withdrawn from the south, the economy of the south is beginning to boom, and most importantly, there is no war, and millions of displaced people are beginning to return to their homes in the south.

The north and south came close to war in October and November 2007 over the failure of the north to implement the more transformational provisions of the Comprehensive Peace Agreement, which would threaten the National Congress Party's (NCP's) hold on power. In July 2007, the north essentially rejected several generous compromises proposed by the south, which went beyond the Comprehensive Peace Agreement to resolve the status of Abyei, the disputed oil-rich area between the north and the south and ancestral seat for centuries of the Ngok Dinka kings (the most powerful southern tribe). These events, particularly the Abyei dispute, led to the south's withdrawal in September from the Government of National Unity, established under the Commonwealth Parliamentary Association. Command and control in both the Sudanese armed forces (SAF) and the SPLA are weak, and the potential for a local commander to initiate hostilities without any higher approval remains a grave risk. Omar Bashir and Salva Kiir, the northern and southern leaders, pulled back their sides from

war by mid-December 2007, just in time to avoid a further escalation of the crisis. In late December, the south rejoined the government, after eight of nine Comprehensive Peace Agreement issues were resolved, at least on paper.

An unavoidable flaw in the design of the agreement is that the northern and southern parties to the agreement charged with its implementation are preparing to unseat each other from power in the elections required by the agreement. Originally scheduled to take place in 2009, the elections have been delayed until at least 2010; the stated reason being that more time is required to conclude census work and establish election committees. Those elections could either reduce the pressure building up in the political system and force leaders to address many of the grievances of the people who live on the periphery of the country, or they could cause the dissolution of the country if the NCP attempts to steal the elections or refuses to leave office if they lose, or if the campaigns generate widespread ethnic violence. A political deal between the Nile River Arabs and Southern Sudanese to run in a coalition offers some chance of reducing the risk that the elections will destabilize the country.

Strategy of the National Congress Party

The ruling National Congress Party (NCP) had its roots in the National Islamic Front, the historic Salafist political party in Sudan, which unseated the last democratically elected government of Sudan in a coup in July 1989, in part to stop that government from signing a peace agreement between the north and south. Although the NCP remains an Islamist party, its driving motivation at this point is simply staying in power.

Successive governments of the Nile River Arabs have pursued a policy for 25 years to maintain themselves in power, which has exacerbated the ethnic, racial, and religious divisions in the country. This policy involved four tactics:

■ arming destitute and poorly educated Arab tribes from the rural areas of the west to do the killing, unleashing them first against the south in the 1980s and then more recently against the Darfuris

■ turning one rebel tribe against another by paying it off, arming one against another, promising land and jobs, and spreading disinformation

■ causing massive population displacement of rebel tribes to destroy their way of life, culture, and value system, undermine their traditional tribal leadership, weaken traditional family life, destroy the structure of their economy, and make them more vulnerable to conversion to radical Salafist teaching

■ keeping the fighting away from Khartoum at all costs, and developing the center (where the Nile River Arabs live) of the country at the expense of the periphery (where the rest of the population lives in poverty and underdevelopment).

This strategy worked for 25 years, but it is now rapidly unraveling. Arab tribes allied with the NCP in Khordofan and Darfur have switched sides or stayed neutral. Southern populations displaced by the war are now returning home angry about what the Nile River Arabs have visited on them. Twice now—once upon southern leader John Garang's death in 2005 and again when a large force of well-armed Darfuri rebels (with 200 vehicles) attacked Omdurman, a suburb of Khartoum, in May 2008—Khartoum has seen widespread violence. The war is now moving to the center. And finally, the south itself has been united, however fitfully and incompletely, and its diverse ethnic groups are now directing frustration and anger on the Arabs in the north. The Nile River Arabs know that they are at risk and that the war threatens to consume them as it approaches their center of power.

The NCP has clearly identified its vital interests and is driven by a nearly obsessive survival instinct. It is strongly believed that the leaders of the ruling party would not endanger their own survival or compromise their essential interests no matter how much international pressure is placed on them, unless that pressure itself posed a greater threat to the survival of the administration.

NCP leaders believe there is a conspiracy in the West in general, and in the United States in particular, to destabilize the country, remove them from power, and ultimately facilitate Sudan's breakup as a nation-state. They see—with some logic—the UN/AU hybrid peacekeeping force as a disguised attempt to carry out this strategy. The more aggressively the international community pursues war crime trials and the Western advocacy movement demands justice in Darfur, the greater and more aggressive the NCP resistance will be to the UN/AU peacekeeping force in Darfur.

The Nile River Arabs are growing more paranoid, defensive, and fearful that they will be unable to resist much longer their adversaries in the west and the south. As a result, they are more obstructionist, difficult to deal with, and insecure.

Economic growth in Sudan, driven by rising oil revenues, has in the past provided the NCP and the Nile River Arabs who run it with the revenue to insulate themselves from outside pressure, allowed them to buy off groups within the country that oppose them, ensured the Arabs in the center of the country are prosperous and unemployment low, guaranteed a growth rate of 12 to 14 percent per year, and allowed them to arm themselves and support a massive internal security apparatus that has kept them in power. Despite this revenue, the forces of dissolution are growing more powerful and are causing unease among the prosperous business community in the center. The U.S. economic sanctions regime put in place during the Clinton administration and then increased, expanded, and extended by President Bush in his Executive order of April 2007 makes it illegal for the United States to do business with or use dollars in trade with dozens of commercial enterprises associated with the Sudanese military and security apparatus, which provides their funding outside the regular budgetary processes. This new sanction has caused enough havoc in the banking and financial system of the country that the Sudanese business community has begun pressing the government for a resolution of the crisis and a normalization of relations with the outside world.

Military Balance of Power

Unlike most authoritarian governments, the Sudanese state does not have a monopoly on the use of violence. The Sudanese People's Liberation Army (SPLA) was formed by John Garang when he began his revolt against the Nile River Arabs in 1983, and now has 22 years of combat experience. It has a larger infantry than the Sudanese government's army does. The Comprehensive Peace Agreement specifically allows international assistance in transforming the southern military, which the U.S. Government has been supporting, though this does not include weapons systems.

Two major factors have led to a serious reduction in the combat readiness of the SAF between 2003 and 2006. The first was a major purge of officers and enlisted men in 2005 and 2006. More than a thousand officers and tens of thousands of enlisted men who had been trained in the west or who displayed strong leadership skills were forced into early retirement because these two groups were seen as those most likely to lead a potential coup.

Secondly, in August 2006, the Bashir government embarked on a major military offensive in Darfur that was a major embarrassment. The SAF were roundly defeated in every battle, as they have been since, demoralizing the military even more. The SAF do maintain a monopoly of airpower, though the air force is modest, and its armored units are much stronger than those of the south. The military power of the Sudanese army, particularly their infantry forces, is now substantially diminished.

Fragility of the State

Military vulnerability is not the north's only weakness at this moment. The Nile River Arabs fear that they are losing control of the country. Khartoum in 2007 and 2008 was pervaded by fear of what might happen if war were to break out between the north and south, or the Darfuri rebels were to take Khartoum. When John Garang died in a helicopter crash—under questionable circumstances—in July 2005, many of the several million southern migrants in Khartoum rioted, burning Arabs and looting their businesses, because they believed the accident was a disguised assassination. Some displaced Darfuri men raped Arab women in Khartoum, telling them this was in retaliation for the rape of their wives, sisters, and daughters.

Some northerners now refer to southerners as a cancer on the country and welcome their potential separation, a sentiment that would have been inconceivable in 2005 or 2006 when the unrelenting refrain of NCP leaders was that Western powers were not doing enough to encourage the unity of the country and to discourage southern secession. The risk of widespread retributive violence in the greater Khartoum area is high if the war in the periphery were brought to the center of the country, a risk that should be the focus of any international or bilateral initiatives trying to resolve the crisis.

The NCP has become more repressive when it has sensed internal or outside threats to its survival. The Western strategy of confrontation has not succeeded in producing a solution to the Darfur crisis. The alternative U.S. approach in dealing with Sudan has been a policy of engagement. That policy produced the Comprehensive Peace Agreement, the one forward-looking accomplishment of the Bashir government, and while it has been erratically implemented, it ended the war between the north and south and stabilized the country.

The United States could now consider a renewed push to resolve the tensions and pull Sudan back from the brink of dissolution. Elements of that "grand bargain" could include:

■ a step-by-step normalization of relations between the United States and Sudan in exchange for full implementation of the Comprehensive Peace Agreement by the NCP, free and fair elections, proper execution of the referendum on southern independence in 2011, and full cooperation in the introduction of the remaining UN/AU troops in Darfur

UN and AU leaders meet with rebel leaders before Darfur peace talks, October 2007

■ resolution of the Abyei dispute through a land-for-oil bargain in which the north would agree to the Abyei Commission boundary sought by the south and the north would get a fixed percentage of the revenues of the oil fields there until they are depleted

■ some way of resolving the International Criminal Court insistence on war crimes trials through some internal judicial process controlled by the Sudanese (which, under court protocols, would obviate the authority of the court)

■ a political agreement of the SPLM (the southern political party) to run in a coalition with one or more of the Nile River Arab parties, which would also include some participation by the NCP in the new government without its control over the security apparatus of the country

■ a broadened and accelerated U.S. Government reconstruction program in southern Sudan, which will increase the chances for southern success.

Chinese engineers unload equipment kits upon arrival at Nyala, Sudan, as part of UN–African Union Mission in Darfur

Challenge of African Development

Helping Africa reduce poverty and achieve self-sustaining development is the greatest humanitarian challenge facing the international community and the United States. It is also an important security challenge. Africa's underdevelopment breeds extremism, crime, and disease, which can spread rapidly with globalization.

Excluding the relatively advanced countries of North Africa, where life expectancy exceeds 71 years, the 48 countries comprising sub-Saharan Africa have an average life expectancy of 50 years. It trails all other regions of the world in terms of virtually all poverty indicators. Twenty-seven percent of children under 5 are malnourished and about 41 percent of the population lives on less than a dollar a day. The primary school enrollment rate is 68 percent.

However, in the past few years, annual economic growth in sub-Saharan Africa has exceeded 5 percent. Since 1996, 25 countries have sustained relatively high growth—at least 4 percent annually—and are making some progress in reducing poverty. More than half have reduced child malnutrition and mortality and increased access to clean water, and a few are reducing the spread of HIV/AIDS.

Background

Underlying the region's underdevelopment is anemic long-term economic growth. Between 1960 and 2005, income per capita grew at about one-fifth the average rate for other developing countries (0.5 versus 2.5 percent). Many factors explain this, starting with the colonial legacy. Borders drawn by European colonial powers resulted in a highly fragmented region: 48 generally very small states, including 15 landlocked and 6 island ones. This resulted in small markets and higher intraregional transportation costs than any other region in the world. The colonial powers left little by way of capable institutions and trained Africans.

However, 40 to 50 years after the African nations gained independence, their disappointing performance should not be laid only at the feet of the colonial powers. With numerous coups, conflicts, and poor policies, many governments have struggled to establish stability and legitimate, effective governance. Donors share responsibility, as foreign aid often promoted Cold War or other foreign policy priorities more than development. In the 1980s, for example, Zaire and Somalia were among the U.S. Government's largest aid recipients. Furthermore, donor efforts have not always been well designed or executed, and some approaches, such as support for import substitution, have been discredited. At the same time, external powers have often exerted overwhelming pressures to shape African governance and actions in the postcolonial era.

Key Issues

Low Economic Growth. Without self-sustaining growth, nations will depend on receiving foreign aid or exploiting their natural resources to reduce

UN (Stuart Price)

poverty. While 13 countries in sub-Saharan Africa have achieved middle-income status, 9 others have regressed since 1960. Growth was especially weak during 1974–1995 but has improved. The two countries with the most remarkable turnarounds were Mozambique and Rwanda, which averaged 8.3 and 7.6 percent annual growth rates respectively, during 1996–2005. Their success is attributable to both stability and improved economic policies.

Low levels and productivity of investment—driven by geography, demography, and government policy—have constrained regional economies. Geographic drawbacks include the region's fragmentation, landlocked and island economies, and disease-prone tropical location. High fertility rates have resulted in a larger and younger population. AIDS has decimated the most productive part of the region's population, especially in southern Africa. Bad policy has helped make the cost of doing business higher than in any other region.

While African governments and donors are working in these areas, regional integration, infrastructure, and higher education require more attention. Redrawing borders to reduce fragmentation is off the table, but regional investment should be promoted to gain cross-border economies of scale, such as the West African gas pipeline network. There should also be increased support to subregional intergovernmental organizations, whose institutional capacity is—with some exceptions, such as ECOWAS—weak, for reducing tariff and nontariff barriers to trade and for research in agriculture and other areas of common interest.

Landlocked countries such as Uganda suffer greatly when coastal countries such as Kenya allow their ports, roads, and rail networks to deteriorate. Greater investment is needed in rural and trunk roads, energy, communications, and ports. Except in a few countries supported by the Millennium Challenge Account, U.S. foreign aid for infrastructure has been insignificant in recent years.

To reduce poverty, investing in primary education, especially for girls, is vital. Here, there has been significant support by African governments and donors, including the United States. With the growing youth bulge, more effort is needed for vocational training to increase productive youth employment and lessen susceptibility to recruitment by extremist or criminal elements. More investment is also needed in higher education to build a larger workforce that can take advantage of new technologies to enhance business productivity. The United States has provided little

foreign aid for higher education in the past decade.

Poor Governance. The World Bank assesses governance according to six indicators:

- voice and accountability
- political stability
- government effectiveness
- regulatory quality
- rule of law
- control of corruption.

Judged against these, performance has generally been dismal; only the former Soviet Union scores worse in a majority of indicators. While half of sub-Saharan African countries are oil or mineral exporters, for most this has been a curse. Resource revenues have reduced incentives to promote other areas of the economy (most particularly agriculture), increased volatility of revenues, and enabled leaders

UN (Stuart Price)

UN–African Union Mission in Darfur officials meet with Arab nomads as part of ongoing efforts to consult with all parties and groups affected by the 5-year conflict

to rely less on taxation from their citizens, and consequently, to be less accountable to them.

Lack of accountability has resulted in inappropriate public expenditure; fewer and less effective government services, such as for education and health; and policies favoring narrow interests. It has also led to legendary corruption, which erodes public trust in government. In Transparency International's

▼ *Continued on p. 330*

Countries with the Largest Numbers of Refugees and Internally Displaced

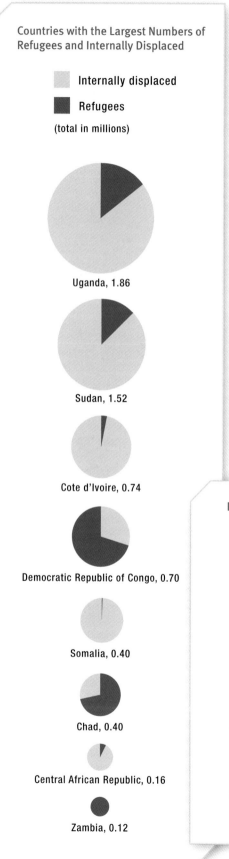

■ Internally displaced

■ Refugees

(total in millions)

Uganda, 1.86

Sudan, 1.52

Cote d'Ivoire, 0.74

Democratic Republic of Congo, 0.70

Somalia, 0.40

Chad, 0.40

Central African Republic, 0.16

Zambia, 0.12

China's Growing Interest In Africa

The United States and the Western European countries have long possessed significant strategic interests in Africa, stemming from its geographic location, valuable resources, historic links, and, since September 11, 2001, its role in the Global War on Terror. But now China, too, perceives a strategic interest in Africa, both as a source of raw materials and a market for manufactured goods. The Chinese have acquired part or majority ownership of oil ventures in Algeria, Angola, Equatorial Guinea, Ethiopia, Libya, Nigeria, and Sudan, and have mining interests in Zambia, Zimbabwe, and the Democratic Republic of the Congo. To promote their objectives, the Chinese have provided favored trading partners with arms, military gear, and military services, causing concern in the United States. Although denying any connection to these Chinese initiatives, the United States is also increasing its military-support activities in Africa, giving the impression of a U.S.-Chinese arms rivalry.

▶ **Recipients of U.S. military aid to Africa include:** *Algeria, Angola, Benin, Botswana, Burkina Faso, Burundi, Cameroon, Cape Verde, Central African Republic, *Chad, Cote d'Ivoire, Democratic Republic of the Congo, Djibouti, Egypt, Ethiopia, Gabon, Gambia, Ghana, Guinea, Guinea-Bissau, Kenya, Lesotho, Liberia, Libya, Madagascar, Malawi, *Mali, *Mauritania, Mauritius, *Morocco, Mozambique, Namibia, *Niger, *Nigeria, Republic of Congo (Brazzaville), Rwanda, Sao Tome e Principe, *Senegal, Sierra Leone, South Africa, Swaziland, Tanzania, Togo, *Tunisia, Uganda, Zambia.

*Member, Trans-Sahara Counter-Terrorism Partnership

▶ **Recipients of Chinese arms sales and military aid to Africa include:** Burkina Faso, Kenya, Niger, Nigeria, Sierra Leone, South Africa, Sudan, Tanzania, Uganda, and Zimbabwe.

Sources: U.S. aid: U.S. Dept. of State, *Congressional Budget Justification for Foreign Operations*, Fiscal Year 2009 (Washington, D.C., 2008). Chinese data: Amnesty International, *People's Republic of China: Sustaining Conflict and Human Rights Abuses: The Flow of Arms Continues* (London, 2006).

Leading Oil Producers in Africa

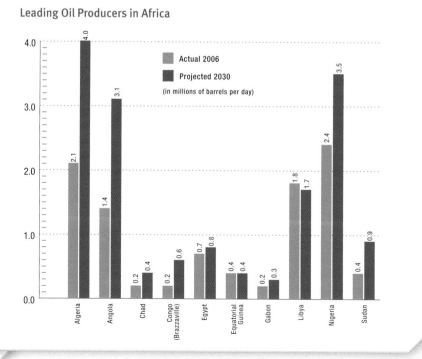

Actual 2006

Projected 2030

(in millions of barrels per day)

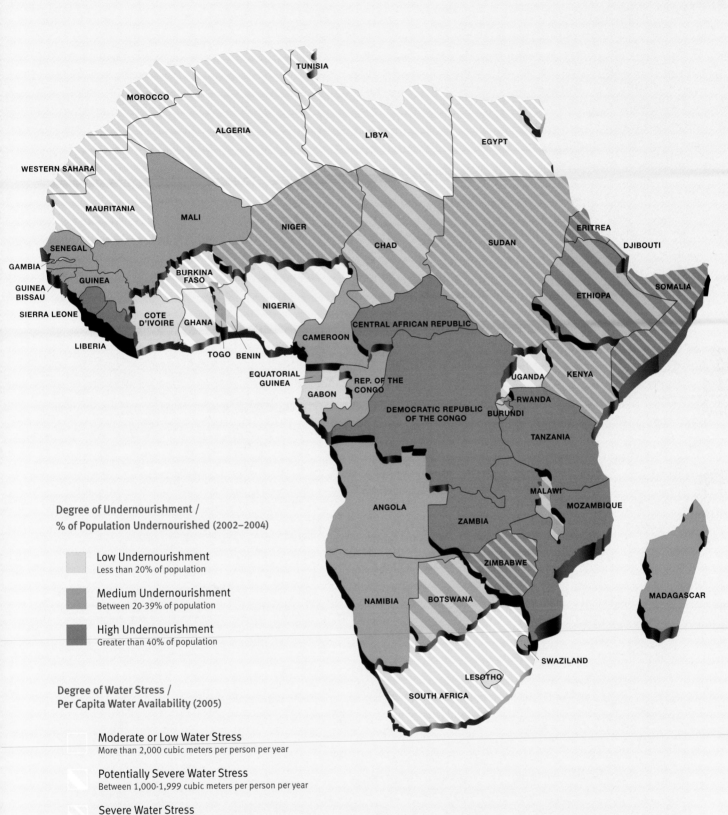

Degree of Undernourishment /
% of Population Undernourished (2002–2004)

Low Undernourishment
Less than 20% of population

Medium Undernourishment
Between 20-39% of population

High Undernourishment
Greater than 40% of population

Degree of Water Stress /
Per Capita Water Availability (2005)

Moderate or Low Water Stress
More than 2,000 cubic meters per person per year

Potentially Severe Water Stress
Between 1,000-1,999 cubic meters per person per year

Severe Water Stress
Less than 1,000 cubic meters per person per year

Source (for both stats): World Development Indicators 2008
Map Creation: UUorld, Inc. with GPO

▲ *Continued from p. 327*

2007 Corruption Perceptions Index covering 179 countries, Botswana was the only African country among the 40 least corrupt. Through elections, a free press, and parliamentary scrutiny, democracy improves accountability. Africa's 8 countries ranked among the 80 least corrupt are all electoral democracies judged free or partly free (in terms of individual political rights and civil liberties) by Freedom House. Yet among sub-Saharan Africa's 16 most corrupt countries, only 5 are electoral democracies and 4 judged free or partly free.

Most regional countries have faltered in building capable government institutions and transparent processes. Brain drain and HIV/AIDS have decimated government ranks in some countries, which have made the economic growth rates in recent years significant and remarkable. Many governments have built complex regulatory systems beyond their capacity to administer and the private sector's ability to comply. Simplification, such as eliminating steps required to start a new business, reduces demands on government, enables more consistent enforcement, and lessens opportunities for corruption.

Botswana demonstrates that good governance is possible in a resource-rich economy. Key to its success has been prudent leadership and concern for accountability and rule of law. Its government has imposed self-discipline in spending mineral revenues, requires minimum rates of return for public investments, and sets standards for service delivery. While the United States and other donors should invest in capacity-building of government institutions, they should focus more on helping governments learn from the experience of Botswana and other good regional performers.

Conflict. If making productive investment in Africa is difficult during stable times, it is nearly impossible in times of conflict. Although the number of conflicts in Africa has fallen in recent years, many remain and others loom. The costs of a civil war worldwide are huge, reducing economic growth by an estimated 2.3 percent per year over the typical 7-year duration. Moreover, conflict spills over to neighboring countries with refugees and loss of transport routes, export proceeds, and remittances. When ethnic violence in Kenya erupted after the elections in December 2007, processing of credit card transactions in Tanzania nearly ground to a halt because they were cleared in Nairobi. In human terms, conflict has been devastating, causing millions of deaths, even more people displaced, destruction of livelihoods, and breakdown in social services.

The largest ongoing conflicts are in Sudan, the eastern Democratic Republic of Congo, and Somalia. The first two have each already resulted in 2 to 4 million lives lost, while all three have resulted in millions more refugees and internally displaced, often leading to conflict being carried into neighboring states, such as (in the case of the Sudanese fighting) Chad. Several neighboring countries have supported or been directly engaged in the fighting. Many other countries have more localized conflicts occurring in regions often distant from their capitals, such as in northern Uganda, Ethiopia's Ogaden, and Nigeria's Niger Delta. Still others, once in conflict but now peaceful such as Sierra Leone, are fragile and could revert to conflict; recidivism within 10 years is about 50 percent.

The causes of conflict are many and complex, and deep understanding of local contexts is imperative if there is to be success in preventing or mitigating them. Conflict in sub-Saharan Africa has become a growth industry for governments and academia. At times, African mediation of conflicts has been superb, but unfortunately, resources available to African leaders to resolve conflicts in their region has too often been lacking. A major case was the inability of African governments to field operational transport aircraft to insert peacekeepers into the Darfur conflict region, a problem which could have been resolved by the provision of C–130 spare parts to the Nigerian air force. The quiet diplomacy of South African President Thabo Mbeki in Zimbabwe has been perceived as ineffective in stemming the plunge of a regional economic powerhouse into abject poverty and chaos, although a significant goal of South Africa in mediating the Zimbabwe dispute was to constrain—rather than inflame—the flow of Zimbabwean refugees to South Africa. In this respect, Mbeki was relatively successful, and conscious of the fact that HIV-initiated diseases, such as new forms of tuberculosis, were being carried into South Africa from Zimbabwe, and potentially could be carried to the world community.

Significantly, African peacekeepers have proven invaluable in resolving regional conflicts, at high casualty costs to the donor forces, such as the high loss of Nigerian personnel in support of U.S. efforts in Somalia, or in taking the lead in Liberian and Sierra Leonean peacekeeping.

Given that it is unlikely that either the United States or European Union wishes to field substantial forces to resolve African conflicts, more needs to be done to support the capabilities of African forces so that they can be easily and efficiently transported in to peacekeeping areas, and then adequately supported there.

The Peace and Security Council of the African Union, the most important arm of the preeminent regional organization on the continent, has a secretariat of just four professional staff. The Intergovernmental Authority on Development, the only subregional organization focusing on conflict in the violence-prone Horn of Africa, is still ineffective 20 years after its creation because of limited funding and staffing as well as interstate conflict. Donors have made efforts to build the capacity of such organizations, and they should do more, but the need for strong African leadership and staffing is paramount.

Seizing the Challenge

Promoting economic growth, improving governance, and reducing conflict in sub-Saharan Africa are long-term challenges that will face the international community and future U.S. administrations. For the United States, effective engagement and progress might focus on four areas: actively engaging in helping resolve conflicts, promoting African leadership in addressing these challenges, building unity of effort among international and U.S. Government agencies engaged in the region, and reestablishing a leading intellectual role for the United States.

Engage in Conflict Resolution. U.S. engagement and leadership in leveraging implementation of agreed obligations under international law, such as in the case of the Eritrea-Ethiopia impasse, could contribute to securing the peace and help reduce or eliminate the regional spillover impact of such seemingly intractable conflicts. Peace, stability, and security would lay a solid foundation for Africa's rapid and sustainable development and allow African states to focus their resources and efforts on addressing their domestic problems.

Promote African Leadership. While some foreign assistance from the United States and other donors has been useful, much has actually undermined African development by fostering dependency and lack of African leadership. For example, programs to fight HIV/AIDS have proven most effective in countries such as Uganda, which have shown strong political leadership from the top. Other African leaders need to do much better, even though, for example, HIV/AIDS had been less of a problem for Nigeria until that country was asked to insert peacekeeping forces into Liberia to resolve the civil war there; this

resulted in homecoming Nigerian troops suffering a 15 percent contagion rate, with consequent impact on Nigerian society, as a penalty for having undertaken the onerous and protracted humanitarian task on behalf of the international community.

The President's Emergency Plan for AIDS Relief should rebalance its efforts to focus less on one-off grants and more on promoting leadership and building capacity of governments to address the HIV/AIDS scourge over the long term and to deal with linked, consequent diseases, such as the new strain of tuberculosis that evolved from the HIV/AIDS pandemic in Zimbabwe. With smart diplomacy and a dose of humility, the U.S. Government should promote African leadership in identifying and resolving African problems. Significantly, Africans responded to the program of "African solutions to African problems," sponsored by Nigeria's leadership under then–President Ibrahim Babangida. The United States should also help strengthen African government institutions and enhance their partnership with private business and civil society. Furthermore, it should promote regional approaches, encouraging Africans to work with each other in attacking common problems, to pressure each other to do better, and to learn from each other what works best and what does not.

Achieve U.S. Unity of Effort. It is not only Africa that is fragmented. So is U.S. Government foreign assistance to the continent, which is now provided by more than 20 governmental agencies and departments. While the U.S. Agency for International Development (USAID) used to provide the majority of U.S. foreign aid to sub-Saharan Africa, its share has declined markedly in favor of the Millennium Challenge Account, President's Emergency Plan for AIDS Relief, and other agencies. Coordination among them is often lacking. At times, policies and assistance programs work at cross purposes, such as subsidies for American cotton growers undermining several African economies, assisted by USAID, that rely on cotton exports. The 2007 creation of the Bureau of Foreign Assistance in the State Department was a positive step in integrating aid provided by State and USAID. It helped make aid more supportive of U.S. strategy, but it does not govern aid channeled through other agencies and its implementation has been flawed. Moreover, it has not reduced congressional earmarks and directives, which result in micromanagement of the aid budget in Africa and a loss of focus. Aid reform needs to encompass all U.S. foreign aid, tie it better to other tools of statecraft, and get the administration and Congress focusing together on fewer priorities. Several commissions and scholars have recently proposed how to accomplish this.

Regain Intellectual Leadership. While the U.S. Government is still the largest donor in Africa, it has ceded intellectual leadership to other donors in many areas. Still strong in health, it lacks capacity in key areas for Africa's development, such as infrastructure and higher education. More broadly, our ability to provide leadership through knowledge and partnerships on the ground has suffered through acute staff shortages, caused by a USAID reduction in force in the late 1990s, insufficient recruitment by State and USAID, and redeployment to Afghanistan and Iraq. Good ideas are often more powerful than funding, but they depend on staff with world-class expertise and local knowledge. They do not all have to be American. Local recruitment of qualified African professionals is highly cost effective and should be expanded. With added expertise, the United States will be better positioned to listen to and work with partners on the ground, monitor developments, and lead in areas of greatest concern. **gsa**

NOTES

[1] By modern definition, the Maghreb as a geopolitical grouping is now taken to include Algeria, Ceuta (a Spanish exclave), Libya, Mauritania, Melilla (a Spanish exclave), Morocco (including Western Sahara), and Tunisia.

[2] Morocco and the United States in 2004 signed a Free Trade Agreement, which was regarded an important step toward President Bush's vision of a Middle East Free Trade Area by 2013. The treaty was ratified by Congress on July 22, 2004.

[3] The revolutionary group, Tigray People's Liberation Front, when it led the coalition that took power in Addis Ababa with the collapse of the Ethiopian Dergue in 1991, agreed voluntarily to cede the Ethiopian territory of Eritrea to the Eritrean People's Liberation Front, which had been an ally in fighting the Dergue government of Ethiopia. Despite the voluntary nature of that redrawing of the national borders, disputes developed between Eritrea and Ethiopia, leading to conventional war between the two. Significantly, however, Ethiopia was not a nation that came into being as a result of European colonization, and therefore could be said to be exempt from the Organization of African Unity/ African Union (OAU/AU) ruling. Similarly, the Kingdom of Swaziland was not a colonial creation, but had voluntarily ceded management of the state to the United Kingdom as a Protectorate, and thus could be said to be exempt from the OAU/AU stricture, and could therefore—as the United Kingdom in fact recommended when it departed in 1960—demand the return of Swazi territory, which had been administratively handed by Britain to South Africa

and Mozambique, without legal authority. Also, the creation of Somalia in 1960 was a voluntary union between two already independent states (the former British Somaliland and former Italian Somaliland), and therefore outside the OAU/AU stricture, which means that when the former British Somaliland withdrew in 1991 from the Somalia union, following the collapse of the Siad Barre administration, Somaliland's legal sovereignty was theoretically intact, although no AU states have yet formally recognized Somaliland's sovereignty. There have been other moves to redraw African boundaries in areas that were covered by the OAU/AU stricture, such as the attempt to create the state of Biafra out of Nigeria's energy-producing region in 1967; the Bakongo ethnic split between Republic of Congo (Brazzaville), Democratic Republic of the Congo (Kinshasa), and Angola remains unresolved since 1975; the contentious Kinyarwanda diaspora from 1959 to the present; and others.

[4] In 2005, the combined gross domestic product for the Economic Community of West African States was estimated at $139 billion.

[5] For example, on January 1, 2006, Bush approved 37 sub-Saharan African countries as eligible for tariff preferences under the African Growth and Opportunity Act (AGOA). This annual determination signifies which countries are making continued progress toward a market-based economy, rule of law, free trade, economic policies that would reduce poverty, and protection of workers' rights. Côte d'Ivoire, Liberia, and Togo were the only countries in the region not approved for the AGOA.

[6] A Bank of America report of April 2006 noted that U.S. imports of African oil reached 921 million barrels, or 18.7 percent of the U.S. total, in 2005. That surpassed imports from the Middle East, which supplied 839 million barrels, or 17 percent. Imports from Africa had increased by 51 percent since 2000 at the same time supplies from the Middle East fell from more than 900 million barrels to 839 million, or from 22 percent to 17 percent of total U.S. imports.

Contributors

The Honorable Dr. Patrick M. Cronin (Chapter Editor) is Director of the Institute for National Strategic Studies (INSS) at National Defense University (NDU), which was established by the Secretary of Defense and Chairman of the Joint Chiefs of Staff in 1984 to conduct strategic assessments for senior Department of Defense officials and decisionmakers. He took up the post at the beginning of 2008 after a 25-year career inside government and academic research centers and spanning areas of defense, security, foreign policy, and foreign assistance. He is simultaneously Director of the Center for the

militaries be needed to address these challenges, but also greater coordination and collaboration with civilian institutions will be central to resolving any immediate crises or finding long-term solutions.

In a region so bound by respect for sovereignty, it will be important to design transnational response mechanisms that encourage solutions that provide appropriate protections for the affected nation while allowing for greater cooperation in the future. This is a tall order. Regional security will depend on the emergence of programs that address the effects of climate change, for example, but also create transregional projects that promote responses to these potentially devastating types of problems.

Finally, as the world becomes increasingly multipolar, the United States will face greater economic and political competition in the region. As emerging powers such as China and India seek to influence the hemisphere, the potential for tension with the

United States will increase. Similarly, Russia is poised to establish a greater role as an arms supplier to the region's armed forces. Iran is also flexing its diplomatic muscle through its recent outreach to Venezuela. The growing influence of Brazil as a major global economic player and potential oil-producing powerhouse presents both opportunities and challenges to U.S. interests. These emerging trends will require new economic and political alliances that can be viewed as an important opportunity for globalization and development, or as a broader threat to U.S. security.

The Economy: Endemic Poverty

Latin America and the Caribbean have the most unequal income distribution in the world, according to the 2008 World Development Indicators from the World Bank. Severe poverty and underdevelopment have led many Latin Americans to engage in illicit activities for employment and sustenance. The

Maritime Zones

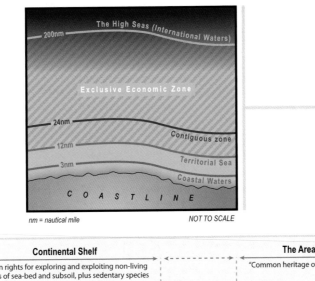

nm = nautical mile   NOT TO SCALE

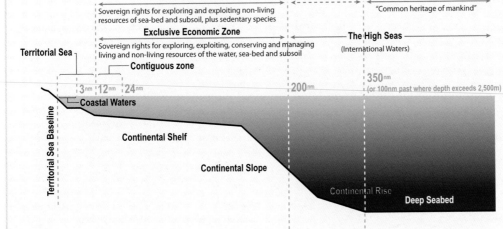

Source: Australian Department of the Environment, Water, Heritage, and the Arts

impact is especially great for countries with a youth bulge, where vast numbers of citizens are under 25 years of age. Such a situation is considered a key indicator of a potentially conflictive environment. While this trend will peak by 2010 in countries such as Brazil and Mexico, it poses a threat to internal security as long as opportunities for economic gain, education, and work do not materialize.

The poverty rate in Latin America has been cut by more than half since 1950 (from 60 percent to perhaps 25 percent in 2007), according to the 2006 World Bank report on Latin America, *Poverty Reduction and Growth: Virtuous and Vicious Cycles.* But as the UN Economic Commission for Latin America has shown, improvement has not been homogeneous. The decline is a product of reduced inflation, remittances, conditional cash transfer programs and other forms of aid, job creation from foreign direct investment, and growing economies. The continued reduction of poverty in Latin America can be helped to some extent by ensuring the region greater access to trade and new markets. This will require more attention to expanding foreign direct investment and promoting new types of industries such as alternative energies and revitalizing agriculture. Prospects for green jobs may help in some countries—especially in the Caribbean and Brazil. Securing titles to property also contributes to the reduction of poverty. Credit scarcity as well as bureaucratic and fiscal barriers to entrepreneurs also need to be addressed. Finally, the empowerment of women through increased educational opportunities and growing employment opportunities is also evident in many countries.

The Role of Energy

Latin America and the Caribbean have abundant energy resources, but they are very unevenly distributed. In 2006, Venezuela, Mexico, and Brazil controlled 90 percent of the region's oil reserves. Natural gas reserves are concentrated in Venezuela (60 percent), Bolivia (9 percent), Trinidad and Tobago (7 percent), Argentina (6 percent), and Mexico (6 percent). A major new oil and natural gas find off the southern coast of Brazil augers potential future supplies, but these new sources are deep underwater and will take billions of dollars to extract. Moreover, they will not be available for at least 5 to 8 years.

The recent price hike of hydrocarbons has not translated into an increase in production. Instead, it has been accompanied by a decline in production in the region's major players, Mexico and Venezuela. This is the product of underinvestment, resulting from both governments' treatment of the national oil companies as "cash cows," combined with legislative and political environments adverse to foreign investment. Ultimately, this decline in production contributes to the continued rise in world oil prices, which puts downward pressure on the economy and disproportionately worsens the quality of life for the poor.

Oil-poor countries of Central America and the Caribbean face a pressing crisis: they are unable to pay for imported oil and gas. As a result, they have come to rely on support from Venezuela through the PetroCaribe initiative. In the short run, this will help save funds needed for social and economic development through reduction in energy costs, but in the long run these states will face an energy crisis that requires investments in renewable energy resources to prevent long-term dependency on one source.

Latin America is distinctive for its vast renewable resources: hydropower, solar, aeolic, geothermal, and biomass. With some exceptions, most of the region's potential in renewables has remained unexplored due to engineering difficulties, lack of economic incentives, environmental concerns, and an absence of governmental support. Brazil is at the forefront of the exploration of renewables in the region. Its success story with ethanol has generated considerable interest in biofuels across Latin America and in the United States, resulting in the U.S.-Brazil Biofuels Pact of March of 2007. This alliance of the two largest ethanol producers should become the foundation of a U.S. energy policy for the Americas.

Given the expected increase in energy demand by 2030, great strides will be needed in the next 4 to 8 years to set down the legal and regulatory mechanisms for broader integration of the region's energy sector. Important decisions in such countries as Mexico, Bolivia, or Venezuela may even be deferred by political obstacles. Different resource endowments make hemispheric uniformity on energy policy impossible, and it may be wiser to think of compatibility in negotiating key aspects of the partnership.

Climate Change, Environmental Degradation, and Food Shortages

Climate change has led to increased natural disasters that will negatively impact the region unless a massive program of environmental adaptation is encouraged immediately. The security dimensions of this problem include sudden massive movements of populations, creating a new category of environmental refugees. Rises in sea level, which are already taking place, compound other environmental threats such as hurricanes and earthquakes, which will demand military rescue operations and humanitarian assistance.

With rising amounts of carbon dioxide in the atmosphere, it is also vital to retain forests, primarily the Amazon. According to recent satellite photographs, nearly 65 of every 100 hectares of forest lost worldwide between 2000 and 2005 were in Latin America. South America showed the largest deforestation in square miles, while Central America lost the highest percentage of forest. The leading cause of deforestation between 2000 and 2005 was the conversion of forest to land for agriculture, particularly to the monoculture of soybeans. Haiti is now 94 percent deforested, and Honduras will lose all its forest cover in 30 years if its rate of deforestation is maintained. On a more positive note, reforestation is under way in countries such as Costa Rica and Saint Vincent. Currently Brazil is the only Latin American country aggressively using real-time high-resolution satellite imagery to track the rate and areas of deforestation. Few other countries can afford such technology without financial assistance. Such investments must be constant and long term if they are to be effective.

Deforestation also negatively affects the region by reducing biodiversity, intensifying flooding, eroding soil, and reducing rainfall and freshwater reserves, creating conditions favorable to the spread of tropical diseases. By affecting the weather in the hemisphere, deforestation also releases large amounts of carbon dioxide and other gases into the atmosphere, increasing the greenhouse gas effect. While many governments are already making some changes, insecurity from global warming needs to be countered with better regional systems for emergency management and strong regional mitigation programs for greenhouse gases.

Predictions of sea level increases over the next 30 to 50 years present a potential crisis as 60 percent of the Caribbean population currently lives on the coastline. Warming will also affect the agricultural cycles as higher temperatures result in different planting seasons and hence a greater need to import food. Recent food riots in Haiti and demonstrations in Mexico over corn prices illustrate the region's vulnerability to disruptions in its food supply chain and underscore the global nature of food security.

The Role of Foreign Actors

Although the United States still is Latin America's most significant partner, it has been consistently losing ground to other actors. Some countries, such as Canada, Japan, South Korea, and Taiwan, have engaged with the region for a significant amount of

time. Others, particularly China, India, and Russia, have only recently been strengthening ties. Finally, there are new actors with little or no historical presence in the region, namely Iran.

The emergence of these new players can be explained by two factors. First, globalization of the economy has pushed the region to a new level of engagement with a wider range of international players from Asia and the Middle East. Second, Washington's geopolitical attention has been diverted from Latin America as a result of the wars in Afghanistan and Iraq. These events created a political vacuum in the United States, making it difficult to address the challenges in the region. This vacuum allowed room for Hugo Chavez, Evo Morales, and Rafael Correa to undermine the U.S. role in the region. In an international environment of heightened competition for natural resources and market access, excluding the European Union and the United States, China has emerged as the most significant partner, in terms of political exchange, trade flows, and investment. China has assumed a pragmatic approach in its relations with the region and has kept the U.S. Government informed of its actions.

Whether for political or commercial interests, Russia is making a strong comeback in Latin America. In 2006, Chavez met with then-President Vladimir Putin, after the acquisition of 100,000 Russian-made Kalishnikov assault rifles, helicopters, and other weaponry. In January 2007, Moscow and Caracas signed an agreement worth $15 million to develop Venezuela's natural gas resources. Russia and Brazil have already achieved a strategic partnership agreement, and Russia is said to be considering launching rockets from the Brazilian spaceport of Alcantara.

Ties with Iran are at present mostly symbolic, but they present a challenge to U.S. policy, especially given Washington's limited dialogue with outlier countries in the Middle East. The influence of Islamic extremism is weak in Latin America but could expand given the region's porous borders. While the current risk of terrorism in the region is relatively low, the United States should work with regional allies to ensure that the breeding ground for recruitment is reduced through programs that promote education, good governance, and inclusion in productive economic activities.

To counter the influence of these new partners in Latin America, the United States needs to continue to engage and make determined demonstrations of goodwill, expand trade and investment offers, and support technological and scientific exchanges. How the United States deals with Iran's engagement in the region will differ from its reaction to the involvement of economic giants such as India and China.

Prospects for Addressing These Issues

If the greatest achievement of post–Cold War Latin America was the expansion of democracy in the hemisphere, with democratic civil-military relations as a cornerstone of that policy, the next decade must build from this base by ensuring that the economic and social problems that dominate the political dialogue are tackled through bilateral and multilat-

President Raul Castro and Vice President Juan Almedia Bosque attend Cuba's National Assembly

eral engagement. Transnational threats cannot be controlled by any one state or external actor and will complicate the picture unless the United States and Latin American and Caribbean states agree on threat assessments and build a common agenda of action to address them. Bringing actors together to solve transnational threats will require the integration of civilian, military, and multilateral organizations to ensure a secure and stable environment.

The Cuba Challenge: The Next 4 to 8 Years

Raul Castro, who has been misunderstood and underestimated for decades, replaced his brother Fidel as Cuba's president on February 24, 2008. His official transition into the presidency followed a 19-month period when Raul acted as provisional president after

Fidel was incapacitated following major surgeries. Since then, Fidel has been too impaired to appear in public or play any real leadership role.

There were no reports of unrest or challenges to the new leadership. Many Cubans, weary of Fidel's 49-year reign, seemed in fact to welcome the change. Raul's collegial and reticent leadership style was particularly appealing after decades of Fidel's grandstanding. His admission that Cuba's dire economic problems were largely self-inflicted was refreshingly candid, and the populace knew that the decentralizing solutions he favored to solve them had been unacceptable to his brother. Raul also abandoned *fidelista* orthodoxy by encouraging relatively unfettered discussions about domestic problems and went on to make clear that his priority is to solve them. He is not known to have travelled abroad in several years and has not closely identified himself with foreign policy priorities.

Soon after being confirmed as president, Raul began to address Cuba's internal problems. Implementing limited economic reforms, he appeared to emulate the Chinese reform model of the early 1980s, with the emphasis on providing liberalizing incentives to farmers and workers to spur productivity. He took steps to alleviate popular grievances by allowing Cubans to visit previously off-limits hotels and restaurants and to buy once-forbidden consumer goods. Although these and other innovations improved the lives of relatively few, they tended to elevate popular expectations for more sweeping change.

Raul has also moved away from some of his brother's draconian social policies. Artists and intellectuals have gained space, and homosexuals, mercilessly oppressed in the past, have been allowed to come out into the open. The death penalty has been largely suspended. Movies and other forms of entertainment incompatible with the regime's traditional values have been aired. And a few remarkably irreverent Web sites that appeal to Cuban youth have been allowed to function.

Nevertheless, consistent with the Chinese model of communism, Raul has no plans to dilute the regime's monopoly of political power. As long as he and his followers are in charge, there will be no democratization, and no opening for the small community of dissident and human rights activists. In 2009, however, the carefully planned release of some political prisoners to win relief from the economic embargo is likely. Raul's more pragmatic policies will probably succeed in winning new support for Cuba in Europe and Latin America, possibly further isolating the United States.

Key Strengths and Vulnerabilities

There has never been another Cuban official below Fidel with power and prestige comparable to what Raul has amassed over the years. Through a network of military and communist party allies, some of whom have been his surrogates and friends since the late 1950s, Raul dominates Cuba's three most powerful institutions:

■ Raul is still the country's only four-star general. After serving 49 years as defense minister, he named his crony and long-time vice minister, General Julio Casas Regueiro, to succeed him.

■ In 1989, Raul also took control of Cuba's second most powerful institution when another of his disciples, General Abelardo Colome Ibarra, was appointed to lead the Ministry of the Interior, which houses all security, police, and intelligence agencies.

■ For years Raul has also been the principal force in the communist party, where his intimate friend Jose Ramon Machado Ventura exercises day-to-day leadership. Together, they plan to strengthen the party by holding a long-delayed congress in late 2009.

These institutions, and the men who lead them, will remain the indispensable bulwarks of Raul Castro's government and of whatever regime or regimes follow it over the next 4 to 8 years.

Paradoxically, this leadership team will also increasingly be the regime's greatest vulnerability. Raul's six vice presidents—who also constitute the inner sanctum of the party—are tough old veterans, many of whom have been at his side for 50 years. He depends on these generals and party apparatchiks because they will support and protect him. He knows how they think and perform and is unlikely to be surprised by any of them. Nevertheless, Raul (who turned 78 in June 2009) and his six vice presidents average slightly more than 70 years of age, constituting a safe, plodding, unimaginative gerontocracy that has no appeal to and little legitimacy with the country's younger generations.

Raul's alter ego, Machado Ventura, epitomizes his patron's aversion to bringing younger men into his inner circle (Machado is several months older than Raul). Machado, the first vice president and next after Raul in the line of succession, has almost no standing with the populace. A former medical doctor with only loose connections to the military high command, his reputation is as a stern disciplinarian and austere party bureaucrat. Seemingly, his only qualification is his closeness to Raul.

Among the five other vice presidents, only one—Carlos Lage, who is in his mid 50s—represents the middle generation of leaders. In a system where Lage's generation is underrepresented and the youth are profoundly alienated, there is a real danger in the leadership choices Raul has made.

Many observers outside of Cuba had expected Raul to name a younger man—Lage for example—as first in the line of succession. A pediatrician with considerable top-tier government and party experience, Lage is reputed to favor liberalizing economic reform and is respected by foreign businessmen and

Cuban refugees depart from port of Mariel, Cuba, bound for Key West, Florida, during mass defection granted by President Fidel Castro, April 28, 1980

diplomats. But he may have been too dependent on Fidel rather than Raul for his standing and perhaps somehow antagonized Raul during the years when he appeared to be Cuba's third most influential civilian leader. By insisting on the faithful but predictable Machado as his designated successor, Raul opted for the safest course in the short term, but one that could have dire consequences just a few years in the future. In effect, Raul gambled that cross-generational tensions can be kept under control.

Cuba's Lost Generation

Cuban youth have become notably more restless over the last few years. Students (and former students expelled because of their activism) claim to be traveling across the island, endeavoring to enlist broader support for their grievances. Some of their professors appear to have allied with them. A new youth-based movement advocating university autonomy, curricular independence, and free speech has attracted a considerable following. A petition to reopen a Catholic university shut down decades ago has been signed by thousands. In February 2008, two university students br ashly challenged a ranking official at an academic forum—an unprecedented act of rebellion.

For some time, Cuban officials have worried openly about the generational divide. In one of his last major speeches, Fidel himself bemoaned the apathy and disassociation of the youth, saying that "the revolution can destroy itself"—a phrase repeated by other leaders and the official media—if the younger generations are not motivated to work enthusiastically for the communist system.

Later, foreign minister Felipe Perez Roque pressed the issue. He complained that alarmingly large numbers of youth (2.5 million in a population of slightly over 11 million) do not identify with the regime's collectivist mentality. They have little or no appreciation of its myths and legends and, in short, are rejectionist. He described them as constituting two large cohorts who were born or came of age after the demise of the Soviet Union in 1991 and the end of the communist subsidies that plunged the Cuban economy into severe depression. Perez Roque's essential point was that Cuban youth today have known little but hardship and deprivation.

Raul shares these concerns. Soon after he assumed provisional power, he met with University of Havana students. In a moment of startling identification with their grievances, he encouraged them to debate and criticize the shortcomings they perceive. Later, when assuming the presidency, he said that Cuba has been "permanently opened to free debate." Then, to clarify his intent, he added that the people must "question everything. . . . The best solutions can come from a profound exchange of differing opinions."

Earlier, Raul had revealed that about 5 million Cubans had engaged in meetings across the island, encouraged by the regime. Anecdotal reports indicate that many of these meetings devolved into strident griping sessions, as Cubans vented their pent-up frustrations with problems including the broken transportation and housing sectors, the lack of jobs (especially for those with the best education), the decrepit state of most of the country's infrastructure, and even the once-sacrosanct educational and public health systems.

Raul and his advisors learned from those communal meetings and soon began to address many of the problems identified. However, by encouraging open debate, they have perhaps dangerously raised expectations for more fundamental change and public engagement. They may be opening the floodgates of rising expectations that the political system itself will be loosened or reformed. They may be inadvertently encouraging antiregime mobilizations. Conversely, any retreat from the promises of greater openness might well induce a popular backlash.

A number of possibilities for change lurk in this generational warp. It is unlikely that the alienation of the youth, and the severe economic problems that fuel it, can be significantly ameliorated within the next few years. A deepening and coalescing of youthful unrest, resulting in organized protests and dissent, will therefore be increasingly likely. So far, no identifiable leaders have emerged from the younger generations, but they will be more likely to appear as the current regime leadership ages. Middle generation figures, now in their late 40s and 50s, will also be likely to embrace the grievances of the youth while trying behind the scenes to force radical departures from the communist party dictatorship. A Cuban Gorbachev, inclined to transform or dismantle the old system, could be just a few years from emerging as successor to Raul and his current circle.

Worst-case Scenarios

Any breakdown in command and control within the armed forces would quickly result in widespread, regime-threatening instability. Tensions within the military hierarchy probably run along generational and other fault lines in an institution where top commanders occupying the same positions for many years are now in their 60s, 70s, and 80s. There has never been a younger officer rebellion in the Castro brothers' armed forces, but the possibility may now be greater than ever before. When Raul selected the colorless and reputedly corrupt General Julio Casas Regueiro to succeed him as defense minister, he may have aggravated underlying animosities and rivalries in the officer corps. Military unity and discipline could also be shattered if large popular demonstrations against the regime broke out. Although police and security personnel would be the first line of defense in that event, military units may also be deployed. In the event that military commanders were ordered to fire on civilians, some commanders would be likely to disobey, possibly sparking internecine conflict between loyalist and rejectionist officers.

The possibility of extensive violence, even civil war, would steadily increase in direct correlation with widening fissures in military command and control. In this case, it would be all but certain that another massive, chaotic seaborne migration to south Florida would ensue as civilians fled unstable conditions and shortages of essential goods. Hundreds of thousands already anxious to migrate to the United States would try to flee on whatever craft might be available. Such a migration could easily exceed the size of the 1980 Mariel boatlift, the largest of three such exoduses that have occurred since 1965, when more than 125,000 Cubans fled. Controlling or deterring such an event with U.S. or any international forces would be unlikely, especially in the early stages.

However, all such previous mass migrations were orchestrated and impelled by Fidel Castro. His successors, now and in the foreseeable future, will be unlikely to take similar action. Raul and his generals would be loath to force another exodus such as Mariel because they know the results would be dangerously destabilizing on the island and could easily become regime-threatening. Thus, if another exodus occurs, it most likely will be the result of regime disarray rather than connivance.

Finally, the possibility of a wrenching succession crisis following Raul's death or incapacitation must be considered. A heavy drinker for many decades, at the age of 78 he probably suffers from serious undisclosed health problems. For years he characteristically has disappeared from public view for weeks, sometimes even months, at a time. It is reasonable to speculate that on at least some of those occasions he was recovering from some health crisis. Given his lifestyle and age, Raul could die suddenly, with almost no warning time for his designated successors to prepare.

The result might well be a chaotic and possibly violent struggle among military, intelligence, and party barons. Machado Ventura, the first vice president, has little or no independent standing with the generals in command of the military and intelligence units. They might or might not agree to recognize him as the Castro brothers' legitimate successor. In either event, a military-dominated regime would likely emerge.

Obviously, given the 4- to 8-year time frame of this analysis, a post-Raul succession seems inevitable. Under almost any conceivable scenario, other than the unlikely sudden disappearance of the communist regime, Cuba's uniformed services and their commanders will dominate its future.

Little is known outside of Cuba about the gener-

als and other senior officers. Thus, it is impossible to estimate with any confidence what policies and priorities they would pursue, how constructively they would be able to collaborate, or where they would turn for external assistance. Similarly, it is nearly impossible to speculate about which commanders would be most likely to emerge dominant after Raul's departure. Cuba's most powerful institution is also the country's most impenetrable.

Securing the Three Borders

The terrorist attacks on September 11, 2001, made it clear that the Atlantic and Pacific Oceans no longer insulate the United States from foreign aggression. It also became clear that an attack on one nation affects the safety, security, economy, and well-being of its neighbors. Hence, new strategies for protecting the country must strengthen its relationships with Canada, Mexico, and The Bahamas in order to meet challenges and common interests.

Before 9/11

The Atlantic and Pacific maritime approaches to North America have been controlled by the U.S. Navy in coordination with the Canadian Maritime Forces since 1940. As members of the North Atlantic Treaty Organization (NATO) and the North American Aerospace Defense Command (NORAD), the United States and Canada had a common doctrine and often trained or operated together in land, sea, and air domains. NORAD, a unique binational command created in 1958, planned and coordinated air sovereignty and aerospace defense missions against strategic threats from the command center in Cheyenne Mountain, Colorado. After the fall of the Berlin Wall, the end of the Cold War, and the liberation of Kuwait in 1991, the United States and Canada had settled into a passive defense and security posture, in part due to the perception of a peace dividend that resulted in reduced military spending throughout the 1990s.

The Commonwealth of The Bahamas cooperates extensively with the United States on counternarcotics interdiction measures. These include participation in Operation *Bahamas and Turks and Caicos* (OPBAT), which targets drug trafficking organizations transiting Bahamian territorial waters. As a maritime state, the Royal Bahamas Defence Force coordinates extensively with the U.S. Coast Guard and Navy.

In contrast to the Canada-U.S. alliance and The Bahamas–U.S. cooperative partnership, the Mexico-U.S. defense and security relationship before 9/11

▼ *Continued on p. 351*

Working with Mexico

Mexico is suffering a crisis of public safety that the United States cannot minimize. Murders, organized kidnappings, and corruption rates have reached some of the highest levels in the world. Mexico's government is locked in a violent struggle against powerful drug cartels that are also fighting each other for control of territory, resources, and manpower. The United States is the largest consumer of illegal drugs and the main source of the cartels' high-powered weapons and kit. It also is beginning to suffer some spillover from the violence. The Bush administration accepted some shared responsibility for Mexico's crisis and, in October 2007, jointly announced the 3-year, $1.4-billion Mérida Initiative (including a small Central American portion) as a new kind of partnership to maximize the efforts against drug, human, and weapons trafficking.

As the level of violence along the U.S.-Mexico border has become sufficiently threatening, President Barack Obama has asked the Chairman of the Joint Chiefs of Staff, Admiral Mike Mullen, to review how Washington might do more to help Mexico's forces. But by only looking south, we ignore the seeds of a future domestic problem that have been planted here. If Mexican and other Latin American narcogangs continue to grow in scope and power within our country, they may become the next-generation irregular challenge to the joint force. The United States and Mexico must find ways to perfect cooperation in the near term and confront a shared security problem together.

Mexico's level of violence escalated in 2008 with nearly 6,300 people killed—many of them tortured and mutilated—up from 2,700 in 2007. The bloodshed and intimidation carried out with impunity suggest that the cartels have sometimes had the upper hand, particularly in the borderlands. In the United States, the gravity of Mexico's situation had little effect on the first tranche of the Mérida Initiative. The package of equipment, software, and technical assistance moved slowly through a reluctant U.S. Congress, where the funding request was reduced significantly and several conditions were imposed. There were few signs of urgency.

These circumstances raise several important questions. Should relations with Mexico be higher on President Obama's foreign policy agenda? How should the administration manifest its commitment to this neighbor, which not only shares intimate ties but also harbors memories of unfair treatment? Are there more meaningful and deeper ways to cooperate in addressing a common problem? Will Washington maintain sta-tus quo commitment to Mérida while concentrating on preventing drug-related violence from spilling across the border? Will Mexico be driven to a level of national desperation that will force it to undertake long-term reforms to improve government performance and ties with the general population?

The crisis has deep roots. In the 1980s and 1990s, successive governments tended to pursue a "live and let live" response to lucrative, brutal, and well-organized regional cartels. Because they provoked violence, jeopardizing public safety, direct confrontations were minimized. With the demise of Colombia's main syndicates in the mid-1990s, Mexican "families," which had worked for the Colombians, took control of domestic drug trafficking. By the end of the decade, higher cocaine flows from Colombia led President Ernesto Zedillo of the Institutional Revolutionary Party to collaborate more aggressively with the United States.

The historic presidential victory of Vicente Fox and his center-right National Action Party (PAN) coincided with dramatic increases in narcotics-related violence. During his administration, drug cartels added profitable methamphetamine and heroin to the more traditional cocaine and marijuana they smuggled in bulk into the United States. New markets appeared in Europe and Mexico itself. The expanding narcotics trade encountered stronger U.S. resistance in the post-9/11 era. Washington's focus on securing the country from terrorists and illegal immigrants resulted in the construction of barriers along the 2,000-mile border with Mexico and more technology and law enforcement personnel to secure it.

Difficulty moving their product into the United States led to a vicious war within and among cartels for control of corridors and local domination of Mexican markets. This clash introduced ruthless militarized gunmen such as Los Zetas, manned with former members of the Mexican and Guatemalan army. President Fox tried unsuccessfully over 6 years to purge and reorganize federal police forces and rein in organized crime, extraditing captured kingpins to the United States. Urban and rural instability escalated sharply, and a general climate of lawlessness encouraged more kidnappings and other types of criminal enterprise.

Felipe Calderón, also from the PAN, succeeded Fox in 2006. Although Mexican military units lacked the necessary training, President Calderón declared war on drug traffickers by committing the loyal armed forces—using more than 45,000 soldiers—in a series of large-scale operations intended initially to restore public order in murder-wracked Ciudad Juárez, Tijuana, and other cities in northern Mexico. It quickly became apparent that the president actually was fighting to reassert state control over cartel-dominated areas. His ability to sustain government presence will be crucial until programs to improve military capabilities and reform the police at all levels can be accomplished.

The Calderón administration faces formidable obstacles to ending Mexico's fragmented sovereignty and regaining public confidence. The extent of drug-related corruption across government, especially in local police forces, far exceeds even pessimistic expectations. The sophistication of the criminal groups with their state-of-the-art military weapons and equipment—much of it smuggled from the United States—often outclasses the Mexican military. Furthermore, the cartels use kidnapping, brutality, and other forms of psychological intimidation effectively. Some community political and business leaders have left their positions or moved their families to the United States.

The seriousness of Mexico's insecurity was captured in the February 2009 State Department travel advisory for Mexico:

Some recent Mexican army and police confrontations with drug cartels have resembled small-unit combat, with cartels employing automatic weapons and grenades. Large firefights have taken place in many towns and cities across Mexico, but most recently in northern Mexico. . . . During some of these incidents, U.S. citizens have been trapped.

Ironically, the advisory appeared as Mexico's tourism industry reported that in 2008, 22.6 million foreign visitors, the majority from the United States, spent $13.3 billion, an increase of 3.4 percent over the previous year.

As the crisis intensifies in Mexico, Americans are not immune from cartel violence and corruption. Mexican ties to U.S. organized crime groups have long been established. Major Mexican syndicates are now thought to be present in at least 230 American cities. Over the last 2 years, U.S. multiagency counternarcotics task forces have arrested more than 750 members of the Sinaloa cartel's distribution network and 500 from the Gulf cartel. Police link recent assassinations and mass graves in Arizona and New Mexico to the cartels. Phoenix is now ranked the second worst place for kidnapping globally, after Mexico City: 359 kidnappings took place there in 2008, all of them linked to trafficking. The feared spillover of Mexican narcotics-related violence has, in fact, taken place—and is getting worse. Alarm bells are ringing, but a U.S. strategic game plan has yet to emerge.

Despite a prickly past and many differences, the United States and Mexico are interdependent, and they formalized that relationship with the North American Free Trade Agreement. Our border is the historic face of this complex relationship. With its network of power plants and transmission lines, gas and oil pipelines, and linked highway and rail systems, the borderland is strikingly vibrant and productive. There is a constant flow of people and vehicles in the millions. Beyond the border, the realization of greater mutual understanding, and an enhanced and trusting relationship, is a work in slow motion.

This raises additional and substantial strategic and policy questions. What are American objectives? The Mérida Initiative can be reduced to assistance and cooperation, but to what end? How far is Washington willing to go to reduce the American demand for drugs, curtail arms smuggling south, exchange intelligence, and work with Mexico (and Central American states) to attack the cartels' supply link to South America? Is integrated sea and air control over the approaches to North America feasible? In turn, how far is Mexico City willing to go to work intimately with its neighbor to the north, from whom Mexico traditionally has sought to remain independent?

▲ *Continued from p. 349*

was distant and noncommitted. Mexico's traditional foreign policy, articulated as the Estrada Doctrine, favored nonintervention in the affairs of other nations. This doctrine was legitimized by article 76 of the Mexican constitution, which empowered the senate to authorize Mexican troops to leave the limits of the country, permitted the passage of foreign troops through national territory, and allowed the stationing of task forces of other powers (for more than a month) in Mexican waters. Even if there was a desire to coordinate with foreign powers, the Senate represented a significant impediment.

In addition to different relationships between the United States and the three border nations, the military organizations of all four nations were organized differently. Since 1986, the United States had a geographic combatant command system wherein a single commander had combatant command of land, sea, and air forces in overseas theaters. Yet the defense of the United States was not assigned to a single geographic combatant command. NORAD focused on air sovereignty and aerospace defense, U.S. Joint Forces Command on maritime defense in the Atlantic, U.S. Pacific Command on maritime defense in the Pacific, and U.S. Army Forces Command on land defense. In Canada, commander, NORAD, commander, Land Forces Command, and commander, Maritime Command, had similar responsibilities for their environments or armed services. The United States and Canada continued to focus on external threats in other theaters.

The Royal Bahamas Defence Force was a naval force with a coastal focus similar to the U.S. Coast Guard. The Defence Act tasks the force to defend The Bahamas, protect its territorial integrity, patrol its waters, provide assistance and relief in times of disaster, maintain order in conjunction with the law enforcement agencies of The Bahamas, and carry out any such duties as determined by the National Security Council.

The Mexican armed forces consist of the Secretariat of National Defense (the army and air force) and the Secretariat of the Navy. The secretariats provide land, sea, and air defense of Mexico, and as required provide defense support to civil authorities in the aftermath of natural disasters. Both organizations have designated geographic regions for their subordinate commands.

Relationships between nations are formalized through the negotiation and approval of treaties and agreements. The number and type of bilateral treaties or agreements in force are key indicators of the maturity of diplomatic relationships between two nations. Starting with the Rush-Baggot Treaty of 1817, Canada and the United States have had a long, cooperative relationship. According to the U.S. State Department, the United States has 42 bilateral agreements with The Bahamas, 205 formal agreements with Mexico, and 252 nation-to-nation agreements with Canada in addition to over 200 Canada-U.S. military-to-military agreements.

As reflected in the table on page 353, the number of defense agreements with Canada and The Bahamas is significant, whereas those with Mexico on defense are much less so (only 5 percent). The majority of agreements with Mexico focus on narcotics. Although all four neighbors are members of the United Nations and the Organization of American States, U.S. relationships with Mexico did not rise to the level of cooperation with The Bahamas and binational interoperability with Canada. During the 1990s, a common threat perception did not stimulate increased diplomacy, military outreach, engagement, or spending among these four nations.

After 9/11

On September 11, a Canadian general officer heading NORAD scrambled U.S. fighters to respond to the aviation threat. On that same day, all civilian flights were grounded and the Canadian people took thousands of stranded travelers into their homes. The day after the attacks, NATO leadership implemented Article 5, which states that an armed attack against one member shall be considered an attack against them all.

On October 7, 2001, the United States and Great Britain initiated Operation *Enduring Freedom*, launch-

U.S. Navy (Jay C. Pugh)

Canadian transport delivers Hurricane Katrina relief supplies to Naval Air Station Pensacola, Florida

ing attacks against the Taliban and al Qaeda. Canadian forces began deployments to Afghanistan in January and February 2002 and continued NORAD flights in support of Operation *Noble Eagle*. In addition to military deployments and operations, on December 12, the governments completed the Canada-U.S. Smart Border Declaration, initiating a 30-point action plan to secure the flow of people and goods. For example, Integrated Border and Marine Enforcement Teams were expanded to other areas of the border to enhance communication and coordination.

Mexican President Vicente Fox expressed empathy for the victims of 9/11 and rejected all forms of violence and terrorism. By March 2002, the governments completed the U.S.-Mexico Border Partnership Action Plan that outlined 22 points to secure infrastructure as well as the flow of people and goods. However, within a year, relations between the United States and Mexico were strained because of a recession that affected the economies of both nations and rising anti-immigration sentiments in the United States. In addition, the lack of tangible support for Operation *Enduring Freedom* and withdrawal from the mutual defense portion of the Rio Treaty in 2002 created negative perceptions of Mexico.

Meanwhile, the General Assembly of the OAS met in Peru on September 11 and within 10 days labeled 9/11 as an attack against all American states. However, The Bahamas, CARICOM, and other members of the Rio Treaty did not provide military support to allied operations in Afghanistan. As a result of the attacks, The Bahamas and CARICOM experienced an economic downturn as decreases in the tourism industry were fueled in part by a fear of flying and new travel restrictions. Unlike the Smart Border initiatives undertaken with Canada and Mexico, the U.S. administration did not attempt to negotiate a similar agreement with The Bahamas or other Caribbean nations. This eventually led to accusations that the United States turned its back on the Caribbean after 9/11.

Two years after the 9/11 attacks, the OAS convened a special conference on security in Mexico City; that conclave affirmed the commitment to promoting and strengthening peace and security in the Western Hemisphere. Adopted on October 28, 2003, the Declaration on Security in the Americas recognized that the states of the Western Hemisphere have different perspectives regarding security threats and priorities. Despite these differences, the declaration achieved a consensus that threats to the Western Hemisphere include terrorism, transnational organized crime, the global drug problem, corruption, asset laundering, illicit trafficking in weapons, and the connections among the aforementioned threats, as well as the possibility of acquisition, possession, and use of weapons of mass destruction and their means of delivery by terrorists.

The conference members acknowledged the responsibilities of the OAS, inter-American, and international forces to develop cooperation mechanisms to address these new threats, concerns, and other challenges based on applicable instruments and mechanisms. Still, the instruments and mechanisms were not well defined.

In addition, the special conference on security occurred 6 months after the March 20, 2003, launch of Operation *Iraqi Freedom*. After 18 months of combat operations in Afghanistan, the United States and allies invaded Iraq to the dismay of all three neighboring governments. Although Canada continued to support combat operations in Afghanistan, Prime Minister Jean Chretien refused to support the Iraq invasion without a clear connection between Saddam Hussein and terrorism. President Vicente Fox of Mexico was against an Iraq invasion without UN Security Council affirmation; and The Bahamas and the majority of Caribbean states failed to support the Bush administration's call for war with Iraq. In 2003, the perceived relationships between the United States and its three neighbors sank to a new nadir.

U.S.–Western Hemisphere Agreements

	Total Agreements	Defense	Percent	Narcotics	Percent
Canada–U.S.	252	67	27	0	0
Mexico–U.S.	205	5	2	44	21
The Bahamas–U.S.	42	16	38	3	7

New Initiatives and Accomplishments

The strained relationship between the United States and its three closest neighbors continued for about 2 years after the invasion of Iraq. Behind the scenes, diplomats from Canada, Mexico, and the United States had been negotiating to improve cooperation on economic and security issues. On March 23, 2005, the Security and Prosperity Partnership of North America initiated cooperative approaches to:

■ secure North America from external threats
■ prevent and respond to threats within North America
■ streamline the secure and efficient movement of legitimate and low-risk traffic across shared borders
■ promote economic growth.

Based on the principle that security and prosperity are mutually dependent, the Security and Prosperity Partnership was the mechanism that facilitated open and frank discussions among government agencies of the three North American Free Trade Agreement partners. The Bahamas and Caribbean Community were not included.

While the U.S. Department of Defense, Canadian Department of National Defence, and the Mexican Secretariat of National Defense are not lead agencies for any partnership initiatives, some progress has been made to enhance military-to-military relations. The United States and Canada created a binational planning group in 2002, which served as a catalyst for enhanced military cooperation. Its effects were multiple:

■ Canada and the United States renewed the NORAD Agreement (2006) expanding the aerospace defense mission to include maritime warning.
■ The Chief of Defence Staff and Chairman of the Joint Chiefs of Staff approved a Basic Defense Document (2006) that identified areas of cooperation.
■ Commanders of U.S. Northern Command (US-NORTHCOM) and Canada Command approved a Civil Assistance Plan (2008) to provide guidance for military-to-military assistance to civil agencies in the event of disasters.
■ NORAD, USNORTHCOM, and Canada Command completed significant work in binational homeland defense and homeland security exercise planning and execution in order to enhance seamless interoperability among staffs, subordinate commands, and over 30 federal agencies.

In September 2005, Mexican armed forces provided immediate assistance to victims of Hurricane Katrina, creating significant goodwill between both nations. However, defense-to-defense contacts between Mexico and the United States progressed slowly until the election of President Felipe Calderon in December 2006. He was the catalyst for enhanced Mexico-U.S. relationships, encouraging his Secretary of National Defense and Secretary of the Navy to reach out to their American counterparts. In February 2007, Mexico provided USNORTHCOM with a naval liaison officer, who has been invaluable in coordination with the Mexican armed forces. In addition, the commander of NORAD and USNORTHCOM has hosted more than 100 distinguished visitors from Mexico for information exchanges, including discussions of how to respond to pandemic influenza.

In 2007, the government of The Bahamas and the U.S. Government launched Operation *Enduring Friendship* to enhance bilateral security and increase capabilities against illicit activities. Recognizing that security vulnerabilities in The Bahamas contribute to vulnerabilities in the United States, *Enduring Friendship* was created to counter illegal drugs, illegal immigrants, or terrorists attempting to traverse The Bahamas' vast marine expanse. *Enduring Friendship* security assistance provides The Bahamas with four 43-foot Interceptor Nor-Tech boats, designed for speed and maneuverability in both the ocean and shallow water, and associated support. The *Enduring Friendship* security assistance initiative also provides much-needed equipment to support the OPBAT work of the Royal Bahamas Defence Force, whether that work is search and rescue or interception of illegal poachers, illegal migration, or drug trafficking.

The Way Ahead

President Bush did not submit the Security and Prosperity Partnership to the U.S. Senate for treaty approval as required by the U.S. Constitution. Consequently, many partnership initiatives continue at the discretion of the sitting administration. Foreign Affairs Canada and the U.S. Department of State would do well to develop a Comprehensive Defence and Security Agreement for approval by the prime minister and the President and ratification by the U.S. Senate. This would provide the needed political vision, legal authority, and overarching guidance for continuous improvement in defense and security on our northern border. In addition, unresolved issues such as the Northwest Passage and ballistic missile defense should not be ignored.

Despite similar culture and customs with other Caribbean Community nations, The Bahamas shares a special relationship with the United States due to geographic proximity and shared concerns about common threats. Therefore, The Bahamas should be invited to participate in bilateral defense and security talks that are focused upon enhanced cooperation against air and maritime threats. The Bahamas and the United States should consider a NORAD-like agreement to establish a binational air and maritime command that ensures seamless information-sharing and synchronized operations against common threats. The Canada-U.S. relationship should serve as this model of interoperability.

The Mexican armed forces once eschewed coordination or cooperation with the U.S. defense establishment. However, senior leaders from Mexico have significantly increased contact and coordination with USNORTHCOM over the past 2 years. Although it may be premature to expect cooperation in homeland defense, bilateral cooperation in air and maritime surveillance and warning against external threats would not raise sovereignty concerns. In addition, the potential exists for cooperation between USNORTHCOM and the Mexican armed forces in bilateral military assistance to civil authorities along our shared border to save lives, prevent human suffering, and mitigate damage to public property.

The OAS gathering in Mexico in October 2008 discussed the Western Hemisphere's security challenges and concluded with the signing of a regional security declaration that aims to improve police education and coordination between law enforcement and other security authorities that combat organized crime. The current U.S. administration must recognize that sovereign neighbors require separate and unique approaches to defense and security relationships. A focus on synchronization, not integration, is the key to accomplishing mutually beneficial goals without violating sovereignty concerns. Following through on this regional security declaration, with coordination and cooperation among all four neighbors, will close gaps and seams currently exploited by transnational threats and drug trafficking organizations.

Responding to the Region's Challenges and Opportunities

Understanding current and past U.S. actions in the Americas requires differentiating between the major challenges facing Latin America and the Caribbean nations and those facing the United States as it loses influence and has to compete with other American

and external powers. Brazil, Venezuela, Russia, and China (as well as increasingly influential regional associations such as CARICOM and UNASUR) have demonstrated that the United States no longer enjoys hegemony in the region. The successful pursuit of interests in a peaceful and stable region will require Washington to find more effective strategies for dealing with the root causes and not just the symptoms of uneven development.

A series of commanders at the U.S. Southern Command, for example, have summarized the region's core challenge in one word: poverty. Combined with a number of pervasive underlying conditions including longstanding social inequities, uneven economic progress, the inequitable distribution of wealth, and significant levels of corruption, the environment for constructive development is inhospitable. Poverty is a key issue, but it is the result of broader developmental shortcomings that directly affect the ability of central governments to protect their citizens. Violent criminal organizations, including gangs and groups engaged in illegal trafficking, take advantage of the region's patchy development to threaten both government operations and human security. The U.S. Government—using its diplomatic, military, developmental, and other instruments of policy—must find cooperative ways to help Latin American and Caribbean governments as they try

Venezuelan President Hugo Chávez addresses UN General Assembly

to correct the major problems related to uneven development. These issues include promoting development, tamping down anti-Americanism, improving civil-military relations, and stemming narcotics trafficking.

Major Issues Related to the Challenge

Development. Most countries in the Americas face the longstanding challenge of uneven development—both domestically and regionally—across political, social, economic, and judicial dimensions. Reversing this trend is a daunting task, but its resolution is imperative for the region to enjoy greater stability and prosperity. The unrepresentative nature of many governments, the character of the economic markets, the inefficiency and corruption of the justice systems, and weak governance contribute to a number of associated security threats including domestic crime and violence as well as transnational criminal networks. Organized crime, gangs, ungoverned spaces, terrorism—both imported and homegrown and related to narcotics—and the trafficking of drugs, persons, and small arms are the effect of an inability of national governments to provide an environment in which democracy thrives, the economy produces both wealth and jobs, and the rule of law pervades. By negotiating and ratifying free trade agreements, including those currently in progress with Colombia and Panama, the United States has an opportunity to assist Latin American and Caribbean governments in their efforts to create stable economies with adequate employment opportunities for their citizens.

Anti-Americanism. The spread of anti-Americanism in the Americas has become a key U.S. concern. The growing wave of populist leaders in Latin America, led by Hugo Chavez and his "21st-century socialism," needs an adversary to succeed. Chavez and his acolytes look outward for a convenient target of blame for their country's economic, social, and political problems. The United States, which is characterized as having a foreign policy of either bullying its neighbors or neglecting the region, is the perfect scapegoat. For those countries with serious internal challenges—Bolivia, Ecuador, and Nicaragua—the idea of socialism for the 21st century, and its associated anti-Americanism, is not without some appeal.

The United States cannot afford to stand idly by, but neither can it overreact aggressively against Chavez and his supporters. Instead, Washington must walk a fine line between engagement with sectors of societies that are in opposition to the government and unintentionally legitimizing the anti-American leaders. Among the positive first steps the United States can take toward improving its relationship with neighbors is to admit mistakes when they have been made. For instance, Secretary of State Condoleezza Rice said that the United States was "shooting ourselves in the foot" by pressuring governments to grant immunity to American Servicemembers (by bilaterally waiving Article 98 of the Rome Statute of the International Criminal Court or risk losing U.S. military assistance). Washington would be wise to continue to move away from similar coercive measures and put forward positive initiatives for the region based on a more subtle use of U.S. soft power.

Civil-Military Relations. To help states consolidate their control over national territory and protect their citizens, the Obama administration will have to work closely with public security and military forces. Such an approach can assist in creating a more secure environment conducive to social and economic development. However, this approach will also raise concerns about the condition of national civil-military relations in various countries of the region. This developmental challenge actually has seen positive, albeit uneven, improvement in the Americas. The attraction and prevalence of military-based authoritarian regimes faded after World War II. By the 1990s, democratically elected civilians governed in most Latin American and Caribbean nations. The past 15 years have seen a further deepening of civilian authority over armed forces, which has largely been accepted. Nonetheless, the continuing need to overcome past distrust between civilians and military officials will require much more time and effort from both sides. The United States can help by continuing to serve as an example of productive civil-military relations and provide ideas for the integration of both civilian and military efforts facing domestic and international security challenges. Education is the key to strengthening this fundamental relationship. The United States could benefit from increasing funding of International Military Education and Training (IMET) programs, which can be used by government and nongovernment civilians as well as military personnel. Latin American and Caribbean ministries of defense also must make better use of these programs, rather than limiting IMET to military personnel.

Narco-trafficking. Narcotics trafficking is a serious security challenge affecting most countries in the Americas. This criminal business recognizes the significant importance of demand—for which the

Alliances, Treaties, and Trading Communities of the Western Hemisphere

Political

ALBA - (*Alternativa Bolivariana para los Pueblos de Nuestra America*, or **Bolivarian Alternative for Latin America**)

ALBA was launched in Havana, Cuba, in 2005 within the framework of the Hemispheric Social Alliance. ALBA challenges the hegemony of neoliberal integration; it is a deliberate response to the proposed Free Trade Area of the Americas and its focus on the market as the source of efficiency and economic growth and prosperity. ALBA is defined as a form of integration that places at its center the fight against poverty and exclusion through social reform.

- Cuba
- Venezuela
- Nicaragua
- Bolivia
- Honduras
- Dominica

- Grenada
- Guyana
- Jamaica
- Nicaragua
- Suriname
- St. Lucia

- St. Kitts and Nevis
- Saint Vincent and the Grenadines
- Haiti
- Honduras
- Guatemala
- Venezuela

PetroCaribe

This Caribbean oil alliance with Venezuela to purchase oil on conditions of preferential payment was launched in June 2005. The payment system allows for a few nations to buy oil on market value, but only a certain amount is needed up front; the remainder can be paid through a 25-year financing agreement at 1 percent interest.

- Cuba
- Dominican Republic
- Antigua and Barbuda

- The Bahamas
- Belize
- Dominica

PetroSur

PetroSur, a political and commercial company promoted by the Bolivarian Republic of Venezuela with the support of other governments of the region, is directed to establish cooperation and integration mechanisms under the basis of complementarity and is called to use, fairly and democratically, the energy resources for the socio-economic improvement of the region.

- Venezuela
- Brazil
- Argentina

PetroAndina

The company, organized as a private company in July 2003 to search for, develop, and produce hydrocarbons in the Southern Cone of South America, has focused its activities in the Neuquen Basin of Argentina and conducts operations from its office in Buenos Aires. It is headquartered in Calgary, Canada.

- Bolivia
- Colombia
- Ecuador
- Peru
- Venezuela

Economic

NAFTA (North America Free Trade Agreement)

This trilateral trade bloc in North America was created by the governments of the United States, Canada, and Mexico.

- Canada
- Mexico
- United States

CAFTA-DR - (Central America-Dominican Republic-United States Free Trade Agreement)

The agreement was designed to eliminate tariffs and trade barriers and expand regional opportunities for workers, manufacturers, consumers, farmers, ranchers, and service providers.

- Costa Rica
- El Salvador
- Guatemala
- Honduras
- Nicaragua
- Dominican Republic
- United States

Mercosur - (*Mercado Comun del Sur*)

The agreement was established by the Treaty of Asuncion in March 1991 and took effect on December 31, 1994. Its purpose was to set up a common market and eliminate trade barriers among the signatory parties.

- Brazil
- Argentina
- Paraguay
- Uruguay

Andean Community - (*Comunidad Andina de Naciones*)

This community is formed of four countries that voluntarily joined to achieve more rapid, better balanced, and more autonomous development through Andean, South American, and Latin American integration.

- Bolivia
- Colombia
- Ecuador
- Peru

SPP - Security and Prosperity Partnership of North America
The partnership was launched in March 2005 as a trilateral effort to increase security and enhance prosperity among the United States, Canada, and Mexico through greater cooperation and information-sharing.

SICA - (*Sistema de Integracion Centroamericana*, or Central American Integration System)
The Central American countries have gone into a process of political, economic, social, cultural, and ecological integration through this system.

UNASUR - Union de Naciones Suramericanas, or Union of South American Nations
UNASUR, set up on the model of the European Union, was made official in May 2008. It aims at the cultural, social, economic, and political integration of the South American peoples.

CARICOM - Caribbean Community and Common Market
The organization's establishment was the result of a 15-year effort to fulfill the hope of regional integration that was born with the establishment of the British West Indies Federation in 1958. The federation came to an end in 1962, but its end may be regarded as the real beginning of what is now the Caribbean Community.

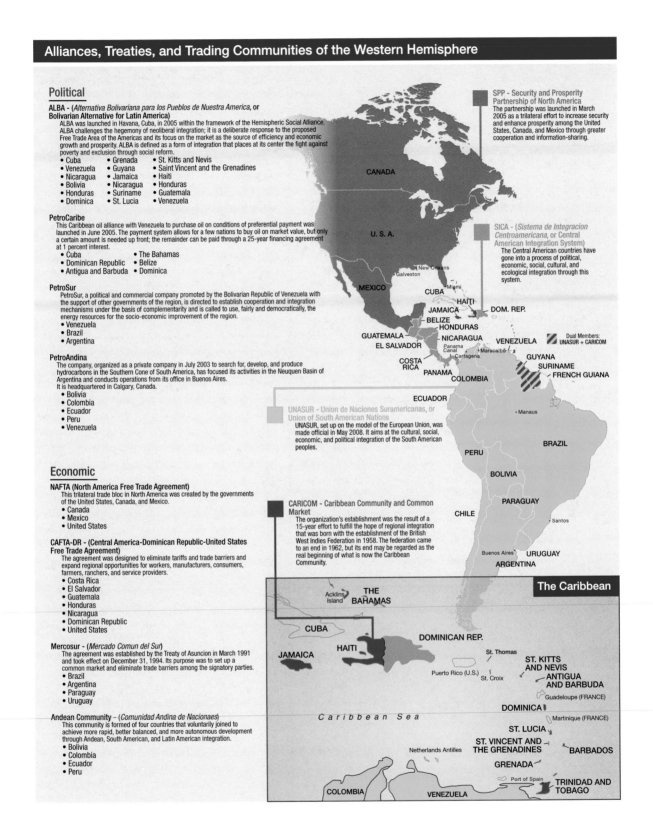

United States is largely responsible—as well as the need for the cultivation, production, and smuggling of illegal substances. The ease with which cartels operate reflects the region's institutional weaknesses. Many governments lack adequate security forces to deter narco-trafficking. Fragile economies are unable to produce sufficient employment and prosperity, leaving farmers few options for supporting their families other than cultivating poppy and coca. Furthermore, judicial systems are often overwhelmed, institutionally weak, or too corrupt to function effectively. Finally, societies themselves have begun to disintegrate, unable to escape the crisis of public order as murders, organized kidnappings, local crime, and corruption mount. With safety deteriorating and the government unable or unwilling to respond, a mix of fear and cynical indifference seizes control of people's lives. The United States has an opportunity to play an active role by implementing broad-reaching, collaborative programs, such as the recent Merida Initiative, to address the multitude of factors that facilitate narcotics trafficking.

Creating Opportunities

While the United States has lost influence in the Western Hemisphere and Washington's leadership is being challenged, Latin America and the Caribbean do not present a completely negative setting for U.S. security and prosperity. On the contrary, many countries have made considerable headway invigorating economic growth, diminishing poverty and inequality, empowering people, deepening democratic roots, and playing responsible roles on the international stage. The fact that Brazil and Mexico are emerging global players does not challenge Washington, nor does Hugo Chavez's brand of radical populism, which most Latin American states have not adopted. In many ways the region presents a positive strategic environment. The issue the United States must address concerns its willingness to adapt to the region-wide sea change taking place in the Americas in order to advance its agenda. Is Washington inclined to redefine its role, build trust with neighbors, and become a partner of choice?

There are things that only states can do together to deal with manmade and natural problems they cannot solve alone. For the foreseeable future, partnership in the international system is less optional than imperative, but close collaboration is not an automatic step for any country, particularly one with the power and tradition of the United States. Its path to partnership necessitates creating the

conditions needed to move forward. The first hurdle is overcoming society's isolationist tendency already visible in debates about immigration and foreign trade and construction of a fence along the border with Mexico. The way ahead also involves reshaping longstanding U.S. concepts and approaches. The patronizing U.S. attitude that only the United States can tutor, provide assistance, and in many ways guide the region's "developing states" persists in many official corridors. This mindset disregards the interests and sensitivities of other states. While anti-Americanism and global economic trends have given many Latin American and Caribbean nations real autonomy in world affairs, this attitude presents a serious obstacle for the United States.

The traditional minimalist U.S. approach to involvement in the hemisphere stitches together a series of country and functional policies. The United States often treats its southern neighbors as if they were united beyond geography and history and a patchwork of common policies could fit all. This will not work today as a basis for regional cooperation. Washington should disaggregate for policy purposes highly diverse Latin American and Caribbean nations, forcing officials to think about and act separately toward individual states and subregional communities.

Without attention to geostrategic perspectives, the U.S. approach deals with subregional groups of countries as collections of bilateral contacts when what is needed are comprehensive, holistic views that draw attention to important policy and planning considerations, such as the nature of political and public security relationships among countries, lines of communication for legal and illegal commerce, and the influence of the zone's geography on land, sea, and air movement. For subregional cooperation to be effective, it needs a comprehensive, unified strategic concept for that area to guide operations, set the direction for programs to strengthen national capacities, and build confidence and mutual trust.

The framework of a new U.S. strategic approach to the Americas should be built on a foundation of three values: respect for the views and sensitivities of other states; a willingness to work with states either individually or as communities in reciprocal ways; and a careful focus on nurturing trust. The structure itself should comprise ways to go about cooperating with Latin American and Caribbean countries or subregional groups. Two potential opportunities, which draw upon the Defense Department's interactive capabilities, include the management of disaster response and joining regional peacekeeping operations. The first opportunity, discussed at the September 2008 Conference of Defense Ministers of the Americas, would involve U.S. participation on a military working group in support of civilian relief agencies and organizations. The aim would be to standardize protocols for the use of the region's military assets to improve communication, coordination, planning, and training for mutual responses to natural or manmade disasters. The second opportunity envisions offering to participate in MINUSTAH. Commanded by a Brazilian, this heavily Latin American peace operation is an important new feature in the region's military collaboration. The U.S. participation consists of 3 military and 49 civilian police. The offer of engineer or medical unit augmentation to MINUSTAH to assist Haiti's painstaking recovery after three hurricanes could demonstrate U.S. willingness to join an existing Latin American force.

The complex challenges facing the Americas cannot be resolved by military means. Moreover, the United States no longer has the political capital or the influence in the Americas to act unilaterally in confronting the challenges facing the region. Instead, a new administration in Washington must be willing to find ways to work collaboratively with partners in order to help them address both their immediate issues and the underlying development problems that provide fertile ground for today's and tomorrow's threats to regional security and stability. gsa

Contributors

Colonel John A. Cope, USA (Ret.) (Chapter Editor), is Senior Research Fellow in the Institute for National Strategic Studies at National Defense University. He is a specialist in Western Hemisphere security affairs (including North American issues), U.S. policy for Latin America and the Caribbean, civil-military relations, and defense education. Before retiring from the Army, Colonel Cope served in the Department of State's Bureau of Inter-American Affairs, U.S. Southern Command, U.S. Army South, U.S. Army War College, and the 101st Airborne Division.

Dr. Thomaz Guedes Da Costa's academic career includes experience teaching international relations theory, strategy, defense issues, and international political economy for the Department of International Relations Department at the University of Brasilia. He worked as a career analyst with Brazil's National Council for Scientific and Technological Development and served as a researcher and advisor in international security, national defense, strategic planning, and foreign intelligence training in the Center for Strategic Studies and the Office of the Brazilian Presidency. Dr. Costa has a degree in international affairs from Indiana University of Pennsylvania and a Ph.D. in Political Science from Columbia University.

Dr. Johanna Mendelson-Forman is a Senior Associate with Americas Program at the Center for Strategic and International Studies, where she works on renewable energy, the Americas, civil-military relations, and postconflict reconstruction. She is a member of the Council on Foreign Relations and serves on the advisory boards of Women in International Security and the Latin American Security Network, RESDAL. She holds a J.D. from Washington College of Law at American University and a Ph.D. in Latin American history from Washington University at St. Louis.

Dr. Brian Latell is a Senior Associate in the Americas Program at the Center for Strategic and International Studies. He has been a Latin America and Caribbean specialist for the last four decades and lectures regularly on these subjects to university, professional, and political groups. In 1998, Dr. Latell retired after three-and-a-half decades as a foreign intelligence officer, having served in the U.S. Air Force and for extended periods as a Latin America specialist at the Central Intelligence Agency and the National Intelligence Council.

Dr. Biff Baker is a Senior Analyst with Science Applications International Corporation, who provides support to U.S. Northern Command Theater Security Cooperation initiatives. Previously, Dr. Baker served as an Army officer and Professor at Colorado Technical University.

Dr. Craig A. Deare is Professor of National Security Affairs in the Center for Hemispheric Defense Studies (CHDS) at NDU. During his tenure at CHDS, he served as the Dean of

Academic Affairs from July 2004 to April 2007. Dr. Deare served in the U.S. Army for 20 years, during which he had a variety of assignments specializing in military intelligence and Latin American Foreign Area Officer duties.

Dr. Caesar D. Sereseres is Associate Dean for Undergraduate Studies, Political Science, School of Social Sciences, at the University of California, Irvine. Professor Sereseres' major fields of interest are U.S. foreign policy and U.S.–Latin American relations. His experience includes a research consultantship in national security studies at the RAND Corporation and service as a Staff Officer in the Office of Policy Planning, Bureau of Inter-American Affairs, at the Department of State from 1985 to 1987.

Dr. Christopher M. Sands is a Senior Fellow at the Hudson Institute, where he specializes in Canada and U.S.-Canada relations, as well as North American economic integration. He serves as a member of the Advisory Committee to the U.S. Section of the North American Competitiveness Council, organized by the U.S. Chamber of Commerce to consult with U.S. Government officials in negotiations under the North American Security and Prosperity Partnership.

Europeans saw Germany with its scientific, economic, and technological strength as the more likely candidate to become the great power of the 20th century. That was certainly how many Germans saw matters, and they attempted to realize that vision at the cost of millions of lives and world wars.

Such attitudes reflected more than European prejudices about a country that had little history or culture, a military that had fought just one war—which was a civil war at that—and a people who consisted of the "tired, poor, huddled masses" from various nations. In contrast, early in the 20th century Germany had a homogenous population, superior technology, premier scientific expertise, leading industries, and a military forged in the wars of German unification that became the most capable fighting force in the world.

By 1918, the United States had become a significant force in the balance of power. Thirty years later with the end of World War II, America became the dominant power in the world. The Nation would continue to dominate the international order during the Cold War. In retrospect, American dominance seems to have been a foregone conclusion, though it was anything but that. Admittedly, the ascendancy of the United States represented a combination of economic strength, geopolitical position, good fortune, gifted leaders, and appalling failures by its opponents. Nevertheless, contingency played a key role in American success. Specifically, there were turning points in the rise of the Nation: World War I, reaction to that conflict, World War II, and finally reaction to that conflict, which differed enormously from how things had unfolded in the 1920s.

U.S. foreign policy in 1900 was one of benign neglect at best. Americans saw themselves as removed from the turmoil of the old world that so many European immigrants had fled in order to escape conscription laws and class prejudice. Moreover, the oceans had protected the United States in the century since it had gained independence. Thus, George Washington's warning against "entangling alliances" made sense to those who paid attention to world affairs. The outbreak of World War I in 1914 mobilized little support in the United States for intervention on either side. National attitudes did move swiftly to favor the Allies after German troops reportedly committed atrocities against civilians in Belgium, Luxembourg, and France. Nevertheless, Americans had no intention of involving their country in a conflict on the other side of the Atlantic.

That disposition began to change when Germany, which was waging unrestricted submarine warfare against ships approaching the British Isles, advertised its aim to sink *Lusitania* on the front page of *The New York Times* in 1915. They achieved that objective and killed 1,198 of the 1,959 people on board the liner, including 128 Americans drowned in the Irish Sea. There is the possibility that if the Republican candidate in 1912, William Howard Taft, or the third party candidate, Theodore Roosevelt, won the election, the United States would have entered the war at that point. Threatened with war, the Germans ceased their unrestricted campaign.

Marine light armored vehicles roll into Kuwait International Airport after retreat of Iraqi forces from Kuwait during Operation *Desert Storm*

But Woodrow Wilson won a divided election in 1912, and was reelected 4 years later with the campaign slogan "He Kept Us Out of War." It turned out to be an ironic catchphrase because Germany resumed unrestricted submarine warfare in early 1917, which led the United States to eventually declare war. The outcome of World War I was close. American forces arrived in substantial numbers only in the summer of 1918, barely in time to tip the balance against the exhausted Reich.

The armistice resulted in a bad peace. The Treaty of Versailles, which attempted to make Germany pay for a war that it had started, was neither sufficiently harsh to keep it down nor mild enough to persuade it to accept defeat. Unfortunately, the Americans then withdrew from Europe, persuaded by intellectuals on both sides of the Atlantic that World War I had been caused by arms merchants and that anything was far better than war. During the 1920s, U.S. leaders refused to accept the notion that the Nation had responsibility even for the health of the world finances and the international economy, much less its security.

Instead, Americans focused on normalcy, isolationism, and the economic bubble of the 1920s. The Smoot-Hawley Tariff Act in 1930 ended international trade and turned a major recession into the Great Depression, which turned rejection of the outside world into national self-indulgence. Then in 1933, Franklin Roosevelt emerged as the leader America desperately needed. However, he only lived to become President because an assassin's shot missed him and instead killed the mayor of Chicago in early 1933. Coincidentally, 2 years earlier, Winston Churchill was almost killed in New York when he looked the wrong way when crossing the street and stepped off the curb into traffic. The survival of both men was essential to the rise of America: Churchill by keeping Britain in the war after the collapse of France, and Roosevelt by taking his country and people into the war. Without those two leaders in power in 1940, it is possible that the Anglo-American alliance may never have existed. Both recognized Adolf Hitler as a great threat. Roosevelt understood the moral danger of Germany. Churchill saw Hitler as not only a moral danger, but as a strategic one as well. He did not come to power until May 1940, at the precise moment when the Western powers had lost nearly all their strategic advantages after the fall of France.

Roosevelt took office almost simultaneously with Hitler becoming the German chancellor and confronted two great strategic problems. First, he had to deal with the upheaval of the Depression, which he could not resolve simply by solving the country's economic crisis. Only through reforms in the financial system and industrial sector could further crises be avoided. Those tasks demanded enormous focus and energy. Second, while Roosevelt recognized that Germany and Japan posed threats, Americans adamantly opposed involvement in world conflicts. Congress underlined that deep sense of isolationism by passing neutrality laws in the mid-1930s that forbade economic dealings with belligerent nations. Thus, as the international situation worsened, Roosevelt had little room to maneuver to provide the Nation's support to those willing to resist aggression.

American isolationist sentiment was so deep that Roosevelt could only muster a small budget allocation for the Navy in 1934 by ordering warships under the Works Progress Administration to ease unemployment. In this sense, Congress willfully

followed the dictates of the people until 1938 when it came to war planning. Only in 1938 did the Navy get substantial funding, and that was intended only for the defense of North America. The Army and Army Air Corps continued to receive only a pittance. The Czech crisis of September 1938 allowed Roosevelt to request funding to improve the Army Air Corps, but the Army itself did not emerge from the doldrums until the fall of France. At that point, some Americans began to recognize the growing danger of the international situation.

The outbreak of a major European war in September 1939 split the country down the middle. Roosevelt was a lame duck because neither he nor most Americans considered the international situation desperate enough for him to seek a third term as President, something that had never happened before. The fall of France changed everything. Roosevelt initially considered that Britain was in a hopeless position. Thus, exchanges with Churchill underlined the desire on the part of Roosevelt to safeguard the Royal Navy if England fell to Germany. But Churchill was clear—he would not surrender. Yet without American economic aid, the British could not stay the course. Moreover, there were others in England willing to make a deal with Hitler.

In the midst of a third campaign for President, with isolationists in full cry, Roosevelt risked his political career by aiding Britain. Overruling his military advisors, Roosevelt ordered surplus armaments, including destroyers, sent to England. This action required great determination in the face of the looming elections that Roosevelt won, which allowed him to guide the United States with immense skill through the major challenges of a world war. In this sense, the serendipity of Roosevelt's survival of the attempt on his life in 1933 takes on added meaning.

Roosevelt ran again for President in 1944, despite failing health. His advisors pressured him to drop Henry Wallace as Vice President and put a relatively unknown senator, Harry Truman, on the ticket. If ever chance were a deciding factor in American history, this was it. Wallace would have been a disaster as President and could have lost the Cold War even before it began.

Truman on the other hand was an extraordinarily successful President. On the surface, he appeared unprepared by virtue of his education or background. But as a voracious reader of history, Truman developed a feel for international relations. Moreover, he was willing to make crucial decisions, such as dropping the atomic bomb. If he had difficulty in understanding Joseph Stalin and the Soviet Union at first, he was a fast learner who chose extraordinarily good advisors. Truman stood fast against Moscow at critical moments, such as the Berlin blockade. The Marshall Plan, written during his administration, represented his willingness to engage in world affairs to a degree that was absent from American leadership after World War I. Yet perhaps his greatest strength as a President was making decisions regardless of public opinion. His motto, "The buck stops here," underscores the readiness to take responsibility. Similarly, the great triumph of his administration was setting the course that established the parameters of the contest with the Soviet Union and ensured that the United States played a role befitting its new economic and financial stature.

Contingency is a difficult matter to identify in retrospect. However, in thinking through the history of the past century, one should not lose sight of the fact that the rise of the United States to its current position was not inevitable. The Nation came close to abstaining from participation in World War I when a German victory would have limited the ability of America to influence European affairs. Then after World War I, the United States almost wrecked the international and global economic system through its shortsighted postwar isolationist policies.

Victory in World War II was the result of con-tingency and chance. It is doubtful if anyone other than Roosevelt could have edged the United States slowly but deliberately into the conflict. He enabled Churchill to maintain a tenuous grip on power after the collapse of France. Finally, the emergence of Truman as a man of stature and substance was dependent on the idiosyncrasies of politicians trying to help Roosevelt win a fourth term. They picked the right man, but largely for the wrong reasons.

What looked nearly certain at the turn of the 20th century—the rise of Germany to dominance in Europe—did not come to pass. Instead, an outlier country that no one expected to rise became the dominant power of the century. Yet even with its large population, favored geographic position, and powerful economy, this section has shown that America's rise to power was not inevitable but grew out of a number of unpredictable events. No matter how certain the future looks, the prudent strategist hedges his bets.

Deterrence and Defense

The North Korean nuclear test in 2006 and the ongoing Iranian quest for nuclear weapons highlight how dramatically the international security environment has changed since the Cold War. Some believe the world is approaching a tipping point where changes in the international arena could have a

Brigadier General Anthony C. McAuliffe gives glider pilots last-minute instructions before takeoff from England, 1944

domino effect with countries scrambling to develop nuclear weapons or hedge capacities to quickly build nuclear arsenals. Under such a scenario, several U.S. allies who have previously renounced nuclear weapons might reconsider the decision, including Japan, South Korea, and Turkey.

Until now, American security guarantees, including extended deterrence in general and extended nuclear deterrence specifically, have been credited with persuading nations to renounce nuclear weapons. The United States is the only country that makes an explicit commitment to use nuclear weapons to protect other nations, 28 in all, including North Atlantic Treaty Organization (NATO) members, Japan, South Korea, and Australia. Testifying before Congress in 1997, Under Secretary of Defense Walt Slocombe stated that:

the role of U.S. nuclear capability in preventing the spread of nuclear weapons often goes unnoticed. The extension of a credible U.S. nuclear deterrent to allies has been an important nonproliferation tool. It has removed incentives for key allies, in a still dangerous world, to develop and deploy their own nuclear forces, as many are technically capable of doing. Indeed, our

strong security relationships have probably played as great a role in nonproliferation over the past 40 years as has the [Non-Proliferation Treaty].

In a world of proliferation challenges, reexamining extended deterrence, including extended prospects for nuclear deterrence, must become a serious priority for the United States.

To *extend* deterrence, the Nation must first be *able* to deter. There have been reassessments of deterrence over the last decade or so, but there is no consensus on what deterrence means, whom to deter, which capabilities to include, and how deterrence could be most effectively accomplished. These questions are coupled with the acknowledgment that there is less confidence in deterrence today than during the Cold War. However, there is recognition in the United States that it makes sense to examine whether and how deterrence concepts could be adapted, adjusted, and applied to the challenges of the 21st century. This assessment must not only look at a range of potential adversaries and threats, but also explore methods and capabilities that would contribute to deterrence. The objective of deterrence operations according to the Joint Operating Concept released in 2006 is to

People's Liberation Army soldiers at Shenyang training base, China

"decisively influence the adversary's decisionmaking calculus in order to prevent hostile actions against U.S. vital interests. . . . An adversary's deterrence decision calculus focuses on their perception of three primary elements." These elements are: first, benefits of a course of action; second, the costs of a course of action; and third, the consequences of restraint (namely, not taking action).

The challenge of altering the decisionmaking calculus of a potential enemy can be examined by looking at three factors. The first requires understanding who makes decisions, how they think and what they care about, how they are affected by domestic politics, what they regard as key objectives, how they weigh risks and gains, and what they believe about the deterrer. All those questions demand expertise on the region, country, group, or leader in question that should depend not only on government agencies, but also on policy centers, academe, allied organizations, and so forth. Furthermore, answers to some of these questions are difficult to discern, and others may never be answered. But learning as much as possible would seem desirable in the case of deterrence. In this way, some of the unknowns will become variables in the planning process.

Second, adapting the capabilities that go beyond nuclear weapons to deter specific actions by specific players in specific situations also is important. Nonnuclear deterrence can include both nonnuclear and nonkinetic passive and active strike defenses as well as nonmilitary tools such as diplomatic efforts, economic assistance, legal means, and even simple restraint.

Third, the clarity and credibility of American messages in the mind of the deteree are critical. U.S. policymakers must have the mechanisms to assess how their words and actions are perceived, how they affect the calculations of each adversary, and how they might mitigate misperceptions that undermine the effectiveness of deterrence. Thus, one aspect of reassurance depends on the trust of allies in the ability of the United States to deter actions against their interests. As the Nation reexamines deterrence, it must consider the requirements for extended deterrence in the evolving security environment. How can America convince allies and friends that it will meet established security commitments so that they do not feel the need to develop nuclear weapons or other capabilities that would be counterproductive? While U.S. views on deterrence emerge, so may those of its allies. Inevitably, differences may arise over whom to deter, the role of offense and defense, and American versus other nations' capabilities to underpin deterrence.

Extended deterrence is more than extended nuclear deterrence. Conventional capabilities are playing a greater role in extended deterrence. Defenses, particularly missile defenses, have gained acceptance and even enthusiasm as a complement to extended deterrence. Forward presence and force projection are also ways to extend deterrence to allies. Beyond military capabilities, extended deterrence rests on the entire fabric of the alliance relationship, including shared interests, dialogue, consultation, coordinated planning, and the overall health of the alliance. In addition, extending deterrence to allies is based on the reputation of America as a security guarantor, which is shaped by its global behaviors. Some allies have been conflicted in this regard, fearing abandonment and wondering if the United States will be there when needed. On the other hand, many fear military entrapment or entanglement by getting pulled into situations against their interests. To be assured, allies first and foremost need to have confidence in American judgment and reliability. Without this basic trust, specific capabilities do not really matter.

In terms of extended nuclear deterrence, however, guaranteeing reassurance and trust is more difficult. To achieve it, America must designate the characteristics of the nuclear forces required to make this contribution to international security. Yet assuring one's allies offers little help in that regard. Establishing reassurance and trust does not define the size or composition of nuclear capabilities. It is impossible to claim that, for example, unless the Nation modernizes with the Reliable Replacement Warhead or retains a certain number of nuclear weapons, allies will no longer be assured.

It is not impossible for allies to feel insecure about the size, composition, and basing of the U.S. nuclear arsenal. That situation occurred in the late 1970s when Chancellor Helmut Schmidt of Germany was concerned that Soviet SS–20 missiles could decouple the U.S. strategic nuclear force from the defense of Europe, which led to fielding Pershing II and ground-launched cruise missiles in Europe. In short, by itself, the deployment of nuclear armed Tomahawk cruise missiles (TLAM–N) off the coast of Europe was insufficient coupling to reassure NATO Allies. Since it guaranteed their security, Allies cared about the precise composition and disposition of U.S. nuclear forces.

Nothing indicates that allies are insufficiently assured about American nuclear forces because of their structure or technical characteristics, but they may be convinced of it by the self-denigration of U.S. nuclear capability. In particular, talk of the United States being self-deterred, which has been used to champion new nuclear weapons, is counterproductive for assurance and deterrence. Granted, it is a Catch-22: changes one thinks are required in a democracy cannot occur without public scrutiny and debate. Yet unless Americans reach a consensus to fill the identified gaps, pointing out gaps in U.S. nuclear capabilities can undermine assurance as well as deterrence.

According to some analysts, questions have arisen in Japan and Turkey about the credibility of the U.S. nuclear guarantee. There is interest in the Japanese defense community in discussing the exact types of conflict scenarios that could put the American nuclear guarantee into play. Such consultations are important in demonstrating the credibility of extended deterrence. For instance, must U.S. nuclear weapons be either deployed or deployable to a given region to reassure allies? At present, the only nuclear weapons deployed on allied territory are the remaining air-delivered bombs in several NATO countries that could be delivered by dual-capable U.S. or allied aircraft. The nuclear weapons in South Korea were removed almost two decades ago, and the extension of nuclear deterrence in the Pacific region since then has been by offshore forces.

The capability to deploy nuclear weapons to assure partners or deter a regional threat has also declined over the years. The Presidential initiatives of 1991 and 1992 eliminated most so-called tactical nuclear weapons. In 1994, the United States announced the decision to permanently give up the deployment of nuclear weapons on carriers or surface ships. While that decision retained the capability to redeploy TLAM–N on attack submarines, there have been budget debates almost every year over the TLAM–N. The Navy has sought to retire the missile because maintaining the capability requires special training for submarine crews and certification of some boats. That represents an allocation of people, time, and money that the Service would prefer to forego. Thus, the TLAM–N system has not been updated for years, and may soon atrophy regardless of the budgetary controversy. Yet Japan places enormous importance on the retention of the Tomahawk missile, even in a reserve status, as evidence of U.S. security guarantees. The question is whether Japan could be reassured about the nuclear guarantee by some other means.

If visible presence is essential for reassurance, perhaps other capabilities can be made visible. For example, the media can cover the deployment of nuclear-capable B–2 bombers to Guam or Diego Garcia. Even nuclear submarines can send a deterrence and reassurance signal, such as when America withdrew intermediate-range missiles from Turkey in 1960 as a consequence of the Cuban missile crisis. In that case, a *Polaris* strategic submarine, which was deployed in the Mediterranean, called at the port of Izmir to demonstrate continuing nuclear presence in the area. Yet the question remains: How much does visibility matter to the credibility of extended nuclear deterrence?

Beyond visible nuclear forces or forces deployable to the region, there could be other ways to demonstrate the credibility of the U.S. extended nuclear deterrent. The options include discussions of nuclear scenarios, as suggested by some Japanese defense officials, or the institutionalization of exchanges on nuclear deterrence matters. Similarly, in light of the importance of the U.S.–NATO nuclear link in the perception of new Alliance members, the best way to promote that linkage in a changed environment also needs to be addressed.

In considering the size and composition of nuclear forces, it is necessary to address the issue of reassuring allies that the extended nuclear pledge remains viable and consider whether or not we will provide it to others who face new nuclear neighbors. However, planners should recognize that aspects of a nuclear posture that assure one ally may frighten another, whether those weapons are deployed on their territory or whether the United States modernizes nuclear weapons or develops new nuclear capabilities. As a result, American officials should consult with allies about what reassures them and which factors are most important to their remaining nonnuclear. Although it is unlikely the specifics of the nuclear arsenal will impact U.S. credibility, the perception of a lack of attention to nuclear issues could add up to allied concern. It is inattention that could undermine the nonproliferation aspects of its posture in providing cover for allies. In the end, if the United States is comfortable with its nuclear posture, it should make the case to allies that its security commitments, including extended nuclear deterrence, remain strong. This alone may reassure allies.

In the long term, the larger question is whether the Nation will continue to play a major role in the world, underpinning global stability and specifically extending nuclear deterrence to other states. In the near term, however, as long as there are nuclear weapons in the hands of others, the United States must sustain a safe and reliable nuclear weapons capability. As long as America has a leading role, its nuclear weapons will be about more than its own security.

Ending Conflict and Promoting Stability

The U.S. military is a far more battle-hardened and battle-weary force than it has been in three decades. As of July 3 2009, there were 130,000 American military personnel in Iraq and roughly 62,000 in Afghanistan. And there are also significant operational commitments in Djibouti, the former Yugoslavia, the Philippines, Thailand, Honduras, and Colombia. The United States has more troops deployed in real-world operations than since the Vietnam War, which involved as many as 500,000 Servicemembers in Southeast Asia. American troops are engaged in what are described as stability operations, which include counterinsurgency, counterterrorism, and nationbuilding—and, contrary to popular belief, are just as challenging and deadly as traditional combat missions of the past.

Although doctrine states that the primary role of the U.S. military is fighting and winning the Nation's wars, history indicates that stability operations have been the more common mission. They have included peacekeeping, counterinsurgency, and nationbuilding from the Western frontier of the 19th century to the South of the Reconstruction era, the Philippines at the end of the Spanish-American War, the Caribbean throughout the early 20th century, Europe and Japan following World War II, Panama, Somalia, Haiti, the Balkans, and current operations. According to the Defense Science Board 2004 Summer Study, the United States has lost more lives and treasure since the Cold War in stability operations than in traditional warfare. Increased emphasis on manmade and natural disasters in weak and failing states suggests that the Nation will have as much difficulty avoiding these crises in the future as it did in the past. Given the likelihood of stability operations, it is important to understand their nature and the factors determining their success or failure.

It may be tempting to ignore theoretical debates over terminology, but it would be a mistake. Words matter because they force us to agree on definitions, a process which in turn forces us to debate and fine tune our understanding about the nature of our environment and how we plan to operate. The term *irregular warfare*, which incorporates such disparate activities as stability operations, counterinsurgency, insurgency, and unconventional warfare in one single

concept, is not useful. A term that means everything actually does not really mean very much at all.

In the Irregular Warfare Joint Operating Concept, *stability operations* are defined as a subset of counterinsurgency or irregular warfare, which is confusing because one is not a subset of the other. Rather, it depends on the level of analysis. Tactically, stability operations represent a set of activities conducted during a mission in which the object is protecting people and establishing or maintaining order. In that context, stability operations could be a subset of a counterinsurgency campaign, conventional conflict, or irregular warfare, if such a thing actually exists. These are tasks in stability operations that the Army references in its full-spectrum doctrine. *Full-spectrum operations* are similar to the three-block war, which was explained by General Charles Krulak, the former commandant of the Marine Corps, in 1997:

In one moment in time, our service members will be feeding and clothing displaced refugees, providing humanitarian assistance. In the next moment, they will be holding two warring tribes apart—conducting peacekeeping operations—and, finally, they will be fighting a highly lethal mid-intensity battle—all on the same day . . . all within three city blocks.[1]

At the strategic level, counterinsurgency can be regarded as a type of stability operation in which systems under stress are returned to or converted to stability. As the Stability Operations Joint Operating Concept of 2006 explained, such operations are mounted in order "to assist a state or region that is under severe stress or has collapsed due to either a natural or man-made disaster."[2]

The causes of systemic stress or failure vary. For instance, a system can fail or come under severe stress because of major interstate or civil war, insurgency, low-grade or chronic political unrest, economic crisis, natural disaster, or a deadly combination involving several factors. Each case also varies with respect to political, cultural, economic, social, and other preconditions, including the relative competence and strength of the local government. When a system is under stress in this way, it is vulnerable to actions by spoilers from low-level criminals and gangs to dangerous warlords to insurgents, all of whom can exploit weak governance to generate chaos, violence, and social unrest. Even normal citizens may turn to crime to survive in such dangerous and anarchic situations. Recent examples include the looting of Baghdad and the chaos in New Orleans in the wake of Hurricane Katrina. In those cases, a vacuum was created by external stresses placed on the system, which was exploited by miscreants of various sorts. In Iraq, a violent insurgency was given space to grow. As both cases demonstrate, either stopping or reversing such pandemonium is extremely difficult, especially for outside forces unfamiliar with the cultural landscape, as occurred in Iraq.

The initial goal of outside intervening forces is stopping chaos and violence. That task is the opposite of traditional military operations (maneuver warfare), which is to create chaos for the enemy forces. In sum, traditional military operations are focused on breaking down a system, whereas stability operations are about strengthening a system of political, economic, and social institutions under stress, preventing or reversing chaotic spirals into violence.

However, outside forces can only do so much. For stability to endure and human security to be maintained, the capacity of the local government must be restored or, in some cases, created in the first place. This may require full-scale nationbuilding depending on indigenous capacities to govern and the extent of damage sustained by existing institutions and resources.

Most successful stability operations have simple albeit not intuitive characteristics. Crafting a strategy for success or deciding to intervene in the first place requires an understanding of what it takes to succeed in a given situation. The following "top five" rules of thumb are derived from current and emerging doctrine, lessons learned, and best practices in recent and historical cases. They provide the basis of a point of departure for making realistic and practical decisions.

1. Start with a Long-term Strategy: "Cheap coats of paint won't work." Success in stability operations is time consuming. A comprehensive multiyear strategy that recognizes this reality must be crafted from the outset. Shortsighted strategies that do not accept what is needed for success fail to do the job, burn resources, and exhaust popular will at home. Moreover, research has indicated that Americans are unsupportive of interventions with strategies that were ill-conceived. Although sustaining domestic support is never easy, leaders stand a better chance if the American people understand the requirements from the beginning and also are convinced that there is an effective strategy in place.

2. Keep the Host Nation in the Lead: "Better [they] do it tolerably, than you do it perfectly." The United States has become the most likely external actor in stability or counterinsurgency operations in a foreign country. Thus, American forces will have either a supporting role with the host-nation government or a brokering role among the warring parties. In any case, local leaders must take the lead substantively as well as publicly. The U.S. goal should be helping the host nation achieve stability and the capacity to sustain peace and govern on its own. In practice, this means integrated planning with local authorities must begin on day one, even before deploying forces. One key reason for such planning is determining whether the host nation will consider legitimate grievances and address them in the political process. Defeating an insurgency without negotiation may be impossible for a democracy in the information age. Intervening in a situation where the local government is unwilling to commit to a political process to resolve the grievances of the people will be ineffectual at best and a great waste of blood and treasure at worst.

3. Put the Population First: "Protect the people where they sleep." When violence breaks out, the people will seek security from whoever can provide it. Ideally, the local government should be the first to offer protection because its legitimacy is derived from the ability to protect the people. Thus, the population is the first priority for an intervening force. This priority should be coupled with the goal of turning over security to local military forces as soon as possible. As General David Petraeus has emphasized, protecting the population involves considerable risk because it means leaving secure bases to "live among the people."

4. Match Ends to Means: The challenge of whole-of-government approach. Helping a nation build durable institutions, including mechanisms for security, governance, and economic development, will require diverse, nonmilitary skills. Currently, civilian experts must synchronize their efforts with military commanders in formulating a coherent whole-of-government strategy. The ability of civilian agencies to provide expertise is limited or lacking in some areas. In filling the gap on an ad hoc basis, the military has gradually developed limited proficiency in these areas. However, to succeed without muddling through in future missions, the United States must build that civilian capacity, which is a process that may take decades. In the meantime, any decision to engage abroad must be made in light of limited civilian expertise and a realistic understanding of the fact that the military must take up the slack. In such cases, there cannot be ambiguity over the fact that the military cannot expect relief since the civilian capacity simply does not exist.

5. Do Not Go It Alone: Victory is easier with friends. Conducting stability operations with allies in sanctioned multinational missions is preferable to unilateral action for two reasons: burdensharing and legitimacy. Americans are more likely to support engagement abroad if they do not have to foot the whole bill and believe that the mission is reasonable and valid. Moreover, local people are more likely to cooperate with outside forces if they regard them as legitimate. The perception of legitimacy is more common when regional or international bodies condone the intervention, recognize local authorities or agreements, publicly denounce insurgents and spoilers, and substantively promote investments in the economic future. Despite challenges in synchronizing tactics, technologies, and strategic objectives, efforts should be made to secure regional and international participation and support for intervention.

This framework and the five rules of thumb are offered as a starting point for leaders charged with deciding when and how to use force abroad. We must keep in mind that it is a delicate balance between the need to learn from experience so as not to repeat old mistakes on the one hand, and the need to avoid the trap of "fighting the last war" on the other. The guidelines presented here reflect a

desire to learn from recent and historical experience. They are presented as a snapshot in time, and like all lessons learned from experience, should be subject to thoughtful revision as circumstances inevitably change.

Iraq Endgame: Internal and Regional Stability

The outlook for Iraq improved greatly because of the substantial decline in violence registered in 2007 and 2008. But serious challenges remain, and continued U.S. engagement will be needed to put the country on a stable footing. An endgame strategy is required for the final phase of the Iraq conflict. The broad challenges for U.S. policy are maintaining and expanding the downward trend in violence and crafting a formula for sustainable security and stability in Iraq and throughout the region. If a lasting peace is to be achieved, it will require Iraqis to reach agreement on questions of power-sharing and resources management in the new political order.

The United States has embarked on a gradual troop withdrawal and transition from combat to training and other security assistance roles. As the process continues, the way that these issues are addressed will affect the long-term outlook for Iraq and the region. In both the political and military realms, the administration faces significant choices

Iraqi soldiers deliver tools to villagers in Bey'a

National Air and Space Museum

Soviet SS–20 and U.S. Pershing-II missiles, regarded as the most threatening missiles in their class, on display in National Air and Space Museum

in crafting its relationship with Iraq. Under a bilateral security agreement that took effect in 2009, U.S. troops are scheduled to leave Iraq no later than the end of 2011. While the combat mission for U.S. troops is ending, the Iraqi government may request assistance from the United States after that. In the formal declaration of principles signed in 2007, Iraq expressed a desire for continued American help to strengthen and professionalize its security forces and enable it to deter foreign threats. However, the bilateral agreement will be put to a referendum in 2009 and a new Iraqi government will be formed after elections at the end of the year. Thus, continuity in the relationship is not assured.

Iraqi security forces have grown in size and competence in recent years but will not become fully self-sufficient for 5 to 10 years. Given the institutions and resources available to Iraq, the expansion and professional development of its military is a straightforward if long-term task. With U.S. assistance, particularly air support and intelligence, surveillance, and reconnaissance, Iraqi security forces should be able to handle the present threat during the transition.

Nonetheless, two critical questions remain. First, will the Iraqis employ their security forces in a nonsectarian and nonpartisan manner? Failing to do so could reignite the conflict. Second, what course will future relations between the United States and the next Iraqi government take? Achieving stability inside Iraq and within the region will require the considered use of American political and military assistance to ensure successful outcomes to these questions.

Coalition and Iraqi forces achieved an amazing turnaround in the war during 2007 and 2008. By the end of 2008, violence in Iraq had fallen to a level not seen since the start of 2004. Various measures contributed to this trend. First, the addition of some 31,000 American troops and doubling of the number of Provincial Reconstruction Teams have been highly successful. Second, and more importantly, the revised objectives of the joint campaign plan as well as changes in the way that U.S. forces are employed were fundamental to reducing the violence. Political accommodation became the main objective of the campaign plan that shifted the focus of the U.S. effort from attacking insurgents to providing security for the population and persuading antagonists to stop fighting. This engagement strategy succeeded in bringing Sunni insurgents and their supporters over to the American side. The resulting increase in human intelligence permitted more effective targeting of so-called irreconcilable elements of the Sunni insurgency, including al Qaeda in Iraq as well as hardcore Shia cells known as special groups. A ceasefire announced by Shia leader Moqtada al-Sadr in August 2007, which followed resolute action by the Iraqi government to check Sadrist provocations in Karbala, also dramatically contributed to the decline in violence.

The most immediate challenge is incorporating Sunnis in the political and economic life of Iraq so that their motivation for fighting is addressed and the insurgency does not resume. The ultimate resolution of the sectarian conflict will require agreement on the federal nature of the state. Additional decisions, legislation, and constitutional revisions also may be necessary. Without such agreements, internal stability will remain elusive and, in turn, affect prospects for regional stability. The ongoing intra-Shia competition must be channeled into the political arena, and Shia militias must be demobilized and employed. The rivalries and substantive differences among Shia groups are likely to continue, but the diversity of Shia opinion may actually promote but not preclude the formation of either multisectarian or nonsectarian coalitions.

The critical decision that the United States must make regarding Iraq is whether its continued assistance will be made contingent on political reconciliation and internal stability. Alternatively, America could either withdraw its support or provide unconditional support. The former choice would be ill advised given the geopolitical importance of the country and the latter could lead to exclusive rule by a Shia majority, which might rekindle the Sunni insurgency. In addition, Arab states would react negatively to the prospect of an alliance between Iraq and Iran.

The United States and other countries have an abiding interest in ensuring that the ceasefire among Iraqi factions is extended and strengthened. This fragile peace could unravel if steps are not taken to preserve it. The most urgent issues include incorporating those Sunnis who stopped fighting the government into the security forces and economic life of the nation; providing basic services and infrastructure to rebuild Sunni areas; and establishing the mechanisms to prevent the use of Iraqi or coalition forces for either sectarian or partisan purposes. While America does not have unlimited leverage, given the Iraqi need for security assistance and its genuine wariness of Iran, the United States should be able to persuade the Iraqi government to take these steps.

Although implementation of the U.S.-Iraqi security agreement will be critical in determining the future of relations, the national elections slated for late 2009 will also have an important impact. The elections may offer an opportunity to broaden representation in the Iraqi parliament, particularly by Sunni and secular groups that previously were not participants. A more broadly representative parliament and government could open the way for compromises on core issues. The United States has a vested interest in free and credible elections under rules that permit new leaders, parties, and coalitions to emerge and share in governing the country.

Even with a broadly representative parliament, it will take a long time to resolve deep-seated differences and past animosity. Outside diplomatic support may be needed to broker enduring compromises. The United States should be prepared together with the international community to appoint envoys and provide sustained diplomatic support to facilitate political solutions to the underlying causes of internal disagreement. America should fashion continuing assistance to the new Iraqi government in a way that facilitates resolution of the most contentious issues.

Iraqi security forces have grown rapidly in recent years, but the Iraqi government estimates that it will be unable to meet all internal and foreign defense needs until sometime between 2012 and 2018. Those forces exceeded 600,000 at the end of 2008 and eventually will number 640,000.[3] The ability of Iraq to plan and execute independent operations and resupply as well as maintain and administer its army and national police forces has grown steadily. Unfortunately, local police capability lags behind. The competence of Iraqi forces will improve over time with experience, even more rapidly if Americans train and advise them. Yet progress is only possible if national identity and military professionalism trump local and sectarian interests.

The growth of the Iraqi security forces has been constrained by a lack of midlevel officers. To meet this shortage, Iraq has mounted a sustained effort, graduating an average of 1,600 cadets annually from its military academies since 2005. Thousands of officers of the former Iraqi army also have been incorporated in the new security forces. However, since these forces have been built from the ground up, commands at brigade, division, and corps levels were formed last and are still in the process of maturing. The Iraqis will be hampered in the midterm by shortfalls in combat enablers, including aviation, combat service support, intelligence, and command

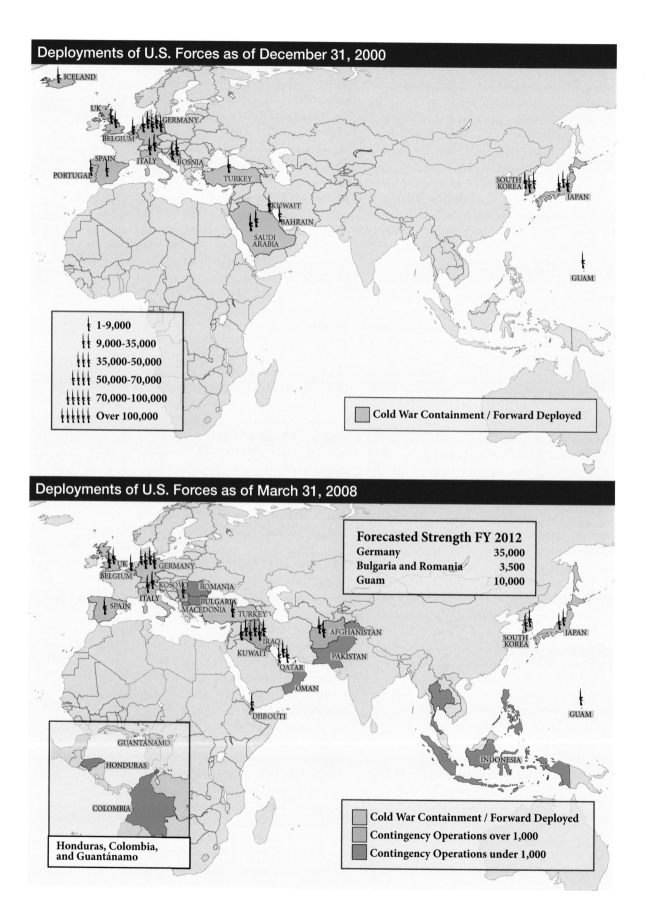

Deployments of U.S. Forces as of December 31, 2000

ICELAND
UK
BELGIUM
GERMANY
SPAIN
PORTUGAL
ITALY
BOSNIA
TURKEY
KUWAIT
BAHRAIN
SAUDI ARABIA
SOUTH KOREA
JAPAN
GUAM

†	1-9,000
††	9,000-35,000
†††	35,000-50,000
††††	50,000-70,000
†††††	70,000-100,000
††††††	Over 100,000

Cold War Containment / Forward Deployed

Deployments of U.S. Forces as of March 31, 2008

Forecasted Strength FY 2012

Germany	35,000
Bulgaria and Romania	3,500
Guam	10,000

UK
BELGIUM
GERMANY
KOSOVO
ROMANIA
SPAIN
ITALY
BULGARIA
MACEDONIA
TURKEY
IRAQ
KUWAIT
QATAR
OMAN
DJIBOUTI
AFGHANISTAN
PAKISTAN
SOUTH KOREA
JAPAN
GUAM
INDONESIA

GUANTÁNAMO
HONDURAS
COLOMBIA

Honduras, Colombia, and Guantánamo

Cold War Containment / Forward Deployed
Contingency Operations over 1,000
Contingency Operations under 1,000

and control. Police and other internal organs of security lack adequate facilities, logistics, leadership, internal affairs, and forensic capabilities. Both the defense and interior ministries have improved their administrative capacity, but remain unable to fully execute their budgets. Although Iraq satisfied most of its defense requirements under the U.S. foreign military sales program, delivery was slow despite efforts by the Pentagon to expedite the process. As a result, Iraq looked for alternative sources of supply.

Pockets of sectarianism remain in the Iraqi security establishment, particularly in the police and facilities protection services. Moreover, there are risks that the government will use these forces as a tool to consolidate the power of one faction or sect, rather than enforce the law equitably for all Iraqis. For example, operational control of Iraqi special operations forces currently resides in the prime minister's office. To minimize the potential of sectarian or partisan use of this asset, which is the most capable of the Iraqi forces, the Independent Commission on the Security Forces of Iraq recommended in September 2007 that the special operations forces be placed under the Iraqi military chain of command, but the recommendation has not been accepted as yet.

Although Iraq continues to build a professional army, it will remain dependent on U.S. forces even as they draw down and assume a supporting role. Under a gradual drawdown and transition plan, U.S. surge brigades completed their tours and have been redeployed, leaving 15 combat brigades and some 155,000 troops in Iraq, and subsequent withdrawals are planned for this year. As outlined in the joint campaign plan, U.S. troops also began shifting from combat missions to tactical, operational, and finally strategic overwatch, as local conditions warranted.

The Multi-National Force plans to continue this gradual transition unless otherwise directed. In October 2008, the security of 13 provinces became the responsibility of Iraqis, and in 2009, all 18 provinces were to come under their control. Iraqi commands are planning and executing operations with U.S. advice when needed. Under the terms of the bilateral security agreement that went into effect in January 2009, the Joint Military Operations Coordination Committee has authority to coordinate all military operations according to Iraqi law and the conditions stipulated in the agreement. This agreement creates a significantly different operating environment from the one that was governed by the United Nations mandate, which expired in 2008. For example, U.S.

▼ *Continued on p. 381*

Darfur: A Complex Conflict

Since 2003, the western Sudanese province of Darfur has been a finger pointed at the conscience of the world. It has gained the attention of governments and humanitarian groups and generated countless pages of political commentary. Yet today the situation is less stable and more difficult than in the past. Civilian deaths reach into the hundreds of thousands, and refugees or internally displaced persons number in the millions. The minority government in Khartoum has adhered to its policy of destruction of the non-Arab population despite little or no support from Arab tribes, and the United States and its allies have passed the ball to the United Nations.

There are many tragedies in Africa and few real successes. Like Somalia, Congo-Kinshasa, and other areas, Darfur has become a humanitarian tragedy. In particular, international inaction and ineffectiveness have humanitarian costs of their own. The failure to stanch the Darfur crisis tarnishes the image of the United States as a world leader and a moral force. At the same time, in its failure to look beyond humanitarian crises, America has neglected to act in its own interest to secure a role in sub-Saharan Africa. The nations in this region are endowed with resources and have potential as U.S. trading and investment partners. The Sahel, which includes part of Sudan, represents a dividing line between the Muslim and non-Muslim world. The form that Islam will adopt in moving south in Africa has import for U.S. security interests. Yesterday's poster child of Africa was a hungry child, while tomorrow's may be the picture of dynamic development that is taking place to prepare countries in the region for active roles around the world.

President Idris Deby of Chad chaired negotiations in 2004 between Sudan and two rebel groups, the Sudanese Liberation Army and the Justice and Equality Movement. The former was represented by Mini Minawi and the latter was headed by Khalil Ibrahim, who did not attend. Chief Salah Gosh led the Sudanese delegation. With only a handful of international observers, the three parties signed a ceasefire agreement on May 8, 2004. Although flawed and reached in an atmosphere of distrust, the agreement offered an opportunity for the international community to resolve the growing Darfur crisis. Yet the region had not gained attention in the United States and Europe where the focus remains on North-South negotiations in Kenya. The actions by the Sudanese government against the non-Arab population in Darfur were unpopular in Sudan, including the army, and Khartoum remained a backwater that had not experienced the oil-driven economic growth that it enjoys today.

Following the signing of the North-South Agreement in 2005, the European Union promised support and asked the African Union to take on the peacekeeping mission. The African Union reluctantly agreed and began the mission with support from the United States and the European Union in an air of cautious optimism. This offered an opportunity for an American initiative to resolve the Darfur crisis with a combination of carrots and sticks, an opportunity that should have been linked to the North-South Agreement. However, the opportunity passed, and the government continued ethnic cleansing unimpeded. The African Union force took on the peacekeeping mission without requisite expertise or assets. Darfur became a popular cause for international celebrities who focus on humanitarian issues. China engaged the government to ensure a share of Sudanese resources, and other parties lined up to make investments in the largest African nation. The United States, devoid of colonial baggage and highly popular in Sudan outside the government, failed to take the lead.

Rebel leaders were hosted in Europe as America decided that the Sudanese Liberation Army must enter into negotiations. Yet rather than insist on compliance with the N'Djamena Agreement (formally known as the Humanitarian Ceasefire Agreement), the international community entered into another round of talks in Nigeria. But despite well-intentioned efforts, the Darfur problem was not resolved and began to deteriorate.

In response to its weak position, the government in Sudan concluded that there would not be strong reactions to the situation in Darfur. So it supported the attacks by the Jinjaweed militia on villages in the region. Aided by the failure of the world community to respond, President Omar al-Bashir and his confederates took the opportunity to divide the rebel groups. The United States tried to get the United Nations to impose tougher and tougher sanctions to no avail. After compelling the parties to the table in 2006, American envoy Robert Zoellick helped broker an agreement that was complex and unenforceable. Under pressure, Minawi signed the agreement but other groups did not. This split resulted in the downfall of Minawi within the Sudanese Liberation Army and in greater internal division. Furthermore, the United States did not engage with the Justice and

Equality Movement, fearful of the earlier relationship between Khalil Ibrahim and Hasan Turabi. But Khalil privately insisted that although he had worked with Turabi in the past, neither Turabi nor any leader had opposed the marginalization of the people of Darfur. He vowed that his only loyalty was to those people. Nevertheless, the international community blithely passed the buck to the United Nations with the result that nothing except bland resolutions ensued.

A forceful international effort headed by the United States could have achieved a great deal. But leaders were focused on humanitarian issues, sanctions, and fears of endangering the North-South Agreement rather than the political and economic consequences of the conflict in Darfur. The result has been a worsened humanitarian situation, sanctions that have had little or no effect, and increasing violence and growing threat. At the same time, interest in Africa and its resources has grown, but America seems not to have grasped the importance of standing firm on Darfur to achieve larger interests in the region. People in sub-Saharan Africa ask why the United States has responded in Bosnia but not in Darfur, especially given the declaration by former Secretary of State Colin Powell concerning the ongoing genocide in Darfur.

The United Nations cannot resolve the problem of Darfur; only America has that capability. As such, the following outlines basic ideas on this humanitarian and security crisis:

■ Call for a meeting of rebel leaders, in limited numbers, from all factions, including Khalil Ibrahim. Only a unified group can negotiate with the Sudanese government. Since unity is the desirable but unlikely outcome, this group should form a council representing all credible factions.

■ Invite the non-Arab and Arab leadership of Darfur including the nomad tribes to meet, preferably in the United States. Although they have suffered, no major Arab tribe supports the government. Ensure humanitarian and development needs are translated into priorities to implement quickly.

■ Invite the Sudanese government to send representatives to the United States for frank discussions. America must be prepared to name an Ambassador, remove Sudan from the list of terrorist states, and end sanctions in return for specific actions. The United States has allies among the Sudanese business leaders, who are Western-educated and prefer to work with American firms. Promoting strong private business ties would be beneficial in eventually affecting change in Khartoum.

■ Host a meeting of decisionmakers from the above groups in a secluded location (such as Dayton).

■ Support a broad-based amnesty since parties threatened with arrest and the International Criminal Court are unlikely to negotiate. Sending a few culprits to The Hague may make some people feel better, but it could work against a lasting resolution. The importance of amnesty is a lesson from the success of the Salvadoran peace agreement in the 1980s.

■ Work within traditional tribal administrative structures to allow for compensation for those groups driven from their homes and lands.

■ Invite only a limited group of international observers to any negotiations to avoid the circus-like atmosphere that was created in Abuja by scores of diplomats, experts, and journalists competing for attention from the rebels and government. A more relevant group of observers might include representatives of the United Nations, European Union, African Union, and Arab League.

The United States has a chance to demonstrate that it is capable of taking a leadership role in the sub-Sahara. America will have to recognize African nations as partners and not only the beneficiaries of humanitarian relief. U.S. resources would be better used to support private investments, agricultural development, water projects, education, health, infrastructure, and the development of human resources.

At stake is the image of America as a moral beacon and its respect for sub-Saharan Africa. Also threatened are relations with Sudan, a bridge between the Muslim north and non-Muslim south. It is the largest country in Africa, a key to the Nile, and a potential ally. The Sudanese people are not anti-American or generally radical. And the Bashir government is unpopular, the military is unenthusiastic, and the Southern Sudan referendum looms near. The United States should take the risk and assume leadership of an international effort to resolve the Darfur crisis.

▲ Continued from p. 379

military personnel come under Iraqi jurisdiction when off duty and off base, Iraqi warrants must be obtained for detentions, and detainees must be turned over to Iraqi custody.

Many questions remain over the implementation of the bilateral security agreement as well as the accompanying strategic framework. The pace of the U.S. troop withdrawal and the nature of future security and diplomatic relations will be determined through further bilateral negotiations. The security agreement provides for the possibility of a quicker withdrawal or revision of the existing agreement. The parliamentary elections may also affect the longer term resolution of these matters.

Despite broad areas of uncertainty, it is likely that U.S. forces will be increasingly dedicated to advisory and training roles for the next year or two. Given continued internal threats, Iraq will need combat enablers and counterterrorism assistance for some time. While American combat units departed urban areas in July 2009, U.S. advisors can be effective if dispersed among Iraqi forces to provide situational awareness. Depending on the threat from neighboring countries, some U.S. forces may be located along the borders as well. These missions and terms of assistance may be revisited in consultations with the new Iraqi government. U.S. force levels should be determined by troop-to-task analyses once missions have been agreed on.

If Iraq retains U.S. military training and advisory assistance, the formation of a multinational transition security command could be the vehicle to train, equip, and advise Iraqi forces. A small counterterrorism unit, if such a presence is desired, could be folded into this command.

Security and stability inside Iraq cannot be achieved if outside actors undermine the efforts to peacefully end the conflict. Diplomatic initiatives as well as other measures are needed to foster regional stability. The so-called neighbors process begun by the United States and Iraq should be enhanced to staunch the flow of insurgents and weapons into Iraq and to prevent tensions and provocations across borders. The United Nations has played a constructive and expanding role in diplomatic efforts both inside Iraq and regionally, and notably in efforts to address the crisis of internally displaced persons and refugees abroad. Despite successes in resettlement and repatriation, more than 4 million Iraqis remain displaced in their own country or are living as expatriates in surrounding nations. Most countries in the region are interested in a security framework that prevents the spillover of conflict in Iraq and creation of a terrorist safe haven. To date, Arab neighbors and members of the Gulf Cooperation Council have been reluctant to support what is perceived as a sectarian-minded Shia government in Baghdad. To the extent the Iraqi government incorporates Sunnis in the police and military and provides services and jobs in areas where they live, regional Arab states should be prepared to support Iraq. The formation of an inclusive government in 2010 will greatly enhance prospects for such support. That will provide Iraq with the influence to counter Iranian efforts to Lebanonize Iraq and control political or military forces inside it.

The goal of regional diplomacy is not to create an anti-Iranian alliance that would destabilize the region or prompt reactions by Tehran, but rather to help defend Iraq and other countries against the destabilizing actions of Iran. Threats in this region demand multilateral and bilateral efforts to avoid war as well as the acquisition of destabilizing weapons of mass destruction. The specter of a poly-nuclear Middle East makes regional engagement a top imperative for U.S. foreign policy. **gsa**

NOTES

[1] Charles C. Krulak, "The Three Block War: Fighting in Urban Areas," speech presented at National Press Club, Washington, DC, December 15, 1997.

[2] Joint Staff, *Military Support to Stabilization, Security, Transition, and Reconstruction Operations Joint Operating Concept* (Washington DC: Department of Defense, December 2004).

[3] This information on the growth and requirements of the Iraqi security forces comes from testimony by Lieutenant General James M. Dubik, USA, to the House Armed Services Committee, July 9, 2008, and an interview by the author with General Nasir Abadi, vice chief of the Iraqi armed forces, on January 4, 2008.

Contributors

Dr. Thomas X. Hammes (Chapter Editor) served 30 years in the U.S. Marine Corps, including duty in Somalia and Iraq. He holds a Master of Historical Research and Ph.D. in Modern History from Oxford University and has lectured widely at U.S. and international staff and war colleges. He is the author of *The*

Sling and the Stone: On War in the 21st Century (Zenith Press, 2004) and over 80 articles and opinion pieces.

M. Elaine Bunn is Distinguished Research Fellow in the Institute for National Strategic Studies (INSS) at National Defense University (NDU).

The Honorable Dr. Patrick M. Cronin is Director of INSS at NDU, which was established by the Secretary of Defense and Chairman of the Joint Chiefs of Staff in 1984 to conduct strategic assessments for senior Department of Defense officials and decisionmakers. He took up the post at the beginning of 2008 after a 25-year career inside government and academic research centers and spanning areas of defense, security, foreign policy, and foreign assistance. He is simultaneously Director of the Center for the Study of Chinese Military Affairs, which serves as a national focal point for multidisciplinary research and analytic exchanges regarding China.

Dr. Janine Davidson is Deputy Assistant Secretary of Defense for Plans. Previously she was Assistant Professor of Public Policy at George Mason University and a nonresident fellow at The Brookings Institution.

Janice Elmore, a retired Foreign Service Officer, was Political Counselor in Khartoum and representative to all Darfur talks in N'Djamena, Addis Ababa, and Abuja.

Williamson Murray is Professor Emeritus at The Ohio State University and co-author of *A War to Be Won, Fighting the Second World War* (Belknap Press, 2001) and co-editor of *The Making of Peace, Rulers, States, and the Aftermath of War* (Cambridge University Press, 2009).

Linda Robinson is an author and consultant. Her latest book, *Tell Me How This Ends: General David Petraeus and the Search for a Way Out of Iraq* (Public Affairs, 2008), was named one of the 100 Notable Books of 2008 by *The New York Times*.

Chapter 17

Alternative Force Structures and Resource Constraints

Designed to provide food for thought rather than policy recommendations or budgetary prescriptions, the following chapter envisions different configurations for different challenges. It starts with a brief overview of how each of the four Services and special operations forces must adjust if we assume hybrid wars are the primary challenges we face. Following that survey, we consider how the U.S. Army must change to deal with continuing counterinsurgency and stability operations while maintaining the capability to fight a conventional opponent.

Next, the chapter examines the Navy's very different set of problems. First, its planned fleet is simply unaffordable. Second, the fleet is a poor match for the challenges the Navy is facing. Thus, this section recalls lessons from the past in how to overcome the cost issues and proposes a different organization to face the second challenge. As always, the Marine Corps literally straddles the two environments and must be prepared to play an active role in both. The

section on the Corps focuses on its role in winning the current conflicts while simultaneously reequipping and modernizing to deal with future threats.

This chapter's discussion of the Air Force highlights how our hard-gained air superiority has been critical to the success of U.S. arms. But it cautions that the Air Force faces major budgetary issues as it tries to replace an aging aircraft fleet while assuming additional duties in space and cyberspace as well as augmenting ground forces in Iraq and Afghanistan.

The next two sections deal with personnel issues and the budget. Demographic and social changes reinforced by persistent conflicts are challenging Service abilities to recruit sufficient high-quality personnel to meet needs. Budgetary pressures from entitlement programs are set to rapidly grow and will force a reassessment of national priorities. The final section discusses how the Pentagon can balance risks and costs in the long run to meet current demands, while posturing the forces to meet future challenges.

U.S. Marine Corps (Keith A. Stevenson)

Amphibious assault vehicles approach beach to disembark Marines and equipment during exercise off Florida coast

Force Structure Implications of Hybrid Warfare

Hybrid warfare is a reaction to the overwhelming superiority of American arms and the leveling impact of globalization. Through its dominance of conventional warfare, America has pushed future opponents to alternative means purposely designed to thwart conventionally oriented Western societies and their military forces. This approach is designed to sidestep America's kinetic forces by changing the rules of the contest. In this new hybrid of war, cunning savagery, continuous organization, and tactical adaptation will be the only constant. As a result, American force planning needs to be examined within a framework that accounts for both the enduring potential of state-on-state conflict and the more likely, but much less threatening, cases of intrastate conflict and failed states.

Army

To meet the complexity of indirect and hybrid threats, the Army envisions developing capabilities to execute decisive combat operations, as well as responding to the unexpected and unpredictable. It intends to balance expeditionary agility and staying power for the long fight regardless of its nature. This moves the Army away from its predisposition to set piece battles against predictable enemy forces. Appropriately, the individual Soldier is the centerpiece of this transformation. In terms of organizing for the future, the Army anticipates the need for greater agility, which will be gained by promoting modularity of brigade-sized units while placing more emphasis on combined arms at lower echelons.

Although the Army appears to be adapting in terms of concept development, force structure changes and the Future Combat System (FCS) do not completely satisfy the requirements of hybrid warfare. The FCS program offers connectivity, surveillance, unmanned systems, and force protection for the battlefield of tomorrow. The principal advantage of this transformation is the evolution from the division-based structure to Brigade Combat Teams (BCTs), which have modularity instead of ad hoc task organization. These units are self-sufficient, cohesive, and readily deployable. Their design also provides improved tactical integration at lower levels, which will be ideal in meeting the challenge of hybrid threats as well as accomplishing future stabilization operations.

However, the Army remains focused on major combat operations and a heavy force structure. In addition, to afford the brigade headquarters over-

head, the Army removed the third maneuver battalion in many brigades. A smaller number of properly manned BCTs would be better suited for operations that call for boots on the ground. Furthermore, the Army has declined to establish dedicated training and advisory groups, which is a decision that must be reconsidered. Besides establishing standing regional headquarters and military advisory groups to conduct stabilization operations, some portion of the force, at least five BCTs, should be assigned as the base component for an increased national capability to conduct preventative or postconflict stability operations in concert with the range of other available instruments of national power.

Navy

After the Cold War ended, Navy leaders optimized the battle force for power projection operations against state opponents with weak navies. They essentially ignored the low end of the conflict spectrum, as indicated by their outsourcing of riverine warfare to the Marines and their plans to eliminate both frigates and Patrol Coastal ships from the battle fleet. As a result, fleet building plans emphasized high-capacity strike platforms, including aircraft carriers and large, expensive, multimission combatants. It was not until 2001 that the Navy inserted the Littoral Combat Ship (LCS)—a small modular combatant—back into its long-range plans. But consistent with the Navy's vision of future warfare at sea, the ship was designed for countermine, antisubmarine, and antisurface warfare during a theater break-in operation, not for operations at the low end of the naval conflict spectrum.

For the past few years, the Navy's principal conceptual approach had been built around an umbrella concept called Sea Power 21, developed by then–Chief of Naval Operations Admiral Vernon Clark. The fleet architecture to bring Sea Power 21 to fruition has been defined in the Navy's shipbuilding program. While revolutionary in its technological base, the program was conventional in its ship mix and leaned heavily toward blue water operations and long-range precision strike from aircraft carriers. In fact, by the time he retired, Admiral Clark concluded that the current Navy fleet was neither balanced nor optimal for making material contributions to the war on terror or against future irregular adversaries.

By 2005–2006, things had begun to change. The long campaign in Iraq, Iran's clever use of submarines and surface ships, advanced antiship weaponry, and small, swarming boats, as well as Hizbollah's ability to employ C–802 antiship cruise missiles in the 2006 Lebanon War, all demonstrated the growing threat of maritime hybrid threats. As a consequence, the Navy reclaimed the riverine mission from the Marines; provided more than 10,000 Individual Augmentees to ground force commanders in Iraq and Afghanistan; scrapped plans to retire the Patrol Coastal ships; modernized 30 frigates to serve through the end of the next decade; converted four *Ohio*-class ballistic missile submarines into conventional cruise mission and special operations transport submarines; expanded its Naval Special Warfare capabilities; and stood up the new Naval Expeditionary Combat Command (NECC), a "type command" responsible for organizing, training, and equipping a variety of forces employed on both the seaward and landward sides of a coastline.

The Navy has explored some innovative ship designs, and is now belatedly looking at its contributions to the war on terror and hybrid threats. It has jumpstarted its regional affairs program, riverine warfare, humanitarian assistance tasks, and Civil Affairs efforts to make a more significant contribution to global campaigns. Nonetheless, despite these welcome moves, maritime hybrid warfare capabilities generally remain at the bottom of the Navy's budgetary priorities. The principal complaint about the Service has been its overemphasis on and overinvestment in deep-water sea control operations, and its heretofore studious avoidance of littoral and riverine operations.

The Navy's program continues to emphasize platforms and capabilities for high-end naval combat against nation-state opponents. As a result, funding for many of the NECC's capabilities is included in supplemental budgets rather than the Department of the Navy base budget. The Navy has stood up only 3 riverine squadrons of 12 boats apiece. Similarly, despite the LCS's great potential, the Navy's program lacks mission packages for special operations support, humanitarian and disaster relief, naval partnership-building, or support for Marine advisory and training teams.

In the midrange, the Navy's major surface investments have focused on a replacement "destroyer," the DDG–1000. This *Zumwalt*-class land attack destroyer is about 50 percent larger in displacement and 5 times more costly than the DDG–51 *Burke*-class vessel that it replaces. It is a technological marvel, with its electric drive engine program, superior radar and signature control, and Advanced Gun System, which provides two fully automated 155mm guns capable of firing global positioning system–guided rounds 83

nautical miles ashore from a 600-round magazine. The Navy is particularly keen on the ship's automation and minimal crew requirements, reduced from 350 to as low as 120. However, the size and cost of the program—$4.4 billion per unit—threaten its survival.

The Navy must not totally ignore the high end of the naval conflict spectrum. The undersea competition is changing, and may be on the verge of a major shift involving unmanned underwater vehicles. Similarly, the Navy is now engaged in an intense, albeit politically understated, naval capability competition in the Western Pacific with the People's Republic of China, including systemic Chinese efforts to develop antinaval theater denial capabilities. Making sure the United States does not

Secretary Gates, Admiral Mullen, General David Petraeus, and General Ray Odierno during change of command ceremony, Baghdad, September 2008

fall behind in that competition is a prerequisite for stability and crisis response in the region. Moreover, as the aforementioned example of Hizbollah's employment of antiship cruise missiles shows, there is a steady, ongoing global proliferation of advanced guided weapons and battle network technologies that will challenge any future U.S. naval operation in ways not seen since World War II. However, it seems fair to say that the Navy's program needs to be better balanced to include additional low-end, hybrid, and high-end naval threats. In other words, emphasis on new hybrid threats should shift some of the focus of the Navy's investment portfolio away from the Global Maritime Commons and traditional deep blue water operations to the more likely contested zones in the world's littorals. A standoff fleet strike capacity will still be important, and the modern aircraft carrier will remain the centerpiece of the U.S. naval power projection fleet. However, the fleet clearly has overcapacity in fleet strike capabilities, and just as clearly lacks capacity in low-end and hybrid naval capabilities.

A key component for any Navy intent on addressing hybrid maritime threats is the naval maneuver fleet, consisting of amphibious warfare ships, maritime prepositioning ships, and joint sealift platforms. This maneuver fleet will have to remain robust, as it is the Navy's most versatile component. The ability to command external lines of communication and operate from the oceanic periphery; to establish sea bases for our forces near crisis areas without having a large footprint ashore; and to put ground forces ashore to deal with pirates and other nonstate maritime actors operating from land will be important components of future naval operations.

Marine Corps

As an expeditionary force, the Marines are well disposed in terms of their culture, doctrine, and force structure to deal with hybrid threats. In particular, the combined arms approach and ability to operate in a decentralized manner set them up for success. Investments that currently position the Marine Corps to retain its unique naval character

Marines from Fleet Antiterrorism Security Team Pacific perform battle drill against simulated base perimeter breech

could be better allocated to fixing chinks in its armor for countering more lethal and irregular enemies.

In adapting to the 21st century, the concept of the Marine Air-Ground Task Force (MAGTF) should be retained but its focus shifted from rare major combat operations to likely deployments requiring sustained expeditionary capabilities in the urban littorals. The Marine Expeditionary Force (MEF) force design must be retained as a reservoir for rapidly tailored forces for various contingencies but must be augmented. MEFs lack an information warfare battalion, a reconnaissance, surveillance, and target acquisition battalion designed to augment reconnaissance companies, and unmanned sensor assets (both ground and aerial systems). In addition, each MEF organization requires a security cooperation group that contains foreign military training and advisory teams and Civil Affairs units.

The second major shift required for a small wars era involves training and manpower paradigms that govern daily operations. The Marine Corps heavily invests in its junior officers but does not make comparable training and education programs available to its enlisted members. If the Corps believes in the strategic impact of small units, then it must invest to make the *strategic corporal* a reality, which some allied militaries have done already, and not simply a bumper sticker.

Current acquisition by the Marine Corps is well settled, particularly the Joint Strike Fighter (JSF) and tactical ground mobility programs. But consideration should be given to limiting purchases of the V–22 Osprey while focusing on assault support assets better suited to urban environments. The Osprey is a superb platform for special operations and deep assaults when speed requires protection and agility. But it may not be nimble enough if urban littorals become the default operating environments in the future. Instead of optimizing its force design for the ship-to-shore challenge, the Marine Corps could focus on deploying more effective forms of force protection once ashore.

Air Force

America's military dominance over the last several decades has been enhanced by its relentless pursuit of aerospace superiority. This capability cannot be taken for granted and needs continuous investment to preserve a competitive advantage. Hybrid threats will not diminish the relevance of airpower. But that dominance must be shaped to provide for

U.S. Navy (Bobbie G. Attaway)

relevant strategic and operational effects necessary for unrestricted warfare. This will require the Air Force to expand its capabilities in space and cyberspace as well as a modern long-range strategic strike capability. Admittedly, there will be fewer threats to air superiority. The current plans for the F–22 Raptor should be curtailed at approximately 200 airframes because its contributions to precision strike and ground attack are dubious at best. U.S. air superiority will rarely be tested in a meaningful way, except by sophisticated air defense systems and even more often by low-tech Man-Portable Air Defense Systems as well as attacks against airfields.

The Air Force has already made some adaptations that prepare for future threats. The Service has improved its expeditionary capability as well as its posture for cyber warfare operations. Its development of unmanned aerial vehicles (UAVs) is first rate. In a completely irregular world, the requirement for precision engagement, especially in urban settings, will continue and perhaps increase in value. Thus, a modernized gunship, either manned or unmanned, has merit given the great success of AC–130s in current operations. Such a vehicle, an airborne Guardian Angel, would combine the advantages of persistent surveillance with pervasive attack.

Special Operations Forces

Afghanistan provided a renaissance for special operations forces. Teams of these warriors built relationships with the Northern Alliance and applied firepower against the Taliban. Subsequently, numerous cases of valor and improvisation testified to the effectiveness of special operations against deft enemies. As a result, these units have developed sophisticated capabilities across a range of operating environments. They must continue to work with foreign militaries and remain agile enough to conduct surveillance and operate against high-value targets even in dense urban areas. Although special operations forces have gotten more resources, they need training, education, staff processes, and aviation assets to enhance their capabilities.

Iraq and Afghanistan have provided an experimental laboratory for potential enemies, who adapt to what works and pursue the fusion of modern capabilities and irregular tactics until they perfect unique styles of warfare. Many if not all capabilities will be required to counter hybrid threats, but the mix of capabilities and force structure should be shaped to better reflect the needs of joint force commanders to defeat potential adversaries located anywhere in the world.

Outlines of a Post-Iraq Army

Shaping virtually all other decisions that President Obama will make about the Army will be U.S. operations in Iraq and Afghanistan. The Army[1] has been rotating combat brigades through both countries at a rate that limits its ability to do, or train to do, anything else. There is no lack of thought in the Army about future directions, but much of that thought will stay on hold if "the future" remains Iraq and Afghanistan.

We assume a situation in which the Service can approximate the mythical 2-year dwell time between unit rotations, giving it time to prepare for the broader array of conflicts that it may face in the future. We begin with the nature of future conflict and the kind of Army we need to handle it. We then turn to the Army's size: how large an Army do we need? And we end by examining the notion of "building partner capacity" and the advisory capability that implies. Army leaders have a good sense of needed change in these areas; the question is whether those ideas can be nurtured and sustained in the debates that surely will follow substantial withdrawal from Iraq. The Obama administration will be instrumental in making sure current directions of change are sustained.

Full-Spectrum Conflict, Full-Spectrum Army

Insurgencies in Iraq and Afghanistan have confronted the Army with a form of conflict that it sought assiduously to ignore in the decades after Vietnam. Against this background, it has picked up counterinsurgency remarkably well—which is useful, since it probably will see more of these messy internal conflicts in the years ahead. If this sounds like refighting the last war, it is worth remembering that the events of 9/11 highlighted the danger of ignoring failing states. Few see Afghanistan as a war of choice, and it makes sense to hedge against other wars of that kind. Meanwhile, post-Saddam Iraq has encouraged the Army to remember that many of its past conflicts were followed by long "governance operations." In asserting that "Establishing a stable peace after an offensive may take longer and be more difficult than defeating enemy forces," the Army's new Field Manual (FM) 3–0, *Operations*, embraces that long-neglected history and the strategic purpose of war: producing a better and more lasting peace.

Some Army critics think that the Service has moved too far toward counterinsurgency and is forgetting how to fight "conventional" conflict.[2] It is a fair point, but it begs the question what future "conventional" conflict will look like. Precisely because the U.S. military does "high-end" maneuver warfare so well, it is hard to imagine future adversaries challenging the United States in that kind of battle. Rather, we should expect them to explore "asymmetric" approaches that neutralize our firepower, draw out conflicts, create civilian casualties, operate aggressive media campaigns, and otherwise frustrate U.S. goals.

Unfortunately, the messiness of today's conflicts is not likely to be confined to insurgencies. We saw hints of "irregular major combat" in the initial invasion of Iraq in 2003, when Saddam's Fedayeen posed a threat to rear areas with significant consequences for U.S. tactics, deployments, and technology. In 2006, Hizbollah employed irregular tactics in confronting Israel's invasion of southern Lebanon. North Korea may seek to do the same should war break out there. These "irregular challenges" can appear in any kind of warfare, perhaps even alongside "regular" warfare. Thus, the Army must plan to meet the "full spectrum" of warfare in the same war, perhaps at nearly the same time.

This means, first, an army with a different balance of skills and capabilities than the balance the Army brought into the present century. It needs less armor and artillery, more military police, Civil Affairs, and support units—the "high-demand, low-density" skills of stability operations—and more infantry, which has wide utility across the spectrum. Whether infantry is "foot" or "medium weight" remains to be seen; the success of Stryker units in Iraq certainly makes the medium weight idea worth exploring.

A more serious challenge of full-spectrum warfare lies in training and leader development. Certain basic Soldier skills and character traits are universally valuable but important skills are unique to areas of the spectrum. More broadly, the mindset of traditional warfare—"destroy the enemy's forces"—differs markedly from "secure the population," the core mindset of counterinsurgency and stability operations. Finally, command in these latter operations tends to be flatter, with lower level commanders and Soldiers facing strategic and often complex ethical decisions. Future full spectrum war will place an enormous premium on leaders (not just officers) who can grasp, quickly, what kind of conflict they are in and shift gears accordingly.

Training takes time. The rapid rotations through Iraq and Afghanistan do not allow for this level of training. The Army has a vision of a 3-year force generation cycle (2 years training, 1 deployed, or pre-

pared to deploy) that is probably the minimum dwell time needed to impart a broad set of full-spectrum skills and then the specific skills needed for the next deployment. Given prevailing constraints on commanders' time, Army trainers must bring training to units at a level that relieves commanders of today's large burden of paperwork.

How Much Army Is Enough?

Given uncertainties about the future and the substantial costs of adding people to the military, questions about force size are almost always controversial. Oddly, today's debate about the size of U.S. ground forces is anchored on the Army's post–Cold War size of 482,000 Active duty personnel. Yet this number was the product of a conception of warfare centered on rapid defeat of enemy forces—conflict in which the entire force can be brought to bear in a military confrontation. In enduring conflicts such as Iraq, by contrast, effective force size is cut by half or two-thirds, depending on rotation rate. Only by accident would the size of today's Army bear any relationship to the likely wars of the future.

Not surprisingly, operations in Iraq and Afghanistan have forced increases in the size of America's ground forces. After allowing a "temporary" increase of 30,000 in the Army's size in January 2004, the Bush administration moved 3 years later to increase the Active Army's authorized end-strength by 65,000 (with Reserve Components increasing by smaller amounts, and the Marine Corps increasing by 47,000), producing an Active Army of 547,000 Soldiers. Although recruiting to this new level initially incurred worrisome (but not catastrophic) declines in the quality of entering Soldiers, a falloff in casualties in Iraq combined with a falloff in economic activity at home seems to have eased recruiting problems. The Army is now nearing the 547,000-Soldier goal.

Is an Army of 547,000 Active duty Soldiers enough? Who knows? This is a case where "muddling through" makes good sense. People are expensive, and there is much uncertainty regarding whether and how "persistent conflict" will be handled in the future. Then again, pursuing the currently authorized increase in size makes sense in terms of present (and perhaps enduring) commitments in Iraq and Afghanistan, and as a hedge against possibly demanding commitments down the road. It is also about all the Army can be expected to recruit and retain in the time allotted. Hopefully some of these uncertainties will be resolved with the passage of time.

Squaring the Size Circle: Building Partner Capacity

If an unstable world becomes less friendly to U.S. interests and more friendly to terrorists (or organized crime, or disease, and so forth), the United States may need to impose stability in countries considerably larger than Iraq or Afghanistan, which have already strained the Nation's ground forces. How does America hedge against such a world? The proffered solution these days is "building partner capacity," which in this case means strengthening the internal security capabilities of weak or threatened states so large U.S. force deployments are not needed.

The latter meaning clearly applies urgently to Iraq and Afghanistan. But Secretary of Defense Robert Gates gave the notion longer term significance in a speech to the Association of the U.S. Army in October of 2007:

[A]rguably the most important military component in the War on Terror is not the fighting we do ourselves, but how well we enable and empower our partners to defend and govern their own countries. The standing up and mentoring of indigenous armies and police, once the province of Special Forces, is now a key mission for the military as a whole.[3]

Gates added that how the "military as a whole" should handle the advise-and-assist mission "remains an open question, and will require innovative and forward thinking."[4] The subject certainly does not lack for that, as proposals for handling training and advising range from building an Army Advisory Corps of 20,000 Soldiers, to taking advisors "out of hide" of deployed brigades, to converting brigades to advisory groups as they go through their predeployment training cycle, to substantially expanding the number of uniformed experts on regions and advising.[5]

Some of these proposals relate directly to the situations in Iraq and Afghanistan, where the capacity-building mission aims to reduce the exposure of deployed U.S. forces. These deserve attention in their own right. But the general goal of this policy is to strengthen governance and security in host nations *instead of* deploying U.S. combat forces. Carving advisors and trainers out of deployed U.S. brigades does not apply.

Advising foreign militaries is the ultimate non-standard requirement. In combat situations such as Vietnam and Iraq, advisors have numbered in the thousands, but in Latin America and Africa, U.S. advisory teams have traditionally been in the tens, occasionally as a result of politically imposed caps on American force levels. Some advisor teams coach host-nation units, some are lodged in the local political organization (Provincial Reconstruction Teams), and some (military training teams) move from situation to situation. The absence of a standard team makes it hard to imagine how Army brigades can consistently be reshaped into advisory teams.

If there is a "standard" requirement amid the variety, it is the need for a far better trained and educated corps of experts than the regular Army (as against the special operations forces) has been able or willing to provide in the past. If it is to have any chance of success, advising must be led by officers and senior enlisted personnel who know the culture and politics of the country to which they deploy, and ideally know the language well. They should be adept at advising (not everyone is), and willing to deploy for more than a year. Those advising foreign military units ideally should have U.S. operational experience; they should be "operator-experts" who advance in the standard command track while also picking up advisory experience. These experts will be the core of advisory teams assembled in accordance with the needs of each particular mission.

This amounts to a call to substantially broaden the education and experience of officers as they rise through the ranks. Leader development actually narrowed after the Cold War ended, with fewer attending graduate school or serving outside Army units.[6] Senior Army officials want to reverse that trend, but they will need support from the civilian leadership. Careers are already stuffed with mandated assignments; if building partner capacity is a top national priority, it has to be given precedence. It may be that the Nation needs to consider lengthening military careers beyond currently mandated lengths. These are not issues that the Army can address by itself.

The Army also will need support in raising the status of "advising" in an organization that has always valued command of U.S. units. In a recent email to the organization, Chief of Staff General George Casey sought, among other things, to "put training on the same footing as other kinds of assignments when it comes to promotions."[7] This is a good move, but it may not be taken seriously; the last time a chief of staff tried this—in the late 1960s—the admonition was forgotten by the time promotions boards met in the early 1970s.[8] If this is the direction in which the Nation wants to move, it will take more than a single Army chief of staff to make the policy stick.

The Future of the Army

The Army does not need to be wrenched around to face in the proper direction. To the contrary, the Army as an institution appears to have a good grasp of what it must do to prepare for the future. The new FM 3–0 embraces history, strategy, and stability operations. The chief of staff's missive on the value of advising recognizes the need to give this function higher status. And of course the Army's performance in Iraq and Afghanistan, adapting to modes of conflict ignored or scorned only a decade ago, lays the groundwork for an Army able to tackle the more complicated and "irregular" forms of conflict the Nation is likely to confront in the future.

Hence the Obama administration's mission should be one of ensuring that the organization sticks to the general course it has chosen. Anyone aware of the Army's history knows how ephemeral many of the changes now proposed may be—particularly amid the national security debates that will follow a substantial withdrawal from Iraq. Field manuals change and dictates from higher headquarters can be amended or quietly forgotten. The Obama administration must ensure that the Army continues to explore the new intellectual and operational territory it now occupies.

Four areas in particular need sustained attention by the Obama administration. First is the effort to broaden officer development paths, ultimately making them richer and more varied than during the Cold War. The administration should be willing to consider lengthening officer careers as a means to this end. Second, and relatedly, the operator-experts that emerge from this broader development process need to be rewarded for service as advisors. Third, rebalancing the force away from the dominance of the combat arms, or at least armor and artillery, will need high-level support. Finally, the way in which the Army delivers "full-spectrum" training as operational tempo allows will need careful attention and analysis.

Table 1. Current and Future Navy Fleets

Ship Type	283-ship Fleet	313-ship Fleet	357-ship Fleet
Aircraft carriers (CVs, CVNs)	11	11	10
Escort carriers (CVEs)	0	0	4
Nuclear-powered ballistic missile submarines (SSBNs, SSBNXs)	14	14	12
Nuclear-powered cruise missile and special operations transport submarines (SSGNs)	4	4	6
Nuclear-powered attack submarines (SSNs)	53	48	48
Guided missile cruisers (CGs, CGXs)	22	19	0
Guided missile destroyers (DDGs, DDGXs, DDG–1000s)	55	69	0
Large Battle Network Combatants	0	0	80
Frigates (FFs)	30	0	0
Mine countermeasure ships (MCMs)	14	0	0
Littoral Combat Ships (LCSs)	1	55	55
Large-deck amphibious assault ships (LHAs, LHDs, LHARs, LHDXs)	10	9	11
Amphibious landing ships (LSDs, LPDs)	21	22	22
Maritime prepositioning future squadron (T–LHA/LHD, T–AKE, LMSR, MLP)	0	12	0
Combat logistics force ships (T–AE, T–AFS, T–AKE, T–AO, T–AOE)	31	30	31
Support ships	17	20	29
Maritime Security Force ships	0	0	49

Source: Naval Vessel Register, available at ‹www.nvr.navy.mil/nvrships/FLEET.HTM›.

A New Competitive Strategy for Enduring Naval Superiority

The U.S. Navy's 283-ship battle force is the most powerful on Earth (see table 1). This force includes 11 aircraft carriers capable of launching and landing conventional jets, and 10 amphibious assault ships capable of operating short takeoff and vertical landing (STOVL) jet fighters, tilt-rotor aircraft, and helicopters. No other navy operates more than four such ships.[9] Its tactical submarine fleet numbers 56 nuclear-powered boats (52 attack boats and 4 cruise missile submarines)—11 more nuclear boats than those found in all foreign navies.[10] Its 77 multimission guided missile destroyers and cruisers carry about the same number of missiles as do the 367 surface combatants operated by the next 20 largest navies. Its 31-ship amphibious warfare fleet can land 2 Marine Expeditionary Brigades, and its 32-ship combat logistics force (CLF)—a mix of fuel tankers, ammunition, and supply ships—gives the Navy a global reach and staying power unmatched by any other navy. Not included in the 283-ship count is a 110-ship prepositioning and sealift fleet operated by the Military Sealift Command, representing 95 percent of the world's militarily useful sealift.[11] Nor does it include approximately 160 Coast Guard cutters and patrol boats.

Despite its great strength, the Navy believes that its battle force is too small given the demands on the fleet. The recently published *Cooperative Strategy for 21st Century Seapower* declares that preventing wars is as important as winning them.[12] As a consequence, it emphasizes persistent global presence and maritime security and humanitarian assistance operations. This strategy entails larger numbers of ships and different types, too, including ships and craft capable of operating in the brown and green waters of the world alongside smaller, less capable navies. Given these tasks, as well as those associated with the current two-war joint standard, the Navy wants its future battle force to be *no less* than 313 ships (see tables 1 and 2).[13]

The likelihood that the Navy will achieve this future goal is low. Since fiscal year (FY) 2003, the Navy has spent about $12.6 billion a year on shipbuilding. The Congressional Budget Office estimates the Navy's FY09 30-year plan to build a 313-ship fleet would cost an average of $27.4 billion a year.[14] Given likely future budgets, few observers believe that the Navy will be able to allocate such large sums to its shipbuilding efforts.[15] Even the Secretary of the Navy has said that unless the Navy designs and builds more affordable ships, the chances that it will be able to build up and sustain a larger fleet are poor.[16]

Table 2. U.S. Navy 313-ship Plan

Type/Class	Required	Description
Aircraft carriers	11	Transitions to CVN 21-class nuclear-powered aircraft carriers
Ballistic missile submarines	14	Comprised of 14 *Ohio*-class nuclear-powered SSBNs
Cruise missile submarines	4	Comprised of 4 *Ohio*-class SSBNs converted to SSGNs
Attack submarines	48	Comprised of nuclear-powered *Los Angeles*-, *Seawolf*-, and *Virginia*-class SSNs
Surface combatants	88	Includes 19 guided missile cruisers (CG[X]s), 7 destroyers (DDG–1000s), and 62 guided missile destroyers (DDGs and DDG[X]s)
Littoral combat ships	55	Sea frames only; program also includes 64 antisurface, antisubmarine, and countermine mission packages
Amphibious warfare ships	31	Includes 9 amphibious assault ships (LHD/LHAs), 10 amphibious transport docks (LPD–17s), 12 dock landing ships (LSDs)
Maritime prepositioned force (future)	12	3 modified LHDs/LHAs, 3 large medium speed RO/RO ships (LMSRs), 3 dry cargo/ammunition ships (T–AKEs), and 3 mobile landing platforms (MLPs)
Combat logistics force	30	Transitions to 4 Fast Combat Support ships (T–AOEs), 11 dry cargo/ammunition ships (T–AKEs), and 15 underway replenishment oilers (T–AOs)
Support vessels	20	Includes 2 command ships (LCCs), 2 submarine tenders (ASs), 4 rescue and salvage ships (ARSs), 4 fleet tugs (T–ATFs), 4 ocean surveillance ships (T–AGOS), 1 high-speed ship (HSS), 3 Joint High Speed Vessels (JHSVs)

The Navy's plans to recapitalize its extensive carrier-based and land-based air forces are similarly challenged. In addition to the F/A–18E/F strike fighters now in production, the Navy must pay for carrier and STOVL versions of the new F–35 Joint Strike Fighter; the E/A–18G electronic attack aircraft; the E–2D airborne early warning aircraft; the P–8A Multimission Maritime Aircraft; the MH–60R and MH–60S shipboard helicopters; and the Broad Area Maritime Surveillance and Firescout unmanned aerial systems. In addition, the Navy must pay for the recapitalization of the Marine Corps' substantial rotary-wing fleet. The steadily growing costs for all these aircraft will continue to put enormous pressure on a Service top line that is already under great strain.

Moreover, it is not yet clear that the Navy's plans are consistent with the emerging competitive environment, which is defined by the ongoing struggle against violent radical Islamist extremists and their terrorist networks, the rise of authoritarian capitalist states, and the prospect of a world in which weapons of mass destruction, especially nuclear weapons, are widely proliferated.[17] In addition, the Navy is witnessing a dramatic expansion in the land, air, and naval power of the People's Republic of China (PRC). At present, the aim of this expansion is to prevent Taiwan from declaring independence. As part of its planning, the PRC must hedge against the possibility of the United States intervening on the side of Taiwan. Accordingly, the PRC is developing a range of capabilities designed to contest U.S. air and naval operations up to 1,600 nautical miles from the Chinese mainland.[18] Foreshadowing the challenges and complexities of naval network warfare, these Chinese capabilities include an over-the-horizon, intelligence, surveillance, reconnaissance, and targeting network; maritime strike aircraft armed with advanced anti-ship cruise missiles (ASCMs); modern ASCM-armed surface combatants; and a qualitatively improved submarine fleet armed with advanced torpedoes and submerged-launched ASCMs. In addition, the PRC is experimenting with land-mobile, maneuverable reentry vehicle–equipped antiship ballistic missiles (essentially coastal artillery with ranges out to 2,500 kilometers), against which U.S. ships may have little defense.[19] This raises an open question: will rapidly improving Chinese maritime anti-access capabilities soon create a broad surface ship "keep out zone" in the far western reaches of the Pacific, and if so, how will the Navy respond?

There may also be a similar ongoing competitive shift in undersea warfare. New undersea target sets such as fiber optic cables and offshore energy platforms may spark new undersea combat missions. Extremely quiet, diesel-electric submarines with air independent propulsion can now patrol for weeks without having to recharge their batteries. Future undersea warfare will involve new types of combat networks composed of sensors, large and small manned submarines, and unmanned underwater vehicles (UUVs) and systems. Because the U.S. ability to project power globally rests on an assumption of continued undersea superiority, the Navy must make sure it is prepared for these changes and that it remains the top competitor when, and if, a major competitive shift occurs.[20]

Based on this quick survey, there are various possible changes to current Navy plans. These changes are shaped by the following assumptions:

■ The Navy can exploit its current comfortable lead in aggregate naval power by determining the direction of the future naval competition before making any dramatic changes to its force structure.

■ Operationally, the Navy must concentrate on improving its ability for forward engagement with smaller navies, fighting hybrid naval adversaries, and supporting U.S. irregular warfare in the near term. Over the long term, it should concentrate on

U.S. Navy (Rebecca Rebarich)

USS *Wyoming*, one of several *Ohio*-class ballistic missile submarines, was designed for Cold War nuclear deterrence but could be refitted for other roles

strengthening its undersea warfighting capabilities and improving the surface fleet's ability to fight from longer range—from beyond the densest defenses along a hostile coast.

■ To strengthen its long-term competitiveness, the Navy must reduce shipbuilding costs, husband resources, sustain the country's naval design and industrial base, and invest in robust research and development.

■ The four best ways to reduce shipbuilding costs and conserve resources are to exploit ship and aircraft designs now in production to the fullest extent possible in order to benefit from learning curve efficiencies; reduce the total number of different ship types to accrue savings in training, maintenance, and logistics; reduce crew sizes, which are the largest driver of a ship's lifecycle costs; and aggressively pursue improved networking capabilities, which provide added combat power well beyond mere numbers of platforms.

Based on these assumptions, the Navy should consider making the following changes to its current plans (see table 2).[21]

Aircraft Carriers. Reduce the carrier force target from 11 to 10 carriers, and shift to a sustained building rate of 1 new carrier every 5 years. At the same time, accelerate the development of a new carrier-based, stealthy, air-refuelable unmanned combat air system (UCAS). The UCAS has the potential to convert the aircraft carrier into a global surveillance-strike system able to fight from long ranges and against the most advanced air defense systems. Because the carrier force will continue to have 11 or 12 carriers through the mid-2030s, the Navy should consider converting one or two into UCAS carriers.[22]

Ballistic Missile Submarines. After completing the ongoing midlife refueling cycle for the first 12 of 14 *Ohio*-class nuclear-powered ballistic missile submarines (SSBNs), reduce the strategic deterrent fleet to 12 boats. This will free up two additional *Ohios* for conversion into nuclear-powered cruise missile and special operations transport submarines (SSGNs) and UUV motherships.[23] The Navy should also begin a concerted effort to design the future SSBN replacement, which will begin replacing the *Ohios* in the mid-2020s, presumably based around a new seabased strategic ballistic missile.

Cruise Missile and Attack Submarines. Forty-eight nuclear-powered attack submarines (SSNs) and 6 SSGNs are a reasonable interim target for the tactical submarine fleet; the ultimate size and character of

the future force will depend entirely on the future undersea competition. The most important requirement is to hedge against a major future undersea warfare challenge by maintaining an industrial base able to build a minimum of two boats per year, sustaining the submarine design base, and continuing a robust undersea warfare research and development program. Accordingly, the Navy should move to two *Virginia*-class SSNs per year as soon as practical, begin designing small manned submarines and UUVs that can perform both Naval Special Warfare and undersea combat network missions, and launch an aggressive undersea warfare experimentation program.

Surface Combatants. As indicated by the Navy's recent decision to truncate the DDG–1000 program to three ships and to restart the Arleigh Burke DDG production line, the Navy's current plan to recapitalize its large surface combatant force is simply too expensive for future shipbuilding budgets. The most important near-term goal is to execute a thorough hull and combat systems upgrade for the 84 guided-missile cruisers and destroyers either in the fleet or being built, to ensure their continued effectiveness. To save costs, the replacement programs for these ships—the CG(X) and DDG(X) programs—should be merged into a single Large Battle Network Combatant program. The new modular ship would be

U.S. Air Force (John M. Foster)

Stryker combat vehicles on patrol, Mosul, Iraq

sized for the cruiser mission, have a 40-year design life, and be affordable enough for a sustained shipbuilding rate of two per year. To maintain the industrial base until the new ship is ready for production, the Navy would continue building the Burke DDGs. Seven would replace the oldest CGs, which cannot be affordably modernized. After that, the Navy would maintain the size of the legacy cruiser and destroyer force at the current target of 88 ships. The long-term goal would be to replace these 88 ships with 80 new Large Battle Network Combatants.[24]

Littoral Combat Ships. The Navy plans to build 55 modular LCSs. Designed as multipurpose battle network combatants, the ships can be configured to perform antisurface, antisubmarine, and countermine duties. The Navy plans to build the ships at a rate of up to six per year, and then stop construction for a decade or more. To sustain the industrial base, a better plan is to build LCSs at a sustained rate of four per year. Once the Navy hits its objective target of 55 ships, it has two options: continue to build four ships per year to expand the size of the LCS force, or continue to build four ships per year, replace the four oldest LCSs on a one-for one-basis, and transfer or sell the excess LCSs to friendly navies. Many small navies seek less complicated and expensive former U.S. warships. Refurbished LCSs would be a good fit for them. Additionally, the Navy should develop additional LCS mission packages to perform additional missions, such as Naval Special Warfare support.

Naval Maneuver Ships. Amphibious warfare ships are perfectly suited for a strategy that emphasizes sustained forward presence and engagement; Maritime Pre-positioning Force (MPF) ships are less so. Accordingly, the Navy should build a force of 33 amphibious ships (11 assault [LHD]/general purpose [LHA], 11 transport dock [LPD–17], and 11 dock landing [LSD]); cancel the proposed MPF (Future) squadron; and retain three legacy MPF squadrons. However, the Navy should build three planned Mobile Landing Platforms, assigning one to each legacy MPF squadron. This ship mix could lift a total of five Marine Expeditionary Brigades. The Navy should also build four additional LHAs to serve as escort carriers (CVEs), with Marine STOVL aircraft aboard, to further distribute fleet aviation capability. To save money, the Navy should replace the LSD force with a variant of the LPD–17 hull now in production.

CLF and Support Ships. The Navy should build 13 large, dry cargo/ammunition ships (T–AKEs), and then build 15 oilers and four Fast Combat Support ships based on variations of the same hull. This would produce a 31-ship CLF fleet with a common hull, which would result in significant savings. Similarly, it should replace its two command ships and two submarine tenders with variations of the LPD–17 hull. The Navy now plans to maintain five ocean surveillance ships, forego building the High Speed Ship, and increase its Joint High Speed Vessel (JHSV) buy to seven ships. These are flexible, inexpensive ships that can serve a variety of engagement and fleet support tasks. The Navy should build a minimum of 5 more for general fleet support, for a total of 12, with 7 dedicated to maritime security duties (see below).

Maritime Security Force Ships. The 313-ship fleet was developed before *A Cooperative Strategy for 21st Century Seapower* was published. The strategy emphasizes persistent presence, maritime security operations, and partnership building capacity. Consistent with this strategy, the Navy should establish seven Global Fleet Stations, each with a command ship (a converted LSD operated by the Military Sealift Command);[25] one Maritime Security Cutter, operated by the Naval Reserve;[26] one JHSV; one riverine squadron; and four Coastal Patrol ships.

For those counting, these recommendations result in a battle force of 357 ships (see table 1). This does not count ships in the Military Sealift Command's prepositioning and sealift fleets, Coast Guard cutters, or other important deployable naval capabilities, such as riverine squadrons. Between now and 2020, the Navy would need to spend approximately $21 billion each year to implement these recommendations. This is about $6 billion less per year than the Congressional Budget Office's estimate for the Navy's FY09 30-year plan to build a 313-ship fleet.

As one can see, these recommended changes lead to less of a radical alternate naval force structure than an alternate competitive strategy for enduring naval superiority. This strategy improves the Navy's ability to engage forward in the near term and prepares it for stiffer challenges in the longer term. It does this by husbanding resources; exploiting the hulls currently in production; reducing ship crews; preserving the naval industrial and design bases; maintaining U.S. undersea superiority; and making sure that future carrier battle forces can fight from longer ranges.

The Marines: From a Force in Readiness to a Force Engaged

This evaluation of the readiness and status of the Marine Corps has three components: winning the current conflict, equipping and modernizing, and posturing the Service for the future.

Winning the Current Fight

The Marines have made material contributions to every major campaign since September 11, 2001. They view Iraq and Afghanistan as part of the generational struggle, and have taken many training, doctrine, and educational initiatives to enhance the ability to prevail in the long war. Some 200,000 members of the Marine Corps have served in Southwest Asia since 2003. Another 49,877 Reservists have been activated since 2001 and 8,142 are deployed today, which represents about 20 percent of the Reserve Component.

The Marine Corps was engaged in Operation *Enduring Freedom* in Afghanistan during 2002, where Task Force 158 operated some 600 miles away from its amphibious shipping and logistics support. Several transition teams also have assisted the Afghan army. To counter the growing Taliban influence, some 3,000 members of the Marine Corps returned to that country in 2008 to engage in aggressive operations in Helmand Province to limit the ability of insurgents to intimidate the Afghan population and undermine the authority of the legitimate government.

The Marines deployed more than 50,000 personnel for Operation *Iraqi Freedom* in 2003, and some 24,000 remained in Iraq over last year. They demonstrated versatility by conducting major operations in Fallujah against foreign fighters and al Qaeda. After that intense urban fighting, the Marines transitioned to stability operations and support of the Iraqi government. They also provided additional battalions and support for the surge in 2007. Operating as part of the larger MAGTF, they performed with agility and demonstrated a wide range of capabilities that negated efforts by the insurgents and supported the Sunni awakening in Al Anbar.

Moreover, the Marine Corps has deployed some 25 training teams in the area of operations of U.S. Central Command, and some 600 Marines in two dozen countries as trainers and advisors. In addition, it executed more than 50 theater engagement events in the past year, including events in Iraq, Central America, the Middle East, and Africa. It also trained more than 400 foreign officers in various Marine Corps educational institutions and programs located in the United States.

In addition to combat operations in distant theaters, the Marine Corps budget has grown to increase its authorized strength from 175,000 to 202,000 by FY11. The commandant insisted on plans to develop all elements of the MAGTF in a balanced manner to meet the challenges of an uncertain future. The additional forces will allow the Service to have sufficient forces to conduct ongoing operations, train new forces for overseas missions, and remain capable of fulfilling both its core competencies and Title 10 responsibilities.

Achieving recruiting, equipment, and construction objectives will cost more than $30 billion over the Future Years Defense Program. Additional end-strength will result in three Marine Expeditionary Forces—balanced in both their capacity and capability. This increase will enable ongoing support to combatant commanders as well as reduce the unsustainable tempo of deployments on Marine personnel.

The increase permitted the addition of three infantry battalions and the equivalent of an artillery and military police battalion, enhanced armor and combat engineer battalions, and air-naval gunfire liaison companies. Current plans call for more logistics units and light attack helicopters. Moreover, the Marines intend to improve the deployment-to-dwell ratio by reducing operating tempo of various units, including military police, UAVs, helicopter, air command and control, combat service support, and explosive ordnance disposal.

Force expansion is being successfully executed. The Marines surpassed the FY08 authorized end-strength objective of 189,000 and also preserved force quality with recruits who have a high school graduation rate of more than 94 percent. The Service also expects to reach its expansion goal ahead of schedule in 2010. The Obama administration must gauge the strategic environment, the likely nature of future conflict, and available resources to determine if this force expansion meets the long-term needs of the Nation. For now, it is apparent that American ground forces have been badly strained by two simultaneous long-term counterinsurgency campaigns.

Equipping and Modernizing

To maintain the current high operating tempo, the budget of the Marine Corps has been substantially increased since the peace dividend of the 1990s. The baseline budget that pays largely for manpower, operations, maintenance, and procurement of ground weapons has increased by 100 percent since FY00 (in current dollars). The Marines also have benefited from substantial funding in Navy accounts, which is known as blue-in-support-of-green funding that provides for aviation. These funds are critical to the Marine Aviation Plan, which will transition more than half of the Marine aviation resources (39 out of

71 squadrons) from 13 legacy types of aircraft to 6 new aircraft models and one unmanned system.

The Expeditionary Fighting Vehicle is designed for operations conducted from the sea and in littoral regions. Although often construed as a niche capability, it has inherent capabilities that provide utility across the conflict spectrum, including riverine and urban operations. The vehicle offers amphibious mobility, cross-country versatility, lethality, enhanced force protection, and communications that will improve joint force operations. This is the largest acquisition program in the Marine Corps, and it has been beset by technical complexities and rising costs. The decision was made to limit the program objective to 574 vehicles in order to invest in a flexible suite of ground vehicles. Although this program survived the last Quadrennial Defense Review (QDR), it will once again be examined for relevance, cost level, and program management challenges.

The F–35B STOVL aircraft is a variant of the JSF that offers basing flexibility and timely support across the full spectrum of warfare. JSF capabilities will integrate combat systems in support of ground forces and be the centerpiece of Marine aviation. Production of the first 19 test aircraft is currently under way. Reflecting the Service's expeditionary orientation, the Marines are committed to an all-STOVL tactical aircraft force, which enables MAGTFs to operate close to supported units under austere conditions.

MV–22 Osprey aircraft are replacing 40-year-old CH–46E helicopters that were introduced during the Vietnam War. The Marines have received 60 aircraft, which are based at Marine Corps Air Station New River, North Carolina; Patuxent River, Maryland; and Al Asad Air Base, Iraq. Ospreys make up one training squadron, one test squadron, and three tactical squadrons. The Marines will transition two CH–46E squadrons to MV–22 squadrons per year through 2012. An Osprey squadron was deployed to Iraq in 2008, and the capabilities of this aircraft have been proven under combat conditions. The range, speed, and durability of the hybrid tilt-rotor aircraft have been ably demonstrated. The MV–22 squadron in Iraq executed operational missions in 6 hours that would have taken some 12 hours in the more vulnerable CH–46 helicopters.

Posture the Service for the Future

The commandant of the Marine Corps has stated that "it is our obligation to subsequent generations of Marines, and to our Nation, to always have an eye to the future—to prepare for tomorrow's challenges to-

day." To further that obligation, he created a task force to produce a new vision and supporting strategy. The vision provides a foundation for operational concepts and identifies the critical steps needed to shape the Service for an increasingly volatile and uncertain future. It is grounded in its role as the Nation's force in readiness, but will guide combat development in the long term to properly organize, train, equip, and prepare the Marine Corps for tomorrow's challenges.

The commandant describes the Marine of tomorrow as a two-fisted fighter capable of destroying enemy formations with flexible air-ground-logistics teams in major contingencies, but equally capable of employing hard-earned irregular warfare skills honed over decades of conflict. The Marine Corps envisions itself as a persistently engaged and multicapable force, drawing on the Total Force to address the full range of contingencies that the future will present.

The Marines aim to become the Nation's expeditionary force of choice. The commandant and his leadership team are committed to maintaining a Marine Corps ready to live hard in uncertain, chaotic, and austere environments with an expeditionary mindset—emphasizing speed of execution, agility, and flexibility. Accordingly, the Service must be lean, agile, and adaptable. Over the last decade, the force has gotten much heavier. A balance must be struck between being heavy enough for expeditionary warfare and light enough for rapid deployment overseas aboard naval ships. Getting lighter will not negatively impact organic sustainability. The vision ensures that the Marines of tomorrow maintain the ability to sustain themselves in operations through the use of a seabase or initial lodgment ashore. The organic sustainability of MAGTFs is a unique and critical force enabler in such conditions, particularly early in an operation.

The vision devotes more attention and resources to education and training for understanding and defeating potential adversaries in complex conflicts involving combat and stability missions. The ability to conduct both types of operations simultaneously represents the essence of that two-fisted fighter—offering a hand to people in need or delivering a precise jab in irregular warfare while wielding a closed fist in major combat operations. The Marine Corps strives to be as effective in counterinsurgencies as it has been in kicking down doors as part of its amphibious operations.

Current operations in Iraq, Afghanistan, and the Pacific basin illustrate the range of operations the Marines must be prepared to conduct in the future. This challenge is nothing new and should not unsettle anyone who understands the history of the Marine Corps or the well-honed crisis response toolkit that the Marines provide worldwide to combatant commanders.

The Nation needs a force in readiness to rapidly and decisively deploy to crises anywhere in the world. But the emerging environment requires the Marines to shift from a "force in readiness" to one that is more engaged and proactive. To do so, the Marine Corps will train, advise, and shape events more directly. Marines should not simply be deployed forward; they should be actively engaged forward supporting theater security plans while also being prepared to conduct complex expeditionary operations. These challenges will require the Service to make changes and adapt to new skill sets. But regardless of resources, the Marines will continue to perform well just as they have done throughout American history.

Critical Decisions for the Air Force

Military strength underpins American diplomacy and its role in the world. The men and women of the Air Force are integral to that strength, standing watch in missile fields and at bases in both Korea and Japan, while serving with distinction in Iraq, Afghanistan, and wherever duty calls. In war and peace, their mission in air, space, and cyberspace as part of joint and coalition forces provides the United States with the capabilities required to project power globally.

Today, the Air Force faces several critical questions. Under new leadership, the Service must address nuclear discipline following two high-profile mishaps. During the 1990s, after Strategic Air Command was dissolved and the conventional role of nuclear bombers was increased, some of that discipline began to erode in the Air Force. In an age of nuclear-armed countries, nuclear weapons remain the ultimate guarantor of U.S. national security, but the organization that the Air Force uses to manage those weapons is no longer up to this critical task.

The Air Force also faces major acquisition problems, which are similar to those confronting other Services but of greater magnitude. As a general rule, the Service is dependent on big-ticket space and air platforms that require decades-long development lead times and remain in the force for decades. Most bombers and tankers flown today were built when General Curtis LeMay led the Air Force, and most fighters were built in the 1970s and 1980s. Added to this problem, after 18 years of maintaining a high operating tempo, including combat sorties and airlift operations to support combat in Southwest Asia, equipment has aged more rapidly than originally anticipated. Recent questions raised by the Government

U.S. Marine Corps (Cherie A. Thurlby)

Marine speaks to villager through translator during civil-military operations training at Marine Base Quantico

Accountability Office about the acquisition process in the Air Force have complicated and postponed recapitalization efforts. Given smaller budgets and a highly charged atmosphere surrounding acquisition matters, solving the recapitalization problem will not be easy but must be tackled under new leadership.

The Air Force also faces serious challenges in regard to its cyber mission. Although analysts increasingly agree that such capabilities will be at the core of conventional and unconventional warfare in the future, budgets do not reflect this priority for any Service. As the Air Force has moved to increase cyber capabilities, the Department of Defense (DOD) has struggled with issues of allocating responsibility for cyber security and warfare among the Services and various agencies. Because it provides 80 percent of land and space command and control infrastructure protection to the Nation, the Air Force is in a position to take the lead in this mission.

Finally, the Air Force faces strategic questions on the allocation of limited resources between unconventional and conventional warfare. Over the next decade, advanced surface-to-air missiles and fourth-generation fighters will be transferred by Russia and China to potentially hostile states. Ensuring the air superiority required to project power globally, and even to utilize UAVs and air-to-ground strike platforms for unconventional warfare, the Air Force must purchase expensive fifth-generation fighters and stealthy long-range bombers. However, doing so will diminish the resources available for assets to support the conduct of current unconventional warfare operations. Squaring this circle will not be easy.

The Air Force is consolidating its nuclear forces under a single command and transforming its procurement system from requirements to acquisition. Moreover, the Service has given cyber assets to the 24th Air Force and, with the Army, Navy, and Intelligence Community, is developing related tactical and strategic efforts at Nellis Air Force Base. Yet budget questions loom large. Given ongoing operations, there is no peace dividend to bank. After a global financial crisis, very large projected deficits, and little in long-range budgets to cover inflation, the Air Force will have to set priorities and make hard decisions.

Fighter Modernization

Along with naval combat assets, Air Force combat aircraft form the basis of U.S. power projection capability. This force is evolving with fifth-generation fighters and next-generation bombers that will replace aging planes. This evolution is important because legacy aircraft and ships are slowly losing the ability to operate against antiaccess technologies. Within the next 10 to 20 years, credible military diplomacy among major powers, and military operations against states capable of buying new Russian and Chinese missiles and aircraft, will require aircraft capable of operating in a high-threat environment. Practically speaking, the Air Force must increase its inventory of fifth-generation fighters as well as develop a new bomber.

As of August 2009, the question of the size of the fifth-generation aircraft appeared to be resolved. The Obama administration decided to end production of the F–22 jet fighter at 187 planes rather than a projected inventory of 243 aircraft as planned in the previous administration. Although some Members of Congress and others continue to support the F–22 program, which began as a response to Soviet aircraft developments in the 1980s, the administration decided to cap the program in order to fund higher priorities. The limited number may make moot the issue of whether the F–22 would ever be sold to allies.

The Air Force must take three steps to develop a successful fighter program. First, it must develop a coordinated acquisition process tied to strategic requirements. In particular, the process requires more focus on the F–35 aircraft. Out-year schedule changes and budget adjustments have made the F–35 program a bill-payer for other acquisitions, which must stop. Second, the JSF program must fully engage those allies investing in program technology. Artificial barriers preventing key partners from fully participating must be dropped. Finally, interoperability of the JSF with allies—equipment, training, information, and combat employment—is the heart of the program and needs top-level attention. Moreover, like fighters, bombers are aging rapidly. The last B–52H came off the production line in 1962. A substantial portion of the fleet is grounded. If the United States intends to maintain the ability to conduct a long-range strike mission, it should continue investment in such aircraft.

Intelligence, Surveillance, and Reconnaissance

While speaking at Maxwell Air Force Base in April 2008, Secretary Gates drew on his experience in the Intelligence Community to challenge the military Services to examine their cultures in order to accomplish future missions. Calling on the tradition of innovation of earlier Air Force thinkers, Secretary Gates urged his audience to consider if the ways in which the military does business continue to make sense.

Nowhere is such thinking more apropos than intelligence, surveillance, and reconnaissance (ISR). The revolution in information technologies, combined with the accuracy of global positioning satellites used for navigation, has introduced highly sophisticated approaches to the application of modern airpower. But the ability to strike targets with precision became limited by the ability to find and identify them, particularly in distinguishing combatants from civilians.

Some of the most critical ISR-related issues the Air Force must address relate to UAVs. Questions continue about balancing the need for persistent ISR capabilities with assets that can survive on the battlefield. If programmers continue to believe that future airspace will be uncontested, they must shift the balance toward vulnerable yet persistent unmanned assets at the expense of more survivable ones in setting their budget priorities. Otherwise, they should give survivability greater weight. The Air Force must develop systems that communicate with ground forces and effectively allocate ISR across continents. Equally important, it must develop methods of cultivating mutual trust and support among Soldiers and Airmen to maximize the effectiveness of Air Force assets. Furthermore, because ISR capabilities involve assembling a cohesive picture with data drawn from multiple domains, the Air Force must increase its ability to process as well as obtain information. Beyond such considerations, the Air Force must seek to improve ISR development in light of the recommendations reported by the Allard Commission in 2008 that indicated the National Reconnaissance Office requires major restructuring.

As new technology has become available, the Air Force has been partnered with commanders on the ground. Over the last 3 years, as ground forces have discovered the value of the Rover platform and other ISR capabilities, requests for persistent surveillance have outstripped assets by levels of magnitude. As joint confidence in ISR as well as guided precision strike grew during the surge in 2007, joint commanders increased the total daily average weight of ordnance dropped by the Air Force in Iraq by more than 1,000 percent. The future demands are likely to be even greater as these capabilities mature and expand.

As the U.S. military learns to utilize ISR-based capabilities, the enemy is also adapting. Increasingly, this problem dominates the news as the enemy seeks to deny precision attack bomb damage with misinformation. Finding targets has become more difficult than striking them. How the joint team deals with this problem will affect the benefit of airpower in future insurgencies. The continuing improvement in ISR assets will require fostering synergism among institutions, people, and technology in the air, space, and cyberspace. It will also mean improving the speed of total feedback and addressing the ability of potential enemies to operate inside a friendly observe-orient-decide-act cycle or the so-called OODA loop. DOD will look to the Air Force to take the lead in finding ISR operational solutions.

Airlift, tankers, and search and rescue platforms that provide logistical support in war are often as important as combat forces. Along with supply ships, airlift plays an important role, not only in supplying war, but also in providing humanitarian relief. The air bridge between Kuwait and Iraq has saved countless lives by delivering supplies without Soldiers having to run the gauntlet of improvised explosive devices, but it has resulted in the premature aging of transport aircraft. Humanitarian airlifts after the Asian tsunami, Pakistani earthquake, Russian attack on Georgia, and natural disasters in the United States have taken a heavy toll on aircraft longevity.

Recapitalizing airlift, tankers, and search and rescue assets has been deferred for many years. In the next 4 years, the Air Force must begin work on combat search and rescue platforms and new tankers. Expanding the airlift capacity will be a fiscal challenge. U.S. Africa Command by itself will demand significant airlift resources to accomplish its interagency mission. In terms of national security priorities, airlift is a capability that joint and coalition operations depend on. The Air Force will be required to identify additional fiscal resources. Prioritizing the mission of the airlift fleet and finding the resources to support it will present a serious challenge.

Space and Cyberspace

Like air assets, space assets are rapidly aging. In an age when states are testing antisatellite weapons, studies point to the increasing vulnerability of large unshielded multipurpose satellites and call for smaller, less costly, and more survivable replacements. With regard to cyberspace where the Air Force has responsibility for most cyber protection, and with defense assets constantly under attack, it is critical to develop an investment plan in this domain. Cyberspace acquisition is being studied in the Electronic Systems Division with support from the Air Force Research Laboratories and should be better framed in the next budget cycle.

Forward Presence

For the Air Force to project global power, it requires international bases to extend its reach and provide aerial refueling of shorter range fighters and transports. Besides projecting national power, basing agreements deter aggression by demonstrating the solidarity of the United States and its allies around the world. As a new generation of antiship missiles has continued to drive aircraft carriers farther from shore, basing will remain important to American defense interests. This requirement has not received the attention that it deserves; thus, basing issues and related power projection considerations must be given a high priority.

People

In recent years, the end-strength of the Air Force has been considerably reduced as missions have increased and its personnel reassigned to in-lieu-of taskings to bolster Army units, which has stressed the force. Resolving this problem will require increasing the size of the force, maximizing value and minimizing waste by streamlining under Air Force Smart Operations, and continuing the focus on quality of life issues. Given the amount of money being allocated to the development of technical skills, Airmen must be retained. Yet given budget pressures, doing so without sacrificing recapitalization or current operations represents a real challenge.

Focus on Energy

Since Jimmy Doolittle helped Shell Oil produce 100-octane aviation fuel in the 1930s, energy has been critical to Air Force research and development. With the price of oil fluctuating and the United States and other nations demanding lower carbon emission from jet fuel, this mission is more important than ever. The Air Force must increase efforts in this area to protect bases from grid interruption and facilitate the transition to alternative fuels in the future. The Air Force Research Laboratory has led the way through innovations that have been extended to commercial partners. The programs are inexpensive and provide a disproportionate return on the investment when the potential of energy security is also factored into the equation.

In the coming decade, the Air Force will face tough choices in rebuilding its nuclear program, defining its cyber mission, and allocating its tight budget across an aging inventory of space and air assets. Its capabilities underpin joint warfighting, from air superiority and aerial refueling to ISR and communications for modern warfare. The future will require hard decisions on the role of the United States in the world and the configuration of the Armed Forces to support national objectives. The global military environment is changing. Policymakers must decide how to structure the Air Force to respond to those changes.

Military Manpower and Personnel Issues

The Armed Forces, particularly the Army, face challenges in both the recruitment and retention of sufficient personnel with requisite qualities. Some factors influencing these challenges—such as the extent of combat operations in Iraq—are likely to abate in the next few years. Others will become more salient. The basic paradigm for manning the force that has existed since the end of the draft in 1973, particularly obtaining recruits, soon may be untenable without major changes and infusions of money. The Obama administration also faces other manpower issues, notably adapting career personnel management to new operational and social realities, dealing with the high cost of military health care, and maintaining capable Reserve Components in an era of mobilization. However, these issues are secondary to finding enough recruits for the Active force.

The All-Volunteer Force instituted some 35 years ago has been extraordinarily successful in both peace and war. The average quality of recruits, both in quantifiable terms and intangibles of character, has been substantially higher than during conscription from 1940 to 1973. This enables the Services to train men and women to higher standards. Disciplinary problems are dramatically lower than during the draft. The higher quality of recruits, coupled with high levels of military compensation that guarantee living standards for career personnel at least equal to their civilian counterparts, has resulted in high-quality career noncommissioned officers. Coupled with force modernization and technological and attitudinal revolutions in unit training, these personnel have brought U.S. forces to a level of readiness unmatched in history. All of this has been seen on the battlefield in the last two decades. Nor are there operational indications that personnel readiness has flagged, almost 8 years after terrorist attacks on the United States, and after 6 years of grinding, repetitive, and frustrating combat operations conducted in Southwest Asia.

The number of new accessions and reenlistments was reduced with the All-Volunteer Force. Active strength was 2.2 million in 1973 and had dropped to only 1.4 million by the mid-1990s. The post-Vietnam Army of 780,000 had declined to 480,000 members on September 11, 2001. Not until the Nation was into the Iraq conflict in 2005 did DOD, prodded by Congress, grudgingly consent to a modest increase in Army strength to 547,000 over several years. The Army has maintained both officer and enlisted strength only by lowering enlistment standards in the last few years and by increasing enlistment, reenlistment, and retention bonuses and special pay. Some enlistment bonuses are figured in five figures and reenlistment bonuses in six. Studies indicate recruits with moral waivers do better by some standards and only slightly worse than other enlistees, while not compromising their overall battlefield performance.

Nonetheless, this state of affairs may not endure. The benefit of paying lump sums to recruit and retain personnel may have reached its useful limit. There has been a decline over the last 15 to 20 years in the propensity of young people to enter the Armed Forces, which not surprisingly has accelerated during the Iraq War. Under existing standards, only about 30 percent of 18-year-old men and women are eligible for military service, with the balance physically or morally unfit because of obesity, health issues, and drug use. More significantly, the rise in college attendance shrinks the pool of youth who have traditionally enlisted. The tendency of African-Americans to enlist has dropped over the past 20 years. This may pose issues for society in general, but it also has the effect of depriving the Services of a reliable manpower pool that formerly enlisted and tended to remain in the military for a career. Some problems may be directly related to Iraq and diminish when the conflict winds down. However, the war on terror and the struggle in Southwest Asia that may require a forward presence for many years suggest that recruitment and retention will take place in a wartime rather than peacetime environment for the foreseeable future.

Reports of an immediate crisis in officer retention, particularly a hemorrhaging of captains in the Army, have turned out to be overstated. However, retention is unquestionably under pressure that is likely to increase. The leadership and knowledge skills of junior officers, many of whom have been combat tested, have led to an unprecedented demand for them in the private sector. The constant transfers, combined with the exhausting pace of Iraq and Afghanistan deployments in both the Army and the Marine Corps, make it difficult for officers to put down roots, marry, and have families. Once married, frequent household moves make it difficult for spouses to establish and maintain their professional careers, which has

▼ *Continued on p. 403*

Integration Initiatives in the Air Force

At a time of increasing competition for scarce resources, the integration of all components makes sense. While the Air Force has been integrating with varying degrees of success for more than 40 years through association constructs, and all components have worked together in combat contingencies for nearly two decades, fiscal imperatives are driving an accelerated rate of association today. It is critical that Airmen look beyond fiscal efficiency and grasp the magnitude of changes in aggressive force structure. Promoting association exclusively for fiscal efficiency risks compromising inherent component attributes and combat effectiveness. Moreover, there are still tough issues that must be resolved. Do association constructs work with operations plans? Do they increase the capability of the joint warfighter? How should they measure that?

Integration represents more than bringing people and equipment together. It means bringing organizations with different cultures together around common equipment and common missions. All organizations and associations are based on relationships that require understanding, respect, and appreciation of them to be successful. The Active Component of the Air Force provides well-trained, highly standardized, dedicated personnel; it comprises 65 percent of the Service. Regular Airmen are available 24 hours a day, 7 days a week, and are able to deploy on short notice for longer periods of time without risking their livelihood. They can move from one duty station to another with few complications. New duty stations and resulting changes in assignments provide these Airmen with a broad perspective on the Air Force and help develop leaders. On the other hand,

U.S. Air Force (Eunique Stevens)

Lt Gen Stenner meets with Active-duty, Reserve, and Guard Airmen in Kirkuk, Iraq frequent moves can make continuity in any given unit mission far more difficult.

Like the Active Component, the U.S. Air Force Reserve and Air National Guard contain well-trained, highly standardized personnel. Most have served in the Active force and have more experience that benefits the younger Airman. They perform a number of the Air Force missions to include some that are not performed by the Active Component, such as aerial spray (Reserve), weather reconnaissance (Reserve), aerial fire fighting (Reserve and Guard), and aerial broadcast operations (Guard). Moreover, members of the Air National Guard perform state-focused, governor-directed missions such as counterdrug operations and disaster response.

Reservists and Guardsmen remain members of the Air Force because they enjoy the mission and are dedicated to the Nation. They strike a balance between commitments to the Service, their families, and their civilian jobs, which is the major source of their income. From their civilian jobs they bring skills, background, and creativity to the military, which are highly valued assets. These Airmen take great pride in their unit and ability to perform the mission. Most have long-term ties in their communities and states, and have little desire to move to another duty station. While this lack of mobility presents difficulties in developing leadership experience over careers, it provides long-term continuity to the unit mission and ultimately to the Air Force.

Members of the U.S. Air Force Reserve and Air National Guard train to the same standards and currencies as the Active duty force at a fraction of the cost. Most are capable of deploying in 72 hours of notification. However, they are not as accessible as their Active counterparts: short of being mobilized, the Reserve Components depend on volunteers to meet wartime taskings. The Reserve and Guard form a smaller percentage of the force (14 and 21 percent, respectively) and thus are less capable than the Active Component of sustaining a high operating tempo.

Such are the attributes of components; they make each unique and successful. The challenge is preserving the culture of each component, improving fiscal efficiency, and adding capabilities. After 40 years of trial and error, some basic truths about association have emerged. Both the host and associate unit should have roughly mirror organizational structures in which each component unit retains a separate administrative chain of control so that promotions, discipline, readiness, training, and so forth remain in the component of the unit. Authority to designate objectives, assign tasks, and provide operational direction to ensure unity of effort in the mission must be resolved by memoranda of agreement. The agreements should provide opportunities for units to develop leaders, not only in terms of administrative control but in operational direction as well.

Because the host unit remains primarily responsible for equipment, there is the potential for an uneven playing field. Moreover, not all missions are the same; some readily lend themselves to training. Equipment can influence how much training can be accomplished. Care should be taken to ensure parity in access to equipment in achieving unit training objectives.

Units must be able to retain their unique and separate identities, which are the source of pride for members of each component and can be the source of motivation in accomplishing missions. If unit identity is compromised, the motivation to perform the mission and serve will be as well. Beyond those basic tenets, associations present new challenges in developing plans to meet the needs of combatant commanders. Often it has been the case that plans were developed for units to deploy together with their equipment in support of a given operation. Associations must be worked into plans. Although progress has been made in developing mobilization plans that deploy equipment separately from units, difficulties will be encountered in executing them. It will be important to find the right mix of Active and Reserve Components when allocating people against missions in the Air and Space Expeditionary Force construct. Determining how long and how best to access Reserve Component personnel for that mix (that is, by mobilizing them or seeking volunteers) provides combatant commanders with the most effectively resourced force.

The Air Force must educate personnel on the unique challenges of associations—at all levels and among components. Advancement in each Service today is premised on joint education and experience. However, it should also be premised on joint component education and experience. Candidates for leadership in associations should be screened and selected based on their ability to get along with other components. Force integration should not be seen as a separate process in and of itself. Properly understood, it is a unified, harmonious, and effective entity.

▲ *Continued from p. 401*

become the norm for a large number of people with college or postgraduate degrees from which most of the officer corps is drawn.

While the existing recruiting model may have outlived its usefulness, the Services probably will continue using it with only marginal adjustments. But other approaches are available. One change would be assigning the same budget priority to recruitment as weapons procurement. The Services spend billions on hardware, but then nickel and dime recruitment in relative terms. The All-Volunteer Force has afforded a good military for the money. Added resources, though, may be needed in the future. Pursuing college-bound youth with educational benefits or paying off student loans of college graduates makes sense. Arguments that educational benefits induce people to leave the military are false. Moreover, recruits should be more carefully selected since about one-third of first-term enlistees do not finish their first term. Rigorous, albeit expensive, drug tests would eliminate some recruits and may deter others from using. The physical fitness standards applied to recruits in meeting training quotas are also problematic. Requiring several more weeks of training makes greater sense than allowing recruits to go on unit assignments only to be separated before completing their first-term enlistment for medical reasons.

The Services should find ways to acquaint young people with military life. Recruiters face *un*military rather than *anti*military attitudes. The option of military service does not dawn on many Americans. While the Pentagon begrudges spending money on the Junior Reserve Officer Training Corps, it does produce a large number of recruits. Moreover, the Services should consider experimenting with programs that enable young people to serve for a few months in the military, similar to the Citizens Military Training Camps operated during the interwar period.

Finally, the President will be subject to enormous pressure to support the admission of admitted homosexuals to the military. This issue reflects a wider debate in society over according full rights to gay men and women. Those who favor ending the statutory ban on gays argue that changed social mores have removed the stigma of homosexuality, and various surveys of military personnel support the admission of gays, plus impressionistic comments by junior and senior officers. If this is the case, it undercuts arguments that openly gay personnel in the ranks negatively affect cohesion and discipline, and buttresses the view that the military, particularly

given a strained recruiting environment, cannot afford to lose the service of capable individuals who happen to be gay or lesbian Americans, although this may be an oversimplification.

Many enlisted personnel are prepared to live and let live with regard to homosexuals who are not out of the closet, but are less well disposed to openly gay men and women. One of the dominant motivations for enlisting in the combat arms is the testing and proving of masculinity, which in the minds of many young men is contradicted by open male homosexuality. Polls and surveys, even those conducted anonymously, may reflect subliminal attempts to conform to popular views rather than actual beliefs, a phenomenon familiar to sophisticated designers of survey research. In addition, there has been virtually no mention of the effect of ending the ban on gays on those who influence potential recruits, principally their parents. These factors suggest that the debate over gays in the military has been framed in a rather limited and restrictive manner.

Defense Budgets: Past and Future

There are a number of critical national security issues that face the Obama administration. The conflicts in Iraq and Afghanistan, rising regional powers, and the ongoing fight to dampen the influence of al Qaeda are daunting tasks. But the most challenging issue may be the badly strained Pentagon fiscal accounts. In the 1990s, defense spending was squeezed to gain a modest peace dividend. Critics predicted a train wreck in military effectiveness as procurement was scaled back. Today, analysts refer to the Pentagon coffers as a poisoned chalice. Stretched by two conflicts in Southwest Asia, these accounts compete within a Federal budget that is increasingly plagued by a weak economic base, changing demographic realities, and ever growing entitlement programs. Resolving such deficiencies, in the midst of ongoing wars, will demand rigorous planning that acknowledges the risk of an overstretched force and judiciously matches ends and means.

The 'war on terror' has resulted in significant increases in the defense budget. Spending in real terms is 30 percent higher today than in 2001, not including funding for the operations in Southwest Asia. At the same time, fiscal constraints have resulted in deferred modernization of the Services. Moreover, higher usage rates of aircraft, vehicles, and weapons increase the cost of resetting the force to previous levels. Supplemental budgets have absorbed the brunt of the reset, but estimates indicate the need for $100 billion to $200 billion in deferred maintenance and repair costs. In addition, the delayed modernization of the Navy and Air Force represents another $200 billion. Filling this gap would increase the defense budget on the order of some 10 to 20 percent.

Beyond qualitative changes in the character of the Armed Forces, there are planned increases in the strengths of the Army and Marine Corps. The Army is authorized to grow by 65,000 to 547,000 and the Marines by 27,000 to 202,000 by FY11. This decision represents a modification to force development guidance that had previously emphasized leap-ahead technology and standoff warfare. Irregular threats in dense urban environments or among "the people" do not present readily identifiable target sets. The combined estimate for these manpower rampup costs comes to almost $108 billion in the FY08 to FY12 period, and $12 billion per year after.

Gauging defense requirements has never been easy. The proverbial question "How much is enough?" has never been satisfactorily answered. U.S. military spending is almost equal to that of the rest of the world combined, or about 47 percent of global defense budgets. The United States spends more on defense than the next 16 nations combined.

As guarantor of international stability, with a range of global interests to protect, it should not be surprising that the U.S. defense budget is the largest. But it begs a key question: why has the Pentagon been unable to provide a sufficient margin of security given that its spending outclasses any rival or com-

bination of rivals by several orders of magnitude? Ultimately, it is a question of how much we can afford and how much potential risk policymakers are willing to accept.

The question "How much is enough?" has been sidestepped by claims that the United States is simply not spending enough. This reasoning rests on arguments comparing past conflicts such as World War II, Korea, and Vietnam to current budget authorizations. Using these comparisons, some argue that the United States is spending far less than in the past and that defense spending has reached an all-time low. These historical comparisons are worthy of a bit of scrutiny. First, historical patterns may not provide a valid basis for comparison, including the Cold War period when a monolithic adversary posed both ideological and existential threats backed by thousands of nuclear warheads as well as tens of thousands of tanks and aircraft. While al Qaeda presents a threat, it is not the same kind as the Soviet Union. Terrorists are committed, and should they acquire weapons of mass destruction, the results could be catastrophic. But the forces and resources needed to check that threat in no way approach levels of past wars.

Is America really spending less? We are spending less of the total Federal budget and less of the gross domestic product (GDP) on the military than in the past. But this does not equate to spending less on defense in terms of absolute resources.

A different story emerges when defense spending is examined in constant dollars adjusted for inflation in past conflicts. Defense budgets grew in both real and absolute terms continuously from 1966 to 2006. What the data fail to capture is the shift to the All-Volunteer Force and the ineluctably higher cost of advanced military technology. These factors are critical elements of our military strategy and the dominant status of our Armed Forces. Both also contribute to a military budget that dwarfs spending in other countries of the world. This is why looking at the defense budget as a percentage of GDP or a share of the Federal budget does not reveal much. In fact, it conceals more than it helps. Such indicators fail to capture growth in the overall economy or steady increases in the budget of the United States; the GDP is an indicator of neither requirements nor national strategy itself, but rather a crude measure of what the Nation can afford.

Defense spending has increased over time in real terms (adjusted for inflation). Although the Pentagon share of the Federal budget has declined, its real or absolute resources have increased. The total top line

Navy southwest region commander visits with Navy Junior Reserve Officer Training Corps students at Carl Hayden High School, Phoenix

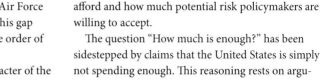

U.S. Navy (Gary Ward)

has grown from $452 billion to 589 billion in constant dollars. So arguments over declining defense budgets need to be clarified. In real terms, almost 30 percent more is being spent today than during the Cold War.

The idea that defense budgets have reached all-time lows is simply not true. America is actually spending more today, much more than other countries in the aggregate. Some increases can be explained by the All-Volunteer Force and rising energy and health care costs, while others support a global basing posture and overwhelming edge in space-based intelligence and warning systems. But a big picture suggests that we should be concerned about the future. The United States has numerous long-term liabilities. The defense share of the Federal budget has declined as entitlements have steadily grown. That share will grow with the retirement of Baby Boomers. The percent of the Federal budget allocated for defense has declined from 43 percent in the early years of the Vietnam War to 28 percent by 1986. Over the last 20 years, it has declined further to 20 percent of the budget, and it will continue to decline on the order of 15 percent by 2026. This will result in spending under 3 percent of GDP.

Demographics and resulting shifts in funding could limit the resources available for defense and make calls for greater military spending moot. Between now and 2030, the number of Americans aged 65 and over will double from 36 million to 72 million. Moreover, the Boomer generation will be roughly 20 percent of the population. Medicare and Medicaid costs will grow from 1 to 25 percent of all Federal spending between 1966 and 2026. Spending on three major entitlement programs consumed over $1 trillion in 2006 or 40 percent of the Federal budget. By 2026, some 13 percent of the GDP and 47 percent of the Federal budget will go to entitlement programs if current trends are not addressed.

Funding increases for such programs pose profound implications for the ability of the Nation to provide for the common defense and other government responsibilities. It has been suggested that given these trends, the only public function left by 2040 will be to mail entitlement checks to pensioners. There will not be money left for anything else, including DOD. The long-term implications of these trends in the American polity could have severe implications for policymakers sooner than anticipated and may contribute to a future perfect storm.

Some national security experts and Members of Congress have called for imposing a floor on defense spending at 4 percent of GDP. The Secretary of Defense and Chairman of the Joint Chiefs of Staff have endorsed such proposals. Today, the Pentagon absorbs nearly 3.7 percent of a $13-trillion-plus economy. The funding currently provided under supplementary requests increases the percentage to roughly 4.2 percent. Given an annual defense budget of over half a trillion dollars, establishing a fixed level of spending would create a stable basis for planning. However, this assumes that the U.S. economy grows and that costs of inflation, personnel, and energy do not erode the added resources. While a 4-percent GDP objective appears reasonable, decisions on making defense investments are going to be difficult to resolve among these many competing demands, even with a stable basis for planning.

Like the Cold War, the 21st century will require substantial investments. A formula will not provide guidance on how to spend constrained resources or what strategy to follow. Investments must be considered on the merits based on the threat and overall strategy, and not simply on what has been done in the past. Avoiding the perfect storm calls for strategic planning and relentless risk management. Balancing Service portfolios and realigning strategic priorities for available resources provided by the budget ultimately will be a test for the Pentagon leadership.

Making Tough Choices on Priorities and Risk

The Obama administration has inherited the most daunting national security challenges in generations. In addition to the conflicts in Iraq and Afghanistan, the President and his team must grapple with a long struggle against violent extremist groups such as al Qaeda; continued proliferation of nuclear and other weapons of mass destruction to hostile states and potentially to nonstate actors; fundamental shifts in the balance of power, particularly in Asia, where China and India are ascendant; competition for and potentially conflict over energy and other resources, from strategic minerals to clean water; the resurgence of a more autocratic and assertive Russia emboldened by petro-wealth; continued globalization but uneven integration, with an increasing potential for state failure as weak states struggle with demographic, economic, health, and environmental pressures to meet basic needs; and the possibility that global climate change will act as an accelerant, causing mass migrations, more frequent and severe natural disasters, and eventual state failures and conflicts.

The administration faces an uncertain security environment in a very different budgetary context than its predecessor. Gone are the days of a booming economy, $128 billion in budget surpluses, and Congresses willing to write a blank check for national security in the wake of the terrorist attacks on September 11, 2001. Instead, the President must confront these challenges in the face of unprecedented financial crises, an American economy in recession, the pending retirement of a generation of Baby Boomers and burgeoning Federal spending on entitlement programs, a national deficit and debt that have both reached historic—and horrific—levels, and a Congress that is increasingly focused on reining in defense spending.

As supplemental funding for operations in Iraq declines and pressures to reduce Federal spending intensify, the defense budget—which represents the largest portion of U.S. discretionary spending—is likely to experience the makings of a perfect storm. Operations and maintenance costs will continue to soar as long as the worldwide operating tempo and the cost of energy remain high or increase. Personnel outlays will continue to skyrocket because of increased health care and pension costs, plus the addition of 92,000 personnel to the Army and the Marine Corps. Reset costs resulting from wartime depletions of equipment stocks will almost certainly be more expensive than originally estimated. Moreover, the costs of modernization will increase as weapons systems reach obsolescence and have to be replaced, existing investment programs continue to grow in cost, and new capabilities required to adapt the Armed Forces for missions in the 21st century are identified.

Looking beyond current conflicts to over the horizon, the administration faces diverse and worrisome challenges. At the same time, it inherits the heavy weight of stressed and unsustainable defense programs, as well as the vice-grip squeeze of the overriding need to get the national economy in order. The combined task of opening the strategic aperture while simultaneously tightening the defense budget will result in some difficult choices about priorities, as well as the allocation and management of risk.

The United States will have to determine how to balance strategic risk in three ways. The first challenge is to determine how best to allocate resources and risk among current strategic priorities, such as the war in Iraq, expanding operations in Afghanistan, prosecuting the global war on terror, and reducing strains on

our overstretched ground forces. The President must conduct a phased transition in the military posture in Iraq while safeguarding American interests; develop a new strategy and campaign plan for Afghanistan, infusing what has long been an economy of force mission with resources to regain momentum; rethink and reframe strategy for combating extremist groups such as al Qaeda, from the tribal areas of Pakistan to the Horn of Africa and the Maghreb; and initiate steps to lessen the operating tempo and increase the at-home dwell time for members of those units who have experienced the greatest strain over the last 7 years.

The second challenge involves deciding how best to allocate risk when investing in future military capabilities. For example, how much emphasis should be placed on developing capabilities for irregular war relative to capabilities to counter high-end asymmetric threats by rising powers and rogue states? And when competing concepts of operations exist for a particular mission set, which one should determine investments? It is this complex and vexing set of choices that is explored here in detail.

The third and most engaging challenge is balancing current demands against future priorities. In wartime, it is tempting for leaders of the defense establishment to focus almost exclusively on meeting operational demands of the day. This is understandable and in some ways appropriate. But even a wartime Secretary of Defense must be the civilian steward of the defense enterprise; part of the job is ensuring that future Presidents will have the military options they need to protect and advance national security in the face of a rapidly changing security environment. Thus, even as Secretary Gates acknowledged early in his tenure that the top priorities were "Iraq, Iraq, and Iraq," in reality, he and his senior civilian and military leadership have spent countless hours wrestling with numerous investment decisions that will shape the size and capabilities of the future force.

For the Secretary and his senior team, balancing risk will involve hard choices about investing in people and materiel for current operations versus protecting investment accounts to ensure the development and procurement of new generations of systems to meet emerging and future challenges. Although there are no right answers to these questions, the defense team must both set priorities and manage risk in developing defense strategy, and make tough calls on resource allocation that have been too long delayed, from rationalizing investments in missile defense to planning investments to recapitalize the Navy's fleet, from enhancing capabilities to check proliferation and use of weapons of mass destruction to developing the cyber warfare capabilities needed to protect U.S. national interests in the 21ˢᵗ century.

Doing so will require careful assessment of the future security environment, judgments about the kinds of demands it may place on the U.S. military, and determination of the options to be developed or preserved for the next President and his successors—and importantly, where the Pentagon can afford to invest less or accept a greater degree of risk.

While it has become commonplace since the first Gulf War to assert that, in the face of the utter dominance of the U.S. military on the conventional battlefield, future adversaries are likely to challenge the United States using asymmetric strategies designed to undermine its strengths and exploit its weaknesses, the DOD program of record has not altered substantially in recognition of this reality. Recent American experience in Afghanistan and Iraq, as well as the recent Israeli combat experience in Lebanon, suggests that future conflicts are likely to assume a hybrid character in which potential adversaries mix traditional, irregular, disruptive, and catastrophic means to best exploit the perceived weakness of the U.S. military.

In practice, this will pull American forces in two very different directions: toward preparing for irregular warfare "among the people" against nonstate actors and weak states that use improvised explosive devices and suicide bombings on the one hand, and toward preparing for high-end asymmetric threats by rising regional powers or rogue states that use cyber attacks, antiair, and antiship weapons—and even antisatellite weapons or weapons of mass destruction—to deny U.S. access to a region or thwart U.S. operations on the other. Moreover, nonstate actors may acquire and use high-end capabilities such as cyber warfare and weapons of mass destruction to advance their objectives.

Making smart investment decisions in this context will require a new type of decisionmaking process in the Pentagon. Ironically, although virtually everything DOD does involves allocating and managing risk, it lacks a rigorous approach to informing strategic choices about risk at the highest levels. It will, therefore, be critical to establish such a process without delay.

Ideally, this priority-setting process should include a number of key elements. The first would be a comprehensive and open-minded assessment of the future security environment with the aim of identifying both known risks—such as terrorists conducting a nuclear attack on U.S. soil or the risk of future adversaries employing antiaccess strategies against us—and potential discontinuities or uncertainties that could impact the U.S. military in some way over the next 20 to 25 years. Potential wildcard scenarios might range from the collapse of a nuclear-armed state such as North Korea or Pakistan to the

Maintenance crew tows Global Hawk UAV

emergence of a game-changing technology or weapons system on the battlefield. This assessment should tee up a series of discussions between the Secretary of Defense, Chairman of the Joint Chiefs of Staff, Joint Chiefs, and combatant commanders, aimed at identifying those future challenges that should be given priority in planning and investments as well as uncertainties and wildcards against which the United States should hedge. This assessment should yield a robust yet finite set of focus areas around which the rest of the process should be structured.

The next step would be to delve into each focus area in an effort to better understand its nature, its associated timelines and indicators, and its implications for the U.S. Armed Forces. Most important, this step in the process would develop alternative strategies and concepts of operations for either dealing with known risks, or for hedging against possible uncertainties and wildcards. For example, if the focus area included penetrating the airspace of a sophisticated regional adversary armed with the most advanced air defenses, competing approaches might range from deploying a larger force of fifth-generation fighters, to developing a new strategic bomber with even more advanced stealth and ISR capabilities, to developing a more robust set of long-range conventional precision-strike options.

The third step would be to undertake a comparative assessment of the alternative approaches to better understand relative strengths, weaknesses, associated risks, possible failure modes, capability requirements, and anticipated costs. In essence, this step would encourage and structure a healthy competition of ideas in an effort to help frame key tradeoffs and concrete choices the Secretary of Defense and his civilian and military leadership team must make over the course of the process.

The fourth step would be to determine which strategies and concepts of operations to prioritize in each focus area. This is likely the most difficult and contentious part of the process, as it is where potential "winners" and "losers" are likely to emerge. In some cases, the Secretary of Defense may choose to pursue a single approach to a given challenge, such as assigning a given mission or set of tasks—for example, providing theater airlift to a particular Service and directing others to get out of the business. In others, the Secretary may determine that there is a need for multiple, even redundant options for dealing with a specific challenge, given either the high stakes involved or the varied conditions under which the challenge might

emerge. For example, in the case of advising, assisting, and building the capacity of partner security forces, the Secretary would almost certainly want to have a Special Operations Force–based option for situations in which a minimal American footprint is required, as well as concepts built around general purpose forces in those situations where the United States is working through military-to-military relationships to rebuild a nation's entire military or a large portion thereof.

The fifth and final step would look across all of the "winners" that have emerged to identify any areas of inconsistency or conflict, and to determine the relative emphasis that should be given to each. In the course of this integrating step, the participants should aim to be as explicit and clear as possible in identifying those areas in which additional risk is being taken, and what might be done to manage or mitigate that risk. The end result of the process would be detailed Secretary guidance for capabilities development and resource allocation.

At every step of this process, it would be useful to incorporate one or more red teams to avoid the trap of group think, to scrutinize underlying assumptions, to question the conventional wisdom of whatever gains traction, to develop solutions that others might not have thought of, and to enrich the range of issues and ideas on the table. Given the highly consequential nature of decisions being made in this process, this would be a prudent way of ensuring that few, if any, stones are left unturned.

Such a process almost certainly would help the Secretary of Defense make better informed decisions. But because even good bets can turn bad, this process would make an even greater contribution by paying more attention to potential wild cards and hedging strategies, thereby improving DOD ability to adapt more quickly to the unexpected.

Although it is crucial for this process to be undertaken early in an administration, it should be more than a one-time exercise. Indeed, it is imperative that the Secretary and Chairman establish an ongoing process of monitoring the changing security environment and conducting net assessments to identify changes that may cause them to rethink their bets. Their staffs also should monitor and evaluate the execution of priority strategies and hedging efforts to determine whether and where adjustments are needed. This does not mean that no decision is final, or that decisions taken can be continually revisited. Rather, the process should be dynamic, with defined and regular feedback into the planning, programming, and budgeting processes of the Pentagon. Although it will not be possible to get the right answer all the time, it should be possible to get much better answers over time.

Some might argue that elements of this approach already exist. Every Secretary goes through some process of setting priorities and translating them into guidance for developing the capabilities he believes the military will need in the future. For their part, the Services and Joint Staff routinely assess concepts of operations and future capability requirements. But there are several attributes of the proposed process that set it apart. It is leader-driven rather than staff-driven. It brings together the most senior civilian and military leaders in a collaborative process. It structures a competition of concepts and ideas with the aim of enabling hard-nosed choices and tradeoffs (rather than making consensus the ultimate objective). And it incorporates red teaming and dynamic feedback throughout the process. Taken together, these various attributes make the proposed process a new, if commonsensical, approach.

During World War II, General Dwight Eisenhower reputedly stated, "plans are nothing [but] planning is everything." Given the immense national security challenges and economic pressures we face, hard choices have to be made and none are devoid of risk. These hard tradeoffs will remain at every feasible budget level; we cannot buy our way out of making these risk allocation decisions. And to defend their budget, at whatever level, defense leaders must demonstrate that they have made the hard-nosed assessments and tough choices. It is, therefore, imperative that, even in the face of the pressures of ongoing operations, the Secretary establish and lead, in partnership with the Chairman, a process that engages his senior civilian and military leaders in a sustained planning effort to identify where to prioritize and how to manage risk.

The QDR is the essential first step in this new planning process. To make it a success, the Secretary must redefine and rescope the QDR process by changing the planning paradigm as described above; by making at least some hard choices to redress the currently unsustainable budgetary posture; and, most important, by laying the groundwork for a sustained effort that will help the U.S. military be better prepared and better able to adapt to the requirements of the 21st century. Whether the next QDR can meet these ambitious expectations and stand the test of time, rigorously working through these issues, and "norming and forming" the Pentagon team in the

process, will be of incalculable value at a time of great consequence. **gsa**

[1] Much of what is asserted here about stress applies to the Marine Corps as well as the Army. Because another section of this chapter focuses on the Marines, this section refers only to the Army.

[2] See, for example, Gian P. Gentile, "Misreading the Surge Threatens U.S. Army's Conventional Capabilities," *World Politics Review Exclusive*, March 4, 2008.

[3] Remarks as delivered by Secretary of Defense Robert M. Gates to the Association of the U.S. Army, Washington, DC, October 10, 2007.

[4] Ibid.

[5] See, for example, John A. Nagl, *Institutionalizing Adaptation: It's Time for a Permanent Army Advisory Corps* (Washington, DC: Center for a New American Security, June 2007); Peter W. Chiarelli with Stephen M. Smith, "Learning From Our Modern Wars: The Imperatives of Preparing for a Dangerous Future," *Military Review* (September-October 2007); Bob Killebrew, *The Left-Hand Side of the Spectrum: Ambassadors and Advisors in Future U.S. Strategy* (Washington, DC: Center for a New American Security, June 2007).

[6] See Leonard Wong, "Fashion Tips for the Field Grade," U.S. Army War College, Strategic Studies Institute, October 4, 2006, available at <www.strategicstudiesinstitute.army.mil/pdffiles/PUB731.pdf>.

[7] Yochi J. Dreazen, "Army to Promote Training as Career Path," *Wall Street Journal*, June 19, 2008, A3. Chief of staff's email accessed at <http://council.smallwarsjournal.com/showthread.php?t=5593>.

[8] See Dreazen for reference to a widely circulating email expressing the skepticism with which many no doubt see the current effort to upgrade the status of advisors.

[9] France operates one aircraft carrier and three helicopter carriers. The United Kingdom has two operational STOVL carriers (and a third in reserve) and one helicopter carrier. Italy operates two STOVL carriers. Russia and Brazil each operate one aircraft carrier. Spain, India, and Thailand each operate one STOVL carrier. South Korea and Japan both operate one helicopter carrier (although both are physically large enough to operate STOVL fighters). See Stephen Saunders, ed., *Jane's Fighting Ships 2007–2008* (Surrey, UK: Jane's Information Group, 2007).

[10] Russia has the largest non-U.S. nuclear-powered fleet, with 18 SSNs and 7 SSGNs. The United Kingdom, France, and China operate nine, six, and five SSNs, respectively. See Saunders.

[11] See "Prepositioning Ships," "Sealift Ships," and Ready Reserve Force Ships," available at <www.msc.navy.mil/inventory/inventory.asp?var=program>. The 110-ship

prepositioning and sealift fleet includes ships maintained in reduced operating status by the Maritime Administration.

[12] See *A Cooperative Strategy for 21st Century Seapower*, October 2007, available at <www.navy.mil/maritime/MaritimeStrategy.pdf>.

[13] *Report to Congress on Annual Long-Range Plan for Construction of Naval Vessels for FY 2007* (Washington, DC: Department of the Navy, n.d.), 5. The table's comments have been updated and modified.

[14] All figures are in FY09 dollars. From Congressional Budget Office, "Resource Implication of the Navy's FY 2009 Shipbuilding Plan," June 9, 2009, available at <www.cbo.gov/ftpdocs/93xx/doc9318/06-09-Shipbuilding_Letter.pdf>.

[15] As Ron O'Rourke, naval analyst at the Congressional Research Service, stated to the American Society for Naval Engineers on June 23, 2008, "The Navy's estimated cost for implementing [its] plan is so large that the Navy no longer appears to have a credible, announced strategy for generating the funds needed to implement [its] 30-year plan."

[16] As Secretary of the Navy Donald Winter stated to the Current Strategy Forum at the Naval War College on June 17, 2008, "We simply cannot afford a 313-ship Navy that averages out to over $3 billion a ship."

[17] For an overview of these strategic challenges, see Andrew Krepinevich, Robert Martinage, and Robert Work, *The Challenges to U.S. National Security* (Washington, DC: Center for Strategic and Budgetary Assessments, 2008).

[18] The Chinese routinely talk about contesting U.S. operations out to the "second island chain," which includes the Japanese Bonin Islands and the Marianas Islands, including the U.S. territory of Guam. Guam sits roughly 1,510 nautical miles from Taiwan and about 1,590 nautical miles from the Chinese mainland. See "[People's Liberation Army] Navy," *Jane's Sentinel Security Assessment—China and Northeast Asia*, June 21, 2007.

[19] See, for example, Roger Cliff et al., *Entering the Dragon's Lair: Chinese Anti-access Strategies and Their Implications for the United States* (Santa Monica, CA: RAND, 2007).

[20] This observation is based on an undersea assessment developed for the Office of Net Assessment, Office of the Secretary of Defense, to which the author contributed.

[21] Unless otherwise stated, these changes refer to the plans outlined in Office of the Chief of Naval Operations, "Report to Congress on Annual Long-Range Plan for Construction of Naval Vessels for FY 2009," February 2008.

[22] See Thomas P. Ehrhard and Robert O. Work, *Range, Persistence, Stealth, and Networking: The Case for a Carrier-based Unmanned Combat Air System* (Washington, DC: Center for Strategic and Budgetary Assessments, 2008).

[23] The SSGNs are optimized as cruise missile submarines. Of the 24 missile tubes on each SSGN, 2 are storage/access tubes; the remaining 22 can each carry 7 Tomahawk land attack cruise missiles. The 22 missile tubes can also be optimized to carry, launch, and recover UUVs.

[24] For a more detailed discussion of this plan, see Robert O. Work, *Know When to Hold 'Em, Know When to Fold 'Em: A New Transformation Plan for the Navy's Surface Battle Line* (Washington, DC: Center for Strategic and Budgetary Assessments, 2007).

[25] By replacing the current LSD force with LPD–17s, the LSDs would be decommissioned before the end of their expected 40-year service lives. The Navy should take the seven in best condition, convert them into auxiliary LSDs, and assign them as command ships for the Global Fleet Stations.

[26] These ships would be variants of the Coast Guard National Security Cutter now in serial production. With Coast Guard law enforcement detachments as part of their crews, they could perform a wide range of maritime and homeland security missions. Operating eight Maritime Security Cutters seems a natural fit for the Naval Reserve, and would be a powerful symbol for the idea of an integrated National Fleet.

Contributors

Dr. Thomas X. Hammes (Chapter Editor) served 30 years in the U.S. Marine Corps, including duty in Somalia and Iraq. He holds a Masters of Historical Research and Ph.D. in Modern History from Oxford University and has lectured widely at U.S. and international staff and war colleges. He is the author of *The Sling and the Stone: On War in the 21st Century* (Zenith Press, 2004) and over 80 articles and opinion pieces.

Michèle A. Flournoy is Undersecretary of Defense for Policy. Prior to this appointment, she was the President and Co-Founder of the Center for a New American Security and previously served as a Distinguished Research Professor at the National Defense University and as Principal Deputy Assistant Secretary of Defense for Strategy and Threat Reduction and Deputy Assistant Secretary of Defense for Strategy.

Robert L. Goldich is an independent consultant on defense issues. When he retired from the Congressional Research Service in 2005 after 33 years of service, he was the senior CRS military manpower and personnel analyst. He holds degrees from Claremont McKenna College and The George Washington University, and is a graduate of the National War College.

Lieutenant Colonel Frank G. Hoffman, USMCR (Ret.), is a Research Fellow in the Center for Emerging Threats and Opportunities at the Marine Corps Combat Development Command.

Dr. Thomas L. McNaugher is a Senior Analyst at the RAND Corporation. He is a former director of the RAND Arroyo Center, and author of *New Weapons, Old Politics: America's Military Procurement Muddle* (The Brookings Institution Press, 1989) and *Arms and Oil: U.S. Military Strategy in the Persian Gulf* (The Brookings Institution Press, 1985).

Lieutenant General Charles E. Stenner Jr. is Chief of Air Force Reserve, Headquarters U.S. Air Force, Washington, D.C., and Commander, Air Force Reserve Command, Robins Air Force Base in Georgia.

Robert O. Work is Under Secretary of the Navy. Previously he was Senior Vice President at the Center for Strategic and Budgetary Assessments. A former Marine colonel, he specializes in defense strategy, revolutions in war, and naval affairs. He is an Adjunct Professor at The George Washington University.

Chapter 18

National Security Reform and the Security Environment[1]

The Three Pillars of Reform

Inadequate interagency coordination[2] could be dubbed the "weather issue" for national security professionals over the past decade; the persistent topic of conversation in the national security community that affects everybody but that nobody can do anything about. Almost all major national security studies note interagency coordination is inadequate (see table 1).[3] Moreover, from the outset of the global war on terror, President George W. Bush made it clear that national strategy would not depend exclusively on military power but rather on the integrated diplomatic, informational, military, economic, and other capabilities of the Nation. Yet in the 7-plus years since the attacks of September 11, 2001, and despite numerous efforts at reform, interagency coordination remains inadequate according to many leaders of the executive and legislative branches, as well as practitioners and experts in the field.

Cross-organizational collaboration thus emerges as a key leadership requirement and an imperative for more effectively managing regional security. Coordination also is a feature of professional military and interagency education, and an essential prerequisite for stabilization operations, intelligence collection, and homeland security activities. Although notable progress has been made in this area, a great deal more still needs to be done.

Growing Concern

The burgeoning consensus on the need to better integrate elements of national power has been a long time coming and dates back to the Cold War. Diplomats once safeguarded national interests in peacetime, while the military assumed that role in wartime. Although a simplification, that division of labor mirrored the American penchant for separating peace and war as different conditions that required either diplomatic or military competencies. Vestiges of the tendency to categorize security problems by discrete elements of national power remain, and that arrangement is not without some merit. However, containment of the Soviet Union

helped cement the notion on the strategic level that all elements of national power had to be integrated to succeed. The National Security Act of 1947 codified this approach by establishing, inter alia, the National Security Council to assist the President in integrating American strategy.

Vietnam and other conflicts during the Cold War, as well as recent threats from proliferation, terrorism, and regional instability in 1980s and 1990s, have extended the consensus on integrating elements of national power from strategic planning to the actual conduct of military operations. A lesson from interventions in Panama, Somalia, Haiti, and Bosnia, for example, was that success required significant cooperation among the government departments and agencies that control diplomatic, informational, military, economic, and other elements of power, not only in Washington, but also in the field. At all levels, this problem involves both efficiency and effectiveness. Some security problems cannot be efficiently resolved by a single instrument of power, irrespective of level and quality of effort, and others cannot be resolved effectively at all without the well-integrated use multiple instruments of power.

Defeating such threats requires not only diverse elements of power, but also command and control assets to make complicated decisions on which instrument takes precedence in which situation. Will collateral damage from bombing terrorist hideouts be justified by the bombing's impact on the enemy? Is marginal financial assistance best spent on training indigenous forces or infrastructure projects to win local support from terrorists? Can short-term manipulation of information in support of military operations be justified when it damages the credibility of local authorities?

The Nation does not have the capacity to make tradeoffs to integrate and apply instruments of power—not for the 'war on terror' or other security challenges that require integrated responses. An increasing number of defense and foreign policy experts believe that the United States must reform the national security system. In fact, in a recent survey of over 250 books, articles, and studies on the subject, only 1 concluded that interagency coordination works well. Many experts have made the case for wholesale changes in the national security system to ensure interagency activities are integrated in the same way as joint military operations were reformed under the Goldwater-Nichols Department of Defense Reorganization Act of 1986 (see table 2).

Various initiatives to improve interagency coordination were undertaken prior to September 11, 2001, but the investigation of those terrorist events proved those initiatives to be insufficient. Similarly, many reforms subsequently enacted are proving inadequate. Before additional reforms with their associated costs are pursued, there must be greater assurance that the reforms will produce the desired outcome. To provide that assurance, recommendations on reforming national security policy must rest on *three fundamental pillars of reform*: rigorous problem analysis, multidisciplinary approaches, and a resolve to embrace solutions regardless of attendant political costs.

Problem Analysis

Although the need for interagency collaboration is clear, the problems involved are complex. Few studies that advocate national security system reform explain the inadequate collaboration of interagency activities. Most of these sources identify problems such as inadequate intelligence or inefficient unity of effort and then go into an exposition of ways to fix the problem. The lack of attention to problem analysis can produce recommendations based on conventional wisdom rather than the careful examination of the facts. For example, popular accounts of the national security system observe its flexibility. They claim that the President changes structures and processes to match his decisionmaking style. This is true, but these changes are superficial and have little impact on the performance of the national security system. Actually, the system is rigid and dominated by powerful bureaucracies that frustrate or veto collaboration when it runs counter to their interests. A number of Presidents have lamented the inflexibility of the system after leaving office.

Some assume that the National Security Council staff would be more efficient if its size was reduced and its bureaucracy eliminated. This observation was popularized during an investigation of the Eisenhower administration by Senator Henry Jackson and has become commonly accepted. Yet it is wrong. Presidents who have reduced the staff have not seen a corresponding increase in effectiveness. Moreover,

such cuts are typically short-lived. The trend following the Cold War has been the slow but sure growth of the staff, not because national security advisors like large staffs but because the workload is crushing. The idea that a staff of 200 or 300 could oversee a national security establishment of approximately 4 million is unrealistic. Compared to other agency headquarters that are supposed to provide integration across functional divisions (such as the Department of Defense and Central Intelligence Agency) and supply a range of services, the National Security Council staff is small and obviously insufficient. It is probably more important to increase its authority than its size, but both reforms are necessary.

Another mistaken bit of conventional wisdom is that leadership matters, while organizations do not.

Customs and Border Protection (James Tourtellotte)

U.S. Customs inspector checks seaport containers from ship at Port of Miami

Strangely, this observation is made in two different and contradictory ways. Some claim that the national security system is effective when managed by a few powerful leaders, perhaps with the President working only with a potent national security advisor (such as Richard Nixon and Henry Kissinger or Jimmy Carter and Zbigniew Brzezinski). Alternatively, it is asserted that the system would function better if top leadership shared decisionmaking and consisted of people who knew, liked, and respected each other. But neither style of leadership ensures interagency collaboration. Strong national security advisors can formulate clear national policy by going around established interagency processes. However, during the policy implementation they encounter resistance from the same agencies and organizations they ignored during policy development. More collegial national security advisors may succeed in keeping organizational differences less public, but interagency frictions persist and still militate against unity of effort.

Table 1. The Need to Reform Interagency Coordination

National Security Reform Studies	Excerpts from Studies (with emphasis added)
Transforming Defense: National Security in the 21st Century, 1997	The national security apparatus established 50 years ago must adapt itself as it takes on a growing list of new challenges and responsibilities. It so far has been *unable to integrate smoothly the resources and organizations needed* to anticipate and mold a more secure international environment.
U.S. Commission on National Security in the 21st Century (Hart-Rudman), 2001	Traditional national security agencies (State, Defense, CIA, NSC staff) *will need to work together in new ways*, and economic agencies (Treasury, Commerce, U.S. Trade Representative) will need to work more closely with the traditional national security community. In addition, other players, especially Justice and Transportation, will *need to be integrated more fully* into national security processes.
Beyond Goldwater Nichols: Phase 1, 2004	The past decade of experience in complex contingency operations, from Somalia to Iraq, has demonstrated that success requires unity of effort not only from the military but also from across the U.S. government and an international coalition. In most cases, however, *such unity of effort has proved elusive*. Time and time again, the United States and its international partners have failed to fully integrate the political, military, economic, humanitarian and other dimensions into a coherent strategy for a given operation— sometimes with disastrous results.
9/11 Commission Report, 2004	In each of our examples, no one was firmly in charge of managing the case. . . . Responsibility and accountability were diffuse. The agencies cooperated, some of the time. But even such cooperation as there was is not the same thing as joint action. . . . *The problem is nearly intractable* because of the way the government is currently structured.
In the Wake of War, Council on Foreign Relations Independent Task Force, 2005	Despite some welcome initial moves, responsibility within the U.S. government for stabilization and reconstruction operations is diffuse and authority is uncertain. Policies delineating the proper role of the military and civilian agencies have yet to be articulated. Further, the civilian agencies involved in stabilization and reconstruction activities operate *without the benefit of a "unified command"* structure ensuring that policy, programs, and resources are properly aligned.
The Commission on the Intelligence Capabilities of the United States Regarding Weapons of Mass Destruction	Everywhere we looked, we found important (and obvious) issues of interagency coordination that went unattended, sensible Community-wide proposals blocked by pockets of resistance, and critical disputes left to fester. Strong interagency cooperation was more likely to result from bilateral "treaties" between big agencies than from Community-level management. This ground was well-plowed by the 9/11 Commission and by several other important assessments of the Intelligence Community over the past decade.
Project Horizon, 2006	U.S. Government *interagency effort too often lacks* effective concentration of attention, resources, action and accountability.
A Smarter, More Secure America, CSIS Commission on Smart Power, 2007	Implementing a smart power strategy will require a strategic reassessment of how the U.S. government is organized, *coordinated*, and budgeted.
America's Role in the World, Institute for the Study of Diplomacy, 2008	The U.S. government *does neither vertical coordination within agencies nor horizontal coordination between agencies well.*
Agency Stovepipes vs. Strategic Agility, U.S. House of Representatives, Committee on Armed Services, Subcommittee on Oversight and Investigations, 2008	The subcommittee found a *lack of unity of direction* and unity of command. This results in a *lack of unity of purpose*. Among the efforts at staffing, training, applying lessons learned, and planning, there is no one person or organization in the lead for the whole of government.

There are two reasons why in-depth problem analysis is uncommon despite its obvious value. First, it is impolitic. It seems uncharitable to dissect the performance of people who are working hard under pressure to produce favorable outcomes. While it is possible to differentiate between the system and the leaders, it proves hard in practice to separate the two. Thus, some studies avoid detailed problem analysis and focus on ways of improving things. Second, problem analysis is difficult. As competing case studies illustrate, it can be hard to agree on the explanation for any given national security event. It is more challenging to explain system performance, since many variables influence outcomes and shift over time. Some experienced practitioners doubt that national security system performance can be explained with any precision. Hence, there is a tendency to identify a range of variables that are influential without assessing their relative merits. Yet the value of any recommendation on reform cannot exceed an understanding of the problems that the reform is intended to fix.

Broad Scope

In-depth problem analysis becomes manageable if its scope is limited. Many studies of national security reform consider some portion of the entire national security system. Although the studies are valuable, the system can only be improved when examined holistically (see figure 1). In national security affairs, this means both the executive and legislative branches. Congress plays a key role in national security, codifying the responsibilities of departments and agencies, providing largesse, confirming officials, and overseeing national policy and its implementation. Yet many studies ignore Congress either because its reform is considered too difficult or because the experts consulted focus exclusively on the activities of the executive branch.

A holistic approach to the national security system requires looking at its diverse ingredients: leadership, structure, processes, human capital, resources, and so-called knowledge management. Some studies of national security reform are based on particular areas of organizational expertise such as human

Table 2. National Security Reform Studies

Pentagon Reforms Mandated by Goldwater-Nichols[1]

Objective	Key Provisions
Strengthen civilian authority	▸ "The secretary has sole and ultimate power within the Department of Defense on any matter on which the secretary chooses to act."
Improve military advice	▸ Designated Chairman of the Joint Chiefs of Staff (JCS) as principal military adviser ▸ Created JCS Vice Chairman position ▸ Directed the JCS Chairman to manage the Joint Staff
Place clear responsibility on combatant commanders for missions	▸ Specified chain of command; removed JCS from the chain of command ▸ Ensured a combatant commander authority is commensurate with his responsibilities ▸ Prescribed authority of unified commanders
Increase attention to strategy formulation and contingency planning	▸ Required Chairman to prepare fiscally constrained strategy ▸ Required Secretary of Defense to provide contingency planning guidance
Provide for the more efficient use of resources	▸ Assigned six new duties to JCS Chairman on resource advice
Improve joint officer management	▸ Established procedures for the selection, education, assignment, and promotion of joint officers
Enhance effectiveness of military operations	▸ Assigned Chairman responsibility for joint doctrine and joint training policies
Improve DOD management	▸ Reduced spans of control ▸ Mandated reductions in headquarters staffs

[1] James R. Locher III, "Goldwater-Nichols II," Powerpoint Briefing, April 14, 2004, National Security Management Course.

capital, and many draw exclusively on practitioners and experts, but rarely do the studies adopt a broad scope of inquiry. Many national security reform efforts focus narrowly on one dimension of the system, particularly infrastructure. One pervading opinion on the inadequacy of reforms that led to the establishment of the Department of Homeland Security was that the consolidation of 22 different agencies was emphasized to the exclusion of many other considerations such as organizational cultures, processes, and personnel incentives.

Another example of an insufficient organizational perspective is the current popularity of the recommendation to combine the National Security Council and the Homeland Security Council. Because concerns such as shipping containers transiting American ports cross the line between domestic and international security affairs, it is assumed that combining these two councils will lead to a seamless approach to national security issues. But it is also important to consider other factors, such as culture, process, and leadership. Decisions are difficult to make in large, formal groups, which explains why the President uses the National Security Council primarily as a sounding board rather than for decisionmaking. Moreover, there are differences in operational cultures of foreign and domestic security organizations that must be accepted. Thus, the idea of combining the councils, which already have large formal and informal memberships, could reduce the willingness of the President to use the structure for decisionmaking. Instead, it would reinforce the pronounced tendency to make decisions in smaller, informal settings.

Figure 1. National Security System

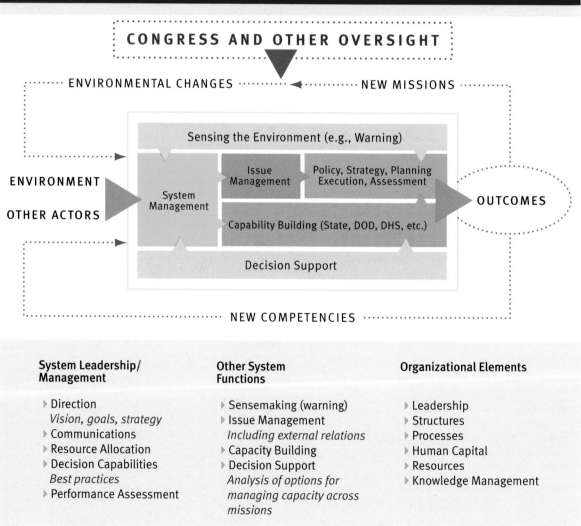

While effective reform of the national security system requires a multidisciplinary approach, the task ought to be distinguished from extant policies. Since reform efforts draw heavily on the experience of experts and practitioners, they tend to concentrate on policy prescriptions. In other words, instead of examining how and why the system functions as it does, most studies offer advice on specific issues. Policy analysis is valuable but, when mixed together with studies of national security reform focused on reorganization, detracts from pinpointing impediments to better performance.

Solutions

Assembling diverse expertise for holistic, multidisciplinary analysis and ensuring that it is grounded in practical knowledge of the national security system is a major challenge. Even when this occurs, there is another pitfall to be avoided: premature compromises that vitiate the impact of proffered solutions. Some national security reform study teams have conducted broad analysis but limit their recommendations to those supported by the team or considered politically practical. In doing so, they reduce the recommendations to half-measures that do not actually solve the problems that have been identified through hard work.

The National Commission on Terrorist Attacks upon the United States (commonly known as the 9/11 Commission) produced a report that serves as a cautionary tale. Well researched and written, the report identified major problems in the system and noted that effective management of transnational counterterrorist operations was missing, which was explained by the inability to collaborate. In the words of the report: "The agencies are like a set of specialists in a hospital, each ordering tests, looking for symptoms, and prescribing medications. What is missing is the attending physician who makes sure they work as a team."

As the commission report indicated, the problems cannot be resolved without adjustments in the authorities of Cabinet officials. The report is worth quoting at length on this point:

The problem is nearly intractable because of the way the government is currently structured. Lines of operational authority run to the expanding executive departments, and they are guarded for understandable reasons: the [Director of Central Intelligence] commands the CIA's personnel overseas; the secretary of defense will not yield to others in conveying commands to military forces; the Justice Department will not give up the responsibility

of deciding whether to seek arrest warrants. But the result is that each agency or department needs its own intelligence apparatus to support the performance of its duties. It is hard to "break down stovepipes" when there are so many stoves that are legally and politically entitled to have cast-iron pipes of their own.

Recalling the Goldwater-Nichols legislation of 1986, Secretary Rumsfeld reminded us that to achieve better joint capability, each of the armed services had to "give up some of their turf and authorities and prerogatives." Today, he said, the executive branch is "stove-piped much like the four services were nearly 20 years ago." He wondered if it might be appropriate to ask agencies to "give up some of their existing turf and authority in exchange for a stronger, faster, more efficient government wide joint effort." Privately, other key officials have made the same point to us.

U.S. Navy (Leah Stiles)

Commander looks at drugs seized by Navy and Coast Guard officials in support of Joint Interagency Task Force–South

Given these conclusions it is surprising the 9/11 Commission did not also recommend circumscribing the authorities of Cabinet officers to ensure that counterterrorism operations would be managed on an interagency basis. Instead, it called for creating the National Counterterrorism Center, which was charged only with planning. The report stipulated that the center would not have responsibility for either policymaking or directing operations. The best recommendation that a consensus would permit was an interagency organization for planning support.

The cumulative effect of national security reforms in recent decades is mixed. The need for greater collaboration and the dismal track record of efforts to provide it underscore the arguments for systemic reform. On the other hand, a degree of reorganization fatigue also has been setting in. While the time is ripe for systemic reform, no plan should be embraced without assurances that it will generate major and lasting improvements. The cost of a failed reform effort would be high, dampening any enthusiasm for changing the system in the future. Organizational reform efforts typically pass through an initial phase of lower productivity before generating better results, so a failure in executing a major overhaul of the current system would be far more costly. For this reason, proponents of systemic reform should be held to the highest standards and required to demonstrate an understanding of impediments to system performance, a holistic plan for reform, and a set of recommendations to solve identified problems.

Refining Jointness

Overall, the joint command system that has evolved since the Goldwater-Nichols Department of Defense Reorganization Act of 1986 has worked well and improved the effectiveness of the Armed Forces. Combatant commanders have clear authority and responsibility for military planning and operations within their regions and have often taken the lead in overall national security strategy in those areas of responsibility. In addition to smaller joint deployments, U.S. forces have been committed to major operations nine times since the Goldwater-Nichols Act became law and the Cold War ended.

The joint reform in the Department of Defense has been so successful that there have been proposals to extend the principles of joint military operations to integrate interagency operations. A study by the Center for Strategic and International Studies made such a recommendation, and the Project on National Security Reform, which is funded by Congress, has issued preliminary findings highlighting the segmented nature of interagency operations and calling for improved collaboration. Although extending the principles of jointness to the national security system has definite merit, it is time to look closely at the state of joint doctrine and organization.

Joint planning and operations can be improved through closer and more formal involvement of Service chiefs and component commanders. The Gold-

water-Nichols Act made the combatant commanders, together with the Chairman of the Joint Chiefs of Staff, responsible to the Secretary of Defense for planning and operations in their areas of responsibility and also relieved the chiefs and subordinate commanders of those responsibilities. The chiefs, who are concerned with the needs of their respective Services, were considered liabilities in joint planning and operations. They were believed to be more interested in Service prerogatives than the overall success of joint operations. The consultations among the Joint Chiefs, based on compromise, were thought to result in watered-down plans that awarded a piece of the action to each Service. During operations, the chiefs were faulted for meddling in the chain of command for the benefit of their Services.

Such concerns were justified by egregious cases in the past, such as the rivalry and confused chain of command during the Vietnam War. Operation *Desert Storm*, less than 5 years after passage of Goldwater-Nichols, showed flashes of inter-Service rivalry as well as moments of inspiring inter-Service integration. Today, senior officers have spent most of their professional careers in the Goldwater-Nichols world and comprise a new generation committed to jointness. By segregating the chiefs in Washington and the component commanders from the joint planning and operations process, the Armed Forces are losing the effectiveness of joint capabilities.

There are three compelling reasons why Service component commanders should be involved in planning at the regional level and Service chiefs should be involved at the national level and personally participate in the monitoring and adjustment of ongoing joint operations:

■ Component commanders and Service chiefs have significant and relevant operational experience and can improve a plan, detect problems with operations, and recommend fixes.

■ Because they are responsible for providing Service forces to the joint task forces that will carry out operations, they have valuable ideas on Service capabilities. With their responsibility for supporting operations, they will have an understanding of the limits of an operation, which are often crucial.

■ If they have been involved in the planning and closely followed the progress of an operation, they will be committed to its success if it runs into difficulties.

There are a number of negative and positive examples in the interaction of joint commanders and

Service components in the decades since the passage of the Goldwater-Nichols Act.

In the months preceding the invasion of Iraq, the primary concern of the chiefs, based on their experience in earlier operations, was weaknesses in the planning of phase four. Their views were expressed in various ways, including the testimony by General Eric Shinseki before the Senate Armed Services Committee. However, without a formal role in the planning process, their views carried little weight, and they had no way to table recommendations to improve the plans. Once Baghdad fell, tensions immediately arose between the newly formed staff of Multinational Force–Iraq and the Service staffs back in Washington. The former group of officers, mostly serving on temporary duty, felt that the coalition was losing control of Iraq and called for additional forces. The Services were concerned about the readiness of personnel and equipment worn down by the deployment and subsequent operations. Had the chiefs been involved in planning for Operation *Iraqi Freedom*, they could have fashioned recommendations to address both concerns.

In Kosovo, the Service chiefs played a more important role, although the process was far from smooth. In that case, the combatant commander launched an air operation that initially failed to achieve its objectives. When he requested that ground units be deployed, and in particular the Army's Apache attack helicopters, the opposition on the Joint Chiefs of Staff played a role in delaying and reducing the effectiveness of the deployed forces. The combatant commander continued the operation using U.S. airpower with the informal cooperation from irregular units of the Kosovo Liberation Army. Eventually, the operation achieved its political objectives. The operation would have been more effective and succeeded more quickly if the original concept had included a branch plan based on the deployment of ground units. The Service chiefs would have participated in approving the plan, come to an agreement with the combatant commander on the conditions under which the branch plan would be activated, and prepared the necessary units to be on call.

When U.S. Pacific Command (USPACOM) organized the U.S. role in Australian-led operations in East Timor, component commanders were fully involved in the planning. One of the conditions of American participation included the decision not to contribute ground forces. The component commanders proposed ways to improve the U.S. contribution to the presence by the United Nations (UN) without

deploying ground forces. In the operation, according to the Australian commanders of UN forces, the capabilities of the American contingent were crucial to its success.

In the wake of the events of September 11, 2001, USPACOM deployed a small joint special operations task force to the southern Philippines to help the indigenous forces combat Abu Sayyaf, a criminal/terrorist gang. Previously, task forces had been quick operations and did not require sustained logistics support. In this case, it was clear the operation would be long and new arrangements would have to be made. After intense discussion with USPACOM and approval from the Department of the Army, U.S. Army Pacific took on the responsibility. As the operation continued and tasks evolved, there was never any issue of providing logistic support. With the long-term commitment of the component commander, the mission continued.

The successes in USPACOM have been on a smaller scale than those of U.S. Central Command in Iraq or U.S. European Command in Kosovo. The command arrangements as well as the personalities were different, but the underlying command and control issue remained the same: reconciling the responsibilities of operational and Service component commanders. Both Service and component commanders fear exhausting operational forces, making them unable to meet new contingencies or build capabilities for the future. Operational commanders always want a comfortable margin to ensure mission success when unexpected but inevitable reverses arise in the field. The best way of reconciling legitimate and important differences in responsibilities is bringing

Emergency vehicles surround Pentagon on September 11

U.S. Air Force (Gary Coppage)

leaders and their staffs into the same process where issues can be aired, analyzed, and decided.

When Service leaders and their staffs are brought into the joint process, the results are good. Gone are the days when leaders assume their Services can fight and win conflicts by themselves. On the contrary, when Service leaders are brought into the joint planning process, they become committed to mission success, and always come up with positive, innovative, and practical ways to integrate their Service with their joint partners to achieve mission success. It is the successful joint commander from joint task force level to the President himself who takes advantage of this joint wisdom of the leadership of the Army, Navy, Marine Corps, and Air Force.

The Evolution of U.S. Southern Command

Problems in Latin America and the Caribbean, from drug cartels to natural disasters, increasingly demand interagency approaches. U.S. Southern Command (USSOUTHCOM) has recognized these dynamics, and at the direction of the Secretary of Defense became an interagency-oriented command. The effects of the information age highlight various policy issues worth examining systematically, especially in light of the Quadrennial Defense Review (QDR). USSOUTHCOM will continue to conduct military operations and security cooperation activities, while enhancing its ability to partner with private and public sector counterparts as well as the interagency community, in order to more effectively and efficiently promote and safeguard U.S. national interests within the region.

Challenges and Opportunities

In the USSOUTHCOM area of focus, which includes the Caribbean, Central America, South America, and adjacent waters, there are two tiers of concern. On one level, there are underlying social and economic challenges such as poverty, corruption, and income inequality. Many countries within the region experience disparities of wealth among their citizens, with attendant corruption problems. These socioeconomic inequalities complicate national development and contribute to instability. On another level, security issues pose serious threats. While the potential for state-to-state conflict remains relatively low, the United States must be vigilant, as incidents in 2008 along the Colombian border with Ecuador demonstrated. In addition, USSOUTHCOM faces

▼ *Continued on p. 422*

Twenty-first Century Diplomacy

The Obama administration has inherited myriad recommendations on addressing challenges to the Nation as well as various plans designed to implement reforms in national security. One issue that all of the proposals have in common is the need for effective diplomatic action. Looking to the future, the United States must focus on emerging trends, threats, and opportunities; examine the means of conducting diplomacy; analyze relevant studies and findings; and prioritize the tasks required to ensure successful efforts to transform the institutions of American diplomacy.

One major challenge to diplomacy in the 21st century is extremism, which includes terrorists and their networks outside war zones. Such groups threaten the democracies that Philip Bobbit calls *nations of consent* by undermining their ways of life. This threat to liberty must be defeated. Another major challenge is extending pluralism and globalization to those people who have not benefited from them. Rising disparities in standards of living around the world that result from globalization are directly connected to the spread of extremism. To stem the rise of extremism in poverty-stricken areas, it is essential to bring processes of democracy and open markets to people who need opportunities to choose their own destiny. A third major challenge is nonproliferation. President John Kennedy predicted that 10 to 15 nuclear powers would emerge in the world. That day is rapidly approaching. Nuclear weapons must not fall into the hands of rogue states or nonstate actors who flout international laws and agreements. Finally, a major challenge is being posed to sustainable living that requires changing some basic attitudes on the environment. Although the current fear over the availability of critical resources is largely focused on energy, there will be concern in the future over supplies of water, food, and other essentials.

Diplomacy will benefit from national security reform that emphasizes collaborative solutions to issues that the Nation cannot address unilaterally. Such an approach calls for a strategic long view of international affairs because it is no longer possible to function on a case-by-case basis. American diplomats must not be reactive—content to report on conditions from abroad and then allow others to make decisions—but proactive. They will be tasked to carry out active policy responsibilities, working inside and outside of Embassies and overseas missions. Americans on the frontlines of diplomacy will have operational roles in dealing with issues such as trafficking in people and drugs. One important aspect of diplomacy in the 21st century will be simultaneity, which requires analyzing issues within the broader context of their overall environment because no single issue holds the key to all others, which must be dealt with simultaneously.

The threat of extremism must be checked by increasing the effectiveness of not only military but also political means, particularly civil-military constructs, such as the Provincial Reconstruction Teams in Afghanistan. The North Atlantic Treaty Organization emphasis on countering narcotics in Afghanistan is one case in point. Promoting democratic pluralism in troubled states, especially given current economic and financial problems, requires going back to fundamentals. An agenda that includes spreading democracy, free market institutions, and rule of law must emphasize American values. Despite other international commitments, the United States must support human rights around the globe. Diplomacy must be retained on the agenda because it has strategic value. To curb the spread of nuclear weapons, the Nuclear Non-Proliferation Treaty must be revised to take account of international developments and persuade emerging nuclear powers to act responsibly. Efforts by Sam Nunn, Henry Kissinger, and other statesmen have been instrumental in focusing attention on this issue. The Comprehensive Test Ban Treaty and the International Atomic Energy Agency must be strengthened and resourced, and regional conflicts that have prompted nuclear proliferation must be mediated. U.S. and allied influence is needed to prevent further proliferation of weapons of mass destruction and to ensure the development and fielding of missile defense systems.

Among the issues confronting the Nation is the sustainability of the environment. Americans are beginning to realize that energy security is not their only domestic problem and that changes in climate are impacting relations with neighbors and allies. For example, the opening by climate change of navigable Arctic sealanes through formerly ice-locked northern regions introduces new international trade and resource considerations in strategic relations with Canada. The east-west energy corridor that reaches from Central Asia to the developed nations of Europe has important consequences for all parties concerned since the uninterrupted supply of oil and natural gas is not only a vital economic necessity but also a critical political and strategic interest. Russia and the Caucasus are leveraging energy issues to influence their regional and international agendas. These is-

sues have led some to suggest extending guarantees under Article 5 of the North Atlantic Treaty to energy security and protecting Alliance members against the manipulation of supplies. Finally, there is the growing issue of climate change. Although once ignored by many countries, its potential danger for humankind has forced governments to consider actions to curb its impact. In sum, there are many ways to change institutions to meet the challenges of the future.

Washington think tanks and policy centers have made a variety of dynamic recommendations on transforming American diplomacy. In a report on what is known as *smart power*, the Center for Strategic and International Studies (CSIS) argued that the image of the United States is linked to how it promotes itself and that the ability to persuade others is as relevant as military strength. Active diplomacy

Admiral Mullen talks with Secretary of State Hillary Clinton at Sather Air Base in Baghdad

provides an opportunity for the Nation to promote its ideals around the globe. Efforts to address global health issues such as HIV/AIDS and malaria illustrate how instruments of so-called soft power (that is, persuasive rather than coercive tools) can influence views of the United States. Another CSIS report, "The Embassy of the Future," stressed the importance of preparing diplomatic personnel and constructing diversified platforms for active frontline missions abroad. In a report entitled "Foreign Affairs Budget for the Future," the Stimson Center drew attention to the crisis in human capital that faces American Embassies and diplomatic missions overseas as well as the Department of State itself at home.

Strengthening agencies such as the U.S. Agency for International Development will be as critical as reforming international institutions such as the United Nations Security Council and the Group of Seven. It is necessary to restructure civilian agencies both to rationalize chains of command and reduce interagency rivalries in the way that the Goldwater-Nichols Act of 1986 reformed the defense establishment. In addition, the Project on National Security Reform has proposed ways to deal with a globalized world in which the United States must protect itself against a range of multidimensional threats. These recommendations offer a solid basis for implementing concepts to reform national security structures and processes and should be considered by the Obama administration.

Among the tasks required to transform American diplomacy is the need to change the attitude of national leaders. Diplomacy has been viewed as a tool of weakness used to make concessions. This negative attitude minimizes the proper role of diplomacy in conducting international affairs. Both civilian and military communities must support the enhancement of diplomatic capabilities. The fact that one of the vocal advocates of building diplomatic efforts is Secretary of Defense Robert Gates is indicative of the need for fundamental change in attitudes toward diplomacy.

Another task needed to revive American diplomacy is accountability. The rapid expansion of responsibilities for conducting diplomatic efforts has diffused accountability among departments, agencies, and special teams with overlapping mandates. When problems do arise, the absence of clear lines of accountability prevents effective decisions from being reached. This deficit must be addressed. There must be real transparency and someone ready to take responsibility.

Finally, there must be sustained efforts to develop the organizations and resources needed to reorient and expand the U.S. diplomatic corps. The prospect of tackling complex international issues raises the question of the availability of skilled people. In addition to career development and educational opportunities to groom the next generation of diplomats, ways must be found to enhance the ability of seasoned diplomats to deal with a changing world. This task involves both expanding knowledge and sharing information. It is essential to adopt new technologies together with practices to maximize the impact of diplomacy. To be effective, American diplomats must venture outside the confines of their Embassies and move into towns and the countryside. This practice will require shifting from risk avoidance to risk management to connect with indifferent or hostile groups and finding ways to communicate with a wider range of audiences.

The success of the Nation depends on pursuing active diplomacy, promoting national values, demonstrating integrity and accountability, and strengthening cooperation with allies and friends, all with the backing of the strongest military in the world. Although the United States has the capacity to act unilaterally in defense of its interests if required, it should strengthen alliances and partnerships as a positive way of enhancing its vital diplomatic role in the world.

Continued from p. 420

transnational security challenges such as narcotrafficking, urban gangs, inadequate disaster preparedness, and illicit movement of people across the region. If unchecked or unaddressed, these security challenges can aggravate traditional animosities and complicate latent bilateral issues, possibly leading to cross-border conflict. These transnational security challenges can destabilize partner nations and weaken fragile civil institutions.

A current that runs through these challenges is the need for a concerted interagency response. Historically, senior leaders have guided those departments, agencies, and related capabilities that protect the Nation from threats and assist partners, a process known as interagency coordination. Although there has been marked progress over the years in this whole-of-government approach, it remains clear that the government is not properly aligned across structural lines to systemically address challenges that the United States and its partners are encountering in the region. Against this backdrop of challenges are cultural, economic, and political trends that form building blocks for new approaches to enhancing national security in the hemisphere. Culturally, the United States and Latin America and the Caribbean share growing demographic links with the potential to alter national security interests over the next few decades. By 2050, nearly one-third of U.S. citizens may have a Latino heritage, which is a twofold increase over the 15 percent figure today. With these changes have come social and cultural trends that will likely increase the emphasis given by U.S. leaders to hemispheric and regional national security issues in the future.

Economically, the United States has vibrant relations with Latin America and the Caribbean, with substantial bilateral trade and commercial exchanges. With the large numbers of both legal and illegal immigrants entering the United States from the region, the nations of Latin America and the Caribbean receive significant financial support from the remittances of these immigrants. For example, Inter-American Development Bank studies estimate that $66.5 billion flowed to the region in remittances during 2007, with about three-quarters of it originating in the United States. Remittances are critical to countries such as Guyana, where the cash flows represent 43 percent of its gross national product. Almost 40 percent of all U.S. foreign trade involves the Americas, more than any other macro region in the

Continued on p. 424

Strategic Leadership

Strategic leadership has many characteristics in common with leadership at lower levels, but it also has some that are distinctive. There are six that we think will be particularly relevant to strategic leaders in the future: intellectual openness, nuance, intellectual agility, integration, teamwork, and ethics.

Intellectual openness. Because the scope of strategic leadership is so wide and the range of opinions on strategic issues is so diverse, leaders must be open to different points of view. Indeed, they should encourage subordinates, peers, and others to express their views as directly as possible—from those in the corridors of power and the public at large to allies and friends abroad. No one has a monopoly on relevant experience and practical wisdom about the complex issues facing American leadership.

Nuance. The problems that occupy the inboxes of strategic leaders involve ambiguity and complexity. If they were unambiguous and simple, they would be solved at lower levels. Strategic leaders must be able to recognize and deal with this ambiguity and complexity and the shades of nuance that they present. This requires effective skills in managing cognitive dissonance, for evidence and argumentation usually send conflicting signals. Denial is *not* one of those skills. Leaders may be able to deny that they perceive cognitive dissonance, but cannot make the conflicting signals disappear by denying them. A well-developed appreciation for nuance would generally reject an either/or approach, which in itself denies ambiguity and complexity. For military leaders in particular, this means that tactics, techniques, and procedures—though important, even necessary—may not always be up to the task at hand, which leads to consideration of another quality.

Intellectual agility. Strategic leaders do not have single-issue inboxes nor do they fully control their agendas. Strategic leaders must be able to transition with little or no warning, and at times turn on a dime, from one problem to another. It is the policy equivalent of the so-called three-block war. In practicing intellectual agility, strategic leaders must be informed and guided by doctrine and past experiences but not become slaves to them. Properly understood, military doctrine is authoritative, but requires judgment in its application. Too often, professional officers remember the former but not the latter and rigidly apply doctrine to situations that may be significantly different from those the doctrine writers envisioned.

Strategic leaders must be adaptable and able to "call an audible" when an unanticipated situation is thrust upon them, or in an anticipated crisis that differs in important ways from the planning scenario, thus rendering the "on-the-shelf" plan not fully appropriate and useful. Since "no war plan survives contact with the enemy," strategic leaders must be able to adapt in the middle of a war or crisis, rather than holding on stubbornly to the plan or policy they began with, even when it no longer seems to be achieving the objectives, or is doing so at unacceptably high costs.

Integration. The problems confronting strategic leaders are rarely unidimensional. Almost by definition, strategic problems are *multi*dimensional, involving military, political, economic, cultural, social, religious, and historical factors and forces that are often difficult to disentangle from each other. Thus, successfully addressing strategic problems involves several instruments of national power, sometimes all of them. Strategic leaders must master the instruments of their own departments or agencies, but must also be able to help integrate and coordinate them with those of other departments and agencies. Strategic leadership requires the skills of an orchestra conductor, not of a soloist, no matter how talented.

Senior Army and Air National Guard officers join officers from other components at Joint Task Force Commander Training Course at U.S. Northern Command, January 2009

Teamwork. Government operations on the strategic level require teamwork. Strategic leaders must build an effective team within their own agencies that includes career officials (both civilian and military) and political appointees. The former are nonpartisan experts and the latter, who also include experts, make administration policy. Strategic leaders must build effective interagency teams to integrate and apply various instruments that the given problem demands. Increasingly in the 21st century, strategic leaders must build effective teams with coalition and alliance partners, whose cultural backgrounds and modes of operation frequently will be greatly different from their own.

Relationships are critical in building effective teamwork on all levels. Organizations do not cooperate or integrate; people do. Building relationships takes time, and new administrations sometimes do not have that luxury because real-world concerns will suddenly intrude. Thus, forming and molding relationships must start on day one. The key to strong and effective relationships is trust. It must be built and earned; it cannot simply be declared. It must be multidirectional, not unidirectional. For trust to take hold in organizations, leaders on all levels must be both trustworthy and trusting. Both are necessary; neither by itself is sufficient.

Ethics. Ethics is always important, but especially given the challenges that the Nation confronts today. Strategic leaders must personally set and periodically recalibrate their own moral compasses. Doing so begins with one's own moral values and principles, those inherited from family (and, for many, from religion) and nurtured in school. Professionals are guided by an ethos that defines and regulates their profession—military, public service, the law. All citizens, but especially public servants, must incorporate national values and principles, which for Americans include those enshrined in the U.S. Constitution and the Declaration of Independence. In an era when the world is shrinking, news is driven by a 24-hour cycle, and coalitions have become the norm, ethics also involve what the Founders called "a decent respect to the opinions of mankind."

Ethics must involve both ethical ends and ethical means, especially for strategic leaders who wrestle with the problems of today. Ethical ends can justify some means, but even the most ethical ends cannot justify any and all means. Leaders will be judged—by themselves and by others—not only by the goals they set, but also by the means they use in trying to achieve those goals. In every organization, regardless of size, leaders set the tone, including the ethical tone. Within military organizations, command climate starts at the top. It is reflected in what strategic leaders say and in what they do, and those who serve in their organizations, as well as those people outside who come into contact with them, pay attention to both words and deeds.

▲ *Continued from p. 422*

world. Technology also integrates the region with the United States. Internet usage in Latin America and the Caribbean over the last 8 years has grown by over 600 percent. In the area of energy interdependence, three of the top four companies that supply half of the oil to the United States are located in the Western Hemisphere, and many future sources of energy for the Nation reside in underexplored areas of the hemisphere.

Two domestic trends affect the potential of the USSOUTHCOM approach to interagency partnering for enhanced security and stability in Latin America and the Caribbean. First, there is a growing political consensus on the need to better integrate military and nonmilitary elements of national power. Second, there have been advances in interagency coordination of civilian and military planning, especially with implementation of the Interagency Management System under Presidential directives on stabilization and reconstruction. Both trends have accelerated thinking about adopting the whole-of-government approach to national security within the region.

Rethinking the Command

With help from the interagency community, US-SOUTHCOM has sought to improve structure and processes to better perform its Title X mission. In 2006, the command was organized on the traditional J level, with slow, hierarchical staff processes, many of which date to Prussian or Napoleonic staff models. Such models were best attuned to a world of relative certainty with industrial age competitors, but they appear out of synch for the military in the 21st century. The command also was fine-tuned for executing joint military operations for a world in which joint operations increasingly needed to become interagency operations.

The value of partnering was evident in Joint Interagency Task Force–South (JIATF–South), with the establishment of effective ways of countering the threat of narcotics from and within Latin America and the Caribbean. With strong interagency and multinational information fusion, a common set of mission objectives, and diverse representation by law enforcement, intelligence, and military personnel, JIATF–South became an effective model of interagency partnership.

At the direction of the Secretary of Defense, with assignment via the Department of Defense Top 25 Transformation Priorities, and authorities under Title X, Section 164, the command has reprised its posture to meet new challenges, including structural changes based on recent lessons from U.S. operations around the world. In addition, this approach called on a command history of adaptation to regional dynamics that dates to the mid-1900s when the organization emerged from its earlier mission as the Panama Canal Department and then Caribbean Command.

The purpose of this approach was to adapt the span of operations to the transnational nature of security challenges today in the region and improve the ability of the command to harmonize its activities and planning with other U.S. Government departments and agencies. There has been significant progress in this area over the last 2 years, and the emerging issues from this process suggest items for the agenda of the congressionally mandated QDR.

Salient Issues

The continuing evolution of USSOUTHCOM will build on strong, existing command and control readiness under Title X to perform combat operations as directed by the President or the Secretary of Defense when circumstances dictate in the defense of U.S. national interests. There are four areas of change that offer new or modified organizational approaches to improving the ability of the command to work with the interagency community.

Integrated Partnering. Under a dual-deputy structure, the civilian deputy will complement the three-star military deputy to the commander by providing increased expertise and oversight of command dealings with its interagency partners. Through the assignment of more interagency personnel (up to approximately 50) across the 1,200 members of the staff, USSOUTHCOM will benefit from the expertise of counterparts from the Department of State and the U.S. Agency for International Development to the Departments of Energy, Commerce, and Justice, many of whom have either served within the region or been focused on regional planning and operations. A partnering directorate that merges the former J9 and J10 staff elements will be focused on the integration of the command with interagency processes and planning to more effectively support the whole-of-government implementation of U.S. regional policy and objectives.

Multinational Cooperation. USSOUTHCOM has reassigned personnel from headquarters to American Embassies in the region to improve support to Ambassadors and their country teams. In addition, in anticipation of occupying a new headquarters building by 2010, the command is expanding partner-nation representation and has begun planning for improved information security protocols to permit broader integration of their international expertise in daily operations.

Strategic Communication. In Latin America and the Caribbean region, the United States must improve its engagement in the marketplace of ideas to advance and protect its security interests. As such, the Office of Strategic Communication, with a developed planning and integration role, is being assigned to the chief of staff to institutionalize strategic communication approaches in all command correspondence and communication, both internally and externally.

Public-Private Collaboration. Just as events in the last few years underscored the importance of working more closely with interagency partners, senior leaders in the Department of Defense have recognized the need to adapt their organizations to better cooperate with the private sector. Whether nongovernmental organizations focused on humanitarian assistance objectives, or even in certain specific instances, multinational corporations with decades of experience in commerce and infrastructure trends in Latin America and the Caribbean, the organizations can share unique insights and perspectives. In some cases, especially in areas such as public health and capacity-building, partnerships can be forged to meet security concerns. USSOUTHCOM has created a public-private cooperation office to explore protocols for collaborative exchanges and identify activities to improve its ability to execute interagency operations in support of regional security objectives. These changes and the approach to reorganization underscore the critical enablers to success and highlight areas to explore in order to improve the capabilities of the command.

This reorganization requires both professional and procedural change in culture and mindset. Although USSOUTHCOM is prepared to lead combat operations, a premium has been put on partnerships and cooperation in support of U.S. civilian counterpart organizations. In addition, with greater coordination with interagency counterparts, training and education is needed across the government. While modest improvement has been made in this area for military personnel, the demand for civilian training, academic courses, and interagency assignments and exchanges is increasing. The 21st century will require greater integration and harmonization of planning, and existing shortfalls in these functions merit early attention and resourcing in the deliberations. This includes language training and area studies, and a system of personnel incentives similar to the changes introduced in the Armed Forces under the Goldwater-Nichols Act.

The promise of increased partnering with nations by building on the cultural, economic, and political linkages in the region has also demonstrated the need for rethinking the basic capacity of USSOUTH-COM within the area of focus. Service components need an improved ability to articulate requirements to support enhanced security cooperation in the region. One example of this approach is the decision to strengthen Naval Forces South by reestablishing the designation of the 4th Fleet. Although no ships will be permanently assigned to the force, this development increases the small planning staff and puts a more senior flag officer in command of this new numbered fleet that will represent maritime requirements across the Navy.

On the Horizon

In refining this reorganization, there are also longer term issues that merit attention in the wider context of the QDR. Progress has been recorded in the developing conceptual options for approaches by the United States within the region. Perhaps it is time to identify concrete steps in establishing regional interagency-led security organizations that would be more effective in unifying efforts by the Nation across regional boundaries.

The position of civilians in combatant commands, whether they represent the Department of Defense or other agencies, should continue to be refined. To understand the linkages and trends within the region, the relationships of combatant command structures in the Western Hemisphere should be reviewed based on previous studies, such as the notion of merging U.S. Northern Command and USSOUTH-COM that was examined in the QDR in 2006. There are both pros and cons to this merger that should be thoroughly vetted in the context of what is best for the peace and security of the Nation and the region in an interagency approach.

U.S. Southern Command will approach the new horizon in Latin America and the Caribbean with one goal in mind: to extend a hand to partner nation militaries in the hemisphere that are seeking positive security cooperation. Working together, the countries of the Americas can bring about positive and lasting changes in this beautiful and vibrant region.

Educating National Security Professionals

With the end of the Cold War and events of the mid-1990s, there was a realization that managing complex contingencies would pose near-term challenges. The threats would be less massive and kinetic in nature, but would stem from sectarian or communal violence leading to ethnic cleansing and internal displacement of peoples, dysfunctional economies, and competition for scarce resources. Both man-made and natural disasters were happening with some frequency, which added urgency to the security policy reviews at the end of the last decade. Based on the resulting critical analyses, Presidential Decision Directive 56, "Managing Complex Contingencies," was issued in 1997 to provide for multidepartmental collaboration and implementation. At its core was the premise that a reinforced program of education and training would replace vertical decisionmaking inside the executive branch with horizontal interagency coordination, planning, and execution.

As integration of national capabilities and resources became the goal for operations in crisis and contingency operations, it became clear that no formal process of education for the managers of these situations existed. The National Defense University, the Foreign Service Institute, and the U.S. Army War College were tasked to begin developing and presenting such a course of studies across the educational activities of Federal departments and agencies. The events of September 11, 2001, and their lessons reinforced the urgency of instituting such education and training. With operations in Southwest Asia embracing asymmetric threats and nation-building, even commanders and planners understood the need for dramatic changes. The transformational nature of building partnership capacity was codified in the QDR, which called for greater interagency representation in future crises and contingencies.

Hurricane Katrina demonstrated the need for a comprehensive and flexible system to address domestic security challenges. Like analyses of developments abroad, the review of the disaster in New Orleans and along the Gulf Coast found that stovepiped responses resulted in abysmal coordination. Assigning comparable priorities to domestic and international security challenges led to a comprehensive definition of national security in the Center for Strategic and International Studies report entitled *Beyond Goldwater-Nichols*, which urged an enhanced structure for interagency integration with attendant education and training.

Subsequently, the QDR process recommended that National Defense University expand its curricula with concentrated studies of interagency affairs. A pilot program was conducted in academic year 2007–2008 to validate instruction intended to produce military and civilian leaders to operate in an interagency environment. At the highest levels within the government, the goal to develop more vigorous programs for civilian managers was extended to senior staffs at both the National Security Council and the Homeland Security Council. These initiatives support a recent directive that has formed civilian national security professionals into a distinct cadre with similar capabilities to their military counterparts for domestic and international crises.

President George W. Bush signed Executive Order 13434 in May 2007, mandating a three-part program of education, training, and relevant experience for developing military as well as civilian national security professional (NSP) officers. The program applied to every department and agency with national security responsibilities and was supplemented by the national security strategy that laid out its principal components and how they were to be implemented. The focus is on a human capital process for selection, promotion, management, and incentivization.

The people known as national security professionals are responsible for developing strategy, implementing strategic plans, and executing missions in support of national security objectives. The Executive Steering Committee of the Office of Management and Budget envisions that the program will supply its members with "the knowledge, skills, abilities, attitudes, and experiences they need to work with their counterparts to plan and execute coordinated, effective interagency national security operations." The individuals in the program will have the potential to function in those contingencies and crises when significant interaction is anticipated between two or more departments, agencies, or other entities. The designation of *national security professional* will be awarded to the occupants of positions who play a role in executing aspects of the National Security Strategy, the National Strategy for Homeland Security, the National Defense Strategy, the National Strategy for Combating Weapons of Mass Destruction, and other national security frameworks and plans. As envisioned, this initiative will not include political appointees, who will receive national security training, education, and experience under a separate effort.

National Commission on Terrorist Attacks Upon the United States presents its report

Understanding competencies that are common to national security professionals is paramount to developing effective training and education programs. Within the broad range of interagency operations, the capabilities that they will require are:

■ strategic thinking—understanding national strategy documentation and being able to envision collaboration with other agencies, think strategically, and engage in interagency planning

■ critical and creative thinking—analyzing issues with other agencies; seeking, evaluating, and synthesizing information from multiple sources; assessing and challenging assumptions; and offering alternative and creative solutions/courses of action

■ leading interagency teams—creating a shared vision and unity of purpose among all players, winning their confidence and trust, and utilizing their knowledge, skills, and resources; developing and mentoring staff from other agencies, ensuring collaborative problem-solving, and managing internal conflicts

■ maintaining global and cultural acuity—maintaining an integrated understanding of factors that influence national security (global/regional/country trends); possessing knowledge of relevant foreign cultures, histories, and languages; and knowing the structures, processes, and cultures of other agencies

■ collaborating—working with agencies to accomplish goals; building and maintaining interagency networks and relationships; and encouraging collaboration, integration and information-sharing

■ planning and managing—developing strategic and operational plans; executing interagency operations (including budgetary and financial management); conducting program management and evaluation; maintaining political and situation awareness; and navigating decisionmaking processes on the technical, policy, and political levels

■ mediating and negotiating—tackling disputes with partners and stakeholders during operations

■ communicating—clearly articulating information, managing expectations of diverse groups, listening actively, and tailoring approaches to different circumstances and audiences.

National security education, like work on shared attributes of national security professionals, is an ongoing, long-term initiative. Future political leadership must ensure that the program, as well as its members, is adequately resourced so that interagency planning and collaboration become institutionalized as opposed to improvised. Personality-driven and ad hoc leadership and procedures are inadequate for the complex challenges of this globalized environment.

The three core elements of the program must become components of personnel development. The training must embrace the above competencies and tailor them for special requirements such as disaster relief, counterinsurgency, strategic communications, and reconstruction. Educational programs must be provided for senior military and civilian leaders, and agencies without a culture of offering education to their personnel must be reoriented. Relationships with civilian academic institutions must be developed to formalize entry-level feeder programs that furnish graduates for the Federal workforce. Moreover, programs will be needed to track national security professionals throughout their careers as they mature and assume positions of greater responsibility.

Work experience, including rotational assignments with other agencies, must become routine for national security professionals. Although human resource considerations in compartmented bureaucracies make that practice challenging, personnel managers must develop procedures and incentives to facilitate such transfers. Only by encouraging promotions will national security as a career field become the foundation of interagency responses to contingencies and crises in the future. Those who receive training, education, and cross-department postings in their careers will be more competitive for designated positions as national security professionals, and these positions will be highly competitive in all departments and agencies of the national security community.

The Importance of Stability Operations

During the Presidential campaign in 2000, Condoleezza Rice said that extended peacekeeping could detract the Nation from its responsibilities in the Persian Gulf and Taiwan Straits, adding that "carrying out civil administration and police functions is simply going to degrade the American capability to do the things America has to do." Moreover, George W. Bush indicated his disdain for stability operations, nationbuilding, and the like prior to the election when he commented: "I'm worried about an opponent who uses nation-building and the military in the same sentence."

But out of the experience of Afghanistan and Iraq came policies and capabilities to meet the requirements of stability operations: National Security Presidential Directive (NSPD) 44, "Management of Interagency Efforts Concerning Reconstruction and Stabilization"; Department of Defense Directive

(DODD) 3000.05, "Military Support for Stability, Security, Transition, and Reconstruction Operations"; and the Civilian Response Corps (CRC) formed by the Department of State.

There is always a temptation to disparage the efforts of past administrations and start anew, but the Nation cannot afford this kneejerk inclination during a time of war. Certainly, there are policies developed in recent years that were poorly conceived or implemented. But some good things have been accomplished, and their momentum should not be lost. Moreover, the eventual withdrawal from Iraq will not mean that the United States can avoid stability operations in the future, and some of the lessons learned in this conflict have come at a high cost. It took over 2 years in Iraq for guidance on stability operations to emerge. Both DODD 3000.05 and NSPD 44 were issued in 2005. Although the latter replaced Presidential Decision Directive 56, "Managing Complex Contingency Operations," which had been signed by President Bill Clinton in 1997, the defense establishment never had been issued anything like DODD 3000.05.

The directive announced that stability operations would be a core American military mission. It recognized that civilian agencies are the most adept at performing many of the tasks involved in stability operations but stated: "Military forces shall be prepared to perform all tasks necessary to establish or maintain order when civilians cannot do so." As the unraveling of the rule of law in Baghdad demonstrated, maintaining order is one of the foremost tasks in stability operations. Yet it is hard to justify building civilian agency capacity to conduct stability operations to Congress when the military is performing those operations. A former defense official pointed out that the directive refers to military *support to* stability operations, but fails to define what is meant by the term and does not clarify command and control in strategically directing such operations.

In theory, NSPD 44 addressed the question of control of stability operations: "The Secretary of State shall coordinate . . . efforts involving all U.S. departments and agencies with relevant capabilities to prepare, plan for, and conduct stabilization and reconstruction activities." The position of Coordinator for Reconstruction and Stabilization was established in August 2004 as focal point in the Department of State for these activities. The decision to place a civilian in charge of stability operations is a sound one because the operations require political solutions.

Yet there is a tension in NSPD 44. The Department of State is supposed to lead an effort of which it is part. Moreover, Foreign Service Officers do not operate in potentially nonpermissive environments alone or with military counterparts. Indeed, the only deployable civilian asset in the national security arsenal is the U.S. Agency for International Development (USAID), which was gutted after Vietnam. In short, NSPD 44 puts the Secretary of State in charge of operational missions outside the normal purview of the department. Indeed, the Secretary of State had to ask for Department of Defense personnel in 2006 to staff the Provincial Reconstruction Teams being organized for Afghanistan, which negated the purpose of providing civilian expertise.

Secretary of Defense Robert Gates urged dramatic increases in civilian instruments of power: "We must focus our energies beyond the guns and steel of the military, beyond our brave Soldiers, Sailors, Marines, and Airmen. We must also focus our energies on the other elements of national power that will be so crucial in the coming years." In an effort to bolster the ranks of civilians available for stability operations, the Department of State officially launched the Civilian Response Corps (CRC) in 2008. This corps provides for 250 full-time first responders who can deploy in a crisis within 48 hours, 2,000 standby members deployable within 30 days, and 2,000 reservists. Whereas the active and standby members will come from the Federal Government, the reservists will be drawn from the private sector as well as state and local governments. Although the Coordinator for Reconstruction and Stabilization based the number of members in the corps on hypothetical planning for small, medium, and large stabilization operations, there have not been any systematic studies that estimate the requirement for civilian capabilities. The lack of holistic resource planning makes Congress dubious about funding such capabilities, especially when the requirements are not based on a compelling strategic narrative.

Issues raised by NSPD 44 regarding the role of the Secretary of State in stability operations should be revisited. Given the political implications of such missions, civilian control is best. Three logical choices exist for this lead civilian role: the Secretary of State, the National Security Advisor, or a new Cabinet-level portfolio established for stability operations. The difficulties of assigning responsibility for an interagency process to the Secretary of State have been discussed. If the National Security Advisor took the lead, there would be disadvantages to giving the National Security Council a more operational role, including detracting from its traditional responsibilities of advising the President and executing policy coordination. As for creating a new Cabinet post, if the creation of the Department of Homeland Security taught us anything, it is that establishing new layers of bureaucracy is not an instant remedy to the problems of the national security community.

The debate on stability operations has not occurred yet, in part because the result will involve uncomfortable tradeoffs. Both civilian and military agencies concur that even after withdrawing from Iraq, the future will be marked by irregular threats. The last QDR argued for shifting the basic mission of the Armed Forces from traditional to irregular warfare. The joint strategic plan issued by the Department of State and USAID also depicts a world filled with nonstate challenges. If this is the case, then the United States must rebalance its toolkit and deepen its civilian capacity. Either the budget for national security will have to grow or money for this adjustment must come from another budget. The huge reset and modernization costs foretell the impending budgetary train wreck.

The CRC is a step in the right direction, but it is difficult to believe that 250 active civilian personnel will fit the bill in a future operating environment. This is especially striking when it is acknowledged that these 250 individuals cannot be deployed all of the time. The military usually plans on two units stateside for every one deployed: one preparing to deploy and the other returning and resetting from deployment. Accordingly, the United States would have about 80 civilians deployed at any time. Any sensible strategy will require far more resources. Even if the CRC is ultimately moved to another department or agency, or if an augmented USAID takes over its roles and absorbs the assets of the corps, greater civilian resources will be needed.

Partisans may assume that the Bush administration got everything about stability operations in Iraq and Afghanistan either right or wrong. As with all complicated things, the truth is really somewhere in between. The standard enunciated by Senator Arthur Vandenberg in 1952 that "politics stops at the water's edge" should be applied to the future of stability operations.

Intelligence Reform

The Intelligence Reform and Terrorism Prevention Act (IRTPA) of 2004 was the most profound reorganization in the management structure of the Intelligence Community in more than 50 years. The

▼ *Continued on p. 433*

Challenges for Intelligence

Congressional and Executive Branch Reforms

President George W. Bush signed the Intelligence Reform and Terrorism Prevention Act (IRTPA) in December 2004. This was the first major restructuring of the Intelligence Community since the National Security Act of 1947, which created the Central Intelligence Agency (CIA) and gave legal basis to the Intelligence Community itself. Fifty-seven years later, the 2004 legislation created the Director of National Intelligence (DNI), who supplanted the Director of Central Intelligence (DCI) as the senior intelligence official, head of the Intelligence Community, and principal intelligence advisor to the President.

In its final report in March 2005, the Commission on the Intelligence Capabilities of the United States Regarding Weapons of Mass Destruction (WMD) made 74 recommendations on how to improve intelligence. The President adopted 70 of the recommendations, and they were added to those changes legislated by the Congress.

The DNI today serves as the head of the Intelligence Community, the 16 intelligence organizations spread across 6 departments and 1 independent agency. He functions as the principal advisor to the President, National Security Council, and Homeland Security Council on matters of intelligence. The IRTPA also expanded DNI responsibilities (beyond those previously held by the DCI) to include those domestic issues that are a part of homeland security. The term *national intelligence* replaced the phrase *national foreign intelligence*. Congress included this provision to address the concern that agencies needed to share intelligence—foreign and domestic—better.

A Tale of Two Men

Ambassador John Negroponte served from April 2005 until January 2007 as the first DNI. Though not an intelligence professional, he had been a consumer of intelligence most of his government career. As his deputy, he had an intelligence professional, National Security Agency (NSA) Director Lieutenant General Michael Hayden, USAF. Working together, they set up the new DNI office.

Negroponte took 6 months to draft the first National Intelligence Strategy (NIS) designed to organize and direct the strategic efforts of the Intelligence Community. This strategy built upon the DCI Strategic Intent for the U.S. Intelligence Community of March 1999. Guided by the new concept of national intelligence defined in the IRTPA, the NIS drew its objectives from the *National Security Strategy of the United States of America*. There are two notable features of the 2005 intelligence strategy. First, it was unclassified. Second, it assigned responsibility for accomplishing each mission and enterprise objective to a specific organization within the office of the DNI or to executive agents among the 16 intelligence components. The mission objectives are outwardly directed at the threats to our nation's security. The enterprise objectives are inwardly directed at improving the capabilities of the Intelligence Community. Both promote greater integration and collaboration among the community's 16 members.

A year later, Negroponte reported to Congress on progress made. High on the list was the establishment of six mission managers to address specific issues of great concern. They serve as the principal Intelligence Community officials overseeing all aspects of intelligence related to both functional and regional areas of focus—counterterrorism, counterproliferation, and counterintelligence, as well as the three regions of Iran, North Korea, and Cuba/Venezuela. Mission managers can call upon the resources of the entire Intelligence Community. They are responsible for understanding the needs of intelligence consumers—key policymakers in the executive branch and Congress. Mission managers provide specific guidance on collection priorities, integration, and gaps; assess analytic quality and needs; share intelligence produced; and recommend funding allocations.

As a second accomplishment, Negroponte cited the creation of new organizations within the CIA and Federal Bureau of Investigation (FBI) to promote better intelligence coordination. The CIA, through the new National Clandestine Service, was given the responsibility to coordinate human intelligence among the CIA, Department of Defense, and FBI. The FBI, as mandated by the 2004 reform law, established a directorate of intelligence to give greater importance to domestic intelligence analysis and collection. Additional recommendations from the WMD Commission led to the creation of the National Security Branch, which combined the functions of intelligence, counterterrorism, counterintelligence, and protection against WMD.

A third accomplishment focused on improvements in analytic tradecraft. The President's Daily Briefing was opened to intelligence contributions beyond the CIA; the Long Range Analysis Unit was created

under the National Intelligence Council to address issues of strategic, long-term concern rather than current intelligence; and the sourcing of national intelligence estimates was improved by including sections on the reliability of, nature of, and gaps in the intelligence used.

When he relinquished his position in January 2007, John Negroponte could point to a number of accomplishments in helping to carry out both the mandates of the IRTPA and recommendations of the WMD Commission. The Office of the DNI was organized, set up, staffed, and moving forward.

Retired Navy Vice Admiral Mike McConnell assumed his position as the second DNI in February 2007. A career naval intelligence officer and former Joint Chiefs of Staff J2, he had finished his military career as the Director of NSA. After retirement, he worked at Booz Allen Hamilton as senior vice president focusing on intelligence and national security issues. This multifaceted experience—in intelligence, the military, and the private sector—prepared him well to deal with the issues he would confront as DNI.

McConnell built on the foundation of the NIS and in mid-April 2007 announced a 100-Day Plan for Integration and Collaboration. Six focus areas to improve the capabilities of the community included promoting a culture of collaboration; improving collection and analysis; building technology leadership and acquisition excellence; adopting modern business practices; accelerating information-sharing; and clarifying DNI authorities.

Possibly the most far reaching measure of the 100-Day Plan was the adoption of the civilian Intelligence Community Joint Duty program, which requires civilians interested in promotion to the senior ranks to complete at least one assignment outside their home agency. In fostering a culture of collaboration, the program gives intelligence professionals the opportunity to broaden and deepen their knowledge of the workings of other agencies. The aim is to create a cadre of senior intelligence professionals better able to understand the complex challenges facing the Nation and to help the Intelligence Community address those challenges in support of the policymakers.

The 100-Day Plan was followed by the 500-Day Plan for Integration and Collaboration. If the former was designed to reinvigorate the process, the latter was designed to sustain, accelerate, and expand the effort.

Two of the most significant accomplishments of the McConnell period were to update the 1978

Foreign Intelligence Surveillance Act (FISA) and Executive Order (EO) 12333, originally issued by President Ronald Reagan in December 1981. The former governs foreign intelligence wiretaps conducted within the United States. The latter is the keystone document outlining the roles and responsibilities of the members of the Intelligence Community.

The FISA update of June 2008 took more than 2 years to accomplish and improves the legal foundations for the Intelligence Community. It also updated domestic electronic surveillance in the era of the Internet and cell phone. After 14 months of negotiation on Capitol Hill, the measure passed in June with substantial bipartisan support: 293–129 in the House of Representatives and 69–28 in the Senate. It was held up over the question of whether to provide legal protection to telecommunication companies that participated in the NSA's warrantless wiretapping program in the aftermath of the terrorist attacks of September 11, 2001. The compromise reached allowed the 40-odd lawsuits to be referred to the U.S. District Courts where they were filed. If the telecommunication companies can prove the Bush Administration authorized the surveillance, the suits will be dismissed.

The update of EO 12333 of July 2008 takes into account the 2004 law that created the DNI. It also allows the 3 years of experience since the enactment of that law to be captured in the effort to better integrate the work of the Intelligence Community. The purpose of the revised executive order is to strengthen the Nation's intelligence capability to give government leaders a greater ability to understand the threats facing the country abroad and at home and to be able to respond to those threats with greater agility and speed with well-informed policy options.

Both measures were important achievements. They helped resolidify foundational pillars of the Intelligence Community that needed updating. Both will help the community do its work, which is to provide better intelligence. The former modernizes how it conducts domestic electronic surveillance; the latter provides clearer guidance on what each of the 16 components of the community is to undertake in the DNI era. Both are designed to provide policymakers a "decision advantage."

Issues for the Future

The Obama administration must confront those threats that we know about today. They include defeating terrorists abroad and at home, preventing and countering the proliferation of WMD, bolstering the growth of democracy and sustaining peaceful democratic states, developing new ways to penetrate and analyze the most difficult targets, and supporting U.S. policy and combat operations in Iraq and Afghanistan. Cyberterrorism is also a topic of keen concern to policymakers and the Intelligence Community. The Internet has helped revolutionize business and economic activity throughout the country and the world; it has also introduced a vulnerability about which we need to know much more. One need only scan the daily newspapers and television/cable news programs for those issues that will require continuous attention.

Equally important as one looks to the horizon and beyond will be anticipating developments of strategic concern and identifying both opportunities as well as vulnerabilities for policymakers. Issues of little policy interest can quickly become matters of state requiring an immediate U.S. response. Others will include those having an impact on U.S. national security: scarcities in energy, food, water; climate change; demographic trends; disruptive civil technologies; financial and economic volatilities; and the reconfiguration of the international system as India, China, Brazil, and Russia claim (or *reclaim* in the case of Russia) a greater voice in international deliberations.

As the Intelligence Community focuses outwardly on the threats of today and tomorrow, it must also focus inwardly to improve capabilities. The following is simply a short list of measures to improve capabilities. It could be expanded. They include:

■ ensuring an integrated information technology network where all members of the Intelligence Community can communicate on the same network. Known as the Single Information Environment, this goal is a key part of the 500 Day Plan.

■ adapting the information-sharing strategy of the traditional Cold War paradigm/culture of "need-to-know" to the 21st-century terrorist threat environment requirement of "responsibility to provide." This is a cultural shift of profound proportions that will take time to institute.

■ supporting the logistical requirements to make the civilian Intelligence Community Joint Duty program function as intended across the 16 intelligence components. A review should examine whether the current support structure is adequate.

- accelerating the security clearance process. It can take anywhere from 12 to 24 months for an individual hoping to work for the Intelligence Community to get a security clearance. A goal has been set to reduce the time to 60 days.

- ensuring that the fundamental changes adopted by the FBI with the establishment of the National Security Branch have taken hold. A review would look at whether integrating the two cultures of intelligence analysis and law enforcement has indeed succeeded. A review would also examine if the full integration of the FBI into the work of the Intelligence Community has occurred.

Concluding Thoughts

The Goldwater-Nichols Department of Defense Reorganization Act of was signed into law in 1986. It took another 10 years for the provisions the act to take full effect. The key word for military reform was *jointness*; the comparable word for intelligence reform has been *integration*. The Intelligence Community is 3 ½ years into its voyage. Its most critical mission today is counterterrorism. Working with military and law enforcement partners, the community has been able to play both offense and defense. Terrorists now have to spend more time worrying about their own security. The higher defensive walls that we have erected at home have made another September 11 event harder to execute—not impossible, but harder.

Most defense experts credit Goldwater-Nichols with having improved the operation of the military Services through a more unified military organization in the years since its passage. The Intelligence Community has made substantial progress. More remains to be done. For those who take the long view, and understand the cultural changes involved, time, patience, and *more* time and *more* patience, will be needed. One day, those supporters of a strong Intelligence Community will point to the changes enacted in 2004 and 2005 as having accomplished what Goldwater-Nichols did for the military. Both efforts, undertaken a generation apart, will be viewed as having been accomplished for the good of the Nation.

▼ *Continued from p. 430*

linchpin of the IRTPA structure is the position of Director of National Intelligence (DNI), who is the senior intelligence advisor to the President. However, unlike the Director of Central Intelligence, this position is separated from other intelligence components. Most observers and some participants characterize the new structure as a work in progress. There are five issues that should be considered in reviewing the state of play of the U.S. Intelligence Community.

Structure

The first issue involves the DNI structure. Can the DNI develop and execute the broad strategic guidance for the Intelligence Community envisioned by the authors of the IRTPA legislation? Most of their attention was centered on perceptions that the Intelligence Community did not collaborate or share information and lacked overarching business practices in personnel, information technology, and other areas. The issue is the apparent disconnect between the responsibilities of the DNI and actual authorities. The relationship with the Secretary of Defense is critical, but it is unlikely that much can be done to improve the role of the DNI by clarifying his authorities vis-à-vis the Secretary of Defense. But there are other things that can be done. A starting point would be to examine the goals of the DNI 100- and 500-day plans and ask: how many of those goals have

U.S. Navy (Holly Boynton)

U.S. Customs agents offload cocaine interdicted during deployment on operation for U.S. Naval Forces Southern Command

been implemented, and among those, what were the impediments? If the hurdles involved turf fights, how can they be surmounted? Here there also is a dilemma. Administrations feel compelled to leave their mark on agencies and policies as quickly as possible. It would be beneficial if the next DNI reviewed the 100- and 500-day plans and asked which of these initiatives should be continued rather than starting over again largely for the sake of novelty. If the DNI structure is not working as intended, the solution must come from Congress since the structure was created in legislation, not by executive order.

Continuity

Closely related to the duties of the DNI is the issue of tenure. Admiral Dennis Blair is the sixth leader of the Intelligence Community in 5 years. It is difficult to run an enterprise, established or new, with that sort of leadership turnover at the very top. The President should provide continuity to the greatest extent possible in filling the senior Intelligence Community positions, ideally making the terms of the position at least 3 to 4 years.

Budget

There are different ways to consider the intelligence budget. Purely in dollar terms, the National Intelligence Program as opposed to the Military Intelligence Program has gone from $26.8 billion to $43.5 billion over the last decade. (As a percentage of the total Federal budget, the national intelligence figure remains unchanged in that period.) There has been a considerable budget feast after nearly a decade of famine in the 1990s. However, the intelligence budget is going down and will undoubtedly become a poor cousin after financial bailouts, domestic needs, and defense and homeland security spending. The DNI should come up with a 5-year budget plan for the Intelligence Community and stick to it. It is difficult if not impossible to plan, build, and manage intelligence activities on a financial roller coaster. This planning is particularly critical when the need for new technical collection systems is considered. A system approved in 2009 will not begin collecting for 10 to 12 years; every start and stop attenuates an already difficult acquisition process.

Personnel

The Intelligence Community is undergoing the most dramatic generational change since its inception. Over half of the analysts serving in its 16 agencies have less than 3 years of experience. These intelligence officers think differently, behave differently, and have different career expectations than their predecessors. If the Intelligence Community cannot accommodate some of these differences, new officers will not stay, perpetuating the inexperience problem. Among the fixes easily achieved are creating a set career path for analysts; tying analyst training and education in their careers to this career path; standing up the National Intelligence University as proposed in the IRTPA; and improving mentoring programs in each component. The Intelligence Community does not put the same emphasis on career development and professional education and training as the Armed Forces, but it is high time for it to catch up.

Standards

Consideration should be given to initiating a discussion among intelligence officers, executive branch policymakers, Members of Congress, and even the media on analytic standards. How often should intelligence be right? What is a set of reasonable (albeit vague) expectations? It is time to get beyond the false legends, misperceptions, and caricatures relating to the tragedies of September 11, 2001, and the search for weapons of mass destruction.

These five issues do not pose daunting tasks. But it should be remembered that the product of intelligence is analysis, which is the result of an intellectual process, not a mechanical one. There are limits on the extent to which this aspect of intelligence can be reformed or improved.

Improving Homeland Resilience

In the aftermath of the terrorist attacks of September 11, President Bush declared a two-front war to confront the threats and vulnerabilities highlighted by the tragic events of that day. One front involved taking the battle to the terrorists and those states that supported or provided them with safe havens. The other front was at home with the establishment of the Department of Homeland Security and U.S. Northern Command. But these fronts did not receive equal attention. Iraq and Afghanistan became the frontline in the global war on terror and have consumed an overwhelming amount of time and resources. For example, the direct costs of the two wars have averaged $300 million per day for 5 years. By contrast, Federal grants since September 11, 2001, to improve security at the sprawling port complexes in New York and New Jersey—which include refineries, chemical plants, and the largest container terminals on the East

Coast—have totaled just $100 million, or the equivalent of what taxpayers have spent every 8 hours to support military operations in Iraq and Afghanistan.

This asymmetry in effort between offensive measures abroad and defensive measures at home suggests the national security community is still attempting to come to grips with three realities highlighted by the al Qaeda attacks on New York and Washington. First, the battleground of choice for current and future U.S. adversaries will more likely be in the civil and economic space than the conventional military domain. Direct engagement with the Armed Forces promises a losing proposition for those who feel compelled to confront U.S. power. However, myriad vulnerabilities, particularly critical infrastructure, translate into alluring targets where a relatively modest investment by terrorists is likely to yield costly societal and economic damage.

The second reality is that international borders are not a barrier to a committed enemy intent on infiltrating and carrying out an attack in the United States. Watch lists and visa restrictions can deter or intercept known terrorists, but they will not stop terrorists without records from entering by crossing the vast land and maritime borders of America. Furthermore, al Qaeda does not need to import weapons of mass destruction. On September 11, 2001, the terrorists converted fully fueled planes into missiles. The third reality is that the only way to safeguard the civil and economic space is by enlisting the participants who occupy it in the effort. Chances are that first preventers and first responders will be ordinary citizens. The only aircraft that did not reach its intended target was United Airlines Flight 93. The terrorists were foiled not by a national security response, but by passengers charging the cockpit. Despite the fact that Washington was defended by the actions of citizens aboard that plane, the Federal Government has not emphasized the importance of mobilizing Americans and the private sector in general to reduce exposure to acts of terrorism. Instead, the focus has been on improving the capacity to detect and intercept terrorists.

The Department of Homeland Security was established in 2003 to improve the coordination of both border and transportation security, and was the largest reorganization since the National Security Act of 1947. The department has three directorates (national protection and programs, science and technology, and management), five offices (policy, health affairs, intelligence and analysis, domestic nuclear detection, and operations coordination), and seven independent agencies (the Transportation Security Administration, Customs and Border Protection, Citizenship and Immigration Services, Immigration and Customs Enforcement, Coast Guard, Federal Emergency Management Agency, and the Secret Service). Its formation involved the merging of functions and operations that were previously performed by 22 distinct agencies. The Bush administration also established the Homeland Security Council within the Executive Office of the President with responsibility for interagency coordination in support of the homeland security mission.

After 5 years, the Department of Homeland Security is struggling to gain its footing. The challenge is compounded by several organizational problems that should be addressed:

■ It has little institutional memory because of the reliance on political appointees and government contractors and the high rates of personnel turnover in its first few years of operation.

■ It has inadequate skilled headquarters-level staffing to improve coordination across components.

■ The major procurement programs have been plagued by technical problems, cost overruns, and missed deadlines that require immediate managerial attention.

■ Its mission requires active participation by other Federal departments that only have collaborated when there has been strong oversight and coordination by the White House.

■ State and local officials and private sector leaders are disenchanted with DHS's penchant for formulating top-down policies without access to requisite expertise and without providing adequate opportunities for input.

■ Congressional oversight is fragmented, intrusive, and disruptive, with a total of 88 committees and subcommittees claiming some jurisdiction over the department or its component agencies.

While addressing these issues will require considerable investments in time and energy, they are only a subset of a critical imperative: to build a more resilient society with the goal of depriving enemies of the mass economic disruptions and fear dividend that they seek to inflict. Militarily, the American infrastructure is too large for terrorists to achieve destruction on a national scale. But an enemy can target vulnerabilities to generate anxiety that will spur Americans to overreact in costly and destructive ways. For instance, in the wake of the attacks on September 11, Federal authorities closed U.S. airspace to foreign and domestic flights, halted the movement of ships entering major seaports, and slowed down traffic across the land borders with Canada and Mexico. These draconian reactions to the commandeering of four airliners by 19 men wielding box-cutters accomplished what no enemy of the United States could have aspired to accomplish by conventional military means: a virtual blockade of American trade and commerce.

Colombians gather at meeting house built as part of a USAID project in Villa Garzon

Promising to win the war on terror is good rhetoric, but the prospects for victory are no more likely than an effort to eliminate the flu virus; there will always be a new strain with each season. As such, it is important to scale back public expectations to containing terrorism when possible and mitigating its consequences when protective measures fail. The counterterrorism prophylactic is building local, regional, and national resilience that arms Americans with greater confidence to prepare for and recover from terrorist attacks and other disasters. Confidence in their resilience would cap their fear and in turn undermine any hope by an enemy that incurring the costs and risks of targeting the U.S. homeland will achieve any meaningful results. In short, there is strength in being able not only to deliver a punch, but to take a punch.

The United States must strive to develop the kind of resilience that Britain displayed during World War II as V–1 flying bombs fell on London. Each night, Londoners headed to the shelters. When the all-clear signal sounded, they put out the fires, rescued wounded from the rubble, and went on about their lives until air raid warnings were sounded again. More than a half-century later, Londoners showed similar resilience when suicide bombers attacked the Underground. The objective of the terrorists may have been to cripple public transportation, but it was foiled by resolute commuters appearing the next morning to board the trains.

Building resilience requires a sustained commitment to four factors. The first is robustness: the ability to keep operating in the face of disaster. In some instances it translates into designing systems or structures, such as buildings and bridges that can withstand hazards. In others, such as energy, transportation, and communications networks, robustness means devising redundant or substitutable systems that can be brought to bear in breakdowns and work stoppages. Robustness also entails investing in and maintaining elements of critical infrastructure, such as dams and levees, so they withstand low-probability but high-consequence eventualities.

The second factor is resourcefulness in managing crises by identifying options, prioritizing means to control and mitigate damage, and communicating those decisions to the responders. Resourcefulness depends primarily on people, not technology. Ensuring that American society is resourceful demands both good contingency plans and well-equipped and trained National Guard units, public health officials, firefighters, police officers, hospital staffs, and emergency planners and responders. It also necessitates close coordination and integration with organizations such as the American Red Cross, the Salvation Army, and increasingly the private sector, to provide personnel, resources, and logistics to deal with the aftermath of catastrophic events.

The third factor is rapidly recovering, or getting things back to normal as quickly as possible after a disaster. If something critical turns out to be either too vulnerable or fragile to withstand an attack or crisis, it should be restored immediately. Competent emergency operations and the ability to deploy the right people and resources to the right place at the right time are crucial.

Finally, resilience means being willing and able to absorb new lessons that can be drawn from catastrophes. Based on experience, public officials, private sector leaders, and individuals must be willing to accept and fund pragmatic changes that improve capabilities before the next crisis. Resilience is based on a traditional American strength: pulling together when disasters strike and volunteering when called on to defend the Nation. Ironically, one barrier to building a resilient homeland in the 21ˢᵗ century is the durability of the concept of national security that served well throughout the Cold War. The U.S.-Soviet struggle with the risk of thermonuclear war required a national security community that was exclusive. Countering espionage necessitated routinely vetting government personnel and sharing information only on a need-to-know basis. However, the resilience imperative requires just the opposite approach. When it comes to the participation of civil society and private sector, the byword of resilience becomes the need-to-have.

The Nation will need to do more than attend to organizational challenges that have hampered the Department of Homeland Security. Of paramount importance is defining both the homeland security and the homeland defense missions to embrace resilience and the necessary investments in outreach and community preparedness. In addition, the private sector that owns and operates much of the critical infrastructure must be given incentives to put in place protective, response, and recovery methods. Resilience is probably the best way to neutralize the chaos and fear that terrorists strive to create. In the age of global terror, it turns out that the best defense might well be a good defense, resting on a solid foundation of societal and infrastructure resilience. **gsa**

NOTES

¹ Some of the material developed for this section was previously published by the Project on National Security Reform, "Forging a New Shield," November 2008.

² *Interagency coordination* is the expression usually used to depict government unity of effort, but many complain that it insufficiently connotes the need to actively integrate efforts as opposed to merely sharing information in an attempt to avoid working at cross purposes. *Interagency collaboration* is used in this chapter to suggest a higher level of integration in which agencies and departments actively and effectively work together in an integrated effort to accomplish common goals.

³ For an overview of such reform studies, see Catherine Dale, Nina M. Serafino, and Pat Towell, "Organizing the U.S. Government for National Security: Overview of the Interagency Reform Debates," RL34455 (Washington, DC: Congressional Research Service, April 18, 2008).

Contributors

Dr. Christopher J. Lamb (Chapter Editor) is a Senior Research Fellow in the Institute for National Strategic Studies (INSS) at National Defense University (NDU). He conducts research on national security strategy and policy, as well as U.S. defense strategy, requirements, plans and programs, and strategic military concepts. His research focuses on global military presence and capabilities-based planning.

Dennis Cutler Blair is Director of National Intelligence (DNI) and a retired U.S. Navy four-star admiral. He was confirmed by the U.S. Senate to serve in the administration of Barack Obama as DNI on January 28, 2009. He was Commander, U.S. Pacific Command. Previously, he was Director of the Joint Staff in the Office of the Chairman of Joint Chiefs of Staff, and served in budget and policy positions on several major Navy staffs and the National Security Council staff. He was also the first Associate Director of Central Intelligence for Military Support.

Stephen E. Flynn is Ira A. Lipman Senior Fellow for Counterterrorism and National Security Studies at the Council on Foreign Relations. Former adviser on homeland security for the U.S. Commission on National Security (Hart-Rudman Commission) and a retired Coast Guard officer, Mr. Flynn is author of *The Edge of Disaster: Rebuilding a Resilient Nation* (Random House, 2007) and *America the Vulnerable: How Our Government Is Failing to Protect Us from Terrorism* (HarperCollins, 2004).

Thomas P. Glakas is an analyst at the National Intelligence Council. Previously he served as a program manager for analytical development for the Central Intelligence Agency, and as a senior intelligence officer for the Defense Intelligence Agency.

Marc Grossman is a retired American Ambassador to Turkey. In 2005, he completed 29 years of public service when he retired from the Department of State as the Under Secretary of State for Political Affairs. Mr. Grossman served as the State Department's third-ranking official, supporting U.S. diplomacy worldwide. He previously served as the Director General of the Foreign Service and Director of Human Resources.

L. Erik Kjonnerod is Director of the Center for Applied Strategic Learning in INSS at NDU. Mr. Kjonnerod is a specialist in politico-military policy exercises and crisis decisionmaking simulations.

Dr. Mark M. Lowenthal is President and CEO of the Intelligence & Security Academy, LLC. He is the former Assistant Director of Central Intelligence for Analysis and Production and former Vice Chairman for Evaluation on the National Intelligence Council. Dr. Lowenthal is a prolific author, having published 5 books and over 90 articles or studies on intelligence and national security. He received his BA from Brooklyn College and his Ph.D. in history from Harvard University. He is an Adjunct Professor in the School of International and Public Affairs at Columbia University.

General Richard B. Myers, USAF (Ret.), served as 15th Chairman of the Joint Chiefs of Staff from 2001 to 2005. In this capacity, he served as the principal military advisor to the President, Secretary of Defense, and National Security Council. He previously served as Vice Chairman of the Joint Chiefs of Staff where he was the Chairman of the Joint Requirements Oversight Council, Vice Chairman of the Defense Acquisition Board, and a member of the National Security Council Deputies Committee and the Nuclear Weapons Council. General Myers is currently the National Defense University (NDU) Colin Powell Chair of Leadership, Ethics, and Character.

Dr. Albert C. Pierce is Director of the Institute for National Security Ethics and Leadership at NDU.

Dr. Tammy S. Schultz is a Fellow at the Center for a New American Security (CNAS). Prior to joining CNAS, she served as a Research Fellow and Director of Research and Policy (Acting) at the U.S. Army's Peacekeeping and Stability Operations Institute. Dr. Schultz also conducts simulations at the Department of State for Foreign Service Officers and is an Adjunct Professor at Georgetown University.

Admiral James G. Stavridis, USN, is North Atlantic Treaty Organization Supreme Allied Commander, U.S. European Command. He previously was Commander, U.S. Southern Command. Admiral Stavridis commanded the USS *Enterprise* Carrier Strike Group, conducting combat operations in the Persian Gulf in support of both Operation *Iraqi Freedom* and Operation *Enduring Freedom*. He has served as a strategic and long-range planner on the staffs of the Chief of Naval Operations and Chairman of the Joint Chiefs of Staff. He has also served as the executive assistant to the Secretary of the Navy and the senior military assistant to the Secretary of Defense.

Chapter 19

Cooperation with Allies and Coalition Partners

One of the most remarkable achievements in diplomatic history was the creation of the network of multilateral, regional, and bilateral institutions and alliances that built, preserved, and solidified peace, prosperity, and stability for the United States and its partners following World War II. Arising out of a shared conviction that only cooperative action could defeat the totalitarian threats posed first by Nazism and later by communism, such bodies as the United Nations (UN), the Bretton Woods financial institutions, the North Atlantic Treaty Organization (NATO), and the European Coal and Steel Community not only endured and evolved, but also spawned similar organizations around the globe and, moreover, shaped the way that much of the world instinctively views international relations.

As power shifts and a complex array of threats and opportunities emerges, the question arises as to the future shape of successful multinational and alliance cooperation. Clearly, the security challenges posed by a globalized world—in which the most serious threats are often not from rival states but from radical organizations and transnational criminal gangs, or arise from impersonal, inchoate trends such as global warming and new, evolving forms of pandemic disease—are very different from those of the era of bipolar superpower confrontation. Ever since the fall of the Berlin Wall and the collapse of the Soviet Union 2 years later, NATO has been grappling to define a new relevance for itself. The end of the Cold War combined with the emergence of North Korea as a nuclear weapons state has also led to changes in

United Nations Headquarters

the shape of U.S. alliances in East Asia. Meanwhile, the Middle East—arguably the most dangerous of the world's regions given that it is the convergence point of many pressing transnational threats and the locus of active conflict involving American forces—remains without any formal alliance structure around which to organize U.S. involvement.

Cooperation with other countries in the 21ˢᵗ century will inevitably take a variety of forms, from multilateralism at the global level down to local, ad hoc cooperation with selected coalition partners that will develop as situations demand. The global economic and financial crisis has accentuated the importance of emerging powers, underscoring the opportunity for new multilateral cooperation even while possibly adding national pressures on existing institutions and alliances. This chapter examines a spectrum of this rich set of possibilities for security cooperation.

Multilateralism

Multilateralism is becoming ever more important in organizing international cooperation on the shared problems facing the world in the 21ˢᵗ century. Yet its misuse over the years has eroded confidence in international organizations. The United States has a strong interest in revitalizing multilateral institutions, but if the Obama administration is going to increase U.S. effectiveness in this important aspect of foreign affairs, it will need to strengthen international law, improve interagency planning, and make significant investments in personnel.

A Globalizing Strategic Environment

After a century of championing international organizations from the Pan American Union to the United Nations, many Americans, who perhaps look for results rather than processes and relationships, have become increasingly skeptical about multilateralism. Former Secretary of State Henry Kissinger put it succinctly in his 1994 book *Diplomacy*: "The United Nations did provide a convenient meeting place for diplomats and a useful forum for the exchange of ideas. It also performed important technical functions. But it failed to fulfill the underlying premise of collective security—the prevention of war and collective resistance to aggression."

U.S. leaders responded to the failures of the United Nations by avoiding it when they needed to deal with critical issues. To some extent, they focused on regional organizations and military alliances such as NATO. But primarily, U.S. leaders relied on bilateral arrangements supplemented as needed by unilateral

measures. Even in trade matters, for instance, where the United States has long used multilateral mechanisms to advance its interests—first the General Agreement on Tariffs and Trade and now the World Trade Organization—the trend has been to pursue regional and bilateral agreements.

As confidence in global multilateralism has declined, regional and subregional organizations have taken on new life, often explicitly building on the advantages of neighborhood. Smaller groupings dealing with narrower agendas are more capable of achieving quick consensus. Furthermore, when disagreements hamper action, it is easy to devolve to even smaller coalitions whose members can agree among themselves to take action.

Under the impact of globalization, however, most problems that affect the security and welfare of the American people no longer respond to unilateral solutions or even to the efforts of narrow ad hoc coalitions. Such coalitions may be preferable to the anarchy of unilateralism, but they lack the broad legitimacy of decisions reached multilaterally within a structured organization, the kind of legitimacy that is necessary to deal effectively with many of the issues that require cooperation beyond U.S. borders: natural disasters, terrorism, arms smuggling, trade, energy, drug trafficking, financial flows, migration, democracy and human rights, development, fragile states, and rising powers. These issues vary widely in their nature. In each case, their management starts at home unilaterally but must become multilateral to succeed.

Why Multilateralism?

Despite its cumbersome nature, multilateralism provides certain advantages that do not accrue through unilateralism or less inclusive forms of international cooperation. Most notably, it creates frameworks for long-term cooperation based on shared principles and precedents that go beyond the bilateral. True multilateralism is more than the temporary agreement of three or more countries on a specific problem; it is, as political scientist Patrick Morgan has defined it, cooperation based on "generalized principles of conduct, rather than . . . considerations linked to specific situations or particular conditions and concerns."[1] When such broad agreement on generalized principles of conduct is turned into a treaty ratified by individual countries, the resulting framework becomes the basis of international law. Today, the UN Charter and the World Court are the cornerstones of global order based on law. Multilateral action under the umbrella of such organizations thus enjoys a special legitimacy in the eyes of many.

Multilateral institutions also have strong potential as means of mass persuasion. The United Nations has been called the "parliament of man" for its presumed ability to embody world public opinion. As Teddy Roosevelt said of the American Presidency, multilateral institutions can serve as "bully pulpits," or as Argentine President Carlos Menem put it in speaking of the Organization of American States (OAS), as *cajas de resonancia*—"sounding boxes." Even if agreement in these forums is not reached, when heads of state and other leaders address key issues in multilateral forums, people listen.

Multilateral forums also play a useful role as consensus-building deliberative mechanisms. The views of the strong and the weak alike can be aired, with the latter often more willing to accede to the needs of the former if they are certain their concerns have been heard. Debates can identify areas of convergence among countries with otherwise different interests. As frustrating as they sometimes are, the delays on action imposed by these debates can also gain time for more carefully considered responses, including ones that are eventually carried out below the multilateral level. Even providing cover for governments to defer problems that cannot be immediately resolved can be useful in international interactions.

Multilateral diplomacy can also lend durability to international agreements, especially in the area of dispute resolution, in ways difficult to achieve on a purely bilateral basis. The multilateral process tends to ensure that the interests of the various parties, whether conflicting or convergent, are identified and reflected in the agreement, thus increasing the likelihood of compliance. Moreover, this process, along with the moral stature generally attributed to multilateral institutions, enhances mutual confidence that all parties will abide by the agreement. It was to capture this sense of moral ratification that the Panama Canal treaties were signed at an OAS meeting in the presence of the hemisphere's heads of state and government; all concerned believed this would discourage cheating on the treaties' provisions.

State-building and economic assistance programs are often both more palatable and more effective when carried out on a multilateral basis. The fragile states most in need of such assistance are also highly vulnerable to charges that bilateral donors exert excessive influence on internal policymaking, further reducing their perceived legitimacy. They can thus benefit from the kind of long-term institutional

support that can be provided impartially through international organizations.

The same applies even to less inherently intrusive forms of assistance. For example, intrinsic tensions in the U.S.-Mexican *Plan Mérida*, an initiative aimed at enhancing cooperation against drug trafficking and other criminal activity, arise out of differing perceptions of whether the nature of the program is assistance or cooperation. Pursuing a similar initiative that would mix assistance and commitments to cooperation in a multilateral rather than bilateral framework might have permitted the participants to finesse or even harmonize such conflicting points of view.

Royal Marine Commandos patrol in Helmand Province, Afghanistan during operation to stabilize and increase security

International organizations have long helped to establish common standards that make possible everything from the mails and trade to the safe operation of flights across borders. The International Telecommunication Union, World Intellectual Property Organization, World Health Organization, and World Bank are all multilateral entities whose neutrality and impartiality enable them to share information and manage technical matters in ways considered relatively free of national biases. Cooperation delivered through international bodies is often better accepted and more effective than assistance through bilateral aid agencies.

On occasion, multilateral institutions are even capable of action to meet threats to the peace. Iraq's August 2, 1990, invasion of Kuwait provided a rare instance. The UN Security Council condemned Iraq's action the very same day as "a breach of international peace and security," and demanded the withdrawal of Iraqi troops. On November 29, 1990, the council authorized the use of "all necessary means to uphold and implement" the previous resolution. Collective security worked quickly and effectively in this case because Iraq had violated a general principle of conduct so vital that no responsible sovereign state could ignore its breach.

The Limits of Multilateralism

In the Kuwait case, as in Korea before that, multilateral authorization provided increased legitimacy at home as well as abroad for U.S.-led military action and facilitated the important contributions made by other countries. The resolutions enabled easier access to the battlefield and better intelligence. This, of course, has not always been the case. Decisive action has sometimes been obstructed by delays or approved only at the cost of giving others influence over U.S. military operations and complicating their implementation. Throughout most of the Cold War, the United Nations was paralyzed by the superpower rivalry. More recently, it has been reduced to peacekeeping missions so weak and numerous that the optimism once associated with the presence of Blue Helmets has been dissipated.

Despite the special moral status that popular opinion in most countries grants to multilateral action, states often give only lip service to the ideal of multilateralism when it comes to practical action. Big countries often worry that working to get broad agreement will delay and interfere with what they believe must be done. Working multilaterally is inconvenient and bureaucratic. The same public opinion that values multilateral consensus tends to dismiss the debates necessary to build that consensus as utopian-chasing talk shops rather than real problem-solving forums.

The numerical prevalence of smaller countries in multilateral forums opens the door to claims that multilateralism is nothing more than the trade unionism of the weak and otherwise irrelevant. The United Nations, when not being characterized as inefficient, corrupt, and anti-American, is particularly vulnerable to this charge. As Eric Shawn put it, the United Nations "opposes and criticizes the U.S. at every opportunity." Roger Cohen of *The New York Times* said much the same thing: "Too often the UN can be no more than the weak lowest common denominator of our collective will, an umbrella that packs up when the storm rises."[2]

Criticism of the United Nations for being too weak on the one hand and for being too strong and overbearing on the other stems from the error of thinking

Session of the Organization of American States Inter-American Commission on Human Rights

of it and similar organizations as having an existence independent of their member states. It is true that multilateral organizations can sometimes articulate common principles in ways that make them the voice of an international community larger than those of its individual member states. But operationally, the UN or the OAS can reflect only what its members are actually willing to do. Sovereign states are still the key units of world politics and thus retain the right to say no. The sovereignty that ensures consideration of the rights and interests of all countries is the same sovereignty that ultimately permits states to opt out or, in the case of the five permanent members of the Security Council, to block action by others. Thus, the suggestion that the solution to the UN's weaknesses lies in giving it the capacity to act independently of its members—such as by acquiring its own independent intelligence-gathering capability—is both unrealistic and inconsistent with the real nature of multilateralism. In that sense, the deficiencies manifested by the United Nations may reflect a need to revise its members' policies more than a need to reform the institution itself.

Making Multilateralism Work

Despite multilateralism's admitted shortcomings, it is increasingly obvious that more and more problems have dimensions that can only be addressed effectively through multilateral diplomacy. Most countries, however, still do not habitually think much, if at all, beyond the bilateral. The United States is among the most culpable in this regard. For much of the recent past, U.S. opinion leaders assumed that they knew what needed to be done and how to do it better than anyone else. That assumption no longer holds true, if it ever did. More than ever before, we must understand and respect the perspectives and interests of those with whom we must cooperate; going it alone cannot suffice for the common effort made possible through multilateral cooperation.

Rule of Law. To some degree, the ineffectiveness of multilateral institutions is the self-fulfilling result of the prevalent U.S. belief that multilateral institutions are inherently ineffective. As the most powerful country in the world, U.S. support for international institutions is essential for them to function effectively, and particularly for them to restrain through international legal norms the behaviors that are most destructive of the peace and stability necessary for the fulfillment of U.S. objectives. Unfortunately, for more than a decade, the United States has shunned or opposed key international agreements, including

the Kyoto Protocol, Ottawa Treaty, Comprehensive Test Ban Treaty, and Law of the Sea Convention. Supreme Court Justice Sandra Day O'Connor commented insightfully that "the decision not to sign on to legal frameworks the rest of the world supports is central to the decline in American influence in the world." Ironically, this lack of U.S. support for international legal agreements not only weakens the capacity of international organizations, but also, by undermining the perceived moral legitimacy of American actions, has the effect of limiting American operational flexibility in interactions with other countries, even in a bilateral setting.

To help restore its credibility, the United States is working to close the Guantanamo Bay prison by the end of 2009, but it could also consider ending sanctions against countries that join the International Criminal Court and ratifying the American Convention on Human Rights and the Inter-American Convention against the Illicit Manufacturing of and Trafficking in Firearms, Ammunition, Explosives, and Other Related Materials. It has already signed both; the Senate should ratify them, with reservations if necessary, because the impact of unimplemented resolutions and unenforced laws is not neutral, but actually negative. Even so, multilateral agreements are not self-enforcing; their implementation depends on the actions of sovereign states. Harmonization of national practices with international law takes time, not merely because of different legal systems and traditions, but because national needs and sovereignty concerns must be satisfied.

Institutional Capacity for Multilateralism. Multilateral approaches are often shunned because the United States believes it lacks the people with the training and expertise to make them work. It is not alone in this concern. But for multilateral solutions to work, sufficient human capital must be invested in them, not only at the high political level of plenary meetings but also, more importantly, at the operational level. Activities involving several countries are inherently complex. They function best when relationships are maintained across countries by a network of professionals who know how to work together. Such networks are the lifeblood of international secretariats: they can both provide early warning of and move to contain issues that might otherwise escalate into problems. In effect, these professional networks serve as valuable insurance policies for progress and peace.

Many studies that have examined interagency processes in the United States have identified a need for an interagency cadre of national security professionals with experience in intelligence, diplomacy, and defense. We need to go beyond that. Every U.S. department and agency should have a corps of public servants who spend part of their careers working in the UN, the OAS, or other international organizations. Stealing a page from the 1986 Goldwater-Nichols Department of Defense Reorganization Act, which requires military officers to have experience and training in joint operations as a prerequisite for promotion to flag rank, a tour working as an international public servant should be a requirement for promotion to the Senior Executive Service or the Senior Foreign Service. Not only would U.S. agencies then be staffed by individuals with international experience, but the international organizations themselves also would be strengthened by the presence of U.S. personnel.

Common standards and training for experts in drug control, terrorism, transnational crime, human rights, civil emergencies, and the mitigation of natural disasters should be greatly increased. All countries should reserve places in their diplomatic and military academies and other advanced schools of public service for counterparts from neighboring countries. In the Western Hemisphere, multilateral training could be increased by creating a new Inter-American Academy of Public Administration, with students nominated by member states. Such international professional training should not be considered foreign aid, but rather a necessary measure to build the technical capacity for effective diplomacy that yields practical, sustainable results across national borders to the benefit of all concerned.

A New Model of Multilateral Security Cooperation. Today's increasingly multipolar world has shifted the focus away from formal alliances based on automatic collective security guarantees toward cooperation in response to specific crises. The multilateral response to the 1995 conflict between Ecuador and Peru may provide a useful model for future cases. To prevent the escalation of fighting, four countries—Argentina, Brazil, Chile, and the United States—acting together as guarantors of an earlier peace treaty, each contributed soldiers to a military observer mission for which the two belligerents shared the costs. The guarantors not only ensured the preservation of the ceasefire, but also shared intelligence, listened to each party's views, and eventually, after 3 years, succeeded against most expectations in hammering out a solution all could support. Close adherence to local, regional, and international laws, respect for

military discipline, and intimate diplomatic-military coordination were the keys to success.

Participation: The Key to Maximizing Power and Stability

The Obama administration must make an urgent start on rebuilding multilateral capacity if the United States is to expand its options for dealing effectively with the era of globalization. The world needs a "diplomatic surge" to revalidate legal frameworks, and a "consultation surge" to forge standards and relationships that will enable the United States to calibrate the application of its power with and toward others. Effectiveness will require participation: without U.S. political participation in the building of consensus and the implementation of decisions, multilateralism cannot live up to its potential.

Enhancing Cooperation among the Atlantic Allies

The post–Cold War transatlantic goal of integrating a Europe that is "whole and free" has been largely accomplished, though with serious ongoing challenges in the Balkans and former Soviet states. Indeed, aggressive Russian behavior in Georgia in summer 2008 elevated NATO concerns about the need to bolster its core function of collective defense. Nevertheless, operating in multinational military coalitions with allies and partners, as in the Balkans and Afghanistan, remains an American security priority. A central challenge is whether NATO will take the lead in organizing these coalitions, or will be limited to laying the political and planning foundations for "coalitions of the willing." Evolving concepts of how coalition operations should look will present both a challenge and an opportunity for President Obama as he seeks to enhance alliance relationships.

The Bosnia, Kosovo, and Afghanistan Experiences

While the militaries of NATO's 28 members remain under national control, the Alliance's integrated military command has provided doctrine and planning for collective military operations for nearly 60 years. During the Cold War, operational guidance concentrated on territorial defense; since 1991, operations have focused on force projection in the Balkans and Afghanistan. While member states make operational decisions via consultation and consensus that reflect shared transatlantic interests, the expansion of NATO's political objectives, membership, and operational mandates has made agreement on the conduct of coalition operations more difficult. NATO can, nonetheless, make multilateral coalitions more effective through an integrated command structure, joint training and exercising, shared intelligence and communications, enabling capabilities, and a culture of common military experience and defense planning.

NATO has transformed its command structure in conjunction with the U.S. realignment of its own troops deployed in Europe to provide a foundation from which to project power beyond the Alliance's area of responsibility. NATO members have built new forces, including a 25,000-member Response Force, and have developed nascent operational ties between NATO and the European Union (EU). The Alliance now emphasizes rapid deployment, sustainability, and jointness in multinational operations that may include any combination of land, maritime, and air assets. Its ability to engage in coalition operations has been forged and tested in Bosnia-Herzegovina, Kosovo, and Afghanistan.

Bosnia-Herzegovina and Peace Enforcement. From 1991 to 1995, NATO could not achieve consensus over how to confront ethnic cleansing in Bosnia-Herzegovina. Allied diplomacy had mostly contained the civil fighting, but NATO procedures blocked intervention. In 1995, NATO finally agreed to airstrikes against Serb forces that were attacking the UN-proclaimed civilian safe havens. This use of airpower, combined with a Croat-Muslim ground offensive, led to a balance of power on the ground and paved the way for American diplomatic initiatives to facilitate a peace agreement. NATO then intervened as a peace enforcer with 60,000 troops, half of which were American. NATO had planned for peace implementation since 1993, a process that included engaging staff officers from Central and Eastern Europe partner countries in command post exercises. This allowed 10,000 troops from non-NATO countries to participate under NATO command—including 2,000 from Russia, with a Russian general posted in the NATO operational planning cell at Supreme Headquarters Allied Powers Europe in Belgium.

The Bosnia mission was successful for several reasons. First, American leadership helped forge a consensus within NATO and included other regional powers acting with a UN mandate. Second, substantial numbers of NATO troops were available for rapid deployment to enforce peace. Third, NATO forces were supported by other international institutions, including the Organisation for Security and Co-operation in Europe, European Union, and World Bank, whose participation allowed the military to focus on primary missions.

Kosovo and Warfighting. In 1998–1999, the United States and NATO used military threats to dissuade Serb forces in Yugoslavia from continuing ethnic cleansing inside Kosovo (then part of Serbia, with a 90 percent majority ethnic Albanian population). NATO agreed through the fall of 1998 to action orders for airstrikes, but these were not implemented. When diplomacy failed to achieve objectives, NATO agreed in March 1999 to launch coalition operations against Yugoslavia. This campaign had six key characteristics. First, it emphasized airpower with no ground element available to combat Serb forces or help with air targeting. Second, senior decisionmakers assumed airpower would produce diplomatic concessions, and thus approved only 3 days of initial bombing. Instead, when bombing commenced, the Serbian army forced most of the Albanian population into fragile neighboring countries. Third, a lack of consensus among the allies limited target selection

UN Security Council votes on resolution condemning aggressive acts by Iraq against Kuwait, September 1990

and how low planes could fly, thus increasing civilian casualties. Fourth, advanced American military technology could not be easily integrated into coalition air operations. For example, to ensure sole control over its assets and prevent operational leaks, the United States did not inform allies in advance about sorties that involved the use of F–117s, B–2s, or cruise missiles. Fifth, NATO's decisionmaking procedures, which some critics called "war by committee," had a negative impact on joint force activation, staff composition, facilities, command and control, logistics, and execution. This lack of decisiveness led to what amounted to "incremental war," while concerns over collateral damage created havens for the enemy. Key decisions were eventually taken outside of NATO by the United States, United Kingdom, France, and Germany, who began to signal preparations for a ground invasion by the United States and the United Kingdom. Finally, the European Union and, most significantly, Russia put diplomatic and economic pressure on Serb leaders to cease attacks on the ethnic Albanian population. Three months after the war began, Serbia capitulated. The Kosovo issue was not "settled," however, until 2008, when the province declared its independence from Serbia; nevertheless, over 15,000 NATO troops remained as peacekeepers, and serious problems regarding the persecution of Serb minorities in Kosovo persist.

Afghanistan and Counterinsurgency. In 2005, NATO assumed command of coalition operations in Afghanistan. In stable areas, European allies contributed to reconstruction and peace support operations, while American-led combat and counterterrorist forces operated as a limited coalition of the willing. These two separate mandates violated a core component of counterinsurgency doctrine: unity of command. The overall operation was further weakened by insufficient NATO force generation; the national caveats placed on many troop deployments, which hindered force generation; and limited command flexibility and situational awareness. Even in peaceful areas, the different levels at which NATO members contributed to the Provincial Reconstruction Teams led to their uneven development and effectiveness. The lack of unity of command even meant that other international organizations and nongovernmental organizations found it difficult to conduct sustained efforts. Major elements that were fundamental to success were outside NATO's area of responsibility, including rebuilding the police force (for which in 2003 the United States initially only budgeted $5 million and Germany sent 50 trainers). Antidrug operations in Afghanistan and political-military trends in Pakistan were also outside NATO's mandate.

By 2007, Taliban forces and al Qaeda were staging sustained attacks against Allied forces in several parts of the country, wearing down public support in Europe and Canada for continued operations. Training the Afghan army represented the best exit strategy, yet by fall 2008, the Afghan army remained poorly trained, rife with desertion, and lacking much of the heavy equipment needed to conduct operations. NATO needed to increase its Mentoring and Liaison Teams from 25 to at least 100 to stay on pace with a goal of 70,000 trained troops—even before a

new target of doubling the Afghan National Army and other security forces was put forth as part of a renewed focus on building Afghan capacity. Training is complicated by Afghan soldiers' and policemen's lack of fluency in English and illiteracy in their own languages. But even trained Afghan troops are difficult to sustain in the field, either because of unclear missions or tribal and ethnic loyalties.[3]

The cases of Bosnia-Herzegovina, Kosovo, and Afghanistan illustrate important areas where NATO has been both essential to and a challenge for coalition military operations. The Bosnia-Herzegovina model of broad-based cooperation on peace operations worked best, while Kosovo and Afghanistan exposed significant political and operational limitations to direct military intervention by NATO. These situations are unique but also instructive of elements for success and dilemmas to avoid when considering the further transformation of NATO for coalition operations.

Issues and Challenges for the United States

The Obama administration has an opportunity to reengage American multilateral leadership during this year marking NATO's 60th anniversary. At the same time that NATO Allies have been reluctant to apply lessons learned from past coalition military engagements as doctrine, the United States is sometimes charged with viewing NATO as a toolbox from which it chooses Allies selectively. Both of these tendencies reduce incentives for states to invest in the institutional foundations that make NATO effective, as well as undermining the principle of shared responsibility. Aligning missions with capabilities will be an essential step toward revitalizing transatlantic security cooperation.

The United States faces several strategic choices. First, Washington must decide whether it wants to cultivate a strong EU military capacity. The United States traditionally has viewed the EU defense and security capabilities as desirable as long as they do not duplicate those of NATO. These institutional architectures can be complementary and are increasingly viewed as such. The European Union provides unique economic and civilian resources, along with multilateral training and exercising for police forces. Meanwhile, the United States dominates force projection capabilities, including air- and sealift, and communications and intelligence infrastructure. How these institutional alignments will complement each other depends on another major strategic challenge, which is to achieve a common threat assessment as the basis for doctrine and planning. Although NATO now supports missile defense systems in Europe, and its members strongly agree about the need to counter weapons of mass destruction proliferation and terrorism, they still cannot settle on the best response.

Reconciling relations with Russia remains a significant challenge for the transatlantic alliance. New geostrategic stresses, especially involving energy and pipelines, are high priorities for the United States and Europe, but developing joint operational doctrine and capabilities remains difficult. NATO has been delegated the tasks of supporting peacekeeping in North Africa, dealing with piracy on the high seas, training Iraqi forces, and bringing peace to Afghanistan. Yet the Balkans, the Caucasus, and the Black Sea remain unstable areas in closer proximity to Europe. It is not clear how steps toward gradual NATO enlargement aimed at consolidating stability in Ukraine and Georgia can be taken without creating further tensions with Russia. Meanwhile, constructive engagement with Russia remains a priority, but has become far more difficult to implement in light of Moscow's decision to intervene militarily outside of its borders. The American bilateral Nunn-Lugar Cooperative Threat Reduction program might serve as a broader multilateral framework for armaments safety and proliferation controls in Eurasia, while arms control and disarmament are given renewed attention. In all these matters, a coherent and sustainable Russia policy is required.

NATO members are willing to undertake coalition missions, but they often have to do so without established doctrinal concepts or sufficient resources. Some initiatives have included command structure reform and the development of the NATO Response Force. The European Union is developing a similar force that could complement NATO missions. NATO also developed emergency response programs for catastrophic terrorism and natural disaster relief. Nonetheless, NATO members are divided about whether the main role of coalition engagement should be peace support or combat operations. In reality, complex security environments such as Afghanistan will likely involve both. Thus, the Obama administration might consider building a consensus for the development of NATO doctrine for coalition operations, including counterinsurgency.

Reaching agreement on operational doctrine within NATO at the multilateral level could prove difficult. Some NATO Allies might prefer the flexibility of ad hoc approaches. Some steps, however, could support a range of coalition operations. NATO could, for instance, develop a substantial facility to train, game,

and exercise coalition and indigenous forces for joint military and civilian operations; such a program could incorporate multinational police forces and nongovernmental organizations, engage the private sector, and develop technology and engineering capacities. Along with this, Brussels also needs to establish an ongoing, NATO-wide net assessment and lessons learned facility, and to expand its information-gathering and analytic capacity by, for example, providing integrated databases for geospatial mapping, shared intelligence and analysis, demographic research, anthropological and sociological cultural awareness, and public opinion survey data. NATO's transformation could include a multinational center to offer large-scale language training and cultural studies for Allied forces and to provide English language training for friendly indigenous forces in conflict zones. With these combined assets, NATO would be well positioned to build an integrated strategic communications capacity. Finally, NATO could develop an integrated capacity linked to coalition deployments for "training the trainers," to carry out sustained local army and police training in stability operations.

Enhancing the Foundations of American Power

Getting more out of NATO Allies and partners will require a renewed spirit of American and European security cooperation. Collective defense remains the core of NATO's purpose, and current missions must be given adequate resources for their successful completion. NATO members, however, would be well served to use the Alliance's 60th anniversary year to bring forward new initiatives and the necessary funding to support a coalition operations doctrine that emphasizes joint military-civilian planning, capabilities, and exercising for peace support, conventional military operations, and counterinsurgency. If NATO fails to adapt, the United States might reassess how it coordinates coalition operations or have to reemphasize crisis containment by exercising power from over the horizon, rather than with deployed forces inside ongoing conflict zones. The United States gains from working with its allies and partners, and the administration will have an immediate opportunity to renew the transatlantic relationship in NATO as a core component of global security.

East Asia and the Pacific: Transforming Alliances

For over half a century, the network of U.S. bilateral security alliances with Australia, Japan, the Philippines, Republic of Korea (ROK), and Thailand has served as the foundation of the region's stability and economic prosperity.

During the Cold War, the alliance structure stood as a vital link in the U.S. global containment strategy, but the Soviet Union's demise did not put an end to interstate tensions and rivalries in East Asia. In the decade that followed the collapse of the Soviet Union, the region experienced a series of challenges to regional stability and security—the 1993 standoff over North Korea's nuclear facilities, the 1996 Taiwan Straits missile crisis, the 1997–1998 Asian financial

Navy guard patrols corridor in Camp Delta section of Joint Detention Group facility, Guantanamo Bay

shock, and North Korea's Taepo Dong missile launch over Japan in 1998—that affected the security interests of the United States, its allies, and its friends.

Today, Cold War legacy issues in East Asia, China-Taiwan relations, and a nuclear-capable North Korea on a still-divided Korean Peninsula continue to pose challenges to longstanding U.S. security interests and commitments. Meanwhile, the terrorist attacks of

September 11, 2001, have reshaped the international security environment and accelerated the global transformation of the U.S. military and the U.S. alliance structure.

The 2001 and 2006 Quadrennial Defense Review (QDR) Reports focused on uncertainty as the defining feature of the international security environment, which was found to be "increasingly complex and unpredictable." Major war, asymmetric warfare, the proliferation of weapons of mass destruction, acts of international terrorism, and terrorists with access to weapons of mass destruction composed a broad and multifaceted set of security contingencies.

Both reports viewed East Asia as a region "susceptible to large-scale military competition." While not specifically mentioning China, the 2001 QDR focused on the requirements for dissuading and deterring a "military competitor with a formidable resource base" in the region. China, with a large and booming economy and an increasingly sophisticated diplomacy combined with notable military restraint, was altering the strategic landscape of the region.

Beyond the military dimension, China's reemergence as the leading power in the region poses a more fundamental and complex strategic challenge for East Asia, the United States, and U.S. allies. In this regard, a sound and strong alliance structure, together with a broad and deep engagement strategy aimed at encouraging Beijing to act as a "responsible stakeholder" in support of international order, plays an important role in managing any risk attendant on China's rise.

The 9/11 attacks ushered in the global transformation of the U.S. military. The 2001 QDR called for the development of joint forces that "must be lighter, more lethal and maneuverable . . . more readily deployable." The 2002 National Security Strategy, referring to operations in Afghanistan, made clear that the United States must be prepared for more and similar deployments and accordingly must develop "transformed maneuver and expeditionary forces." The Transformation Planning Guidance, issued in April 2003, made clear that the United States could not afford to have "large forces tied down for lengthy periods," and that transformed forces would "take action from a forward position and rapidly reinforce from other areas."

The post-9/11 requirements also ushered in the transformation of the Asian alliances. In addition to existing alliance commitments to the defense of Japan and the Republic of Korea, and a similar, but nontreaty, commitment to the security of Taiwan, U.S. forces now would also be tasked with operations relating to global counterterrorism. At the same time, transformation required the allies to do more in their own defense and in support of international order.

Although the process of alliance transformation has focused on the two key Northeast Asian countries, the Republic of Korea and Japan, where the U.S. military presence was concentrated during the Cold War, the United States has also undertaken capacity-building with Thailand and the Philippines to enhance their abilities to deal with internal threats posed by Islamic militants and separatist movements. In 2003, the government of then–Prime Minister John Howard invoked Article V of the Australia–New Zealand–United States security pact (known as ANZUS) to deploy Australian forces to Afghanistan and Iraq in support of the United States.

Transforming the U.S.–ROK Alliance

The East Asia Strategy Initiative. Alliances, as instruments of national policy, are dynamic elements in a constant process of evolution: adjusting roles, missions, and capabilities to adapt to an ever-changing international environment. At times, changes in the international environment are transforming events, requiring a restructuring of alliance relationships.

The East Asia Strategy Initiative (EASI) of 1990 and 1991 was aimed at gradually reducing the U.S. force presence in the Asia-Pacific region and restructuring alliance relationships at the end of the Cold War. On the Korean Peninsula, EASI aimed to manage a three-stage reduction in U.S. forces over a 10-year period, starting with a Phase I reduction of 7,000 personnel. The overall objective was to move U.S. forces from a leading to a supporting role in the defense of the ROK; in this process, the United States would be prepared to consider necessary changes in command relationships. EASI also supported the relocation of U.S. military forces out of downtown Seoul.

EASI, however, did not survive the first North Korean nuclear crisis in the early 1990s. In November 1991, Secretary of Defense Dick Cheney postponed the implementation of Phase II.

Transforming the Alliance Post-9/11. The 9/11 attacks led U.S. leaders to conclude that the heavy American forces stationed along the demilitarized zone (DMZ) between North and South Korea would have to be transformed to meet new challenges in the global security environment. In addition to the Cold War mission of deterring North Korea, U.S. forces were now required to be able to deploy from the peninsula for missions elsewhere.

Meanwhile, with the 2002 election of South Korean President Roh Mo-hyun, whose political agenda aimed to address inequalities in the alliance relationship, and in light of an increasingly capable ROK military, the process of transformation furthered the longstanding U.S. objective of moving from a leading to a supporting role in the defense of the ROK, and shifting the alliance toward a more equal partnership.

The two objectives were realized through a bilateral negotiating structure, the Future of the Alliance (FOTA) initiative, which was followed by the Security Policy Initiative (SPI).

Collectively, the two initiatives resulted in:

■ The relocation of U.S. forces from forward positions at the DMZ to two hubs south of the Han River, Osan-Pyongtaek and Taegu-Pusan. Redeploying south of Seoul rather than being tied down at the DMZ complicates Pyongyang's planning and enhances U.S. counterstrike options in the event of a North Korean attack. It also facilitates the deployment of U.S. forces from the peninsula to deal with contingencies elsewhere, including those related to international terrorism.

■ The relocation of U.S. forces to garrisons south of Seoul will permit the return of the Yongsan Base, located in the middle of downtown Seoul, and some 50 other facilities to the ROK. The Yongsan relocation in particular will accomplish a longstanding U.S. objective, going back to EASI, of eliminating the political tensions inherent in a large U.S. troop presence in the heart of the capital.

The two initiatives also accomplished the enduring goal of moving the United States from a leading to a supporting role in the defense of the ROK. Primary responsibility for the defense of South Korea now rests with the ROK army, supported principally by U.S. air and naval assets. In line with the rebalancing of defense responsibilities, Washington and Seoul agreed in February 2007 to transfer wartime operational control to the ROK no later than April 12, 2012. In the process, the U.S.–ROK Combined Forces Command will be disestablished and replaced by a new bilateral command structure.

The effectiveness of the new security framework will be enhanced by projected ROK increases in defense spending under the Defense Reform 2020 plan and by U.S. provision of interim bridging capabilities in areas such as intelligence and command and control.

Reaching agreement on these changes required overcoming a number of sensitive issues. Many South Korean officers considered the initial U.S. target date for the transfer of operational control to be premature. This was accommodated by extending the date to no later than April 12, 2012. Likewise, many South Koreans were concerned that the U.S. concept of "strategic flexibility," involving the deployment of U.S. forces from the peninsula to deal with contingencies linked to international terrorism, would weaken deterrence against North Korea. There were also apprehensions that the deployment of U.S. forces from the peninsula to the Taiwan Strait in a China-Taiwan contingency might involve the ROK in a U.S.-China conflict. These concerns were dealt with through an exchange of diplomatic notes between Secretary of State Condoleezza Rice and Foreign Minister Ban Ki-moon in January 2006, whereby the two governments expressed their understanding of each other's requirements and respect for their positions.

In two summit meetings, President George W. Bush and the ROK's current president, Lee Myung-bak, agreed to develop a 21st Century Strategic Alliance to extend cooperation from the peninsula to the region and beyond.

Transforming the U.S.-Japan Alliance

Article VI of the United States–Japan Security Treaty reads, "For the purpose of contributing to the security of Japan and the maintenance of international peace and security in the Far East, the United States of America is granted the use by its land, air, and naval forces of facilities and areas in Japan." The early 1990s nuclear standoff on the Korean Peninsula revealed the U.S.-Japan alliance to be woefully unprepared to deal with a potential contingency there. U.S. access to ports, airfields, and hospitals ran into legal barriers at the national, prefectural, and local levels, calling into question the degree to which Japan could fully support U.S. military operations in the event of a regional war.

To address the issues, the United States and Japan entered into negotiations that resulted in the Tokyo Declaration of April 1996, which updated the alliance for the post–Cold War world. The Tokyo Declaration and the subsequent implementing legislation, signed in 1997–1998, committed Japan to provide the United States with rear-area support "in contingencies in areas surrounding Japan." The Ministry of Foreign Affairs defined "areas surrounding Japan" as being functional, as opposed to geographic, in nature and application. The ambiguity and flexibility of the ministry's definition later facilitated the deployment of Japan's Maritime Self-Defense Force to the Indian Ocean and Persian Gulf region in support of Operation *Enduring Freedom* (2003) in Afghanistan.

In October 2000, the Institute for National Strategic Studies published *The United States and Japan: Advancing Toward a Mature Partnership*, the findings of a study group on the U.S.-Japan relationship chaired by Richard Armitage and Joseph Nye. The report called for an across-the-board strengthening of both the relationship and the bilateral alliance. Under President George W. Bush and Japan's Prime Minister Junichiro Koizumi, the report would serve as a blueprint for the Defense Policy Review Initiative, a process intended to guide the continued development of the alliance.

Since 2002, the Defense Policy Review Initiative has informed the transformation of the U.S.-Japan alliance to meet the requirements of the 21st century. Since 9/11, the alliance has advanced based on convergent strategic assessments of the international security environment and a strong mutual conviction that the alliance enhances the security of both countries and the Asia-Pacific region. Moreover, it fosters global security and stability. These assessments are reflected in several key national security documents of the alliance partners. On the U.S. side, these are the 2001 and 2006 QDR reports and the 2002 and 2006 National Security Strategies. The corresponding Japanese documents include the 2002 Defense White Paper, the October 2004 report of the Council on Security and Defense Capabilities, and the December 2004 New Defense Guidelines.

The joint statements issued by the bilateral U.S.-Japan Security Consultative Committee, a forum for meetings between the U.S. Department of State and the Japanese Ministry of Foreign Affairs, are also important blueprint documents in the process of alliance transformation. The February 2005 joint statement conceptualized the alliance as global in scope, and as a force in support of international stability and security; it also identified common strategic objectives both in East Asia and globally. Subsequently, the committee issued additional joint statements, including Alliance Transformation and Realignment for the Future (October 2005), Roadmap for Realignment (May 2006), and Alliance Transformation: Advancing United States-Japan Security and Defense Cooperation (May 2007).

Relocation and collocation, concentration, and missile defense cooperation characterize transformation in the U.S.-Japan alliance. The following are a few recent examples:

■ The U.S. Army I Corps relocated from Washington State on the Pacific Coast to Camp Zama, Japan, where it is collocated with the Ground Self-Defense Force Readiness Command.

■ The U.S. Navy carrier air wing stationed at Atsugi Air Base in the Tokyo metropolitan area was transferred to the Marine Corps Air Station at Iwakuni, and the KC–130 tanker squadron will be based at Iwakuni but deploy to the Kanoya Self-Defense Force base in Kyushu and Guam for training and operations.

■ On Okinawa, transformation involves the relocation of the Futenma U.S. Marine Corps Air Station to the shoreline areas of Camp Schwab and Henoko Bay; the relocation of the Marine Corps III Marine Expeditionary Force Headquarters and 8,000 Marine personnel and dependents to Guam; and the concentration of the remaining Marine presence, resulting in a reduced footprint on Okinawa. Japan has agreed to provide $6.9 billion of the total cost of $10.27 billion involved in the Guam relocation.

Progress in the Futenma-Guam relocation has been halting, however, owing to issues in Tokyo-Okinawa relations, internal Okinawa politics, and debates over the location and shape of the runways at Camp Schwab. Failure to effect the Futenma relocation, which has a target date of 2014 for completion, is likely to undermine the entire Guam realignment initiative.

Missile defense cooperation has involved the deployment of the U.S. X-Band radar at the Air Self-Defense Force Shariki Air Base, the sharing of X-Band data with Japan, and setting up of the Bilateral Joint Operations Coordination and Control Center at Yokota Air Base. The United States has also deployed a Patriot PAC–3 battalion to the Kadena Air Base and continued to add Standard Missile (SM–3) capabilities to forward-deployed naval forces, while Japan has accelerated the modification of its Aegis ships to make them SM–3-capable. The United States and Japan are also cooperating in the development of the next generation SM–3 interceptor. In September 2008, the Air Self-Defense Force reported the successful testing of its PAC–3 interceptor in White Sands, New Mexico.

The U.S.-Australia Alliance

The United States–Australia alliance has served to enhance stability in the Asia-Pacific region. Australia has played a major role in supporting stability in East Timor, Papua New Guinea, and the Solomon Islands, and in combating international terrorism in the Asia-Pacific region. A substantial convergence in the two nations' strategic perspectives and security policies in recent years has extended alliance cooperation beyond the region.

In the wake of the 9/11 attacks, Australia invoked Article V of the ANZUS treaty, defining the attacks on the United States as an attack on Australia. Under Prime Minster John Howard, Australia deployed forces to both Afghanistan and Iraq. Howard's successor, Kevin Rudd, subsequently withdrew Australia's combat forces from Iraq, while continuing military support in Afghanistan.

Cooperation also extends to combating the spread of weapons of mass destruction and Australia's participation in exercises related to the 2003 U.S. Proliferation Security Initiative. The alliance partners are also working to enhance bilateral cooperation in intelligence matters, as well as in humanitarian assistance and disaster relief.

U.S.-Philippine Alliance

Counterterrorism has been at the top of the U.S.-Philippine security cooperation agenda. The United States provides security assistance and training to the Philippine armed forces for their campaign against Abu Sayyaf, a Muslim separatist organization on Basilan Island, and for improvements to maritime border security. The Philippines was among the first countries to send troops to support the United States in Operation *Iraqi Freedom*, and was designated a major non-NATO ally in 2003. Despite the early withdrawal of the Philippine contingent, counterterror cooperation remains strong.

The United States is also supporting the Philippine Defense Reform program, which is aimed at transforming the Philippine defense establishment and improving the leadership and training of the Philippine armed forces. In accordance with the bilateral Mutual Defense Treaty, the annual Balikatan exercise combined U.S.-Philippine exercises in order to improve crisis action planning and the counterterrorism capabilities of the Philippine armed forces, and to enhance interoperability with U.S. forces.

U.S.-Thailand Alliance

This alliance relationship emphasizes capacity-building in the Thai military to develop doctrine, education, and training. U.S. defense and security assistance enhances the ability of the Thai military to meet transnational challenges as well as to deal with internal instability caused by Muslim separatist groups in the southern provinces.

The United States conducts over 40 training exercises annually with Thailand. The centerpiece of these is the multinational Cobra Gold exercise, which aims to strengthen regional cooperation in disaster relief as well as global peacekeeping operations. Also, Thailand has participated in Operations *Enduring Freedom* and *Iraqi Freedom*.

Looking Ahead

The bilateral alliance system is irreplaceable for dealing with the hard security issues confronting the East Asia region, from the Korean Peninsula to the Taiwan Strait. This will remain true for the foreseeable future. Meanwhile, trilateral security dialogues, now taking root among the United States, Japan, and South Korea, and among the United States, Australia, and Japan, are expanding the scope for alliance-based cooperation. A quadripartite strategic dialogue encompassing the United States, Japan, Australia, and India has been under consideration and may yet materialize.

At the same time, the alliances should be seen as the building blocks for multilateral coordination with nonallies to deal with a myriad of nontraditional security issues confronting the region, ranging from disaster relief to climate change, from nonproliferation to containing the spread of infectious diseases. The habits of cooperation and coordination developed over the years within the alliances can provide a firm foundation for initiatives aimed at dealing with issues of common concern on an ad hoc basis.

Strengthening Middle East Partnerships

U.S. strategic partnerships in the Middle East have been under enormous strain over the last two decades, strains even more severe than those long inherent in the fundamental differences between the goals and perspectives of the United States and those of regional states. These strains at the government-to-government level reflect those existing in U.S. relations with all levels of Arab society.

Perceptions that the U.S.-led wars in Iraq and Afghanistan war are aspects of a broader American war against Islam, that the Guantanamo and Abu Ghraib prisons reflect the hypocrisy of American rhetoric, and that the United States is now supporting Shia dominance over Sunnis, combine with longer standing complaints that the United States applies a double standard to the Israeli-Arab conflict and is only involved in the Middle East to obtain its resources. Grievances against U.S. policy are not always internally consistent—America is criticized both for

supporting authoritarian regimes and for pushing democratization too hard—but the grievances are no less deeply felt for being contradictory.

These contradictions are typical of the complexities of the Middle East. Unlike parts of the world where the United States has a long history of involvement in regional security, there is no framework of alliances to lend structure and predictability to strategic relations in the Middle East. Instead, the United States has a web of bilateral partnerships that reflect the great diversity in the economic and political environment in which each partner exists. To deal effectively with this complexity, the United States needs to learn to approach the Middle East with greater nuance and sophistication than it has in the past.

The Importance of U.S. Middle East Partnerships

Strong cooperative partnerships with the countries of the Middle East are central to almost all the U.S. national objectives that have been set forth by successive administrations, from defeating terrorism and preventing the proliferation of weapons of mass destruction to promoting economic and overall human development, defusing conflicts, and expanding the chances for greater economic and political freedom. Following are some key areas in which U.S.-Middle Eastern cooperation is particularly important.

Energy. Over 65 percent of the world's petroleum reserves and a large percentage of its natural gas are in the Middle East. As is widely recognized, until a replacement for hydrocarbon fuels is found, these resources will remain vital to economic growth throughout the entire, increasingly interdependent world. What is less well understood is the Middle East's own heavy reliance on these resources to generate income, not only in the oil- and gas-producing states themselves, but also in those countries that depend on remittances from expatriate workers. This raises serious questions about how the region will be able to cope with an ultimately inevitable post-oil world. It is important that the transition to the post-oil world does not increase the instability and tensions in the region.

Lines of Communication. Transport networks and nodes of critical importance to the global economy crisscross the Middle East, from the Strait of Gibraltar in the west to the Strait of Hormuz in the east. These waterways and the pipelines and port facilities that serve them are nearly as important to global energy markets as the region's hydrocarbon resources themselves. Moreover, the waterways also play a key role in the trade of other goods between Europe and Asia and are crucial to the ability of the United States to move troops and military equipment from one theater to another in a crisis. The same is true of the air routes linking Asia and Europe and, in military terms, the overflight agreements that permit military use of those routes. Road networks in some of these countries are also essential to both commercial and military movements.

U.S.-Muslim Relations and Countering Terrorism. Although the people of the Middle East are a minority of the world's Muslims, the region is a fulcrum for U.S. relations with that wider Muslim community. Because of globalization, what happens in the region, whether in Abu Ghraib or Gaza, reverberates throughout predominantly Muslim communities everywhere. The effect of the Iraq War on violent extremism is certainly profound, even if difficult to delineate. What seems clear is that terrorism is a threat that can only be countered by cooperation with the states in which extremist organizations operate, a partial list of which would include Iraq, Algeria, Morocco, Saudi Arabia, Jordan, and Egypt.

Proliferation of Weapons of Mass Destruction. Apart from North Korea, the countries of most pressing current concern with respect to the proliferation of nuclear and other weapons of mass destruction lie within the Middle East or on its immediate periphery. India's and Pakistan's de facto entry into the nuclear club in 1998 inevitably affected the calculations of their neighbors to the west. Many Arab states have struck deals with France, the United States, and others on nuclear energy development. Others have shown interest in developing their own nuclear programs. Aside from the obvious safety and environmental concerns that may arise from such programs, there are proliferation concerns. Speculation is rife about what other Arab states will do if Iran acquires nuclear weapons. Preventing Iran from crossing that line promises to be difficult enough; forestalling the ensuing ripple effect will only be possible through strong strategic relationships with the other countries of the region.

Strengthening Partnerships: The Way Ahead

The Israeli-Palestinian Conflict and U.S.-Israel Relations. However much some may dispute it—and perhaps fewer do after the fighting in Gaza in early 2009—the one thing on which Arab leaders and their strongest critics on the right and left all agree is that U.S. favoritism toward Israel is the main obstacle to better relations. If the United States truly wants to strengthen its partnerships in the Middle East and to alleviate the negative state of its interactions with

UN (Mark Garten)

UN Security Council issues presidential statement on launch of long-range rocket by North Korea

the Islamic world at large, it needs to work energetically and visibly toward comprehensive, durable, wise, and fair solutions to the Israeli-Palestinian and related conflicts. Even the perception of *positive intent* to solve a problem can go a long way in the Middle East, but mere lip service can be counterproductive. Arab audiences are well able to distinguish empty pledges from serious intentions. Promising to address the conflict without putting serious muscle behind the promise will only make the U.S. reputation worse, not better. Those Arabs who have been arguing for moderation and negotiation on this issue are losing ground in the "Arab street" to those who are arguing for more aggressive measures. As one Arab leader said recently, "We need to show our people some progress on this. The moderates are on the ropes." The Obama administration's swift appointment of former Senator George Mitchell as a special envoy for the Middle East was a helpful signal of Washington's intent to find a diplomatic solution to longstanding tensions.

Israel obviously enjoys a special status as a U.S. partner, one to whose security successive administrations have pledged themselves. Despite these close ties, U.S. relations with Israel are sometimes strained. More importantly, they complicate U.S. relations with other regional actors. Israelis increasingly recognize that the threats their country faces are changing in ways that require fundamentally rethinking many strategic premises. If the United States can help shape this rethinking with the new Netanyahu government, it may be possible to enhance Israel's security while at the same time promoting broader U.S. interests, including improving its relations with the other countries in the region.

Iraq and Afghanistan. U.S. partnerships with the Arab world are also under stress because of the long-running wars in Iraq and Afghanistan. Muslims, whether Arab or non-Arab, react angrily to these conflicts not because they support terrorism but out of concern with the conduct of the wars. While most Middle Eastern governments are not democracies by any means, their ability to provide the kind of cooperation that is crucial to U.S. success in countering terrorism is nevertheless bounded by public opinion, which is in turn shaped by U.S. actions in the region.

It is no secret that there is, in many Middle Eastern countries, a widening divide between rulers and ruled, in some cases leading to deadly violence. Regimes are acutely aware of this sense of alienation and understand that antiterrorism cooperation with the United States, while helpful in countering

near-term threats, can aggravate anti-regime and anti-Western trends in the long run. If the United States could focus its efforts more on what Arabs would call the "roots of terrorism," it could go a long way toward alleviating popular concerns and thus permitting closer cooperation. If the United States is once again seen as a country that produces jobs and freedom rather than conflict and oppression, it could start to turn the tide of disfavor that faces it in much of the Muslim world.

Winding down U.S. military involvement in Iraq will alleviate tensions somewhat, depending on the level of political stability left behind. In the meantime, the United States needs to ensure that its actions do not unnecessarily fuel the sense that America is "anti-Islam." This is a matter of deeds, not words, although the newly inaugurated President's Arab-media interview on January 26, 2009, put down a marker about Washington's desire to improve relations throughout the Arabic-speaking world. The President's speech in Cairo in June 2009 provided another compelling statement, but the United States also needs to change realities on the ground. The symbolic importance of the decision to shut down the Guantanamo prison cannot be overstated.

The United States can also do things at home to mitigate its anti-Islamic image, including trying harder to manage anti-Muslim sentiments in the United States better. What Americans say to each other reverberates in the Middle East more than many realize.

Finding Areas for Nonsecurity Cooperation. Many countries in the Middle East are facing water shortages, high unemployment, stagnating economies, and increasing socioeconomic stress. Working with regional states as equal partners to address these problems could go a long way toward putting U.S. relations on a stronger footing. For example, desalination technology could form the centerpiece of a major U.S. effort to promote sustainable development in the region. At the same time, it is also necessary to enhance personal ties by means of development cooperation, even if it means incurring some risk. A recent initiative to establish a Peace Corps program in rural Egypt was stopped before receiving full consideration, ostensibly due to security concerns. Such concerns, on the face of it, seem exaggerated, but in any case, such programs are exactly what are needed in places such as the Egyptian countryside. Fixing an old woman's eyes and helping clean up water supplies will go further toward improving relations with the Arab people than all the strategic communications Washington could ever fund.

Cooperation with regional states is also the best way to develop much-needed expertise on the Middle East within the United States. Programs that send American students, scholars, and scientists abroad should be bolstered. Arabic, Farsi, Turkish, and other language programs should be given greater funding and focus. Centers of excellence should be developed with an eye toward long-term relations with the region.

Working with Other Allies. Recent history clearly demonstrates that the United States cannot solve the problems of the Middle East on its own. It needs to share information and resources not only with partners within the region but with those outside as well. Given their history of involvement in the Middle East, many European governments have considerable long-term knowledge and expertise on the region (although in some cases, the history also entails unwelcome baggage). The United States is accustomed to asking for allied contributions when it comes to military operations in the Middle East; it needs to think more broadly than that. Many members of the European Union as well as the EU itself are involved in development, education, and other projects in the region. The United States and the EU may have different perceptions on some issues, but they need each other to promote their mutual fundamental interests in the Middle East.

In a different way, the U.S. Asian allies, particularly Japan and South Korea, are also playing an increasingly important role in the Middle East, especially economically. While U.S. relations with other major players, such as China, Russia, and India, are sometimes strained, focusing on shared interests and objectives like the importance of Middle Eastern oil and gas might help illuminate previously overlooked opportunities for cooperation. The United States should not throw caution to the wind, but does need to recognize that its potential competitors are gaining influence. If it can adjust its expectations, policies, and actions to this reality, cooperation in such areas as development of energy and other resources, sea lane security, and alleviation of the conditions fostering extremism could lead to that most elusive of Middle Eastern outcomes, a win-win situation.

Seeing Past the Similarities

The Middle East is a complex place. Arab cultures and societies are not monolithic. Even the one thing that is said to unite all Arabs—the Arabic language—is actually quite different across and within the countries of the region, with the version spoken in one country often almost unintelligible to natives of another. Middle Easterners' perceptions of the United States and the rest of the world, as well as of their own region and what is important in that region, vary even more widely than the language.

While many of the region's countries face similar sets of challenges, each of them also has its own unique problems. To improve its partnerships, the United States must work not only on the cross-cutting issues, but on the country-specific ones as well. Indeed, the region is so diverse that Americans should probably stop seeking a unified theory to explain the entire Middle East, and instead start fully incorporating its kaleidoscopic complexity into strategic planning. Instead of aiming for a grand strategic vision that would provide a single, simple set of solutions, the United States should start rebuilding strained relations on a bilateral and subregional level. It should build flexibility into its regional policies and be ready to adjust and adapt to evolving realities, rather than relying on tried and true formulas that may have outlived their usefulness.

The one overarching exception, documented time and again, is the Israeli-Palestinian conflict. If a more hopeful diplomatic trajectory were to be seen, then it might be possible to work with religious and other leaders to bridge the gaps between Muslim communities around the world and the United States. The key will be to demonstrate a sense of the progress that cooperation with America can yield economically, politically, and socially.

Economic Development and Conflict Management: Priorities for the Future

Many believe that the United States should pay more attention to the problems of global poverty and fragile states, and increase its reliance on "soft power." The George W. Bush administration moved in this direction by creating the President's Emergency Plan for AIDS Relief and the Millennium Challenge Account, and by increasing aid to Africa. The administration warned that "weak states, like Afghanistan, can pose as great a danger to our national interests as strong states." The Iraq and Afghanistan wars have led to billions of dollars being spent on stabilization and reconstruction in those countries. While these programs set some directions for the future, however, the U.S. Government has not defined clear priorities to guide foreign assistance and conflict management efforts in the medium to long term. Officials in the new administration should be asking several questions as they consider the directions they want foreign policy to take in the next several months and years:

■ Are we doing enough to promote economic growth?
■ What is the best way to support growth?
■ What can economic assistance contribute to the struggle against extremism?
■ What capabilities do we need to prevent or manage conflicts?
■ Who should pay for them?

Current Views

Afghanistan and Pakistan. There is widespread agreement that the security situation in Afghanistan has deteriorated and will require expanded troop commitments from the United States and NATO soon if it is to be brought under control. Many also believe that the Afghan government will need large and sustained economic assistance if it is to build its legitimacy, find alternatives to the poppy economy, and undercut support for the Taliban. The growing problem of sanctuary for the Taliban and al Qaeda in Pakistan's tribal areas has also convinced U.S. national security officials that Pakistan, too, will require major economic assistance and diplomatic engagement to help the fragile civilian government gain control over its territory and the many rival factions that threaten its stability.

U.S. Air Force (Delia A. Castillo)

F–16 takes off from Aviano air base during NATO Operation *Allied Force*

Countering Extremism. To reduce support for extremism in Islamic countries, the Bush administration relied mainly on diplomacy (belated attention to the Middle East peace process, pressure on authoritarian governments to democratize, and pressure on governments to support U.S. security objectives

in the region). As the previous section makes clear, however, public opinion in most Arab countries nevertheless remains overwhelmingly critical of U.S. policy. One option that has not been extensively explored is to use aid directly to help citizens. The U.S.–Middle East Partnership Initiative tried to do some of this, with uneven results. The new administration needs to consider a much more ambitious effort that targets one of the big underlying problems in the Middle East: the youth bulge.

Bottom Billion. There is growing support in Western countries for stronger efforts to relieve poverty and improve living conditions in the developing world, demonstrated by international support for the UN's Millennium Development Goals and the popularity of antipoverty movements led by pop singer Bono and others. In his book, *The Bottom Billion,* Paul Collier has called attention to the special problems faced by the billion or so people who live in countries in Africa, Central America, and Central Asia who have been left behind by global growth. National security officials have also become more concerned about economically stagnant and unstable countries, whose borders often contain "ungoverned spaces" where terrorists can operate or maintain bases. All these problems will be made worse by rapid population growth in poor countries, which the UN Population Division predicts will add 2.5 billion people by 2050. (The populations of Afghanistan, Liberia, Niger, and the Democratic Republic of the Congo will likely triple in this period.) The Group of Seven countries have agreed to increase aid for Africa and other poor regions. While some of the increased American aid has gone to support economic growth (especially through Millennium Challenge), the largest portion has concentrated on HIV/AIDS, health, and education. While those are all important areas, the United States and other leading donors are not doing enough to support growth. Without economic growth, poverty cannot be reduced, social programs cannot be sustained, and stability and security are jeopardized.

Fragile States and Conflict. Concern is growing about the problems of fragile states and civil conflict in the developing world. Paul Collier has shown that risk of conflict is associated with poverty and economic stagnation, and that conflict is extremely destructive to development. There is broad agreement that fragile states pose a major foreign policy challenge, but little consensus on what to do about them. This is a long-term problem. The United States and the international community need to agree on general principles that can guide their efforts in this area.

New Initiatives

The new era we are entering can be viewed as the second stage of the struggle against extremism. The first stage began on 9/11 and has been dominated by the wars in Afghanistan and Iraq. These conflicts can be compared to the Korean War, whose nature and outcome shaped the early years of the Cold War. As in that earlier time, the world faces a global threat, this time in the form of violent nonstate extremism. The ability to use military force remains critically important to countering terrorism, but there is a growing consensus that military means alone will not be sufficient. It was only 8 years after the signing of the 1953 Korean armistice that the Kennedy administration, for reasons having to do with Cold War geopolitical competition in the Third World, embarked on a substantial expansion of American investment in international economic development. President John Kennedy essentially created the modern field of development assistance, and established a new agency to manage it—the U.S. Agency for International Development (USAID). To deal with current threats, we need a new vision no less bold than Kennedy's, developed in closer partnership with other nations and international institutions.

Following are some specific suggestions for future U.S. policy initiatives in the four areas described above.

Afghanistan and Pakistan. Afghanistan will require large amounts of aid for at least several decades to help it raise low income levels, develop alternatives to the poppy economy, strengthen the capacity of the government to deliver services, and build the government's legitimacy. The government in Kabul needs to introduce political reforms, reduce the power of the warlords, and improve security and stability. None of this will be cheap—or quick. It will require sustained assistance from donors, including the United States, Europe, and others.

A daunting new set of challenges has arisen in Pakistan, due in part to that country's failure to control its border with Afghanistan. That failure, however, is linked to the broader problems of a fragile political order, severe economic strains (short-term in the macroeconomy and long-term in endemic poverty), and local political support for the Taliban, especially in the tribal areas. To address these problems, the government in Islamabad will have to not only make hard political choices, but also find a way to sell them to the people. Neither seems likely to occur without concerted diplomatic and economic support from outside the country. The U.S. administration should consider a large economic package that focuses on short-term macroeconomic stabilization and long-term improvements in the welfare of poor people and the tribal areas. The latter should emphasize education and health, but also include programs to improve business and employment opportunities (infrastructure, business regulations, credit programs, and training). The United States will have to assume the largest share of the costs of such a package, but should also seek support from Europe and the Persian Gulf states, which have both the ability to contribute and a clear interest in Pakistan's stability. The United States should also seek to involve China and Iran in regional diplomacy to stabilize Pakistan.

Islamic Youth. One of the biggest problems in the Middle East is the so-called youth bulge, a demographic group that includes both the large number of young people who cannot find good jobs today, and the growth in their numbers projected for the next 20 years. The persistent poverty and lack of education that characterize the youth bulge contribute to popular support for extremism and threaten to destabilize governments. To reduce support for extremism and address the Arab public perception that the United States "doesn't care" about Arab countries, the United States should work with European and other nations to help unemployed young people in non-oil-rich countries in the Middle East get the education they need and find productive employment. Even rich Gulf states have youth employment problems, but they have the resources to deal with them, and should pay for any Western help they receive. But in countries such as Jordan, Egypt, Yemen, Afghanistan, and Pakistan, and areas such as the West Bank, the United States and Europe should take the lead, even if the Gulf states are willing to contribute financing.

The program should emphasize education and training, with a focus on practical business skills. It should aim to help both those who have formal academic credentials but lack the skills and values (for example, team orientation) that businesses seek and those who lack even basic academic training. It should include practical skill-building for unemployed university graduates, vocational training for less educated youth, business assistance for startups, support for existing or new local business schools, and Western-standard bachelor's and master's degree programs for the best and brightest (ideally through study at Western institutions, but if necessary done locally by Western educators). Although international programs always run the risk of local opposition,

American programs should be run, to the extent possible, by USAID missions, working with Western and local nongovernmental organizations and companies, not through host government ministries. Past experience has shown that there is strong local interest in such training and education and that young people will not be overly concerned that the training might have an American label, which it should have: "from the people of the United States of America."

The Bottom Billion. The United States should work with other donor countries, the World Bank, and the UN to put in place major new initiatives to help "bottom billion" countries advance and join the global economy. These initiatives should stress three themes. First, donor countries should increase their support for economic growth. Over the last 40 years, there has been a trend toward giving more aid for the social sectors and less for agricultural development, infrastructure, and other programs to support growth. This trend has been due in part to the success of such aid in improving health and education outcomes, and its relative lack of success in spurring growth in Africa and other regions. If Washington wants to reduce poverty and make social services sustainable, however, policymakers have to find ways to help poor countries grow faster, which means putting a greater focus on economic growth programs.

Second, to make aid for growth support more effective, we should take lessons from the successful development experiences of Asian countries, including China. Two of the most important lessons are that growth pushes have to be led from within by leaders who are dedicated to economic advancement and export promotion; and that the most successful growth strategies did not follow the Washington Consensus model of imposing comprehensive economic reforms at the outset and then letting business develop naturally. Rather, they involved incremental reforms over time that brought tangible gains in business development and exports along the way—what the Chinese call "crossing the river by feeling for stones." Many of those governments intervened actively to promote exports.

These principles suggest that aid for growth support should emphasize the following:

■ **Selectivity.** It should concentrate on those countries doing the most to help themselves.
■ **Business Development.** Donors should not impose a rigid ideological model, but look at who is doing the best job of improving business conditions and give them aid to support the development of local businesses, agriculture, and nontraditional exports.
■ **Regional Models.** The goal should be to help leading-edge countries advance so they can be models for their regions.

Millennium Challenge embodies many of these principles, but does not pay enough attention to helping countries develop their own growth and export strategies. It focuses on those countries with the best development conditions today, but ignores many states where the bottom billion are found. In none of these bottom billion countries can the conditions for growth truly be called good—some are just further along than others. All need to make continuous changes over decades to advance (as China did). The political commitment has to come from local leaders, but they need technical and business advice.

Third, the advanced countries should consider new and possibly more intrusive methods to encourage the responsible management of mineral wealth. As Collier makes clear, when high mineral wealth is combined with very low levels of economic development, the risks of corruption, "Dutch Disease" (when a sudden influx of foreign currency, usually resulting from the discovery of an exportable resource, destabilizes a country's currency and balance of trade), and long-term economic stagnation are overwhelming. The incentives for predation are too powerful to be overcome locally. The only chance to break these vicious cycles is for the international community to press for greater transparency in oil payments, auctions for oil contracts, transparency in the uses of mineral proceeds, and prudent management of mineral wealth for the long term. The Group of Eight's (G–8's) July 2008 endorsement of the Extractive Industries Transparency Initiative is a promising first step, but actually getting the countries concerned to implement the initiative will be a challenging task that requires closely coordinated international pressure and incentives.

Conflict and Fragile States. Helping fragile states stabilize and develop is one of the great challenges of our time, one that requires a multinational response, as is explained in more detail in the next section. Unfortunately, because advanced countries often find little national interest or any imperative to take on the high costs and uncertainties of assisting individual fragile states, they tend to look to the UN or regional bodies to lead these efforts. That strategy will not work, however, unless the rich countries are willing to provide more resources to the UN and other organizations. The rich countries should view fragile states as a global "public goods" problem that requires shared funding.

While fragile states vary greatly in the types of help they need (one size does not fit all), there is one broad initiative that could help with the problems of weak government institutions and weak private sectors: institute a long-term education program for people who commit to work in their government ministries for agreed periods of time. This should include overseas and local degree training (with outside academic help) in economics, management, public administration, and technical fields. The United States funded thousands of scholarships for this type of education in East and Southeast Asia in the 1960s and 1970s, which helped recipient countries strengthen their governments and advance economically.

States that have fallen into civil conflict occupy a special category. They often suffer from deep-rooted divisions and internal weaknesses that are very hard to resolve at the level of the antagonists. Outside interventions are often ineffective because they assume that the task is peacekeeping, when the real problem is that there is no peace to be kept. When a leading power intervenes—as Britain did in Sierra Leone in 2000—it can sometimes suppress violence fairly easily. In many cases, however, no leading power wants to take that responsibility, which leaves the task to the UN or regional actors. In these cases, it is again incumbent on rich countries to give the UN, African Union, and other organizations the needed support to do the job. They should consider the following actions:

■ **Sovereignty.** The UN and regional bodies should develop new procedures and criteria for intervening in situations where conflict or government abuses are creating humanitarian crises or threatening regional stability. State sovereignty should not be unconditional.

■ **Peace Enforcement.** The advanced countries should help the UN and regional bodies strengthen their conflict mediation and peace enforcement capabilities. The UN needs standby forces that can intervene proactively, with much better equipment, training, and pay than peacekeeping forces have today.

■ **Expeditionary Assistance Capacities.** The international institutions and major powers need to develop new civilian expeditionary capacities that

combine the ability to deliver social services and create employment quickly with the capacity to support development over the longer term.

Meeting the Challenge, Paying the Bill

Finding the funds to pay for these initiatives will be difficult, especially as Western budgets come under strains due to economic slowdowns and the need for government interventions to manage the credit crisis. The United States cannot pay for everything by itself, but must do its share. It will have to work cooperatively with Europe and Japan, the international institutions, and, it is to be hoped (over the long term), with China, India, and other emerging market countries to find common ways forward. We need a new vision of national security in the post-9/11 world—one that recognizes that stability is linked to economic opportunity.

Stabilizing Fragile States

As explained above, fragile states pose a wide range of problems for the United States and its allies and coalition partners. They produce instability that extends far beyond their own borders and can threaten the security of countries around the world. And, as discussed above, the United States and its allies must make strategic adjustments, including adjustments to their assistance programs, if they are to become more effective at reversing state failure. The best way to address these problems is to help fragile states rebuild their governance capacity, but such efforts require plentiful resources and long-term political commitments. International cooperation is a vital part of most of these efforts, but capacity shortfalls remain and problems of multinational coordination tend to emerge. The U.S. administration faces a number of constraints on its ability to conduct state-building operations, and it must select priorities for improvement to meet the full range of security challenges that the United States and its allies are likely to face in the future.

Why Is International Cooperation Necessary?

Weak and failed states suffer from a wide range of problems that can all be traced to what Ashraf Ghani and Clare Lockhart call the "sovereignty gap," which is the wide difference between formal sovereignty and the actual ability to govern. These governments have the legal right to govern their own affairs, but they lack the administrative capacity to do so effectively. The sovereignty gap leads to numerous problems whose effects extend far beyond their own borders, including criminality, terror, arms proliferation, and refugee flows, to name a few.

Closing the sovereignty gap, particularly in states emerging from conflict, is difficult. It involves rebuilding state capacity or, in some cases, building state capacity for the first time, across a wide range of sectors. Reestablishing the security sector is arguably the most important first task, since few other efforts can progress until order has been established and effective justice and correctional systems are in place. Other high-priority areas include restoring the government's administrative capacity; providing such essential services as public utilities, health care, and education; stabilizing the economy; and developing a regulatory framework that encourages local and international commerce.

These are all enormous endeavors. None of them can be accomplished quickly, so they require long-term commitments of money, people, and political will. The United States simply cannot do this on its own in most cases, even if it wanted to, because the scope of the efforts involved in recreating the basic governing structures of a state is simply too large for any single country to take on by itself. Nationbuilding requires coordinated international cooperation for success. Efforts to stabilize fragile states must leverage the capabilities and resources of the international community, to maximize the number of assets that are brought to bear, and to help sustain political will over the long time horizons involved.

Key Issues for the Obama Administration

The new administration will face a number of challenges throughout its term in office that may limit its ability to work with partner countries to stabilize fragile states. These challenges are likely to persist in some form during the next 4 to 8 years even if the administration tries to address them, especially because many of them involve structural capacity problems that do not lend themselves to quick fixes.

Civilian Capacity Is Vital but Lacking. Most of the security challenges that emanate from fragile states cannot be addressed primarily through military means. Though military force will remain an important component of any national security strategy, these challenges cannot be addressed without extensive civilian efforts. Reducing terrorism and insurgencies, for example, can require intelligence and law enforcement efforts as much as, if not more than, the use of military force. And the reestablishment of effective governance capacity in failed or fragile states requires primarily civilian involvement in the areas of law and order, justice and prison systems, public health, and education, to name just a few critical areas.

Unfortunately, the international community lacks anywhere near the civilian capacity required for sustained and successful state-building efforts. In most countries, civilian expertise in this wide range of areas is dispersed across government departments and agencies, and bureaucratic politics often impede the interagency coordination that would be necessary to integrate these efforts into coordinated state-building strategies. Many countries, including the United States, United Kingdom, Canada, and Germany, have sought to improve capacity in this area by reforming bureaucratic structures. Although these efforts have led to marginal improvements, they have remained limited by ongoing turf wars and poor organizational placement. As a result, even the bureaucracies of the most highly developed countries have had a difficult time fulfilling mandates.

Moreover, such civilian capacity as exists can seldom be readily deployed to zones of conflict and instability. Building state capacity cannot be done from afar; experts need to be present on the ground for a long period of time to provide advice and assistance. Yet civilians cannot be ordered to deploy in the same way that military forces can, and few countries have invested in civilian capacity for long-term international aid work. The United States, Canada, and many European countries are all experimenting with developing rosters of deployable civilian personnel, but these efforts still involve relatively limited numbers of personnel who are unlikely to be able to meet the demands for their services in future operations. The enduring nature of these problems will constrain the ability of the United States and its partners to address the needs of weak and failed states, and suggests that limited civilian capacity for state-building operations will remain a key challenge well into the Obama administration, and perhaps beyond.

Everyone Wants to Coordinate, but No One Wants to Be Coordinated. Even when civilian capacity does exist, there are major obstacles to the integration of those capabilities into a coordinated state-building strategy. It is difficult enough to coordinate all of the relevant actors from a single country, but the problem gets exponentially harder in multinational operations. Participating countries usually have their own policies and priorities in such operations, and they often prefer to maintain national control of their programs rather than subordinate them to others. At best, this failure to coordinate leads to wasted resources and duplication; at worst, it leads to contradictory approaches that undermine the very objectives of the operations.

Afghanistan provides a case in point. NATO commands all multinational military forces through the International Security Assistance Force, but no comparable structure exists on the civilian side. Dozens, if not hundreds, of workers on the ground are providing humanitarian relief, conducting development activities, and assisting governments at the district, provincial, and national levels. Virtually all of these actors agree that their activities need to be better coordinated to prioritize programs and use their limited resources more effectively, but formal efforts to coordinate international approaches have not been successful. The coordination efforts that do exist occur on an ad hoc basis in the field, and do not address the fundamental strategic questions—even though most of the actors on the ground agree that a more coordinated approach is crucial for the overall success of their efforts in Afghanistan.

Iraq Will Frame the Terms of the Debate. For better or worse, debates about whether or how to stabilize fragile states in the coming years will almost inevitably involve some sort of comparison to Iraq. Iraq has been the most ambitious, the most expensive, and the most controversial state-building project in recent years, and so it will shape public perceptions around the world about the feasibility and desirability of such efforts. Although it seems unlikely that future state-building efforts will approach the scale of Iraq, people—both in the United States and among its partners and allies—will tend nevertheless to generalize from that experience and oppose future attempts at state-building, even if they occur under very different circumstances.

Building Capacity for the Long Term

These obstacles will not be easy to overcome, and may well limit the enthusiasm in the United States and abroad for engaging in new state-building efforts. Nevertheless, fragile states pose so many different security threats to the international community that improving worldwide capacity to address them should be a high priority for the new administration.

The U.S. Government should continue recent initiatives to improve civilian capacity. The Civilian Response Corps is an important step in the right direction, and Congress has recently demonstrated a newfound willingness to fund this initiative. It

U.S. Navy (John Gay)

General David McKiernan, commander, ISAF, congratulates residents of De Rawod district in Afghanistan for completion of Chutu Bridge

must continue to develop so that the government can deploy qualified civilians to future state-building operations. The administration must also ensure that the U.S. Armed Forces, and the Army in particular, do not lose all of the lessons about training foreign security forces that they paid such a high price to learn in Iraq. Since this will be a vital mission in many future state-building missions, particularly in postconflict situations, the military must institutionalize this training capacity so that it can be quickly mobilized when future demands emerge.

The administration should also encourage partners and allies to improve their own capacities for state-building operations, especially in areas where they have a comparative advantage. Police training is one such area; many European countries have national police forces that more closely resemble the police forces being rebuilt than does the decentralized policing system in the United States. The administration should also encourage multilateral organizations, including the European Union and the African Union, to develop their own capacities for these missions, so that they can pool the contributions of smaller nations and use them more effectively.

Finally, the administration should engage neighboring states early and often. Neighbors always have direct security interests at stake when they border a weak or failed state, and they will act to further those interests. If they believe that international state-building efforts will help, they can be a positive force for success. If they believe that their interests are threatened, however, they can easily play the role of a spoiler and undermine the efforts of the international community. The challenge for the administration and its partners, then, will be to engage neighbors with adept diplomacy, so that they become constructive supporters of any international state-building efforts.

Rethinking Security Assistance

Security assistance, as a category of foreign aid, has meant many things to many people over the years. To some recipient countries, it has represented a lifeline to help lift them from circumstances of vulnerability, and a bridge that links their military officers with the special organizational culture, prestige, and high standards of the U.S. Armed Forces through military education, training, exercises, and force modernization programs via arms transfer relationships.

Not all observers have viewed U.S. assistance to foreign countries with unabashed enthusiasm. The late Senator Jesse Helms famously termed U.S.

foreign assistance the equivalent of throwing money "down a rat hole." U.S. programs to train and equip foreign military forces have periodically drawn criticism when the recipient country's track record for human rights and democratic practices has been found wanting. While many legislators on either side of the political aisle have held more positive views about the purposes and the results of U.S. security assistance, Senator Helms was not alone in his concern that American tax dollars have not always translated into maximum gains for the U.S. national interest when spent assisting foreign countries.

What "measures of effectiveness" for the U.S. security assistance process would satisfy the highest expectations of policy practitioners and their legislative overseers? Reduced to their essence, they are few:

■ The intended uses of assistance funds must be likely to benefit the U.S. national interest—indeed, more likely to do so than any alternative use of the funds, including not spending them at all.

■ The process of determining funding allocations should capture and reflect the judgments of the most expert and best-informed participants regarding the urgency of need and anticipated effects of these expenditures.

■ The resulting worldwide program of assistance should reflect the sensible expectation that, notwithstanding the wisdom embodied in these budget plans, fast-developing circumstances bearing consequences for the U.S. national interest will merit unanticipated resource allocations.

The goal, in sum, is to maximize the prospect that the expenditure of U.S. security assistance funds will translate, on a day-to-day basis and over time, into effective U.S. influence on foreign individuals, societies, governments, events, and trends. Those who believe most strongly in the value of security assistance should be the most anxious that these performance parameters be met, and demonstrably so, the better to assure a broad and reliable congressional constituency for such assistance.

The Current System: Falling Short of Expectations

By these measures, the existing security assistance process must be judged less than satisfactory. Merely to recite the above metrics is to highlight the gap between the status quo and what could and should be. The deficiencies of the system, however, are not a reflection of the quality of individual inputs from hard-working officials so much as an indictment of a process overloaded by inputs that fails to preserve and capture the best among them. Indeed, for many senior U.S. military, diplomatic, and policymaking practitioners with recent experience in this arena, several conclusions seem unassailable.

First, the civilian and military managers of U.S. foreign relations operating on the frontlines around the world are perennially frustrated by significant revisions that occur well after they have developed and rendered their budget recommendations to Washington. It is true that the President, advised by the Office of Management and Budget, has a leadership role in managing the level of overall Federal expenditures; more often than not, however, explicit budgetary restraint on behalf of the President is exercised at the back end of the process rather than being clearly advertised at the beginning as a planning parameter. For its part, Congress, constitutionally empowered in matters of Federal expenditure, introduces its own significant alterations by earmarking some allocations and changing others without being obliged to explain its actions. While Members of Congress are fully capable of improving upon the best efforts of the executive branch, the absence of transparency can give rise to unfortunate perceptions about the influence exercised by recipient governments on Capitol Hill directly or through lobbyists.

Second, the country-specific security assistance allocations that emerge from final congressional deliberations and are sent each year to the President's desk for signature bear scant resemblance to the collective recommendations made months earlier at the front end of the budget-building process by the most senior empowered U.S. officials at American Embassies or geographic combatant commands around the world. On its face, the disparity in priorities between senior decisionmakers in Washington and their internationally deployed representatives signals some disunity of perspective and effort between the two groups. What many veteran policymakers find symptomatic of a dysfunctional budget process is the absence of dynamic movement year-on-year in traditional security assistance budget accounts. There has been modest movement in most countries' Foreign Military Financing (FMF) and International Military Education and Training allocations, even in the face of strategically momentous world events accompanied by urgent demands from senior professionals in the field for more latitude and scope to deploy these tools of American influence. It is hard to justify the enormous bureaucratic effort expended in develop-

ing country-specific and regional security assistance allocation recommendations when the most urgent of these recommendations—for significant changes in support of priority security goals—are so clearly unlikely to survive all the way to the final product that reaches the President for signature.

Third, security assistance funding has proven time and again inflexible, tied by law to specified countries and programs, and hence unavailable for fast-breaking crises where such a tool would clearly be the policy option of choice. Senior policy officials in Republican and Democratic administrations alike have experienced the same predicament wherein the President seeks to exert immediate political influence on an important situation but finds that the preferred tool—security assistance—cannot be reallocated in the necessary amounts due to legislative earmarks. Very often, Peacekeeping Operations (PKO) funds, which are by design more flexible than FMF, are diverted to the crisis of the moment and thus removed from whatever purposes had been painstakingly planned in coordination with foreign governments, the UN Secretariat, regional multilateral organizations such as the African Union, and others over the preceding 12 to 24 months. Such was the case in 2005 when PKO funds promised and dedicated to a 5-year, G–8–approved Global Peace Operations Initiative to train competent foreign military units on several continents for peacekeeping duty were suddenly reallocated in response to the breaking crisis in Darfur. There are costs to the national interest when the United States develops and codifies formal budget allocations backed by diplomacy, and then abandons a long-declared priority as the price of responding to an unanticipated higher priority.

There are long-term costs to perpetuating a system where the budget development process for security assistance funding is, at best, poorly attuned to the strategic perspectives of the country's leading civil and military operators overseas, not optimized to the realities of policy engagements around the world as they emerge, and therefore not configured to be as potent a tool of real-time political influence as leading U.S. policymakers inevitably want and need. In business terms, this would be the equivalent of losing touch with one's customer; many would agree that U.S. foreign policy needs to pay closer attention to the "market" of international trends, opinions, beliefs, and ideology if it is to retain the mantle of leadership in this century.

A recipient country whose assistance funds have been earmarked by Congress will ignore the voice of the American Ambassador with impunity, comforted by the certainty that the "check" of U.S. assistance is already "in the mail," since the by-name country appropriation is written into law. This represents a potentially wasted expenditure, a gift without gratitude, as the funds may not translate into a lever of policy influence for the U.S. Government on a day-to-day basis. American taxpayers are entitled to a system that affords the highest potential political return on their assistance investment. Congress has never been compelled to justify its preservation of earmarks other than the commitments connected to established U.S. strategic equities such as Israel's peace treaties with Egypt and Jordan.

The paucity of discretionary funds, other than a small emergency account in the hands of every U.S. Ambassador around the world, is another opportunity lost. Washington has an understandable desire to minimize malfeasance by limiting discretionary funds in the hands of government employees abroad; however, this desire becomes unreasonable when junior military officers in Iraq have as much or more cash resources at their discretion to dispense as an engagement tool than highly experienced, Senate-confirmed senior diplomats representing the President of the United States to entire sovereign countries. These latter officials must be trusted and empowered to expend modest discretionary funds on a routine basis to capitalize on politically, culturally, and economically significant opportunities to win goodwill and long-term influence for the United States among foreign populations.

The objective, it bears repeating, is a political outcome—influence—without which foreign countries are more likely to act in ways adverse to our national interest. When the American officials that a foreign government or population sees in the field are perceived only as implementers of Washington budget decisions rather than empowered decisionmakers in their own right, this tool of national influence is not being used to maximum effect.

By far the clearest symptom of a security assistance process in distress has been the frequent scramble for funds by the Department of State, on behalf of the President, in response to exigent new circumstances facing the United States. The fact is that urgent scrambles to shift funds from existing budget accounts have occurred repeatedly in response to critical needs since 9/11, and most of the time, ad hoc alternative funding arrangements were necessitated by the absence of reprogrammable State Department funds. When U.S. diplomats and military commanders needed to secure the active

cooperation of countries close to areas of current or prospective hostilities involving American forces, the list of unanticipated and unbudgeted needs was long, from runway improvements on foreign airbases to accommodate U.S. aircraft, to defraying the expenses incurred by host-country military forces facilitating a U.S. combat mission in the vicinity of terrorist strongholds. Many friendly forces needed hot weather gear, weapons and ammunition, and even specialized training as a condition of joining the military coalitions conducting missions in Afghanistan and Iraq.

The chronic inability of existing security assistance authorities and funds under the control of the Secretary of State to service these urgent U.S. national security interests led to the establishment of precedents for the Pentagon to fill the void with its budget resources. Quickly enough, these precedents became workable patterns of funding, and what had begun as ad hoc became the most efficacious budget option, such that the overall trend produced a shift of security assistance program responsibilities away from the Department of State to the Department of Defense (DOD).

This shift in program stewardship was not by design; congressional overseers of State Department appropriations repeatedly warned State officials against the mounting trend even while producing no relief to the conditions that caused it. Time and again in this decade, the Secretary of State's authorities and responsibilities have not been matched by available resources to address unanticipated, top-priority strategic issues of the day. Time and again, the Secretary of Defense has stepped in to address the need by arranging with his oversight committees the reprogramming of funds from the defense budget to accomplish what had traditionally been State Department functions.

Seven years after 9/11, a host of new DOD security assistance authorities has arisen, some of them under the control of military commanders in the field, some others managed by officials within the Office of the Secretary of Defense. The Secretary of State retains a voice in approving security assistance country allocations for activities that are now essentially DOD programs. Foreign policy authority, predictably, has migrated along with resources, leaving the State Department and its oversight committees comparatively much diminished in their respective roles, and agonizing even more over how to use those authorities and apportion the discretionary resources that remain under their purview.

Many would say, with reason, that the new Pentagon security assistance franchise meets the needs of U.S. foreign policy in a timely, accountable, and effective way. It is also the case that the more ready availability of DOD funding elevates the Pentagon's policy voice with governments around the world seeking cooperation and support—a consequence not necessarily foreseen or intended when these new DOD authorities were created out of wartime necessity. The larger question raised is whether the United States, having placed the policy responsibility for arms transfers and security assistance under the Secretary of State for four decades in stark contrast to many other governments where the military or its parent defense ministry operates unchallenged in such matters of state, should now wish to emulate the model that it has been urging others to change for so many years.

In a further irony, as State's primacy in security assistance management has eroded, the department has simultaneously built up its internal financial management bureaucracy and process, which includes the establishment of the Bureau of Resource Management. There are undoubtedly merits in having one or more seasoned business executives overseeing the organization's budget, as indeed there is merit in any system that seeks to align expenditures with declared national policy goals. The paucity of discretionary resources under State Department management, however, now leads to more time-consuming and hence inefficient reallocation processes when events conspire, as they frequently do, to change the priorities of the day. There are more bureaucratic players contesting decisions over fewer assistance funds.

There is a further disadvantage to having a professional "budget management" cadre in the State Department. Foreign policy officials with advanced skills in many areas of diplomacy are not the primary stewards over the budget resources of the programs for which they are ultimately responsible. Without the clear responsibility to manage assistance resources, some of these officials will try to pull from the system the maximum amount for their areas of operation at every opportunity, rather than weighing tradeoffs and conserving resources with the confidence that saved monies will be available for more important needs later in the budget year. It is worth asking whether this represents the optimal business practice for an enterprise whose unified focus at all times should be on achieving benefits to the national interest far from the Washington Beltway.

Nor are these problems limited to the executive branch. On Capitol Hill, the culture of deference between Members and particularly committees regarding their respective jurisdictions leads to a set of bureaucratic "seams" much worse than those found in the executive branch. The State Department's authorizing and appropriating committees, who are well versed on arms control and nonproliferation policies as well as human rights concerns, are mindful not to tread on the "turf" of the Armed Services and Defense Appropriations Committees, who alone deliberate on the operational goals and challenges managed by the Secretary of Defense and the combatant commanders. Whereas the top executive branch officials convene regularly to assess intelligence, diplomatic, and military options, from which flow arms transfer and military deployment decisions, each congressional committee handles a subset of the national policy "toolkit," and no more. An administration's focus on achieving counterterrorist and warfighting objectives through the judicious use of tools such as security assistance is therefore informed, and its policy judgments animated, by a far wider azimuth of political-military perspectives than that available to its various congressional overseers.

The U.S. Government's management challenge on security assistance, as with many tools of engagement and influence, is that there are a lot of "cooks in the kitchen." Some of this is by design. One would expect to find independent positions requiring negotiation and compromise between the executive as policy implementer and Congress as the Federal funding authority. Moreover, there is an appropriate tension between the practitioners seeking to use assistance to advance important policy objectives on the one hand, and the budget managers seeking to limit Federal expenditures in service of effectiveness and efficiency objectives on the other hand.

Beyond these structural checks and balances, however, there are distortions that detract from the achievement of optimal outcomes. Authority over resources can be the cause of unhealthy bureaucratic friction between and within departments and agencies. The scarcity of discretionary funds only exacerbates the competition for influence between policy offices and financial management offices. Too often, efforts to maintain secrecy about budget decisions work against the goal of an open, collaborative process that seeks consensus among all stakeholders.

After so many internal iterations and such an expenditure of effort to build an assistance budget in the executive branch, the fact that Congress may take a different view of global strategic priorities and the favor in which certain governments and leaders should be held reflects constitutional design, and hence should be seen as a strength of the U.S. system. The fact remains, however, that executive branch negotiators will, more often than not, accept these congressional preferences without debate, even at considerable expense to the President's policy priorities; the legislative liaison offices at the State and Defense Departments rarely advise arguing against Congress's wishes and risking programmatic retribution from those authorities with the "power of the purse" over all of their operations. This argues for a more robust and continuous dialogue between the executive and Congress from the outset.

All of the distortions described here in the nearly 2-year cycle from initial plans to eventual disbursement of assistance funds, and the corresponding failure of the process to capitalize on the quality time and effort expended early on by frontline practitioners in the field, may be a cost that the U.S. Government can no longer afford. These assistance accounts, after all, concern U.S. relations with other governments and their military and security sectors. In the 21st century, it is increasingly apparent that the international security environment features multiple actors with growing influence, both good and bad.

A Washington budget process capable of exerting effective influence on the security challenges of this century will do well to begin with a top-level political consensus on the goals to be pursued and the national interests at stake in our success or failure to achieve them. Only on such a foundation can a more efficient, flexible, transparent, and collaborative planning and allocation process be forged, one that, by better defining the national interest, places it further above political or personal consideration.

Living with Coalitions

Just as cooperation between companies in the business world can take many forms, from full-blown joint ventures to short-term cooperative advertising campaigns, so can cooperation between countries. The modes of cooperation that two firms or two governments might choose from time to time depend in part on habit, but also in part on a clear-eyed calculation of what each hopes to achieve from the cooperation, and what it is willing to sacrifice to achieve it.

Companies and countries alike can get into ruts, falling back on forms of behavior that are familiar and comfortable. In a stable, established environment, being proficient at doing the same thing over and over again can serve a company or a country

well. But, in business, the companies that are most successful in rapidly changing sectors are generally those open to breaking old habits and embracing less familiar, more innovative approaches. Again, the same is true of countries.

Coalitions vs. Alliances

The United States has been just as susceptible as any other country to becoming entrenched in habitual approaches to international cooperation. For 150 years, the United States adhered so faithfully to George Washington's declaration that "it is our true policy to steer clear of permanent alliances" that the Nation not only steered clear of permanent alliances but also of any alliances at all, including the temporary emergency alliances that Washington said would be acceptable. Even the dispatch to Europe of the million-strong American Expeditionary Force in World War I was carried out not as an "ally" but as an "associated power."

This sustained refusal to enter into alliances, however, did not mean that the U.S. Armed Forces never worked in concert with foreigners. On the contrary, they frequently operated during this period as part of what we would today call "coalitions of the willing"— with Britain's Royal Navy to suppress piracy in the Caribbean and the slave trade off the coast of West Africa, and with a shifting variety of European powers to protect Western lives and interests during riots and revolutions in places from South America to the Middle East to—most notably—China.

That the United States ultimately abandoned its historic antialliance stance, first for the short-term, emergency purpose of winning World War II and then for the longer term purpose of containing Soviet expansionism, did not mean that President Washington's cautions had been wrong, but rather that circumstances had changed. There were (and still are) sound reasons to steer clear of permanent alliances. They do, as Washington warned, limit freedom of action. They can make it more difficult to sustain good relations with those outside the alliance, even in nonmilitary spheres. They can put one's own peace and prosperity at the mercy of the "ambition, rivalship, interest, humor or caprice" of others, and may, if an ally behaves recklessly, even ensnare a country in a conflict against its own wishes. They are, in a word, "entangling."

These drawbacks were and are just as applicable to the North Atlantic Treaty, ANZUS, and the Rio Pact as to any other permanent alliance. American statesmen entered into these alliances anyway because they recognized the global circumstances that once made Washington's advice so enduringly applicable had been radically transformed. In the late 1940s, the global situation was dire enough that the advantages of alliances were seen (although not unanimously) to outweigh the disadvantages. In the face of a clear, massively threatening, and commonly recognized threat, nations recognized mutual "entanglement" as a source of strength. In a bipolar world, formal alliance structures provided dependability and predictability and sent the adversary a signal of resolve. A shared understanding that the threat was an enduring one made the institutions of a permanent alliance desirable for creating habits of cooperation, for harmonizing and even standardizing many aspects of terminology, command, control, communications, logistics, and legal status. The problem is that, as in the 1940s, global circumstances have again been transformed.

Why Coalitions?

Three generations of American diplomats, soldiers, and policymakers have now lived their entire professional lives in an international security system of which the collective defense alliances created in the 1940s have been the dominant organizing principle. U.S. comfort with alliances as the normal means of international security cooperation has been reinforced by the remarkable success these alliances have enjoyed and by their apparent adaptability to the challenges presented by the post–Cold War stra-

tegic environment, the kind of nonpolar world order contemplated in the opening chapter of this volume.

Institutions such as NATO may be sufficiently malleable to survive the transition from the bipolar Cold War order for which they were created to a new world in which the most pressing challenges may arise from shifting arrays of nonstate movements and other unfamiliar and evolving dangers, a world in which there is no single, enduring threat toward which to direct long-term attention and long-term investment. But it does not follow that NATO-like institutions will necessarily be the most effective means to meet such challenges. Nor is it clear that the political contortions necessary for NATO in particular to undertake operations outside the geographic area prescribed by its charter will necessarily redound to the long-term health of the organization, particularly if the erosion of the consensus rule turns NATO into merely a pre-assembled collection of nations from which coalitions can be easily be configured.

If most analysts' expectations are correct, and the security environment of the 21st century turns out dramatically more fluid and rapidly changing than the one for which the great alliances of the 20th century were created, it is only logical that the United States and "like-minded" countries—a category likely to shift kaleidoscopically from one issue to another—would look for more flexible instruments of cooperation to meet the strategic surprises of the

Coalition forces return to base near Tarmiyah, Iraq, following an air assault mission

U.S. Army (Jacob H. Smith)

new age. It was in the context of just such a strategic surprise, Iraq's 1990 invasion of Kuwait, that the term *coalition* entered the modern American national security lexicon. The *Desert Storm* coalition was so labeled precisely to convey a sense of temporariness and flexibility. Many countries whose contribution to the common effort was enormously valuable for political reasons never would have signed up if the coalition had even been portrayed as an alliance, let alone if it had taken that international legal form. Some countries saw the commonality of interests with the United States as transient, or they feared that alliance with America would ipso facto mean alliance with certain other American "allies," such as Israel. In other cases, they shied away from too open-ended a defense commitment to other members of the coalition.

Similar reservations are likely to apply in the way countries regard the challenges of the future. We already see them in connection with what the United States has viewed since 9/11 as a "war" on terrorism. Many traditional U.S. allies simply do not see the struggle as a war, especially those in Europe for whom the threat is largely domestic, and thus a matter for internal security agencies, not military forces. Conversely, many traditional U.S. partners in the Muslim world do see the struggle very much as a war—albeit one being fought in many cases against their own citizens—but calculate that overt alliance relationships with the United States to prosecute the war would do the adversary more good than harm.

Working Effectively in Coalitions

For the United States to make the most effective use of coalitions in meeting the challenges of the 21st century will take more than a simple lexicon shift; it will require American officials to relearn an old political calculus. Unconstrained by the interlocking moral and legal commitments of which alliances are made, and often lacking the shared goals and values from which such commitments derive, coalition partners are likely to be more transparently driven by calculations of self-interest than many Americans have been accustomed to in dealing with allies. Other countries will be with us on some matters and not on others. This implies a style of coalition management that:

■ segregates issues that can be segregated. In alliances, framing a multitude of particular issues as manifestations of a single systemic challenge can be unifying. In coalitions, it tends to drive away

partners willing to cooperate on one front (for example, suppressing al Qaeda) but not on another (such as regime change in Iraq).

■ embraces pragmatism. If the United States had insisted on NATO-style unity of command in Operation *Desert Storm*, it would never have been able to assemble the broad-based coalition necessary to counter Saddam Hussein's claims that he was standing up for the Arab world against the West.

■ does not hold a grudge. In an alliance, it is reasonable to fault a member that fails to carry its fair share of the burden, because alliances are governed by a "one for all, all for one" ethic. This does not apply in coalitions; partners owe the coalition no more than what they sign up for in the case at hand. Those that choose not to take part in a particular endeavor may make a different calculation the next time they are needed. The door should always be left open.

Beyond this change of mindset, the United States can also take a number of concrete steps to improve its ability to manage coalitions effectively.

Laying the Political Foundation. A perennial problem faced by democracies when a need for collective military action arises is how to persuade a skeptical public that such action is in their own country's interest and not only that of the partner states—that their leaders are not acting like the "poodles" of a foreign master, as the British colorfully describe the matter. Established alliances, in which all the governments share an interest in building popular support, and in which the justification for cooperation can be reinforced continuously over a period of years, are more easily able to build a reservoir of popular support on which to draw in the face of setbacks. By contrast, when a coalition has to be assembled on short notice, governments often face an uphill struggle to generate consensus, and may find public support evanescent if the mission is more costly than expected.

The U.S. Government must therefore be directly involved in generating elite and mass consensus in other countries in anticipation of possible contingencies. It cannot depend on partners to carry out this task, for some will become fully vested in the success of any given mission only after the fact. Besides public diplomacy, this will require broad-based, labor-intensive, time-consuming consultations with a wide range of potential partner states on emerging dangers that might ultimately never require collective action. They must begin well in advance of any specific request for commitments—when action is impending, it is too late to build the conceptual consensus that must underlie a political decision to move forward.

Attracting Meaningful Contributions. It may be familiarity with the all-for-one, one-for-all ethic of formal alliances that is responsible for the mentality that seems to place greater stock in the number of "flags in the sand" than in what partners can realistically bring to the operation. In the long run, this approach undermines the ability of the United States to assemble future coalitions. "Donor fatigue" sets in as the same countries are tapped time and again to provide contributions that turn out to be underutilized. Eventually, donors will stop stepping forward in response to calls for troops, all the sooner if the dispatch of troops is seen to have had a deleterious effect on the donors' ability to meet its own needs at home. U.S. decisionmakers should target requests for coalition contributions in any given situation to a tailored selection of countries that have specific military, civil, or cultural capabilities relevant to each given situation.

Clearing Procedural Underbrush. Every time a coalition is put together, it is necessary to solve anew the same set of issues related to command structures, terminology, rules of engagement, and doctrine. In an alliance such as NATO, issues similar to these are addressed in advance through well-defined institutional arrangements. In coalitions, dealing with them is inevitably a more haphazard process that depends on political decisions to be made by contributing governments at the time. Having gone through the process repeatedly, however, it should be possible to clear away some of the procedural underbrush in advance, or at least to identify those matters that will require addressal.

To that end, U.S. Joint Forces Command (USJFCOM) should be tasked to develop a formal, combined lessons-learned process with past coalition partners to identify the most common and troublesome issues. The command should also design a set of combined, civil-military staff planning exercises to build contacts, develop familiarity, and identify potential roadblocks to cooperation with a wide range of prospective coalition partners. Having USJFCOM rather than the geographic combatant commands lead this process is essential precisely because coalitions, unlike traditional alliances, will invariably draw participation without regard to regional boundaries. Scenarios need not have real-world relevance; if they are too realistic, prospective partners will often be reluctant to participate. The purpose is to

provide a substitute means of building habits of cooperation at the working level that has traditionally been possible only within permanent alliances.

Sensitivity to the Limits of Coalitions. One key advantage that regional security organizations such as NATO and OAS have over ad hoc coalitions is that their place in the international order is enshrined in the UN Charter, and that they thus enjoy a degree of legitimacy in the eyes of many that an ad hoc coalition can never possess. This legitimacy is not everything—the opponents of the bombing of Serbia in 1999 did not find it any more acceptable for having been carried out under NATO auspices than if it had been done by an unaffiliated "coalition of the willing." Nevertheless, it is politically and legally easier for many countries to participate in military operations if they are endorsed by the UN or a recognized regional organization, whether the EU, African Union, Arab League, or Association of Southeast Asian Nations. The United States should be prepared to work through any of these bodies as circumstances warrant. Moreover, U.S. policymakers must be acutely attuned to the perception in many quarters that, by operating through coalitions rather than alliances, America has somehow abandoned its commitment to collective security in favor of assertive unilateralism. As should be clear from the above, nothing could be further from the truth; correctly seen, coalitions are merely another manifestation of America's fundamentally collective approach to security.

Can We Learn to Love Coalitions?

As suggested above, U.S. officials are apt to find the investment of time and effort required for the management of shifting coalitions tiresome. Sometimes it may even seem pointless. Certainly an era of international security cooperation through short-term coalitions will leave few tangible, enduring achievements comparable to NATO and the Organization of American States, institutions whose continued relevance should not be undervalued even if they are not as well suited to present-day challenges as they were to those for which they were created. The same could be said of the 19th century, and yet great things were accomplished through exactly the kind of coalitions that are likely to dominate the landscape of international security in the coming decades.

Some might think it desirable if we could somehow get coalitions to behave more like alliances. But even if that were possible, whatever it might yield in increased predictability could only come at a cost in flexibility and responsiveness to fluid, evolving challenges. We must simply accept that adaptive instruments require close, attentive management. American leaders may never learn to love coalitions, but they must learn to live with them. **gsa**

NOTES

[1] John G. Ruggie, *Multilateralism Matters* (New York: Columbia University Press, 1993), 333.

[2] *International Herald Tribune*, February 21, 2007.

[3] For details on the Afghan army and police situation as it stood in 2008, see Anthony Cordesman, "The Ongoing Lessons of the Afghan and Iraq Wars," Center for Strategic and International Studies, April 2008.

Contributors

Joseph McMillan (Chapter Editor) is Principal Deputy Assistant Secretary of Defense for International Security Affairs. Previously, he served as Senior Research Fellow in the Institute for National Strategic Studies (INSS) at National Defense University (NDU). A specialist on regional defense and security issues in the Middle East and South Asia, and on transnational terrorism, Mr. McMillan has more than two decades of experience as a civilian official in the Department of Defense, and he also has served as academic chairman of the Near East South Asia Center for Strategic Studies.

Dr. Paul J. Sullivan is Professor of Economics in the Industrial College of the Armed Forces (ICAF) at NDU and Adjunct Professor of Security Studies at Georgetown University. Dr. Sullivan teaches courses on Middle Eastern economics and politics, U.S.-Islamic relations, energy security, resources, and security and has been an active participant in a wide range of U.S.-Arab and U.S.-Muslim dialogues, policy panels, and working groups.

Dr. Nora Bensahel is a Senior Political Scientist at the RAND Corporation and Adjunct Professor of Security Studies at Georgetown University, specializing in military strategy and doctrine. Dr. Bensahel's recent work has examined stability operations in Iraq and Afghanistan, postconflict reconstruction, military coalitions, and multilateral intervention.

Lincoln P. Bloomfield, Jr., is President of Palmer Coates LLC and Chairman of the Henry L. Stimson Center in Washington, DC. In addition to serving as Assistant Secretary of State for Political-Military Affairs from 2001 to 2005, Ambassador Bloomfield has held other senior positions in the White House, Department of State, and Department of Defense, most recently as special envoy for man-portable air defense systems threat reduction.

Dr. R. Stephen Brent is a Senior Foreign Service officer in the U.S. Agency for International Development (USAID) and Chair of the Department of Economics in ICAF at NDU. Prior to joining the Industrial College, Dr. Brent led USAID support for the Millennium Challenge Account.

Luigi R. Einaudi is a Distinguished Visiting Fellow in INSS at NDU. His diplomatic career spans more than 30 years, including assignments as U.S. Ambassador to the Organization of American States (OAS) and Special Envoy to the Ecuador-Peru peace talks. In 2000, Ambassador Einaudi was elected Assistant Secretary General of the OAS and subsequently served as Acting Secretary General from 2004 to 2005.

Dr. Sean Kay is Professor of Politics and Government and Chair of International Studies at Ohio Wesleyan University, and Mershon Associate in the Mershon Center for International Security Studies at Ohio State University. Dr. Kay specializes in globalization, international organizations, and U.S. foreign and defense policy and is the author of *Global Security in the Twenty-First Century: The Quest for Power and the Search for Peace* (Rowman and Littlefield, 2006).

Dr. James J. Przystup is Senior Research Fellow in INSS at NDU, specializing in Asian security issues, particularly those involving Japan and Korea. He has worked on Asia-related issues for more than 20 years in both the public and private sectors, including assignments with the Policy Planning Staff at the Department of State, Office of the Secretary of Defense, and Subcommittee on Asian and Pacific Affairs of the House Foreign Affairs Committee.

Chapter 20

Competitive Strategies for U.S. Engagement

After 9/11, the United States reduced its role in the world to one big idea: prosecuting the "global war on terrorism." Inevitably, terrorism, which is a tactic, not a philosophy, failed to provide a universal organizing principle for U.S. security. Now American leaders face a wicked dilemma: how to recalibrate America's strategy to meet myriad complex challenges with diminished power.

A sobering agenda besets today's crisis managers: leaving Iraq more secure; stanching Afghanistan's declining order; closing down Pakistan's safe havens; preventing an Indo-Pakistan war; averting the stark choice between an "Iranian bomb or bombing Iran";

rebuilding a fractured Arab-Israeli peace; balancing North Korea's twin dangers of proliferation and instability; forging a limited nuclear partnership with Russia while tightrope-walking over its "near abroad"; preserving the non-use of weapons of mass destruction; overhauling the international financial architecture; forging new approaches to complex global challenges such as energy and environmental security—and others, including strategic surprises—will require tailored approaches, in-depth knowledge, and strategic patience.

Conflating disparate challenges under a single banner will not make them more manageable. We

President Obama approaches media to make statement on Capitol Hill

AP Images (Lawrence Jackson)

will have to do many things well, and we might begin by recognizing that today's immediate "crises" are inseparable from larger tectonic shifts.

This Global Strategic Assessment has focused on eight global trends driving tomorrow's complex security environment and five pathways to dealing with them. The challenges amount to a paradigm shift, and policymakers may increasingly find themselves operating in terra incognita.

First, even prior to the subprime mortgage crisis and Wall Street meltdown, a gradual global redistribution of economic power from the West to "the Rest" was under way. The saliency of this swing is rooted in history: Economic power is the bedrock of enduring military and political power. Unless some rising nations that have spent decades on the sidelines of the world's economic and trading system are engaged and bound by a common set of rules, the available means for dealing with security will shrink.

Second, we are on the cusp of, but not yet in, a multipolar world. Cold War bipolarity is moribund, even if major-power hostility is not. Unipolarity was derived from subtraction, but the world leaped into multiplication. No single power can mobilize others around its parochial agenda. And handling 21st-century challenges with 20th-century international machinery is Sisyphean. But while political power has fragmented, emerging or resurgent powers—including China, Russia, India, and Brazil—lack the desire or capacity to assume the mantle of leadership.

Third, the globalization of communications is challenging more than the virtual foundations of the information society. Technology is shifting power to the edge, allowing dispersed but networked groups, including terrorists and transnational criminals, to compete with the state's hierarchical structures. Personal, national, and international security are all jeopardized by the heightened risk of pernicious cyber attack. Networks are vulnerable; the wider the network, the wider the vulnerability.

Fourth, energy and environmental security have reached a tipping point. The industrial-era system based on cheap hydrocarbons and scant ecological regard is finished. Volatility in the price of oil and gas weakens the global economy, creates potential flashpoints, and transfers wealth to autocratic oil-exporting regimes. Even with energy conservation and innovation, the world faces another looming resource crisis over water. Consider just one fact: A person's access to fresh water in the Middle East is half of what it was 20 years ago, and it will be half again less in another two decades.

Fifth, the 9/11 tragedy and growing insecurity in Afghanistan today remind us of the growing challenge posed by fragile states and "ungoverned" spaces. There is no surefire way to build effective states. And there are too many weak states to address them at once or to consider investing everything in a solitary problem. There are some billion people in some 60 countries, especially in sub-Saharan Africa, left behind in dire poverty. While weak states are not automatically threats, fragile states may aid and abet a host of other problems, from piracy to trafficking to incubating terrorism and pandemics.

Transnational terrorism poses a sixth global trend. Stateless actors can inflict unprecedented damage, and we must be on our guard against catastrophic terrorism. Meanwhile, we will have to brace ourselves for conventional terror strikes, not only from al Qaeda central and the general Salafi jihadist movement but also by aggrieved local groups, as the November 2008 attack on Mumbai reminds. But passion is not strategy, and overreaction strengthens terrorists. Extensive use of military force will make our strongest instrument the leading liability.

Seventh, the character of war is changing. Low-level uses of force and greater civil-military integration, whether to interdict traffickers or conduct humanitarian operations, are becoming more necessary. Meanwhile, "modern" wars in Afghanistan, Iraq, and Lebanon have produced a renaissance in counterinsurgency and irregular warfare. In the future, capable opponents may seek to pursue "hybrid warfare"—combining conventional, irregular, and catastrophic forms of warfare. Hedging against potential peer competitors means balancing immediate demands with future requirements, not least with respect to conventional forces and space power.

An eighth trend shaping tomorrow's security environment is the proliferation of weapons of mass destruction. Our worst fears regarding mass-disruption weapons have not been realized, but important developments have made it increasingly possible that nuclear or biological weapons may be used in the coming years. Iran's prospective status as a nuclear "threshold" state may be the leading indicator that we are on the verge of a second nuclear age. Meanwhile, there is a growing danger that flourishing life sciences may spawn uncontrolled biological agents.

There is nothing foreordained about another American Century. Constraints on the Nation's resources preclude costly trial and error. Global order is not something managed on a budget. The Obama administration will be hard pressed to manage global disorder without a game-changing strategy. Here are five pathways to initiate recalibration.

Heal thyself. To a remarkable degree, security hinges on America having its house in order. A stable economy is the first step. Restoring legitimacy will lower U.S. transaction costs around the world. Americans need to export hope, not fear, preparing as much for a long search for peace and prosperity as for a long war. Over time, better national education is the prerequisite for joining a globalized world.

Redefine problems. Ends should be realistic. In seeking to transform a region, one is more likely to be transformed; in a quixotic search for definitive victory or permanent peace, one is more apt to hasten exhaustion and failure. Preventing a 9/11 sequel is hard, but it need not produce bankruptcy. A broader definition of security will be needed, recognizing emerging interrelationships, for instance, among energy, the environment, food, and climate change.

Surge civilians. Complex challenges require a larger whole-of-government team of national security professionals, with particular new investments in diplomats and development specialists, as well as the arts of planning, implementation, and assessment. It is time to construct a serious civilian expeditionary corps for complex operations, including conflict prevention. A permanent surge of civilian capacity within the career bureaucracy might enhance government's ability to be more strategic, better trained, and more integrated.

Countermobilize. The United States can use its considerable standing to mobilize emerging power centers into action through not only bilateral alliances and coalitions of the willing but also multilateral institutions. Only a multitude of actors has a chance of tackling complex challenges. Some problems can become opportunities around which society and international actors may be catalyzed into action. For example, when it comes to countering a general threat such as terrorism, the most important partners are Muslims, who are best placed to marginalize a radical Salafi jihadist ideology.

Exercise strategic restraint. The United States cannot afford quagmires that drain resources without providing lasting security. The temptation to play world policeman from the Potomac is seductive; its allure is encouraged by inertia and by free riders. But it is neither America's sole responsibility nor its remit. A strong military is the U.S. ace in the hole, but better still are indirect approaches, strategies of leverage, and "smart power."

America cannot afford to be the world's exclusive security guarantor, but the world is ill prepared for American retrenchment. A shrewd and realistic strategy that balances broadening strategic ends with narrowing national means will require visionary leadership and the best that America has to offer.

The Greek poet Archilochus said that the fox knows many things and the hedgehog knows one big thing. Any "Obama Doctrine" will have to be as clever as the fox. Above all, the United States must keep its eye on multiple challenges, taking care not to exert its finite resources on any single problem.

This final chapter provides several specific approaches for the United States to recalibrate its strategy in the decade ahead: using a smarter blend of soft and hard power to pursue foreign policy and security objectives, as Professor Joseph Nye relates; reflecting on past experience to inform us about future policy, as Mark Kramer endeavors to do; countermobilizing against al Qaeda to turn its weaknesses against it, as Dr. Audrey Kurth Cronin prescribes; linking smarter policies to effective public diplomacy and strategic

U.S. Marine Corps (Andrew J. Carlson)

Marine patrols in Helmand Province, Afghanistan, as part of International Security Assistance Force

communications, as Robert Reilly recommends; rediscovering psychological operations and information operations against specific threats, as Dr. Jerrold Post writes; following policy with careful policy implementation, as Ambassador Ronald Neumann expresses based on considerable first-hand experience; and, as Harlan Ullman suggests, adopting a comprehensive new strategy based on peace, prosperity, and partnership. These are but a few ideas. But as written above and suggested throughout this assessment, the task is to know how to grapple with many challenges, threats, and opportunities at the same time.

Restoring American Leadership through Smart Power

American soft power has declined in recent years. Soft power is the ability to obtain preferred outcomes through attraction rather than either coercion or largesse. Public opinion polls indicate a serious decline in the attractiveness of the United States in Europe, Latin America, and most dramatically, across the entire

General David Petraeus, commander, U.S. Central Command, testifies at Senate Armed Services Committee hearing about U.S. policy toward Pakistan and Afghanistan, April 2009

Muslim world. One important exception is non-Muslim countries of the East Asian region. There, a recent survey by the Pew Research Center shows that, despite Chinese efforts to increase its soft power, America remains dominant in all soft power categories.

The resources that produce soft power for a country include culture (attractiveness to others), values (demonstrated consistency), and policies (perceived inclusiveness and legitimacy). When pollsters ask why American soft power has declined, the respondents cite policies over culture or values. Since it is easier to change policy than culture, there is the possibility that the Nation can advocate new policies that will contribute to recovering some of its soft power.

Some analysts have drawn analogies between the global war on terror and the Cold War. Most instances of transnational terrorism in the last century took a generation to burn out. However, that characterization ignores one aspect of the analogy. Despite numerous problems, Cold War strategy involved a smart combination of hard coercive power and the soft attractive power of ideas. The Berlin Wall fell not to an artillery barrage but to sledgehammers and bulldozers wielded by millions of people who had lost faith in communism.

It is improbable that the United States could ever attract the likes of Osama bin Laden. Hard power is necessary in such cases. But there is enormous diversity in the Muslim world. Witness Iran, where mullahs regard America as "The Great Satan," but many young people want American videos to watch in the privacy of their homes. Many Muslims disagree with American values as well as policies, but that does not mean they side with the bin Ladens. At the strategic level, soft power can isolate extremists and deprive them of recruits. Even tactically, as Malcolm Nance has recently indicated, "soft power tools—giving small cash gifts; donating trucks, tractors, and animals to communities; and granting requests for immigration, education, and healthcare—can be vastly more effective than a show of force [given the] fluid diversity of the enemy."

Success in the information age is not the result of whose army wins, but whose story wins. The current struggle against extreme Islamist terrorism is not a clash of civilizations, but a civil war within Islam. The United States cannot win unless the Muslim mainstream wins. Although hard power is needed in combating extremists, the soft power of attraction is required to win the hearts and minds of the majority. There has not been sufficient debate on the role of soft power. It is an analytical term of art and not a political slogan, which may explain why it has taken hold in academe in Europe, China, and India, but not America. In the current political climate, it makes a poor slogan—emotions after September 11, 2001, left little room for anything described as soft. The Nation needs soft power, but it is a difficult sell for politicians.

Soft power is not the solution to all problems. Although North Korean dictator Kim Jong Il watches Hollywood movies, they are unlikely to affect his nuclear weapons program. Moreover, soft power got nowhere in changing Taliban support for al Qaeda during the 1990s. But other goals such as promoting democracy and human rights are better achieved by soft power.

The term *smart power* describes strategies that combine the resources of hard and soft power. The Smart Power Commission, which was comprised of Members of Congress, retired diplomats and military officers, and heads of nonprofit organizations, concluded that America's image and influence had declined in recent years, and that the Nation had to move from exporting fear to inspiring optimism and hope. This bipartisan commission is not alone in that conclusion. Last year, Secretary of Defense Robert Gates recommended committing more money and effort to soft power, including diplomacy, economic assistance, and communications, because the military alone cannot protect U.S. interests. He noted that defense spending totals almost $500 billion annually compared with $36 billion for the Department of State. "I am here to make the case for strengthening our capacity to use soft power," Secretary Gates remarked, "and for better integrating it with hard power." He conceded that having the Pentagon seek additional resources for Foggy Bottom was like a man-bites-dog story, but these are not normal times.

Smart power is the ability to successfully combine the hard power of coercion with the soft power of attraction into a strategy. By and large, the United States managed such a combination during the Cold War, but more recently has overly relied on hard power because it is the visible source of American strength. The Pentagon is the best trained and resourced arm of government, but there are limits to what hard power can achieve on its own. The promotion of democracy, human rights, and civil society is not best dispensed from the barrel of a gun. Although the military has impressive operational capabilities, the practice of turning to the Pentagon because it can get things done in the field leads to a perception of an overmilitarized foreign policy.

Diplomacy and foreign assistance are often underfunded and neglected, in part because of the difficulty of demonstrating a short-term impact on critical challenges. In addition, wielding soft power is difficult because many of its resources reside in the private sector and civil society and in bilateral alliances, multilateral institutions, and transnational contacts. Moreover, American foreign policy institutions and personnel are fractured and compartmentalized, and there are also inadequate interagency processes for developing and funding a smart power strategy.

The Smart Power Commission acknowledged that terrorism is a continuing threat, but pointed out that over-responding to the provocations by extremists does more damage than the terrorists do. The commission argued that success against terrorism means developing a new central premise for U.S. foreign policy to replace the theme of a war on terror. A commitment to providing for the global good can provide that premise. America should become

a smart power by investing in global public goods—providing what people and governments around the world seek but are unable to attain without the leadership of the largest economy. By complementing military and economic might with greater investments in soft power, and focusing on global public goods, the United States can rebuild the framework needed to tackle tough global challenges.

U.S. Navy (John Kipp, Jr.)

Admiral Mullen greets Pakistan army chief of staff aboard USS *Abraham Lincoln* in North Arabian Sea

Specifically, the Smart Power Commission emphasized the following critical areas:

- **Alliances, Partnerships, and Multilateral Institutions.** Many of these important relationships have fallen into disarray in recent years, and a renewed investment in institutions will be essential.
- **Global Development.** Elevating the role of development in U.S. foreign policy can align interests with people around the world. An initiative on global public health would be the place to start.
- **Investment.** Public diplomacy should rely less on broadcasting and more on face-to-face contacts and exchanges. A new international understanding could be focused on young people.
- **Economic Integration.** Resisting protectionism and continuing engagement in the global economy are necessary for both growth and prosperity. Maintaining an open international economy requires attention to the inclusion of those that market changes leave behind both at home and abroad.

■ **Energy Security and Climate Change.** Global goods will be increasingly important on the agenda of world politics. A new foreign policy should develop an international consensus, and innovative technologies will be crucial in meeting the challenges of energy and environment.

Implementing a smart power strategy will require reassessing how government organization, coordination, and budgeting interact. The Nation should consider various creative solutions to maximize the ability to succeed, including appointing officials who can reach across bureaucracies to align resources in a smart power strategy. Leadership matters in foreign policy. Nations follow their interests, but their leaders define them in different ways. For a powerful nation such as the United States, the structure of world politics allows degrees of freedom in such definitions. It may be true, as some structuralists argue, that the most powerful state is like the big kid on the block who engenders jealousy and resentment in others, but it also matters whether that kid is seen as a bully or a helpful friend. Both substance and style matter. In terms of substantive policies, if the most powerful actor is seen as producing global public goods, it is likely to develop legitimacy and soft power.

Style matters even when public goods are the substance of policy. Charles Krauthammer argued for a new unilateralism that recognized America as the only superpower, strong enough to decide what is right and expectant that others would follow because they have little choice. But this idea is counterproductive. For instance, when an American delegate to the United Nations (UN) conference on climate change stated that "The [United States] will lead, and we will continue to lead, but leadership requires others to fall into line and follow," the comment became a sore point that set back diplomatic efforts. It illustrates how insensitivity to the style and temperament of beholders undercuts the impact of soft power even when directed at producing global public goods.

Consultation and listening are key to soft power. The United States must learn to generate soft power, and relate it to hard power in smart strategies. The bad news is that the Nation is facing a difficult international environment. The good news is that it has used hard, soft, and smart power in equally difficult contexts in the past. In 1970, during the Vietnam War, America was viewed as unattractive in many parts of the world, but with changed policies and the passage of time, it was able to recover its soft power. It can do so again today.

Cold War Myths and Realities

Global politics from the late 1940s to the late 1980s was dominated by the Cold War. Four-and-a-half decades of competition between the United States and Soviet Union sparked crises and led both parties to deploy large military forces, including tens of thousands of nuclear weapons. While American and Soviet leaders managed to avoid all-out war, the lingering repercussions of the Cold War will be felt for decades to come. The collapse of the Soviet Union brought change to the international system, but aspects in the standoff between the superpowers are still relevant. Understanding the past is critical to foreign policy, but history rarely provides lessons on how to approach current issues. Policymakers are tempted to look for lessons that fit their preconceived notions. As a result, misleading myths about the Cold War persist. They should be discarded in favor of broad guidance for future foreign policy.

One tenacious myth about the Cold War is that America consistently adhered to the strategy of containment in seeking to deter and, when necessary, to challenge the expansion of communist influence beyond areas occupied by Soviet forces in 1944–1945 (Eastern Europe and North Korea). Not only op-ed writers, but also scholars of international relations and even some historians have depicted American strategy during the Cold War as based solely on the doctrine of containment. In an article published in July 2008, two experts on international affairs claimed that U.S. foreign policy during the long twilight struggle against its only heavyweight rival was shaped by a single template for global relations: the overarching strategy to contain Soviet communism.

In reality, U.S. foreign policy during the Cold War was not guided by an inflexible template. In some instances, America did not attempt to contain the spread of Soviet influence, but acquiesced in the victories by communist and leftist forces. For example, after the Soviet-backed regimes seized power in Czechoslovakia in 1948 and China in 1949, the United States undertook no military or covert action to reverse them. American inaction in these cases, whether wise or not, entailed significant costs. Declassified documents reveal that the failure to try to oppose the takeover of China emboldened Joseph Stalin, and subsequently contributed to the decision by the Soviet Union in 1950 to condone North Korean plans for the invasion of South Korea.

When the United States did attempt to contain the spread of Soviet influence, the record was mixed. America successfully rebuffed the North Korea invasion and countered the Soviet Union in Western Europe and Japan, but in other cases U.S. efforts to deal with communist advances in places such as Cuba and Vietnam were unsuccessful. Even in Afghanistan in the 1980s, U.S. covert aid to anti-communist guerrillas for limited objectives oriented toward the Soviet Union did not actually succeed in dislodging the regime. Although the U.S.-backed resistance helped spur Mikhail Gorbachev to pull Soviet troops out of Afghanistan, the regime in Kabul survived for several years after the Soviet withdrawal was completed, in part because Moscow continued to provide vast quantities of military and economic support. Not until the Soviet Union collapsed and the successor Russian government abruptly ended assistance to the Afghan government did the communist regime in Kabul collapse.

The notion that containment was the single template for U.S. foreign policy in the Cold War is also belied by instances when America went beyond attempting to curb the spread of Soviet or leftist influence. At various points in the Cold War, the United States tried to roll back Soviet or pro-Soviet forces through covert operations (Iran, Guatemala, Indonesia, and Chile) or unilateral military action (the Dominican Republic and Grenada). The Nation also used diplomatic means, economic aid, and military assistance to forge amicable ties with states that

broke with the sphere of influence dominated by the Soviet Union, notably Yugoslavia, China, and Egypt.

The common view that American foreign policy meant to or could pursue a single approach in the Cold War is inaccurate. U.S. policymakers often showed flexibility, and could not rigidly adhere to a single template. No such template would have been feasible because there was often no consensus on key aspects of foreign policy. Both inside and outside the government, debate raged over the nature of the threat (internal and external) and the best means of responding. Protests against the Vietnam War and the controversy over aid to anti-communist forces in Nicaragua are cases in point. The bipartisanship of the 1950s was more the exception than the norm.

What does all this imply about U.S. foreign policy in the 21st century? First, no overarching strategy or template would be feasible or desirable. If a uniform template was impractical during the Cold War, it is all the more inappropriate today. Second, consensus on the goals and means of foreign policy is almost never guaranteed in advance, and would not necessarily be desirable even if it was. The best way to create a durable consensus is by pursuing policies that are successful. In the run-up to the Gulf War in 1991, for example, public and congressional opposition was strong. After the U.S. military deployed overwhelming force and drove the Iraqis out of Kuwait,

Iraqi soldiers patrol on joint air assault mission with coalition forces near Tarmiyah

support for the war soared. By contrast, public and congressional support for the Vietnam War was solid at the outset but waned as the conflict was escalated without any conclusive outcome. Consensus is not a prerequisite for the success of foreign policy, but success is a prerequisite for consensus. Third, most of the supposedly new challenges and threats of the post–Cold War era—international terrorism, anti-Americanism, Alliance crises, and nuclear proliferation—are not new. Nearly all the following threats were actually more severe during the Cold War:

International Terrorism. The number of international terrorist attacks was higher in the late 1960s and early 1970s than it has been since 1989. In the span of 1 year in 1971–1972, Black September launched spectacular terrorist attacks, including the assassination of the Jordanian prime minister, the simultaneous hijacking of multiple passenger aircraft and other individual hijackings, a massacre at Lod Airport by the Japanese Red Army, and the kidnapping and murder of Israeli athletes at the Munich Olympics. No comparable string of attacks in such a short time has occurred in the post–Cold War era.

Anti-Americanism. The notion that the United States enjoyed popularity during the Cold War is a myth. Anti-Americanism is cyclical, and its surge in the late 1960s has never been surpassed. Demonstrations occurred in nearly all parts of the globe in 1968 against U.S. foreign policy. An unofficial war crimes tribunal convened in Stockholm put the Lyndon Johnson administration on trial not only over Vietnam, but also for covert action in Greece in 1967. In late 1979, in the wake of the revolution in Iran, anti-American attacks roiled the Islamic world. The United States, as the dominant nation in the world, is bound to be the target of resentment and hostility regardless of its policies. The choice of policies can influence the degree of hostility, but the notion that the United States was once loved around the world and could be loved again if only it adopts the right policies is a will o' the wisp.

Crises in the Alliance. The idea that the North Atlantic Treaty Organization (NATO) was cohesive in the face of the Soviet threat is another myth. In reality, the Alliance was almost constantly in crisis and nearly collapsed in the late 1960s when France pulled out of the integrated military command. The challenge led the Johnson administration to begin planning to disband the Alliance. NATO members overcame numerous intra-Alliance crises during the Cold War, and they are likely to experience periodic crises in the post–Cold War era.

Nuclear Terrorism. Threats of nuclear terrorism existed throughout the Cold War. After 1950, there were concerns that the Soviet Union might secretly transfer a nuclear bomb to an anti-American terrorist group or smuggle nuclear explosives through a U.S. port and detonate them in a crisis. From the early 1950s to the late 1980s, U.S. intelligence agencies and the RAND Corporation undertook many classified analyses of nuclear terrorism, some of which warned in dire terms of the likelihood of a near-term attack. The threat should not be discounted today, but concern over this threat is hardly something new.

Nuclear Proliferation. The spread of nuclear weapons was a concern for the United States in the Cold War, starting with the Soviet acquisition of nuclear weapons in 1949, some 2 to 3 years ahead of U.S. intelligence estimates. So great was the concern over the impending Chinese acquisition of nuclear weapons in 1964 that the Johnson administration secretly debated whether to conduct a preemptive strike on its nuclear facilities. Nuclear proliferation was much greater during the Cold War than in the years since it ended. In addition, Great Britain, France, China, and India tested and deployed nuclear weapons during the Cold War. In the post–Cold War era, Pakistan and North Korea have tested them, making a net increase of one nuclear weapons state since 1989. During the Cold War, a nuclear weapons state emerged roughly every 5 years, whereas since then the rate has been less than half that. Nuclear proliferation remains a serious threat, but the threat has existed for some 60 years.

In attempting to prevent Soviet expansion and communist subversion, the United States often faced tradeoffs in its commitment to democratic values. The Cold War led to a vast expansion of national security, and American efforts to counter threats had some moral consequences. The excesses of the McCarthy era, narcotics and mind-control experiments, and wiretapping and infiltration of protest movements were among the notable examples. The Nation often supported authoritarian regimes in Latin America and Asia that fought communist insurgencies. Although U.S. officials encouraged those regimes to accept democratic reforms, their leaders were usually immune to such overtures and compromises were required. Similar tradeoffs are bound to arise today as the United States deals with countries in the Middle East and Southwest Asia.

The Cold War also forced America to make choices on the treatment of enemy combatants and terrorists. The Nation signed and ratified the four Geneva Conventions of 1949, but during the Vietnam War was unsure whether to extend those protections to Viet Cong prisoners of war. The administration ultimately decided to accord full coverage to all prisoners (Viet Cong as well as North Vietnamese), but the fact that the issue was debated indicates the challenges that arise when fighting guerrillas who do not abide by the laws of war. The United States at times was implicated in the abuse of insurgents in Latin America, notably when intelligence operatives distributed guidance on torture. But when U.S. political leaders learned about the torture manual, they regarded it as antithetical to American values. Despite compromises that the United States made during the Cold War, officials were unwilling to emulate the Soviet Union in resorting to torture. The underlying spirit of this episode in the Cold War is worth reviving today.

War of Ideas

The National Strategy for Combating Terrorism in 2006 stated that "in the long run, winning the War on Terror means winning the battle of ideas." That emphasis seems to be reflected in every strategic document since then, including the *National Defense Strategy of the United States of America* in 2005, which called directly for "countering ideological support for terrorism."

But the emphasis has not produced any results. In fact, the American side in the war of ideas has not yet shown up. Strategic communications or public diplomacy, which is intended to win such wars, has been the single weakest instrument of national strategy since September 11, 2001. By almost any index, the United States is not doing well; some even say it has already lost. After traveling 6 months in the Muslim world, Akbar Ahmed, who chairs Islamic Studies at American University, stated, "I felt like a warrior in the midst of the fray who knew the odds were against him but never quite realized that his side had already lost the war." There are two reasons why the Nation is not winning this war: organizational dysfunction and intellectual confusion.

During the Cold War, the U.S. Information Agency (USIA) was charged with conducting the war of ideas. At one time, it had 10,000 employees, including foreign nationals, and an annual budget of $1 billion. After the collapse of the Soviet Union, the agency was dismantled. Public diplomacy, it seemed, was obsolete, a relic of the Cold War. During the

▼ *Continued on p. 481*

Thinking Strategically about al Qaeda

As a terrorist movement, al Qaeda has sought to commit violence on a scale and at a pace never before encountered by the United States and its allies and friends around the world. A countermobilization strategy could be developed to combat al Qaeda by setting it apart from other jihadi groups, exploiting its internal divisions, hiving off its followers and supporters, calling attention to its wanton brutality, and facilitating a backlash to discredit and diminish the movement.

Devising such a counterstrategy requires understanding the classic approaches of terrorism—namely, compellence, provocation, polarization, mobilization, and eroding legitimacy. The first three use leverage to turn the traditional formulation of ends-ways-means of strategy on its head. For terrorists, strategy is not matching ends and means, since the reaction of target audiences can be the means or ends, or both. Moreover, these five strategies are not mutually exclusive.

Compellence normally seeks to influence one party to do something that another wants it to do. Ascribing the motives of terrorist groups to that of state activity is natural but can be misleading. Terrorists normally oversimplify complex situations through messages targeted at their audiences, not least of all in the West, which are disseminated on the Internet and over the news media.

Provocation attempts to force a state to react, to do something—usually not a specific policy but some type of firm action that works against its own interests. Compared to war, terrorism may be unimportant, but when it manages to provoke a state to act, it can indirectly cause even greater death and destruction.

Polarization can drive states to the right, fragmenting societies to the extent that moderate governance becomes impossible. It is particularly effective when used against democracies with guaranteed civil liberties and domestic support, but it can have unintended consequences that prevent a group from achieving its aims.

Mobilization is suited for a globalized world in which democratized communications, public access, reduced cost, frequent messaging, and visual exploitation afford groups such as al Qaeda the capabilities to leverage the effects of terrorist activities in an unprecedented way.

Eroding legitimacy isolates and undermines the state both at home and abroad, discredits its foreign and defense policies, and also complicates its ability to maintain its alliances with other states.

Because terrorism is often the instrument of weak nonstate actors, there are more examples of strategies of leverage than any other type. A terrorist group may use a combination of several approaches, but how the state responds certainly matters. Terrorism is the weak strategy of the weak, drawing strength from the actions of the state. Reactions by a government in the narrow framework of one strategy may be counterproductive with respect to defeating the others.

In terms of frequency and effectiveness, these strategies are temporal, reflecting the political contexts in which they arise. Compellence best fit the mid-20th century because it aligned well with nationalism, whose aims could be expressed in terms of territory. Provocation was suited to the 19th century because of the condition of declining autocratic regimes. Polarization figured in the early days of Marxism and reemerged at the end of the 20th century with terrorism designed to polarize racial, religious, tribal, linguistic, or ethnic groups. And mobilization is well adapted to the current world with changes in political organizations, communications, and trade.

The histories of terrorist groups point to various ways in which they may end: the destruction of leadership, failure to transition between generations, achieving their stated cause, negotiating a settlement, succumbing to military or police repression, losing popular support, and transitioning to other malignant activities such as criminality or war. Not all these pathways are probable for every group, and they are not all relevant to al Qaeda. For example, it is clear that al Qaeda will not end if Osama bin Laden is killed. Groups that have ended in this way have been hierarchical, reflecting to some degree a cult of personality, and lacking a viable successor, none of which describes al Qaeda. It will also not die out between generations, as al Qaeda has transitioned beyond its original structure and is a multigenerational threat. Likewise, achieving its cause or reaching a negotiated settlement is a pathway that does not apply to al Qaeda. Groups that have achieved their ends have limited goals. At least as articulated in recent years, al Qaeda seeks to mobilize the *umma* to rise up, throw off the influence of the West, eliminate its support for Arab regimes, and establish a new world order (sometimes called a caliphate).

Such objectives could not be achieved without overturning the international political system, and there is no evidence that al Qaeda has moved closer to achieving them. As for negotiations, engaging in a legitimate political process has historically required feasible, negotiable terms and a sense of stalemate. And terrorists seeking negotiations often have an incentive to find a way out of what they consider a losing cause. But none of this describes al Qaeda.

The remaining pathways deserve greater scrutiny. Although the campaign against al Qaeda has yielded results, the limits of driving the group into hiding and reducing its capacity to operate have been demonstrated. Democracies find it hard to sustain a policy of repression, which can undermine civil liberties and domestic support. American use of force signified Western resolve, killed al Qaeda leaders, and prevented attacks, but force alone cannot drive this group to its end. That would require a scorched-earth policy

that the United States would not tolerate.

The loss of popular support has ended many terrorist groups, and it is a plausible scenario for al Qaeda. Support can be compromised through miscalculation, especially in targeting. Attacks may cause revulsion among actual or potential constituencies: at least one-third of the victims of al Qaeda have been Muslims, the same people the group claims to protect. Another pathway is failing to convey a positive image or progress toward its goals, which applies to al Qaeda.

Finally, groups can transition from terrorism to criminal behavior or escalate to insurgency or conventional warfare, especially with state sponsorship. Some argue that this may have already happened in the case of al Qaeda, which would be unfortunate. In this connection, it is counterproductive to regard this group as a global insurgency because the term bestows legitimacy on al Qaeda, emphasizes territorial control, and puts the United States into a dichotomous strategic framework that precludes clear-eyed analysis of the strategies of leverage that are being used against America and its allies.

The question for policymakers in the midst of a terrorist campaign is not to ask how they are doing, but rather how they will it end. And the second question is not when the next attack will occur, but rather what comes after that event. Terrorism arises in political, social, and historical contexts that constantly evolve. But terrorist groups traditionally end in certain discernible ways. The challenge is knowing which ending fits a given terrorist group, to work synergistically with the process as it unfolds, and to push it further in that direction. Governments who get caught up in the short-term goals and spectacle of terrorist attacks overlook broader historical perspectives, that are crucial to reasserting state power and legitimacy, and the strategies of leverage exploit such mistakes. Driving a terrorist movement such as al Qaeda toward its end is much smarter than responding in a cause-and-effect manner to its tactical actions as they occur.

▲ *Continued from p. 479*

brief end-of-history fantasy, it was thought that the ideas of democratic, constitutional political order and free markets stood uncontested throughout the world. The war of ideas was over—and America had won.

The functions of USIA were relegated to the Department of State and Broadcasting Board of Governors. The senior official responsible for the war of ideas became the Under Secretary of State for Public Diplomacy and Public Affairs, a third-tier position—which speaks volumes about the extent of the demotion of this activity as a consequence of the peace dividend. Within the State Department, public diplomacy functions were dispersed among regional and other bureaus, making coordination and control a major problem.

The attempt to situate public diplomacy in State has failed. One reason is that the department's role is diplomacy, *not* public diplomacy. It should not be expected to perform both, since these roles sometimes conflict. Public diplomacy attempts to reach people in other nations directly over the heads of their governments. This can complicate the job of the State Department, which has the responsibility of maintaining good relations with those governments. The difficulty of placing both roles in one institution was recently summarized by a commentator from the U.S. Advisory Commission on Public Diplomacy: "State does not recruit for public diplomacy; State does not test for public diplomacy; State does not train for public diplomacy; State has a glass ceiling for public diplomats."

The Broadcasting Board of Governors assumed responsibility for non-defense government broadcasting, including the Voice of America. It became a standalone agency run by part-time board members, most of whom have had no experience in either foreign policy or public diplomacy. The eight-member board exercises executive power and is not directly accountable to anyone. Since the professional experience of the governors has been mainly in the national mass media, they have sought to impose that media culture on government broadcasting by refashioning much of it using American pop culture. Radio Sawa is the prime example of this approach.

Coordination through the White House Communications Office, National Security Council, and interagency bodies has made few improvements to this unsatisfactory situation. Lack of both an executive authority and a chain of command to execute strategic communications plans has hampered well-intend-

ed efforts. The Department of Defense occasionally has tried to fill the gap, but it is neither organized nor authorized to conduct public diplomacy except in a support role and on a reimbursable basis. The Pentagon was even prohibited from supporting a project involving posters to be displayed in 100 Embassies to publicize military relief efforts for the tsunami victims in Southeast Asia. This occurred because of a conflict between Title 10 and Title 22 responsibilities, resulting in the banning of images of U.S. forces rescuing and aiding victims in the region portrayed.

Philippine civilians attend medical civic action program in Juban to receive veterinarian aid for animals during exercise Balikatan 2009

No government agency has possessed the capability to implement a sustained multifaceted strategy to win the war of ideas since USIA was dismantled. The events of September 11, 2001, revealed that the assumption on which the agency had been abolished, namely that the world embraced democratic pluralism, was not universally accepted by those to whom it applied. Seven years later, there are many individuals across the U.S. Government with the expertise to successfully conduct the war of ideas, but there still is no organization to execute this instrument of national power.

Secretary Gates stated in November 2007 that America is "miserable at communicating to the rest of the world what we are about as a society. . . . Al-Qaeda is better at communicating its message on the Internet than America." Several days later, former Secretary of Defense Donald Rumsfeld observed that "U.S. institutions of public diplomacy and strategic communications . . . no longer exist," adding, "when the U.S. Information Agency became part of the

State Department in 1999, the country lost what had been a valuable institution capable of communicating America's message to international audiences powerfully and repeatedly." The consensus is that something is wrong, particularly within the Department of Defense, because this serious deficiency in national capabilities has grave consequences for the Armed Forces.

It may be time to create an organization that can propagate American ideals and institutions to the world and counter hostile propaganda. A strategic communications agency could maintain a focus on aiding liberals and moderates in Muslim-majority countries, and not get lost in daily spin control. It would have responsibility for developing and reinforcing an anti-authoritarian social and cultural network in the Islamic world. It would be independent of the Department of State, which could be inclined to downplay differences for the sake of relations with particular countries or regions. Moreover, it would be independent of the Department of Defense and Central Intelligence Agency to avoid entanglement in their respective missions. Its director would report to the President and be responsible for the interagency coordination of all strategic communications efforts.

This agency should be funded to promote the free exchange of ideas in the Islamic world and beyond and to support allies in those regions. To put present efforts in budgetary perspective, current spending on U.S. public diplomacy is about the same as the McDonald's restaurant chain's worldwide advertising budget, and half of what Saudi Arabia gives annually to spread Wahhabism throughout the Muslim world and elsewhere. The approximately $1.3 billion being spent on public diplomacy is 1/450th of the entire Pentagon budget.

An agency dedicated to the war of ideas would only be as effective as its understanding of the ideas that it propagates and the hostile ideas that it contests. Wars of ideas are fought over contending interpretations of reality such as the meaning of life for which people are willing to die.

Every threat to the existence of the United States has come on the level of moral principle, whether it has been Nazis and their racial theory or communists and their class theory. Both explicitly denied American moral principles as articulated in the Declaration of Independence. Today, radical Islamists deny those same principles with their own deformed theology. The resulting conflicts are conducted in terms of moral legitimacy. Defending one's ideas and attacking those of the enemy depend upon a moral rhetoric and appeal to a moral comparison, such as the Axis of Evil and the Great Satan.

America is failing in this war of ideas because it has not seriously addressed the larger issue of moral legitimacy—its own and the enemy's—which is the real nub of the conflict. One needs compelling ideas to fight countervailing ideas. The United States has not engaged at the level on which this moral conflict is being waged. Instead, its message to the Islamic world has been preempted by American pop culture. It is not strange that the United States should turn to entertainment media, but it cannot entertain or advertise its way through a war of ideas. While pop culture itself creates enough problems, the U.S. Government ironically spreads it through the broadcasts of Radio Sawa and Radio Farda to the Arab and Persian worlds. By doing so, the Nation has inadvertently projected the image of itself as an adolescent, and is not taken seriously where it counts. An adolescent superpower is not a source of comfort to allies, and it is much less a magnet for those nations addressing the crisis of the day.

The image of America as an adolescent superpower is particularly troubling in light of the upheaval in the Muslim world, which will have enormous consequences. The unavoidable clash of values spawned by the forces of globalization challenges Islam. The loss of faith makes life meaningless and therefore intolerable for most Muslims. The majority of Muslims interpret the threat of secular influences that are exacerbated by multiple nonstop satellite television channels as an attack on Islam itself. This conclusion has been responsible for a wave of vociferous responses.

In terms of this larger crisis in the Islamic world, the exiled Iranian philosopher Abdulkarim Soroush has said that "Muslims would like to live in a democratic milieu, and at the same time they would like to keep their faith as well. They do not want to live in a democratic atmosphere at the expense of their beliefs and convictions." The United States should not go out of its way to convince them that this is an impossibility. Rather, it ought to demonstrate that this is an American truism and that faith and freedom are by no means mutually exclusive in the modern world.

American pop culture does not depict freedom as an essential constituent of the moral order, but often as something inimical to it. In pop culture, the United States appears to offer young Muslims the choice between either greater freedom with no purpose, or personal submission to a higher purpose espoused by radical Islamists. So long as adversaries continue to frame the question in those terms, America will contribute to its own defeat in the war of ideas.

The United States has not demonstrated that freedom has an indispensable moral meaning. In fact, it often unintentionally does the opposite. While serving as the Under Secretary of State for Public Diplomacy, Karen Hughes lauded American diversity, which is not effective against the divine mission of some adversaries. When the popular notion of American diversity becomes the message, it conveys the idea that the United States does not discriminate among various claims to truth. To many Muslims, diversity equals relativism and moral decline. Slogans simply do not reflect the moral principles on which American tolerance of diversity is based. These principles are not found on the Department of State Web site or in the *U.S. National Strategy for Public Diplomacy and Strategic Communication*, which reflect no sense of subtlety or awareness. As Professor Harry Jaffa has commented, the United States is "telling others to accept the forms of our own political institutions, without any reference to the principles or convictions that give rise to those institutions."

The first step in reinvigorating public diplomacy is reestablishing U.S. moral legitimacy and undermining adversaries through the serious exposition and promotion of ideas. Anything done in the name of public diplomacy that is not related to one of these

objectives is not relevant to the war of ideas and should be rejected. Under this standard, 85 percent of the activities listed in the current State Department Public Diplomacy Update would be eliminated. Moreover, the selection of target audiences should shift from those consumers of mass culture abroad to the educated and influential groups in foreign societies. These audiences should be reached via media that they take seriously—books, journals, films, theater, dialogues, and substantive exchanges. If the Nation wants to be taken seriously, it must win the war of ideas; but that war can be won only if the Nation takes *it* seriously.

Information Operations to Counter Terrorism and Rogue States

The end of the Cold War did not bring on the long-anticipated peace dividend. Rather, following the fall of the Berlin Wall and subsequent demise of the Soviet Union, there was a rise in ethnic conflict. The relative stability of the superpower rivalry has been succeeded by political-military crises precipitated by rogue states. The media have been filled with the names of leaders such as Saddam Hussein, Slobodan Milosevic, Kim Jong Il, Mahmoud Ahmadinejad, Hugo Chavez, and Robert Mugabe, several of whom seek or already have weapons of mass destruction.

Low-intensity conflict and transnational terrorism are prominent features of the 21st-century security

U.S. Air Force (Eric Harris)

Provincial Reconstruction Team member talks with administrators at school that provides training for trades

environment. The last two decades have been punctuated by a series of terrorist events: the bombing of the World Trade Center in 1993; the Aum Shinrikyo sarin gas attack on Tokyo subways in 1995; the coordinated bombings of U.S. Embassies in Kenya and Tanzania in 1998; the attack on the USS *Cole* in 2000; the attacks on the World Trade Center and the Pentagon in 2001; and the everyday suicide bombings by radical Palestinian groups in Israel. With few exceptions, these attacks were designed to cross the mass-casualty threshold. Terrorism is a vicious form of psychological warfare, waged through the media. One of the key goals in terrorist strategy is influencing selected audiences, including its potential

Iraqi army commander presents plaque to imam and Sunni leader in Mosul, Iraq

recruits, in the West and throughout the political establishment. As has been seen in the case with rogue states, the United States and its allies have been insufficiently responsive to conducting psychological operations to counter them.

The strategy of deterrence and the doctrine of mutually assured destruction, which relied on the rationality of the Soviet Union, were formulated during the Cold War but are no longer relevant. To extrapolate from deterrence a new way of dealing with potential adversaries will inevitably lead to erroneous policies. What deters a superpower rival may be counterproductive in the case of an outlaw nation or terrorist group; indeed, it may prove to be an incentive rather than a deterrent. And yet all too

frequently, this is exactly what strategic thinking has proposed doing.

There is no one-size-fits-all model for deterrence. Rather, the approach should be tailored to the nature of an enemy—based on what one expert has called an actor-specific behavioral model. In countering terrorists and rogues, models of their psychologies, decisionmaking processes, and strategic cultures are an absolute necessary. Threats arise from relatively unknown and unfamiliar sources. One cannot optimally deter a potential enemy that one does not understand. And yet appropriate models and the requisite understanding are often unavailable. The nuanced political profiles of personalities are particularly important in the case of leader-dominant societies.

In the overreliance on technology, social science expertise has been insufficiently applied to the war for hearts and minds, leaving adversaries to operate on a relatively uncontested information battlefield. This has profoundly disadvantaged American national security. Individual terrorists are psychologically normal people, not crazed fanatics. It is not psychopathology, but rather group and collective psychology that is important in this sort of conflict, with a particular emphasis on collective identity that is vital to understanding the mind of the terrorist.

If indeed terrorism is a vicious species of psychological warfare, waged through the media, it must be countered by psychological warfare. Core elements of integrated information operations guided by understanding of the dynamics of terrorist groups include inhibiting potential terrorists from joining groups in the first place, producing tension within groups, facilitating the means to exit groups, reducing support for groups, and delegitimizing the leaders of groups.

Stemming the flow of recruits on which terrorist groups depend is the most critical challenge. The reservoir of hatred is deep, and hatred is bred especially among nationalist-separatist terrorists. Recruitment can be inhibited by deromanticizing terrorism, providing secular education to counter radical Wahabi *madrassa*s, offering alternate means to redress legitimate grievances, and opening otherwise autocratic societies. Dissension can be promoted by exploiting the fact that underground groups are emotional pressure cookers, fostering paranoia by injecting rumors of traitors within the ranks, and alienating followers from their leaders. The means of facilitating an exit from groups include introducing amnesty programs, allowing reduced sentences for those who cooperate, using defectors as a source of rumors, and challenging the ideological basis of extremism. One difficulty has been the relative silence of moderate voices in countering the language of extremism, which otherwise pervades the societies in question. In sermons at mosques, the behavior of martyrs is honored, just as those who martyr themselves for the cause of Tamil independence are honored.

Countering the voices of extremism is a tough job, one that cannot be plausibly carried out by the West, but must be addressed within Islam. The voices of moderation are beginning to be heard. Of particular note is the growing conflict among Islamic extremists led by Sayid Imam al-Sharif (also known as Dr. Fadl), a founding ideologue of al Qaeda and the former leader of the Egyptian terrorist group al Jihad. Fadl, a brilliant medical school classmate of Ayman al-Zawahri (deputy and putative successor to Osama bin Laden) renowned for his knowledge of Islamic jurisprudence, formalized the rules of holy war in *The Essential Guide for Preparation*. This work by Fadl became the definitive ideological underpinning of al Qaeda, including axioms such as "jihad is the natural state of Islam" and that "Muslims must always be in conflict with non-believers." In another of his texts, *The Compendium of the Pursuit of Divine Knowledge*, which is more than 1,000 pages long, Fadl provided al Qaeda with the theological justification for violence against all who opposed its extremist path, labeling them as nonbelievers.

But by 1994, Fadl was becoming disillusioned with al Qaeda because of its use of violent excesses that seemed to go beyond theological justification. As members of the Islamic Group imprisoned in Egypt began to consider other interpretations of jihad, they came to believe they had been manipulated into pursuing the path of violence. This rethinking culminated in the startling declaration by one revolutionary leader at a military trial in 1997 that the Islamic Group would cease all violent activity, and a series of publications was produced to explain their new thinking. One of the leaders asserted that "the Islamic Group does not believe in the creed of killing by nationality."

After September 11, 2001, the Egyptian government exposed the debate taking place within its prisons, a move that threatened the foundation of al Qaeda. In 2007, Fadl undermined the agenda of bin Laden and Zawahiri in a rejection of al Qaeda doctrine that he faxed from jail that asserted, "We are prohibited from committing aggression even if the enemies of Islam do that." The statement, which appeared in Egyptian and Kuwaiti media, was rejected by Zawahiri: "I wonder if they now have fax machines in Egyptian jail cells? I wonder if they're connected to the same line as the electric shock machines?" But the effect was damaging since it came from Fadl. Controversy over the theological justification of the extremism of al Qaeda doctrine arose, and increasing numbers of committed jihadists began repenting sins committed while they were misinformed. In addition to Egypt and Kuwait, deradicalization is under way in Saudi Arabia, Jordan, Yemen, Singapore, and Indonesia. Although success has not been fully evaluated, the results are encouraging in Egypt. The program includes reducing support by society at large and potential recruits, marginalizing

U.S. Navy (Cristina R. Morrison)

Sailors deliver bags of rice to citizens in Sumatra, Indonesia, in wake of tsunami

the influence of al Qaeda, and delegitimizing the likes of bin Laden and Zawahiri.

Identifying the theological basis of Islamist extremism as dubious can undermine its dogmatic certitude, but for the most part it has gone unchallenged. One challenge has been countering the viral spread of extremist ideology via the Internet. Although this debate is taking place among scholars, the message reaches an estimated 5,000 radical Islamist Web sites. This is a major factor as young people are increasingly being radicalized over the Internet.

Ironically, despite condemning globalization and its attendant evils, the Islamist extremists employ modern information technology to propagate their message. And these Islamists have a clear strategy on using the Internet, as revealed in the following directive on an al Qaeda Web site:

Due to the advances of modern technology, it is easy to spread news, information, articles and other information over the Internet. We strongly urge Muslim Internet professionals to spread and disseminate news and information about the Jihad through e-mail lists, discussion groups, and their own websites. If you fail to do this, and our site closes down before you have done this, you may hold you to account before Allah on the Day of Judgment. . . . This way, even if our sites are closed down, the material will live on with the Grace of Allah.

Four months prior to the Madrid bombings in 2004, this posting appeared on the Internet:

In order to force the Spanish government to withdraw from Iraq, the resistance should deal painful blows to its forces. . . . It is necessary to make the utmost use of the upcoming general election in March next year. We think that the Spanish government could not tolerate more than two, maximum three blows, after which it will have to withdraw as a result of popular pressure. If its troops remain in Iraq after these blows, the victory of the Socialist Party is almost secured, and the withdrawal of the Spanish forces will be on its electoral program.

But words alone will not suffice. Our words must be complemented by our actions.

Public Diplomacy in Countering Adversaries

Just as an understanding of terrorist psychology is required in targeting information operations, public diplomacy and strategic communication programs designed to counter rogue states must be informed by a nuanced appreciation of leaders and their strategic culture. Importantly, public diplomacy and information operations must be thematically coordinated. A White House speech intended for a domestic audience can be counterproductive if delivered to an international audience.

The first Gulf War and invasion of Iraq illustrate opportunities taken and lost. An aggressive psychological operations (PSYOP) campaign was planned and executed for Operation *Desert Storm* by the 4th Psychological Operations Group with Army Reserve PSYOP units. These 650 Soldiers made a major contribution to the coalition psychological warfare effort. They developed and delivered 29 million

leaflets, which were distributed by balloons and from B–52s, and even smuggled some into Baghdad. Partly as a result of this campaign, 44 percent of the Iraqi army deserted, 17,000 defected, and more than 87,000 surrendered. It is judged that as a consequence of this successful PSYOP effort, tens of thousand of lives were saved. This was effective tactical battlefield PSYOP, derived from techniques developed and refined during World War II.

Effectively countering Saddam Hussein psychologically required a nuanced understanding of his political personality. Rather than being the madman of the Middle East, Saddam was a rational political actor who often miscalculated because he was surrounded by sycophants who for good reason were afraid to criticize him for fear of losing their jobs or lives. Thus, he could remain in touch with reality psychologically while being out of touch with it politically. Saddam had a traumatic background that left him wounded psychologically, so that criticism, no matter how constructive, was capable of wounding his fragile self-esteem at the peril of critics.

His residences provide an apt metaphor for the layers of his psychology. He was born in a mud hut in Tikrit, which symbolized the social and economic poverty in his early life. Despite the abuse and deprivation of those early years, at the age of 8, an uncle named Khayrallah filled him with compensatory dreams of glory, telling him that one day he would play a major role in Iraqi and Arab history by following the path of Saladin and Nebuchadnezzar, who had rescued Jerusalem from the Crusaders. Symbolizing his grandiose self-concept were the lavish palaces, which he built throughout Iraq. But what underlay the palaces? Underground bunkers of steel and reinforced concrete, bristling with weapons and communications equipment, symbolizing the siege state in Saddam's psychology, ready to be attacked, ready to lash back. But by the time he was discovered in a spider hole, ironically beneath a simple mud hit, his life was shattered.

Saddam wrapped himself in the Palestinian flag after a UN resolution called for him to pull out of Kuwait, indicating he would abide by the resolution when earlier resolutions on Israel and the occupied territories were honored, which made him a hero to the Palestinians. It was dreams of glory realized as he became a major world leader. He had the world by the throat.

Saddam probably could not have been deterred or reversed himself, for he had painted himself into a corner. But he had abruptly changed direction in the past when it was pragmatic to do so, and could do so again, if and only if—a double contingency—he could retain his power base and not lose face. In the event, the emphatic statement made by President George H.W. Bush while pounding on the table—"There will be no face saving"—seemed designed to leave Saddam with no way out. It may have contributed to his decision that he could not withdraw without being humiliated and that he had to stand up to the coming massive air attack. As it was, Saddam declared victory on the fifth day of that attack. Since it had been predicted he could survive only 3 to 4 days, he could claim victory in the Arab context because he courageously resisted a superior adversary, and each succeeding day of defiance only magnified that achievement.

Saddam was surprised by the breadth of the coalition that President Bush assembled. In the period leading to the invasion of Kuwait, Saddam misjudged not only the impact of his action on his Arab neighbors but also the support of Russia and France. An adaptive leader who learned from experience, Saddam set out to unravel the coalition and the unanimity among the nations arrayed against him. With economic incentives, he eventually wooed Russia, China, and France without whose support the United States would be unable to rally UN action for coercive diplomacy and sanctions against Iraq. With carrots and sticks, he bullied his Arab neighbors and restored relations with them, as demonstrated by the call of Saudi Prince Abd Allah in 1997 for the Gulf Cooperation Council to "overcome the past with its events and pains." The prodigal son was back. The United States failed to counter this aggressive diplomatic offensive with a strategic information operation and public diplomacy campaign, leading essentially to the unraveling of the coalition that had been so effective in stemming aggressive behavior by Saddam.

After the 1991 conflict, Saddam was obsessed with loyalty of the military, which had been fractured by the war. Those who showed any enthusiasm for his overthrow were jailed, tortured, and executed with their families. In the 2003 conflict, this significantly inhibited defection from within the senior ranks. There was fear of reprisal until Saddam was captured. It was loyalty at the barrel of a gun. His brutal revenge against those suspected of disloyalty was a highly effective psychological instrument designed to retain the allegiance of his own military leaders.

President George W. Bush and Secretary of Defense Donald Rumsfeld delivered a particularly adroit series of public diplomacy speeches in late 2002 during the run-up to Operation *Iraqi Freedom*. Convinced of the danger to U.S. troops from Iraqi use of weapons of mass destruction, Secretary Rumsfeld indicated that the military had a major role to play in reconstruction. But he went on to say that if such weapons were used, all bets were off. Several weeks later, President Bush indicated that Saddam might well order the use of weapons of mass destruction. He added that in that event, Iraqi generals would be advised to disobey such an order. Such comments were designed both to inhibit the use of weapons of mass destruction and split Saddam from the Iraqi military leadership. Splitting leaders from their followers should be central to influence campaigns. But it can be particularly difficult to achieve in closed societies such as North Korea where the information environment is tightly controlled.

The Case of North Korea—Unlike Father, Unlike Son

Kim Il Sung, founding father of the Democratic People's Republic of Korea (DPRK), was a noted guerrilla leader who rose to power under Soviet patronage. He created the *juche* (independence) ideology of North Korea and consistently declared the goal of unifying Korea under his leadership. It was his son, Kim Jong Il, beginning with his first position at age 30 as director of the Bureau of Propaganda and Agitation, who created the cult of personality around his charismatic father as well as the notion of himself as the successor in that charismatic role. Kim Jong Il created the myth of the man born on Mount Paektu, a sacred Korean mountain from which the nation sprang, when in fact he was born in a hovel in the Soviet Union under Russian protection.

Kim Jong Il is a pale imitation of his father. He is not a nationbuilder or a guerrilla fighter, nor did he create an ideology. It is a case of unlike father, unlike son. Thus, the giant shadow of his father, the Eternal President, looms over the son. It is difficult enough succeeding a powerful father; it is impossible psychologically to step into the shoes of a godlike figure. That continuing pretense remains the daunting reality that challenges the ruler of North Korea. Disparities between the father and son contribute to profound insecurity of Kim Jong Il, who is trapped by the ideology of *juche* and reunification—"majesty sits uncomfortably on his shoulders."

By the early 1970s, it became clear that Kim Il Sung was grooming Kim Jong Il to take over. The son worked behind the scenes while his father remained the political face of the country. Kim Jong Il became Secretary of the Korean Workers Party in 1973 and a full member of the Politburo in 1974. He announced the Ten Principles that required absolute loyalty to his father. By early 1980s, Kim Jong Il had assumed daily control of the nation, including the intelligence apparatus, but he has never taken the title of President. He and his cronies enjoy a hedonistic lifestyle in Pyongyang. Kim Jong Il is insecure about his political and physical stature, once commenting that he "resembled the droppings of a midget." Despite his grandiosity and egotism, this statement reveals his extreme insecurity about stepping into the godlike shoes of Kim Il Sung.

Kim Jong Il lives in a seven-story pleasure palace and recruits young girls from junior high school for so-called joy brigades to provide rest and relaxation for hardworking senior officials. While average North Koreans earn between $900 and $1,000 annually, he reportedly spent from $650,000 to 800,000 annually during the 1990s on expensive cognac. Addicted to motion pictures, he supposedly has a collection of some 10,000 to 20,000 films. His concept of leadership may be influenced by images of Western movie heroes.

His sensitivity to criticism influences his leadership style. He is at the center of a starburst, receiving policy analysis from various groups on the United States, China, South Korea, Russia, and Japan, but without any coordination among the groups. Moreover, although he scans the Web for several hours daily and reportedly watches CNN, he has only an imperfect understanding of political reality, and his subordinates are reluctant to criticize him.

Kim Jong Il's lack of empathy also affects his leadership style, including with his own people. He once recounted with pride the story of a disagreement with Kim Il Sung when his father plaintively asked: "Must we spend so much on the military? Can we not provide more to our people?" To which Kim Jong Il replied: "No, father, the military requires these funds." This lack of empathy also contributes to his misunderstanding of potential adversaries, such as the United States.

The official policy of the DPRK is that the military has the top priority. Defense spending comes before the economy and the general population. The economy is broken and cannot be fixed. Pyongyang has not made the change from a centrally controlled communist-style economy, and the disproportionate military spending is leading to an implosion. As many as 3 million North Koreans have starved to death in famines. Hundreds of thousands lost their lives in subsequent relocation to government-run camps. Kim Jong Il asks

Secretary Gates and General James Cartwright, Vice Chairman of the Joint Chiefs of Staff, brief press on plans for fiscal year 2010 at Pentagon, April 2009

DOD (Cherie Cullen)

the people to endure continuing hardships at the same time that he and the elites live in the lap of luxury.

Kim Jong Il overestimates his prowess and may have succumbed to his own propaganda as conveyed in the slogan "1 a match for 100," suggesting that 1 North Korean soldier is a match for 100 from any other country. He looks to nuclear weapons as compensation for his weakened conventional forces, believing the United States to be casualty-averse. He exaggerates the strain in the relationship between Washington and Seoul and the popular dissent and political instability in South Korea, while underestimating potential internal dissent. Kim values his personal safety, wealth, and regime survival, the stability of Pyongyang, the comfort of the elites on whom he must rely, and the maintenance of total domestic control.

If the current diplomatic offensive becomes unraveled and Kim Jong Il again fails to live up to his commitments on dismantling the nuclear weapons program, information operations could well be incorporated in a coordinated and consistent national strategy. Communication must be clear and backed by deeds. If the violation of Agreed Framework had been overlooked and the shipment of heavy oil continued, America would have been seen as all bark and no bite.

An information operations campaign intended to split Kim and his leadership elite from their followers would include identifying Pyongyang as a prime military target by extensive overt surveillance, countering the 1-a-match-for-100 slogan by displaying American military capabilities, and educating lower level military and civilian audiences on the gap between their deprivation and the hedonism of national elites. Because of the major information blackout, this would require satellite communication and shortwave radio. No information operations campaign against North Korea can proceed unilaterally, but must involve close coordination with U.S. allies in the region and the concurrence of the Republic of Korea.

There has been insufficient attention to information warfare in dealing with adversaries and potential adversaries, thus leaving the information battlespace virtually uncontested. Actor-specific behavioral models are required to counter adversaries, from international terrorists to rogue states. One cannot fight adversaries who are not understood. And what deters one given adversary could incite another. The actor-specific behavioral models in turn should be the foundation for tailored psychological warfare programs, designed to sever the links between leaders and their followers.

Implementing Complex Operations

Washington is a policy town. For many great issues, from the Marshall Plan to global warming, policy decisions are critical. But focusing on policy can lead to the notion that a decision taken is an action completed. In complex situations, this can be a dangerous assumption because it can limit understanding of time lags in what local people accept as reality to which they can react. Similarly, there is only beginning to be a focus on the need for the implementation of hundreds or thousands of subordinate actions that do not flow automatically from policy decisions.

One example of the illusionary quality of policy is the lag time between fiscal decisions and their impact in the field. The Bush administration decided to recommend additional funding for Afghanistan's economic development in 2006. The recommendation, divided into a base budget and supplemental request, went to Congress in 2007. Votes occurred in the summer and autumn and funds were released to the U.S. Agency for International Development (USAID) and the Embassy in Kabul. For road work, for example, contracts had to be awarded, engineering studies written, and so forth. In many areas, winter halted construction. Dirt could not fly until spring 2008—18 months *after* the decision, which is a long time in war. Finding ways to move funds more quickly is a recurring problem in Afghanistan, Iraq, and other contingencies. It is a problem that will occur again unless more thought is given to solving it.

Another implementation issue is planning. Much has been said about the missed opportunity for greater prewar planning on Iraq. But a second area of tension is largely unstudied—namely, between the need to plan and need to act. The Afghan war could not have been foreseen before September 11, 2001, and once it began there was no time for detailed planning. Reconstruction needs were huge; in many cases, new construction was required since nothing was there beforehand. International knowledge of the country was fragmentary and telling the Afghans to wait a year or two for a plan was unacceptable. Performance had to begin with planning following behind. This meant that plans would change as the knowledge grew and mistakes were discovered.

The Office of Management and Budget pressed for a comprehensive, 5-year development plan, but there were two major problems. First, there was no way of realistically gauging what other donors would do in the out years, and resources might have to be shifted to cover their projects if they did not perform. The second problem was that needs were seen differently as lessons were being learned. At the outset, infrastructure was not made a high priority. Then the requirement for a major ring road around the country became obvious. Later, a series of secondary roads were seen as basic building blocks in economic development. By 2006, the insurgency was growing and the need for tertiary roads in combat areas became more critical than earlier developmental criteria indicated. A long-term plan could have been written at any point along the way, but it would have been dated within 6 months. Under such conditions, planning must remain flexible, which is the antithesis of the kind of comprehensive plan that is usually called for.

When problems mount, certain proposals frequently reoccur—they are not inherently wrong, but they overpromise. The most common of these proposals are the calls for a new strategy, for a single point of coordination, and for a wiring diagram of the chain of command to bring about improvements on the ground. Efforts to achieve such policy fixes to implementation problems waste a great deal of time that could have been better used to make real improvements.

The national need for clear strategic direction is an important responsibility of the President. But in multinational operations, agreed strategy is usually developed at a high level of generality. In strategic planning in World War II, NATO strategy in Afghanistan, and international strategy in Bosnia, strategic direction were only the starting points, and rather general ones at that. The devil is in the details that must be sorted by national representatives on the ground, which include militaries, embassies, development agencies, international organizations, support groups, and local government where it exists. Agreement in any capital on the major goals does not automatically lead to agreement on how to achieve them any more than it will at Cabinet level in the U.S. Government. Lack of agreement leads to wasted motion, work conducted at cross purposes, gaps in meeting essential needs, inefficient use of available resources, and a great deal of finger pointing.

The response to these problems is usually to call for a coordinator or single point of control. A designated senior person can help the situation, but less than is popularly supposed. National authorities do not just salute and take orders. Development organizations in many countries do not report to foreign ministries, nor do they necessarily agree on priorities. Military commanders may be subordinate in theory to senior multinational commanders, but

the latter must deal with nationally imposed limits on their forces, or *caveats* in NATO parlance. In addition to caveats, these commanders must consult their national headquarters before executing orders. Although senior-level coordinators may be helpful, they are not panaceas. Another concern is the chain of command. In Afghanistan, there is a particularly murky chain with some U.S. forces reporting to U.S. Central Command and others under NATO reporting to U.S. European Command, and some even reporting to both. And all of them have responsibilities that overlap with the Ambassador.

The need for improvement is clearer than the solution. In Bosnia, Iraq, and Afghanistan, as well as more traditional peacekeeping missions, actions by the military influence what civilians accomplish, and the reverse is true as well. The military refusal to arrest war criminals in Bosnia undercut the civilian authorities. Lack of progress in development and effective government in Afghanistan complicates the military task. The point is simply that while improving the chain of command will help, it will not remove overlapping responsibilities. And when the operation is multinational, the problem increases geometrically.

There are many lessons about implementation that have been learned but generally not acted upon, including the following:

■ Washington needs a different interactive process with the field. Strategic guidance needs to be clearer and micromanagement lessened. Differences between agencies need resolution. Often what happens is bureaucratic compromise and excessive management of action plans instead of decisions taken to the President. Field views that should govern implementation are lost.

■ Military and civilian leaders either have to reach comfortable working relationships, or Washington needs to replace leaders. Fruitful cooperation with successive military commanders in Afghanistan but disagreements in the early period of operations in Bosnia and Iraq were never resolved.

■ The need to plan and implement simultaneously requires getting more staff and more qualified staff into the field quickly and keeping the numbers high enough, with good people, both to oversee project implementation and handle strategic planning. We continue to try to do both jobs with a staff adequate for only one of the two functions.

■ USAID needs a substantially increased ability to move money faster. Accomplishing this will mean many changes, but a few of the basic ones are more staff and more ability to contract directly with local contractors without ponderous, gigantic American umbrella contracts.

■ We need a way to find money faster and shift it between needs. Our current process is designed for long-term debate with two exceptions: emergency relief and certain military funds, which have the twin result of involving the military more and more in economic operations for which they lack long-term competence while draining military manpower and attention from key warfighting tasks. Congress must be part of the solution since they hold the purse strings.

■ Expand the staff of the Department of State (and USAID). Having more flexible tools and putting them in civilian hands only makes sense if there are hands to wield them; right now, there are not enough.

■ Non-U.S. coordinators have a particular importance to improving operation coordination on the ground if they have the right personality, mandate, and staff. They are not a simple solution but have a role because they avoid the reactions that come if America is perceived as trying to run everything. Too often, the personality gets the focus but lacks the mandate and the resources. All three must be seen as a package or major mismatches between means and ends will continue.

Better implementation by itself is insufficient; it is just muddling through by another name. In principle, there is no reason that both policy and implementation cannot be done, although the reality is that it is not. The U.S. military is drawing lessons on using its capabilities on the ground, but the civil sector is behind. Neither Congress nor previous administrations have changed funding levels, legal authorities, or staffing to increase efficiency. Until policy direction and implementation are improved to provide authority and resources, these problems will continue.

Peace, Prosperity, and Partnership

To tackle crucial issues of national security, it is necessary to develop an overarching framework to bring together disparate elements of potential solutions and organize them around the common aims of peace, prosperity, and partnership. After 8 years of polarizing foreign policy, the Nation must chart a fundamentally new course to maintain national security. Some may argue for a return to a more prag-

matic, interest-based approach to policymaking while other observers call for greater emphasis on soft or smart power as the best means of achieving national objectives. And still other perspectives cannot be discounted.

It is tempting to critique the Bush administration in the area of national security. But the reality is grim. Iraq and Afghanistan are failing states not salvageable by military force alone. Pakistan is fragile and hindered by a new government that cannot overcome past animosities and govern in its best interests. Moreover, Americans are ambivalent over the prospects of a different form of a cold war with China and Russia. The future of NATO hangs in the balance in Afghanistan and in the transformation from a military to a security-based alliance. Even in

Railway workers and police examine debris of destroyed train at Madrid's Atocha station, March 2004

this hemisphere, the United States seems incapable of fashioning rational policies toward its neighbors whether in reforming immigration statutes, fighting narcotraffickers, or normalizing relations with Cuba. And the concern over the health of the domestic economy—given the crises in the banking, mortgage, and investment sectors—often relegates foreign policy to the political back-burner.

Virtually every international organization created to improve security, including economic development, arose either from World War II or in the early years of the Cold War. The UN, NATO, the World Bank, and other mature institutions were designed in, as well as for, a bygone era. Whether these aging organizations can be modernized, redirected, or supplanted presents a global challenge for the 21st century.

Despite the harshness of this assessment, the United States has opportunities to exploit. First, it can adopt global and regional instead of bilateral approaches to conducting foreign and defense policy. For example, Iraq cannot be secured without regional cooperation. Neither Afghanistan nor Pakistan can become stable unless both states tackle their common threats. And dealing with the nuclear weapons ambitions of Iran will require other powers to be coopted in this process. Hence, cooperation by states, international organizations, and nongovernmental organizations is crucial. That demands a global perspective, with effective outreach to regional components.

A new administration offers the opportunity to restore American prestige, influence, and reputation. Discarding past shibboleths such as the *global war on terror* and the *with-us-or-against-us* mentality is crucial to changing the perception of the United States throughout the world. Developing a viable strategic communications plan to explain American policy will be vital in this effort, which is something that the Bush administration failed to accomplish.

It will be necessary to harness governmental assets as well as appropriate resources from the private sector to advance foreign and defense policy. This also will require incorporating allies, friends, and other states, as well as nongovernmental organizations. Unilateral action has a place, but multilateralism in the broadest sense must become the new watchword. With new leaders in many capitals of the world, opportunities exist to either improve or restore relations. There are also opportunities in the fact that virtually every nation has major common and shared interests. No state wants nuclear war, not even Iran. None supports ruining the environment or destroying the planet. Few states advocate terrorism, although the definition of what actually constitutes terror is not universally accepted. By identifying shared interests and building on them as a basis for foreign and defense policy, America should create new or exploit old opportunities.

The United States and its allies and friends are fortunate in having very capable populations. The issue is mobilizing them to serve. This is something that the military has done although the strain of constant deployments to Iraq and Afghanistan is taking a toll. The Nation must find a way to galvanize the public resolve and use it. People have been, are, and will be the most precious national asset. Too often governments only give lip service to this reality.

Before laying out a framework and strategy for foreign and defense policy, an assessment of the hier-archy of challenges, choices, and priorities is crucial. Obviously, debate over each item is warranted, but some consensus can be reached over the major issues that will shape the future even if dealing with each one may spark sharply different opinions of how to proceed.

Four categories apply to the hierarchy of challenges, choices, and priorities. First, there are some issues that are common to or shared by states. A state is an entity with a duly constituted government that adheres to the rule of law and has rational leadership, though not always defined in American terms. Iran and North Korea would be considered states. Common interests fall into this category. The next category contains issues common to both allies and friends beyond the shared interests. The third category includes unique issues that reflect unilateral preferences or dictates arising from specific laws or domestic constituencies. Finally, there is a category of issues that are important to others but that can generate indifference, ignorance, or disagreement. Parts of the Arab and Islamic world fall into this category, where a clash of values and cultures frequently arises over misperception or misunderstanding can lead to conflict. In some cases, the United States assigns little or no legitimacy or rationality to opposing views and attitudes.

It will be necessary to deal with the environment, climate change, population, resources, regional instability, weapons of mass destruction, radical extremism, and so forth. What is important is that most of these issues are linked, and the solutions to one set have consequences for the others that too often are ignored. The conclusion is that policies and solutions must be comprehensive. An example of comprehensiveness is found in the way combatant commanders execute their responsibilities. The Unified Command Plan established 10 geographic and functional commands: U.S. Northern Command (homeland defense), U.S. Southern Command (Latin America), U.S. Central Command (Greater Middle East), U.S. European Command (Europe, Russia, and former Soviet republics), U.S. Pacific Command (Asia), U.S. Africa Command, U.S. Joint Forces Command (transformation, doctrine, training, and experimentation), U.S. Special Operations Command, U.S. Strategic Command, and U.S. Transportation Command.

U.S. Southern Command (USSOUTHCOM) is a case in point. USSOUTHCOM has few warfighting responsibilities, although it is waging the so-called war on drugs. Its major task is preventing conflicts and crises before they erupt. But because prevention